WORLD TRADE ORGANIZATION

Dispute Settlement Reports

2013
Volume I

Pages 1-468

CAMBRIDGE
UNIVERSITY PRESS

University Printing House, Cambridge CB2 8BS, United Kingdom

Cambridge University Press is part of the University of Cambridge.

It furthers the University's mission by disseminating knowledge in the pursuit of education, learning and research at the highest international levels of excellence.

www.cambridge.org
Information on this title: www.cambridge.org/9781107112391

First published 2015

Printed in the United Kingdom by Clays, St Ives plc

A catalogue record for this publication is available from the British Library

Library of Congress Cataloguing in Publication data

ISBN 978-1-107-11239-1 Hardback

THE WTO DISPUTE SETTLEMENT REPORTS

The *Dispute Settlement Reports* of the World Trade Organization (the "WTO") include panel and Appellate Body reports, as well as arbitration awards, in disputes concerning the rights and obligations of WTO Members under the provisions of the *Marrakesh Agreement Establishing the World Trade Organization.* The *Dispute Settlement Reports* are available in English. Volumes comprising one or more complete cases contain a cumulative list of published disputes. The cumulative list for cases that cover more than one volume is to be found in the first volume for that case.

This volume may be cited as DSR 2013:I

TABLE OF CONTENTS

CANADA - CERTAIN MEASURES AFFECTING THE RENEWABLE ENERGY GENERATION SECTOR /

CANADA - MEASURES RELATING TO THE FEED-IN TARIFF PROGRAM

Reports of the Appellate Body
WT/DS412/AB/R, WT/DS426/AB/R

Adopted by the Dispute Settlement Body on 24 May 2013[*]

Canada, *Appellant/Appellee*

Japan, *Other Appellant/Appellee/ Third Participant*

European Union, *Other Appellant/Appellee/ Third Participant*

Australia, *Third Participant*

Brazil, *Third Participant*

China, *Third Participant*

El Salvador, *Third Participant*

Honduras, *Third Participant*[1]

India, *Third Participant*

Korea, *Third Participant*

Mexico, *Third Participant*

Appellate Body Division:

Present:

Ramírez-Hernández, Presiding Member

Bhatia, Member

Unterhalter, Member

---

* Note by the Secretariat:
The Appellate Body is issuing these Reports in the form of a single document constituting two separate Appellate Body Reports: WT/DS412/AB/R and WT/DS426/AB/R. The cover page, preliminary pages, sections 1 through 5 and the annexes are common to both Reports. The page header throughout the document bears the two document symbols WT/DS412/AB/R and WT/DS426/AB/R, with the following exceptions: section 6 on pages JPN-217 to JPN-219, which bears the document symbol for and contains the Appellate Body's findings and conclusions in the Appellate Body Report WT/DS412/AB/R; and section 6 on pages EU-220 to EU-221, which bears the document symbol for and contains the Appellate Body's findings and conclusions in the Appellate Body Report WT/DS426/AB/R.

Norway, *Third Participant*

Saudi Arabia, *Third Participant*

Separate Customs Territory of Taiwan, Penghu, Kinmen and Matsu, *Third Participant*

Turkey, *Third Participant*[2]

United States, *Third Participant*

TABLE OF CONTENTS

1 In DS412 only.

2 In DS426 only.

CASES CITED IN THESE REPORTS

Short Title	Full Case Title and Citation
Australia – Salmon	Appellate Body Report, *Australia – Measures Affecting Importation of Salmon*, WT/DS18/AB/R, adopted 6 November 1998, DSR 1998:VIII, p. 3327
Brazil – Retreaded Tyres	Appellate Body Report, *Brazil – Measures Affecting Imports of Retreaded Tyres*, WT/DS332/AB/R, adopted 17 December 2007, DSR 2007:IV, 1527
Canada – Aircraft	Appellate Body Report, *Canada – Measures Affecting the Export of Civilian Aircraft*, WT/DS70/AB/R, adopted 20 August 1999, DSR 1999:III, 1377
Canada – Aircraft (Article 21.5 – Brazil)	Appellate Body Report, *Canada – Measures Affecting the Export of Civilian Aircraft – Recourse by Brazil to Article 21.5 of the DSU*, WT/DS70/AB/RW, adopted 4 August 2000, DSR 2000:IX, p. 4299
Canada – Autos	Appellate Body Report, *Canada – Certain Measures Affecting the Automotive Industry*, WT/DS139/AB/R, WT/DS142/AB/R, adopted 19 June 2000, DSR 2000:VI, 2985
Canada – Autos	Panel Report, *Canada – Certain Measures Affecting the Automotive Industry*, WT/DS139/R, WT/DS142/R, adopted 19 June 2000, as modified by Appellate Body Report WT/DS139/AB/R, WT/DS142/AB/R, DSR 2000:VII, 3043
Canada – Dairy	Appellate Body Report, *Canada – Measures Affecting the Importation of Milk and the Exportation of Dairy Products*, WT/DS103/AB/R, WT/DS113/AB/R and Corr.1, adopted 27 October 1999, DSR 1999:V, p. 2057
Canada – Feed-in Tariff Program	Panel Report, *Canada – Measures Relating to the Feed-in Tariff Program*, WT/DS426/R and Add.1, circulated to WTO Members 19 December 2012

Short Title	Full Case Title and Citation
Canada – Periodicals	Appellate Body Report, *Canada – Certain Measures Concerning Periodicals*, WT/DS31/AB/R, adopted 30 July 1997, DSR 1997:I, 449
Canada – Renewable Energy	Panel Report, *Canada – Certain Measures Affecting the Renewable Energy Generation Sector*, WT/DS412/R and Add.1, circulated to WTO Members 19 December 2012
Canada – Wheat Exports and Grain Imports	Appellate Body Report, *Canada – Measures Relating to Exports of Wheat and Treatment of Imported Grain*, WT/DS276/AB/R, adopted 27 September 2004, DSR 2004:VI, p. 2739
Canada – Wheat Exports and Grain Imports	Panel Report, *Canada – Measures Relating to Exports of Wheat and Treatment of Imported Grain*, WT/DS276/R, adopted 27 September 2004, upheld by Appellate Body Report WT/DS276/AB/R, DSR 2004:VI, 2817
Chile – Price Band System	Appellate Body Report, *Chile – Price Band System and Safeguard Measures Relating to Certain Agricultural Products*, WT/DS207/AB/R, adopted 23 October 2002, DSR 2002:VIII, 3045 (Corr.1, DSR 2006:XII, 5473)
China – Auto Parts	Appellate Body Reports, *China – Measures Affecting Imports of Automobile Parts*, WT/DS339/AB/R / WT/DS340/AB/R / WT/DS342/AB/R, adopted 12 January 2009, DSR 2009:I, p. 3
China – Intellectual Property Rights	Panel Report, *China – Measures Affecting the Protection and Enforcement of Intellectual Property Rights*, WT/DS362/R, adopted 20 March 2009, DSR 2009:V, 2097
China – Publications and Audiovisual Products	Panel Report, *China – Measures Affecting Trading Rights and Distribution Services for Certain Publications and Audiovisual Entertainment Products*, WT/DS363/R and Corr.1, adopted 19 January 2010, as modified by Appellate Body Report WT/DS363/AB/R, DSR 2010:II, 261

Short Title	Full Case Title and Citation
China – Raw Materials	Appellate Body Reports, *China – Measures Related to the Exportation of Various Raw Materials*, WT/DS394/AB/R / WT/DS395/AB/R / WT/DS398/AB/R, adopted 22 February 2012
EC – Asbestos	Appellate Body Report, *European Communities – Measures Affecting Asbestos and Asbestos-Containing Products*, WT/DS135/AB/R, adopted 5 April 2001, DSR 2001:VII, 3243
EC – Bananas III	Appellate Body Report, *European Communities – Regime for the Importation, Sale and Distribution of Bananas*, WT/DS27/AB/R, adopted 25 September 1997, DSR 1997:II, 591
EC – Bananas III	Panel Reports, *European Communities – Regime for the Importation, Sale and Distribution of Bananas, (Ecuador)* WT/DS27/R/ECU, *(Guatemala and Honduras)* WT/DS27/R/GTM, WT/DS27/R/HND, *(Mexico)* WT/DS27/R/MEX, *(United States)* WT/DS27/R/USA, adopted 25 September 1997, as modified by Appellate Body Report WT/DS27/AB/R, DSR 1997:II, p. 695 to DSR:1997:III, p. 1085
EC – Export Subsidies on Sugar	Appellate Body Report, *European Communities – Export Subsidies on Sugar*, WT/DS265/AB/R, WT/DS266/AB/R, WT/DS283/AB/R, adopted 19 May 2005, DSR 2005:XIII, p. 6365
EC – Hormones	Appellate Body Report, *EC Measures Concerning Meat and Meat Products (Hormones)*, WT/DS26/AB/R, WT/DS48/AB/R, adopted 13 February 1998, DSR 1998:I, p. 135
EC – Sardines	Appellate Body Report, *European Communities – Trade Description of Sardines*, WT/DS231/AB/R, adopted 23 October 2002, DSR 2002:VIII, 3359
EC – Selected Customs Matters	Panel Report, *European Communities – Selected Customs Matters*, WT/DS315/R, adopted 11 December 2006, as modified by Appellate Body Report WT/DS315/AB/R, DSR 2006:IX-X, p. 3915

Short Title	Full Case Title and Citation
EC and certain member States – Large Civil Aircraft	Appellate Body Report, *European Communities and Certain Member States – Measures Affecting Trade in Large Civil Aircraft*, WT/DS316/AB/R, adopted 1 June 2011
India – Autos	Panel Report, *India – Measures Affecting the Automotive Sector*, WT/DS146/R, WT/DS175/R and Corr.1, adopted 5 April 2002, DSR 2002:V, p. 1827
Indonesia – Autos	Panel Report, *Indonesia – Certain Measures Affecting the Automobile Industry*, WT/DS54/R, WT/DS55/R, WT/DS59/R, WT/DS64/R and Corr.1 and 2, adopted 23 July 1998, and Corr. 3 and 4, DSR 1998:VI, 2201
Japan – Alcoholic Beverages II	Appellate Body Report, *Japan – Taxes on Alcoholic Beverages*, WT/DS8/AB/R, WT/DS10/AB/R, WT/DS11/AB/R, adopted 1 November 1996, DSR 1996:I, p. 97
Japan – DRAMs (Korea)	Appellate Body Report, *Japan – Countervailing Duties on Dynamic Random Access Memories from Korea*, WT/DS336/AB/R and Corr.1, adopted 17 December 2007, DSR 2007:VII, p. 2703
Korea – Alcoholic Beverages	Appellate Body Report, *Korea – Taxes on Alcoholic Beverages*, WT/DS75/AB/R, WT/DS84/AB/R, adopted 17 February 1999, DSR 1999:I, 3
Korea – Various Measures on Beef	Appellate Body Report, *Korea – Measures Affecting Imports of Fresh, Chilled and Frozen Beef*, WT/DS161/AB/R, WT/DS169/AB/R, adopted 10 January 2001, DSR 2001:I, 5
Philippines – Distilled Spirits	Appellate Body Reports, *Philippines – Taxes on Distilled Spirits*, WT/DS396/AB/R / WT/DS403/AB/R, adopted 20 January 2012
Turkey – Rice	Panel Report, *Turkey – Measures Affecting the Importation of Rice*, WT/DS334/R, adopted 22 October 2007, DSR 2007:VI, 2151
US – Anti-Dumping and Countervailing Duties (China)	Appellate Body Report, *United States – Definitive Anti-Dumping and Countervailing Duties on Certain Products from China*, WT/DS379/AB/R, adopted 25 March 2011

Short Title	Full Case Title and Citation
US – Carbon Steel	Appellate Body Report, *United States – Countervailing Duties on Certain Corrosion-Resistant Carbon Steel Flat Products from Germany*, WT/DS213/AB/R and Corr.1, adopted 19 December 2002, DSR 2002:IX, 3779
US – Certain EC Products	Appellate Body Report, *United States – Import Measures on Certain Products from the European Communities*, WT/DS165/AB/R, adopted 10 January 2001, DSR 2001:I, p. 373
US – COOL	Appellate Body Reports, *United States – Certain Country of Origin Labelling (COOL) Requirements*, WT/DS384/AB/R / WT/DS386/AB/R, adopted 23 July 2012
US – Gasoline	Appellate Body Report, *United States – Standards for Reformulated and Conventional Gasoline*, WT/DS2/AB/R, adopted 20 May 1996, DSR 1996:I, p. 3
US – Large Civil Aircraft (2nd complaint)	Appellate Body Report, *United States – Measures Affecting Trade in Large Civil Aircraft (Second Complaint)*, WT/DS353/AB/R, adopted 23 March 2012
US – Section 211 Appropriations Act	Appellate Body Report, *United States – Section 211 Omnibus Appropriations Act of 1998*, WT/DS176/AB/R, adopted 1 February 2002, DSR 2002:II, p. 589
US – Softwood Lumber IV	Appellate Body Report, *United States – Final Countervailing Duty Determination with Respect to Certain Softwood Lumber from Canada*, WT/DS257/AB/R, adopted 17 February 2004, DSR 2004:II, 571
US – Softwood Lumber IV	Panel Report, *United States – Final Countervailing Duty Determination with Respect to Certain Softwood Lumber from Canada*, WT/DS257/R and Corr.1, adopted 17 February 2004, as modified by Appellate Body Report WT/DS257/AB/R, DSR 2004:II, p. 641

Short Title	Full Case Title and Citation
US – Tuna II (Mexico)	Appellate Body Report, *United States – Measures Concerning the Importation, Marketing and Sale of Tuna and Tuna Products*, WT/DS381/AB/R, adopted 13 June 2012
US – Upland Cotton	Appellate Body Report, *United States – Subsidies on Upland Cotton*, WT/DS267/AB/R, adopted 21 March 2005, DSR 2005:I, p. 3
US – Upland Cotton	Panel Report, *United States – Subsidies on Upland Cotton*, WT/DS267/R, Corr.1, and Add.1 to Add.3, adopted 21 March 2005, as modified by Appellate Body Report WT/DS267/AB/R, DSR 2005:II, p. 299
US – Upland Cotton (Article 21.5 – Brazil)	Appellate Body Report, *United States – Subsidies on Upland Cotton – Recourse to Article 21.5 of the DSU by Brazil*, WT/DS267/AB/RW, adopted 20 June 2008, DSR 2008:III, 809
US – Wheat Gluten	Appellate Body Report, *United States – Definitive Safeguard Measures on Imports of Wheat Gluten from the European Communities*, WT/DS166/AB/R, adopted 19 January 2001, DSR 2001:II, 717
US – Wool Shirts and Blouses	Appellate Body Report, *United States – Measure Affecting Imports of Woven Wool Shirts and Blouses from India*, WT/DS33/AB/R, adopted 23 May 1997, and Corr.1, DSR 1997:I, p. 323

ABBREVIATIONS USED IN THESE REPORTS

Abbreviation	Description
CES	Clean Energy Supply
CHP	Combined Heat and Power
complainants	Japan and the European Union
DSB	Dispute Settlement Body
DSU	Understanding on Rules and Procedures Governing the Settlement of Disputes
Electricity Act of 1998	Electricity Act, 1998, *Service Ontario 1998*, Chapter 15, Schedule A, as amended (Panel Exhibit JPN-5)
Electricity Restructuring Act of 2004	An Act to amend the Electricity Act, 1998 and the Ontario Energy Board Act, 1998 and to make consequential amendments to other Acts, *Service Ontario 2004*, Chapter 23 (Panel Exhibits CDA-18 and JPN-8)
EU Panel Report	Panel Report, *Canada – Measures Relating to the Feed-in Tariff Program* (WT/DS426/R)
FIT	feed-in tariff
FIT Programme	Ontario Power Authority Feed-in Tariff Program
FIT Programme Interpretations	FIT Program Interpretations of the Domestic Content Requirements (Panel Exhibit EU-7)
FIT Standard Definitions	Ontario Power Authority, Feed-in Tariff Appendix 1 – Standard Definitions (version 1.5.1), 15 July 2011 (Panel Exhibit JPN-135)
GA	Global Adjustment
GATT 1994	General Agreement on Tariffs and Trade 1994
GPA	Agreement on Government Procurement
Green Energy and Green Economy Act of 2009	An Act to enact the Green Energy Act, 2009 and to build a green economy, to repeal the Energy Conservation Leadership Act, 2006 and the Energy Efficiency Act and to amend other statutes, *Service Ontario 2009*, Chapter 12 (Panel Exhibit JPN-101)
HCI	Hydroelectric Contract Initiative

Abbreviation	Description
HEPCO	Hydro-Electric Power Commission of Ontario
HOEP	Hourly Ontario Energy Price
Hogan Report	Professor William W. Hogan, Harvard University, "Overview of the Electricity System in the Province of Ontario", 21 December 2011 (Panel Exhibit CDA-2)
IESO	Independent Electricity System Operator
IESO Market Manual	Independent Electricity System Operator, Market Manual
IESO Market Rules	Independent Electricity System Operator, Market Rules for the Ontario Market
IPP	Independent Power Producer
Japan Panel Report	Panel Report, *Canada – Certain Measures Affecting the Renewable Energy Generation Sector* (WT/DS412/R)
kW	kilowatts
kWh	kilowatt hour
LDC	Local Distribution Company
MCP	market clearing price
Memorandum of Agreement	Memorandum of Agreement between Her Majesty the Queen in Right of the Province of Ontario as Represented by the Minister of Energy and Hydro One Inc., 27 March 2008 (Panel Exhibit CDA-107)
Minister's 2009 FIT Direction	Direction dated 24 September 2009 from the Deputy Premier and Minister of Energy and Infrastructure to the Chief Executive Officer, Ontario Power Authority to develop a feed-in tariff (FIT) programme (Panel Exhibit JPN-102)
MW	megawatts
NUG	Non-Utility Generator
OEB	Ontario Energy Board
OEFC	Ontario Electricity Financial Corporation
OPA	Ontario Power Authority

Abbreviation	Description
OPA Proposed FIT Price Schedule Presentation	OPA, Presentation on "Proposed Feed-in Tariff Price Schedule Stakeholder Engagement – Session 4", 7 April 2009 (Panel Exhibit CDA-46)
OPG	Ontario Power Generation
Panel Reports	Panel Report, *Canada – Certain Measures Affecting the Renewable Energy Generation Sector* (WT/DS412/R) and Panel Report, *Canada – Measures Relating to the Feed-in Tariff Program* (WT/DS426/R)
PJM Interconnection	Mid-Atlantic region of the United States
PV	photovoltaic
RES	Renewable Energy Supply
RESOP	Renewable Energy Standard Offer Program
RPP	Regulated Price Plan
SCM Agreement	Agreement on Subsidies and Countervailing Measures
SSS	Standard Supply Service
TRIM	trade-related investment measure
TRIMs Agreement	Agreement on Trade-Related Investment Measures
TRIPS Agreement	Agreement on Trade-Related Aspects of Intellectual Property Rights
Working Procedures	Working Procedures for Appellate Review, WT/AB/WP/6, 16 August 2010
WTO	World Trade Organization
WTO Agreement	Marrakesh Agreement Establishing the World Trade Organization

PANEL EXHIBITS CITED IN THESE REPORTS

Exhibit	Description
CDA-2	Professor William W. Hogan, Harvard University, "Overview of the Electricity System in the Province of Ontario", 21 December 2011
CDA-6	Government of Ontario, *Ontario's Long-Term Energy Plan* (Queen's Printer for Ontario, 2010)
CDA-16	Ontario Energy Board webpage, "Electricity Prices: ... OEB's Role in Electricity Prices", available at: <http://www.ontarioenergyboard.ca/OEB/Consumers/Electricity/Electricity+Prices#role>
CDA-18	An Act to amend the Electricity Act, 1998 and the Ontario Energy Board Act, 1998 and to make consequential amendments to other Acts, *Service Ontario 2004*, Chapter 23
CDA-46	Ontario Power Authority, Presentation on "Proposed Feed-in Tariff Price Schedule Stakeholder Engagement – Session 4", 7 April 2009
CDA-52	Ontario Ministry of Energy, Request for Proposals for 300 MW of Renewable Energy Supply (RES I), issued 24 June 2004
CDA-53	Ontario Ministry of Energy, Request for Proposals for 1,000 MW of Renewable Energy Supply (RES II), issued 17 June 2005
CDA-54	Ontario Ministry of Energy, Request for Proposals for approximately 500 MW of Renewable Energy Supply (RES III), issued 22 August 2008
CDA-55	Ontario Power Authority, Joint Report to the Minister of Energy: Recommendations on a Standard Offer Program for Small Generators connected to a Distribution System, 17 March 2006
CDA-59	Electricity Conservation & Supply Task Force, Tough Choices: Addressing Ontario's Power Needs, Final Report to the Minister of Energy (January 2004)
CDA-64	Ontario Energy Board, EB-2009-0084, Report of the Board on the Cost of Capital for Ontario's Regulated Utilities, 11 December 2009
CDA-85	S. Arrowsmith, "Government Procurement in the WTO", *Studies in Transnational Economic Law*, Vol. 16 (Kluwer Law International, 2002), p. 53
CDA-106	Independent Electricity System Operator, Market Rules for the Ontario Market, Chapter 11 of the 7 March 2012 issue

Exhibit	Description
CDA-107	Memorandum of Agreement between Her Majesty the Queen in Right of the Province of Ontario as Represented by the Minister of Energy and Hydro One Inc., 27 March 2008
CDA-128	S. Arrowsmith, "Government Procurement in the WTO", *Studies in Transnational Economic Law*, Vol. 16 (Kluwer Law International, 2002), p. 51
CDA-129	A. La Chimia and S. Arrowsmith, "Addressing Tied Aid: Towards a More Development-Oriented WTO?", *Journal of International Economic Law*, Vol. 12 (September 2009), pp. 707-747
EU-4	Ontario Power Authority, Feed-in Tariff Program Rules (version 1.5.1), 31 October 2011
EU-5	Ontario Power Authority, Feed-in Tariff Contract (version 1.5.1), 31 October 2011
EU-6	Ontario Power Authority, microFIT Contract (version 1.6.1), 31 October 2011
EU-7	FIT Program Interpretations of the Domestic Content Requirements
EU-20	European Wind and Energy Association, *The Economics of Wind Energy* (March 2009) (extracts)
JPN-5	Electricity Act of 1998, *Service Ontario 1998*, Chapter 15, Schedule A, as amended
JPN-7	Blake, Cassels & Graydon webpage, "Overview of Electricity Regulation in Canada", accessed at: <http://www.blakes.com/english/legal_updates/reference_guides/Overview%20of%20Electricity%20in%20Canada.pdf> (no longer available)
JPN-8	An Act to amend the Electricity Act, 1998 and the Ontario Energy Board Act, 1998 and to make consequential amendments to other Acts, *Service Ontario 2004*, Chapter 23
JPN-11	IESO webpage, "Global Adjustment Archive", available at: <http://www.ieso.ca/imoweb/b100/ga_archive.asp>
JPN-26	Ontario Power Authority, A Progress Report on Electricity Supply: Fourth Quarter 2010
JPN-30	FIT Price Schedule, 3 June 2011
JPN-31	microFIT Price Schedule, 13 August 2010
JPN-32	FIT Price Schedule, 13 August 2010

Exhibit	Description
JPN-33	FIT Price Schedule, 2 July 2010
JPN-34	FIT Price Schedule, 24 September 2009
JPN-38	Ontario Power Authority, Micro Feed-in Tariff Program: Program Overview (2010)
JPN-41	Hydro One, News Release, "Hydro One Releases 2010 Year-End Financial Results", 10 February 2011, available at: <http://www.hydroone.com/OurCompany/Media Centre/Documents/NewsReleases2011/02_10_2011_Year-End_Financials.pdf>
JPN-43	Hydro One webpage, "Our Subsidiaries", available at: <http://www.hydroone.com/OurCompany/Pages/OurSubsidiaries.aspx>
JPN-44	Independent Electricity System Operator webpage, "The Power System", available at: <http://www.ieso.ca/imoweb/siteShared/power_system.asp>
JPN-46	Electricity Distributors Association webpage, "Delivering Safe, Reliable and Environmentally Responsible Electricity to Ontarians", July 2010, available at: <http://www.eda-on.ca/eda/edaweb.nsf/0/762d9f4c8b3b490385257331004c49ba/$FILE/DELIVERING_ECONOMIC_BENEFITS.pdf>
JPN-47	IESO webpage, "Find Your Local Utility", available at: <http://www.ieso.ca/imoweb/siteshared/local_dist.asp?sid=ic>
JPN-48	Department of Justice Canada, Constitution Acts, 1867 to 1982, Part VI – Distribution of Legislative Powers, Sections 91-95
JPN-49	Government of Ontario webpage, "All Agencies List", available at: <http://www.pas.gov.on.ca/scripts/en/BoardsList.asp>
JPN-50	Government of Ontario webpage, "Agency Details, Ontario Power Authority", available at: <http://www.pas.gov.on.ca/scripts/en/BoardDetails.asp?boardID=141181>
JPN-51	Government of Ontario webpage, "Agencies: Boards, Commissions, Councils, Authorities and Foundations", available at: <http://www.ontario.ca/en/your_government/ONT06_018949.html>
JPN-52	Government of Ontario webpage, "About the Ministry of Energy", available at: <http://www.energy.gov.on.ca/en/about/>

Exhibit	Description
JPN-55	Ontario Power Authority webpage, "Directives to OPA from Minister of Energy", available at: <http://www.powerauthority.on.ca/about-us/directives-opa-minister-energy-and-infrastructure>
JPN-57	Government of Ontario webpage, "Agency Details, Independent Electricity System Operator", available at: <http://www.pas.gov.on.ca/scripts/en/BoardDetails.asp?boardID=128220>
JPN-59	Independent Electricity System Operator webpage, "About the IESO", available at: <http://www.ieso.ca/imoweb/about/about_the_ieso.asp>
JPN-62	Independent Electricity System Operator, Settlement Statements and Invoices: Marketplace Training (December 2010)
JPN-63	Government of Ontario webpage, "Agency Details, Ontario Energy Board", available at: <http://www.pas.gov.on.ca/scripts/en/BoardDetails.asp?boardID=764>
JPN-64	Ontario Energy Board webpage, "What We Do", available at: <http://www.ontario energyboard.ca/OEB/Industry/About+the+OEB/What+We+Do>
JPN-71	Ontario Energy Board, Retail Settlement Code, 1 October 2011 revision
JPN-75	IESO webpage, "Global Adjustment", available at: <http://www.ieso.ca/imoweb/b100/b100_ga.asp>
JPN-79	Independent Electricity System Operator, Market Rules for the Ontario Market, Chapters 7 and 9 of the 12 October 2011 issue
JPN-80	Independent Electricity System Operator, Introduction to Ontario's Physical Markets: IESO Training (October 2011)
JPN-82	Independent Electricity System Operator, Market Manual, Part 5.5
JPN-84	Independent Electricity System Operator, *HST Guide for IESO Transactions*, Issue 26.0 (12 October 2011)
JPN-90	Independent Electricity System Operator webpage, "Retail Contracts", available at: <http://www.ieso.ca/imoweb/siteshared/retailers.asp>

Exhibit	Description
JPN-91	Independent Electricity System Operator brochure, "What You Need to Know About Changes to Electricity Prices Coming November 1, 2009: A Guide For Ontario's Public Sector"
JPN-101	An Act to enact the Green Energy Act, 2009 and to build a green economy, to repeal the Energy Conservation Leadership Act, 2006 and the Energy Efficiency Act and to amend other statutes, *Service Ontario 2009*, Chapter 12
JPN-102	Direction dated 24 September 2009 from the Deputy Premier and Ontario Minister of Energy and Infrastructure to the Chief Executive Officer, Ontario Power Authority to develop a feed-in tariff (FIT) program
JPN-119	Ontario Power Authority, Feed-in Tariff Program Rules (version 1.5.1), 15 July 2011
JPN-120	Ontario Power Authority, Feed-in Tariff Program Rules (version 1.1), 30 September 2009
JPN-121	Ontario Power Authority, Feed-in Tariff Program Rules (version 1.2), 19 November 2009
JPN-122	Ontario Power Authority, Feed-in Tariff Program Rules (version 1.3.0), 9 March 2010
JPN-123	Ontario Power Authority, Feed-in Tariff Program Rules (version 1.3.1), 2 July 2010
JPN-124	Ontario Power Authority, Feed-in Tariff Program Rules (version 1.3.2), 29 October 2010
JPN-125	Ontario Power Authority, Feed-in Tariff Program Rules (version 1.4), 8 December 2010
JPN-126	Ontario Power Authority, Feed-in Tariff Program Rules (version 1.5), 3 June 2011
JPN-127	Ontario Power Authority, Feed-in Tariff Contract (version 1.5.1), 15 July 2011
JPN-128	Ontario Power Authority, Feed-in Tariff Contract (version 1.1), 30 September 2009
JPN-129	Ontario Power Authority, Feed-in Tariff Contract (version 1.2), 19 November 2009
JPN-130	Ontario Power Authority, Feed-in Tariff Contract (version 1.3.0), 9 March 2010

Exhibit	Description
JPN-131	Ontario Power Authority, Feed-in Tariff Contract (version 1.3.1), 2 July 2010
JPN-132	Ontario Power Authority, Feed-in Tariff Contract (version 1.3.2), 29 October 2010
JPN-133	Ontario Power Authority, Feed-in Tariff Contract (version 1.4), 8 December 2010
JPN-134	Ontario Power Authority, Feed-in Tariff Contract (version 1.5), 3 June 2011
JPN-135	Ontario Power Authority, Feed-in Tariff Appendix 1 – Standard Definitions (version 1.5.1), 15 July 2011
JPN-145	Ontario Power Authority, FIT Application Form, 1 December 2009
JPN-154	Ontario Regulation 578/05 made under the Ontario Energy Board Act, 1998, entitled "Prescribed Contracts Re Sections 78.3 and 78.4 of the Act", as amended
JPN-157	Ontario Power Authority, microFIT Rules (version 1.6.1), 10 August 2011
JPN-158	Ontario Power Authority, microFIT Rules (version 1.1), 30 September 2009
JPN-159	Ontario Power Authority, microFIT Rules (version 1.2), 19 November 2009
JPN-160	Ontario Power Authority, microFIT Rules (version 1.3), 10 December 2009
JPN-161	Ontario Power Authority, microFIT Rules (version 1.4), 2 July 2010
JPN-162	Ontario Power Authority, microFIT Rules (version 1.5), 25 August 2010
JPN-163	Ontario Power Authority, microFIT Rules (version 1.6), 8 December 2010
JPN-164	Ontario Power Authority, microFIT Contract (version 1.6.1), 10 August 2011
JPN-165	Ontario Power Authority, microFIT Contract (version 1.1), 30 September 2009
JPN-166	Ontario Power Authority, microFIT Contract (version 1.2), 19 November 2009

Exhibit	Description
JPN-167	Ontario Power Authority, microFIT Contract (version 1.3), 10 December 2009
JPN-168	Ontario Power Authority, microFIT Contract (version 1.4), 2 July 2010
JPN-169	Ontario Power Authority, microFIT Contract (version 1.5), 25 August 2010
JPN-170	Ontario Power Authority, microFIT Contract (version 1.6), 8 December 2010
JPN-171	Ontario Power Authority, Conditional Offer of microFIT Contract (version 1.6.1)
JPN-229	Canada Energy webpage, "Mid and Peak Tier Time-of-Use Rate Rises 8% on May 1", news article posting, *The Toronto Star*, 19 April 2012, available at: <http://www.canadaenergy.ca/>
JPN-230	My Rate Energy Ontario, Canada webpage, "Price Protection for Electricity", available at: <http://myrateenergy.ca/electricity-info.php>

1. INTRODUCTION

1.1 Canada, Japan, and the European Union each appeals certain issues of law and legal interpretations developed in the Panel Reports, *Canada – Certain Measures Affecting the Renewable Energy Generation Sector*[3] and *Canada – Measures Relating to the Feed-in Tariff Program*[4] (Panel Reports).[5] The Panel was established[6] to consider complaints by Japan[7] and the European Union[8] (the

---

[3] WT/DS412/R, 19 December 2012 (Japan Panel Report (DS412)).

[4] WT/DS426/R, 19 December 2012 (EU Panel Report (DS426)).

[5] The Panel issued its findings in the form of a single document containing two separate reports, with a common cover page, table of contents, and sections I through VII (including the Panel's findings), and with separate conclusions and recommendations in respect of the dispute initiated by Japan and in respect of the dispute initiated by the European Union.

[6] At its meetings held on 20 July 2011 and 20 January 2012, the Dispute Settlement Body (DSB) established two panels pursuant to, respectively, Japan's request in document WT/DS412/5 and the European Union's request in document WT/DS426/5, in accordance with Article 6 of the Understanding on Rules and Procedures Governing the Settlement of Disputes (DSU). (Panel Reports, para. 1.4)

On 6 October 2011, the Director-General composed the Panel in DS412. With respect to DS426, following the agreement of the parties, the Panel was composed, on 23 January 2012, with the same persons as in DS412. Following consultations with the parties, the Panels in the two disputes decided to harmonize their timetables to the greatest extent possible, in accordance with Article 9.3 of the

complainants) with respect to certain domestic content requirements in the feed-in tariff programme (FIT Programme) established by the Canadian Province of Ontario.

1.2 The measures at issue in these disputes, as identified by the Panel[9], are the following:

a. the FIT Programme, as evidenced by the following measures:

i. the Electricity Act of 1998[10], as amended, including in particular Part II – Independent Electricity System Operator, Part II.1 – Ontario Power Authority, and Part II.2 – Management of Electricity Supply, Capacity and Demand, including in particular Section 25.35 – Feed-in tariff program;

ii. an Act to enact the Green Energy Act of 2009 and to build a green economy, to repeal the Energy Conservation Leadership Act of 2006 and the Energy Efficiency Act and to amend other statutes[11] (Green Energy and Green Economy Act of 2009), including in particular Schedule B, amending the Electricity Act of 1998;

iii. an Act to amend the Electricity Act of 1998 and the Ontario Energy Board Act of 1998 and to make consequential amendments to other Acts[12] (Electricity Restructuring Act of 2004), including in particular Schedule A, Sections 29-32, enacting Part II.1 of the Electricity Act of 1998, and Sections 33-38, enacting Part II.2 of the Electricity Act of 1998, and Schedule B, Sections 17-18, enacting Sections 78.3-78.4 of the Ontario Energy Board Act of 1998;

iv. Ontario Regulation 578/05, made under the Ontario Energy Board Act of 1998, entitled "Prescribed Contracts Re Sections 78.3 and 78.4 of the Act"[13];

v. the Independent Electricity System Operator (IESO) Market Manual, including in particular Part 5.5 – Physical Markets Settlement Statements[14];

DSU. As in the Panel Reports, the Panels in DS412 and DS426 are herein collectively referred to as the "Panel". (See *Ibid.*, paras. 1.6 and 1.7 and fn 5 thereto)

7 Request for the Establishment of a Panel by Japan, WT/DS412/5.

8 Request for the Establishment of a Panel by the European Union, WT/DS426/5.

9 Panel Reports, para. 2.1.

10 *Service Ontario 1998*, Chapter 15, Schedule A (Panel Exhibit JPN-5).

11 *Service Ontario 2009*, Chapter 12 (Panel Exhibit JPN-101).

12 *Service Ontario 2004*, Chapter 23 (Panel Exhibits CDA-18 and JPN-8).

13 As amended (Panel Exhibit JPN-154).

14 IESO, Market Manual, Part 5.5 (Panel Exhibit JPN-82).

vi. the IESO Market Rules, including in particular Chapter 7 – System Operations and Physical Markets, Chapter 9 – Settlements and Billing, and Chapter 11 – Definitions[15];

vii. Direction dated 24 September 2009 from George Smitherman, Deputy Premier and Minister of Energy and Infrastructure, to Colin Andersen, Chief Executive Officer, Ontario Power Authority (OPA), directing the OPA to 0develop a feed-in tariff (FIT) programme and include a requirement that the applicant submit a plan for meeting the domestic (i.e. Ontario) content goals in the FIT Rules[16] (Minister's 2009 FIT Direction);

viii. all versions of the FIT Rules[17] and microFIT Rules[18] issued by the OPA since the inception of the FIT Programme;

ix. all versions of the FIT Contract, including General Terms and Conditions, Exhibits, and Standard Definitions[19], and microFIT Contract, including Appendices and the Conditional Offer of microFIT Contract[20], issued by the OPA since the inception of the FIT Programme;

x. all versions of the FIT Application Form[21] and online microFIT Application issued by the OPA since the inception of the FIT Programme;

xi. all versions of the FIT Price Schedule[22] and microFIT Price Schedule[23] issued by the OPA since the inception of the FIT Programme; and

xii. all versions of the FIT Program Interpretations of the Domestic Content Requirements[24] (FIT Programme Interpretations) issued by the OPA since the inception of the FIT Programme;

b. the individual FIT Contracts for wind or solar photovoltaic (PV) sources executed by the OPA since the inception of the FIT Programme; and

---

[15] IESO, Market Rules for the Ontario Market, Chapters 7 and 9 of the 12 October 2011 issue (Panel Exhibit JPN-79), and Chapter 11 of the 7 March 2012 issue (Panel Exhibit CDA-106).

[16] Panel Exhibit JPN-102.

[17] Panel Exhibits JPN-119 through JPN-126 and EU-4.

[18] Panel Exhibits JPN-157 through JPN-163.

[19] Panel Exhibits JPN-127 through JPN-134 and EU-5.

[20] Panel Exhibits JPN-164 through JPN-171 and EU-6.

[21] See Panel Exhibit JPN-145.

[22] Panel Exhibits JPN-30, JPN-32, JPN-33, and JPN-34.

[23] See Panel Exhibit JPN-31.

[24] See Panel Exhibit EU-7.

c. the individual microFIT Contracts for solar PV source executed by the OPA since the inception of the FIT Programme.

1.3 The FIT Programme is a scheme implemented by the Government of the Province of Ontario and its agencies in 2009, through which generators of electricity produced from certain forms of renewable energy are paid a guaranteed price per kilowatt hour (kWh) of electricity delivered into the Ontario electricity system under 20-year or 40-year contracts.[25] Participation in the FIT Programme is open to facilities located in Ontario that generate electricity exclusively from one or more of the following sources of renewable energy: wind, solar PV, renewable biomass, biogas, landfill gas, and waterpower.[26] It is administered by the OPA and implemented through the application of a standard set of rules, standard contracts, and, for each class of generation technology, standard pricing.[27] The FIT Programme is divided into two streams: (i) the FIT stream – for projects with a capacity to produce electricity that exceeds 10 kilowatts (kW), but is no more than 10 megawatts (MW) for solar PV projects or 50 MW in the case of waterpower projects; and (ii) the microFIT stream – for projects having a capacity to produce up to 10 kW of electricity.[28] The microFIT stream is intended to provide "'a simplified approach for enabling the development of renewable micro-generation projects in Ontario', with a view to attracting participants such as homeowners, farmers and small businesses".[29] Only projects that satisfy all of the specific eligibility requirements, and that can be connected to the Ontario electricity system, will be offered a FIT or microFIT Contract by the OPA, and thereby permitted to participate in the FIT Programme.[30]

1.4 Under the FIT stream, electricity generation facilities utilizing windpower and solar PV technologies must comply with "Minimum Required Domestic Content Levels", which must be satisfied in the development and construction of these facilities.[31] The microFIT stream also imposes Minimum Required Domestic Content Levels, but only on generation facilities utilizing solar PV technology.[32] The "Domestic Content Level" of a facility participating in either stream of the FIT Programme is calculated pursuant to a methodology that

[25] Panel Reports, para. 7.64.

[26] Panel Reports, para. 7.66 (referring to FIT Rules (version 1.5.1), Section 2.1(a); and OPA, Feed-in Tariff Appendix 1 – Standard Definitions (version 1.5.1), 15 July 2011 (FIT Standard Definitions) (Panel Exhibit JPN-135), Definition Nos. 215 and 216).

[27] Panel Reports, para. 7.67.

[28] Panel Reports, para. 7.66 (referring to FIT Rules (version 1.5.1), Section 2.1(a)(iii); and microFIT Rules (version 1.6.1), Section 2.1(a)(iv)).

[29] Panel Reports, para. 7.209 (quoting OPA, Micro Feed-in Tariff Program: Program Overview (2010) (Panel Exhibit JPN-38), p. 1 and Section 1.2(a); and microFIT Rules (version 1.6.1), Section 1.1).

[30] Panel Reports, paras. 7.68 (referring to FIT Rules (version 1.5.1), Sections 2, 3, and 5.2; and microFIT Rules (version 1.6.1), Sections 2, 3, and 4.1).

[31] Panel Reports, para. 7.9.

[32] Panel Reports, para. 7.64.

identifies a range of different "Designated Activities" and an associated "Qualifying Percentage".[33] For each Designated Activity that is performed in relation to a facility, an associated Qualifying Percentage will be achieved. A project's Domestic Content Level "will be determined by adding up the Qualifying Percentages associated with all of the Designated Activities performed in relation to that particular project".[34] The Minimum Required Domestic Content Levels prescribed under both streams of the FIT Programme are set out in Table 1.

Table 1: Minimum Required Domestic Content Levels Prescribed under the FIT Programme

	Wind (FIT)		**Solar PV (FIT)**		**Solar PV (microFIT)**	
Milestone Date for Commercial Operation	2009-2011	2012-	2009-2010	2011-	2009-2010*	2011-
Minimum Required Domestic Content Level	25%	50%	50%	60%	40%	60%

* Solar PV microFIT applications received by the OPA on or before 8 October 2010 may satisfy the 40% domestic content requirement.

Source: Panel Reports, para. 7.158, Table 1, and fn 310 thereto.

1.5 Further information about the factual aspects of these disputes is set forth in greater detail in paragraphs 2.1 and 7.9-7.68 of the Panel Reports, and in section 4 of these Reports.

1.6 Both complainants claimed that the challenged measures are inconsistent with Articles 3.1(b) and 3.2 of the Agreement on Subsidies and Countervailing Measures (SCM Agreement), Article 2.1 of the Agreement on Trade-Related Investment Measures (TRIMs Agreement), and Article III:4 of the General Agreement on Tariffs and Trade 1994 (GATT 1994). More specifically, Japan put forward the following claims:

a. through the FIT Programme, as well as individually executed FIT and microFIT Contracts for wind and solar PV projects, Canada grants and maintains prohibited subsidies that are contingent upon the use of domestic over imported goods, in violation of Articles 3.1(b) and 3.2 of the SCM Agreement;

---

[33] Panel Reports, para. 7.159.

[34] Panel Reports, para. 7.160.

b. the domestic content requirements of the FIT Programme, as well as individually executed FIT and microFIT Contracts for wind and solar PV projects, accord less favourable treatment to Japanese renewable energy generation equipment than accorded to like products of Ontario origin, in violation of Article III:4 of the GATT 1994; and

c. the FIT Programme and individually executed FIT and microFIT Contracts for wind and solar PV projects constitute trade-related investment measures (TRIMs) inconsistent with the provisions of Article III of the GATT 1994, and therefore in violation of Article 2.1 of the TRIMs Agreement.[35]

1.7 For its part, the European Union claimed:

a. Canada violates Articles 3.1(b) and 3.2 of the SCM Agreement since the FIT Programme and its related contracts established by the Government of Ontario are subsidies within the meaning of Article 1.1 of the SCM Agreement that are provided contingent upon the use of domestic over imported goods, namely, contingent upon the use of equipment and components for renewable energy generation facilities produced in Ontario over such equipment and components imported from other Members of the World Trade Organization (WTO), including the European Union;

b. Canada violates Article 2.1 of the TRIMs Agreement, in conjunction with paragraph 1(a) of its Annex, because the FIT Programme and its related contracts established by the Government of Ontario are TRIMs that require the purchase or use by enterprises of equipment and components for renewable energy generation facilities of Ontario origin or source; and

c. Canada violates Article III:4 of the GATT 1994 because the FIT Programme and its related contracts established by the Government of Ontario are TRIMs falling under paragraph 1(a) of the Annex to the TRIMs Agreement and, in any event, because they impose domestic content requirements on wind and solar PV electricity generators that affect the internal sale, purchase, or use of renewable energy generation equipment and components, according less favourable treatment to like products of European Union origin.[36]

1.8 The Panel Reports were circulated to WTO Members on 19 December 2012.

[35] Panel Reports, para. 3.1.

[36] Panel Reports, para. 3.4.

1.9 In its Reports, the Panel explained that it decided first to assess the complainants' claims under the TRIMs Agreement and the GATT 1994 before entertaining the claims under the SCM Agreement. The Panel explained, in this regard, that "the complainants assert, and Canada does not contest, that the measures at issue are trade-related investment measures affecting imports of renewable energy generation equipment and components."[37] This suggested to the Panel that, "compared with the SCM Agreement and Article III:4 of the GATT 1994, it is the TRIMs Agreement that deals most directly, specifically and in detail, with the aspects of the FIT Programme, and the FIT and microFIT Contracts, that are at the centre of the complainants' concerns."[38] The Panel stated that it would therefore proceed as follows:

> In this light, we will commence our evaluation of the complainants' claims by focusing on those made under the TRIMs Agreement. However, it is apparent from the terms of Article 2.1 of the TRIMs Agreement that, in undertaking this evaluation, we will also necessarily have to come to a view about the merits of the complainants' allegations concerning the consistency of the challenged measures with Article III:4 of the GATT 1994. Thus, in the section that follows we will simultaneously evaluate the merits of both of the complainants' claims under Article 2.1 of the TRIMs Agreement and Article III:4 of the GATT 1994.[39]

1.10 In response to the complainants' claims under the TRIMs Agreement and the GATT 1994, Canada invoked Article III:8(a) of the GATT 1994, arguing that the FIT Programme is not subject to the obligations of Article III. Canada argued that this is because the laws and requirements that create and implement the FIT Programme are laws and requirements that govern the procurement of renewable electricity for the governmental purpose of securing an electricity supply for Ontario consumers from clean sources, and "not with a view to commercial resale or with a view to use in the production of goods for commercial sale".[40] Both Japan and the European Union disagreed with Canada that the measures at issue fall within Article III:8(a) of the GATT 1994.[41] The European Union additionally countered that Article III:8(a) does not apply to measures that fall within the scope of Article 2.2 of the TRIMs Agreement and paragraph 1(a) of the Illustrative List annexed thereto.[42]

---

37 Panel Reports, para. 7.70.

38 Panel Reports, para. 7.70 (referring to Appellate Body Report, *EC – Bananas III*, para. 204).

39 Panel Reports, para. 7.70. (fn omitted)

40 Panel Reports, para. 7.86 (referring to Canada's first written submission to the Panel (DS412), para. 67).

41 See Panel Reports, paras. 7.74-7.77 and 7.81-7.85.

42 See Panel Reports, para. 7.80.

1.11 The Panel thus considered that it had to resolve the following three issues:

a. whether the measures at issue are TRIMs within the meaning of Article 1 of the TRIMs Agreement[43];

b. if so, whether paragraph 1(a) of the Illustrative List in the Annex to the TRIMs Agreement precludes the application of Article III:8(a) of the GATT 1994 to the challenged measures[44]; and

c. to the extent that paragraph 1(a) of the Illustrative List does not remove the possibility of applying Article III:8(a) to the challenged measures, whether those measures are of the kind described in Article III:8(a) of the GATT 1994.[45]

1.12 First, the Panel found that "the FIT Programme, and the FIT and microFIT Contracts, to the extent they envisage and impose a 'Minimum Required Domestic Content Level', constitute TRIMs within the meaning of Article 1 of the TRIMs Agreement."[46] Second, the Panel rejected the European Union's argument about the applicability of Article III:8(a) of the GATT 1994 to measures falling within the scope of paragraph 1(a) of the Illustrative List annexed to the TRIMs Agreement. The Panel considered that, "[g]iven the language of Article 2.1, it would ... be inappropriate to infer from Paragraph 1(a) of the Illustrative List that TRIMs having the characteristics described in that paragraph will *always* be inconsistent with Article III:4 of the GATT 1994, irrespective of whether they may be covered by the terms of Article III:8(a) of the GATT 1994."[47]

1.13 Next, the Panel assessed the measures in the light of the various elements of Article III:8(a) of the GATT 1994. The Panel found that: (i) "the Government of Ontario's purchases of electricity under the FIT Programme constitute 'procurement', within the meaning of that term in Article III:8(a)"; and (ii) "the 'Minimum Required Domestic Content Level' prescribed under the FIT Programme, and effected through the FIT and microFIT Contracts, is one of the 'requirements governing' the Government of Ontario's 'procurement' of electricity".[48] However, the Panel found that "the Government of Ontario's 'procurement' of electricity under the FIT Programme is undertaken 'with a view to commercial resale'."[49] In the light of the last intermediate finding, the Panel concluded:

---

43 Panel Reports, para. 7.108.
44 Panel Reports, para. 7.113.
45 *Ibid.*
46 Panel Reports, para. 7.112.
47 Panel Reports, para. 7.120. (original emphasis)
48 Panel Reports, para. 7.152.
49 Panel Reports, para. 7.151.

> [W]e find that the measures at issue are not covered by the terms of Article III:8(a), and that consequently, Canada cannot rely on Article III:8(a) of the GATT 1994 to exclude the application of Article III:4 of the GATT 1994 to the "Minimum Required Domestic Content Level" that the complainants challenge.[50]

1.14 Having found that the measures at issue are not covered by the terms of Article III:8(a), the Panel turned to the assessment of these measures under paragraph 1(a) of the Illustrative List of the TRIMs Agreement. The Panel found that:

> ... compliance with the "Minimum Required Domestic Content Level" not only involves the "purchase or use" of products from a domestic source, within the meaning of Paragraph 1(a) of the Illustrative List, but also that such compliance "is necessary" for electricity generators using solar PV and windpower technologies to participate in the FIT Programme, and thereby "obtain an advantage", within the meaning of Paragraph 1 of the Illustrative List. We are therefore satisfied that the challenged measures are TRIMs falling within the scope of Paragraph 1(a) of the Illustrative List, and that in the light of Article 2.2 and the chapeau to Paragraph 1(a) of the Illustrative List, they are inconsistent with Article III:4 of the GATT 1994, and thereby also inconsistent with Article 2.1 of the TRIMs Agreement.[51]

1.15 Hence, as regards Japan's and the European Union's claims under the TRIMs Agreement and the GATT 1994, the Panel concluded:

> In the light of the findings we have made in this Section of these Reports, we conclude that the FIT Programme, and the FIT and microFIT Contracts, are inconsistent with Article 2.1 of the TRIMs Agreement and Article III:4 of the GATT 1994.[52]

1.16 As regards the complainants' claims under the SCM Agreement, the Panel noted Japan's position that the measures at issue are "direct transfer[s] of funds" and "potential direct transfers of funds" within the meaning of Article 1.1(a)(1)(i) of the SCM Agreement. Alternatively, Japan submitted that the measures are "income or price support" within the meaning of Article 1.1(a)(2).[53] The European Union's "primary" argument was that the challenged measures constitute "income or price support". The European Union also argued that the measures at issue could be characterized as "direct transfer[s] of funds". In the alternative, the European Union contended that the measures at issue are "potential direct transfers of funds" under subparagraph (i)

[50] Panel Reports, para. 7.152.
[51] Panel Reports, para. 7.166.
[52] Panel Reports, para. 7.167.
[53] Panel Reports, para. 7.169.

or "entrust[ment] or direct[ion"] within the meaning of subparagraph (iv) of Article 1.1(a)(1).[54] Conversely, Canada asserted that the FIT Programme and related contracts can only be legally characterized as financial contributions in the form of government "purchases [of] goods".[55]

1.17 The Panel determined that the appropriate legal characterization of the FIT Programme and the FIT and microFIT Contracts is as a "financial contribution" in the form of government "purchases [of] goods" within the meaning of Article 1.1(a)(1)(iii) of the SCM Agreement.[56] Furthermore, the Panel disagreed with the complainants' argument that they could also be legally characterized as "direct transfer[s] of funds" for the purposes of the SCM Agreement.[57] The Panel also concluded that the measures at issue cannot be "potential direct transfers of funds" under subparagraph (i) or a form of financial contribution involving government entrustment or direction within the meaning of subparagraph (iv) of Article 1.1(a)(1).[58] Moreover, on the grounds of judicial economy, the Panel decided to make no findings on whether the measures at issue may be legally characterized as "income or price support" under Article 1.1(a)(2) of the SCM Agreement.[59]

1.18 Having determined that the measures constitute a financial contribution, the Panel proceeded to examine whether they confer a "benefit" within the meaning of Article 1.1(b) of the SCM Agreement. The Panel observed, in this regard, that the complainants' main line of argumentation was that, in the absence of the FIT Programme, a competitive wholesale market for electricity in Ontario could not support commercially viable operations of the contested FIT generators. To substantiate this argument, the complainants advanced a number of proposed competitive wholesale market electricity price benchmarks, or proxies for this benchmark, that they submitted demonstrate that the FIT Programme provides "more than adequate remuneration" for the OPA's purchases of electricity under the FIT and microFIT Contracts.[60]

1.19 The Panel agreed with the complainants that "there can be only *one* relevant market for the purpose of the benefit analysis, namely, the market for electricity that is generated from all sources of energy, including solar and wind energy."[61] The Panel then examined the complainants' claim that the IESO-administered wholesale electricity market would be the appropriate "market" benchmark to conduct the analysis under Article 1.1(b). In this context, the Panel had found that "the IESO-administered wholesale market does not arrive at its equilibrium price (the HOEP) through forces of supply and demand that are

[54] Panel Reports, para. 7.176.
[55] Panel Reports, para. 7.181.
[56] Panel Reports, para. 7.222.
[57] Panel Reports, para. 7.243.
[58] Panel Reports, para. 7.248.
[59] Panel Reports, para. 7.249.
[60] Panel Reports, para. 7.276.
[61] Panel Reports, para. 7.318. (original emphasis)

unaffected by the policies of the Government of Ontario."[62] Therefore, the Panel found that:

> ... the wholesale electricity market that currently exists in Ontario is not a market where there is effective competition. Rather, Ontario's wholesale electricity market is perhaps better characterized as a part of an electricity system that is defined in almost all aspects by the Government of Ontario's policy decisions and regulations pertaining to the supply mix needed to ensure that Ontario has a safe, reliable and long-term sustainable supply of electricity, as well as how the costs of that system will be recuperated.[63]

1.20 Accordingly, the Panel found that the "Hourly Ontario Energy Price" (HOEP) and all of the HOEP-derivatives that the complainants had advanced[64] could not serve as appropriate benchmarks for the purpose of the benefit analysis.[65] The Panel also rejected four out-of-province electricity markets – namely, Alberta, in Canada, and New York State, New England, and the Mid-Atlantic region (PJM Interconnection), in the United States – that the complainants had submitted as possible proxies for the wholesale market price in Ontario.[66]

1.21 Next, the Panel found that the application of a competitive wholesale market standard would ignore that a competitive wholesale electricity market would fail to attract the degree of investment to secure a reliable supply of electricity, and that, at present, this goal could only be achieved by means of government intervention in what would otherwise be unacceptable competitive market outcomes. Based on this reasoning, the Panel found that it would not be appropriate to determine whether the FIT Programme and the FIT and microFIT Contracts confer a benefit within the meaning of Article 1.1(b) of the SCM Agreement by comparing the terms and conditions of participation in the FIT Programme with those that would be available to generators participating in a wholesale electricity market where there is effective competition.[67] Therefore, the Panel found that Japan and the European Union failed to establish that the challenged measures confer a benefit within the meaning of Article 1.1(b) of the SCM Agreement.[68]

---

62 Panel Reports, para. 7.298.

63 Panel Reports, para. 7.308.

64 Namely, the weighted-average "wholesale rate" during 2010 for generators other than FIT and Renewable Energy Standard Offer Program (RESOP) generators, and the price paid by retail consumers under the "Regulated Price Plan" (RPP) in 2010.

65 Panel Reports, para. 7.308 and fn 610 thereto.

66 Panel Reports, para. 7.308.

67 Panel Reports, para. 7.312.

68 Panel Reports, para. 7.328(ii).

1.22 Having rejected the benchmarks proposed by the complainants and found that the complainants had failed to establish the existence of a benefit, the Panel made its own suggestion as to what it considered could be an appropriate benchmark in the circumstances of this case. The Panel stated that "one way to determine whether the challenged measures confer a benefit ... would involve testing them against the types of arm's length purchase transactions that would exist in a wholesale electricity market whose broad parameters are defined by the Government of Ontario."[69] In the Panel's view, this approach could be used to determine whether the challenged measures confer a benefit by comparing "the rate of return obtained by the FIT generators under the terms and conditions of the FIT and microFIT Contracts with the average cost of capital in Canada for projects having a comparable risk profile in the same period".[70] However, the Panel stated that "the record of these disputes does not contain any appropriate information" to conduct this analysis.[71]

1.23 In the light of the above findings, the Panel concluded, in the Japan Panel Report (DS412), that:

a. Japan had established that the Minimum Required Domestic Content Levels prescribed under the FIT Programme, and implemented through the individual FIT and microFIT Contracts executed since the FIT Programme's inception, placed Canada in breach of its obligations under Article 2.1 of the TRIMs Agreement and Article III:4 of the GATT 1994[72]; and

b. Japan had failed to establish that the FIT Programme, and the individual solar PV and windpower FIT and microFIT Contracts executed since the FIT Programme's inception, constituted subsidies, or envisaged the granting of subsidies, within the meaning of Article 1.1 of the SCM Agreement, and thereby that Canada had acted inconsistently with Articles 3.1(b) and 3.2 of the SCM Agreement.[73]

1.24 In the EU Panel Report (DS426), the Panel concluded that:

a. the European Union had established that the Minimum Required Domestic Content Levels prescribed under the FIT Programme, and implemented through the individual FIT and microFIT Contracts executed since the FIT Programme's inception, placed Canada in breach of its obligations under Article 2.1 of the TRIMs Agreement and Article III:4 of the GATT 1994[74]; and

---

69 Panel Reports, para. 7.322. (fn omitted)

70 Panel Reports, para. 7.323.

71 Panel Reports, para. 7.326.

72 Japan Panel Report (DS412), para. 8.2.

73 Japan Panel Report (DS412), para. 8.3.

74 EU Panel Report (DS426), para. 8.6.

b. the European Union had failed to establish that the FIT Programme, and the individual solar PV and windpower FIT and microFIT Contracts executed since the FIT Programme's inception, constituted subsidies, or envisaged the granting of subsidies, within the meaning of Article 1.1 of the SCM Agreement, and thereby that Canada had acted inconsistently with Articles 3.1(b) and 3.2 of the SCM Agreement.[75]

1.25 The Panel made the following recommendation in both the Japan Panel Report (DS412) and EU Panel Report (DS426):

> We recommend that Canada bring its measures into conformity with its obligations under the TRIMs Agreement and the GATT 1994.[76]

1.26 On 5 February 2013, Canada notified the Dispute Settlement Body (DSB), pursuant to Articles 16.4 and 17 of the Understanding on Rules and Procedures Governing the Settlement of Disputes (DSU), of its intention to appeal certain issues of law covered in the Panel Reports and certain legal interpretations developed by the Panel and filed a Notice of Appeal[77] and an appellant's submission pursuant to Rule 20 and Rule 21, respectively, of the Working Procedures for Appellate Review[78] (Working Procedures). On 11 February 2013, Japan and the European Union each notified the DSB, pursuant to Articles 16.4 and 17 of the DSU, of its intention to appeal certain issues of law covered in the respective Panel Report and certain legal interpretations developed by the Panel and each filed a Notice of Other Appeal[79] and an other appellant's submission pursuant to Rule 23 of the Working Procedures. On 25 February 2013, Canada, Japan, and the European Union each filed an appellee's submission.[80] On 26 February 2013, Australia filed a third participant's submission and, on 27 February 2013, Brazil, China, Saudi Arabia, and the United States each filed a third participant's submission.[81] On the same day, El Salvador, Honduras[82], India, Korea, Mexico, Norway, the Separate Customs

---

75 EU Panel Report (DS426), para. 8.7.

76 Japan Panel Report (DS412), para. 8.5; EU Panel Report (DS426), para. 8.9.

77 WT/DS412/10, WT/DS426/9 (attached as Annex 1 to these Reports).

78 WT/AB/WP/6, 16 August 2010.

79 WT/DS412/11 (Japan) (attached as Annex 2 to these Reports); WT/DS426/10 (European Union) (attached as Annex 3 to these Reports). On 12 February 2013, the European Union sent a letter to the Appellate Body Secretariat indicating that there was a "clerical mistake" in its Notice of Other Appeal, and requesting authorization to correct it. In accordance with Rule 18(5) of the Working Procedures, the Appellate Body Division hearing this appeal provided Canada, Japan, and the third parties with an opportunity to comment in writing on this request. No objections to the European Union's request were received. On 15 February, the Division authorized the correction to the European Union's Notice of Other Appeal, as requested in its letter of 12 February 2013.

80 Pursuant to Rules 22 and 23(4) of the Working Procedures.

81 Pursuant to Rule 24(1) of the Working Procedures.

82 In DS412 only.

Territory of Taiwan, Penghu, Kinmen and Matsu, and Turkey[83] each notified its intention to appear at the oral hearing as a third participant.[84] Also on 27 February 2013, Japan and the European Union each notified that it intended to appear at the oral hearing as a third participant in the dispute initiated by the other.[85]

1.27 On 12 February 2013, the Appellate Body received letters from Canada, Japan, and the European Union requesting the Appellate Body to allow observation by the public of the oral hearing in these appellate proceedings. Canada requested the Appellate Body to allow public observation of the oral statements and answers to questions of the participants, as well as those of third participants that agree to make their statements and responses to questions public. Canada proposed that public observation be permitted via simultaneous closed-circuit television broadcasting with the option for the transmission to be turned off should the participants find it necessary to discuss confidential information, or if a third participant had indicated its wish to keep its oral statement confidential. In its letter, Japan supported Canada's request, indicating that it also wished to make public its statements and answers to questions by the Appellate Body in the course of the hearing, and that it agreed with Canada's request that the Appellate Body hold an open hearing in this appeal. Japan further agreed that public observation be allowed by means of simultaneous closed-circuit video broadcasting. For its part, the European Union stated that it agreed and associated itself with Canada's request for an open hearing.

1.28 On 13 February 2013, the Appellate Body Division hearing this appeal invited the third parties to comment in writing on the requests of the participants to open the hearing to public observation. On 18 February 2013, the Division received responses from Australia, Brazil, China, El Salvador, India, Mexico, Norway, Saudi Arabia, Turkey, and the United States. In their respective comments, Brazil, China, El Salvador, India, Mexico, Saudi Arabia, and Turkey stated that they did not object to allowing public observation of the oral hearing in the present disputes. Brazil, China, India, Mexico, and Turkey emphasized that this was without prejudice to the systemic views each has on the issue of public observation of panel and Appellate Body hearings. Saudi Arabia stated that it did not object to allowing public observation of the oral hearing in these disputes. Australia, Norway, and the United States stated their support for the participants' request to allow public observation of the oral hearing. China, India, and Saudi Arabia indicated that they wished to maintain the confidentiality of their statements and responses to questions during the hearing.

1.29 On 19 February 2013, the Division issued a Procedural Ruling authorizing the requests of Canada, Japan, and the European Union to open the

---

[83] In DS426 only.

[84] Pursuant to Rule 24(2) of the Working Procedures.

[85] *Ibid.*

hearing to public observation and adopting additional procedures for the conduct of the hearing. The Procedural Ruling is attached as Annex 4 to these Reports.

1.30 On 7 and 12 March 2013, the Appellate Body received, respectively, unsolicited *amicus curiae* briefs from an energy company and an academic. The participants and third participants were given an opportunity to express their views on these briefs at the oral hearing. The Division did not find it necessary to rely on these *amicus curiae* briefs in rendering its decision.

1.31 The oral hearing in this appeal was held on 14-15 March 2013.[86] Public observation took place via simultaneous closed-circuit television broadcast to a separate room. Transmission was turned off during statements made by those third participants that had indicated their wish to maintain the confidentiality of their submissions. The participants and eight of the third participants (Australia, Brazil, China, India, Norway, Saudi Arabia, Turkey[87], and the United States) made opening statements.[88] The participants and third participants responded to questions posed by the Members of the Division hearing the appeal.

1.32 On 30 April 2013, Japan and the European Union requested the Appellate Body to issue two reports in one single document with separate sections containing findings and conclusions for each complainant.[89] On 1 May 2013, Canada was afforded an opportunity to comment on Japan's and the European Union's requests, and raised no objection.

[86] On 5 February 2013, the Appellate Body received a letter from Japan requesting that the oral hearing not be scheduled during the period 11-13 March 2013. Because the Working Schedule for Appeal drawn up by the Division provided for the oral hearing to be held on 14-15 March 2013, it was unnecessary for the Division to consider further Japan's request.

[87] Because Turkey was a third party in the Panel proceedings in DS426 only, it was requested to limit its statement to that dispute. Honduras was a third party in the Panel proceedings in DS412 only, and was therefore requested to limit its statement to that dispute. Honduras, however, did not make an oral statement.

[88] On 6 March 2013, Japan sent a letter to the Appellate Body Secretariat in which it indicated that the time-limit of 20 minutes allocated by the Division to Japan for the delivery of its oral statement was not sufficient for it to address the many points raised by Canada in its appellee's submission. The Division decided to grant an additional 5 minutes to Japan, as well as to Canada and to the European Union, for the delivery of their oral statements.

[89] In a letter dated 13 February 2013, Japan indicated that it agreed with the consolidation of the appellate proceedings in these two disputes, in which all third parties were invited to participate. However, Japan said it understood that the Division had invited all third parties in both disputes to participate in these consolidated appellate proceedings on the condition that, in their submissions and oral statements, the third participants would address only the issues appealed in the dispute(s) to which they were third parties in the Panel proceedings.

2. ARGUMENTS OF THE PARTICIPANTS AND THIRD PARTICIPANTS

2.1 Claims of error by Canada – Appellant

2.1.1 Article III:8(a) of the GATT 1994

2.1 Canada requests the Appellate Body to reverse the Panel's conclusion that the FIT Programme and related FIT and microFIT Contracts are inconsistent with Article III:4 of the GATT 1994 and Article 2.1 of the TRIMs Agreement, and to find instead that the FIT Programme and Contracts satisfy the prerequisites of Article III:8(a) and are therefore not subject to the obligations of Article III:4 of the GATT 1994 or Article 2.1 of the TRIMs Agreement.[90] Canada alleges that the Panel erred in finding that the measures at issue do not fall within the scope of Article III:8(a) of the GATT 1994 because the Government of Ontario's purchases of electricity generated from renewable sources under that programme are "with a view to commercial resale", and raises two allegations of error with respect to the Panel's interpretation of this phrase.

2.2 First, Canada asserts that the Panel erred in its interpretation of Article III:8(a) by focusing on whether there is "commercial resale" of electricity by the Government of Ontario while it neglected to interpret properly the term "with a view to" in Article III:8(a). Canada alleges that the Panel failed to examine the ordinary meaning of the words "with a view to" and thus failed to give effect to this term. Canada notes that the ordinary meaning of "with a view to" is "with the aim or object of attaining, effecting, or accomplishing something".[91] According to Canada, this ordinary meaning was never challenged by the complainants or the Panel. Thus, Canada asserts that a purchase "with a view to commercial resale" is a purchase with an aim to "commercial resale".

2.3 Furthermore, Canada argues that the Panel failed to take into account the term "governmental purposes" as immediate context for the phrase "not with a view to commercial resale". Canada refers to the Panel's statement that the phrase "and not with a view to commercial resale" serves specifically to inform and limit the otherwise relatively broad meaning of the term "governmental purposes", and argues that this phrase can only inform the meaning of the term "governmental purposes" if it is interpreted to require an "inquiry into the 'purpose' and 'view' behind the purchase".[92] Canada contends that, under the FIT Programme and Contracts, the Government of Ontario purchases electricity with a view "to help ensure a sufficient and reliable supply of electricity for

---

[90] Canada's appellant's submission, paras. 7, 8, and 83.

[91] Canada's appellant's submission, para. 34 (quoting Oxford English Dictionary online, <*http://www.oed.com/viewdictionaryentry/Entry/223303*>, p. 5, No. III.17.b).

[92] Canada's appellant's submission, para. 32.

Ontarians and to protect the environment"[93], and that it does not purchase electricity with a view to commercial resale.

2.4 Second, Canada alleges that the Panel misinterpreted the words "commercial resale" in Article III:8(a). Canada asserts that the Panel based its assessment solely on interpretations advanced by the parties rather than developing its own analysis. Canada further alleges that, in doing so, the Panel misstated the interpretations advanced by the parties. In particular, while the Panel initially properly acknowledged the complainants' position that the phrase "with a view to commercial resale" means "with a view to being sold or introduced into the stream of commerce, trade or market, regardless of any profit"[94], the Panel subsequently, in its application, focused on whether Hydro One Inc.[95] and "Local Distribution Companies" (LDCs or distributors) compete with retailers. The Panel also misstated Canada's interpretation of the term "commercial resale". While Canada explained that "commercial resale" means resale with an underlying intent to profit, the Panel incorrectly stated that Canada interpreted "commercial resale" as a resale for profit. Canada contends that, had the Panel properly interpreted this term, it would have concluded that "commercial resale" means resale with the underlying intent to profit.

2.5 For Canada, the interpretation of the word "commercial" by the Appellate Body in *US – Anti-Dumping and Countervailing Duties (China)* in the context of Article 14(b) of the SCM Agreement, the interpretation of the term "commercial scale" in Article 61 of the Agreement on Trade-Related Aspects of Intellectual Property Rights (TRIPS Agreement) by the panel in *China – Intellectual Property Rights*, and the interpretation of the term "commercial considerations" in Article XVII:1(b) of the GATT 1994 by the panel in *Canada – Wheat Exports and Grain Imports*, confirm that the meaning of "commercial resale" is a resale with the underlying intent to profit.[96] Canada contends that this meaning is also consistent with academic commentary, stating that, in the context of Article III:8(a), a resale is commercial if the activity is carried out as a profit-making activity, and not where only a nominal fee is charged.[97]

---

93 Canada's appellant's submission, para. 34.

94 Canada's appellant's submission, para. 37 (quoting Panel Reports, para. 7.146).

95 We note that Hydro One Inc. is wholly owned and controlled by the Government of Ontario and operates 97% of the transmission system in Ontario. (See Panel Reports, para. 7.34)

96 Canada's appellant's submission, paras. 40-44 (referring to Appellate Body Report, *US – Anti-Dumping and Countervailing Duties (China)*, paras. 465-490; and Panel Reports, *China – Intellectual Property Rights*, paras. 7.534, 7.535, 7.544, and 7.577; and *Canada – Wheat Exports and Grain Imports*, paras. 6.87-6.89, 6.96, 6.123, and 6.129).

97 Canada's appellant's submission, paras. 44 to 46 (referring to Canada's comments on the European Union's and Japan's responses to Panel questions (second set), para. 108, in turn referring to A. La Chimia and S. Arrowsmith, "Addressing Tied Aid: Towards a More Development-Oriented WTO?", *Journal of International Economic Law*, Vol. 12, No. 3 (2009) (Panel Exhibit CDA-129), p. 719); Canada's first written submission to the Panel (DS412), para. 90; and Canada's comments on the European Union's and Japan's responses to Panel questions (second set), para. 86, in turn referring

2.6 With respect to the FIT Programme and Contracts, Canada submits that there is no suggestion that the Government of Ontario purchases electricity with an aim to resell for profit. Rather, the Government of Ontario purchases electricity under the FIT Programme to help ensure a sufficient and reliable supply of electricity for Ontario consumers and to protect the environment. Canada further submits that the Electricity Act of 1998 prevents the OPA from doing anything with the aim to profit, because it stipulates that the business and affairs of the OPA shall be carried on without the purpose of gain.[98] Accordingly, Canada requests the Appellate Body to reverse the Panel's finding that the Government of Ontario purchases electricity under the FIT Programme "with a view to commercial resale" and to find instead that the Government of Ontario's purchases of electricity are not "with a view to commercial resale".

2.7 Finally, Canada requests the Appellate Body to complete the analysis under Article III:8(a) of the GATT 1994 with respect to the requirement of "not ... with a view to use in the production of goods for commercial sale"; to find that the Government of Ontario purchases electricity "not ... with a view to use in the production of goods for commercial sale"; and to reverse the Panel's conclusion that the FIT Programme and Contracts are inconsistent with Article III:4 of the GATT 1994 and Article 2.1 of the TRIMs Agreement. Canada asserts that the Government of Ontario is not using the electricity purchased by the OPA to make any goods, because the Government of Ontario does not make any goods. Moreover, regardless of what is done with the electricity purchased, the Government of Ontario does not purchase that electricity with the aim of producing goods to sell for profit. For Canada, the measures at issue satisfy all elements of Article III:8(a) and therefore fall within the scope of this Article. Consequently, they are not subject to the obligations of Article III of the GATT 1994 or the TRIMs Agreement.

2.8 In response to questioning at the oral hearing, Canada clarified its position regarding the interpretation of the term "governmental purposes" in Article III:8(a). For Canada, the context provided by the words "not with a view to commercial resale" suggests that the inquiry under "governmental purposes" needs to go beyond the stated aim of the government, and must include an assessment of whether a government has traditionally supplied a certain product, whether it has a constitutional mandate to do so, and it must take account of the role of government in a particular country, focusing on the history, constitution, and legislation of a particular government.

2.9 Furthermore, also in response to questioning at the oral hearing, Canada addressed the European Union's objection to Canada's request that the Appellate Body complete the analysis and reverse the Panel's conclusion that the FIT Programme and Contracts are inconsistent with Article III:4 of the

---

to S. Arrowsmith, "Government Procurement in the WTO", *Studies in Transnational Economic Law*, Vol. 16 (Kluwer Law International, 2002), p. 51 (Panel Exhibit CDA-128)).

[98] Canada's appellant's submission, para. 47 (referring Electricity Act of 1998, Section 25.2(2)).

GATT 1994 and Article 2.1 of the TRIMs Agreement, because Canada did not expressly request this in its Notice of Appeal. Canada argued that such requests relate to the "nature of the decision or ruling sought" and that, pursuant to Rule 22(2)(b)(iv) of the Working Procedures for Appellate Review, they must be included in the appellant's submission but not in the notice of appeal. Canada also argued that its Notice of Appeal and appellant's submission were provided to the European Union simultaneously, and that, when both documents are read together, the errors alleged and relief sought by Canada are clear.

2.1.2 Article 11 of the DSU – "Commercial resale"

2.10 Canada claims that the Panel failed to make an objective assessment of the matter before it, contrary to Article 11 of the DSU, when finding that the Government of Ontario purchases electricity under the FIT Programme "with a view to commercial resale" within the meaning of Article III:8(a) of the GATT 1994.

2.11 First, Canada asserts that the Panel failed to "consider evidence before it in its totality" or "'evaluate the relevance and probative force' of all the evidence" when it concluded that Hydro One Inc. and distributors compete with electricity retailers.[99] Canada explains that Hydro One, distributors, and retailers have very different roles in the Ontario electricity system and do not compete with each other. Hydro One and distributors provide the service of physical transmission and distribution of electricity. Conversely, retailers do not transmit or distribute electricity; rather, they sell a financial product – a hedge on electricity prices. Retailers enter into contracts with consumers for a fixed price for the HOEP portion of their electricity bill over a certain period.[100] Canada underscores that it explained to the Panel that "[r]etailers make their profits through their separate financial contracts with end-users" and "guarantee[] some price certainty".[101] Canada further observes that the Panel acknowledged that "retailers 'sell *contracts* to businesses and consumers'".[102] Thus, according to Canada, retailers have a different function from Hydro One and distributors.

---

[99] Canada's appellant's submission, para. 54 (quoting Appellate Body Reports, *US – COOL*, para. 299 (fn omitted)).

[100] Canada's appellant's submission, para. 50 (referring to the following two retailer websites: Canada Energy webpage, "Mid and Peak Tier Time-of-Use Rate Rises 8% on May 1", news article posting, *The Toronto Star*, 19 April 2012 (Panel Exhibit JPN-229), available at: *<http://www.canadaenergy.ca/>*, p. 2; and My Rate Energy Ontario, Canada webpage, "Price Protection for Electricity" (Panel Exhibit JPN-230), available at: *<http://myrateenergy.ca/electricity-info.php>*, p. 2).

[101] Canada's appellant's submission, para. 51 (quoting, respectively, Canada's opening statement at the second Panel meeting, para. 56; and comments on European Union's and Japan's responses to Panel questions (second set), para. 51).

[102] Canada's appellant's submission, para. 51 (quoting Panel Reports, para. 7.147, in turn quoting Government of Ontario, *Ontario's Long-Term Energy Plan* (Queen's Printer for Ontario, 2010) (Panel Exhibit CDA-6), Appendix One). (emphasis added by Canada)

2.12 In addition, Canada states that Hydro One and distributors continue to perform their services to a consumer regardless of whether that consumer chooses to enter into a contract with a retailer. Hydro One still transmits the electricity and distributors still distribute it to a consumer with a retailer contract.[103] The consumer is still billed by the distributor and must still pay a fee for the transmission (by Hydro One) and for the distribution (by the distributor) of the electricity.[104] Canada argues that, since consumers must still pay Hydro One and distributors for the transmission and delivery of electricity, regardless of whether a consumer chooses to enter a price-hedging contract with a retailer, the revenues of Hydro One and distributors are not affected by this choice. Consequently, Hydro One and distributors are indifferent as to whether a consumer enters into a contract with a retailer, and they do not compete with these retailers.

2.13 Second, Canada asserts that the evidence on which the Panel relied does not support its conclusion that Hydro One and distributors compete with retailers. Furthermore, Canada argues that the Panel failed to provide "'reasoned and adequate explanations and coherent reasoning' to support its findings".[105]

2.14 Canada identifies three exhibits on which the Panel allegedly based its conclusion about competition between, on the one hand, Hydro One and distributors and, on the other hand, retailers. Canada has reviewed each exhibit and observes that none mentions Hydro One. Moreover, while the exhibits mention distributors, none suggests that those distributors compete with retailers.

2.15 The first exhibit identified by Canada is Section 29 of the Electricity Act of 1998.[106] Canada notes that Section 29 merely states that distributors must sell electricity to a consumer in the event that a retailer with which a consumer has contracted is unable to do so. In Canada's view, this statement reinforces the role of distributors to ensure a stable supply of electricity and is inconsistent with the conclusion that distributors compete with retailers for business. Canada further notes that the only mention of competition in Section 29 is in paragraph 4, which addresses "competition *among retailers*".[107] This paragraph does not address competition between retailers and distributors.

---

[103] Canada's appellant's submission, para. 52 (referring to Electricity Act of 1998, Section 26(1): "A transmitter or distributor shall provide generators, retailers and consumers with non-discriminatory access to its transmission or distribution systems in Ontario in accordance with its licence"; and Section 29(1): "A distributor shall sell electricity to every person connected to the distributor's distribution system, except a person who advises the distributor in writing that the person does not wish to purchase electricity from the distributor"). Canada also refers to the Canada Energy website (Panel Exhibit JPN-229), *supra*, fn 100, p. 2.

[104] Panel Reports, para. 7.57.

[105] Canada's appellant's submission, para. 55 (quoting Appellate Body Reports, *US – COOL*, para. 299, in turn quoting, with approval, Appellate Body Report, *US – Upland Cotton (Article 21.5 – Brazil)*, fn 618 to para. 293).

[106] Panel Exhibit JPN-5.

[107] Canada's appellant's submission, para. 60. (emphasis added by Canada)

2.16 The second exhibit is the Ontario Energy Board (OEB) Retail Settlement Code[108], in particular Sections 1.1, 2.7, 10.1, and 12. Canada recognizes that Section 1.1 does refer to a "competitive retailer". However, Canada asserts that such retailer is not one that competes with distributors. Canada explains that the term "competitive retailer" is defined as "a person who retails electricity to consumers who do not take SSS"[109]; and "SSS", or "Standard Supply Service", is "the service approved by the [OEB] ... which ... establishes the minimum conditions that a distributor must meet in carrying out its obligations to sell electricity under section 29 of the *Electricity Act*."[110] Thus, Canada states that a "competitive retailer" is just a retailer – an entity that offers fixed prices for the HOEP portion of a consumer's electricity bill over a certain period of time (the length of the contract between the consumer and a retailer) instead of the regulated fluctuating prices. As regards Section 2.7, Canada points out that it requires distributors to enter into contracts with retailers when requested by the retailer. This undermines, rather than supports, a conclusion that distributors compete with retailers. Moreover, Canada notes that Section 10.1 identifies the service transaction requests to which the Retail Settlement Code applies. It underlines that consumers can choose to contract with a retailer and pay a fixed price for the HOEP portion of their electricity bill over a fixed period of time instead of paying the fluctuating price. Hence, it does not suggest that there is competition between distributors and retailers. Lastly, Canada refers to Section 12 as simply confirming the obligation of distributors to enter into contracts with retailers and as therefore inconsistent with the contention that they are competing.

2.17 The third exhibit identified by Canada is an extract from a page on the IESO's website.[111] According to Canada, this webpage merely confirms that, unlike distributors, retailers sell a price-hedging contract. In sum, Canada asserts that neither the IESO website, nor Sections 1.1, 2.7, 10.1, and 12 of the Retail Settlement Code, nor Section 29 of the Electricity Act of 1998, supports the Panel's statement that distributors compete with retailers. Canada thus considers that, in relying on these exhibits to support its conclusion, the Panel failed to make "an objective assessment of the facts", as required by Article 11 of the DSU, "by failing to 'ensure that its factual findings have a proper basis in [the] evidence'."[112]

2.18 Consequently, Canada asserts that the Panel erred when relying on the findings that Hydro One and distributors compete with retailers and that the

---

108 1 October 2011 revision (Panel Exhibit JPN-71).

109 Retail Settlement Code, Section 1.2, p. 7.

110 Retail Settlement Code, Section 1.2, p. 11.

111 IESO webpage, "Retail Contracts" (Panel Exhibit JPN-90), available at: <*http://www.ieso.ca/imoweb/siteshared/retailers.asp*>.

112 Canada's appellant's submission, para. 71 (quoting Appellate Body Report, *US – Tuna II (Mexico)*, para. 254 (fn omitted); and referring to Appellate Body Reports, *US – Carbon Steel*, para. 142; and *US – Wheat Gluten*, paras. 161 and 162).

Government of Ontario and the municipalities profit from the resale of electricity procured under the FIT Programme to conclude that there is a "commercial resale" of renewable electricity in Ontario.

2.19 Canada also challenges the Panel's finding that the Government of Ontario and municipal governments profit from the resale of electricity that is purchased under the FIT Programme. Canada explains that Hydro One's "core mandate is to ensure 'safe, reliable and cost-effective transmission and distribution of electricity to Ontario electricity users'"[113] and that "it must 'prioritize investments in transmission and distribution capacity to support projects necessary to maintain ongoing grid security and reliability'."[114] It is by maintaining this grid that Hydro One earns its revenue. The OEB, which regulates aspects of the Ontario electricity system[115], calculates the cost of maintaining the assets and adds a rate of return.[116] This sum is then recovered from consumers through the delivery component on their electricity bills.[117] Thus, Canada argues, Hydro One's profits are unrelated to the amount of electricity that it transmits to the distribution grid or to consumers.

2.20 Canada adds that distributors similarly profit from maintaining their assets. The OEB determines the cost of maintaining the distribution assets and then adds a rate of return.[118] This sum is also recovered from end-users through the delivery charges on their electricity bills. Hence, as in the case of Hydro One and the transmission of electricity, the revenues of distribution companies are unrelated to the amount of electricity that they deliver.[119]

2.21 Canada submits that, even if Hydro One and distributors were to profit from any resale of electricity, they do not profit from any resale of the electricity purchased under the FIT Programme. Hydro One and distributors are paid for maintaining their assets, regardless of the source of the electricity that is transmitted and distributed by those assets. Therefore, according to Canada, their revenues are unaffected by the FIT Programme and the Government of Ontario's purchase of renewable electricity under the Programme.

---

[113] Canada's appellant's submission, para. 74 (quoting Memorandum of Agreement between Her Majesty the Queen in Right of the Province of Ontario as Represented by the Minister of Energy and Hydro One Inc., 27 March 2008 (Memorandum of Agreement) (Panel Exhibit CDA-107), p. 1 (also quoted in Canada's response to Panel question No. 13(a) (second set), paras. 41 and 42)).

[114] Canada's appellant's submission, para. 74 (quoting Memorandum of Agreement, p. 2).

[115] Canada's appellant's submission, para. 74 (referring to Canada's first written submission to the Panel (DS412), para. 23).

[116] Canada's appellant's submission, para. 74 (referring to Canada's response to Panel question No. 15 (first set), para. 80; and OEB, EB-2009-0084, Report of the Board on the Cost of Capital for Ontario's Regulated Utilities, 11 December 2009 (Panel Exhibit CDA-64)).

[117] Panel Reports, para. 7.57.

[118] Canada's appellant's submission, para. 75 (referring to Canada's response to Panel question No. 15 (first set), para. 81).

[119] Canada's appellant's submission, para. 75 (referring to Canada's comments on the Interim Panel Reports, p. 3; and Panel Reports, para. 7.149).

2.22 For these reasons, Canada considers that, by finding that Hydro One and distributors profit from the resale of electricity purchased under the FIT Programme, the Panel failed to make "an objective assessment of the facts". Therefore, the Panel failed to comply with Article 11 of the DSU, by failing to "ensure that its factual findings have a proper basis in [the] evidence"[120], by failing to "consider evidence before it in its totality"[121], and by failing to "'evaluate the relevance and probative force' of all of the evidence".[122]

2.2 Arguments of Japan – Appellee

2.2.1 Article III:8(a) of the GATT 1994

2.23 Japan requests the Appellate Body to uphold, albeit under different reasoning, the Panel's finding that the FIT Programme and related FIT and microFIT Contracts involve procurement of electricity "with a view to commercial resale" within the meaning of Article III:8(a) of the GATT 1994. Japan contends that Canada's appeal will be rendered moot if the Appellate Body finds, pursuant to Japan's claims as other appellant, that the FIT Programme and Contracts are not "procurement by governmental agencies of products purchased for governmental purposes" under Article III:8(a). This is so because an assessment of the element "with a view to commercial resale" appealed by Canada presupposes an affirmative finding by the Appellate Body on the existence of "procurement" by the Government of Ontario "for governmental purposes". Japan submits that, therefore, the Appellate Body should, following the fundamental structure and logic of Article III:8(a), commence its analysis by addressing the claims raised by Japan relating to the existence of "procurement" by the Government of Ontario "for governmental purposes". If the Appellate Body were to agree with Japan either that the FIT Programme and Contracts do not involve "procurement by governmental agencies of products purchased" or that such purchases are not "for" governmental purposes, then Canada's entire appeal would be rendered moot.

2.24 In response to Canada's allegations of error, Japan disagrees, first, with Canada's interpretation of the words "with a view to" and, second, with its reading of "commercial resale". First, Japan argues that, under Canada's position that the phrase "with a view to commercial resale" requires intent to make a profit, a WTO Member could exclude from its obligations under Article III of the GATT 1994 any resale of goods previously purchased simply by stating that

---

[120] Canada's appellant's submission, para. 76 (quoting Appellate Body Report, *US – Tuna II (Mexico)*, para. 254 (fn omitted); and referring, in fn 109, to Appellate Body Reports, *US – Carbon Steel*, para. 142: "[N]or may panels make affirmative findings that lack a basis in the evidence contained in the panel record" (fn omitted); and *US – Wheat Gluten*, paras. 161 and 162).

[121] Canada's appellant's submission, para. 76 (quoting, as an example, Appellate Body Reports, *US – COOL*, para. 299).

[122] Canada's appellant's submission, para. 76 (quoting Appellate Body Reports, *US – COOL*, para. 299 (fn omitted)).

such resale was not aimed at generating returns or profit. Japan alleges that this approach would ignore the context of Article III because it would allow WTO Members to circumvent the national treatment obligation and thus render Article III:4 meaningless. Moreover, to the extent profit was earned, the Member could argue that it earned such profit from carrying out its assigned governmental purposes, and not from its commercial resale activity. This would give Members an unlimited ability to override the national treatment disciplines in Article III by simply asserting that the measures at issue were not undertaken with the aim to make profit.

2.25 Second, in response to Canada's contention that the Panel misinterpreted the term "commercial resale", Japan submits that the Panel correctly found that "commercial resale" need not necessarily involve profit. Japan asserts that, regardless of whether any profit is earned, the phrase "with a view to commercial resale" means that the product at issue is purchased with a view to being sold or introduced into the stream of commerce, trade, or market. Japan argues that WTO panels have found the term "commercial" to mean "engaged in commerce; of, pertaining to, or bearing on commerce"[123], and that nothing in this meaning entails a requirement of intent to profit. In response to Canada's reliance on the Appellate Body report in *US – Anti-Dumping and Countervailing Duties (China)*, Japan argues that the term "commercial" was considered in the context of the interpretation of the term "commercial loan" in Article 14(b) of the SCM Agreement, and that the context of the present case is very different. What makes the resale of electricity purchased by the Government of Ontario under the FIT Programme and Contracts "commercial" is the fact that this electricity is injected into the transmission grid, comingled with all the other electricity generated within Ontario, and delivered to consumers in Ontario. For Japan, the Panel's observation that "electricity purchased under the FIT Programme is consumed through precisely the same channels as electricity supplied from all other generating sources" is the critical fact that supports the conclusion that electricity is purchased by the Government of Ontario under the FIT Programme and Contracts "with a view to commercial resale".[124]

2.2.2 Article 11 of the DSU – "Commercial resale"

2.26 If the Appellate Body considers that competition with other entities is relevant for purposes of assessing whether a "commercial resale" exists, Japan submits that the Panel did not err in finding that Hydro One Inc. and distributors face private-sector competition in the Ontario electricity market.

---

[123] Japan's appellee's submission (DS412), para. 35 (referring to Panel Reports, *Canada – Wheat Exports and Grain Imports*, para. 6.84; and *China – Intellectual Property Rights*, para. 7.534; both, in turn, quoting *The New Shorter Oxford English Dictionary*, 4th edn, L. Brown (ed.) (Clarendon Press, 1993), Vol. 1, p. 451).

[124] Japan's appellee's submission (DS412), para. 35 (quoting Panel Reports, para. 7.147).

2.27 Japan argues that the fact that the Panel recognized and took into account that private-sector retailers "sell contracts"[125] does not detract from or make non-objective the Panel's conclusion that such retailers compete with Hydro One and distributors to sell electricity to consumers in Ontario. As the Panel stated in its review of the factual background, "[r]etail consumers either purchase electricity based on use from their LDCs, or they enter into contracts for electricity with an LDC or [a private-sector] licensed electricity retailer".[126] In other words, consumers in Ontario have a choice as from whom they purchase their electricity – either distributors or private-sector retailers. Thus, Japan asserts that distributors and private-sector retailers compete to sell electricity to consumers in Ontario.

2.28 Japan recalls the Panel's finding that four private companies own and operate 3% of the transmission system[127], and three out of 80 distributors are private companies.[128] Thus, Japan submits that Ontario has established an electricity system in which Hydro One and municipally owned distributors may compete with private transmission and distribution companies in the resale of electricity to consumers. The Panel recognized these facts in its evaluation of whether electricity is purchased under the FIT Programme "with a view to commercial resale".

2.29 Moreover, if the Appellate Body were to agree with Canada that the term "commercial resale" entails a profit element, Japan submits that the Panel correctly found that the Government of Ontario earns financial returns from its "resale" of electricity to consumers in Ontario, thereby making the "resale" a "commercial" one under Canada's own definition of the term. Japan observes that Canada's appeal simply repeats its previous argument that the OPA is intended to carry out its functions without the purpose of gain, which the Panel rejected when it noted that, "although the OPA does not profit from the resale of electricity through Hydro One and the LDCs, it is evident that the Government of Ontario and Ontario's municipal governments will profit from these operations".[129] Moreover, the Panel noted that this was a fact taken from Canada's own responses to the Panel's questions.[130] Japan points out that Canada itself agrees in its appeal with this aspect of the Panel's analysis, stating that "Hydro One profits" and that "[d]istributors also profit".[131]

---

125 Japan's appellee's submission (DS412), para. 37 (quoting Canada's appellant's submission, para. 51, in turn quoting Panel Reports, para. 7.147).

126 Japan's appellee's submission (DS412), para. 37 (quoting Panel Reports, para. 7.57).

127 Japan's appellee's submission (DS412), para. 38 (referring to Panel Reports, para. 7.34 and fn 104 thereto).

128 Japan's appellee's submission (DS412), para. 38 (referring to Panel Reports, para. 7.35).

129 Japan's appellee's submission (DS412), para. 40 (quoting Panel Reports, para. 7.150).

130 See Panel Reports, para. 7.149.

131 Japan's appellee's submission (DS412), para. 40 (quoting, respectively, Canada's appellant's submission, paras. 74 and 75).

2.30 Japan asserts that the evidence on the record also shows that Hydro One operates as a "commercial" company that makes "commercial profits", even though its only shareholder is the Government of Ontario. For example, Hydro One's financial report for 2010 (which was cited by the Panel) indicates that it had the following key financial results: (i) total revenue of Can$5,124 million; (ii) net revenue of Can$232 million; (iii) net income of Can$591 million; and (iv) dividend payment of Can$28 million to its shareholder, the Province of Ontario.[132] Any profits made by Hydro One, if not reinvested in the company, will eventually flow back to the government and, therefore, the Panel was correct to conclude that the Government of Ontario profits from the resale of renewable electricity.

2.31 Japan observes that, in its appeal, Canada attempts to exclude Hydro One and local distributors from its own definition of "commercial" by characterizing their profits, not as profits from their transmission or distribution activities (i.e. from the commercial resale of renewable electricity), but as profits derived from the "maintenance of their assets".[133] At the same time, however, Canada admits that such profits are earned through "delivery charges" on the electricity bills paid by consumers. Japan recalls that it primarily argues that these facts indicate that Hydro One does not "purchase" electricity "for governmental purposes". However, if the Appellate Body disagrees with Japan on this argument, it should logically find that those "delivery charges" are assessed on a per-kWh basis, and therefore are deemed to be inextricably linked to the amount of electricity delivered to and consumed by consumers. The sources cited by Canada also specify that these charges or rates are meant to allow distribution utilities to "recover their distribution costs"[134] (i.e. the cost of distributing electricity to consumers). Japan therefore considers that this cannot be reconciled with Canada's assertion that "Hydro One's and LDCs' 'profits do not depend on the amount of electricity that they transmit and distribute and, therefore, [that] they do not profit from any resale of electricity'."[135]

2.32 Therefore, Japan requests the Appellate Body to find that the Panel did not fail to make an objective assessment of the facts as required by Article 11 of the DSU by concluding that Hydro One and distributors face private-sector

---

[132] Japan's appellee's submission (DS412), para. 41 (quoting Hydro One, News Release, "Hydro One Releases 2010 Year-End Financial Results", 10 February 2011 (Panel Exhibit JPN-41), available at: <*http://www.hydroone.com/OurCompany/MediaCentre/Documents/NewsReleases2011/02_10_2011_Year-End_Financials.pdf*>).

[133] Japan's appellee's submission (DS412), para. 42 (referring to Canada's appellant's submission, paras. 74-76).

[134] Japan's appellee's submission (DS412), para. 42 (quoting Canada's appellant's submission, para. 20, in turn quoting OEB webpage, "Electricity Prices: ... OEB's Role in Electricity Prices" (Panel Exhibit CDA-16), available at: <*http://www.ontarioenergyboard.ca/OEB/Consumers/Electricity/Electricity+Prices#role*>).

[135] Japan's appellee's submission (DS412), para. 42 (quoting Canada's appellant's submission, para. 76).

competition, including from private-sector electricity retailers, in the resale of renewable electricity in Ontario and that the Government of Ontario profits from the resale of electricity allegedly purchased under the FIT Programme and FIT and microFIT Contracts.

2.3 Arguments of the European Union – Appellee

2.3.1 Article III:8(a) of the GATT 1994

2.33 The European Union requests the Appellate Body to uphold the Panel's finding that the FIT Programme and related FIT and microFIT Contracts involve procurement of electricity "with a view to commercial resale" within the meaning of Article III:8(a) of the GATT 1994. The European Union disagrees, first, with Canada's interpretation of the term "with a view to" and, second, with Canada's reading of "commercial resale". In addition, the European Union objects to Canada's request that the Appellate Body complete the analysis and reverse the Panel's conclusion that the FIT Programme and Contracts are inconsistent with Article III:4 of the GATT 1994 and Article 2.1 of the TRIMs Agreement.

2.34 First, in response to Canada's allegation that the Panel neglected to interpret properly the term "with a view to" in Article III:8(a), the European Union contends that the Panel's analysis demonstrates that the Panel interpreted the terms "commercial resale" and "not with a view to" together, and that the Panel's conclusion relates to purchases "with a view to commercial resale".[136] For the European Union, the Panel's description of the FIT Programme shows that the very purpose of the Programme is the delivery of a certain type of electricity into Ontario's electricity market. In particular, the FIT Programme and the OPA's operations thereunder are specifically intended to ensure that electricity from renewable sources is introduced into the electricity market in order to replace electricity from other generation sources.

2.35 The European Union agrees with the Panel's finding that the stated intention as to why the Government of Ontario purchases electricity could not be dispositive of the question whether such purchase was made "with a view to commercial resale", because this would be a purely subjective, and thus not appropriate, standard. Instead, the interpretation should be based on an objective standard focusing on the actual circumstances of each case. Governments may characterize any given transaction as responding to multiple policy objectives, but, in order to characterize a transaction as "with a view to commercial resale", it is sufficient to establish that the goods are intended for the market at the time of their purchase.

[136] European Union's appellee's submission (DS426), para. 21 (referring to Panel Reports, paras. 7.146 and 7.151).

2.36 Furthermore, the European Union disagrees with Canada's contention that the Panel based itself solely on interpretations advanced by the parties rather than developing a proper analysis of the term "with a view to". The Panel agreed with the interpretation suggested by the European Union while explicitly disagreeing with the interpretation proposed by Canada.[137] The European Union acknowledges that the Panel could have developed its reasoning in more detail; nonetheless, it is clear that the Panel did interpret the term "with a view to" in this case.

2.37 Second, the European Union disagrees with Canada's interpretation of the words "commercial resale". The European Union maintains that the clause "not with a view to commercial resale or with a view to use in the production of goods for commercial sale" in Article III:8(a) serves to avoid circumvention of the disciplines of Article III of the GATT 1994 by prohibiting governments to purchase on a discriminatory basis in cases where the purchased product will return to the market either directly or indirectly as an input into another product. The European Union contends that this objective, as well as the French and the Spanish versions of the text of Article III:8(a) – in particular the words *"revendus dans le commerce"* and *"reventa comercial"* – provide support for its proposition that the term "commercial resale" does not necessarily require that the product in question be resold for profit, but that it merely requires that the purchased product be sold or introduced into the market through the ordinary channels of commerce. The European Union adds that sales at a loss are no less commercial than sales for profit, and reselling a product at a price lower than the price at which it was purchased does not make the former transaction "non-commercial".

2.38 Furthermore, the European Union submits that the word "commercial" is used in Article III:8(a) in order to distinguish purchases made for government use from purchases made with a view to be further traded and introduced into commerce. The term "commercial" was not added to the provision in order to include an idea of "profit", but rather to highlight that Article III:8(a) would cover purchases for governmental purposes. Interpreting "commercial resale" as requiring a profit would permit WTO Members to circumvent the disciplines of Article III, because governments could discriminate against imported products and then introduce the purchased domestic product into the market thereby causing results that the national treatment principle is meant to avoid. With regard to Canada's references to the Appellate Body report in *US – Anti-Dumping and Countervailing Duties (China)*, the panel report in *China – Intellectual Property Rights*, and the panel report in *Canada – Wheat Exports and Grain Imports*, the European Union responds that those panel and Appellate Body reports did not interpret the word "commercial" in

[137] European Union's appellee's submission (DS426), para. 26 (referring to Panel Reports, paras. 7.148 and 7.151).

Article III:8(a), and that the same term can have different meanings depending on its specific context.

2.39 In addition, the European Union requests the Appellate Body to reject Canada's requests for completion of the analysis under Article III:8(a) of the GATT 1994 and reversal of the finding that the FIT Programme and Contracts violate Article 2.1 of the TRIMs Agreement and Article III:4 of the GATT 1994. The reason adduced by the European Union is that Canada's Notice of Appeal does not contain a request that the Appellate Body either reverse the Panel's finding that the FIT Programme and Contracts are inconsistent with Articles 2.1 of the TRIMs Agreement and Article III:4 of the GATT 1994 or that the Appellate Body complete the analysis with respect to the two elements "with a view to commercial resale" and "with a view to use in the production of goods for commercial sale" in Article III:8(a).

2.40 The European Union asserts that Canada's failure to include these requests in its Notice of Appeal means that such requests are outside the Appellate Body's jurisdiction. The European Union explains that Canada failed to provide a brief statement of the nature of the appeal, including a reference to paragraph 7.167 of the Panel Reports and paragraph 8.6 of the EU Panel Report, and that it also failed to include the nature of the decision or ruling sought with respect to those paragraphs, contrary to Rule 20(2)(d) of the Working Procedures for Appellate Review. The European Union further asserts that the Appellate Body should refrain from examining Canada's request for completion of the analysis under Article III:8(a), because it is not framed as a request to complete the analysis, but as an allegation of failure by the Panel to have made a particular finding.

2.41 In the event that the Appellate Body decides to complete the analysis pursuant to Canada's request, the European Union asserts that it should find that the Government of Ontario purchases electricity "with a view to use [it] in the production of goods for commercial resale" and that therefore the requirements of Article III:8(a) are not met. The European Union maintains that electricity purchased by the Government of Ontario is injected into the grid to be used by consumers in Ontario. Many of them are industrial consumers, who then also manufacture other products for sale on the market using this electricity. The European Union disagrees with Canada that the phrase "with a view to use in the production of goods for commercial sale" should be understood as referring to the actions of the government, rather than actions of other operators, because the terms of Article III:8(a) of the GATT 1994 do not refer to "use by the government" but rather to "use" without further qualification.

2.3.2 Article 11 of the DSU – "Commercial resale"

2.42 The European Union asserts that Canada's allegations that the Panel failed to make an objective assessment of the matter including the facts, as required by Article 11 of the DSU, when finding that (i) Hydro One Inc. and distributors compete with private retailers and (ii) Hydro One and distributors profit from any resale of renewable electricity are unfounded.

2.43 At the outset, the European Union observes that the Appellate Body would only have to examine Canada's claim under Article 11 of the DSU if, as a consequence of those errors, the Panel's ultimate finding that the Government of Ontario purchases electricity through the FIT Programme "with a view to commercial resale" cannot stand. The European Union considers that the Panel's finding is not dependent on any of the factual findings contested by Canada. The European Union notes, in this regard, that the Panel properly determined that "commercial resale" does not always necessarily involve profit. Under the same interpretation, the Appellate Body may consider it unnecessary to examine the second factual matter raised by Canada, namely, whether Hydro One and distributors profit from any resale of renewable electricity.

2.44 The European Union submits that the same conclusion can be reached regarding the first factual matter challenged by Canada, that is, the finding that Hydro One and distributors are in competition with retailers. The European Union points out that Canada does not contest the Panel's finding that electricity purchased under the FIT Programme is consumed through precisely the same channels as electricity supplied from all other generating sources. Likewise, Canada does not contest the Panel's finding that the Government of Ontario's purchases of electricity, through the FIT Programme, "may be considered to be a first step in the resale of electricity to retail consumers, and thereby the introduction of electricity into commerce".[138] The Panel agreed that the facts at issue (in particular the fact that the electricity purchased under the FIT Programme is consumed through the same channels as electricity supplied from all other generating sources and thus reintroduced into commerce) support the characterization of the measures at issue as undertaken "with a view to commercial resale", thereby not falling under Article III:8(a) of the GATT 1994. Consequently, the European Union argues that the Panel's ultimate finding was not dependent on the factual issues Canada challenges in its appeal.

2.45 Having said that, the European Union recalls that the Appellate Body has clarified that a panel is "entitled, in the exercise of its discretion, to determine that certain elements of evidence should be accorded more weight than other elements".[139] In doing so, the Appellate Body has further noted that a panel "is not required to discuss, in its report, each and every piece of evidence"[140], and that, "in view of the distinction between the respective roles of the Appellate Body and panels", the Appellate Body will not "interfere lightly" with

---

[138] European Union's appellee's submission (DS426), para. 44 (quoting Panel Reports, para. 7.148).

[139] European Union's appellee's submission (DS426), para. 45 (quoting Appellate Body Report, *EC – Asbestos*, para. 161).

[140] European Union's appellee's submission (DS426), para. 45 (quoting Appellate Body Report, *Brazil – Retreaded Tyres*, para. 202).

the panel's fact-finding authority[141] and "cannot base a finding of inconsistency under Article 11 simply on the conclusion that [it] might have reached a different factual finding from the one the panel reached".[142] Thus, the European Union underscores that not every error allegedly committed by a panel amounts to a violation of Article 11 of the DSU.

2.46 The European Union considers that the Panel properly concluded that, as a matter of fact, (i) Hydro One and distributors compete with private retailers and (ii) Hydro One and distributors profit from the resale of renewable electricity.

2.47 The European Union asserts that the Panel's factual finding that Hydro One and distributors compete with private retailers is well supported by the evidence on the record and, consequently, the Appellate Body should not interfere with the Panel's discretion as a trier of facts. First, contrary to what Canada alleges, private-sector licensed electricity retailers do not merely sell hedge-contracts, but also the electricity that comes with them. The European Union observes that, elsewhere, the Panel noted that there was "evidence suggesting that an electricity 'marketer' takes title to electricity (and therefore in our view possession), by virtue of purchasing electricity for resale from power generators and wholesalers".[143] Also, as noted by the IESO, retailers purchase electricity in the market and through contracts with generators. The OEB posts a list on its website of energy providers licensed to sell electricity in the province[144], and retail contracts are described as another way to purchase the electricity, but they do not cover other charges such as delivery charges.[145] Likewise, Canada itself recognized that "[c]ustomers that contract with competitive electricity retailers have wholesale electricity and related products and services purchased on their behalf by their electricity retailer and are subject to the rates set in their retail contracts".[146] This suggests that private-sector licensed electricity retailers do take title of the electricity they purchase from generators/distributors in order to resell it to final consumers. At any rate, there is resale of electricity (possibly bundled with electricity services) to final consumers.

---

[141] European Union's appellee's submission (DS426), para. 45 (quoting Appellate Body Reports, *US – Wheat Gluten*, para. 151; *EC – Sardines*, para. 299; and *US – Carbon Steel*, para. 142).

[142] European Union's appellee's submission (DS426), para. 45 (quoting Appellate Body Report, *US – Wheat Gluten*, para. 151).

[143] European Union's appellee's submission (DS426), para. 49 (quoting Panel Reports, fn 462 to para. 7.239).

[144] IESO webpage, "The Power System" (Panel Exhibit JPN-44), available at: <*http://www.ieso.ca/imoweb/siteShared/power_system.asp*>.

[145] IESO brochure, "What You Need to Know About Changes to Electricity Prices Coming November 1, 2009: A Guide For Ontario's Public Sector" (Panel Exhibit JPN-91).

[146] European Union's appellee's submission (DS426), para. 49 (quoting Professor William W. Hogan, Harvard University, "Overview of the Electricity System in the Province of Ontario", 21 December 2011 (Hogan Report) (Panel Exhibit CDA-2), p. 29).

2.48 Furthermore, the European Union explains that, in the background section of the Panel Reports, the Panel noted that retail consumers that do not fall under the "Regulated Price Plan" (RPP) may enter into a retail contract with a distributor or licensed electricity retailer, paying a contracted price for electricity for a fixed period.[147] Indeed, final consumers in Ontario can choose to pay the RPP of the OEB and purchase their electricity from distributors, or may decide to purchase it from private-sector licensed electricity retailers.[148] In other words, final consumers can choose whether to buy from distributors (and pay the fluctuating regulated prices under the RPP) or from private-sector licensed electricity retailers (and pay fixed hedged prices not dependent of the RPP for a particular period of time). The European Union thus asserts that, in this sense, private-sector licensed electricity retailers compete with Hydro One and other distributors in selling electricity and electricity services to consumers.

2.49 Consequently, the European Union argues that, as a matter of fact, private-sector licensed electricity retailers do not merely sell hedge-contracts to consumers. Indeed, retailers compete with Hydro One and distributors in selling electricity and electricity services to final consumers, who can choose between purchasing such electricity at the fluctuating regulated prices under the RPP or at fixed prices from retailers.

2.50 The European Union additionally asserts that the evidence cited by the Panel in footnote 297 of its Reports – that is, Section 29 of the Electricity Act of 1998[149], the Retail Settlement Code[150], and the IESO website page[151] – properly supports its finding that Hydro One and distributors sell electricity in competition with private-sector licensed retailers. Section 29 of Ontario's Electricity Act of 1998 contains the distributor's obligation to sell electricity. Contrary to what Canada alleges, Section 29 does not merely reinforce the role of distributors in ensuring a stable supply of electricity, but also shows that there is actual competition between distributors and private-sector licensed electricity retailers. In particular, Section 29 contemplates the possibility that a consumer does not purchase electricity from the distributor but from private-sector licensed electricity retailers, and yet imposes the obligation on the distributor to sell electricity to the final consumer in case the private-sector licensed electricity retailer is unable to do so for any reason. In other words, Section 29 reflects the fact mentioned before that consumers in Ontario can choose to purchase electricity and electricity services from distributors or from private-sector licensed electricity retailers.

---

[147] Panel Reports, para. 7.59.

[148] Panel Reports, para. 7.42.

[149] Panel Exhibit JPN-5.

[150] Panel Exhibit JPN-71.

[151] IESO webpage, "Retail Contracts" (Panel Exhibit JPN-90), available at: <*http://www.ieso.ca/imoweb/siteshared/retailers.asp*>.

2.51 The European Union adds that Sections 1.1, 2.7, 10.1, and 12 of the Retail Settlement Code, referred to by the Panel, equally support the Panel's conclusion as to the existence of competition between Hydro One and distributors, on the one hand, and private-sector licensed electricity retailers, on the other hand. In those sections, it is made clear that consumers in Ontario can choose between purchasing electricity and electricity services from distributors (under the SSS, and then be subject to the OEB's RPP) and purchasing electricity from private-sector licensed electricity retailers. In particular, Section 10 explains how to deal with consumer requests to switch from electricity supplied to a consumer through the SSS to electricity supplied by a competitive retailer. In this sense, it is evident that Hydro One and distributors compete with private retailers in order to sell electricity and provide electricity services.

2.52 Finally, the European Union states that the IESO website page, referred to by the Panel, explains that consumers in Ontario can also purchase their electricity from private-sector licensed electricity retailers, and provides detailed information as to when such an option could be attractive to final consumers.

2.53 In sum, the European Union considers that the evidence cited by the Panel in footnote 297 of its Reports adequately supports its factual finding that Hydro One and distributors sell electricity in competition with private-sector licensed electricity retailers. Thus, contrary to what Canada alleges, the Panel did not make an error.

2.54 As regards the Panel's second finding challenged by Canada under Article 11 of the DSU – that is, that the Government of Ontario profits from the resale of electricity – the European Union responds that the Panel rejected Canada's argument because "[d]istributors profit from their service of distributing electricity to the end-user, rather than any on-sale of the renewable electricity, itself".[152] According to the Panel, to the extent that the service of electricity distribution is necessarily tied to, and inseparable from, the sale of electricity as a "commodity", there was no basis to conclude that the resale activities of Hydro One and almost all of the distributors did not result in making profits. In other words, the Panel concluded that, as a matter of fact, it was not possible to distinguish between remuneration (and profits) generated by electricity distribution services (for which the maintenance of the grid is necessary) and the remuneration (and profits) generated by the sale of electricity itself (flowing through such grid). The European Union observes that Canada has not indicated any factual elements that the Panel would have disregarded or wilfully distorted and that would contradict the Panel's observations in this regard.

[152] European Union's appellee's submission (DS426), para. 59 (quoting Panel Reports, para. 7.150, in turn quoting Canada's opening statement at the second Panel meeting, para. 55).

2.55 Consequently, in the European Union's view, the Panel did not err in finding that Hydro One and distributors profit from the resale of electricity purchased by the Government of Ontario through the FIT Programme.

2.56 In view of the foregoing, the European Union submits that the Panel did not fail to make an objective assessment of the matter under Article 11 of the DSU, and properly concluded that (i) electricity is sold to consumers by Hydro One and distributors in competition with private retailers and that (ii) the Government of Ontario profits from the resale of renewable electricity. In any event, the European Union submits that these factual findings were not essential for the Panel's ultimate finding that the Government of Ontario's purchases of electricity through the FIT Programme are undertaken "with a view to commercial resale". Even if they were essential, the Panel provided adequate reasoning and supported its conclusion on the basis of the evidence on the record.

2.4 Claims of error by Japan – Other appellant

2.4.1 The order in which the Panel dealt with Japan's claims under the SCM Agreement and its claims under the TRIMs Agreement and the GATT 1994

2.57 Japan submits that the Panel improperly decided to commence its evaluation with Japan's claims under the TRIMs Agreement and the GATT 1994, instead of Japan's claims under the SCM Agreement.

2.58 Japan recognizes that, in *Chile – Price Band System*, the Appellate Body said that "arguments regarding the order of analysis chosen by the Panel [do not] amount to a separate 'allegation of error'".[153] However, it notes that the Appellate Body suggested in that dispute that an improper order of analysis may result in an improper appreciation by a panel of the factual and legal issues in a particular dispute.

2.59 Japan recalls that it had argued before the Panel that the evaluation should commence with Japan's claims under the SCM Agreement, because that Agreement "deals specifically, and in detail, with" the measures at issue in this dispute.[154] According to Japan, the reason why this is so is because the target of Japan's challenge in this dispute has been the provision of subsidies to FIT generators contingent on their use of renewable energy generation equipment produced in Ontario over such equipment imported from abroad.

2.60 Japan notes that the Panel dismissed Japan's argument because no party had contested that "the measures at issue are trade-related investment measures

---

[153] Japan's other appellant's submission (DS412), para. 10 (quoting Appellate Body Report, *Chile – Price Band System*, para. 182).

[154] Japan's other appellant's submission (DS412), para. 11 (quoting Appellate Body Report, *EC – Bananas III*, para. 204).

affecting imports of renewable energy generation equipment".[155] Thus, the Panel concluded that it is the TRIMs Agreement that "deals most directly, specifically and in detail, with"[156] the measures at issue. Japan fails to see how the fact that no party had contested that the measures at issue are TRIMs makes the TRIMs Agreement the agreement that "deals most directly, specifically and in detail, with" those measures. Rather, Japan submits that the Panel conducted no actual analysis of which agreement deals most specifically, and in detail, with the measures at issue. By failing to conduct such an analysis, the Panel therefore erred.

2.61 Japan points out that the Panel appeared to agree that the SCM Agreement deals most specifically with the measures at issue given that the Panel based the interpretation of government "purchases" in Article III:8(a) of the GATT 1994 on its finding on "the proper legal characterization of the measures at issue under Article 1 of the SCM Agreement".[157] Japan is thus "puzzled"[158] by the Panel's decision not to commence its evaluation with Japan's claims under the SCM Agreement, which would have led the Panel to a correct appreciation of the factual and legal issues in this dispute.

2.62 In addition, Japan argues that the Panel should have commenced with the SCM Agreement, because a remedy under Article 4.7 of that Agreement would resolve this dispute more promptly than the remedy under Article 19.1 of the DSU that would result from a violation of the GATT 1994 or the TRIMs Agreement. Pursuant to Article 3.7 of the DSU, the aim of dispute settlement is "to secure a positive solution to a dispute" and, moreover, Article 3.3 provides that the "prompt settlement" of disputes is "essential to the effective functioning of the WTO". In the present dispute, such "prompt settlement" would be achieved by a remedy under Article 4.7 of the SCM Agreement, which obliges the responding Member to act "without delay" and within a time period specified by the panel, which are not obligations pursuant to Article 19.1 of the DSU, which requires the respondent Member to bring into conformity measures found to be inconsistent.

2.63 For these reasons, Japan requests the Appellate Body to find that the Panel improperly began its evaluation with Japan's claims under the TRIMs Agreement and the GATT 1994. Further, Japan asserts that, instead of following the Panel's approach, the Appellate Body should begin its evaluation with Japan's claims under the SCM Agreement.

2.64 At the oral hearing, Japan acknowledged that it did not consider that the Panel had a legal obligation to commence its evaluation with the SCM Agreement. Japan also confirmed that it is not requesting the Appellate Body to find that the Panel erred, nor is it requesting reversal of a

155 Japan's other appellant's submission (DS412), para. 12 (quoting Panel Reports, para. 7.70).
156 Panel Reports, para. 7.70. (fn omitted)
157 Japan's other appellant's submission (DS412), para. 13 (quoting Panel Reports, para. 7.136).
158 Japan's other appellant's submission (DS412), para. 13.

finding of the Panel. Thus, Japan's sole request is that the Appellate Body itself commence the evaluation with its claims under the SCM Agreement.

2.4.2 Claims under Article III:8(a) of the GATT 1994

2.65 Japan requests the Appellate Body to uphold the Panel's conclusion that the FIT Programme and related FIT and microFIT Contracts are inconsistent with Article III:4 of the GATT 1994 and Article 2.1 of the TRIMs Agreement and to modify, reverse, or declare moot and of no legal effect several intermediate findings by the Panel.

2.4.2.1 The Panel's finding that the FIT Programme and Contracts involve "procurement by governmental agencies of products purchased"

2.66 Japan alleges that the Panel erred in finding that the Government of Ontario "purchases" electricity. Japan also alleges that the Panel erred in finding that the Government of Ontario "purchases" electricity in the context of Japan's claim relating to Article 1.1(a)(1)(iii) of the SCM Agreement. Japan maintains that, if the Appellate Body agrees with Japan's proposition in the context of its claim that the Panel erred in finding that the Government of Ontario "purchases" goods in the sense of Article 1.1(a)(1)(iii) of the SCM Agreement, then it must on the same grounds reverse the Panel's finding under Article III:8(a) of the GATT 1994 that the measures at issue involve "procurement by governmental agencies of products purchased for governmental purposes".

2.67 Japan argues that the structure of the energy system in Ontario – in particular the unbundling of generation, transmission, and distribution of electricity and the allocation of each of these functions together with corresponding regulatory functions to separate entities – suggests that the Government of Ontario does not engage in the physical supply or sale of electricity. In particular, Japan submits that the OPA serves as a financing entity to provide financial support to those generators the government desires to promote. In contrast, issues relating to the stable supply of electricity are addressed by other entities, but not through purchases of electricity by the government.[159] In addition, Japan argues that the fact that the government permits privately owned entities to take a role in the generation, transmission, and distribution of electricity supports the proposition that the Government of Ontario "need not"[160] purchase electricity in order to achieve a stable supply of electricity in the province of Ontario.

[159] Japan's other appellant's submission (DS412), paras. 167, 165, and 40.

[160] Japan's other appellant's submission (DS412), para. 41.

2.4.2.2 The Panel's interpretation of the word "for" in term "for governmental purposes"

2.68 In the event that the Appellate Body does not reverse the Panel's finding that the measures at issue involve "procurement by governmental agencies of products purchased", Japan appeals, conditionally, the Panel's interpretation and application of the term "purchased for governmental purposes", and requests the Appellate Body to complete the analysis and find that the FIT Programme and related FIT and microFIT Contracts do not involve "purchase[s] for governmental purposes". Japan alleges that the Panel failed to interpret the meaning of this phrase because it concluded merely that a purchase of goods by a governmental agency for governmental purposes could not at the same time constitute a government purchase of goods with a view to commercial resale, and applied the provision based on this assumption rather than on a proper interpretation of the term "for governmental purposes".

2.69 Japan contends that, by assuming that a purchase for "governmental purposes" could not at the same time amount to a government purchase of goods "with a view to commercial resale" under Article III:8(a), the Panel neglected to analyze whether purchases under the FIT Programme were made "for" governmental purposes. As a result, the Panel failed to analyze whether there was "a true and genuine connection between the 'purchase' ... and 'governmental purpose[]' at issue" and whether purchases of electricity were in fact made "truly and genuinely" in order to obtain or achieve the securing of a stable electricity supply from clean sources.[161]

2.70 Japan argues that electricity is "purchased for governmental purposes" only if the purchase is made "in order to obtain certain governmental purposes or with the objective of achieving such governmental purposes".[162] Japan refers to Canada's proposition that the governmental purpose behind the FIT Programme and Contracts is "to help secure the supply of adequate and reliable electricity in Ontario from clean sources".[163] Accordingly, Japan contends that, in order for the Government of Ontario's purchases of electricity under the FIT Programme to fall within the scope of Article III:8(a), the Panel would have had to find that those purchases were made truly and genuinely in order to obtain or achieve the securing of a stable electricity supply from clean energy sources. However, Japan argues that, within the framework of the Ontario electricity market, in which generation, transmission, and distribution of electricity are carried out by distinct governmental entities, the Government of Ontario does not have to purchase electricity in order to achieve a stable supply of electricity. For Japan, the purpose of securing a stable electricity supply itself does not require that a governmental entity generate, supply, or sell electricity to consumers. Moreover,

---

[161] Japan's other appellant's submission (DS412), paras. 171 and 174, respectively.

[162] Japan's other appellant's submission (DS412), para. 174.

[163] Japan's other appellant's submission (DS412), para. 174 (quoting Canada's first written submission to the Panel (DS412), para. 88).

Japan contends that the fact that Ontario allows the operation of privately owned entities to distribute electricity to consumers confirms that the Government of Ontario does not need to take possession of electricity in order to achieve its stated purpose of ensuring a stable supply of electricity to Ontario consumers.

2.71 Japan also refers to the Appellate Body reports in *Philippines – Distilled Spirits* and *Korea – Alcoholic Beverages* for the proposition that the object and purpose of the GATT 1994 as reflected in Article III is to "avoid[] protectionism, requiring equality of competitive conditions and protecting expectations of equal competitive relationships".[164] For Japan, an interpretation of Article III:8(a) in line with this object and purpose must ensure that the exclusion from the obligation of Article III for products purchased for governmental purposes is not so expansive that it allows WTO Members to avoid the obligations under Article III simply by assigning a "governmental purpose" to a particular measure. Japan contends that, therefore, Article III:8(a) must be interpreted to require that a government's purchase of products is made "truly and genuinely" in order to obtain or achieve a particular governmental purpose.[165]

2.72 Finally, Japan asserts that the domestic content requirements of the FIT Programme undermine the governmental purpose of securing electricity supply from clean sources, because these requirements have the effect of limiting generators' access to the best available technology from the global marketplace.

2.4.2.3 The Panel's interpretation and application of the term "with a view to commercial resale"

2.73 In the event that the Appellate Body rejects both Japan's appeal relating to the Panel's finding that the Government of Ontario "purchases" electricity and Japan's appeal that the measures at issue involve "purchase[s] for governmental purposes", Japan requests the Appellate Body to find that the Panel failed to interpret properly the term "commercial resale" by concluding that profit earned by the government as a result of the "resale" was relevant evidence of its "commercial" nature. In place of this erroneous conclusion, the Appellate Body should find that the phrase "with a view to commercial resale" means "with a view to being sold in the stream of commerce or trade"[166] and that, to the extent the FIT Programme and Contracts involve purchases of electricity by the Government of Ontario, such purchases are "with a view to commercial resale" because the electricity is purchased with a view to being sold or introduced into

164 Japan's other appellant's submission (DS412), para. 175 (quoting Appellate Body Reports, *Philippines – Distilled Spirits*, para. 221, in turn quoting Appellate Body Report, *Korea – Alcoholic Beverages*, para. 120).

165 Japan's other appellant's submission (DS412), para. 175.

166 Japan's other appellant's submission (DS412), para. 188. (emphasis omitted)

the stream of commerce, trade, or market, without regard to whether the government makes a profit from the resale.

2.74 Japan takes issue with the Panel's consideration of "profit" when it concluded that "the Government of Ontario purchases electricity under the FIT Programme 'with a view to commercial resale' based partly on the fact that 'the Government of Ontario and the municipal governments ... profit from the resale of electricity'."[167] Referring to dictionary definitions of the words "commercial" and "commerce", Japan contends that the definitions of these words do not include any element of profit. Furthermore, Japan refers to the panel reports in *Canada – Wheat Exports and Grain Imports* and *China – Intellectual Property Rights* in support of its proposition that the word "commercial" means "engaged in commerce; of, pertaining to, or bearing on commerce"[168] and that these definitions do not include an element of "profit".

2.75 In addition, Japan makes reference to the Appellate Body report in *Japan – Alcoholic Beverages II* for the proposition that the purpose of Article III of the GATT 1994 is to avoid protectionism in the application of internal tax and regulatory measures, and contends that an interpretation of "not with a view to commercial resale" as not aiming to resell for profit would allow Members to adopt protectionist measures contrary to the objective of Article III.[169] Under this interpretation, a Member that wished to exclude a particular foreign product from its domestic market could declare an aim to secure a stable supply of that product for the benefit of its consumers' welfare, establish a non-profit government agency to purchase quantities of that product subject to the requirement that the product be produced domestically, and then resell that product to consumers without earning profit from the resale.

2.4.3 The Panel's decision to exercise judicial economy with respect to Japan's "stand-alone" claim under Article III:4 of the GATT 1994

2.76 Japan submits that the Panel failed to make an objective assessment under Article 11 of the DSU and exercised false judicial economy by failing to examine separately Japan's claim that the FIT Programme and related FIT and microFIT Contracts are inconsistent with Article III:4 of the GATT 1994. Japan notes that the Panel found that the challenged measures are TRIMs falling within the scope of paragraph 1(a) of the Illustrative List in the Annex to the TRIMs Agreement, and are therefore inconsistent with the national treatment

[167] Japan's other appellant's submission (DS412), para. 184 (quoting Panel Reports, para. 7.151).

[168] Japan's other appellant's submission (DS412), para. 186 (quoting Panel Reports, *Canada – Wheat Exports and Grain Imports*, para. 6.84; and *China – Intellectual Property Rights*, para. 7.534; both, in turn, quoting *The New Shorter Oxford English Dictionary*, Lesley Brown (ed.) (Clarendon Press, 1993), Vol. 1, p. 451).

[169] Japan's other appellant's submission (DS412), para. 187 (referring to Appellate Body Report, *Japan – Alcoholic Beverages II*, p. 16, DSR 1996:I, p. 109).

obligation of Article III:4 of the GATT 1994. Having made this finding, the Panel declined Japan's request to undertake a separate analysis of the elements of Article III:4. Japan argues that the Panel's exercise of judicial economy was improper and contrary to the Panel's duty under Article 11 of the DSU in two respects.

2.77 First, Japan asserts that the Panel was not entitled to exercise judicial economy, because a separate finding under Article III:4 of the GATT 1994 was required for securing the prompt settlement of this dispute in accordance with Article 3.3 of the DSU, in the case that the Appellate Body were to disagree with the Panel's characterization of the FIT Programme and Contracts as TRIMs, or as TRIMs falling within the scope of paragraph 1(a) of the Illustrative List.

2.78 Second, Japan points out that the terms of paragraph 1(a) of the Illustrative List of the TRIMs Agreement and Article III:4 of the GATT 1994 are different, such that the Panel did not examine Japan's primary claim that the incentive to use domestic parts and components in preference to imported ones resulting from the domestic content requirements of the FIT Programme and Contracts provides less favourable treatment to imported products than that accorded to domestic like products, which is inconsistent with Article III:4. Japan explains that the Panel analyzed whether, in all situations, the operation of the Minimum Required Domestic Content Levels under the FIT Programme and Contracts require that at least some Ontario-sourced goods must be used, and concluded that such a requirement does indeed exist.[170] While Japan agrees with this conclusion, it notes that the standard under Article III:4 is different and, in fact, broader.7 Japan submits, in this regard, that the incentive to use domestic supplies resulting from a domestic content requirement that may be satisfied by using goods or services, as it exists under the FIT Programme and Contracts, is sufficient to meet the broader "less favourable treatment" standard of Article III:4. According to Japan, the Panel's failure to reach a conclusion under Article III:4 affects the implementation that may be required, and thus may "provide only a partial resolution of the matter at issue".[171]

2.79 Japan requests the Appellate Body to complete the analysis and reach the finding under Article III:4 that the Panel erroneously failed to make. To assist the Appellate Body in reaching a separate finding under Article III:4, Japan briefly reviews the arguments it put forward during the Panel proceedings, while noting that Canada did not contest that, should Article III:8(a) of the GATT 1994 not apply, the FIT Programme and Contracts are inconsistent with Canada's obligations under Article III:4.

2.80 As regards whether renewable energy generation equipment manufactured domestically in Ontario and imported from Japan are "like

[170] Japan's other appellant's submission (DS412), para. 149 (referring to Panel Reports, paras. 7.158-7.163).

[171] Japan's other appellant's submission (DS412), para. 143 (quoting Appellate Body Report, *US – Tuna II (Mexico)*, para. 403).

products", Japan argues that these products are in a directly competitive relationship in the market. Japan submits that there is no substantial difference between such domestic and imported equipment in terms of their physical properties, end-uses, consumer perceptions, and tariff classifications – i.e. they share all four categories of "characteristics" identified by the Appellate Body as relevant in an analysis of "likeness".[172]

2.81 Next, Japan submits that the domestic content rules of the FIT Programme and Contracts are "requirements". Japan explains that a renewable energy generator that wishes to obtain the subsidized rates offered by the FIT Programme voluntarily accepts, through the application for and execution of a FIT or microFIT Contract, the obligation to comply with a variety of conditions, including the Minimum Required Domestic Content Level relevant to its solar PV (FIT and microFIT) or wind (FIT) project.

2.82 Japan further asserts that the domestic content requirements of the FIT Programme and Contracts "affect[]" the "internal" "sale", "purchase", or "use" of renewable energy generation equipment.[173] This is because the domestic content requirements incentivize Ontario-based wind and solar PV energy generators to choose renewable energy generation equipment manufactured in Ontario over such equipment produced abroad. These requirements thereby modify the conditions of competition in favour of such goods made in Ontario and have "an effect on"[174] the sale, purchase, or use of those goods in Ontario.

2.83 Finally, Japan argues that the domestic content requirements of the FIT Programme and Contracts accord less favourable treatment to imported renewable energy generation equipment than that accorded to like products of Ontario origin. Japan observes that the focus of this analysis is on whether the FIT Programme and Contracts modify the conditions of competition in the relevant market to the detriment of imported products.[175] It then explains that, by requiring the use of goods or services of Ontario origin in order to obtain above-market electricity rates, the FIT Programme necessarily creates incentives, or a purchasing preference, among Ontario-based wind and solar PV electricity generators to use renewable energy generation equipment produced in Ontario, which in turn stimulates domestic production of such equipment. The "Domestic Content Grids" require that any such generator use at least some Ontario-origin goods to achieve the Minimum Required Domestic Content Levels, thereby confirming the preference for locally produced goods over goods of foreign

---

[172] See Appellate Body Report, *EC – Asbestos*, paras. 99 and 101.

[173] Japan's other appellant's submission (DS412), para. 147.

[174] Japan's other appellant's submission (DS412), para. 147 (referring to Panel Reports, *Turkey – Rice*, paras. 7.221 and 7.222; and *Canada – Autos*, para. 10.80; and Appellate Body Report, *Canada – Autos*, para. 158).

[175] Japan's other appellant's submission (DS412), para. 148 (referring to Appellate Body Report, *Korea – Various Measures on Beef*, para. 135; and Panel Reports, *Turkey – Rice*, para. 7.232; and *China – Publications and Audiovisual Products*, para. 7.1532).

origin. Japan notes that the Panel itself concurred on this latter point in its analysis under paragraph 1(a) of the Illustrative List of the TRIMs Agreement.[176]

2.84 Therefore, Japan requests the Appellate Body to find that the Panel's exercise of judicial economy with respect to Japan's claim under Article III:4 of the GATT 1994 was improper and contrary to Article 11 of the DSU. Japan additionally requests the Appellate Body to complete the analysis and find that, because the FIT Programme and Contracts impose domestic content requirements on wind and solar PV electricity generators that affect the internal sale, purchase, or use of renewable energy generation equipment, resulting in less favourable treatment to like products of Japanese origin, they are inconsistent with Article III:4 of the GATT 1994, independent of any conclusion under the TRIMs Agreement.

2.85 At the oral hearing, Japan clarified how Canada's implementation obligations could be different if the Panel had made a finding of violation under Japan's "stand-alone" claim under Article III:4. According to Japan, Canada could lower the FIT Programme's domestic content requirements to a point where such requirements could be met exclusively through the use of local services. Japan was of the view that such a situation would not be addressed by the Panel's finding under Article III:4 and the TRIMs Agreement, but that such situation would have been covered had the Panel made a "stand-alone" finding under Article III:4 of the GATT 1994.

2.4.4 Claims under the SCM Agreement

2.4.4.1 Article 1.1(a) – "Financial contribution" or "income or price support"

2.86 Japan argues that the Panel erred in its interpretation and application of Article 1.1(a) of the SCM Agreement in characterizing the FIT Programme and related FIT and microFIT Contracts as government "purchases [of] goods". Japan does not dispute the Panel's findings that: (i) the OPA pays for "delivered electricity"; (ii) the Government of Ontario (through its agent Hydro One Inc., which operates 97% of the transmission lines in Ontario) takes possession of the electricity during its transmission to end-consumers; and (iii) Ontario laws, regulations, and contracts characterize the challenged measures as "procurements" or "purchases [of] electricity".[177] However, Japan submits that the Panel failed to determine the proper legal characterization of the challenged measures on the basis of an evaluation of their most principal and relevant characteristics. To identify and elucidate the true nature or principal characteristics of a measure, a panel must fully appreciate all relevant facts and surrounding circumstances, which may include whether and to what extent such

---

176 Japan's other appellant's submission (DS412), para. 148 (referring to Panel Reports, para. 7.163).

177 Japan's other appellant's submission (DS412), paras. 30 and 31.

measure would serve to achieve a stated policy goal. In particular, Japan claims that the Panel overlooked the Government of Ontario's policy decision to unbundle the generation, transmission, and distribution of electricity to achieve its goal of ensuring a stable supply of electricity in Ontario, as well as the design and operation of the FIT Programme and Contracts within the framework of the Ontario electricity market. Japan adds that neither the OPA nor the Government of Ontario makes payments for electricity generated under the FIT Programme for the government's own consumption or for use in providing public services to Ontario residents.

2.87 Japan argues that the measures at issue are not appropriately characterized as government "purchases [of] goods" for three reasons. First, the OPA serves as a financing entity, instead of a purchasing entity, because it never takes possession of electricity. Hydro One, a different governmental entity, is the one receiving the delivered electricity. Second, the Government of Ontario's goals regarding its electricity system are addressed through the roles allocated to the different entities in the Ontario electricity system and programmes and not through purchases of electricity by the government. In this regard, the promotion of environmentally friendly generation is achieved through financing provided under the Renewable Energy Standard Offer Program (RESOP) and the FIT Programme. Third, the fact that the Government of Ontario permits privately owned entities to carry out the role of supplying electricity to consumers in Ontario reveals that the Government of Ontario need not take possession over (i.e. purchase) electricity in order to achieve its objective of ensuring the stable supply of electricity to Ontario consumers.

2.88 Japan contends that the measures at issue are properly characterized as "direct transfer[s] of funds" and "potential direct transfers of funds" under Article 1.1(a)(1)(i) of the SCM Agreement. In the first place, Japan elaborates that the measures constitute "direct transfer[s] of funds" because the OPA collects the "Contract Payments" it owes under FIT and microFIT Contracts from consumers through the "Global Adjustment" (GA) and distributes them to FIT generators. In the second place, Japan specifies that the measures are "potential direct transfers of funds" since FIT generators are entitled to guaranteed payments for delivered electricity for the entire duration of a FIT or microFIT Contract. In the alternative, Japan argues that the FIT Programme and Contracts may also be characterized as "income or price support" under Article 1.1(a)(2) of the SCM Agreement because the Government of Ontario contributes to the prices and income enjoyed by FIT generators and incentivizes the domestic production of equipment used to produce energy from FIT generators.

2.89 Consequently, Japan argues that the Panel committed legal error under Article 1.1(a) of the SCM Agreement in determining that the appropriate legal characterization of the FIT Programme and Contracts was as government "purchases [of] goods" under Article 1.1(a)(1)(iii). Japan requests the Appellate Body to reverse the Panel's finding and that it conclude instead that the FIT Programme and Contracts are appropriately characterized as "a government practice [that] involves a direct transfer of funds ... [or] potential direct transfers of funds" or "any form of income or price support".[178] In the alternative, if the Appellate Body agrees with the Panel that these measures are properly characterized as "purchases [of] goods", Japan requests the Appellate Body to modify the Panel's finding in this regard to find that these measures may be characterized in addition as "direct transfer[s] of funds", "potential direct transfers of funds", or "income or price support" under Article 1.1(a) of the SCM Agreement.

2.90 Furthermore, Japan argues that, in rejecting the complainants' arguments that the measures at issue may also be characterized as "direct transfer[s] of funds" or "potential direct transfers of funds", the Panel in effect found subparagraphs (i) and (iii) of Article 1.1(a)(1) of the SCM Agreement to be mutually exclusive. In Japan's view, this finding derives from the Panel's observation that: "[w]e see no way of reading Articles 1.1(a)(1)(i) and (iii) in a way that enables us to conclude that government 'purchases [of] goods' could also be legally characterized as 'direct transfer[s] of funds'".[179] Japan asserts that nothing precludes a panel from determining that a measure may be characterized in multiple ways under Article 1.1(a)(1) of the SCM Agreement, as long as the panel's findings are based on a proper understanding of the measure's relevant characteristics and an objective assessment of the facts. Japan alleges that this conclusion follows from the Appellate Body report in *US – Large Civil Aircraft (2nd complaint)*, where the Appellate Body stated that "Article 1.1(a)(1) ... does not explicitly spell out the intended relationship between the constituent subparagraphs" and that the structure of this provision "does not expressly preclude that a *transaction* could be covered by more than one subparagraph".[180] Japan argues that, despite these findings by the Appellate Body, the Panel's finding in this dispute amounts to a conclusion that Article 1.1(a)(1) does expressly preclude government "purchases [of] goods" from also being characterized as "direct transfer[s] of funds" or "potential direct transfers of funds".

2.91 Moreover, Japan rejects the Panel's reliance on the principle of effective treaty interpretation for precluding the possibility that government "purchases [of] goods" could also be characterized as "direct transfer[s] of funds" or "potential direct transfers of funds". In Japan's view, the Panel itself recognized that "there exist distinct situations where a purchase of goods may not also be a direct transfer of funds, namely the situation where the payment for the purchase is not monetary in nature."[181] Japan further contends that the principle of

---

[178] Japan's other appellant's submission (DS412), para. 48.

[179] Japan's other appellant's submission (DS412), para. 49 (quoting Panel Reports, para. 7.246).

[180] Japan's other appellant's submission (DS412), para. 50 (quoting, respectively, Appellate Body Report, *US – Large Civil Aircraft (2nd complaint)*, para. 613 and fn 1287 thereto). (emphasis added by Japan)

[181] Japan's other appellant's submission (DS412), para. 53 (referring to Panel Reports, para. 7.246).

effective treaty interpretation does not preclude the use of treaty text in a confirmatory manner. Indeed, had the drafters omitted the term "purchases goods" from Article 1.1(a)(1)(iii), "it would have left open the possibility for some Members to argue that the omission of 'purchases [of] goods', particularly in an exhaustive list such as Article 1.1(a)(1), should be interpreted to mean that government transfers of funds in exchange for the receipt of goods should *not* be considered financial contributions."[182]

2.92 According to Japan, the Panel's finding that it could not conclude that government "purchases [of] goods" could also be legally characterized as "direct transfer[s] of funds" is a legal error, and Japan requests the Appellate Body to declare it moot and of no legal effect. Thus, Japan requests the Appellate Body to find that the FIT Programme and Contracts may be characterized as "direct transfer[s] of funds" or "potential direct transfers of funds", regardless of whether they may also be characterized as government "purchases [of] goods".

2.93 Finally, Japan argues that the Panel improperly exercised judicial economy with respect to Japan's claim that the FIT Programme and Contracts constitute "income or price support" under Article 1.1(a)(2) of the SCM Agreement, and thereby failed to make an objective assessment of the matter as required by Article 11 of the DSU. In particular, Japan argues that the Panel's exercise of judicial economy was improper because it failed to explain why its findings (i.e. reasoning and conclusion) with respect to Japan's benefit argument in connection with its "financial contribution" claims are exactly applicable to Japan's benefit argument in connection with its "income or price support" claim. Japan requests the Appellate Body to find that the challenged measures may be characterized as "income or price support", and to find that a benefit exists with respect to this characterization of the FIT Programme and FIT and microFIT Contracts.

2.4.4.2 Article 1.1(b) – "Benefit"

2.94 Japan claims on appeal that the Panel erred in its interpretation and application of Article 1.1(b) of the SCM Agreement, and failed to make an objective assessment as required by Article 11 of the DSU, in finding that the complainants did not establish an appropriate benchmark or counterfactual against which to assess "benefit", and in dismissing various benchmarks proposed by Japan and a further alternative described by the Panel.

2.95 Japan asserts that the Panel concluded that various proposed alternatives were not appropriate benchmarks because the relevant market "must be 'a market where there is effective competition' in which prices are 'established through the operation of unconstrained forces of supply and demand, and not by means of government intervention'"[183] and that certain objectives – namely, securing a

---

[182] Japan's other appellant's submission (DS412), para. 54. (original emphasis; fn omitted)

[183] Japan's other appellant's submission (DS412), para. 65 (quoting Panel Reports, para. 7.275).

reliable electricity system and pursuing health and environmental objectives – could only be achieved in a market with "government intervention", which, in turn, makes competitive markets unsuitable for use as a benchmark. Japan contends that, in addition to being an erroneous interpretation and application of Article 1.1(b), this results in a prejudiced (i.e. non-objective) examination of the issue of benefit, which is inconsistent with Article 11 of the DSU.

2.96 Japan considers that the proper counterfactual is simply one that reflects a situation "but for" the policy in question. For Japan, the history of the Ontario electricity market and the design, structure, and operation of the FIT Programme allow for only one conclusion: the FIT Programme allows wind and solar PV electricity generators to operate in the Ontario market that would otherwise not do so. This alone constitutes a benefit. Japan states that the Panel majority failed to address why this was not so.

2.97 For Japan, whether or not the measures are contributing to certain policy goals should have no relevance in determining the appropriate benchmark. Japan considers that, as suggested by the dissenting member of the Panel, a subsidy may allow a government to achieve certain policy goals that would not be achieved under market conditions prevailing in the absence of that subsidy. Japan notes that "governments regularly use subsidies or other forms of benefits in order to achieve outcomes that 'the market' alone cannot fulfil."[184] Japan agrees with the dissenting opinion that the necessity of the measures at issue for producers to operate at all confirms the fact that such measures constitute a benefit under prevailing market conditions. Japan argues that the Panel majority's approach would leave unregulated subsidies granted to achieve a governmental purpose, thus creating a "large .loophole"[185] in the SCM Agreement. Japan also notes that obligations such as the prohibition against subsidies contingent on the use of local goods in Article 3 of the SCM Agreement do not limit Members in their ability to provide subsidies for environmental or health purposes.

2.98 Japan asserts that in finding that no benefit had been established, solely in the light of the guidelines set by Article 14(d) of the SCM Agreement, the Panel erroneously focused on the degree or amount of benefit, rather than on the existence of a benefit. Japan notes that Article 14(d) does not preclude a finding of the existence of a benefit, but provides a particular methodology for calculating the amount of benefit that Members must specify in their own domestic law for the purpose of the imposition of countervailing duty measures. According to Japan, the Panel majority appeared to recognize the limits of Article 14(d) and that there may be more than one way to demonstrate the existence of a benefit.[186] Japan considers that, even relying on the framework of

[184] Japan's other appellant's submission (DS412), para. 84.

[185] Japan's other appellant's submission (DS412), para. 72.

[186] Japan's other appellant's submission (DS412), para. 99 (referring to Panel Reports, paras. 7.271 and 7.272).

Article 14(d), a comparison of the FIT rates with the weighted-average wholesale rate or the RPP commodity charge would itself establish the existence of a benefit.

2.99 Japan argues that the Panel failed to appreciate the significant difference between what non-renewable energy producers expect to receive and what FIT producers receive. For example, Japan contends that FIT producers currently receive two to eleven times higher rates than the weighted-average wholesale rate. In Japan's view, the magnitude of the difference between the rates received by FIT and non-FIT producers leaves no doubt as to the existence of a benefit. According to Japan, there is no reason to believe that in a less-regulated, "competitive" market, the non-FIT rates would be anywhere close to the FIT rates.

2.100 Additionally, Japan claims that, after improperly deciding to rely exclusively on the framework of Article 14(d) of the SCM Agreement, the Panel chose an improper market benchmark. Japan contends that this resulted in a prejudiced examination of the issue of benefit, inconsistent with Article 1.1(b) of the SCM Agreement and Article 11 of the DSU.

2.101 First, Japan submits that the proper counterfactual or market benchmark would be Ontario's current electricity market except for wind and solar PV FIT producers, as these "would not exist" absent the FIT Programme.[187] Japan submits that the Panel's rejection of this possible benchmark as distorted by government regulation is based on an incorrect understanding of the Appellate Body's finding in *US – Softwood Lumber IV*. In that dispute, Japan notes, the main question was about the size of a benefit, not its existence. Japan observes that, to measure the size of a benefit, it clearly matters if the market price with which the current price is compared is itself influenced by government policies. To show the existence of a benefit, however, it is sufficient that the alternative sales price is lower than the current price. Japan considers that the comparison would be "circular" only if the market price were distorted solely because of the FIT Programme or any other government intervention targeted at FIT generators. In Japan's view, that is "clearly not the case" in this dispute.[188]

2.102 Turning to the Panel majority's alternative benchmark, Japan argues that such a benchmark would also require that a subsidy had been granted. Japan contends that the Panel majority's "erroneous view of the appropriate benchmark" led it to suggest an alternative approach to benefit based on "an artificial market for wind and solar PV energy", that is, one in which commercial distributors would act under a government-imposed obligation to acquire electricity from generators operating solar PV and windpower plants.[189] While

[187] Japan's other appellant's submission (DS412), para. 104.

[188] Japan's other appellant's submission (DS412), para. 104 (quoting and referring to Appellate Body Report, *US – Softwood Lumber IV*, para. 93).

[189] Japan's other appellant's submission (DS412), para. 108.

Japan considers that this methodology would nevertheless lead to the conclusion that a benefit exists, Japan objects to the use of such an artificial market. In Japan's view, this simply replaces the current government intervention with another: an obligation for commercial distributors to purchase wind- and solar PV-generated electricity.

2.103 Japan also argues that there is no textual basis in Article 1.1(b) for the consideration of environmental protection in a benefit analysis. Japan states that there is no legal basis in the SCM Agreement to justify an otherwise prohibited subsidy under Article 3.1 on grounds such as environmental protection, which, according to Japan, "is understandable because domestic content requirements are irrelevant for purposes such as protection of the environment or promotion of human health".[190] Japan clarifies that it has "no objection whatsoever to Canada promoting renewable energy, which can be a crucial tool to reduce greenhouse gas and other emissions", but that "the promotion of renewable energy must be consistent with Members' WTO obligations."[191] Japan considers that the Panel majority's consideration of environmental protection in its assessment of the appropriate benchmark was a legal error under Article 1.1(b) of the SCM Agreement.

2.104 Moreover, according to Japan, the Panel's approach is essentially based on costs, and erroneously ignores the demand-side of the electricity market. Japan contends that the Panel majority erroneously ignored the "market reality" that "demand does not necessarily exist for every good or service at a price higher than, or even equal to, its *cost*."[192] Japan considers that, under this approach, commercial distributors would have to pay a price that covers generators' production costs plus a reasonable rate of return, but the Panel majority ignored whether the demand-side in Ontario would actually support a price that fully covers these costs. In Japan's view, no rational consumer would in fact ever buy electricity at prices above the costs of solar PV and wind energy producers. Japan further argues that a "cost-based" interpretation of "benefit" "would subvert the central idea of how subsidies are regulated in the SCM Agreement and lead to absurd results".[193]

2.105 Japan also notes that the Panel's alternative counterfactual approach relies on artificially created separate markets, in contradiction to its own finding regarding the existence of only one market for electricity in Ontario. Japan considers this contradiction to amount to a breach of Article 11 of the DSU.

2.106 Finally, Japan submits that the Panel made contradictory findings under the SCM Agreement and the TRIMs Agreement. On the one hand, the Panel stated that mere participation in the FIT Programme may be viewed as an "advantage" within the meaning of the Illustrative List of the

[190] Japan's other appellant's submission (DS412), para. 107.

[191] *Ibid.*

[192] Japan's other appellant's submission (DS412), para. 109. (original emphasis)

[193] Japan's other appellant's submission (DS412), para. 113.

TRIMs Agreement.[194] On the other hand, it did not find that participation in the FIT Programme alone would ensure economically viable operations and constitute a "benefit" for the purposes of the SCM Agreement. Japan submits that this contradiction evidences that the Panel majority failed to make an objective assessment of the facts under Article 11 of the DSU.

2.4.4.3 Article 11 of the DSU – "Benefit"

2.107 Japan presents an additional conditional appeal under Article 11 of the DSU in the event that the Appellate Body rejects its principal benefit argument under Article 1.1(b) of the SCM Agreement. Japan requests the Appellate Body to find that the Panel failed to make an objective assessment under Article 11 of the DSU when it concluded that it could not resolve the question of benefit under its suggested alternative approach to the issue.[195]

2.108 Although Japan considers that the Panel majority's alternative benchmark is flawed because it effectively results in a benefit analysis based on costs, Japan submits that the Panel could have found the existence of benefit by conducting an analysis under its proposed alternative benchmark. In this respect, Japan contends that the Panel record does contain sufficient evidence for the Panel to have completed its proposed analysis. Japan argues that the Panel determined that, under the terms of the FIT and microFIT Contracts, solar PV and wind projects will receive a steady stream of income over a 20-year period, provided that the Government of Ontario does not default on the payments required under the Contracts. Japan submits that the "principal risk"[196] under which FIT generators operate is the sovereign risk of default by the Government of Ontario, which would allow a comparison with the Ontario Government long-term bond yield. While the Panel recognized that the pre-tax rate of return on equity used to develop the FIT Price Schedule in 2009 was 15.8%, it failed to compare the 15.8% with the Ontario Government long-term bond yield that was 4.25% in 2009.[197]

2.109 Japan observes that, instead, the Panel's analysis focused on a comparison of the target rates of return for FIT generators and Ontario's regulated utilities (base-load nuclear and hydro facilities). Japan submits that, even under this analysis, the Panel should have found a benefit to exist. First, Japan notes that the Panel stated that the rate of return on other regulated utilities "could be as high as 12.96%", which Japan notes is "below OPA's 15.8% pre-tax target rate

[194] Japan's other appellant's submission (DS412), para. 117.

[195] Japan's other appellant's submission (DS412), para. 119 (referring to panel Reports, paras. 7.322-7.327).

[196] Japan's other appellant's submission (DS412), para. 122.

[197] Japan's other appellant's submission (DS412), para. 123 (referring to Panel Reports, paras. 7.325 and 7.326 and fns 636 and 641 thereto).

of return" of FIT generators.[198] Second, "the 12.96% figure is based on the *most extreme* estimate of an appropriate risk premium for electricity utilities".[199] Japan considers that 9.75% – the OEB's calculation of an average risk premium for all energy generation technologies – would be the appropriate benchmark. Japan notes that this is even lower than the OPA's 11% after-tax rate of return on equity for FIT generators.[200] Third, Japan objects to the Panel's conclusion that a comparison of rates of return for wind and solar PV electricity generators with Ontario's regulated electricity utilities "is not appropriate because of the 'major technical differences' between the operations".[201] Japan submits that the Panel found that: solar PV and windpower facilities "resemble base-load generation"[202]; Ontario's regulated utilities have a higher risk than wind and solar PV FIT projects because they do not receive government-backed guaranteed prices for 20 years; and the regulated utilities receive lower rates of return than wind and solar PV FIT projects. For Japan, the existence of a benefit in this case is undeniable. In Japan's view, the Panel's failure to conclude that a benefit exists under its alternative approach constitutes a failure by the Panel to make an objective assessment of the matter as required by Article 11 of the DSU.[203] Japan requests the Appellate Body to complete the analysis if it rejects Japan's main benefit argument under Article 1.1(b) of the SCM Agreement.

2.110 Should the Appellate Body find that the challenged measures constitute subsidies within the meaning of Article 1.1 of the SCM Agreement, Japan requests the Appellate Body to complete the analysis and find that the challenged measures are inconsistent with Articles 3.1(b) and 3.2 of the SCM Agreement.

2.111 Japan states that Canada has never disputed that, if the FIT Programme and Contracts are "subsidies", they are inconsistent with Articles 3.1(b) and 3.2. Nonetheless, Japan recalls its arguments before the Panel that, as the challenged measures are prohibited subsidies under Article 3 of the SCM Agreement, they are "deemed to be specific" pursuant to Article 2.3 of the SCM Agreement. Japan submits that the FIT subsidies are "contingent ... upon the use of domestic over imported goods", both in law and in fact, because they are conditional or dependent upon satisfying the domestic content requirements of the

[198] Japan's other appellant's submission (DS412), para. 124 (referring to Panel Reports, para. 7.326 and fn 641 thereto).

[199] Japan's other appellant's submission (DS412), para. 124. (original emphasis)

[200] Japan's other appellant's submission (DS412), para. 124 (referring to OEB, EB-2009-0084, Report on the Cost of Capital for Ontario's Regulated Utilities (Panel Exhibit CDA-64), Table 1, p. 38).

[201] Japan's other appellant's submission (DS412), para. 124 (quoting Panel Reports, para. 7.326).

[202] Japan's other appellant's submission (DS412), para. 124 (quoting Panel Reports, para. 7.19).

[203] Japan's other appellant's submission (DS412), para. 124 (referring to Panel Reports, paras. 7.19 and 7.326 and fn 641 thereto; and OEB, EB-2009-0084, Report of the Board on the Cost of Capital for Ontario's Regulated Utilities, 11 December 2009 (Panel Exhibit CDA-64), Table 1, p. 38).

FIT Programme (specifically, the Minimum Required Domestic Content Levels).[204]

2.5 *Claims of error by the European Union – Other appellant*

2.5.1 *The relationship between the TRIMs Agreement and Article III:4 of the GATT 1994*

2.112 The European Union submits that the Panel erred in the interpretation and application of Articles 2.1 and 2.2 of the TRIMs Agreement, read in conjunction with paragraph 1(a) of the Illustrative List in the Annex to the TRIMs Agreement, when finding that these provisions do not preclude the application of Article III:8(a) of the GATT 1994 to the challenged measures.

2.113 The European Union considers that the GATT 1994 and the TRIMs Agreement must be read harmoniously and in a holistic manner in order to give meaning and effect to all of their provisions. As the Panel noted[205], Article III:8 of the GATT 1994 is a "scope" provision. Article III:8(a) excludes certain measures adopted by governments from the national treatment obligation contained in Article III of the GATT 1994. In other words, measures falling under Article III:8(a) can never be said to be inconsistent with any part of Article III (including Article III:4), because Article III does not apply to such measures.

2.114 According to the European Union, the characterization of Article III:8(a) of the GATT 1994 as a "scope" provision has significant consequences when examining the text of Article 2 of the TRIMs Agreement. In this regard, the European Union draws a contrast between the text of Article 2.1 and Article 2.2 of the TRIMs Agreement. Article 2.1 refers to Article III of the GATT 1994, and in doing so includes Article III "as a whole".[206] For its part, Article 2.2 of the TRIMs Agreement sets out an illustrative list of measures that are necessarily inconsistent with Article III:4 of the GATT 1994. Article 2.2 of the TRIMs Agreement does not refer to Article III of the GATT 1994 "as a whole", nor does it qualify in any way the plain language "are inconsistent with" (e.g. it does not say "inconsistent with the terms of Article III:4"). The European Union understands this difference in language to mean that the Panel's reasoning holds only in relation to TRIMs other than the specific measures defined through the Illustrative List. For those measures that fall within the scope of the Illustrative List, the question whether they could escape a violation through the applicability of Article III:8(a) of the GATT 1994 no longer presents itself because the

---

[204] Japan notes that this is expressly stated in, *inter alia*, the Green Energy and Green Economy Act of 2009, the Minister's 2009 FIT Direction, and every version of the FIT and microFIT Rules and FIT and microFIT Contracts. (Japan's other appellant's submission (DS412), paras. 128-130)

[205] Panel Reports, fn 263 to para. 7.113.

[206] European Union's other appellant's submission (DS426), para. 31 (referring to Panel Report, *Indonesia – Autos*, para. 14.61).

TRIMs Agreement has conclusively settled the issue. In the European Union's view, paragraph 1 of the Illustrative List contains the understanding of Members that the type of measures listed therein would under no circumstances escape a violation under Article III:4 of the GATT 1994 and Article 2.1 of the TRIMs Agreement.

2.115 The European Union alleges that the Panel's interpretation "alters the nature and function"[207] of Articles 2.1 and 2.2 and the Illustrative List of the TRIMs Agreement. This is because the Panel's approach largely nullifies the effects of Article 2.2 and the Illustrative List in relation to the general obligation in Article 2.1. The European Union explains that Article 2.2 and the Illustrative List aim at introducing detail and specificity to the general obligation in Article 2.1. Being more specific and precise, Article 2.2 and the Illustrative List inform the application of Article 2.1 (and not the other way around, as contended by the Panel). By contrast, the European Union observes that its proposed interpretation is not "inconsistent with the clear terms of Article 2.1"[208], because the application of a specific rule, aimed at identifying explicitly a subset of measures that are inconsistent with Article III of the GATT 1994 (in particular, in relation to the fourth paragraph of Article III), is not contradictory in any way to the nature of Article 2.1 of the TRIMs Agreement as a horizontal obligation that applies to all TRIMs.

2.116 In addition, the European Union asserts that the Panel's interpretation "ignores" the object and purpose of the TRIMs Agreement, which is "to 'elaborate' 'further' or 'additional' provisions to the already existing ones".[209] The European Union notes that, if Article 2.2 and the Illustrative List were to be read "as merely stating the obvious"[210] – that is, that the types of measures listed in the Annex discriminate against imported goods – with no other implications, they would largely be redundant.

2.117 In sum, the European Union argues that a proper interpretation of Articles 2.1 and 2.2, read in conjunction with paragraph 1(a) of the Illustrative List, should lead to the conclusion that the TRIMs listed in the Annex to the TRIMs Agreement are inconsistent with Article III:4 of the GATT 1994. In those cases, Article III:8(a) of the GATT 1994 does not apply.

2.118 Based on the foregoing, the European Union submits that the Panel wrongly interpreted and applied Articles 2.1 and 2.2, read in conjunction with paragraph 1(a) of the Illustrative List in the Annex to the TRIMs Agreement, when finding that these provisions do not preclude the application of Article III:8(a) of the GATT 1994 to the challenged measures. Accordingly, the European Union requests the Appellate Body to reverse that Panel finding.

---

207 European Union's other appellant's submission (DS426), para. 33.

208 Panel Reports, para. 7.119.

209 European Union's other appellant's submission (DS426), para. 35. (fn omitted)

210 European Union's other appellant's submission (DS426), para. 35.

2.119 The European Union additionally requests the Appellate Body to complete the analysis and correctly apply the legal interpretation set out above to the Panel's factual findings and uncontested facts on the record. The European Union asserts that the measures at issue in the present dispute match exactly the description set out in paragraph 1(a) of the Illustrative List, namely, that these are measures "compliance with which is necessary to obtain an advantage, and which require ... the purchase of or use by an enterprise of products of domestic origin or from any domestic source".[211] The European Union observes that the Panel reached the same conclusion. Consequently, the European Union requests the Appellate Body to find that Article III:8(a) of the GATT 1994 is not applicable in the present case. Furthermore, as a consequence of this finding, the European Union requests the Appellate Body to uphold, although modifying the reasoning, the Panel's ultimate finding that the challenged measures are TRIMs falling within the scope of paragraph 1(a) of the Illustrative List, and that, in the light of Article 2.2 and the *chapeau* to paragraph 1(a) of the Illustrative List in the Annex to the TRIMs Agreement, they are inconsistent with Article III:4 of the GATT 1994, and thereby also inconsistent with Article 2.1 of the TRIMs Agreement.

2.5.2 Claims under Article III:8(a) of the GATT 1994

2.120 The European Union requests the Appellate Body to uphold the Panel's conclusion that the FIT Programme and related FIT and microFIT Contracts are inconsistent with Article III:4 of the GATT 1994 and Article 2.1 of the TRIMs Agreement, but also to modify, reverse, or declare moot and of no legal effect several intermediate findings by the Panel.

2.5.2.1 The Panel's finding that the domestic content requirements "govern" procurement of electricity

2.121 The European Union requests the Appellate Body to reverse the Panel's finding that the domestic content requirements with respect to windpower and solar PV generation equipment under the FIT and microFIT Contracts "govern" the alleged procurement of electricity for the purpose of Article III:8(a) of the GATT 1994. The European Union alleges that the Panel erred in the interpretation and application of Article III:8(a) in making this finding. The European Union further requests the Appellate Body to complete the analysis and to find instead that the domestic content requirements do not "govern" procurement of electricity. For the European Union, the Panel failed properly to consider the link between the words "procurement" and "products purchased". In the European Union's view, "laws, regulations or requirements" in the sense of

---

[211] European Union's other appellant's submission (DS426), para. 38 (referring to European Union's first written submission to the Panel (DS426), paras. 148-153).

Article III:8(a) must be related to the subject matter of the procurement – that is, the "products purchased for governmental purposes" – in order to "govern" such procurement. Article III:8(a) does not cover requirements or conditions that are not connected with "intrinsic characteristics" or the nature of the product purchased.[212] Otherwise, Article III:8(a) would allow discriminatory requirements extending far beyond the actual object of the procurement at stake and affecting broad areas of economic activity, thereby circumventing the objective of Article III of the GATT 1994.

2.122 The European Union contends that the domestic content requirements of the measures at issue are not covered by Article III:8(a) because they relate to generation equipment, a product that is different and "completely disconnected" from the product purchased by the government, which is electricity.[213] The European Union alleges that the Panel erred in finding that there is a close relationship between the domestic content requirements and the electricity purchased by the government because the domestic content requirements relate to "the very same equipment that is needed and used" to produce the energy purchased by the government and because compliance with the domestic content requirements is a "necessary prerequisite" for the alleged procurement of electricity by the Government of Ontario.[214] The Panel ignored that domestic content requirements imposed in relation to generation equipment have nothing to do with the intrinsic characteristics or the nature of the final products.

2.123 In its opening statement at the oral hearing, the European Union submitted that not every condition relating to procurement automatically falls under the terms of Article III:8(a) of the GATT 1994. The European Union argued that rules governing procurement activity, such as rules imposing deadlines or thresholds, or determining the type of procedure to follow in the context of a bidding process, are covered by Article III:8(a). In addition, conditions regulating the product and its characteristics, such as "technical specifications", are also covered. However, the European Union argues that conditions exogenous to the subject matter of the contract, such as the requirements relating to the origin of equipment used to generate electricity procured under the FIT Programme, do not fall under Article III:8(a) because they have "no rational link" with the attributes of the electricity procured.[215] In response to questioning at the oral hearing, the European Union responded to Canada's argument based on Article XVI of the Agreement on Government Procurement (GPA) that, because the signatories to the GPA are all bound by the obligations in the GATT, they would not have needed to prohibit domestic content requirements on inputs into products that are purchased by governments

[212] European Union's other appellant's submission (DS426), para. 51.

[213] European Union's other appellant's submission (DS426), para. 53.

[214] European Union's other appellant's submission (DS426), para. 56 (quoting Panel Reports, para. 7.127).

[215] European Union's other appellant's submission (DS426), para. 53.

if those requirements fall outside the scope of Article III:8(a) and therefore are, in any event, prohibited by Article III:4 of the GATT 1994. The European Union responded that Canada's reference to "inputs" is inapposite, because the FIT Programme and related Contracts do not involve inputs incorporated into the final product (electricity). Instead, the domestic content requirements at issue relate to equipment and components used to generate electricity. The European Union added that the scope of Article III:8(a) of the GATT 1994 and Article XVI of the GPA are different, because the latter provision covers not only goods and suppliers, but also services, and because it extends beyond the issue of domestic content.

2.5.2.2 The Panel's interpretation of the term "governmental purposes"

2.124 The European Union requests the Appellate Body to reverse or to declare moot and of no legal effect the Panel's statement that the term "governmental purposes" in Article III:8(a) may be read to encompass any government purchase "for a stated aim of the government".[216] In the event that the Appellate Body, in response to Canada's appeal, reverses the Panel's finding that the Government of Ontario's purchases of electricity under the FIT Programme are undertaken "with a view to commercial resale", the European Union requests the Appellate Body to reverse or modify the Panel's reasoning as to the meaning of "governmental purposes", to complete the analysis, and to find that the Government of Ontario's procurement of electricity under the FIT Programme is not undertaken for "governmental purposes".[217]

2.125 The European Union maintains that the term "purchased for governmental purposes" in Article III:8(a) refers only to "government purchases of goods that are needed to sustain the work and functions of the government".[218] Thus, they will have to "be actually used or consumed by the government in the context of its administrative tasks or in the context of the exercise of its public functions".[219] The European Union notes that the word "purposes" in the English version of Article III:8(a) corresponds to the word "*necesidades*" and "*besoins*" in the Spanish and French versions of the covered agreements. The meanings of these terms are not entirely identical and, therefore, in order to interpret the provision in a manner honouring Article 33(3) of the Vienna Convention on the Law of Treaties[220] (Vienna Convention), Article III:8(a) of the GATT 1994 must be understood as referring to purchases for "purposes" or "needs" of the government, or for purchases of goods that will

---

[216] European Union's other appellant's submission (DS426), para. 60 (quoting Panel Reports, para. 7.138 (fn omitted)).

[217] European Union's other appellant's submission (DS426), para. 61.

[218] European Union's other appellant's submission (DS426), para. 60.

[219] *Ibid.*.

[220] Done at Vienna, 23 May 1969, UN Treaty Series, Vol. 1155, p. 331.

be used by a government for its own consumption or used in the performance of its functions.[221]

2.126 For the European Union, the decisive factor is whether or not the purchased goods will be utilized in some way by the government. The word "purposes" in Article III:8(a) should be understood as referring to a situation in which different government bodies and structures would be unable to perform their functions without the actual use of the good purchased. Such purposes or needs may include government purchases of goods in order to be able to provide government services to citizens. The European Union contends that the functions a government typically performs are delimited by its own constitutional powers. Different governments may have different purposes or needs depending on the different roles that governments may play in different societies. While the scope of the governmental functions covered under Article III:8(a) should not be defined in the abstract, it may be useful to consider typical governmental functions in the Member concerned. The European Union submits that the Appellate Body took a similar approach in *US – Anti-Dumping and Countervailing Duties (China)* with respect to the question of whether an entity is vested with governmental authority in interpreting Article 1.1(a)(1) of the SCM Agreement.[222]

2.127 The purposes or needs of the government cannot include purchases aimed at complying with any stated public policy objective, regardless of whether the goods will be used by the government, because otherwise government purchases aimed at "protecting local producers against imports" as a stated policy would escape the national treatment obligation in Article III of the GATT 1994.[223] The European Union contends that Article XVII:2 of the GATT 1994 provides relevant context and that the negotiating history suggests that Article III:8(a) and Article XVII:2 should be interpreted in a harmonious manner, in the sense that the terms "for governmental purposes" and "government needs" are coterminous with the phrase "products for immediate or ultimate consumption in governmental use".[224]

2.128 Finally, in the event that the Appellate Body reverses the Panel's finding that the Government of Ontario's purchases of electricity under the FIT Programme are "with a view to commercial resale" as requested by Canada, the European Union requests the Appellate Body to complete the analysis and find that the Government of Ontario's purchases of electricity under the FIT Programme are not undertaken "for governmental purposes". In this regard, the European Union argues that the Government of Ontario's purchases of electricity are not undertaken "for governmental purposes" because the

---

[221] European Union's other appellant's submission (DS426), paras. 74 and 75.

[222] European Union's other appellant's submission (DS426), para. 77 (referring to Appellate Body Report, *US – Anti-Dumping and Countervailing Duties (China)*, para. 297).

[223] European Union's other appellant's submission (DS426), para. 80.

[224] European Union's other appellant's submission (DS426), para. 85.

electricity is not used by the Government of Ontario. If the electricity purchased by the government is not used for its own consumption, or in the performance of governmental functions such as the provision of public services, such purchases do not fall under Article III:8(a) of the GATT 1994. The European Union contends that the creation of an electricity system with a stable, reliable, and sufficient supply of electricity from renewable sources is a legitimate policy objective, but it is not in itself a provision of a public service.

2.5.3 Claims under the SCM Agreement

2.129 The European Union did not appeal the Panel's finding that the challenged measures amount to government "purchases [of] goods" within the meaning of Article 1.1(a)(1)(iii) of the SCM Agreement.

2.5.3.1 Article 1.1(b) – "Benefit"

2.130 The European Union claims that the Panel erred in applying Article 1.1(b) of the SCM Agreement. In particular, the European Union calls into question the Panel's analysis of whether there was a "benefit" relative to a market benchmark. The European Union requests the Appellate Body to reverse the Panel's findings that the European Union failed to establish the existence of a benefit and to declare moot and of no legal effect the Panel's findings and observations in paragraphs 7.276-7.327 of the Panel Reports. The European Union also requests that the Appellate Body complete the analysis to find that, as the FIT generators would not obtain remuneration on the market absent the FIT Programme, the challenged measures confer a benefit under Article 1.1(b) of the SCM Agreement. The European Union submits that, as the Panel's findings of benefit are in error, so too is the Panel's ultimate conclusion that the European Union failed to establish that the FIT Programme and Contracts constitute subsidies or envisage the granting of subsidies inconsistent with Articles 3.1(b) and 3.2 of the SCM Agreement. The European Union requests the Appellate Body to reverse the Panel's finding and to complete the analysis to find that the challenged measures amount to subsidies prohibited under Articles 3.1(b) and 3.2 of the SCM Agreement, and to recommend that Canada withdraw its prohibited subsidies without delay, as required by Article 4.7 of the SCM Agreement.

2.131 The European Union takes issue with the Panel's finding that the European Union could not establish whether the remuneration provided to FIT generators was "adequate" in relation to a "market standard" – that is, a competitive wholesale market for electricity. The Panel found that the actual prices found in Ontario could not be used as a relevant market benchmark as they were distorted by government intervention. Thus, a hypothetical "market" counterfactual based on a competitive wholesale market for electricity could not be used either as it would not achieve the government objectives established in Ontario.[225] The European Union submits that the Panel wrongly engaged in examining market counterfactuals in order to make a comparison to determine the adequacy of remuneration where, in reality, the determination of benefit was much simpler.

2.132 According to the European Union, the Panel ignored the actual "prevailing market conditions" in Ontario that already showed that, absent the FIT Programme, the remuneration provided by the FIT Programme to FIT generators was not, and could not be, available. The European Union contends that the "mere justification for the existence" of the FIT Programme "manifestly showed" that such government incentives were necessary in a marketplace like Ontario where the supply of electricity generated from windpower and solar PV technologies cannot be achieved by market forces alone and thus necessitates government support.[226] Thus, according to the European Union, the Panel wrongly found that the European Union did not establish whether the remuneration provided to FIT generators was "adequate".

2.133 The European Union recalls that Article 14(d) of the SCM Agreement, which may be relevant in instances where the challenged measures amount to a financial contribution in the form of a government "purchase[] [of] goods", provides that the "purchase[] [of] goods" by a government shall not be considered as conferring a benefit unless the purchase is made for more than adequate remuneration. The European Union argues that, in making a comparison under Article 14(d), there may be no need to have recourse to hypothetical market counterfactuals or proxies in cases where it is uncontested that, absent the government purchase, the "prevailing market conditions" show that such a product could not be sold since, for instance, there are identical or similar substitutable products being sold at much lower prices.

2.134 Turning to the facts of the present dispute, the European Union argues that the Panel failed to apply the relevant standard correctly when examining the "prevailing market conditions" in Ontario. The European Union observes that the Panel found that the relevant product market for the purposes of determining the existence of a benefit should be the market for electricity, rather than the segment corresponding to electricity generated from windpower and solar PV technologies. The European Union states that "'what the recipient would have obtained from the market' in Ontario was, simply, no remuneration at all (hence the need for government support through the FIT Programme)", and that this was "unambiguously clear from the record of the case".[227] The European Union argues that, where the same or substitutable goods produced by other generating

---

[225] European Union's other appellant's submission (DS426), paras. 146 and 147 (referring to Panel Reports, para. 7.313(b) and (c)).

[226] European Union's other appellant's submission (DS426), para. 147.

[227] European Union's other appellant's submission (DS426), para. 160.

technologies were much less remunerated, the Panel should have arrived at a conclusion as to the existence of a benefit "with little difficulty".[228]

2.135 For the European Union, the mere nature of the FIT Programme indicates that it was introduced to achieve a policy objective of a particular energy supply-mix including renewable generation sources that the "prevailing market conditions" in Ontario could not accomplish. According to the European Union, Canada's submissions indicate that the FIT Programme was created to induce new renewable energy generation, since Ontario's established market structure did not invite sufficient entry of new generators, particularly generators using alternative and renewable energy sources. The European Union notes that the stated objectives of the FIT Programme include to "[i]ncrease capacity of renewable energy supply to ensure adequate generation and reduce emissions", to "[p]rovide incentives for investment in renewable energy technologies", and to "[e]nable new green industries through new investment and job creation", as well as to "facilitate the increased development of Renewable Generating Facilities of varying sizes, technologies and configurations".[229] The European Union notes that the Panel recognized that "[the] prevailing conditions of supply and demand in Ontario suggest that a competitive wholesale electricity market would fail to attract the degree of investment in generating capacity needed to secure a reliable supply of electricity, and that, at present, this goal can only be achieved by means of government intervention in what would otherwise be unacceptable competitive market outcomes".[230]

2.136 The European Union states that, as regards Article 14(d), what the recipient would have obtained from the market is not limited to only the price level but includes all the terms and conditions of the transaction as part of such "remuneration". The European Union states that, on the one hand, the FIT Programme provides remuneration to FIT generators in the form of "guaranteed rates at a certain level and ... for a period of 20 years, including generous price escalation conditions, thereby shielding the FIT generators from any market risks".[231] The European Union highlights that these conditions are provided regardless of the scale or generation capacity of the project, noting that there is a guarantee to purchase as much as the FIT generators can produce. On the other hand, the European Union argues, such remuneration was not available in the relevant marketplace of Ontario in view of the fact that there are other competing generation technologies with lower operating costs also producing electricity. The European Union argues that the elements included in the FIT remuneration would not be available to FIT generators in the market, absent

[228] European Union's other appellant's submission (DS426), para. 162. (fn omitted)

[229] European Union's other appellant's submission (DS426), para. 161 (quoting, respectively, Minister's 2009 FIT Direction, p 1; and FIT Rules (version 1.5.1), Section 1.1).

[230] European Union's other appellant's submission (DS426), para. 161 (referring to Panel Reports, para. 7.312).

[231] European Union's other appellant's submission (DS426), para. 163.

the FIT Programme. The European Union considers that the dissenting opinion seemingly agreed with this proposition.

2.137 Further, the European Union notes that, in cases involving prohibited subsidies under Article 3 of the SCM Agreement, there is no need to quantify the amount of benefit. The European Union observes that the Appellate Body does not need to identify the relevant benchmark to establish the amount of benefit conferred by the FIT Programme, but rather it suffices to conduct an analysis that permits a determination of the existence of a benefit under Article 1.1(b) of the SCM Agreement, regardless of its amount.

2.138 The European Union considers that the dissenting opinion agreed with the European Union's view that the fact that the market in Ontario alone cannot achieve all policy objectives (such as positive environmental externalities that the market does not capture) does not mean that such "market" should be dismissed as the relevant point of comparison to determine the existence of a benefit. According to the European Union, it is precisely such a "marketplace" that is relevant in determining the existence of a benefit.[232] The European Union points to Article 8.2(c) of the SCM Agreement as reflecting the intention of the drafters of the Agreement that financial contributions provided by the government to achieve a particular policy objective that cannot be achieved by market forces alone may constitute subsidies within the meaning of the SCM Agreement.

2.139 Finally, the European Union points to the Panel's finding in the context of the claims under the TRIMs Agreement that "*mere participation* in [the] FIT Programme may be viewed as obtaining an 'advantage'".[233] The European Union fails to understand on what basis the Panel found that the remunerating conditions provided by the FIT Programme *per se* amount to an "advantage" under the *chapeau* of paragraph 1(a) of the Illustrative List in the Annex to the TRIMs Agreement, but not a "benefit" under the SCM Agreement, considering that the Appellate Body has stated that the term "benefit" encompasses some form of "advantage".[234] In the European Union's view, the same analysis that had permitted the Panel to find that the FIT Programme provided an advantage under the TRIMs Agreement should have led the Panel to conclude that the FIT Programme confers a benefit under Article 1.1(b) of the SCM Agreement.

2.140 The European Union requests the Appellate Body to complete the analysis on the basis of the fact that, absent the FIT Programme, under the "prevailing market conditions" in Ontario, FIT generators would not obtain the remuneration provided by the FIT Programme.

---

[232] European Union's other appellant's submission (DS426), para. 166.

[233] European Union's other appellant's submission (DS426), para. 168 (quoting Panel Reports, para. 7.165). (original emphasis)

[234] European Union's other appellant's submission (DS426), para. 169 (referring to Appellate Body Report, *Canada – Aircraft*, para. 153).

2.5.3.2 Article 11 of the DSU – "Benefit"

2.141 In the alternative, the European Union submits that the Panel did not make an objective assessment of the matter in accordance with Article 11 of the DSU. The European Union submits that the Panel failed to consider the totality of the evidence, as presented and argued by the European Union, when finding that, even on the basis of its alternative counterfactual, the European Union failed to establish the existence of "benefit". According to the European Union, the Panel's refusal to consider the European Union's arguments and evidence that would have allowed it to complete its analysis under its own hypothetical "market" counterfactual was based on incoherent reasoning and the exercise of false judicial economy.

2.142 The European Union recalls that, in its observations about a possible alternative approach to the determination of benefit under Article 1.1(b) of the SCM Agreement, the Panel "relied on a hypothetical 'market' counterfactual where the policy objective of securing an adequate supply-mix was achieved under a government-imposed obligation on distributors to purchase electricity from generators operating solar PV and windpower technologies"[235], but where regulation would not prevent effective competition among generators of wind and solar PV electricity.

2.143 The European Union considers that there is sufficient evidence on the record for the Panel to have found the existence of a benefit, even under the hypothetical market counterfactual suggested by the Panel, or another counterfactual based on price negotiations between potential generators and the government. The European Union points to its submissions before the Panel that, where the State can select producers, it can "obtain the lowest possible price from each producer through direct negotiation or through a bidding process that will ensure purchases at no more than the specific costs plus profit expectation by each bidder"[236], and that "the predecessors of the FIT Program were administered based on the best prices offered by generators through a bidding process".[237]

2.144 According to the European Union, this, and other evidence on the record, shows that remuneration provided as a result of a bidding process in Ontario led to much lower rates. In particular, the European Union observes how the predecessor of the FIT Programme (the Renewable Energy Supply (RES) Initiatives) in 2004-2008 followed a competitive procurement process. The highest competitive prices proposed in the context of those tenders (a disclosed

---

[235] European Union's other appellant's submission (DS426), para. 182.

[236] European Union's other appellant's submission (DS426), para. 186 (referring to European Union's closing statement at the second Panel meeting (DS426), para. 11).

[237] European Union's other appellant's submission (DS426), para. 185 (referring to European Union's second written submission to the Panel (DS426), para. 85).

average of 8.4 cents per kWh and an estimated highest bid of 9.4 cents per kWh) were "way below any of the rates guaranteed under the FIT Programme".[238]

2.145 The European Union highlights that the FIT Programme "guarantees a minimum of profits to the FIT Generators regardless of the market, unlike the case of any producer, which has to compete on price".[239] The European Union considers that an analysis of the "structural elements" of the FIT Programme (namely, the standard rate and guarantee conditions) should have allowed the Panel to complete the analysis and find "benefit" under the Panel's own alternative counterfactual. The European Union recalls that at the Interim Review stage it raised the point that, even under the approach suggested by the Panel, there was sufficient information on the record to determine the existence of a benefit, and requested the Panel to complete its analysis on the basis suggested by the European Union, "or on any other alternative" basis, "in view of the information already available on the record".[240]

2.146 In addition, the European Union alleges that the Panel's failure to consider the totality of the evidence was based on incoherent reasoning and the exercise of false judicial economy. The European Union states that the Panel's only reasoning as to why it did not consider the European Union's evidence was that, having rejected Canada's argument that there was a separate market for wind- and solar PV-generated electricity, it was not necessary to evaluate the merits of the European Union's alternative arguments advanced to demonstrate that, even according to Canada's line of argument, the FIT and microFIT Contracts amounted to financial contributions that confer a benefit.[241]

2.147 Moreover, the European Union argues that, on the one hand, the Panel found that a separate wholesale market for electricity generated by windpower and solar PV technologies "would not be the appropriate focus" of the benefit analysis in the present dispute, while, on the other hand, it applied a standard that would require a comparison between the remuneration under the FIT Programme and the remuneration that specifically solar PV and windpower generators would obtain within a hypothetical "market" counterfactual.[242] The European Union considers that this constitutes incoherent reasoning and false judicial economy contrary to the Panel's obligations under Article 11 of the DSU. The European Union requests the Appellate Body to reverse the Panel's finding that the European Union failed to establish the existence of a benefit, to

[238] European Union's other appellant's submission (DS426), paras. 189 and 190 (quoting OPA, Joint Report to the Minister of Energy: Recommendations on a Standard Offer Program for Small Generators connected to a Distribution System, 17 March 2006 (Panel Exhibit CDA-55), pp. 17 and 20; and Hogan Report, p. 34).

[239] European Union's other appellant's submission (DS426), para. 187 (referring to European Union's comments on Canada's response to Panel question No. 17 (second set), para. 19).

[240] European Union's other appellant's submission (DS426), paras. 191 and 192 (referring to European Union's comments on Interim Panel Report, pp. 6-7).

[241] European Union's other appellant's submission (DS426), para. 197.

[242] European Union's other appellant's submission (DS426), paras. 198 and 199.

complete the analysis on the basis of the uncontested arguments and evidence submitted by the European Union, and to find that the challenged measures confer a benefit under Article 1.1(b) of the SCM Agreement.[243]

2.148 The European Union claims that, as a consequence of the Panel's errors regarding "benefit", the Panel's ultimate conclusion that the European Union failed to establish that the challenged measures constitute subsidies or envisage the granting of subsidies inconsistent with Articles 3.1(b) and 3.2 of the SCM Agreement is also in error. The European Union requests the Appellate Body to reverse this finding, to complete the analysis, and to find that the measures amount to prohibited subsidies. Moreover, the European Union requests the Appellate Body to recommend that Canada withdraw its prohibited subsidies without delay as required by Article 4.7 of the SCM Agreement. Should the Appellate Body be unable to complete the analysis under any of the requests made by the European Union, the European Union requests the Appellate Body to declare moot and of no legal effect the Panel's findings and conclusions in paragraph 7.328(ii) of its Reports, and in paragraph 8.7 of the EU Panel Report (DS426).[244]

2.6 Arguments of Canada – Appellee

2.6.1 The order in which the Panel dealt with Japan's claims under the SCM Agreement and its claims under the TRIMs Agreement and the GATT 1994

2.149 Canada did not address in its appellee's submission Japan's claim that the Panel erred by commencing its evaluation with Japan's claims under the TRIMs Agreement and the GATT 1994, rather than with its claims under the SCM Agreement.

2.6.2 The relationship between the TRIMs Agreement and Article III:4 of the GATT 1994

2.150 Canada asserts that the Panel correctly found that the TRIMs Agreement does not preclude the application of Article III:8(a) of the GATT 1994 to the FIT Programme's domestic content requirements.

2.151 Canada notes the European Union's argument that the Panel "ignored" the difference in the terms used in paragraphs 1 and 2 of Article 2 of the TRIMs Agreement.[245] According to Canada, rather than support the European Union's interpretation, the reference to Article III:4 of the GATT 1994 in Article 2.2 of the TRIMs Agreement undermines it. Canada explains that, by

---

243 European Union's other appellant's submission (DS426), para. 204.

244 European Union's other appellant's submission (DS426), para. 206.

245 Canada's appellee's submission, para. 28 (referring to European Union's other appellant's submission (DS426), paras. 31 and 32).

characterizing the measures in the Illustrative List of TRIMs in the Annex to the TRIMs Agreement as inconsistent with "the obligation of national treatment provided for in paragraph 4 of Article III" of the GATT 1994, instead of "Article III", Article 2.2 does not address the consistency of the measures listed in the Annex to the TRIMs Agreement with Article III of the GATT 1994, as a whole, including Article III:8(a).

2.152 Canada also rejects the European Union's argument that the Panel's interpretation renders Article 2.2 of the TRIMs Agreement and the Illustrative List "essentially redundant".[246] Canada submits that "just because a measure obviously discriminates against imported goods does not mean that the measure satisfies all the elements of Article III:4."[247] Canada adds that Article 2.2 of the TRIMs Agreement not only identifies measures that are inconsistent with Article III:4 of the GATT 1994 but, more specifically, measures that are inconsistent with that Article and that can also be characterized as TRIMs. Furthermore, it notes that the list is "illustrative" and, therefore, apart from any other function, provides an illustration of the types of measures that are both TRIMs and inconsistent with the national treatment obligation in Article III:4 of the GATT 1994.

2.153 In addition, Canada argues that the European Union "overlooks"[248] that the context to paragraph 1 of the Illustrative List undermines its interpretation of that paragraph. Canada points out that the Illustrative List also contains, in paragraph 2, examples of TRIMs that are inconsistent with Article XI:1 of the GATT 1994. It further notes that Article XI:2 contains a "scope" provision similar to Article III:8(a) of the GATT 1994. Canada draws an analogy between Articles XI:2 and III:8(a) in their relation to the Illustrative List of the TRIMs Agreement. Consequently, Canada submits that, if the European Union's interpretation of the effect of the Illustrative List of TRIMs that are inconsistent with Article III:4 is correct, then this must also be the effect of the Illustrative List of TRIMs that are inconsistent with Article XI:1 of the GATT 1994. In other words, under the European Union's reasoning, the TRIMs that are listed in the Illustrative List as inconsistent with Article XI:1 must fall outside the scope of Article XI:2. Yet, Canada submits that a comparison between Article XI:2 and the TRIMs listed in the Illustrative List as inconsistent with Article XI:1 of the GATT 1994 reveals that this proposition "is untenable".[249] Canada emphasizes that the Illustrative List contains measures that "clearly"[250] could fall within the scope of Article XI:2 of the GATT 1994. As an example, Canada refers to measures that "restrict the importation by an enterprise of products used in or

---

246 Canada's appellee's submission, para. 30 (quoting European Union's other appellant's submission (DS426), para. 27).

247 Canada's appellee's submission, para. 30.

248 Canada's appellee's submission, para. 32.

249 Canada's appellee's submission, para. 33.

250 *Ibid.*

related to its local production". Canada argues that such measures can "clearly"[251] fall within the scope of Article XI:2(c)(ii), which states that "[t]he provisions of paragraph 1 of this Article shall not extend to ... [i]mport restrictions on any agricultural or fisheries product ... necessary to the enforcement of government measures which operate ... to remove a temporary surplus of the like domestic product".

2.154 Therefore, Canada asserts that the European Union's interpretation of Article 2.2 and paragraph 1 of the Illustrative List in the Annex to the TRIMs Agreement is inconsistent with the text and its context. Canada thus submits that the European Union has failed to provide grounds to overturn the Panel's decision that the TRIMs Agreement does not preclude the application of Article III:8(a) of the GATT 1994 to the FIT Programme's domestic content requirements.

2.6.3 Claims under Article III:8(a) of the GATT 1994

2.155 Canada requests the Appellate Body to uphold the Panel's findings with respect to the issues raised under Article III:8(a) of the GATT 1994 in the other appeals by the European Union and Japan.

2.6.3.1 The Panel's finding that the FIT Programme and Contracts involve "procurement by governmental agencies of products purchased"

2.156 Canada maintains that the Panel correctly found that the Government of Ontario "purchases" electricity under the FIT Programme. For Canada, the Panel properly considered the facts that the funds transferred to suppliers are intended to pay for the electricity that is delivered into Ontario's electricity grid; that the Government of Ontario takes "possession" of the electricity because it directs the movement of that electricity to and throughout the grid by means of IESO instructions; and that the Electricity Act of 1998, the Minister's 2009 FIT Direction, the FIT and microFIT Contracts, and other related documents all characterize the challenged measures as a "procurement" or "purchase" of electricity.

2.157 In response to Japan's argument that the allocation of the generation, transmission, and distribution of electricity to different entities in Ontario suggests that the Government of Ontario does not "purchase" electricity, Canada argues that it is irrelevant which specific agency within the Government of Ontario takes physical possession of the electricity, as long as the Government of Ontario takes possession. Canada further submits that Japan overlooks that the Panel found that an entity can purchase a product even if it does not take "physical possession" of it. According to the Panel, even if there is no transfer of

[251] *Ibid.*

physical possession of a product, there can be a "purchase" if the purchaser obtains "an entitlement"[252] to the product, and Canada asserts that the Panel effectively found that the OPA has an entitlement to electricity delivered under the FIT and microFIT Contracts.

2.6.3.2 The Panel's finding that the domestic content requirements "govern" the procurement of electricity

2.158 Canada contends that the Panel correctly found that the domestic content requirements "govern" the procurement of electricity. For Canada, the Panel correctly considered that, because the domestic content requirements must be satisfied by generators wanting to participate in the FIT Programme, these requirements "govern" procurement of electricity by the Government of Ontario under the FIT Programme. The European Union argues that the Panel's interpretation allows discriminatory requirements to extend far beyond the actual object of the procurement at stake, affecting broad areas of economic activity that would be irreconcilable with the objective of Article III of the GATT 1994. In response to this argument, Canada asserts that the European Union overlooks the objective of paragraph 8(a) of Article III, which supports the inclusion of domestic content requirements on the inputs into products that are purchased by the government. Canada maintains that this provision was included in Article III in order to enable Members to pursue public policy through government procurement.

2.159 Furthermore, Canada refers to Article XVI:1 of the GPA, which prohibits conditions on the inputs into the product that is purchased. Canada argues that, since the signatories to the GPA are all bound by the obligations in the GATT, they would not have needed to prohibit domestic content requirements on inputs into products that are purchased by governments if those requirements fall outside the scope of Article III:8(a) and, therefore, are in any event prohibited by Article III:4 of the GATT 1994. Furthermore, Canada refers to Article XVI:2 of the GPA, which allows developing countries to negotiate exemptions from the disciplines on domestic content requirements on inputs into products that are purchased by the government. Canada argues that there would have been no need to include this exemption if developing countries nevertheless faced such disciplines under the GATT 1994. In addition, Canada alleges that the European Union overlooks academic commentary, suggesting that "it is clear"[253] that requirements imposed on the inputs into products purchased by the government fall within the scope of Article III:8(a) of the GATT 1994.

---

[252] Canada's appellee's submission, para. 38 (referring to Panel Reports, paras. 7.228 and 7.229).

[253] Canada's appellee's submission, para. 54 (quoting S. Arrowsmith, "Government Procurement in the WTO", *Studies in Transnational Economic Law*, Vol. 16 (Kluwer Law International, 2002), p. 53 (Panel Exhibit CDA-85)).

2.6.3.3 The Panel's interpretation of the term "governmental purposes"

2.160 Canada submits that the Panel correctly interpreted the term "governmental purposes". In particular, Canada supports the Panel's statement that the ordinary meaning of "governmental purposes" is relatively "broad"[254] and may encompass all three of the meanings advanced by the parties, including the meaning proposed by Canada that a purchase for "governmental purposes" is a purchase for a stated aim of the government. Canada maintains that the European Union's interpretation of the word "purposes" as "needs" is not supported by dictionary definitions of the word "purpose". For Canada, the term "governmental purposes" must be interpreted in context with the phrase "and not with a view to commercial resale or with a view to use in the production of goods for commercial sale", and that this phrase confirms that the term "governmental purposes" also refers to the "view" or "aim" behind the purchase. Thus, Canada argues that the inquiry must be into the "purpose", "view", or "aim" behind the purchase and whether it is governmental or commercial.

2.161 Canada further submits that, even if the term "governmental purposes" refers to "needs" of the government, as the European Union argues, it is not clear why purchases for the "needs" of the government are only those for consumption or physical use by the government. With respect to the European Union's reference to the negotiating history of Article III:8(a) and its argument that the provision originally referred to purchases for "governmental use", Canada asserts that the European Union has failed to explain why the negotiators of the provision ultimately chose the word "purposes" instead of "use".

2.162 Moreover, in response to the European Union's argument that the context of Article XVII:2 of the GATT 1994 lends support to its reading of the term "governmental purposes", Canada argues that the inclusion of the word "use" in Article XVII:2 highlights that negotiators chose not to include this word when describing the purchases falling within the scope of Article III:8(a) of the GATT 1994.

2.6.3.4 The Panel's interpretation of the word "for" in the term "for governmental purposes"

2.163 Canada contends that the Panel correctly interpreted the word "for" in the term "for governmental purposes". In response to Japan's argument that the Panel neglected to analyze whether there was a "true and genuine connection between the 'purchase' ... and 'governmental purpose[]' at issue"[255], Canada maintains that Japan is raising a new argument and that it is therefore challenging neither an "issue[] of law covered in the panel report" nor a "legal interpretation[] developed by the panel" as required under Article 17 of the

[254] Canada's appellee's submission, para. 59 (quoting Panel Reports, para. 7.140).
[255] Japan's other appellant's submission (DS412), para. 171.

DSU. Canada asserts that this issue is outside the scope of the Appellate Body's mandate under Article 17.6 of the DSU, because the Panel was never asked to define the word "for" in the manner now advanced by Japan. Canada submits that the appeal of this issue is also outside the scope of Article 17.6 because there are insufficient facts on the Panel record for the Appellate Body to assess it, given that the issue was not pleaded before the Panel.

2.164 Alternatively, if the Appellate Body finds this issue to be properly before it, Canada asserts that the dictionary definition of the word "for" provided by Japan does not support its interpretation of this word in Article III:8(a) of the GATT 1994. In response to Japan's argument that the object and purpose of the GATT 1994 suggests that an interpretation of Article III:8(a) should "ensure that the exclusion for products 'purchased for governmental purposes' is not so expansive that it allows WTO Members to avoid their obligations under Article III simply by assigning a 'governmental purpose' to a particular trade-restrictive measure"[256], Canada agrees. In Canada's view, "Article III:8(a) should be interpreted 'to require that a government's purchase of products is made truly and genuinely *in order to obtain or achieve* a particular governmental purpose,' as argued by Japan."[257] For Canada, however, this does not mean that only those purchases that are necessary to achieve a particular governmental purpose fall within the scope of Article III:8(a). Canada submits that the decision of the negotiators of the GATT not to include a necessity test in Article III:8(a) was a deliberate choice.

2.6.3.5 The Panel's interpretation of the term "with a view to commercial resale"

2.165 Canada alleges that both Japan and the Panel misinterpreted the term "commercial resale". Canada refers to the arguments set out in its appeal of the Panel's interpretation of the phrase "with a view to commercial resale", where it submits that "commercial resale" is a resale with the underlying intent to profit. Canada argues that the Appellate Body report in *US – Anti-Dumping and Countervailing Duties (China)*[258] supports its interpretation of the term "commercial resale". In response to Japan's challenge of the Panel's interpretation of this term, Canada argues that Japan's interpretation of "commercial resale" as resale "into the stream of commerce, trade or market"[259] is incorrect, because dictionary definitions of "commerce" include transactions with intent to realize a profit.

---

[256] Canada's appellee's submission, para. 71 (quoting Japan's other appellant's submission (DS412), para. 175).

[257] Canada's appellee's submission, para. 71 (quoting Japan's other appellant's submission (DS412), para. 175 (original emphasis)).

[258] Appellate Body Report, *US – Anti-Dumping and Countervailing Duties (China)*, para. 478. (fn omitted)

[259] Canada's appellee's submission, para. 10 (referring to Japan's other appellant's submission (DS412), paras. 182-188).

2.166 In addition, Canada asserts that Japan's interpretation "overlooks"[260] that the word "commercial" qualifies the word "resale" in Article III:8(a). A "resale" of a product necessarily means that the product will be "sold into the stream of commerce or trade". Hence, a "commercial resale" cannot mean the same thing. The addition of the word "commercial" must qualify the "resale" in some way. For Canada, the word "commercial" qualifies the "resale" in that it stipulates that it must be for an underlying intent to profit. Furthermore, Canada alleges that Japan's interpretation ignores relevant context provided by the term "governmental purposes". Intent to introduce a product "into the stream of commerce or trade" can still be "governmental". Canada presents the example of a government purchasing books for community libraries and medical vaccines. That the government recovers some of the cost for the purchase of those products does not diminish the governmental nature of that purchase. In Canada's view, the purchase only loses its governmental character and becomes commercial if the government seeks to profit from it.

2.167 Canada argues that both Japan and the Panel misinterpreted the term "with a view to" in Article III:8(a) of the GATT 1994. Canada refers to the arguments set out in its appeal of the Panel's interpretation of the phrase "with a view to commercial resale". Canada maintains that both Japan and the Panel failed to examine the meaning or effect of the term "with a view to" and instead focused solely on the meaning of the term "commercial resale". As a result, Japan and the Panel incorrectly focused on whether there is commercial resale of the electricity that is purchased under the FIT Programme, rather than the view to which that electricity is purchased.

2.168 Canada refers to Japan's argument that Canada's interpretation is contrary to the object and purpose of the GATT 1994 because it would allow a Member that wished to exclude a particular foreign product from its domestic market to declare an aim to secure a stable supply of that product for the benefit of its consumers' welfare, establish a non-profit government agency to purchase quantities of that product subject to the requirement that the product be produced domestically, and then resell that product to consumers without earning profit from that resale. Canada contends that this is not correct, because Japan overlooks that a purchase must be for "governmental purposes and not with a view to commercial resale", and that the purpose of excluding a foreign product from a domestic market cannot be a governmental purpose.

2.169 Canada further submits that the governmental nature of a purchase will partly depend on the role that a government plays in a particular country and the government's role in supplying the product at issue. Canada maintains that, if the government has not traditionally supplied the product and has no constitutional mandate to do so, then this will indicate that the purchase of the product for the alleged benefit of consumers is not actually for a governmental purpose.

---

[260] Canada's appellee's submission, para. 77.

2.6.3.6 Canada's request for completion of the analysis

2.170 In the event that the Appellate Body completes the analysis under Article III:8(a) of the GATT 1994, Canada submits that the evidence on the record demonstrates that the Government of Ontario purchases solar PV- and wind-generated electricity under the FIT Programme "for governmental purposes and not with a view to commercial resale or with a view to use in the production of goods for commercial sale". Canada maintains that the relevant factors for characterizing the aim behind the purchase are the role of the government within a particular country (including its constitutional and legislative mandate), the stated aims of the government behind the purchase, and whether the government has an intention to profit from the resale or use of the product. For Canada, the application of these three elements demonstrates that the Government of Ontario's purchases of electricity under the FIT Programme are "for [a] governmental purpose[] and not with a view to commercial resale or ... use in the production of goods for commercial sale".

2.171 Regarding the first element, Canada maintains that the aim behind the purchase of electricity under the FIT Programme is the governmental aim of helping to ensure a sufficient and reliable supply of electricity from clean sources for Ontarians. With respect to the second element, Canada argues that the Government of Ontario plays a significant role in ensuring the provision of a sufficient and reliable supply of electricity from clean sources. Canada submits that the Canadian Constitution Act of 1982[261] gives Canadian provinces, including Ontario, the power to "make laws in relation to ... development, conservation and management of sites and facilities in the province for the generation and production of electrical energy"[262], and asserts that the Government of Ontario has relied on this power expressly to commit in legislation to pursue for Ontarians a reliable and sufficient supply of electricity from clean sources. Canada argues that the Government of Ontario plays a significant role in all aspects of the province's electricity system. The Ontario Government, along with local municipal governments, owns the vast majority of the transmission and distribution network that physically supplies electricity to Ontario consumers. It controls the flow of electricity through its agent, the IESO, and regulates the price of electricity and the cost of physically supplying electricity through its agent, the OEB. Canada further submits that the Government of Ontario owns the majority of electricity-generating assets in Ontario through its agent, Ontario Power Generation (OPG), and that the

[261] The Constitution Act, 1982 was enacted as Schedule B to the Canada Act, 1982 (UK) 1982, Chapter 11, which came into force on 17 April 1982.

[262] Canada's appellee's submission, para. 90 (referring to Department of Justice Canada, Constitution Acts, 1867 to 1982, Part VI – Distribution of Legislative Powers (Panel Exhibit JPN-48), Section 92A(1)(c)).

Government also supplements its generation of electricity by purchasing electricity through its agent, the OPA.

2.172 As to the third element, Canada submits that the OPA is prevented from profiting from any aspect of its operations, including the purchase of electricity under the FIT Programme. In that respect, Canada notes that Section 25.2(2) of the Electricity Act of 1998, entitled "Not for profit", states that "[t]he business and affairs of the OPA shall be carried on without the purpose of gain". In sum, for Canada, the role of the Government of Ontario, the stated aims of the government when purchasing renewable electricity, and the government's "not for profit" mandate with regard to the purchase and any resale or use of the electricity, all confirm that the aim of the Government of Ontario behind the purchase of electricity under the FIT Programme is governmental and not commercial.

2.173 Canada maintains that this conclusion is supported by findings of the Panel. Canada submits that the Panel did not directly address the purpose behind the Government of Ontario's purchase of electricity under the FIT Programme, but that it did acknowledge that the FIT Programme serves two fundamental objectives, namely, encouraging the participation of new generation facilities using renewable sources of energy into the Ontario electricity system, and stimulating local investment in the production of renewable energy generation equipment. In addition, Canada refers to the Panel's findings that the objectives of the FIT Programme "are pursued through the execution of the FIT and microFIT Contracts"[263] and to the Panel's finding that "one of the fundamental objectives of the FIT Programme is to secure investment in new generation facilities *for the purposes* of diversifying Ontario's supply-mix and helping to fill the supply gap that is expected from the closure of Ontario's coal-fired facilities by 2014."[264]

2.6.4 The Panel's decision to exercise judicial economy with respect to Japan's "stand-alone" claim under Article III:4 of the GATT 1994

2.174 Canada did not address in its appellee's submission Japan's claim that the Panel erred by failing to make a finding with respect to Japan's "stand-alone" claim under Article III:4 of the GATT 1994. At the oral hearing, Canada noted that the Panel did make a finding under Article III:4 of the GATT 1994 and said that it did not see why it would have been necessary for the Panel to have made an additional finding under Japan's "stand-alone" claim under Article III:4.

---

[263] Canada's appellee's submission, para. 96 (quoting Panel Reports, para. 7.216).

[264] Canada's appellee's submission, para. 96 (quoting Panel Reports, para. 7.223 (original emphasis)).

2.6.5 Claims under the SCM Agreement

2.6.5.1 Article 1.1(a) – "Financial contribution" or "income or price support"

2.175 With respect to Japan's challenge to the Panel's finding that the measures at issue constitute government "purchases [of] goods", Canada submits that the Panel was correct in finding that the FIT Programme and related FIT and microFIT Contracts constitute a "financial contribution" in the form of government "purchases [of] goods". Canada submits that this finding by the Panel is in accordance with the relevant legal standard, which requires a factual assessment of the transaction at issue to determine its "inherent or essential quality".[265] In this regard, Canada points to the Panel's "extensive analysis of the FIT Program, its legal basis, the mandate and powers of the OPA, the FIT and microFIT Contracts, the intangible nature of electricity, and the role of Hydro One Inc. and the IESO to find that the OPA pays for 'delivered electricity' into Ontario's electricity system".[266] Canada emphasizes that the Panel found that "fundamental" to the FIT and microFIT Contracts was an "exchange" of certain core obligations between generators and the OPA.[267] In particular, FIT and microFIT suppliers must deliver electricity into the Ontario electricity system and, in return, the OPA agrees to make the payments called for under the FIT and microFIT Contracts.

2.176 Canada disagrees with Japan's arguments that the Panel erred in characterizing the measures at issue as government "purchases [of] goods". In response to Japan's claim that "it is other government entities and not the OPA that actually takes possession of the FIT-generated electricity"[268], Canada submits that the Panel correctly found that possession by the actual purchasing entity was not necessary for a finding of government "purchases [of] goods". According to the Panel, there can be a purchase even if there is no transfer of physical possession of a product if the purchaser obtains "an entitlement"[269] to the product. In Canada's view, the Panel effectively found that the OPA has an entitlement to electricity pursuant to the FIT and microFIT Contracts that it directs be fed into the system. It is not important which government entity takes physical possession of the electricity, because physical possession is not necessary for a purchase to be made.

2.177 With respect to Japan's arguments that "Ontario's stated objective of ensuring a stable supply of electricity does not require that the government

---

[265] Canada's appellee's submission, para. 108.

[266] Canada's appellee's submission, para. 111 (referring to Panel Reports, paras. 7.223 and 7.224).

[267] Canada's appellee's submission, paras. 103 and 104.

[268] Canada's appellee's submission, para. 113 (referring to Japan's other appellant's submission (DS412), para. 39).

[269] Panel Reports, paras. 7.228 and 7.229.

purchase the electricity"[270], and that the presence of private parties in Ontario's electricity system "demonstrates that Ontario does not need to take possession of or purchase electricity to meet the need of ensuring a stable supply"[271], Canada argues that whether a government purchase is necessary or whether private entities supply electricity is irrelevant for purposes of the proper legal characterization of the FIT Programme and Contracts under Article 1.1(a)(1) of the SCM Agreement.[272]

2.178 With respect to Japan's assertion that the Panel erred in finding subparagraphs (i) and (iii) of Article 1.1(a)(1) to be mutually exclusive, Canada submits that the Panel correctly found that the FIT Programme could not properly be characterized as both "direct transfer[s] of funds" and government "purchases [of] goods". In Canada's view, the customary rules of interpretation do not permit a blurring of the distinction between "direct transfer[s] of funds" and government "purchase[s] [of] goods" as this would make the explicit reference to government "purchase[s] [of] goods" in subparagraph (iii) meaningless. Canada recalls the Panel's conclusion that the Appellate Body's statement in *US – Large Civil Aircraft (2nd complaint)* does not amount to a finding that "transactions properly characterized as 'purchases [of] goods' can also constitute 'direct transfer[s] of funds'".[273] In Canada's view, the Panel's finding is entirely consistent with the Appellate Body's statement. In particular, while, in a general sense, "[t]he structure of [Article 1.1(a)(1)] does not preclude that a transaction could be covered by more than one subparagraph"[274], Canada points out that, in the present case, where the same aspects of the same measure are at issue, one cannot properly characterize them both as government "purchases [of] goods" and "direct transfer[s] of funds".

2.179 Canada submits that the Panel properly exercised judicial economy with respect to Japan's characterization of the measures at issue as "income or price support". Canada notes that the Appellate Body has clarified that panels are not required to examine each legal claim made by a complainant. The exercise of judicial economy is proper where a finding is not necessary to resolve fully the matter at issue. Canada argues that Japan's appeal of this issue should be rejected because the complainants' "benefit" arguments with respect to "income or price support" were "essentially the same" as those related to "financial contribution". In this regard, Canada points out that Japan's "benefit" argument with respect to "income or price support" is entirely based on the alleged "market" benchmarks proposed in the context of establishing whether a "benefit" was conferred by a

270 Canada's appellee's submission, para. 113 (referring to Japan's other appellant's submission (DS412), para. 40).

271 Canada's appellee's submission, para. 113 (referring to Japan's other appellant's submission (DS412), para. 41).

272 Canada's appellee's submission, paras. 39 and 114.

273 Canada's appellee's submission, para. 116 (quoting Panel Reports, para. 7.247).

274 Canada's appellee's submission, para. 117.

"financial contribution".[275] Given that the Panel majority rejected the entirety of Japan's "benefit" claim with respect to "financial contribution", including all of the alleged "market" benchmarks, the entire basis on which Japan's "income or price support" "benefit" allegation rests was rejected by the Panel. Therefore, the outcome of the dispute would have been no different if the Panel had not exercised judicial economy with respect to Japan's "income or price support" claim.

2.180 In the alternative, if the Appellate Body decides to reverse the Panel's exercise of judicial economy, Canada argues that Japan has failed to establish that the FIT Programme constitutes a form of "income or price support". In Canada's view, the term "income or price support" not only means that incomes or prices must be maintained through government measures, but also implies that income or price levels were determined by supply and demand (i.e. by a market) prior to the government's intervention. Canada highlights that the OPA is not responding to some market signal indicating when it must intervene in the market to purchase enough renewable electricity to maintain a certain price level under the FIT Programme.[276] Finally, in the context of the requirement in Article XVI of the GATT 1994 that income or price support "operates directly or indirectly to increase exports of any product ... or to reduce imports", Canada argues that Japan has provided no evidence suggesting that imports of wind or solar electricity into Ontario have declined as a result of the FIT Programme or that exports of wind or solar electricity have increased. Consequently, the conditions to find that the challenged measures are "income or price support" within the meaning of Article 1.1(a)(2) have not been met by Japan.

2.6.5.2 Article 1.1(b) – "Benefit"

2.181 Canada states that both the European Union and Japan adopt the dissenting member of the Panel's "but for" conclusion with regard to "benefit": that is, a "benefit" may be found because, absent the FIT Programme, windpower and solar generators under the FIT Programme "would not otherwise be present".[277] Canada submits that the question of whether a benefit is conferred must, instead, turn on whether the terms of the transaction reveal that the government has paid more than an "adequate" price, for that specific form of electricity, with its specific inherent qualities.

2.182 Canada alleges that a proper approach to assessing whether a benefit is conferred should reflect the ordinary meaning of Article 1.1(b) of the SCM Agreement, in the relevant context of Article 14 and the related jurisprudence. Canada refers to the Appellate Body's jurisprudence regarding the relevance of

---

275 Canada's appellee's submission, para. 125.

276 In addition, Canada points out that price support should also alter the market price for the good in question for other sellers in that market and that Japan has made no such allegation. (Canada's appellee's submission, para. 132)

277 Canada's appellee's submission, para. 138 (quoting Panel Reports, para. 9.23).

Article 14(d) of the SCM Agreement as a guideline in interpreting Article 1.1(b). It recalls that, in *EC and certain member States – Large Civil Aircraft*, the Appellate Body stated that Article 14(d) "highlights that a proper market benchmark is derived from an examination of the conditions pursuant to which the goods ... at issue would under market conditions, be exchanged".[278] Canada further recalls that, in respect of the term "adequate remuneration", "'[r]emuneration' is defined as 'reward, recompense; payment, pay'. Thus, a benefit is conferred when a government provides goods to a recipient and, in return, receives insufficient payment".[279] Canada submits that, in a case of a government "purchase[] [of] goods", a benefit is conferred only when a government purchases goods from a recipient and makes more than sufficient payment or compensation for those goods.

2.183 With respect to the question of whether Article 14(d) of the SCM Agreement is concerned with the existence or with the amount of benefit, Canada stresses that Article 14(d) begins with the phrase "purchase of goods by a government *shall not* be considered as conferring a benefit *unless* the ... purchase is made for more than adequate remuneration".[280] Canada considers that Article 14(d) demonstrates that whether a benefit is being conferred depends on the price paid by the government and that this provision deals with the existence of a benefit in the context of a government "purchase[] [of] goods" and not merely how to calculate the amount of benefit.

2.184 Canada agrees that, in a general sense, the Appellate Body has found that a benefit is an "advantage" conferred on a recipient and is determined by a comparison based on whether the recipient is "better off" than it would be absent the contribution. However, the actual comparison required in a specific benefit analysis is to be conducted by comparing the terms of a government's "financial contribution" to terms available in the market for a comparable transaction. In Canada's view, a proper benefit analysis assumes a counterfactual market purchase and the central question is whether the terms of a financial contribution are more beneficial than a similar transaction between two arm's-length private entities on the market. In Canada's view, the most appropriate benchmark to test "adequacy of remuneration" of the FIT rates would be rates for both wind and solar electricity established through an arm's-length transaction between private entities in Ontario. At the oral hearing, Canada stated that the Panel record contains no such evidence.

2.185 Canada alleges that the complainants' approach ignores the distinction between a "financial contribution" and a "benefit ... conferred". Canada states that the architecture of Article 1.1 is clear and that there are two discrete

---

[278] Canada's appellee's submission, para. 163 (quoting Appellate Body Report, *EC and certain member States – Large Civil Aircraft*, para. 975).

[279] Canada's appellee's submission, para. 164 (quoting Appellate Body Report, *US – Softwood Lumber IV*, para. 84 (fn omitted)).

[280] Canada's appellee's submission, para. 179. (emphasis added by Canada)

components to the definition of a "subsidy". Canada submits that, under the approach advocated by the complainants, the mere provision of a "financial contribution" by a government becomes the "benefit". Every time a government purchases a good for which there is no private-sector demand, the fact of that purchase itself would demonstrate a benefit conferred regardless of the price at which that purchase is made. Canada gives the example of the government purchase of armoured vehicles or vaccines, noting that, under the complainant's approach, if these goods would not be purchased on the market absent the government's purchase, then there would be a benefit conferred regardless of the purchase price. To Canada, this would render Article 1.1(b) meaningless.

2.186 Canada disagrees with the European Union's contention that, where the "prevailing market conditions" show that such a product could not be sold, the comparison is between "something" and "nothing", and there is a benefit. According to Canada, the standard to find "benefit" is quite clear – "more than adequate remuneration". Hence, Japan and the European Union have failed to prove that Ontario's purchase of wind and solar electricity under the FIT Programme "is made for more than adequate remuneration".[281]

2.187 Canada reiterates its view that, in limited circumstances where prices are distorted by a government's predominant position as a purchaser of goods, alternative benchmarks may be used. However, such proxies must nevertheless relate to the "prevailing market conditions" in the country of purchase. Canada contends that the European Union ignores that it was a finding of distortion in *US – Softwood Lumber IV* that led the Appellate Body to recognize that prices from such a market could not be used in a proper comparison. Canada states that the dissenting opinion agreed "with the majority that all of the complainants' proposed benchmarks are inappropriate", and that "the price outcomes of the IESO-administered wholesale market (the HOEP) are significantly distorted by the actions and policies of the Government of Ontario".[282] Canada highlights also that the dissenting member of the Panel stated that the proposed benchmarks do not represent prices established on a competitive wholesale electricity market in Ontario.

2.188 Canada alleges that the approach advocated by the complainants ignores factual findings made by the entire Panel (including the dissenting member of the Panel) on the nature of the Ontario electricity system. In particular, the complainants' "benefit" arguments (that are premised on the dissenting conclusions) assume that the FIT Programme brings into the market generators that would be otherwise excluded due to competition. In this respect, Canada disagrees with the European Union and Japan that it is an uncontested fact that, absent the FIT Programme, FIT generators would not have entered the market. According to Canada, this ignores the Panel's findings of fact that absent the

---

281 Canada's appellee's submission, para. 180.

282 Canada's appellee's submission, para. 149 (referring to Panel Reports, para. 9.10).

FIT Programme new entrants would probably negotiate a price for wind and solar electricity with Ontario and that the IESO-administered "market" based mechanism is not a "market" appropriate for the purposes of a "benefit" analysis. Canada points out that, in Ontario, the government represents the demand-side of the relevant purchase transaction and determines which generators can participate in the Ontario electricity system and that generators, regardless of the form of generation, do not compete with each other.

2.189 With respect to the European Union's claim that the existence of a benefit should have been made "with little difficulty"[283] and its reference to the panel's decision in *US – Large Civil Aircraft (2nd complaint)*, Canada distinguishes that situation from the present one. Canada notes that the panel in that dispute dealt with "revenue foregone" pursuant to Article 1.1(a)(1)(ii) of the SCM Agreement. Canada recognizes that certain forms of government "financial contribution" do not have terms that require any comparison to market terms. They "do not have terms *per se* in the same sense that equity capital, loans, loan guarantees, provision of goods and services and the purchase of goods do."[284] According to Canada, in the case of grants and revenue forgone, "the fact of the government action (i.e. the 'financial contribution' itself) may very well demonstrate the conferral of a benefit."[285] However, Canada considers that, consistent with the Appellate Body's treatment of such "financial contributions" as "purchases [of] goods", that is not the case with "financial contributions" that have terms.

2.6.5.3 Article 11 of the DSU – "Benefit"

2.190 In response to the European Union's and Japan's arguments that there was sufficient evidence on the record for the Panel to find "benefit" on the basis of the Panel majority's observations on how an appropriate benefit analysis might have been conducted, Canada responds that, while the Panel offered "observations" in response to specific requests from the complainants, it is clear that these "observations" were not findings. Canada considers that the Panel recognized that the complainants bear the burden of making their case and that this is not the Panel's role. Moreover, Canada observes that these observations are simply the Panel majority's views on an alternative approach to "benefit" made at the complainants' urging.

2.191 Responding to the European Union's claim that the Panel acted inconsistently with Article 11 of the DSU by not making a finding as to the existence of a benefit on the basis of the European Union's arguments, Canada states that the Panel majority was correct in stating that the "observations" raise "a number of important questions and factual issues [that] would [have] need[ed]

---

283 Canada's appellee's submission, para. 185 (quoting European Union's other appellant's submission (DS426), para. 162 (fn omitted)).

284 Canada's appellee's submission, para. 186.

285 *Ibid.*

to be explored and resolved in order for any such analysis to be undertaken".[286] Considering that these observations are not findings, Canada argues that the European Union's claim under Article 11 of the DSU "is of no effect".[287]

2.192 Canada also rejects Japan's claims made before the Panel that the weighted-average wholesale rate and the RPP commodity charge could support the finding of a benefit because, absent the FIT Programme, the generators in question would not be in Ontario's wholesale electricity "market".[288] Canada contends that Japan's statement that the unaffected rates are significantly lower than the FIT rates, given the magnitude of difference between Japan's original benchmarks and the FIT rates, "ignores the fact that the entire Panel, including the dissent, comprehensively rejected all these benchmarks because they do not represent prices determined by market forces".[289] In this regard, Canada recalls that the Panel found that price offers by generators in this "market" are "not motivated by the need to cover marginal costs of production (as would typically be the case in a competitive wholesale electricity market ...)".[290] Rather, the primary motivation for generators is to ensure they are dispatched in order to receive their regulated or contract-based rates of remuneration. Canada argues that, "[o]n this basis, the Panel rejected the HOEP and HOEP derivative benchmarks proposed by Japan and the European Union", finding that the IESO-administered wholesale market clearing mechanism that generates the HOEP was actually "best characterized as a tool for the IESO to make the dispatch decisions needed to balance *physical* supply and demand for electricity".[291] Canada states that the dissenting member of the Panel agreed that the HOEP is "directly related to the electricity pricing policy and supply-mix decisions of ... Ontario"[292] and concluded that the HOEP, its derivatives, and the proposed out-of-province benchmarks "do not represent a price established on a competitive wholesale electricity market in Ontario".[293]

2.193 For these reasons, Canada requests the Appellate Body to reject the complainants' other appeals and uphold the Panel's finding that they have failed to demonstrate that Ontario's purchase of wind and solar electricity under the FIT Programme constitutes a "subsidy" that is inconsistent with Articles 3.1(b) and 3.2 of the SCM Agreement.

---

286 Canada's appellee's submission, para. 206 (quoting Panel Reports, para. 7.327).

287 Canada's appellee's submission, para. 206.

288 Canada's appellee's submission, para. 208 (referring to Japan's other appellant submission (DS412), para. 85).

289 Canada's appellee's submission, para. 210 (referring to Panel Reports, paras. 7.293-7.298 and 9.8-9.10).

290 Canada's appellee's submission, para. 211 (quoting Panel Reports, para. 7.298).

291 Canada's appellee's submission, para. 211 (quoting Panel Reports, para. 7.298 (original emphasis)).

292 Canada's appellee's submission, para. 212 (referring to Panel Reports, para. 9.10).

293 *Ibid.*

2.7 Arguments of the third participants

2.7.1 Australia

2.194 With respect to the claims raised under Article III:8(a) of the GATT 1994, Australia shares the concerns raised by the European Union regarding the Panel's interpretation of the term "governmental purposes". Australia supports the European Union's request that the Appellate Body reverse or declare moot and of no legal effect the Panel's statement that the term "governmental purposes" is relatively broad and may encompass the meaning proposed by Canada – that is, that a purchase for "governmental purposes" may exist whenever a government purchases a product for a stated aim of the government.[294] In Australia's view, the Panel's interpretation of the term "for governmental purposes" is not consistent with the ordinary meaning of the word "purposes", the French and Spanish versions of Article III:8(a), or the negotiating history of Article XVII:2 of GATT 1994, all of which denote the concept of practical advantage or use by the government, rather than a purchase for an aim of the government. Australia agrees with Japan that, if any purchase by a governmental agency for a stated aim of the government were to be covered by Article III:8(a), as Canada suggests, then a WTO Member could circumvent the disciplines of Article III simply by inserting itself as an intermediary in any given market.

2.195 As to the determination of "benefit" under Article 1.1(b) of the SCM Agreement, Australia stated at the oral hearing that it considered that the relevant inquiry is whether the financial contribution is provided on terms that confer an advantage on the recipient. Australia emphasized that there is nothing inherently wrong with a subsidy; the SCM Agreement simply requires that Members avoid recourse to subsidies that are prohibited or cause adverse trade effects. Australia submitted, however, that, if the burden of establishing the existence of a subsidy is too high, many government programmes that were intended to be disciplined by the SCM Agreement would escape scrutiny. Australia submitted that, if the decision of the Panel majority stands, then it could be difficult for any government support programme to be captured by the SCM Agreement. Indeed, the determination of a market benchmark would become difficult and the evaluation of whether there is a subsidy could be unduly constrained in any market where the government intervenes with regard to price.

2.196 At the oral hearing, Australia added that the guidance in Article 14(d) of the SCM Agreement does not provide an exclusive standard for determining whether a benefit is conferred. Australia recalled that, in *Canada – Aircraft*, the Appellate Body found that the ordinary meaning of "benefit" clearly encompasses some form of advantage, and that, in *EC and certain member States – Large Civil Aircraft*, the Appellate Body explained that, in identifying

[294] Australia's third participant's submission, para. 6 (referring to Panel Reports, para. 7.139).

such advantage, a comparison is required to determine whether the recipient of the financial contribution is made "better off"[295] than it would otherwise have been, absent the government action. In Australia's view, this jurisprudence provides the appropriate legal standard and should have provided the basis for the Panel's inquiry, rather than seeking to determine whether FIT generators were given more than adequate remuneration under Article 14(d) of the SCM Agreement. Australia submitted that, given the Panel's finding of an advantage under the TRIMs Agreement, a finding of "benefit" under the SCM Agreement should have been made with little difficulty.

2.197 Finally, Australia indicated at the oral hearing that it agreed with the approach of the dissenting member of the Panel to determining "benefit". In particular, Australia stated that the FIT Programme confers a benefit because electricity generators supplying wind- or solar PV-sourced electricity would not be able to enter the market unless the Government of Ontario purchased this electricity at elevated prices through FIT and microFIT Contracts. Thus, the FIT Programme accords an advantage on FIT generators and thereby confers a benefit under Article 1.1(b) of the SCM Agreement.

2.7.2 Brazil

2.198 Brazil alleges that the Panel's interpretation of the terms "governmental purposes" and "not with a view to commercial resale" in Article III:8(a) of the GATT 1994 conflates two different legal requirements into a single one and thereby renders part of the text of this provision redundant and without legal effect. For Brazil, the Panel's failure to consider the use of the word "and" joining these two terms in Article III:8(a) amounts to establishing that the simple existence of a "commercial resale" is enough to set aside the applicability of this provision altogether, regardless of its rationale or its relation with the first requirement of this provision, that is, the purchase of goods for "governmental purposes". Brazil considers that, should this interpretation prevail, the term "governmental purposes" would be rendered inutile. In the present case, the Panel never arrived at a conclusion with regard to the question of whether purchases of electricity under the FIT Programme were made for "governmental purposes". In Brazil's view, in order to assess if a measure falls outside the purview of Article III:8(a), it would be necessary to analyze both requirements separately.

2.199 Moreover, Brazil considers that the purpose of any governmental action can only be assessed on a case-by-case basis, and should be informed by the functions performed by a given government in each sector of its economy. Brazil submits that most governments have the constitutional or legal responsibility to provide certain services to their citizens – such as health, education, water,

[295] Australia's opening statement at the oral hearing.

electricity, transportation, and public security – and that providing these services constitutes a "governmental purpose" within the meaning of Article III:8(a).

2.200 Brazil further submits that, if the negotiators had intended to restrict the meaning of the term "governmental purposes" to purchases made by governmental agencies for their own use or consumption, they would have done so expressly, as they did in Article XVII:2 of the GATT 1994. Brazil contends that not all purchases of goods made by the government qualify as purchases for "governmental purposes" within the meaning of Article III:8(a), because this would allow the government of a WTO Member to circumvent the disciplines of Article III by inserting itself as an intermediary in any given market. Rather, Brazil submits that the appropriate analysis under Article III:8(a) requires comparing the overall design, structure, and architecture of a procurement programme with the legal and regulatory framework of the responding Member to determine "whether the purchase of goods under scrutiny genuinely pertains to a governmental function in the specific sector of that Member's economy, in light of the legitimate policy objectives within that State's society".[296]

2.201 At the oral hearing, Brazil further stated that the jurisprudence developed in the context of Article XX of the GATT 1994 provides useful guidance for assessing whether a government procurement programme pursues a governmental purpose. For Brazil, this guidance calls for an examination of whether the measure makes a contribution to its objective. Brazil argued that the other two elements of the "necessity test" – i.e. the "restrictiveness" of the measure and the importance of the objective pursued – are not as relevant in the context of Article III:8(a), given that a discriminatory government procurement programme will necessarily be restrictive, and that there seems to be no criteria to establish a hierarchy between different governmental purposes in the context of this provision.

2.202 With respect to the determination of "benefit" under Article 1.1(b) of the SCM Agreement, Brazil argues that the conclusion reached by the Panel majority that the FIT Programme does not confer a benefit was based on a flawed analysis of the Ontario electricity market. In particular, Brazil contends that the Panel majority's conclusion that none of the benchmarks presented by the complainants were appropriate to evaluate the existence of a benefit is "at odds" with prior decisions of the Appellate Body.[297] Brazil agrees with the dissenting opinion that the fact that a competitive market might not exist in the absence of government intervention, or that it may not achieve all of the objectives set by a government, does not mean that it cannot be used as a benchmark for the benefit analysis.

---

[296] Brazil's third participant's submission, para. 27.

[297] Brazil's third participant's submission, para. 36 (referring to Appellate Body Reports, *EC and certain member States – Large Civil Aircraft*, paras. 982 and 1122 (the latter para. referring in turn to Appellate Body Report, *US – Upland Cotton*, para. 480); and *Japan – DRAMs (Korea)*, para. 172).

2.203 According to Brazil, it "seems rather obvious" that, "if a producer that increases its market share as a result of a financial contribution is 'better off' in relation to the 'prevailing market conditions', then a producer that did not have an economically viable enterprise [that] enters the market through a financial contribution will also be 'better off' in relation to 'prevailing market conditions'."[298] For Brazil, it is "clear" that, in this case, the producers of solar PV and windpower electricity are "better off" in relation to the "prevailing market conditions" for the simple fact that they became market participants with a long-term, guaranteed participation in the market.[299] This provides a strong indication that the FIT and microFIT Contracts confer a benefit within the meaning of Article 1.1(b) of the SCM Agreement.

2.204 Brazil emphasizes that subsidies are not, in and of themselves, inconsistent with the covered agreements, provided they are not prohibited under Article 3.1(b) of the SCM Agreement, and may be appropriate to promote legitimate objectives.

2.7.3 China

2.205 With respect to the claims raised under Article III:8(a) of the GATT 1994, China supports the European Union's appeal of the Panel's finding that the Minimum Required Domestic Content Levels are "requirements governing" the procurement of electricity within the meaning of this provision. China argues that, because the word "procurement" in Article III:8(a) is linked to the words "products purchased", the provision does not apply to procurement of any product, but only to the procurement of products falling within the scope of Article III. China maintains that the Minimum Required Domestic Content Levels with respect to generation equipment under the FIT Programme are only remotely related to the procurement of electricity by the Government of Ontario, and that the Government of Ontario may purchase electricity without such Minimum Required Domestic Content Levels. China submits that it is therefore difficult to justify the application of Article III:8(a) with respect to the local content requirements concerning generation equipment.

2.206 Moreover, China disagrees with Canada's proposition that the phrase "with a view to commercial resale" in Article III:8(a) must be interpreted as referring to the intention behind a purchase. For China, this requirement requires an examination of evidence, rather than of the intention asserted by a governmental agency. China contends that Canada's interpretation may lead to the "absurd situation"[300] that a transaction would fall within the scope of Article III:8(a) as long as a governmental agency claims not to have an intention of commercial resale, even if that agency actually conducts commercial resale.

[298] Brazil's third participant's submission, para. 46.

[299] Brazil's third participant's submission, para. 44.

[300] China's third participant's submission, para. 15.

China also disagrees with Canada's interpretation of the term "commercial resale" as referring to resale with the underlying intent to profit. China submits that a resale may be considered "commercial" under Article III:8(a) even if it does not involve a profit. In addition, China alleges that Canada's interpretation of the phrase "with a view to commercial resale" renders the words "with a view to" redundant, because, for Canada, both the term "commercial resale" and the term "with a view to" refer to the aim or intent of the government. China submits that, when determining whether a resale is "commercial" within the meaning of Article III:8(a), the existence of profit should not be the legal standard that resolves the issue, but only one factor to be taken into account.

2.7.4 India

2.207 Pursuant to Rule 24(2) of the Working Procedures, India chose not to submit a third participant's submission. At the oral hearing, India stated that the Panel was correct in finding that, under Article III:8(a) of the GATT 1994, a purchase for "governmental purposes" may exist whenever a government purchases goods for a stated aim of the government. India considered that Japan's contention that the scope of the term "government purpose" is limited to purchases for the government's own use unduly limits the scope of this term. With respect to the interpretation of the term "commercial resale" in Article III:8(a), India indicated that the focus should be on the nature of the sale, that is, whether it is an action that is in pursuance of a government policy objective.

2.208 Moreover, India expressed its disagreement with Japan's claim that the measures at issue constitute "income or price support" within the meaning of Article 1.1(a)(2) of the SCM Agreement. For India, acceptance of Japan's interpretation would mean that any price regulation of public utilities or services could be susceptible to challenge as a subsidy, irrespective of the nature and intent of such price intervention. In India's view, regulatory oversight that simply ensures pricing based on market principles cannot be characterized as a subsidy.

2.209 With respect to the determination of "benefit" under Article 1.1(b), India contested Japan's and the European Union's argument that the FIT Programme confers a benefit because, in India's view, absent the FIT Programme, there would be no demand for renewable energy. India urged the Appellate Body to reject this claim since, under this reasoning, there would be no marketplace for renewable energy. For India, the alternative benchmark proposed by the Panel majority was appropriate and should be upheld by the Appellate Body. India observed that, while it may have been possible to determine whether a benefit is conferred by examining whether rates of return are significantly above average cost of capital in Canada for projects having a comparable risk profile, the facts on the record do not support such a finding.

2.7.5 Norway

2.210 Pursuant to Rule 24(2) of the Working Procedures, Norway chose not to submit a third participant's submission. At the oral hearing, Norway expressed its concern with the Panel's interpretation that the term "governmental purposes" in Article III:8(a) of the GATT 1994 is relatively broad and may encompass all situations where a government purchases a product for a stated aim of the government. In Norway's view, this interpretation would allow every single purchase made by a government to constitute a purchase for "governmental purposes", as every such purchase will have some sort of aim.

2.211 Norway agreed with the Panel that a purchase "with a view to commercial resale" cannot, at the same time, be considered a "product purchased for governmental purposes". However, as the term "governmental purposes" has independent meaning, Norway considered that the Panel erred by basing its joint assessment of the two requirements only on its conclusion of the meaning of the phrase "with a view to commercial resale", and thereby not concluding on the interpretation of the term "governmental purposes".[301]

2.7.6 Saudi Arabia

2.212 With respect to the determination of "benefit" under Article 1.1(b) of the SCM Agreement, Saudi Arabia asserts that the Panel correctly considered Article 14(d) of the SCM Agreement to be relevant in these disputes. Saudi Arabia points out that Article 14(d) describes how the adequacy of remuneration is to be determined in relation to "prevailing market conditions" for the goods in question in the country of purchase. Saudi Arabia submits that the word "market" in Article 14(d) is intended to refer to the in-country market in which the government measure in question has been adopted and that the word "prevailing" means "existing" market conditions.[302]

2.213 Saudi Arabia submits that the term "adequate remuneration" does not mean profit maximization, nor does it require that a transaction seek the highest price for the seller or the lowest price for the purchaser. Saudi Arabia agrees with the Panel that "[t]he relevant 'market' need not be a 'pure' marketplace that is devoid of any degree of government intervention".[303] At the oral hearing, Saudi Arabia requested the Appellate Body to affirm that government intervention does not preclude the use of a domestic price benchmark.

2.214 Moreover, Saudi Arabia states that the Panel's rejection of external benchmarks was sound because such benchmarks are appropriate only in "very

[301] Norway's opening statement at the oral hearing.

[302] Saudi Arabia's third participant's submission, para. 9.

[303] Saudi Arabia's third participant's submission, para. 15 (quoting Panel Reports, para. 7.274 (fn omitted)).

limited"[304] situations. Saudi Arabia cautions that an external benchmark that does not reflect domestic market conditions is an arbitrary measure that could negate the comparative advantages of the country under investigation. According to Saudi Arabia, in-country cost-based benchmarks have distinct advantages as alternatives to in-country price benchmarks, especially in contrast with external benchmarks. For instance, in-country cost-based benchmarks can be tailored to the unique circumstances of the country, industry, and enterprises concerned to reflect the prevailing market conditions in the country of purchase. Thus, Saudi Arabia requests the Appellate Body to affirm, as a general rule, and consistent with the text of Article 14(d), that in-country cost-based benchmarks are to be preferred over external benchmarks because the latter inevitably require speculative adjustments to reflect prevailing in-country market conditions.

2.7.7 Turkey

2.215 Pursuant to Rule 24(2) of the Working Procedures, Turkey chose not to submit a third participant's submission. At the oral hearing, with respect to Article III:8(a) of the GATT 1994, Turkey argued that the measures that are excepted from the obligations of Article III by virtue of the application of Article III:8(a) also include measures that breach Article III:4, such as those set forth in the Illustrative List in the Annex to the TRIMs Agreement. Moreover, Turkey stated that, although they constitute a single requirement, the terms "governmental purposes" and "not with a view to commercial resale or with a view to use in the production of goods for commercial sale" need to be analyzed separately. Therefore, Turkey does not agree with the Panel that a purchase of goods for "governmental purposes" cannot at the same time amount to a governmental purchase of goods "with a view to commercial resale".[305]

2.7.8 United States

2.216 The United States addresses five aspects of the Panel's interpretation and application of Article III:8(a) of the GATT 1994. First, the United States disagrees with the Panel's finding that there was a "close relationship"[306] between the product procured by the government (i.e. electricity) and the products affected by the domestic content requirements (i.e. generation equipment) under the FIT Programme. For the United States, the use of the word "governs" in Article III:8(a) indicates that the "laws, regulations or requirements" must directly pertain to the procurement by a government of a specific product.

---

[304] Saudi Arabia's third participant's submission, para. 19 (quoting Appellate Body Report, *US – Softwood Lumber IV*, para. 102).

[305] Turkey's opening statement at the oral hearing (DS426).

[306] United States' third participant's submission, para. 18 (quoting Panel Reports, para. 7.127).

2.217 Second, the United States agrees with the European Union that the products purchased by the government must be for use in pursuit of its functions, including consumption by the government, or in the provision of goods or services to its citizens. Third, the United States contends that the Panel correctly interpreted and applied the term "with a view to" in Article III:8(a) of the GATT 1994. The United States argues that the Panel considered the "aim" or "purpose" of the purchase and correctly concluded that the Government of Ontario purchases electricity with an aim to commercial resale, because it purchases electricity in the full knowledge and intent that the electricity will be resold on the market to private consumers rather than put to a governmental purpose.

2.218 Fourth, the United States argues that the words "commercial resale" should be interpreted to mean "to be sold into the market".[307] By including in its ambit government purchases made "for governmental purposes" and excluding those made for "commercial resale", Article III:8(a) seeks to distinguish between purchases made for "governmental" reasons and those made for "commercial" reasons, and thus clarifies that "a purchase leading to a commercial resale is not a purchase for governmental purposes, and *vice versa*."[308] Fifth, regarding the phrase "use in the production of goods for commercial sale", the United States argues that this provision is not limited to use in the government's production of goods for commercial sale, but that it applies equally to goods purchased by a government for use in private production of goods for commercial sale.

2.219 With respect to the relationship between the TRIMs Agreement and Article III:4 of the GATT 1994, the United States agrees with the Panel that a measure excepted from the obligations of Article III of the GATT 1994 by paragraph 8(a) would not breach the national treatment obligation in paragraph 4 by virtue of being included in the Illustrative List in the Annex to the TRIMs Agreement. The United States observes that Article 2.2 of the TRIMs Agreement and the Illustrative List do not establish independent obligations. Rather, a national treatment breach under Article 2 of the TRIMs Agreement only occurs in the event of a breach of Article III of the GATT 1994, which will not arise if one of its exceptions applies.

2.220 With respect to the determination of whether the measures at issue confer a benefit within the meaning of Article 1.1(b) of the SCM Agreement, the United States considers that the Panel majority erred in several respects. First, the United States considers that the Panel majority's finding that the FIT generators would be "unable to conduct viable operations"[309] in a competitive wholesale market in Ontario in the absence of the FIT Programme should have led the Panel to find that the FIT Programme and FIT and microFIT Contracts are financial contributions with terms "more favourable to what is

---

307 United States' third participant's submission, para. 10.

308 United States' third participant's submission, para. 12.

309 United States' third participant's submission, para. 24 (quoting Panel Reports, para. 7.311).

available to the recipient on the market"[310] and thus confer a benefit. Moreover, like the European Union and Japan, the United States notes that the Panel found the price guarantee to be an "advantage"[311] in relation to the TRIMs Agreement, and considers that this should have informed the question of whether the guarantee of those rates conferred a benefit for the purposes of the SCM Agreement.

2.221 Second, the United States submits that there is no requirement in Article 1.1(b) that "benefit" be demonstrated on the basis of such a purely competitive market, nor is there any context provided by Article 14 that would lead to that conclusion. The United States recalls that the Panel majority concluded that the word "market" in Article 14(d) refers to "a market where there is effective competition"[312] solely on the basis of the Appellate Body's findings in *US – Softwood Lumber IV* concerning the acceptable use by an investigating authority of benchmarks other than in-country private prices. The United States emphasizes that the task of a panel under Article 1.1(b) is to determine the existence of a benefit, not to calculate its amount. The United States also notes that, in *US – Softwood Lumber IV*, the Appellate Body used the phrase "*may* use a benchmark other than private prices"[313], and that the Appellate Body did not find that an investigating authority must rely on a benchmark solely based on a theoretical competitive market or resort to an actual competitive market outside the market at issue. Further, the United States points out that, even if the HOEP alone is an inappropriate basis for a benchmark, it may still play a role as part of a benchmark. Thus, the Panel majority erred in rejecting any benchmarks that derived from the HOEP.

2.222 The United States argues that a benefit benchmark is not required to include a government's policy choices. In particular, the United States objects to the position expressed by the Panel majority that a suitable benefit benchmark must "reflect 'the particular situation in Ontario', namely policy decisions ... with regard to the level of supply and sources of energy"[314], as this amounts to a requirement that a suitable benchmark must "reflect certain policy choices made by a government".[315] The United States sees no textual basis for such an interpretation and observes that every subsidy reflects a policy decision. The United States thus agrees with Japan that "[t]o require that the applicable

---

[310] United States' third participant's submission, para. 24 (quoting Appellate Body Report, *EC and certain member States – Large Civil Aircraft*, para. 974).

[311] United States' third participant's submission, fn 28 to para. 23 (referring to Panel Reports, paras. 7.165 and 7.166).

[312] United States' third participant's submission, para. 31 (quoting Panel Reports, para. 7.275).

[313] United States' third participant's submission, fn 53 to para. 34 (quoting Appellate Body Report, *US – Softwood Lumber IV*, para. 103). (underlining added by the United States)

[314] United States' third participant's submission, para. 38 (quoting Panel Reports, para. 7.312).

[315] United States' third participant's submission, para. 38.

benchmark be adjusted to reflect the government's policy would ... threaten to make the finding of a subsidy impossible."[316]

2.223 The United States observes that, where a government mandate to purchase a given level of green-sourced electricity is enough by itself for green-sourced electricity to enter the market, there will not necessarily be an impact on electricity prices. This would be so, for instance, in cases where the cost of producing green-sourced electricity – albeit higher – is close to the cost of producing electricity from traditional sources. The United States considers that the hypothetical benchmark proposed by the Panel majority involving a government-imposed mandate to acquire solar PV and windpower energy in fact illustrates the error in its approach. Even with such a mandate, if the cost is significantly higher than the cost of producing electricity from traditional sources, a rational producer will not enter the green energy sector unless the prices are sufficiently high to cover the cost of producing green-sourced electricity (including a return on investment).

2.224 Moreover, recalling that the Panel rejected the benchmarks put forth by the complainants based on the HOEP, the United States contends that the Panel majority erred when it rejected wholesale and retail prices because they were "derived" from the HOEP.[317] The United States points out that the wholesale and retail prices are derived not just from the HOEP but also from the Global Adjustment (GA).[318] The United States considers that the Panel majority should have considered these benchmarks rather than simply dismissing them on the basis that they are "HOEP-derivative".[319]

2.225 At the oral hearing, the United States argued that, by purchasing electricity produced from solar PV and windpower sources, the Government of Ontario is creating demand that would otherwise not exist. This is supported by the fact that solar PV- and wind-powered generators would not enter the market "but for" the FIT Programme, due to their higher costs. The United States pointed out that, by making a financial contribution that allows otherwise unviable producers to enter the market, the FIT Programme confers a benefit within the meaning of Article 1.1(b) of the SCM Agreement.

---

316 United States' third participant's submission, para. 40 (referring to Japan's other appellant's submission (DS412), para. 97).

317 United States' third participant's submission, para. 47.

318 United States' third participant's submission, para. 47 (referring to Panel Reports, para. 7.55).

319 United States' third participant's submission, para. 48.

3. ISSUES RAISED IN THIS APPEAL

3.1 The following issues are raised in this appeal:

a. Whether the analysis of Japan's claims in this appeal should commence with Japan's claims under the SCM Agreement (raised by Japan);

b. With respect to the relationship between Article III of the GATT 1994 and the TRIMs Agreement, whether the Panel erred in the interpretation and application of Articles 2.1 and 2.2 of the TRIMs Agreement, read in conjunction with paragraph 1(a) of the Illustrative List in the Annex to the TRIMs Agreement, when finding that these provisions do not preclude the application of Article III:8(a) of the GATT 1994 to the challenged measures (raised by the European Union);

c. With respect to the Panel's interpretation and application of Article III:8(a) of the GATT 1994, whether the Panel:

   i. erred in finding that the domestic content requirements at issue "govern" the procurement of electricity (raised by the European Union);

   ii. erred in finding that the FIT Programme and related FIT and microFIT Contracts involve "procurement by governmental agencies of products purchased" (raised by Japan);

   iii. erred in the interpretation and application of the terms "for governmental purposes" (conditional appeals raised by Japan and the European Union);

   iv. erred by considering evidence of profit as a relevant factor in assessing whether the Government of Ontario's purchases of electricity under the FIT Programme are undertaken "with the view to commercial resale" (conditionally raised by Japan);

   v. erred in finding that the Government of Ontario's purchases of electricity under the FIT Programme are undertaken "with the view to commercial resale" (raised by Canada); and

   vi. failed to make an objective assessment of the matter before it, contrary to Article 11 of the DSU, when finding that the measures at issue involve purchases "with a view to commercial resale". More specifically, whether the Panel acted inconsistently with Article 11 of the DSU in finding that:

- Hydro One Inc. and Local Distribution Companies sell electricity in competition with private-sector licensed retailers (raised by Canada); and
- the Government of Ontario and the municipal governments profit from the resale of electricity purchased under the FIT Programme to consumers (raised by Canada);

d. Whether the Panel failed to comply with its duties under Article 11 of the DSU and exercised false judicial economy by failing to make a finding of inconsistency with Article III:4 of the GATT 1994 independent of its findings relating to the TRIMs Agreement (raised by Japan);

e. With respect to Article 1.1(a) of the SCM Agreement, whether:

   i. the Panel erred in finding that it could not conclude that government "purchases [of] goods" could also be legally characterized as "direct transfer[s] of funds" (raised by Japan);

   ii. the Panel erred in finding that the FIT Programme and related FIT and microFIT Contracts are government "purchases [of] goods" (raised by Japan); and

   iii. even if the FIT Programme and related FIT and microFIT Contracts are characterized as government "purchases [of] goods", then whether they may also be characterized as "direct transfer[s] of funds", "potential direct transfers of funds", or "income or price support" (raised by Japan);

f. Whether the Panel erred in exercising judicial economy with respect to the Japan's claim that the measures at issue may be legally characterized as "income or price support" under Article 1.1(a)(2) of the SCM Agreement, and thereby acted inconsistently with its obligations under Article 11 of the DSU (raised by Japan); and

g. With respect to the Panel's interpretation and application of Article 1.1(b) of the SCM Agreement, whether the Panel:

   i. erred in finding that the European Union and Japan failed to establish that the challenged measures confer a benefit (raised by Japan and by the European Union); and

   ii. failed to make an objective assessment of the matter under Article 11 of the DSU in finding that the European Union and Japan failed to establish that the challenged measures confer a benefit (raised by Japan and by the European Union).

4. BACKGROUND AND OVERVIEW OF THE MEASURES AT ISSUE

4.1 Electricity networks

4.1 Before addressing the claims raised by the participants on appeal, we provide an overview of the measures at issue and outline certain relevant facts identified by the Panel. For additional details in this regard, recourse should be had to the Panel Reports.[320] We note that some of the Panel's factual findings seem to refer generally to electricity markets, while others seem to refer to the Ontario electricity market in particular. To the extent we reproduce the Panel's statements that seem to relate generally to electricity markets, we do so because we consider them to be of particular application to the circumstances of these disputes and not necessarily because we are of the view that they necessarily reflect the characteristics of all electricity markets.

4.2 Electricity is delivered to consumers through high-voltage transmission lines, which connect generators to distributors and large consumers, and through lower-voltage distribution lines, which deliver electricity to individual consumers. In order to ensure the integrity of the electricity system as a whole, it is necessary to maintain a continuous supply-demand balance between generators and consumers. Electricity delivery networks may fail if the quantity of electricity demanded (known as "load") is greater or less than the quantity of electricity supplied for any length of time. In particular, when important imbalances occur, electricity networks may be destabilized, leading to brownouts, blackouts or, in extreme cases, the interruption of power to all consumers.[321] Due to the need to maintain a continuous supply-demand balance across an entire electricity system, uncoordinated bilateral trades between buyers and sellers of electricity cannot take place.[322] As a consequence, "electricity systems require some kind of central coordination mechanism to ensure that the output of generators is exactly equal to the amount demanded by consumers".[323]

4.3 Given that electricity cannot be stored in large quantities and that demand for electricity fluctuates over any given day[324], electricity systems generally satisfy demand by utilizing a mix of generation technologies, each with different cost structures and operational requirements. The Panel found that electricity

---

320 See, in particular, Panel Reports, paras. 7.9-7.68 and 7.195-7.219.

321 Panel Reports, para. 7.11.

322 Panel Reports, para. 7.12.

323 Panel Reports, para. 7.12 (referring to Professor William W. Hogan, Harvard University, "Overview of the Electricity System in the Province of Ontario", 21 December 2011 (Hogan Report) (Panel Exhibit CDA-2), p. 13).

324 The Panel found that, as there are no close substitutes for electricity, electricity demand is largely unresponsive to prices in the short run (i.e. it is relatively price inelastic). Thus, electricity demand fluctuates over the course of a day, week, month, or year when factors other than price (e.g. air temperature and hours of daylight) cause the demand for electricity to change. (Panel Reports, para. 7.13)

"facilities may be described as 'base-load', 'intermediate' or 'peaking', depending upon when and for how long they operate, whether they can raise or lower their output rapidly in a controlled manner ('dispatchability'), and whether their costs are mostly fixed or variable."[325] In particular, the Panel found that base-load generation is that portion of an electricity system's supply-mix that is expected to be able to operate during both low- and high-demand periods.[326] Typical examples of base-load generation are hydroelectric[327] and nuclear stations.[328] This function, however, may also be performed by other technologies (e.g. coal) depending on the supply-mix in a given jurisdiction and on the cost of fuel.[329] In turn, intermediate-load generation supplies power when system demand is above its minimum level but still below its maximum level.[330] Coal and natural gas plants are frequently used for intermediate-load generation.[331] Finally, peak-load generators tend to have a high degree of dispatchability and may only run infrequently, usually at times when demand is near the system-wide capacity limit.[332] Single-cycle gas-combustion turbines are an example of peak-load generators. The ability of generators to adjust their level of output quickly (i.e. their dispatchability) tends to be lowest for base-load generators and highest for peak-load generators.[333] Furthermore, the Panel found that electricity generation produced from solar photovoltaic (PV) and windpower technologies resemble base-load generation in that most of their costs are capital costs, but they differ in that their capacity utilization is lower due to intermittent output.[334]

4.4 The Panel noted that "[n]on-dispatchable loads account for most of the energy consumed in Ontario".[335] It further explained that electricity demand is largely unresponsive to prices in the short run (i.e. it is relatively inelastic).[336]

---

[325] Panel Reports, para. 7.14.

[326] Panel Reports, para. 7.15.

[327] Base-load generators tend to have limited dispatchability. However, hydroelectric plants are an exception in that their output can be raised or lowered on relatively short notice. (Panel Reports, para. 7.15)

[328] Panel Reports, para. 7.15.

[329] *Ibid.*

[330] Panel Reports, para. 7.16.

[331] *Ibid.*

[332] Panel Reports, para. 7.17.

[333] Panel Reports, para. 7.280. The Panel noted, however, that "[a]lthough hydroelectricity is usually classified as base load power, certain types of hydroelectric facilities can be dispatched". (*Ibid.*, (referring to Hogan Report, p. 5))

[334] Panel Reports, paras. 7.19 and 7.280. The Panel found that generation facilities utilizing solar PV and windpower technologies are considered intermittent generators because power is produced only during certain times of the day and/or night. In particular, wind turbines only produce electricity when the wind is blowing, and electricity from solar PV sources is only produced during the day. (*Ibid.*)

[335] Panel Reports, fn 526 to para. 7.279 (quoting IESO, Introduction to Ontario's Physical Markets: IESO Training (October 2011) (Panel Exhibit JPN-80), p. 4).

[336] Panel Reports, para. 7.279 (referring to IESO, Introduction to Ontario's Physical Markets: IESO Training (October 2011) (Panel Exhibit JPN-80), p. 4). In particular, the Panel explained that

Thus, the demand curve can be represented by a (nearly) vertical line in a traditional supply/demand diagram.[337] In addition, the Panel found that plotting the bids submitted by generators in a wholesale electricity market where there is effective competition against their output defines the electricity supply curve.[338] The Panel described the supply curve of a typical mix of generators "as an upward sloping step function that rises sharply as output approaches the market's capacity limit".[339] The Panel further explained that the intersection of supply and demand determines the market clearing price (MCP) and quantity of electricity.[340] Due to the steepness of the supply and demand curves in typical electricity markets, prices may be extremely volatile, rising or falling sharply in response to small changes in demand and/or supply.[341] According to the Panel, "[t]his is not necessarily an undesirable feature in an electricity market."[342] The Panel cited as an example a situation where high prices encourage households and businesses to consume less of the scarce commodity, as well as provide incentives for incumbent generators to increase their output and for new firms to enter the market by investing in new generation.[343] Therefore, the Panel found that, although a "well-designed" electricity market would provide adequate incentives for investment in new electricity generation, "this theoretical market ideal has not yet been achieved in many electricity systems, including in Ontario".[344] The Panel stated that "one of the main reasons for this is the complexity of incorporating appropriate demand-side responsiveness to supply-side price signals in times of scarcity".[345]

4.5 The Panel explained that, partly because of the absence of a more responsive demand in electricity markets, many governments have sought to control price volatility by intervening in the market. Consequently, many countries have experienced insufficient investment in generation because the prices set in their "organized" wholesale market are not allowed to rise to a level that, in the long run, fully compensates generators for the all-in cost of their investments (including fixed and sunk costs).[346] In such situation, referred to in the Hogan Report and by the Panel as the "missing money" problem, "[p]rivate investors will not be willing to finance construction of new generation under such conditions; and in the absence of such investment, an electricity market will

electricity demand is relatively inelastic because there are no close substitutes for electricity and there is a lack of easily observable price signals on the demand-side. (*Ibid.*)

337 Panel Reports, para. 7.279.

338 Panel Reports, para. 7.281 (referring to Hogan Report, p. 16).

339 Panel Reports, para. 7.281.

340 Panel Reports, para. 7.282.

341 *Ibid.*

342 Panel Reports, para. 7.282.

343 *Ibid.*

344 Panel Reports, para. 7.282 (quoting Hogan Report, pp. 16 and 17, respectively).

345 Panel Reports, para. 7.282 (referring to Hogan Report, p. 16).

346 Panel Reports, para. 7.283 (referring to Hogan Report, pp. 13 and 15-19).

be unable to reliably meet future electricity demand."[347] The Panel found that the "missing money" problem affects both conventional generation technologies and the more expensive solar PV and windpower generation technologies.[348]

4.2 Ontario's electricity market

4.6 The Government of Ontario established the Hydro-Electric Power Commission of Ontario (HEPCO) in 1906.[349] HEPCO, which was renamed Ontario Hydro in 1974, was organized as "a vertically integrated public utility with generation, transmission and distribution functions".[350] The Energy Competition Act of 1998, which enacted the Electricity Act of 1998[351], authorized the "unbundling"[352] of Ontario Hydro into five successor entities: (i) the Independent Market Operator, later renamed the Independent Electricity System Operator (IESO), which is an "agency" of the Government of Ontario[353] that "administers Ontario's electricity markets and operates and maintains the IESO-controlled grid to ensure real-time coordination between electricity supply and demand"[354]; (ii) Ontario Power Generation (OPG), which inherited Ontario Hydro's generation assets; (iii) Hydro One Inc., which received Ontario Hydro's transmission network and rural local distribution businesses; (iv) the Ontario Electricity Financial Corporation (OEFC), which inherited other Ontario Hydro assets and liabilities, including contracts with "Non-Utility Generators" (NUGs); and (v) the Electrical Safety Authority, which was tasked with regulating the system's safety.[355]

4.7 In addition, the Panel found that the Ontario Energy Board Act of 1998 designated the Ontario Energy Board (OEB), an "agency" of the Government of Ontario, as the regulator of "Ontario's electricity and natural gas sectors in

---

347 Panel Reports, para. 7.283 (referring to Hogan Report, pp. 17-19).

348 Panel Reports, para. 7.283 (referring to Hogan Report, p. 17).

349 Panel Reports, para. 7.21.

350 Panel Reports, para. 7.22.

351 *Service Ontario 1998*, Chapter 15, Schedule A, as amended (Panel Exhibit JPN-5).

352 Panel Reports, para. 7.22 (referring to Government of Ontario, *Ontario's Long-Term Energy Plan* (Queen's Printer for Ontario, 2010) (Panel Exhibit CDA-6), p. 5).

353 As an "agency" of the Government of Ontario, the IESO falls under the "legislative responsibility" of the Government of Ontario's Ministry of Energy. (Panel Reports, para. 7.39 (referring to Government of Ontario webpages, "All Agencies List" (Panel Exhibit JPN-49), available at: <*http://www.pas.gov.on.ca/scripts/en/BoardsList.asp*>; "About the Ministry of Energy" (Panel Exhibit JPN-52), available at: <*http://www.energy.gov.on.ca/en/about/*>; and "Agency Details, Independent Electricity System Operator" (Panel Exhibit JPN-57), available at: <*http://www.pas.gov.on.ca/scripts/en/BoardDetails.asp?boardID=128220*>; and IESO webpage, "About the IESO" (Panel Exhibit JPN-59) , available at: <*http://www.ieso.ca/imoweb/about/about_the_ieso.asp*>))

354 Panel Reports, para. 7.40 (referring to Electricity Act of 1998, Section 5). The Panel found that, in particular, the IESO manages Ontario's wholesale electricity market, which involves monitoring and directing the movement of electricity across the IESO-controlled grid and the settlement of payments between market participants. (*Ibid.*, para. 7.40)

355 Panel Reports, para. 7.22 (referring to Hogan Report, pp. 20-21).

conformity with the public interest".[356] In the electricity sector, the OEB sets the transmission and distribution rates, determines the prices that will be received by OPG's "regulated" assets for electricity delivered into Ontario's electricity grid, and maintains the "Regulated Price Plan" (RPP), which establishes the prices paid by retail consumers that purchase electricity from "Local Distribution Companies" (LDCs).[357]

4.8 In May 2002, the Ontario wholesale electricity market was opened to competition.[358] It was expected that the restructuring of the electricity sector would attract private investment into electricity generation. However, although electricity prices rose 30% in the months following the market opening[359], the anticipated investment failed to materialize.[360] Instead, according to the Panel, the relatively high electricity prices led the Government of Ontario temporarily to freeze electricity prices for residential, institutional, and small business consumers.[361] In particular, the Panel found that, "in addition to the price volatility problems associated with the inherent attributes of competitive wholesale electricity markets, a combination of other factors shaping the interaction of supply and demand for electricity in Ontario affected the operation of the competitive wholesale market that existed between May and November 2002".[362] These factors included: very high temperatures during the summer of 2002, which drove up demand to levels that could not be satisfied by existing suppliers without significant price increases; the delay in re-establishing production at the Pickering Unit 4 nuclear plant; the impact of Enron's collapse on financial markets and the temporary failure of the long-term energy trading market; and the retreat of financial markets from the electricity industry.[363]

---

[356] Panel Reports, para. 7.42 (referring to Government of Ontario webpages, "All Agencies List" (Panel Exhibit JPN-49), available at: <*http://www.pas.gov.on.ca/scripts/en/BoardsList.asp*>; and "Agency Details, Ontario Energy Board" (Panel Exhibit JPN-63), available at: <*http://www.pas.gov.on.ca/scripts/en/BoardDetails.asp?boardID=764*>; and OEB webpage, "What We Do" (Panel Exhibit JPN-64), available at: <*http://www.ontarioenergyboard.ca/OEB/Industry/About+the+OEB/What+We+Do*>).

[357] Panel Reports, para. 7.42.

[358] Panel Reports, para. 7.285 (referring to Canada's first written submission to the Panel (DS412), para. 25) Between May and November 2002, electricity generated from facilities accounting for 94% of Ontario's generation capacity was bought and sold on the wholesale market at prices set through a market clearing mechanism administered by the Independent Market Operator. (*Ibid.* (referring to Canada's response to Panel questions Nos. 1 and 19 (second set); and first written submission to the Panel (DS412), para. 22(iv)) The mix of electricity generation technologies that operated in 2002 included nuclear, coal, hydroelectric, and oil/gas facilities, which together accounted for over 99% of total available capacity (29,523 megawatts) and total electricity output (149,690 gigawatt hours) in 2002. (*Ibid.*, para. 7.286 (referring to Canada's response to Panel question No. 1 (second set))

[359] Panel Reports, para. 7.287 (referring to Government of Ontario, *Ontario's Long-Term Energy Plan* (Queen's Printer for Ontario, 2010) (Panel Exhibit CDA-6), p. 6).

[360] Panel Reports, para. 7.23.

[361] *Ibid.*

[362] Panel Reports, para. 7.289. (fn omitted)

[363] Panel Reports, paras. 7.287-2.289 (referring to Government of Ontario, *Ontario's Long-Term Energy Plan* (Panel Exhibit CDA-6), p. 6; Canada's response to Panel Question No. 1(g) (second set);

4.9 The Panel found that, due to the problems encountered during the 2002 market opening experience, the Government of Ontario decided to once again restructure Ontario's electricity system in 2004 by enacting the Electricity Restructuring Act of 2004.[364] This Act created the Ontario Power Authority (OPA) as "an 'agency' of the Government of Ontario responsible for managing Ontario's electricity supply and resources in order to meet its medium and long-term needs".[365] The OPA is under the "legislative responsibility" of the Government of Ontario's Ministry of Energy and receives and executes directives from the Minister of Energy.[366] The Panel found that the OPA's statutory objectives include engaging in:

> [A]ctivities in support of the goal of ensuring adequate, reliable and secure electricity supply and resources in Ontario; [and]
>
> ... activities to facilitate the diversification of sources of electricity supply by promoting the use of cleaner energy sources and technologies, including alternative energy sources and renewable energy sources; ...[367]

The Panel further found that, in order to achieve these objectives, the OPA was given the power to:

> [E]nter into contracts relating to the procurement of electricity supply and capacity in or outside Ontario; [and]
>
> ... enter into contracts relating to the procurement of electricity supply and capacity using alternative energy sources or renewable energy sources to assist the Government of Ontario in achieving goals in the development and use of alternative or renewable energy technology and resources; ...[368]

4.10 In its current form, Ontario's electricity system is a partially liberalized "hybrid" system where both public and private entities participate in generation,

---

Japan's first written submission to the Panel (DS412), para. 25; and Electricity Conservation and Supply Task Force, Tough Choices: Addressing Ontario's Power Needs, Final Report to the Minister of Energy (January 2004) (Panel Exhibit CDA-59), p. 84).

[364] An Act to amend the Electricity Act, 1998 and the Ontario Energy Board Act, 1998 and to make consequential amendments to other Acts, *Service Ontario 2004*, Chapter 23 (Panel Exhibits CDA-18 and JPN-8). See Panel Reports, para. 7.24.

[365] Panel Reports, para. 7.37 (referring to Government of Ontario webpages, "All Agencies List" (Panel Exhibit JPN-49), available at: <*http://www.pas.gov.on.ca/scripts/en/BoardsList.asp*>; and "Agency Details, Ontario Power Authority" (Panel Exhibit JPN-50), available at: <*http://www.pas.gov.on.ca/scripts/en/BoardDetails.asp?boardID=141181*>).

[366] Panel Reports, para. 7.37 (referring to Government of Ontario webpage, "About the Ministry of Energy" (Panel Exhibit JPN-52), available at: <*http://www.energy.gov.on.ca/en/about/*>; and OPA webpage, "Directives to OPA from Minister of Energy" (Panel Exhibit JPN-55), available at: <*http://www.powerauthority.on.ca/about-us/directives-opa-minister-energy-and-infrastructure*>).

[367] Panel Reports, para. 7.37 (quoting Electricity Act of 1998, Section 25.2(1)(c) and (d)).

[368] Panel Reports, para. 7.37 (quoting Electricity Act of 1998, Section 25.2(5)(b) and (c)).

transmission, distribution and retail activities.[369] The Government of Ontario, however, "continues to play a critical role in all aspects of the system's functioning".[370] There are three groups of generators in Ontario: (i) the government-owned assets of OPG, which is a wholly owned corporation of the Government of Ontario[371]; (ii) NUGs, which are private generators that entered into supply contracts in the 1980s and 1990s with Ontario Hydro[372]; and (iii) "Independent Power Producers" (IPPs), which include all the other generators in Ontario that have started to operate since the wholesale market was restructured.[373] The Panel set out in a table the mix of electricity generation that existed in Ontario in 2010:

369 Panel Reports, para. 7.25 (quoting Hogan Report, p. 21).

370 Panel Reports, para. 7.25.

371 OPG produced approximately 58% of all electricity generated in Ontario in 2010. OPG's nuclear and base-load hydroelectric generation facilities are classified as "OPG Regulated Assets" and receive a price for electricity set by the OEB. Other "unregulated" hydroelectric and coal-fired facilities owned by OPG receive the Hourly Ontario Energy Price (HOEP) for the supply of electricity. (Panel Reports, para. 7.27)

372 Panel Reports, para. 7.26. The Panel found that the prices paid to NUGs for delivered electricity, which were negotiated 20 years ago, are known to be generally higher than the HOEP. (*Ibid.*, para. 7.31)

373 Panel Reports, para. 7.26. The Panel found that IPPs, which generate around 40% of Ontario's electricity supply, receive prices that are negotiated or set under different types of OPA initiatives and contracts including: the Clean Energy Supply (CES) contracts for natural gas; the Renewable Energy Supply (RES) Requests for Proposals I, II, and III; the Hydroelectric Contract Initiative (HCI) for grid-connected non-OPG-owned hydro facilities; the Combined Heat and Power (CHP) Requests for Proposals I, II, and III; the Renewable Energy Standard Offer Programme (RESOP); and the FIT Programme. (*Ibid.*, para. 7.28)

Table 2: Ontario Electricity Generation Mix

Generation technology	Share of 2010 installed capacity	Approximate share of 2010 projected generation	Type of capacity	Relative capital cost	Relative operating cost per kWh	Relative dispatchability
Nuclear	31%	52%	base-load	high	low	low
Hydropower	22%	19%	base-load, peak-load, renewable	high	low	low for run-of-river, high for pondage
Coal	12%	8%	intermediate	medium	low	high
Gas and oil	25%	15%	peak-load	low	high	high
Wind	4%	2%	intermittent, renewable	very high	very low	low
Solar PV	0.3%	<0.1%	intermittent, renewable	very high	very low	low
Bioenergy	0.7%	1%	intermediate, renewable	medium	low	low
Conservation	5%	4%	base-load, peak-load	n/a	n/a	n/a

Source: Panel Reports, para. 7.280, Table 2.

4.11 Generators with capacity greater than 10 megawatts (MW) typically connect to the transmission system.[374] The Panel found that 97% of the transmission system in Ontario is owned and operated by Hydro One Networks Inc., a subsidiary of Hydro One Inc.[375] The remaining 3% is owned and operated by four other private companies. Generators that are connected to the transmission system must register with the IESO. Generators with capacity of 10 MW or less generally connect to the distribution system via an LDC.[376] Hydro One owns and operates approximately one quarter of Ontario's distribution system. The remainder of Ontario's distribution system is operated by 80 LDCs, 77 of which are owned by municipal governments.[377]

---

[374] Panel Reports, para. 7.33.

[375] Panel Reports, para. 7.34 (referring to Hydro One Website, "Our Subsidiaries" (Panel Exhibit JPN-43), available at: <*http://www.hydroone.com/OurCompany/Pages/OurSubsidiaries.aspx*>. The Panel found that "Hydro One is a holding company wholly-owned by the Government of Ontario and an 'agent' of the Government of Ontario." (Panel Reports, para. 7.147)

[376] Panel Reports, paras. 7.33 and 7.35 (referring to Hydro One Website, "Distribution-connected Generators" (Panel Exhibit JPN-45); and Electricity Transmission and Distribution in Ontario (Panel Exhibit JPN-36), p. 4).

[377] Panel Reports, para. 7.35 (referring to Hydro One webpage, "Our Subsidiaries" (Panel Exhibit JPN-43), available at: <*http://www.hydroone.com/OurCompany/Pages/OurSubsidiaries.aspx*>; Electricity Distributors Association webpage, "Delivering Safe, Reliable and Environmentally Responsible Electricity to Ontarians", July 2010 (Panel Exhibit JPN-46), available at: <*http://www.eda-on.ca/eda/edaweb.nsf/0/762d9f4c8b3b490385257331004c49ba/$FILE/ DELIVERING_ECONOMIC_BENEFITS.pdf*>; Blake, Cassels & Graydon webpage, "Overview of Electricity Regulation in Canada" (Panel Exhibit JPN-7), pp. 11 and 16, accessed at: <*http://www.blakes.com/english/legal_updates/reference_guides/Overview%20of%20Electricity%20*

4.12 The Panel found that the price for electricity sold at the wholesale level in Ontario is established by the IESO through the operation of a mechanism that uses supply and demand "stacks"[378] to determine for every five-minute interval: (i) which generators supply electricity and which consumers consume electricity; (ii) the amount of electricity to be supplied and consumed; and (iii) the MCP for that electricity.[379] The MCP is thus set every five minutes at the intersection between electricity supply and demand stacks in the IESO wholesale market. In turn, the average of the twelve MCPs set during the course of an hour is the "Hourly Ontario Energy Price" (HOEP).[380]

4.13 Generators in Ontario's electricity market whose rates are not regulated or contracted receive the MCP/HOEP for the electricity they deliver into the system. The Panel found that "[t]he only generators that receive the HOEP *alone* are the OPG's unregulated hydroelectric facilities and two of its coal-fired generation facilities"[381], which account for 8% of electricity generation in Ontario.[382] By contrast, facilities accounting for 92% of Ontario's 2010 generation capacity do not receive the HOEP, but a contracted or regulated rate.[383] These generators are subject to an adjustment to account for the difference between the MCP/HOEP and the generators' contracted or regulated price.[384] This adjustment is known as the "Global Adjustment" (GA) and it is a charge borne by either final electricity consumers or electricity generators depending on the relationship between the MCP/HOEP and the contracted or regulated rate. For instance, if the MCP/HOEP is lower than the regulated or contracted price, the GA will be a positive number representing a charge to consumers that must be paid to generators. However, if the MCP/HOEP is higher than the regulated or contracted price, the GA will be a negative number

---

in%20Canada.pdf>, (no longer available); and IESO webpage, "Find Your Local Utility" (Panel Exhibit JPN-47), available at: <*http://www.ieso.ca/imoweb/siteshared/local_dist.asp?sid=ic*>).

378 The Panel understood the functioning of the IESO "stack system" to be as follows:

> The IESO "stack system" is established on the premise that certain generators are capable of easily varying their electricity production while others are not, and likewise that certain consumers are capable of easily varying their electricity consumption while others are not. Generators and consumers that can easily vary their electricity production or consumption are termed "dispatchable", and receive "dispatch" instructions from the IESO every five minutes stating the quantity to be supplied or consumed. Those generators and consumers that cannot easily vary their electricity production or consumption are termed "non-dispatchable"; they do not receive "dispatch" instructions from the IESO, but rather their supply and demand is considered fixed and automatically placed by the IESO at the front of the supply and demand stacks.

(Panel Reports, para. 7.46)

379 Panel Reports, para. 7.45.

380 Panel Reports, para. 7.51.

381 Panel Reports, para. 7.296 (referring to Canada's first written submission, para. 38). (original emphasis)

382 Panel Reports, para. 7.27.

383 Panel Reports, para. 7.296.

384 Panel Reports, para. 7.53.

representing a charge to generators that must be paid to consumers. The Panel found that "[t]he GA has been consistently positive since at least 2009."[385]

4.14 Due to the fact that most generators participating in the IESO-administered wholesale market do not receive the HOEP alone, but a higher price established by the OEB (50% of capacity) or under contracts with the OPA or the OEFC (42% of capacity)[386], the primary motivation behind a generator's price offers is to be selected to dispatch electricity, and not to cover its marginal costs of production.[387] Thus, the Panel found that:

> ... the price offers attached to a generator's supply bids in the IESO-administered wholesale market are not motivated by the need to cover marginal costs of production ... but rather by the need for each generator to be chosen to supply electricity into the Ontario grid in order to receive its contracted or regulated prices. Thus, the IESO-administered wholesale market does not arrive at its equilibrium price (the HOEP) through forces of supply and demand that are unaffected by the policies of the Government of Ontario.[388]

4.15 The IESO is also responsible for settling the "physical" electricity market in which participants buy and sell energy, which involves collecting electricity payments from consumers and distributing these funds to electricity generators.[389]

4.16 Retail prices are generally determined by adding up the MCP/HOEP, the GA, other fees and charges, and the additional distribution charge to cover the cost of delivering electricity to the consumer.[390] Consumers at the retail level either purchase electricity based on use from their LDCs or they enter into contracts for electricity with an LDC or licensed electricity retailer.[391] The Panel found that "[t]he former retail consumers pay for the electricity commodity according to the OEB's RPP, and the latter retail consumers pay for the electricity commodity according to a retail contract."[392] Under this retail

---

385 Panel Reports, para. 7.55 (referring to IESO webpage, "Global Adjustment Archive" (Panel Exhibit JPN-11), available at: <*http://www.ieso.ca/imoweb/b100/ga_archive.asp*>). The Panel explained that "[t]he total GA owed to generators is allocated to consumers pro-rata based on the amount of electricity (kWh) they consume, regardless of which generators are supplying electricity at the time of their consumption." (*Ibid.*, para. 7.56 (referring to IESO, *HST Guide for IESO Transactions*, Issue 26.0, 12 October 2011 (Panel Exhibit JPN-84), Section 8.11, p. 35))

386 Panel Reports, para. 7.296 (referring to Canada's first written submission to the Panel (DS412), para. 37).

387 Panel Reports, para. 7.297.

388 Panel Reports, para. 7.298.

389 Panel Reports, para. 7.60 (referring to IESO, Settlement Statements and Invoices: Marketplace Training (December 2010) (Panel Exhibit JPN-62), p. 1).

390 Panel Reports, para. 7.57.

391 *Ibid.*

392 Panel Reports, para. 7.57. (fn omitted) The Panel further noted that RPP prices vary according to the type of meter used by the customer (conventional or smart). (*Ibid.*, para. 7.58)

contract, consumers "pay[] a contracted price for electricity for a fixed period, plus the GA".[393]

4.3 *The FIT Programme*

4.17 The feed-in tariff programme (FIT Programme)[394] is a scheme implemented by the Government of Ontario in 2009 to increase the supply of electricity generated from certain renewable sources of energy into the Ontario electricity system.[395] It is the third in a series of initiatives adopted by the Government of Ontario since 2004 to diversify its energy supply-mix and help replace coal-fired facilities.[396] The FIT Programme was formally launched by the OPA in 2009 pursuant to the Direction of the Ontario Minister of Energy and Infrastructure[397] (Minister's 2009 FIT Direction) acting under the authority of the Electricity Act of 1998, as amended by the Green Energy and Green Economy Act of 2009.[398] Generators participating in the FIT Programme "are paid a guaranteed price per kWh of electricity delivered into the Ontario electricity system under 20-year or 40-year contracts with the OPA".[399] Participation in the FIT Programme is open to facilities located in Ontario that produce electricity from the following renewable energy sources: wind, solar PV, renewable biomass, biogas, landfill gas, and waterpower.[400]

---

[393] Panel Reports, para. 7.59 (referring to IESO webpage, "Global Adjustment" (Panel Exhibit JPN-75), available at: <*http://www.ieso.ca/imoweb/b100/b100_ga.asp*>).

[394] The complainants challenge the WTO-consistency of the FIT Programme, the individual FIT Contracts utilizing wind and solar PV sources and the individual microFIT Contracts utilizing a solar PV source executed by the OPA since the FIT Programme's inception. The complainants argue that the FIT Programme is evidenced by a number of measures listed *supra* in para. 1.2.

[395] Panel Reports, para. 7.65.

[396] The Panel found that the two earlier initiatives were the RES I (2004), II (2005), and III (2008), and the RESOP (2006). The Panel further determined that:

> [u]nder the RES initiative, the OPA awarded supply contracts through a competitive bidding process which set prices for delivered electricity at the levels of the lowest bids meeting the specified conditions. ... Under the RESOP, the prices paid to solar PV generators are based primarily on the principle of cost recovery. For non-solar RESOP generators, prices are based on those applied under the RES initiative.

(Panel Reports, para. 7.29 (fn omitted))

[397] Direction dated 24 September 2009 from George Smitherman, Deputy Premier and Minister of Energy and Infrastructure, to Colin Andersen, Chief Executive Officer, Ontario Power Authority (OPA), directing the OPA to develop a feed-in tariff (FIT) programme (Panel Exhibit JPN-102), and to include a requirement that the applicant submit a plan for meeting the domestic (i.e. Ontario) content goals in the FIT Rules.

[398] An Act to enact the Green Energy Act, 2009 and to build a green economy, to repeal the Energy Conservation Leadership Act, 2006 and the Energy Efficiency Act and to amend other statutes, *Service Ontario 2009*, Chapter 12 (Panel Exhibit JPN-101). See Panel Reports, paras. 7.65 and 7.195.

[399] Panel Reports, para. 7.64.

[400] Panel Reports, para. 7.66. Under the FIT Programme, all renewable fuels other than waterpower are awarded 20-year contracts. Waterpower facilities are awarded 40-year contracts. (*Ibid.*, paras. 7.64 and 7.195)

4.18 The FIT Programme is divided into two streams: (i) the FIT stream – for all renewable energy projects with a capacity to produce electricity over 10 kilowatts (kW), except for solar PV projects, which must have a capacity of over 10 kW and no more than 10 MW, and waterpower projects, which must have a capacity of over 10 kW and no more than 50 MW; and (ii) the microFIT stream – for projects having a capacity to produce up to 10 kW of electricity. Participants under the microFIT stream are typically small household, farm, or business generation projects.[401]

4.19 The OPA implements the FIT Programme through the application of a standard set of rules, standard contracts (i.e. FIT and microFIT Contracts) and, for each class of generation technology, standard pricing. The standard rules are found in a series of instruments, including the FIT and microFIT Rules developed by the OPA[402], the IESO Market Rules[403], and the IESO Market Manual.[404] The Panel found that, in order fully to understand the parties' contractual rights and obligations, the FIT and microFIT Contracts must be read together with, respectively, the FIT and microFIT Rules.[405]

4.20 An entity that enters into a FIT or microFIT Contract is required to, *inter alia*, build, operate, and maintain the approved generation facility in accordance with all relevant laws and regulations, and deliver the electricity produced into the Ontario electricity system. In return for performing these and other contractual obligations, such entity will be remunerated, over the term of the particular contract, in accordance with a formula that is based on a standard "Contract Price" established by the OPA.[406]

4.21 In addition to these obligations, the FIT Programme imposes "Minimum Required Domestic Content Levels" that must be satisfied in the development and construction of solar PV electricity generation facilities participating in both streams of the FIT Programme and of windpower electricity generation facilities taking part in the FIT stream. The Minimum Required Domestic Content Levels do not apply to qualifying projects using any of the other renewable energy

---

401 Panel Reports, para. 7.66 (referring to FIT Rules Exhibit (version 1.5.1), Section 2.1(a)(iii); and microFIT Rules (version 1.6.1), Section 2.1(a)(iv)).

402 The FIT and microFIT Rules set out, *inter alia*: (i) the project eligibility and application requirements; (ii) the tests for the connection of the project to the Ontario electricity system; and (iii) an overview of some of the key aspects of the respective contract, such as the duration, price, and settlement of payments. (Panel Reports, paras. 7.199 and 7.210)

403 The Panel found that "[t]he IESO Market Rules govern the IESO-controlled grid, including the terms and conditions pursuant to which payments due to electricity generators participating in the 'IESO-administered markets' will be settled." (Panel Reports, para. 7.204)

404 Panel Reports, para. 7.67. The Panel found that Part 5.5 of the IESO Market Manual provides detailed instructions on how the GA is to be determined and settled. (*Ibid.*, para. 7.54 (referring to IESO Market Manual, Part 5.5 (Panel Exhibit JPN-82), Sections 1.6.7 and 1.6.11))

405 Panel Reports, paras. 7.199 and 7.210.

406 Panel Reports, para. 7.68 (referring to FIT Rules (version 1.5.1), Sections 7.1(a), 7.1(b), and 10.1(a); FIT Price Schedule, 3 June 2011 (Panel Exhibit JPN-30); FIT Contract (version 1.5.1), Article 3.1 and Exhibit B; and microFIT Price Schedule, 13 August 2010 (Panel Exhibit JPN-31).

sources covered by the FIT Programme.[407] The applicable Minimum Required Domestic Content Levels prescribed under both streams of the FIT Programme are summarized in Table 1 at paragraph 1.4 of these Reports.

4.22 Under the FIT stream, the "Domestic Content Level" of a facility is calculated pursuant to the methodology set out in Exhibit D of the FIT Contract. Exhibit D contains four different Domestic Content Grids, each of which identifies a range of different *Designated Activities* and an associated *qualifying percentage*.[408] The two Domestic Content Grids under the microFIT stream are set forth in Appendix C to the microFIT Contract.[409] For each Designated Activity that is performed in relation to a "Contract Facility", an associated qualifying percentage will be achieved.[410] A project's Domestic Content Level is determined by adding up the qualifying percentages associated with all of the Designated Activities performed in relation to that particular project. The Panel found that, pursuant to the Minimum Required Domestic Content Levels imposed by the FIT Programme, at least some Ontario-sourced *goods* (in particular, renewable energy generation equipment and components) must be used by FIT and microFIT suppliers utilizing solar PV technology and by FIT generators using windpower technology.[411]

4.23 The FIT and microFIT Contract Prices are established by the OPA and published in the FIT and microFIT Price Schedules.[412] Such prices are intended to cover the development costs plus a reasonable rate of return over the duration of the FIT and microFIT Contracts.[413] The Panel found that "[t]he after tax rate

---

[407] Panel Reports, para. 7.64.

[408] Panel Reports, para. 7.159 (referring to FIT Contract (version 1.5.1), Exhibit D).

[409] Panel Reports, paras. 7.159 and 7.161 (referring to microFIT Rules (version 1.6.1), Definitions, pp. 14-16).

[410] By way of example, the Panel explained that "where the wind turbine blades of a windpower project have been 'cast in a mould in Ontario' and the 'instrumentation that is within the blades has been assembled in Ontario', the Contract Facility will achieve a Qualifying Percentage of 16%." (Panel Reports, para. 7.160)

[411] Panel Reports, para. 7.163.

[412] Panel Reports, paras. 7.202 and 7.213 (referring to FIT Rules (version 1.5.1), Sections 7.1(a), 7.1(b), and 10.1(a); microFIT Rules (version 1.6.1), Section 5.2 and Definitions; FIT Price Schedule, 3 June 2011 (Panel Exhibit JPN-30); and microFIT Price Schedule, 13 August 2010 (Panel Exhibit JPN-31)).

[413] Panel Reports, paras. 7.202 and 7.213. The Panel found that:

> [t]he Contract Prices applicable to the measures at issue were determined using a discounted cash flow model taking into account "reasonable" capital costs (i.e. "project development, construction and equipment costs"), "reasonable" operating and maintenance costs (i.e. "project staffing and maintenance costs, including on-going capital expenditures and property taxes") and "reasonable" connection costs (i.e. "project connection costs, no significant upgrade costs assumed").

(*Ibid.*, para. 7.202 (fn omitted))

The Panel further determined that, "[f]or certain technologies, a specified percentage of the Contract Price will escalate annually based on increases in the consumer price index". (Panel Reports, para. 7.202 (fn omitted)) Prices for electricity produced by windpower projects are eligible for annual

of return on equity used to develop the FIT Price Schedule in 2009 was 11%."[414] The OPA has ultimate contractual liability for all FIT and microFIT "Contract Payments". However, in practice, the actual payments are made by a combination of the OPA, the IESO, and relevant LDCs.[415] In particular, under the settlement process for payments to transmission-connected FIT suppliers, in the event that the GA is positive, the IESO transfers the MCP/HOEP directly to FIT generators, while the GA is paid to generators by the OPA.[416] By contrast, distribution-connected FIT and microFIT suppliers receive their full Contract Payments (i.e. the HOEP plus the GA) from the relevant LDC to which they are connected. The relevant LDC then seeks reimbursement of the GA from the OPA via the IESO.[417]

5. ANALYSIS OF THE APPELLATE BODY

5.1 The order in which the Panel dealt with Japan's claims under the SCM Agreement and its claims under the TRIMs Agreement and the GATT 1994

5.1 We begin with Japan's allegation concerning the proper sequence of analysis of its claims under the GATT 1994 and TRIMs Agreement[418], on the one hand, and the SCM Agreement, on the other hand.

5.2 Before the Panel, Japan and the European Union brought claims under the SCM Agreement, the TRIMs Agreement, and the GATT 1994. The complainants requested the Panel to evaluate these claims by first focusing on those made under the SCM Agreement, because that Agreement deals most specifically and in detail with the measures at issue, including with respect to the nature of the remedy that is available in the event of a finding of violation. By contrast, Canada argued that the Panel should first address the claims under Article III:4 of the GATT 1994, because this provision deals most specifically, and in detail, with the focus of the complainants' challenge, namely, the

escalation, whereas the ones applicable to projects utilizing solar PV technologies are not eligible for such escalation. (*Ibid.*, para. 7.30)

[414] Panel Reports, para. 7.29. See also para. 7.202 (referring to Canada's response to Panel question No. 26 (first set) and No. 12 (second set); and OPA, Presentation on "Proposed Feed-in Tariff Price Schedule Stakeholder Engagement – Session 4", 7 April 2009 (Panel Exhibit CDA-46) (OPA Proposed FIT Price Schedule Presentation), slide 30).

[415] Panel Reports, paras. 7.68, 7.204, and 7.213.

[416] Panel Reports, paras. 7.62 and 7.204.

[417] Panel Reports, para. 7.63. The Panel found that, after paying a supplier its full Contract Payment, "the relevant LDC will ... seek to recover any amounts paid in excess of the wholesale price of electricity for the electricity delivered by the Supplier in question, from the OPA, through the IESO." (*Ibid.*, para. 7.205 (fns omitted))

[418] In this part of its appeal, Japan is not suggesting that there is a particular sequence of analysis as between the TRIMs Agreement and the GATT 1994.

Minimum Required Domestic Content Levels prescribed under the FIT Programme and related FIT and microFIT Contracts.[419]

5.3 The Panel first noted that Canada did not contest the complainants' assertion that the measures at issue are trade-related investment measures (TRIMs) affecting imports of renewable energy generation equipment and components. In the Panel's view, "[t]his suggests that, compared with the SCM Agreement and Article III:4 of the GATT 1994, it is the TRIMs Agreement that deals most directly, specifically and in detail, with the aspects of the FIT Programme, and the FIT and microFIT Contracts, that are at the centre of the complainants' concerns."[420] On this basis, the Panel decided to commence its evaluation of the complainants' claims by focusing on those made under the TRIMs Agreement. The Panel noted, however, that examining the claims under Article 2.1 of the TRIMs Agreement also entailed evaluating the merits of the complainants' claims under Article III:4 of the GATT 1994. Consequently, the Panel simultaneously evaluated the merits of both claims brought by the complainants.[421]

5.4 In its other appellant's submission, Japan argued that the Panel should have commenced its evaluation with Japan's claim under the SCM Agreement.[422] However, at the oral hearing, Japan clarified that its request in this appeal was limited to asking us to commence our own analysis with the allegations of error relating to the SCM Agreement. Japan is not suggesting that we reverse or modify a finding or legal interpretation of the Panel, or that the Panel's decision to commence its evaluation with the SCM Agreement constituted legal error or resulted in the Panel failing to conduct an objective assessment of the matter contrary to Article 11 of the DSU.[423]

5.5 Both the national treatment obligations in Article III:4 of the GATT 1994 and the TRIMs Agreement, and the disciplines in Article 3.1(b) of the SCM Agreement, are cumulative obligations. Article III:4 of the GATT 1994 and the TRIMs Agreement, as well as Article 3.1(b) of the SCM Agreement, prohibit the use of local content requirements in certain circumstances. These provisions address discriminatory conduct. We see nothing in these provisions to indicate that there is an obligatory sequence of analysis to be followed when claims are made under Article III:4 of the GATT 1994 and the TRIMs Agreement, on the one hand, and Article 3.1(b) of the SCM Agreement, on the other hand. Nor has Japan argued that the disposition of its claim under Article 3.1(b) of the SCM Agreement would somehow pre-empt our assessment under Article III:4 of the GATT 1994 and the TRIMs Agreement.

---

419 Panel Reports, para. 7.69.

420 Panel Reports, para. 7.70. (fn omitted)

421 Panel Reports, para. 7.70.

422 Japan's other appellant's submission (DS412), paras. 10-15.

423 Japan's response to questioning at the oral hearing.

5.6 We are aware that, in a series of previous disputes, issues concerning the sequence of analysis have been dealt with by seeking to identify the agreement that "deals specifically, and in detail, with" the measures at issue.[424] Japan and the European Union both emphasized before the Panel that the focus of their complaints is the domestic content requirements that form part of the FIT Programme and FIT and microFIT Contracts.[425] We note that the TRIMs Agreement deals specifically with investment measures related to trade in goods or TRIMs. It does not regulate anything else. Domestic content requirements are one type of TRIM regulated under the TRIMs Agreement. One of the examples in the Illustrative List annexed to the TRIMs Agreement refers specifically to requirements relating to "the purchase or use by an enterprise of products of domestic origin or from any domestic source, whether specified in terms of particular products, in terms of volume or value of products, or in terms of a proportion of volume or value of its local production".[426] The SCM Agreement deals specifically with subsidies. It defines what government conducts constitute subsidies, classifies different kinds of subsidies, and establishes different regulations for each type of subsidy. The SCM Agreement also sets out the remedies available to WTO Members affected by subsidies and provides detailed guidance on how domestic countervailing duty investigations should be conducted. The local content requirements of the FIT Programme and related FIT and microFIT Contracts are being challenged by Japan under Article 3.1(b) of the SCM Agreement. This provision regulates so-called import-substitution subsidies, which are one of only two kinds of subsidies prohibited under the SCM Agreement. At the same time, the SCM Agreement regulates a broader universe of measures. Thus, based on the above discussion, we are not persuaded that, compared to the GATT 1994 and the TRIMs Agreement, the SCM Agreement can be described as regulating more "specifically, and in detail,"[427] the measures challenged in this dispute.

5.7 Japan has emphasized the differences in the remedies foreseen under the SCM Agreement and the remedy foreseen in Article 19 of the DSU.[428] The specific remedy provided under Article 4.7 of the SCM Agreement is an important consideration. In *EC – Export Subsidies on Sugar*, the remedy provided under Article 4.7 was the reason why the Appellate Body found that the panel had improperly exercised judicial economy when it failed to make findings under the SCM Agreement once it had found a violation of the Agreement on Agriculture.[429] While the difference in remedy would be relevant

424 Appellate Body Report, *EC – Bananas III*, para. 204. See also Panel Reports, *Indonesia – Autos*, paras. 14.61-14.63; *EC – Bananas III*, paras. 7.185-7.187; *Canada – Autos*, paras. 10.63 and 10.64; and *India – Autos*, paras. 7.157-7.162.

425 Panel Reports, paras. 7.6, 7.7, and 7.70.

426 TRIMs Agreement, Annex (Illustrative List), para. 1(a).

427 Appellate Body Report, *EC – Bananas III*, para. 204.

428 Japan's other appellant's submission (DS412), para. 14.

429 Appellate Body Report, *EC – Export Subsidies on Sugar*, paras. 332-335.

to a decision as to whether or not there would be a need to address the claims under the SCM Agreement, having made findings under the GATT 1994 and the TRIMs Agreement, we do not see its relevance in this case for the question of which claim to address first. In any event, this was not a case in which the Panel exercised judicial economy; the Panel made findings under Article III:4 of the GATT 1994 and the TRIMs Agreement. It then examined Japan's claims under the SCM Agreement and found that Japan had failed to establish that the challenged measures confer a benefit within the meaning of Article 1.1(b) of the SCM Agreement.[430] Japan has appealed the Panel's finding on benefit, and we address Japan's appeal in section 5.5.2 of these Reports.

5.8 Issues of sequencing may become relevant to a logical consideration of claims under different agreements. However, no such issues arise in this case. The Panel examined the claims under Article III:4 of the GATT 1994 and the TRIMs Agreement, and then the claims under the SCM Agreement. Japan has not indicated why commencing the analysis with the SCM Agreement could lead to a different outcome than commencing with the GATT 1994 and the TRIMs Agreement, as the Panel did in this case. We see no obligation in this case to begin the analysis with the claims under the SCM Agreement. Ultimately, the decision in this case as to whether to commence the analysis with the claims under the SCM Agreement or those under the GATT 1994 and the TRIMs Agreement was within the Panel's margin of discretion.[431] The Panel opted to commence the analysis with the claims under the GATT 1994 and the TRIMs Agreement. We see some practical value in following the same sequence as the Panel. Therefore, we *decline* Japan's request that we commence our evaluation with the allegations of error relating to the SCM Agreement.

5.2 The applicability of Article III:8(a) of the GATT 1994 to measures falling under Article 2.2 of the TRIMs Agreement and the Illustrative List annexed thereto

5.9 We now turn to the European Union's claim that Article III:8(a) of the GATT 1994 is applicable to measures that fall under Article 2.2 of the TRIMs Agreement and the Illustrative List annexed thereto. Before assessing the European Union's claim, we summarize the Panel's findings and the arguments raised on appeal.

5.2.1 The Panel's findings

5.10 The Panel began its analysis of this issue with Article 2.1 of the TRIMs Agreement. The Panel noted that Article 2.1 expressly refers to "the provisions of Article III ... of GATT 1994" and understood this to include

430 Panel Reports, para. 7.328(ii).

431 See Appellate Body Report, *Canada – Wheat Exports and Grain Imports*, para. 126.

Article III:8(a) of the GATT 1994. From this, the Panel reasoned that "any government procurement transactions covered by the terms of Article III:8(a) of the GATT 1994 will be removed from the scope of the obligations set out in Article III, including Article III:4" and "where a particular TRIM involves the same kind of government procurement transactions described in Article III:8(a), it cannot be found to be inconsistent with the obligation in Article 2.1 of the TRIMs Agreement."[432]

5.11 Turning to Article 2.2 of the TRIMs Agreement, the Panel observed that this provision "does not impose any obligations on Members, but rather informs the interpretation of the prohibition set out in Article 2.1".[433] The Panel then addressed the relationship between Article 2.2 of the TRIMs Agreement and Article III:8 of the GATT 1994 as follows:

> Article 2.2 explains that the TRIMs described in the Illustrative List of the Annex to the TRIMs Agreement are to be considered inconsistent with Members' specific obligations under Articles III:4 and XI:1 of the GATT 1994. It does not follow, however, that TRIMs having the same characteristics as those described in Paragraph 1(a) of the Illustrative List must be automatically found to be inconsistent with Article III:4 of the GATT 1994 *when they would otherwise be covered by the terms of Article III:8(a) of the GATT 1994*. Such a reading of Article 2.2 would be inconsistent with the clear terms of Article 2.1, which explicitly state that there will be a violation of Article 2.1 of the TRIMs Agreement whenever a measure is inconsistent with Article III of the GATT 1994. This refers to *the whole of Article III, including Article III:8(a)*.[434]

5.12 The Panel went on to dismiss the European Union's argument because it did not "reflect the proper sequence of the legal analysis that is envisaged under Articles 2.1 and 2.2 of the TRIMs Agreement".[435] The Panel explained what it considered to be the proper sequence of analysis as follows:

> Where in a particular case it is found that the national treatment obligation in Article III:4 applies to a challenged measure, the Illustrative List may be used to determine whether the challenged measure is inconsistent with that obligation through the operation of Article 2.1 of the TRIMs Agreement. Where such a measure has the characteristics that are described in Paragraph 1(a) of the Illustrative List, it follows from the clear language of this provision that it will be in violation of Article III:4 of the

---

[432] Panel Reports, para. 7.118.

[433] Panel Reports, para. 7.119.

[434] Panel Reports, para. 7.119. (original emphasis)

[435] Panel Reports, para. 7.120.

> GATT 1994, and thereby also Article 2.1 of the TRIMs Agreement. Given the language of Article 2.1, it would, in our view, be inappropriate to infer from Paragraph 1(a) of the Illustrative List that TRIMs having the characteristics described in that paragraph will *always* be inconsistent with Article III:4 of the GATT 1994, irrespective of whether they may be covered by the terms of Article III:8(a) of the GATT 1994.[436]

5.13 On the basis of the above, the Panel concluded that:

> Paragraph 1(a) of the Illustrative List in the Annex to the TRIMs Agreement does not obviate the need for us to undertake an analysis of whether the challenged measures are outside of the scope of application of Article III:4 of the GATT 1994 by virtue of the operation of Article III:8(a) of the GATT 1994.[437]

5.2.2 Claims and arguments on appeal

5.14 On appeal, the European Union asserts that the Panel erred in the interpretation and application of Articles 2.1 and 2.2 of the TRIMs Agreement, read in conjunction with paragraph 1(a) of the Illustrative List in the Annex to the TRIMs Agreement, when finding that they do not preclude the application of Article III:8(a) of the GATT 1994 to the challenged measures.

5.15 The European Union distinguishes the text of Article 2.1 and Article 2.2 of the TRIMs Agreement. It notes that, while Article 2.1 refers to Article III of the GATT 1994, Article 2.2 sets out an Illustrative List of measures "that are necessarily 'inconsistent with Article III:4'".[438] The European Union understands this difference in language to mean that the Panel's reasoning holds only in relation to TRIMs other than the specific measures defined through the Illustrative List. For those that fall within the scope of the Illustrative List, the question of whether they could escape a violation through the applicability of Article III:8 of the GATT 1994 no longer presents itself, because the TRIMs Agreement has conclusively settled the issue.

5.16 The European Union requests us to complete the analysis and correctly apply the legal interpretation set out above to the Panel's findings and uncontested facts on the record.

5.17 Canada asserts that the Panel correctly found that the TRIMs Agreement does not preclude the application of Article III:8(a) of the GATT 1994 to the FIT Programme's domestic content requirements.[439] Canada explains that, by describing the measures in the Illustrative List of TRIMs as inconsistent with

---

[436] Panel Reports, para. 7.120. (original emphasis)

[437] Panel Reports, para. 7.121.

[438] European Union's other appellant's submission (DS426), para. 31. (fn omitted)

[439] Canada's appellee's submission, para. 27.

"the obligation of national treatment provided for in paragraph 4 of Article III", instead of "Article III", "Article 2.2 does not address the consistency of the measures listed in the Annex with Article III, as a whole, including Article III:8(a)."[440]

5.18 In addition, Canada argues that the European Union "overlooks"[441] that the context of paragraph 1 of the Illustrative List undermines its interpretation of that paragraph. Canada points out that the Illustrative List annexed to the TRIMs Agreement also contains, in paragraph 2, examples of TRIMs that are inconsistent with Article XI:1 of the GATT 1994. It further notes that Article XI has a scope provision similar to Article III:8(a) of the GATT 1994. This scope provision is found in Article XI:2, which states that "[t]he provisions of paragraph 1 of this Article shall not extend to the following ...". Consequently, Canada submits that, if the European Union's interpretation were correct, then this interpretation would also hold for TRIMs that are inconsistent with Article XI:1 of the GATT 1994. In other words, under the European Union's reasoning, the TRIMs that are listed in the Illustrative List as inconsistent with Article XI:1 must fall outside the scope of Article XI:2. Yet, Canada submits that a comparison between Article XI:2 of the GATT 1994 and the TRIMs listed as inconsistent with Article XI:1 of the GATT 1994 in the Annex reveals that this proposition "is untenable".[442] Canada emphasizes that the Annex contains measures that "clearly"[443] could fall within the scope of Article XI:2 of the GATT 1994. Therefore, Canada asserts that the European Union's interpretation of Article 2.2 of the TRIMs Agreement and paragraph 1 of the Annex is inconsistent with the text and its context. Canada thus submits that that the European Union has failed to provide grounds to overturn the Panel's decision that the TRIMs Agreement does not preclude the application of Article III:8(a) of the GATT 1994 to the FIT Programme's domestic content requirements.

5.2.3 *Is Article III:8(a) of the GATT 1994 applicable to measures falling within the scope of Article 2.2 of the TRIMs Agreement and the Illustrative List annexed thereto?*

5.19 We begin our analysis with Article 2 of the TRIMs Agreement, which provides:

---

440 Canada's appellee's submission, para. 29.

441 Canada's appellee's submission, para. 32.

442 Canada's appellee's submission, para. 33.

443 *Ibid.*

National Treatment and Quantitative Restrictions

> 1. Without prejudice to other rights and obligations under GATT 1994, no Member shall apply any TRIM that is inconsistent with the provisions of Article III or Article XI of GATT 1994.
>
> 2. An Illustrative List of TRIMs that are inconsistent with the obligation of national treatment provided for in paragraph 4 of Article III of GATT 1994 and the obligation of general elimination of quantitative restrictions provided for in paragraph 1 of Article XI of GATT 1994 is contained in the Annex to this Agreement.

5.20 Article 2.1 of the TRIMs Agreement prohibits Members from applying a TRIM – that is, an investment measure related to trade in goods[444] – "that is inconsistent with the provisions of Article III or Article XI of GATT 1994". The cross-reference in the latter part of Article 2.1 to Article III of the GATT 1994 is unqualified. We understand this to be a reference to Article III of the GATT 1994 in its entirety, including Article III:4. Thus, as the Panel explained, a measure that is inconsistent with Article III:4 of the GATT 1994 would also be a TRIM that is incompatible with Article 2.1 of the TRIMs Agreement.[445] Importantly, the cross-reference to Article III also includes paragraph 8(a) of that provision. As we discuss in more detail in section 5.3 of these Reports, a measure that falls within the scope of paragraph 8(a) cannot violate Article III of the GATT 1994. This, in turn, means that a Member applying such a measure would not violate Article 2.1 of the TRIMs Agreement. We note, in this respect, that the relationship between Article 2.1 of the TRIMs Agreement and Article III of the GATT 1994 is not a point of contention between the participants.[446]

5.21 The issue that is contested, and that we need to resolve in this appeal, concerns the relationship between, on the one hand, Article 2.2 and the Illustrative List of the TRIMs Agreement and, on the other hand, Articles III:4 and III:8(a) of the GATT 1994. The European Union takes the position that TRIMs that fall within the scope of Article 2.2 and the Illustrative List of the TRIMs Agreement are inconsistent with Article III:4 of the GATT 1994, irrespective of whether they also fall within Article III:8(a) of the GATT 1994. According to the European Union, Article 2.2 and the Illustrative List of the TRIMs Agreement establish that measures falling within their scope and that violate the national treatment obligation in Article III:4 of the GATT 1994 cannot be justified because the derogation in Article III:8(a) is unavailable. The

---

[444] See Article 1 of the TRIMs Agreement. The Panel found that "the FIT Programme, and the FIT and microFIT Contracts, to the extent they envisage and impose a 'Minimum Required Domestic Content Level', constitute TRIMs within the meaning of Article 1 of the TRIMs Agreement." (Panel Reports, para. 7.112) This finding has not been appealed.

[445] Panel Reports, para. 7.117.

[446] European Union's and Canada's responses to questioning at the oral hearing.

Panel rejected the European Union's interpretation, and Canada supports the Panel's interpretation in this appeal.

5.22 Article 2.2 refers to the obligation of national treatment provided for in paragraph 4 of Article III of the GATT 1994, as well as the obligation of general elimination of quantitative restrictions provided for in paragraph 1 of Article XI of the GATT 1994. Article 2.2 also refers to an illustrative list of TRIMs that is found in the Annex to the TRIMs Agreement. The term "illustrative" indicates that the examples in the list do not constitute a closed list. In other words, there can be other types of TRIMs that are inconsistent with the national treatment obligation in Article III:4 and the obligation of general elimination of quantitative restrictions in Article XI:1 of the GATT 1994. The use of the term "include" in paragraph 1 of the Illustrative List further supports this understanding.[447]

5.23 Turning to the Illustrative List referred to in Article 2.2, we note that the Panel found that the measures fall within the coverage of paragraph 1(a), which provides:

> 1. TRIMs that are inconsistent with the obligation of national treatment provided for in paragraph 4 of Article III of GATT 1994 include those which are mandatory or enforceable under domestic law or under administrative rulings, or compliance with which is necessary to obtain an advantage, and which require:
>
> (a) the purchase or use by an enterprise of products of domestic origin or from any domestic source, whether specified in terms of particular products, in terms of volume or value of products, or in terms of a proportion of volume or value of its local production; ...

5.24 By its terms, a measure that falls within the coverage of paragraph 1(a) of the Illustrative List is "inconsistent with the obligation of national treatment provided for in paragraph 4 of Article III of GATT 1994". Thus, like Article 2.2 of the TRIMs Agreement, paragraph 1(a) of the Illustrative List refers to the obligations in Article III:4 of the GATT 1994.

5.25 The European Union draws attention to the differences in language between Article 2.2 of the TRIMs Agreement and the Illustrative List, on the one hand, and Article 2.1 of the TRIMs Agreement, on the other hand. It underscores that the latter provision refers to Article III of the GATT 1994 "as a whole"[448], while Article 2.2 and the Illustrative List refer specifically to Article III:4 of the GATT 1994.

---

[447] Article 1(e) of the Agreement on Agriculture defines "export subsidies" as "subsidies contingent upon export performance, including the export subsidies listed in Article 9 of this Agreement". In *US – Upland Cotton*, the Appellate Body noted that the use of the word "including" in Article 1(e) of the Agreement on Agriculture suggests that the list of export subsidies in Article 9 is not exhaustive. (Appellate Body Report, *US – Upland Cotton*, para. 615)

[448] European Union's other appellant's submission (DS426), para. 30.

5.26 In our view, Article 2.2 provides further specification as to the type of measures that are inconsistent with Article 2.1. The operative part of Article 2.2 is the reference to the Illustrative List, which provides examples of measures that are inconsistent with the national treatment obligation. While Article 2.2 and the Illustrative List focus on the specific provisions where such obligation is reflected – that is, Article III:4 of the GATT 1994 – we do not believe it responds to the question of whether such measures are inconsistent with Article III of the GATT 1994 in its entirety. Where a measure falls within the scope of Article III:8(a), the measure is not inconsistent with Article III overall. Thus, we agree with the Panel that Article 2.2 and the Illustrative List must be understood as clarifying to which TRIMs the general obligation in Article 2.1 applies.[449] Furthermore, we understand the absence of a reference to Article III:8(a) of the GATT 1994 in Article 2.2 of the TRIMs Agreement and in the Illustrative List as indicating that these provisions are neutral as to the applicability of the former provision. This results in a harmonious interpretation of Articles 2.1 and 2.2 of the TRIMs Agreement and Articles III:4 and III:8(a) of the GATT 1994. By contrast, the interpretation advocated by the European Union would result in different obligations for those TRIMs that fall within the Illustrative List and those that do not.

5.27 We find additional support for this interpretation in the initial clause of Article 2.1 and Article 3 of the TRIMs Agreement. The opening clause of Article 2.1 reads: "Without prejudice to other rights and obligations under GATT 1994". This language suggests that the provision is not intended to curtail other rights that Members have under the GATT 1994. The right to discriminate in government purchases – subject to the conditions and requirements of Article III:8(a) – is one such right recognized in the GATT 1994. Moreover, Article 3 of the TRIMs Agreement, entitled "Exceptions", provides contextual support for our interpretation. It states that "[a]ll exceptions under GATT 1994 shall apply, as appropriate, to the provisions of this Agreement." As the title and text of Article 3 indicate, this provision refers to "exceptions". The Panel and the participants have characterized Article III:8(a) as a "scope" provision.[450] Even though Article III:8(a) is not one of the exceptions that "apply, as appropriate," to the TRIMs Agreement, Article 3 further suggests that the provisions of the TRIMs Agreement are not intended to constrain other rights that Members have under the GATT 1994.

5.28 The European Union argues that the Panel's interpretation "alters the nature and function of Articles 2.1, 2.2 and the Illustrative List" and "largely

[449] Panel Reports, para. 7.119: "Article 2.2 of the TRIMs Agreement does not impose any obligations on Members, but rather informs the interpretation of the prohibition set out in Article 2.1. In particular, Article 2.2 explains that the TRIMs described in the Illustrative List of the Annex to the TRIMs Agreement are to be considered inconsistent with Members' specific obligations under Articles III:4 and XI:1 of the GATT 1994."

[450] Panel Reports, fn 263 to para. 7.113; Canada's response to questioning at the oral hearing.

nullifies the effects of Article 2.2 and of the Illustrative List in relation to the general obligation in Article 2.1."[451] Under the Panel's interpretation, Article 2.2 and the Illustrative List continue to provide examples of TRIMs that involve discrimination and that are inconsistent with the national treatment obligation in Article III:4, and consequently would violate the obligation in Article 2.1 of the TRIMs Agreement. Contrary to the European Union's assertion, Article 2.2 and the Illustrative List continue to "introduc[e] detail and specificity to the general obligation in Article 2.1".[452] We agree that the Panel's interpretation means that a limited set of measures that fall both within one of the examples of the Illustrative List of the TRIMs Agreement and Article III:8(a) of the GATT 1994 ultimately would not be found to be inconsistent with Article III:4 of the GATT 1994 and Article 2.1 of the TRIMs Agreement. Yet, we do not see this as nullifying the effects of Article 2.2 and the Illustrative List. Rather, it is a result of interpreting Article 2.2 and the Illustrative List harmoniously with the other provisions of the TRIMs Agreement and with Article III of the GATT 1994. In any event, the broader subset of TRIMs that fall within the Illustrative List and do not qualify for derogation under Article III:8(a) of the GATT 1994 remains inconsistent with the national treatment obligation in Article III:4 of the GATT 1994 and Article 2.1 of the TRIMs Agreement.

5.29 We note that Canada has pointed out that the European Union's interpretation would apply equally to the examples in paragraph 2 of the Illustrative List of the TRIMs Agreement. Canada asserts that this would mean that measures falling within this paragraph 2 would be inconsistent with Article XI:1 of the GATT 1994 and that Article XI:2 would be unavailable to justify such measures.[453] At the oral hearing, the European Union referred to some of the requirements in Article XI:2 and questioned whether such provision would apply to the measures described by Canada. It would appear that the reasoning set out above in relation to Articles 2.1 and 2.2 of the TRIMs Agreement and Article III:4 of the GATT 1994 would apply *mutatis mutandis* to the relationship between Articles XI:1 and XI:2 of the GATT 1994. Nevertheless, we need not determine this issue conclusively in this case because we have already determined that the application of Article III:8(a) of the GATT 1994 is not precluded where the challenged measure falls within the scope of Article 2.2 and paragraph 1(a) of the Illustrative List of the TRIMs Agreement.

5.30 The European Union emphasizes the language in the first paragraph of the preamble of the TRIMs Agreement, stating that "the object and purpose of the TRIMs Agreement was precisely to 'elaborate' 'further' or 'additional' provisions to the already existing ones."[454] The European Union adds that the Panel's interpretation contradicts the TRIMs Agreement's object and purpose

[451] European Union's other appellant's submission (DS426), para. 33.
[452] *Ibid.*
[453] Canada's appellee's submission, para. 33.
[454] European Union's other appellant's submission (DS426), para. 35. (fn omitted)

because, "[i]f Article 2.2 and the Illustrative List were to be read as merely stating the obvious i.e. that the types of measures listed in the annex discriminate against imported goods, with no other implications, they would largely be redundant."[455]

5.31 The first paragraph of the preamble of the TRIMs Agreement quotes the negotiating mandate of the Punta del Este Declaration[456], referring to the "trade restrictive and distorting effects of investment measures" and calling for negotiations to "elaborate, as appropriate, further provisions that may be necessary to avoid such adverse effects on trade". The fourth paragraph recognizes that "certain investment measures can cause trade-restrictive and distorting effects".

5.32 We do not find the European Union's reliance on the language of the Punta del Este negotiating mandate to be persuasive. Looking at the TRIMs Agreement as a whole, we consider that the "further" provisions that it contains mainly clarify the application of Articles III and XI of the GATT 1994 to a specific set of measures – namely, TRIMs. In doing so, however, there is little, if any, indication that the provisions of the TRIMs Agreement were intended to override rights recognized in the GATT, such as the right provided in Article III:8(a). On the contrary, several provisions of the TRIMs Agreement – particularly the initial clause of Article 2.1, and Articles 3 and 4 – would seem to reflect reiterative attempts to safeguard rights recognized in the GATT, rather than to override them.

5.33 For the reasons stated above, we consider that the Panel correctly rejected the European Union's argument that Article III:8(a) of the GATT 1994 is not applicable to measures that fall within the scope of Article 2.2 of the TRIMs Agreement and the Illustrative List annexed thereto. Therefore, we *uphold* the Panel's finding, in paragraph 7.121 of the Panel Reports, that "Paragraph 1(a) of the Illustrative List in the Annex to the TRIMs Agreement d[id] not obviate the need for [the Panel] to undertake an analysis of whether the challenged measures are outside of the scope of application of Article III:4 of the GATT 1994 by virtue of the operation of Article III:8(a) of the GATT 1994." As we have upheld the Panel's finding, there is no basis for us to entertain the European Union's request that we complete the analysis and find that Article III:8(a) of the GATT 1994 is not applicable in the present case because the measures fall within Article 2.2 and the Illustrative List of the TRIMs Agreement.[457]

---

455 European Union's other appellant's submission (DS426), para. 35.

456 Ministerial Declaration adopted at Punta del Este, Uruguay on 20 September 1986 to launch the Uruguay Round of Multilateral Trade Negotiations.

457 European Union's other appellant's submission (DS426), para. 38.

5.3 Article III:8(a) of the GATT 1994

5.34 We turn to Article III:8(a) of the GATT 1994. The three participants challenge on appeal different aspects of the Panel's interpretation and application of this provision.

5.35 Canada alleges that the Panel erred in finding that the FIT Programme and related FIT and microFIT Contracts are not covered by Article III:8(a) and that, consequently, Canada cannot rely on that provision to exclude the application of Article III:4 of the GATT 1994 to the Minimum Required Domestic Content Levels.[458] Canada requests us to reverse this finding, complete the legal analysis under Article III:8(a), and find that the FIT Programme and Contracts fall within the scope of Article III:8(a). Consequently, Canada requests us to find that the FIT Programme and Contracts do not breach Article III:4 of the GATT 1994 or Article 2.1 of the TRIMs Agreement.[459]

5.36 The European Union and Japan request us to uphold the Panel's finding that the FIT Programme and Contracts are not covered by Article III:8(a) and that, consequently, Canada cannot rely on that provision to exclude the application of Article III:4 of the GATT 1994. The European Union and Japan also support the Panel's conclusion that the FIT Programme and Contracts are inconsistent with Article 2.1 of the TRIMs Agreement and Article III:4 of the GATT 1994. However, in their other appeals, they each appeal several aspects of the Panel's interpretation and application of Article III:8(a) of the GATT 1994 and request us to modify certain intermediate findings by the Panel.

5.37 The Panel's findings are summarized in subsection 5.3.1. The claims and arguments of the participants are set out in subsection 5.3.2. Subsection 5.3.3 provides our interpretation of Article III:8(a) of the GATT 1994. Finally, in subsection 5.3.4, we address the Panel's application of Article III:8(a) to the facts of these disputes.

5.3.1 The Panel's findings

5.38 At the outset of its analysis, the Panel addressed the question of whether the FIT Programme and related FIT and microFIT Contracts are "trade-related investment measures" (TRIMs) within the meaning of Article 1 of the TRIMs Agreement. The Panel found that one aim of the FIT Programme and Contracts is to encourage investment in the local production of equipment associated with the generation of electricity from renewable sources in Ontario.[460] Furthermore, the Panel found that the FIT Programme and Contracts "compel[] [electricity generators] to purchase and use certain types of renewable energy generation equipment sourced in Ontario in the design and construction

---

[458] Panel Reports, para. 7.152.

[459] Canada's appellant's submission, para. 7.

[460] Panel Reports, para. 7.109 (referring to Minister's 2009 FIT Direction, p. 1).

of their facilities".[461] On this basis, the Panel concluded that the FIT Programme and Contracts constitute TRIMs "to the extent they envisage and impose" domestic content requirements.[462]

5.39 The Panel then assessed whether the FIT Programme and Contracts are consistent with Article 2.1 of the TRIMs Agreement. The Panel noted that this provision contains a reference to Article III of the GATT 1994 and, consequently, it assessed whether the FIT Programme and Contracts fall within the scope of Article III:4 of the GATT 1994, or whether they are "outside the scope of application of Article III:4 ... by virtue of the operation of Article III:8(a)".[463] In this respect, the Panel addressed three issues, namely:

a. whether the FIT Programme and Contracts can be characterized as "laws, regulations or requirements governing procurement" of electricity;

b. whether the FIT Programme and Contracts involve "procurement by governmental agencies of products purchased"; and

c. whether "procurement" is undertaken "for governmental purposes and not with a view to commercial resale or with a view to use in the production of goods for commercial sale".

5.40 Regarding the first issue, the Panel found that a measure "governing" procurement is one that "controls, regulates or determines that procurement".[464] With respect to the FIT Programme and Contracts, the Panel found that the domestic content requirements for renewable energy generation equipment are a condition that must be satisfied by generators utilizing solar PV or windpower technologies in order to participate in the FIT Programme. The Panel explained that the domestic content requirements thus compel the purchase and use of certain generation equipment originating in Ontario as a necessary prerequisite for the procurement of electricity by the Government of Ontario to take place. The Panel found that, consequently, the domestic content requirements are requirements "governing" the procurement of electricity by the Government of Ontario under the FIT Programme and Contracts.[465] The Panel found further support in the fact that the electricity procured by the Government of Ontario is produced using the very same generation equipment that is subject to the domestic content requirements. Thus, for the Panel, there was a "close relationship" between the products affected by the domestic content requirements (renewable energy generation equipment) and the product procured (electricity).[466]

---

461 Panel Reports, para. 7.111.

462 Panel Reports, para. 7.112.

463 Panel Reports, para. 7.113.

464 Panel Reports, para. 7.124 (referring to Canada's first written submission to the Panel (DS412), para. 83, in turn referring to Panel Report, *EC – Selected Customs Matters*, para. 7.529).

465 Panel Reports, para. 7.124.

466 Panel Reports, para. 7.127.

5.41 Second, with respect to the question of whether the FIT Programme and Contracts involve "procurement by governmental agencies of products purchased" within the meaning of Article III:8(a), the Panel stated that the term "procurement", when interpreted in its immediate context, should be understood to have the same meaning as the term "purchase".[467] Turning to its assessment of whether the FIT Programme and Contracts involve "purchases" of electricity, the Panel referred to its analysis of the phrase "a government ... purchases goods" in Article 1.1(a)(1)(iii) of the SCM Agreement. In that respect, the Panel found government "purchase" of goods to mean the action by which the government obtains possession (including via obtaining an entitlement) over goods through some kind of payment. The Panel stated that this interpretation was "equally applicable to guide [the Panel's] analysis ... under Article III:8(a) of the GATT 1994".[468] Accordingly, the Panel concluded that the FIT Programme and Contracts involve "procurement by governmental agencies of products purchased" within the meaning of Article III:8(a) of the GATT 1994.

5.42 Third, with regard to the issue of whether procurement by the Government of Ontario is "for governmental purposes and not with a view to commercial resale or with a view to use in the production of goods for commercial sale" within the meaning of Article III:8(a), the Panel noted that the parties had advanced different meanings of the term "for governmental purposes". Canada had suggested that a purchase "for governmental purposes" may exist whenever a government purchases a product for a stated aim of the government. Japan, on the contrary, had proposed that a purchase "for governmental purposes" covers only purchases of products for governmental use, consumption, or benefit; and the European Union had submitted that the term "for governmental purposes" refers to purchases for governmental needs, including the purchase of products consumed by the government itself and products necessary for a government's provision of public services.[469]

5.43 The Panel stated that the ordinary meaning of the term "for governmental purposes" was relatively broad and that it may encompass all three meanings advanced by the parties.[470] The Panel, however, also considered that the immediately following phrase "and not with a view to commercial resale" informs and limits the otherwise relatively broad ordinary meaning of the term "governmental purposes", and that procurement of products purchased "for governmental purposes" could not at the same time be "procurement ... with a view to commercial resale or with a view to use in the production of goods for commercial sale".[471] The Panel then stated that, if it found that procurement of electricity by the Government of Ontario is undertaken "with a view to

[467] Panel Reports, paras. 7.131 and 7.135.

[468] Panel Reports, para. 7.136 (referring to Panel Reports, section VII.C.2(c)(iii), pp. 98-107).

[469] Panel Reports, para. 7.138.

[470] Panel Reports, para. 7.139.

[471] Panel Reports, para. 7.140.

commercial resale or with a view to use in the production of goods for commercial sale", such procurement would not be covered by Article III:8(a). Without making a finding on whether the FIT Programme and Contracts involve purchases "for governmental purposes", the Panel turned to assess whether the Government of Ontario purchases electricity "with a view to commercial resale or with a view to use in the production of goods for commercial sale".

5.44 The Panel noted that the parties had advanced different meanings also of the phrase "with a view to commercial resale". While Canada had argued that the phrase referred to a purchase with the "aim to resell for profit", the complainants had submitted that it meant "with a view to being sold or introduced into the stream of commerce, trade or market, regardless of any profit".[472] The Panel stated that, under the interpretation advanced by the complainants, the Government of Ontario's purchases of electricity under the FIT Programme and Contracts are undertaken "with a view to commercial resale", because the purchased electricity is introduced into commerce in competition with private-sector electricity retailers.[473] The Panel then addressed the interpretation advanced by Canada that the phrase "with a view to commercial resale" refers to resale with the underlying intent to profit. In this respect, the Panel found it evident that the Government of Ontario and municipal governments profit from the resale of electricity, and, consequently, the Panel found that Canada's argument that the Government of Ontario does not purchase electricity with a view to commercial resale failed even on the terms of Canada's own interpretation of the term "commercial resale".[474] The Panel emphasized that it was not of the view that "commercial resale" will always necessarily involve profit, but that, because the Government of Ontario and municipal governments profit from the resale of electricity under the FIT Programme and Contracts, and because the resales of electricity are made in competition with licensed electricity retailers, the purchases of electricity by the Government of Ontario are undertaken "with a view to commercial resale".

5.45 On this basis, the Panel concluded that the FIT Programme and Contracts are not covered by Article III:8(a) and that they are therefore subject to the disciplines of Article III:4 of the GATT 1994.[475] The Panel then found that the FIT Programme and Contracts are inconsistent with Article III:4 of the GATT 1994 and Article 2.1 of the TRIMs Agreement because they require the purchase or use of products of Canadian origin, and because compliance with that requirement is necessary in order to participate in the FIT Programme.[476]

---

[472] Panel Reports, para. 7.146. (fns omitted)
[473] Panel Reports, para. 7.148.
[474] Panel Reports, para. 7.151.
[475] Panel Reports, para. 7.152.
[476] Panel Reports, para. 7.167.

5.3.2 Claims and arguments on appeal

5.46 Canada alleges that the Panel erred in finding that the measures at issue do not fall within the scope of Article III:8(a) of the GATT 1994 because the Government of Ontario's purchases of electricity generated from renewable sources under the FIT Programme are "with a view to commercial resale", and raises two allegations of error with respect to the Panel's interpretation of this phrase. First, Canada asserts that the Panel erred in its interpretation of Article III:8(a) by focusing on whether there is "commercial resale" of electricity by the Government of Ontario while it neglected to interpret properly the term "with a view to" in Article III:8(a). Canada contends that, under the FIT Programme and Contracts, the Government of Ontario purchases electricity with a view "to help ensure a sufficient and reliable supply of electricity for Ontarians and to protect the environment"[477], and that it does not purchase electricity with a view to commercial resale. Second, Canada alleges that the Panel misinterpreted the term "commercial resale" in Article III:8(a). Canada contends that, had the Panel properly interpreted this term, it would have concluded that "commercial resale" means resale with the underlying intent to profit. With respect to the FIT Programme and Contracts, Canada submits that there is no suggestion that the Government of Ontario purchases electricity with an aim to resell for profit.

5.47 Canada additionally claims that the Panel failed to make an objective assessment of the matter, contrary to Article 11 of the DSU, in finding that the Government of Ontario's procurement of electricity under the FIT Programme is undertaken "with a view to commercial resale" within the meaning of Article III:8(a) of the GATT 1994.[478] Canada challenges two findings of the Panel in this respect. First, Canada challenges the Panel's finding that Hydro One Inc. and distributors sell electricity in competition with private-sector licensed retailers.[479] Second, Canada challenges the Panel's finding that the Government of Ontario and the municipal governments profit from the resale of electricity that is purchased under the FIT Programme.[480]

5.48 Japan and the European Union request us to uphold the Panel's conclusion that the FIT Programme and Contracts are inconsistent with Article 2.1 of the TRIMs Agreement and Article III:4 of the GATT 1994. However, in their other appeals, they each appeal several aspects of the Panel's interpretation and application of Article III:8(a) of the GATT 1994 and request us to modify certain intermediate findings of the Panel.

5.49 Japan alleges that the Panel erred in finding that the Government of Ontario "purchases" electricity. Japan argues that the structure of the energy system in Ontario, in particular the unbundling of generation, transmission, and

---

477 Canada's appellant's submission, para. 34.
478 Canada's appellant's submission, para. 48.
479 Canada's appellant's submission, para. 72.
480 Canada's appellant's submission, paras. 76 and 77.

distribution of electricity and the allocation of each of these functions together with corresponding regulatory functions to separate entities, suggests that the Government of Ontario does not engage in the physical supply or sale of electricity.

5.50 In the event that we do not reverse the Panel's finding that the measures at issue involve "purchases" by the Government of Ontario, Japan appeals, conditionally, the Panel's interpretation and application of the term "purchased for governmental purposes", and requests us to complete the analysis and find that the FIT Programme and Contracts do not involve "purchase[s] for governmental purposes". Japan alleges that the Panel failed to interpret the meaning of this phrase because it concluded merely that a purchase of goods by a governmental agency for governmental purposes could not at the same time constitute a government purchase of goods with a view to commercial resale, and applied the provision based on this assumption rather than based on a proper interpretation of the term "for governmental purposes". Japan argues that electricity is "purchased for governmental purposes" only if the purchase is made "in order to obtain certain governmental purposes or with the objective of achieving such governmental purposes".[481]

5.51 In the event that we reject both Japan's appeal relating to the Panel's finding that the Government of Ontario "purchases" electricity and Japan's appeal that the measures at issue involve "purchase[s] for governmental purposes", Japan requests us to find that the Panel failed to interpret properly the term "commercial resale" by concluding that profit earned by the government as a result of the "resale" was relevant evidence of its "commercial" nature. Japan submits that, in place of this erroneous conclusion, we should find that the phrase "with a view to commercial resale" means "with a view to being sold into the stream of commerce or trade"[482] and that, to the extent the FIT Programme and Contracts involve purchases of electricity by the Government of Ontario, such purchases are "with a view to commercial resale", because the electricity is purchased with a view to being sold or introduced into the stream of commerce, trade, or market, without regard to whether the government makes a profit from the resale.

5.52 The European Union requests us to reverse the Panel's finding that the domestic content requirements with respect to windpower and solar PV generation equipment under the FIT and microFIT Contracts "govern" the alleged procurement of electricity for the purpose of Article III:8(a) of the GATT 1994. In the European Union's view, "laws, regulations or requirements" within the meaning of Article III:8(a) must be related to the subject matter of the procurement – that is, the "products purchased for governmental purposes" – in order to "govern" such procurement. Article III:8(a) does not cover requirements

[481] Japan's other appellant's submission (DS412), para. 174.

[482] Japan's other appellant's submission (DS412), para. 188. (emphasis omitted)

or conditions that are not connected with "intrinsic characteristics"[483] or the nature of the product purchased. The European Union argues that conditions exogenous to the subject matter of the contract, such as the requirements relating to the origin of equipment used to generate electricity procured under the FIT Programme, do not fall under Article III:8(a) of the GATT 1994 because they have "no rational link" with the attributes of the electricity procured.[484]

5.53 The European Union also requests us to reverse or to declare moot and of no legal effect the Panel's statement that the term "governmental purposes" in Article III:8(a) may be read to encompass any government purchase "for a stated aim of the government".[485] In the event that we reverse, in response to Canada's appeal, the Panel's finding that the Government of Ontario's purchases of electricity under the FIT Programme are undertaken "with a view to commercial resale", the European Union requests us to reverse or modify the Panel's reasoning as to the meaning of "governmental purposes", to complete the analysis, and to find that the Government of Ontario's procurement of electricity under the FIT Programme is not undertaken for "governmental purposes".[486] The European Union maintains that the term "purchased for governmental purposes" in Article III:8(a) refers only to "government purchases of goods that are needed to sustain the work and functions of the government".[487] Thus, such goods will have to "be actually used or consumed by the government in the context of its administrative tasks or in the context of the exercise of its public functions".[488] In that event, the European Union also requests us to complete the analysis and find that the Government of Ontario's purchases of electricity under the FIT Programme are not undertaken "for governmental purposes". In this regard, the European Union argues that the Government of Ontario's purchases of electricity are not undertaken "for governmental purposes" because the electricity is not used by the Government of Ontario. If the electricity purchased by the government is not used for its own consumption, or in the performance of government functions such as the provision of public services, such purchases do not fall under Article III:8(a) of the GATT 1994. The European Union contends that the creation of an electricity system with stable, reliable, and sufficient supply of electricity from renewable sources is a legitimate policy objective, but it is not in itself a provision of a public service.

---

[483] European Union's other appellant's submission (DS426), para. 51. (fn omitted)

[484] European Union's other appellant's submission (DS426), para. 53.

[485] European Union's other appellant's submission (DS426), para. 60 (quoting Panel Reports, para. 7.139 (fn omitted)).

[486] European Union's other appellant's submission (DS426), para. 61.

[487] European Union's other appellant's submission (DS426), para. 60.

[488] *Ibid.*

5.3.3 Interpretation of Article III:8(a) of the GATT 1994

5.54 The three participants challenge on appeal different aspects of the Panel's interpretation of Article III:8(a) of the GATT 1994. This is the first time that the Appellate Body is called upon to interpret this provision. Article III:8(a) of the GATT 1994 stipulates:

> The provisions of this Article shall not apply to laws, regulations or requirements governing the procurement by governmental agencies of products purchased for governmental purposes and not with a view to commercial resale or with a view to use in the production of goods for commercial sale.

5.55 We observe that Article III:8(a) begins with the words "The provisions of this Article shall not apply to ...". This introductory clause establishes a linkage with the remainder of Article III. The title of Article III is "National Treatment on Internal Taxation and Regulation". The national treatment principle enshrined in Article III has been a cornerstone of the multilateral trading system since its inception. This general principle, which is articulated in the first paragraph of Article III, postulates that internal measures "should not be applied ... so as to afford protection to domestic production".[489] Other paragraphs of Article III "constitute specific expressions" of this "overarching, 'general principle'".[490]

5.56 The opening clause of Article III:8(a) uses the term "apply" in the negative, thus precluding the application of the other provisions of Article III to measures that meet the requirements of that paragraph. Article III:8(a) therefore establishes a derogation from the national treatment obligation of Article III for government procurement activities falling within its scope. Measures satisfying the requirements of Article III:8(a) are not subject to the national treatment obligations set out in other paragraphs of Article III. Article III:8(a) is a derogation limiting the scope of the national treatment obligation and it is not a justification for measures that would otherwise be inconsistent with that obligation. At the same time, we note that the characterization of the provision as a derogation does not pre-determine the question as to which party bears the burden of proof with regard to the requirements stipulated in the provision.[491]

5.57 Article III:8(a) contains several elements describing the types and the content of measures falling within the ambit of the provision. Some of the terms qualify other terms used in the same provision, or provide guidance for the interpretation of those terms. Indeed, the participants have emphasized the relationships between the various terms in Article III:8(a), although they do not agree on the interpretation of all of them. We consider that Article III:8(a)

---

[489] Appellate Body Report, *Japan – Alcoholic Beverages II*, p. 18, DSR 1996:I, p. 111.

[490] Appellate Body Report, *EC – Asbestos*, para. 93.

[491] We recall that, in *China – Raw Materials*, the Appellate Body distinguished between "exceptions" (such as the general exception of Article XX) and limitations of the scope of an obligation (such as Article XI:2(a)). (Appellate Body Reports, *China – Raw Materials*, para. 334)

should be interpreted holistically. This requires consideration of the linkages between the different terms used in the provision and the contextual connections to other parts of Article III, as well as to other provisions of the GATT 1994. At the same time, the principle of effective treaty interpretation requires us to give meaning to every term of the provision.[492]

5.58 Article III:8(a) describes the types of measures falling within its ambit as "laws, regulations or requirements governing the procurement by governmental agencies of products purchased". We note that the word "governing" links the words "laws, regulations or requirements" to the word "procurement" and the remainder of the paragraph. In the context of Article III:8(a), the word "governing", along with the word "procurement" and the other parts of the paragraph, define the subject matter of the "laws, regulations or requirements". The word "governing" is defined as "constitut[ing] a law or rule for".[493] Article III:8(a) thus requires an articulated connection between the laws, regulations, or requirements and the procurement, in the sense that the act of procurement is undertaken within a binding structure of laws, regulations, or requirements.

5.59 The term "procurement" may refer generally to "[t]he action of obtaining something; acquisition", or it may refer more specifically to "the action or process of obtaining equipment and supplies".[494] In a more technical sense, procurement usually refers to formal procedures used by governments to acquire goods or services.[495] In Article III:8(a), the word "procurement" is related to the words "products purchased". In this respect, the Panel found that the term "procurement" in Article III:8(a) should be given the "same essential meaning" as the word "purchased" and *vice versa*.[496] However, in our view, the concepts of "procurement" and "purchase" are not to be equated. As we see it, "procurement" is the operative word in Article III:8(a) describing the process and conduct of the governmental agency. The word "purchased" is used to describe the type of transaction used to put into effect that procurement. Not every procurement needs to be effectuated by way of a purchase, and not every purchase is part of a process of government procurement. The use of the word "purchased" in the same provision suggests reading the word "procurement" as referring to the process of obtaining products, rather than as referring to an acquisition itself, because, if procurement was understood to refer simply to any acquisition, it would not add any meaning to Article III:8(a) in addition to what is already expressed by the word "purchased". We therefore understand the word "procurement" to refer to the process pursuant to which a government acquires

---

492 See Appellate Body Report, *US – Gasoline*, p. 23, DSR 1996:I, p. 21.

493 Oxford English Dictionary online, *<http://www.oed.com/view/Entry/80304>*.

494 Oxford English Dictionary online, *<http://www.oed.com/view/Entry/151913>*.

495 Such procedures typically express principles, such as efficiency or transparency. See e.g. the 2011 Model Law on Public Procurement prepared by the United Nations Commission on International Trade Law (UNCITRAL).

496 Panel Reports, para. 7.131.

products. The precise range of contractual arrangements that are encompassed by the concept of "purchase" is not a matter we need to decide in this case.

5.60 Article III:8 further specifies what is procured and by whom. The subject matter of the procurement is a "product", and it is being procured by a "governmental agency". The term "agency" is defined as "[a] business, body, or organization providing a particular service, or negotiating transactions on behalf of a person or group".[497] The word "agency" is used in connection with the word "governmental" and, accordingly, Article III:8(a) refers to entities acting for or on behalf of government. The Appellate Body has held that the meaning of "government" is derived, in part, from the functions that it performs and, in part, from the authority under which it performs those functions.[498] We therefore consider that the question of whether an entity is a "governmental agency", in the sense of Article III:8(a), is determined by the competences conferred on the entity concerned and by whether that entity acts for or on behalf of government.

5.61 We consider that Articles XVII:1 and XVII:2 of the GATT 1994 provide relevant context for the interpretation of the term "governmental agency" in Article III:8(a). Article XVII:1 stipulates obligations for state trading enterprises and Article XVII:2 sets out a derogation from those obligations for certain government procurement transactions. In contrast to Article III:8(a), the provisions of Article XVII relate to "state trading enterprises" and not to "governmental agencies". According to Article XVII:1, this includes state enterprises and enterprises that are conferred exclusive or special privileges from the state. It follows that the GATT 1994 recognizes that there is a public and a private realm, and that government entities may act in one, the other, or both. Governments may limit the actions of entities to the public realm or give entities competences to act in the private realm. In our view, the term "governmental agencies" refers to those entities acting for or on behalf of government in the public realm within the competences that have been conferred on them to discharge governmental functions. This further confirms our understanding that a "governmental agency" is an entity acting for or on behalf of government and performing governmental functions within the competences conferred on it.

5.62 We turn next to the term "products purchased" within the meaning of Article III:8(a). A "product" in the sense of this provision is something that is capable of being traded. The term "product" is also found in other provisions of Article III of the GATT 1994 that provide relevant context. Paragraphs 2 and 4, in particular, focus on the treatment accorded to "products". Article III:4 prohibits discrimination against imported products, that is, it prohibits a Member from treating imported products less favourably than like products of national origin. In the context of Article III:2, the national treatment obligation applies

[497] Oxford English Dictionary online, <*http://www.oed.com/view/Entry/3851*>.

[498] Appellate Body Reports, *Canada – Dairy*, para. 97; and *US – Anti-Dumping and Countervailing Duties (China)*, para. 290.

also to the treatment of imported products that are directly competitive to or substitutable with domestic products.

5.63 We have found above that Article III:8(a) stipulates conditions under which derogation from the obligations in Article III takes place. The derogation in Article III:8(a) becomes relevant only if there is discriminatory treatment of foreign products that are covered by the obligations in Article III, and this discriminatory treatment results from laws, regulations, or requirements governing procurement by governmental agencies of products purchased. Both the obligations in Article III and the derogation in Article III:8(a) refer to discriminatory treatment of products. Because Article III:8(a) is a derogation from the obligations contained in other paragraphs of Article III, we consider that the same discriminatory treatment must be considered both with respect to the obligations of Article III and with respect to the derogation of Article III:8(a). Accordingly, the scope of the terms "products purchased" in Article III:8(a) is informed by the scope of "products" referred to in the obligations set out in other paragraphs of Article III. Article III:8(a) thus concerns, in the first instance, the product that is subject to the discrimination. The coverage of Article III:8 extends not only to products that are identical to the product that is purchased, but also to "like" products. In accordance with the Ad Note to Article III:2, it also extends to products that are directly competitive to or substitutable with the product purchased under the challenged measure. For convenience, this range of products can be described as products that are in a competitive relationship. What constitutes a competitive relationship between products may require consideration of inputs and processes of production used to produce the product. In its rebuttal of Canada's claim under Article III:8(a), the European Union acknowledges that the cover of Article III:8(a) may also extend to discrimination relating to inputs and processes of production used in respect of products purchased by way of procurement.[499] Whether the derogation in Article III:8(a) can extend also to discrimination of the kind referred to by the European Union is a matter we do not decide in this case.[500]

5.64 We now turn to the next element of Article III:8(a). The provision refers to purchases "for governmental purposes". The participants have put forward divergent views as to the meaning of the term "for governmental purposes" in Article III:8(a). Canada advocates a broad interpretation that may encompass any

[499] The European Union explains that, when it refers to product "characteristics", it does so not as necessarily referring to physically detectable characteristics, but as referring to elements that define the nature of the product more broadly. The European Union submits that the environmental profile or the environmental attributes that a particular product may incorporate, even if they do not materialize into any particular physical characteristic, could legitimately form part of the requirements of the product purchased that are closely related to the subject matter of the contract. (European Union's other appellant's submission (DS426), fn 43 to para. 51)

[500] We do not address in this case rules for determining the origin of products purchased. It has not been alleged in this case that the Minimum Required Domestic Content Levels are rules of origin.

purchase for a stated aim of the government.[501] Canada claims that its interpretation was accepted by the Panel.[502] In response to questioning at the oral hearing, Canada clarified that the inquiry under "governmental purposes" needs to go beyond the stated aim of the government, and must include an assessment of whether a government has traditionally supplied a certain product, whether it has a constitutional mandate to do so, and that it must take account of the role of government in a particular country, focusing on the history, constitution, and legislation of a particular government. The European Union considers Canada's interpretation to be overly broad. For the European Union, the key issue is whether the "products purchased" are needed to sustain the work and functions of the government and therefore will genuinely by utilized in some way by the government in the exercise of its public functions (including the provision of public services).[503] The European Union accepts that "products purchased for governmental purposes" need not be confined to those for the consumption or physical use by the government.[504] Japan emphasizes the word "for", which it considers requires an inquiry into whether there is a true and genuine connection between the "purchase" and the "governmental purpose" at issue.[505]

5.65 Contrary to what Canada alleges, it is not apparent to us that the Panel developed its own interpretation of the term "for governmental purposes". The Panel did suggest that the "ordinary meaning" of the term "governmental purposes" is "relatively broad" and could encompass all three meanings put forward by the parties, including Canada's interpretation.[506] Yet, the Panel did not stop there. Immediately after this statement, the Panel indicated that it had to "interpret this expression within its context".[507] Ultimately, however, the Panel did not define "governmental purposes". Instead, the Panel stated that "the term 'governmental purposes' should be interpreted in juxtaposition to the expression 'not with a view to commercial resale or with a view to use in the production of goods for commercial sale' that appears in Article III:8(a)."[508] Based on the proposition that a purchase "for governmental purposes" cannot at the same time amount to a government purchase of goods "with a view to commercial resale", the Panel did not come to a conclusion on whether the FIT Programme and Contracts involve purchases of electricity for "governmental purposes". Rather, the Panel turned to the question of whether those purchases are made with a view to commercial resale, based on the assumption that, if it found that to be the

501 Canada's appellee's submission, para. 59.
502 Canada's appellee's submission, para. 59 (referring to Panel Reports, paras. 7.138 and 7.139).
503 European Union's opening statement at the oral hearing.
504 *Ibid.*
505 Japan's other appellant's submission (DS412), para. 171.
506 Panel Reports, para. 7.139.
507 *Ibid.*
508 Panel Reports, para. 7.145.

case, this would also imply that the purchases are not made for "governmental purposes".[509]

5.66 The word "purpose" may refer to "an object in view; a determined intention or aim" or it may refer to "the end to which an object or action is directed".[510] In Article III:8(a), the word "purpose" is used in conjunction with the word "governmental". Accordingly, the term "governmental purposes" may refer either to the intentions or aims of a government, or it may refer to government as the end to which the product purchased is directed. We note that in Article III:8(a) the word "governmental" is used once in connection with "purposes", and again in connection with the word "agencies". The reference to "governmental agencies" defines the identity of the entity carrying out the procurement. Yet, because governmental agencies by their very nature pursue governmental aims or objectives, the additional reference to "governmental" in relation to "purposes" must go beyond simply requiring some governmental aim or objective with respect to purchases by governmental agencies.

5.67 We further note that the French version of Article III:8(a) refers to "*les besoins des pouvoirs publics*" and the Spanish version of the provision refers to "*las necesidades de los poderes públicos*". The term "purposes" thus corresponds to the terms "*besoins*" and "*necesidades*", respectively, in the French and the Spanish texts. Both the French and the Spanish terms correspond closely to the English term "needs".[511] As such, the French and the Spanish text can be read harmoniously[512] with an interpretation of the word "purposes" in English as referring to purchases of products directed at the government or purchased for the needs of the government in the discharge of its functions. By contrast, the words "*besoins*" or "*necesidades*" cannot be read harmoniously with the definition of the term "purpose" as "objectives" or "aims" of the government, because neither the word "*besoins*" in French, not the word "*necesidades*" in Spanish encompass the notion of an aim or objective.[513]

5.68 Article XVII:2 of the GATT 1994 provides relevant context for the interpretation of the words "governmental purposes" in Article III:8(a). The provision refers to "imports of products for immediate or ultimate consumption in governmental use". By referring to immediate and ultimate consumption in

[509] *Ibid.*

[510] Oxford English Dictionary online, <*http://www.oed.com/view/Entry/154972*>.

[511] *The Oxford Spanish Dictionary*, B. Galimberti and R. Russell (eds.) (Oxford University Press, 1994), p. 523; *Le Nouveau Petit Robert*, P. Varrod (ed.) (Dictionnaires Le Robert, 1993), pp. 246-247.

[512] Article 33 of the Vienna Convention reflects the principle that the treaty text is equally authoritative in each language, unless the treaty provides or the parties agree that, in case of divergence, a particular text shall prevail. For the covered agreements, Article XVI of the WTO Agreement provides that the English, French, and Spanish language each are authentic. Consequently, the terms of Article III:8(a) of the GATT 1994 are presumed to have the same meaning in each authentic text.

[513] *Diccionario de la Lengua Española*, 22nd edn (Real Academia Española, 2001), p. 1065.

governmental use, Article XVII:2 identifies instances in which a product may be said to be purchased for governmental purposes. An obvious example is where a governmental agency purchases a good, uses it to discharge its governmental functions, and the good is totally consumed in the process. None of the participants disputes that this would constitute an example of a good purchased for governmental purposes. We also note that Article XVII:2 is phrased more narrowly than Article III:8(a), as the former provision refers to "immediate or ultimate consumption in governmental use". This in turn suggests that, where products purchased are consumed in governmental use, Article III:8(a) does not require that this be "immediate or ultimate". Therefore, we are of the view that the phrase "products purchased for governmental purposes" in Article III:8(a) refers to what is consumed by government or what is provided by government to recipients in the discharge of its public functions. The scope of these functions is to be determined on a case by case basis.[514] Finally, we recall that Article III:8(a) refers to purchases "*for* governmental purposes".[515] The word "for" relates the term "products purchased" to "governmental purposes", and thus indicates that the products purchased must be intended to be directed at the government or be used for governmental purposes. Thus, Article III:8(a) requires that there be a rational relationship between the product and the governmental function being discharged.

5.69 We turn next to the analysis of the last element of the text of Article III:8(a), namely, the phrase "and not with a view to commercial resale or with a view to use in the production of goods for commercial sale". In the context of Article III:8(a), the words "with a view to commercial resale" relate back to the "products purchased" and thus attach to the same textual element as the clause "for governmental purposes". Both the terms "for governmental purposes" and "not with a view to commercial resale" further qualify and limit the scope of "products purchased". These two requirements are linked by the words "and not", which suggests that the requirement of purchases not being made with a view to commercial resale must be met in addition to the requirement of purchases being made for governmental purposes. Accordingly, a purchase that does not fulfil the requirement of being made "for governmental purposes" will not be covered by Article III:8(a) regardless of whether it complies with the requirement of being made "not with a view to commercial resale". These are cumulative requirements. We therefore disagree with the Panel's proposition that where a government purchase of goods is made "with a view to commercial resale", it is for that reason also not a purchase "for governmental purposes".

[514] At the oral hearing an example was discussed, in which a public hospital purchases pharmaceuticals and provides them to patients. Both Canada and the European Union accepted that this could qualify as a purchase "for governmental purposes".
[515] Emphasis added.

5.70 Turning then to the meaning of the words "commercial resale", we note that the term "resale" is defined as the "sale of something previously bought".[516] In the context of Article III:8(a), the word "resale" refers to the term "products purchased". Accordingly, the product not to be "resold" on a commercial basis is the product "purchased for governmental purposes". As we see it, "commercial resale" is a resale of a product at arm's length between a willing seller and a willing buyer. Much of the debate in this case has focused on whether procurement "with a view to commercial resale" must involve profit. Canada, in particular, has argued that procurement "with a view to commercial resale" is procurement "with the aim to resell for profit".[517] Japan and the European Union reject the proposition that profit, or an intent to profit, is a required element.[518] Although the Panel ultimately found the existence of profit in this case[519], it seemed unpersuaded by Canada's argument that a profit element is required for a resale to be "commercial".[520] The Panel observed, in this regard, that "it is a fact that loss-making sales can be, and often are, a part of ordinary commercial activity."[521]

5.71 As we see it, whether a transaction constitutes a "commercial resale" must be assessed having regard to the entire transaction. In doing so, the assessment must look at the transaction from the seller's perspective and at whether the transaction is oriented at generating a profit for the seller. We see profit-orientation generally as an indication that a resale is at arm's length. Profit-orientation indicates that the seller is acting in a self-interested manner. Yet, as the Panel noted, there are circumstances where a seller enters into a transaction out of his or her own interest without making a profit. There are different circumstances in which a seller may offer a product at a price that does not allow him or her to make a profit, or sometimes even fully to recoup cost. In such circumstances, it may be useful to look at the seller's long-term strategy. This is because loss-making sales could not be sustained indefinitely and a rational seller would be expected to be profit-oriented in the long term, though we accept that strategies can vary widely and thus do not see this as applying axiomatically. The transaction must also be assessed from the perspective of the buyer. A commercial resale would be one in which the buyer seeks to maximize his or her own interest. It is an assessment of the relationship between the seller and the buyer in the transaction in question that allows a judgement to be made whether a transaction is made at arm's length.

5.72 Finally, we turn to the clause "not ... with a view to use in the production of goods for commercial sale" in Article III:8(a). Where the provision uses the

---

516 Oxford English Dictionary online, <*http://www.oed.com/view/Entry/163370*>.

517 Panel Reports, para. 7.146.

518 *Ibid.*

519 This finding has been appealed by Canada under Article 11 of the DSU. See *infra*, paras. 5.83 and 5.84.

520 Panel Reports, para. 7.151.

521 *Ibid.*

same words as in the phrase "not with a view to commercial resale", we consider that these words have the same meaning in both clauses. Furthermore, while the penultimate clause of Article III:8(a) refers to commercial "resale", the last clause refers simply to "sale". To us, this is due to the fact that the penultimate clause addresses the sale of the product previously bought by the governmental agency and the last clause addresses the sale of a product that is different from the product previously bought by the government. However, we consider that both clauses refer essentially to the same type of sales transactions.

5.73 The provision further refers to "use in the production of goods". The word "use" is defined as "[t]he act of putting something to work, or employing or applying a thing, for any (*esp.* a beneficial or productive) purpose".[522] The relevant purpose in the sense of the provision is then specified by the words "in the production of goods". The preposition "in" expresses a relation of inclusion and thus suggests that the product has a role in the production of goods. Finally, we note that the clause "not with a view to commercial resale" and the clause "with a view to use in the production of goods for commercial sale" are connected with the word "or", which suggests that the provision covers only products that are neither purchased with a view to commercial resale, nor purchased with a view to use in the production of goods for commercial sale.

5.74 In sum, we consider that Article III:8(a) sets out a derogation from the national treatment obligation contained in Article III of the GATT 1994. The provision exempts from the national treatment obligation certain measures containing rules for the process by which government purchases products. Under Article III:8(a), the entity procuring products for the government is a "governmental agency". We have found above that a "governmental agency" is an entity performing functions of government and acting for or on behalf of government. Furthermore, we have found that the derogation of Article III:8(a) must be understood in relation to the obligations stipulated in Article III. This means that the product of foreign origin must be in a competitive relationship with the product purchased.[523] Furthermore, Article III:8(a) is limited to products purchased for the use of government, consumed by government, or provided by government to recipients in the discharge of its public functions. On the contrary, Article III:8(a) does not cover purchases made by governmental agencies with a view to reselling the purchased products in an arm's-length sale and it does not cover purchases made with a view to using the product previously purchased in the production of goods for sale at arm's length.

[522] Oxford English Dictionary online, <*http://www.oed.com/view/Entry/220635*>.

[523] Whether the derogation in Article III:8(a) can extend also to discrimination relating to inputs and processes of production used in respect of products purchased by way of procurement is a matter we do not decide in this case. (See *supra*, para. 5.63)

5.3.4 *Application of Article III:8(a) of the GATT 1994 to the facts of these disputes*

5.75 We now turn to consider whether the Panel erred in finding that the FIT Programme and related FIT and microFIT Contracts are not covered by Article III:8(a) and that they are therefore subject to the disciplines of Article III:4 of the GATT 1994.[524] We note that the product that is subject to the Minimum Required Domestic Content Levels of the FIT Programme and Contracts challenged by the complainants as discriminatory under Article III:4 of the GATT 1994 and the TRIMs Agreement is certain renewable energy generation equipment.[525] The product purchased by the Government of Ontario under the FIT Programme and Contracts, however, is electricity and not generation equipment.[526] The generation equipment is purchased by the generators themselves. Accordingly, the product being purchased by a governmental agency for purposes of Article III:8(a) – namely, electricity – is not the same as the product that is treated less favourably as a result of the Minimum Required Domestic Content Levels of the FIT Programme and Contracts.

5.76 We observe that the Panel noted the difference between the product subject to the Minimum Required Domestic Content Levels and the product subject of procurement.[527] However, the Panel found that, in the present case, purchases of electricity nonetheless fall within the scope of the derogation of Article III:8(a), because the generation equipment "is needed and used" to produce the electricity, and therefore there is a "close relationship" between the products affected by the domestic content requirements (generation equipment) and the product procured (electricity).[528]

5.77 Canada supports the Panel's finding that there is a "close relationship" between the product affected by the domestic content requirements (generation equipment) and the product procured by the Government of Ontario (electricity), because the domestic content requirements for electricity generation equipment are a condition that must be satisfied by generators utilizing solar PV or windpower technologies in order to participate in the FIT Programme, and because the electricity procured by the Government of Ontario is produced using the very same generation equipment that is subject to the domestic content requirements.[529]

5.78 We recall our finding above that laws, regulations, or requirements "governing" procurement must articulate a connection between those legal instruments and procurement in the sense that the act of procurement is taken

---

524 Panel Reports, para. 7.152.

525 Panel Reports, para. 7.124. See also paras. 7.158-7.160.

526 Panel Reports, para. 7.64.

527 Panel Reports, paras. 7.125 and 7.126 and fn 271 thereto.

528 Panel Reports, para. 7.127.

529 Canada's appellee's submission, paras. 47-57.

within a binding structure of laws, regulations, or requirements. We acknowledge that, under the challenged measures, a connection is articulated between the procurement of electricity and the Minimum Required Domestic Content Levels regarding generation equipment. However, in our view, this connection under municipal law is not dispositive of the issue, because Article III:8(a) imposes also other conditions.

5.79 We have found above that the conditions for derogation under Article III:8(a) must be understood in relation to the obligations stipulated in the other paragraphs of Article III. This means that the product of foreign origin allegedly being discriminated against must be in a competitive relationship with the product purchased. In the case before us, the product being procured is electricity, whereas the product discriminated against for reason of its origin is generation equipment. These two products are not in a competitive relationship. None of the participants has suggested otherwise, much less offered evidence to substantiate such proposition. Accordingly, the discrimination relating to generation equipment contained in the FIT Programme and Contracts is not covered by the derogation of Article III:8(a) of the GATT 1994.[530] We therefore *reverse* the Panel's findings, in paragraphs 7.127, 7.128, and 7.152 of the Panel Reports, that the Minimum Required Domestic Content Levels of the FIT Programme and related FIT and microFIT Contracts are laws, regulations, or requirements governing the procurement by governmental agencies of electricity within the meaning of Article III:8(a) of the GATT 1994. Instead, we *find* that the Minimum Required Domestic Content Levels cannot be characterized as "laws, regulations or requirements governing the procurement by governmental agencies" of electricity within the meaning of Article III:8(a) of the GATT 1994.

5.80 We recall that both Japan and the European Union directed claims to various parts of the Panel's analysis regarding Article III:8(a). In particular, Japan claims that the Panel erred in finding that the Government of Ontario's purchases of electricity under the FIT Programme constitute "procurement" within the meaning of Article III:8(a)[531], because the structure of the energy system in Ontario, in particular the unbundling of generation, transmission, and distribution of electricity and the allocation of each of these functions together with corresponding regulatory functions to separate entities, suggests that the Government of Ontario does not engage in the physical supply or sale of electricity. The European Union contends that the domestic content requirements of the measures at issue are not covered by Article III:8(a) because they relate to

---

[530] We recall that we do not address in this case rules for determining the origin of products purchased. It has not been alleged in this case that the Minimum Required Domestic Content Levels are rules of origin.

[531] Panel Reports, para. 7.136.

generation equipment, a product that is different and "completely disconnected" from the product purchased by the government, which is electricity.[532]

5.81 Both Japan and the European Union have raised additional claims but have done so on a conditional basis. Japan and the European Union conditionally appeal the Panel's interpretation and application of the term "for governmental purposes".[533] Japan conditionally appeals the Panel's interpretation and application of the term "commercial resale".[534]

5.82 We have addressed the various elements of Article III:8(a) to which the claims of Japan and the European Union relate in a holistic interpretation of this provision set out above. Having found that the Minimum Required Domestic Content Levels do not fall within the ambit of the derogation in Article III:8(a), we need not address these further allegations of error raised by the European Union and Japan seeking reversal of intermediate findings by the Panel. These findings are moot.

5.83 Canada claims that the Panel erred in finding that the Government of Ontario's purchases of electricity under the FIT Programme are undertaken "with a view to commercial resale". It additionally makes two claims under Article 11 of the DSU in connection with this finding. In particular, Canada argues that the Panel failed to make an objective assessment of the matter before it, contrary to Article 11 of the DSU, when finding that the measures at issue involve purchases "with a view to commercial resale" within the meaning of Article III:8(a) of the GATT 1994. More specifically, Canada claims that the Panel acted inconsistently with Article 11 of the DSU in finding that: (i) Hydro One Inc. and distributors sell electricity in competition with private-sector licensed retailers; and (ii) the Government of Ontario and the municipal governments profit from the resale of electricity purchased under the FIT Programme to consumers.

5.84 Our conclusion that the measures at issue are not covered by Article III:8(a) of the GATT 1994 is not premised on a finding that the Government of Ontario's procurement of electricity under the FIT Programme is undertaken "with a view to commercial resale". Rather, it is based on our finding that Article III:8(a) does not cover discriminatory treatment of the equipment used to generate the electricity that is procured by the Government of Ontario. Furthermore, we have mooted the Panel's intermediate findings, including the finding that the Government of Ontario's procurement of electricity under the FIT Programme and Contracts is undertaken "with a view to commercial resale". Thus, we do not consider it necessary to address further Canada's claims.

5.85 In the light of our finding that the Minimum Required Domestic Content Levels do not fall within the ambit of Article III:8(a), and in the light of the fact

---

532 European Union's other appellant's submission (DS426), para. 53; Panel Reports, para. 7.128.

533 Panel Reports, para. 7.145.

534 Panel Reports, para. 7.151.

that Canada has not appealed the Panel's finding that the FIT Programme and Contracts are inconsistent with Article III:4 of the GATT 1994 and Article 2.1 of the TRIMs Agreement[535], the Panel's conclusion, in paragraph 8.2 of the Japan Panel Report and in paragraph 8.6 of the EU Panel Report, that the Minimum Required Domestic Content Levels prescribed under the FIT Programme and related FIT and microFIT Contracts are inconsistent with Article 2.1 of the TRIMs Agreement and Article III:4 of the GATT 1994 stands.

5.4 Did the Panel properly exercise judicial economy when it declined to make a finding under Japan's "stand-alone" claim under Article III:4 of the GATT 1994?

5.86 We now turn to Japan's allegation that the Panel failed to comply with its duties under Article 11 of the DSU and exercised false judicial economy by failing to make a finding with respect to Japan's claim under Article III:4 of the GATT 1994, which was independent of Japan's claim involving both Article III:4 of the GATT 1994 and the TRIMs Agreement.

5.87 We recall briefly how this issue was argued before the Panel. Japan claimed that the measures at issue are inconsistent with Article III:4 of the GATT 1994 because they impose "requirements" on renewable energy generators "affecting" the "internal" "sale", "purchase", and "use" of renewable energy generation equipment, and accord imported equipment treatment less favourable than "like products" of Ontario origin.[536] This claim was independent from, and additional to, its claim of violation of the TRIMs Agreement, which also included Article III:4.[537] For convenience, we refer below to the first claim as Japan's "stand-alone Article III:4 claim". We refer to the second claim as Japan's "TRIMs–Article III:4 claim".

5.88 As described in Section 5.2, the Panel decided to "simultaneously evaluate the merits of both of the complainants' claims under Article 2.1 of the TRIMs Agreement and Article III:4 of the GATT 1994".[538] The Panel explained that it was "apparent from the terms of Article 2.1 of the TRIMs Agreement" that, in undertaking its evaluation under the TRIMs Agreement, it would "also necessarily have to come to a view about the merits of the complainants' allegations concerning the consistency of the challenged measures with Article III:4 of the GATT 1994."[539]

---

[535] Panel Reports, para. 7.167. Canada did not contest before the Panel that the measures at issue are TRIMs. (*Ibid.*, para. 7.70) Also, the Panel noted that, "apart from Canada's reliance on Article III:8(a) of the GATT 1994, Canada has not advanced any specific arguments to reject the complainants' claims under Article 2.1 of the TRIMs Agreement and Article III:4 of the GATT 1994." (*Ibid.*, fn 254 to para. 7.107)

[536] Japan's first written submission to the Panel (DS412), para. 262.

[537] Japan's first written submission to the Panel (DS412), para. 295 et seq.

[538] Panel Reports, para. 7.70.

[539] *Ibid.*

5.89 At the end of its analysis, the Panel found that "the challenged measures are TRIMs falling within the scope of Paragraph 1(a) of the Illustrative List, and that in the light of Article 2.2 and the chapeau to paragraph 1(a) of the Illustrative List, they are inconsistent with Article III:4 of the GATT 1994, and thereby also inconsistent with Article 2.1 of the TRIMs Agreement."[540] The Panel then concluded:

> In the light of the findings we have made in this Section of these Reports, we conclude that the FIT Programme, and the FIT and microFIT Contracts, are inconsistent with Article 2.1 of the TRIMs Agreement and Article III:4 of the GATT 1994.[541]

5.90 At the interim review stage, Japan requested the Panel to "address Japan's other argument and that it do so by undertaking a separate analysis of Article III:4 of the GATT 1994."[542] Japan argued that "this separate analysis is necessary in order for the Panel to discharge its responsibilities under Articles 3 and 11 of the DSU."[543] Canada did not comment on Japan's request.[544]

5.91 The Panel responded as follows:

> [W]e have found that the challenged measures are TRIMs falling within the scope of Paragraph 1(a) of the Illustrative List, and that in the light of Article 2.2 of the TRIMs Agreement and the chapeau to Paragraph 1(a) of the Illustrative List, the challenged measures are inconsistent with both Article 2.1 of the TRIMs Agreement and Article III:4 of the GATT 1994. Having made this finding, we do not believe it is necessary for the purpose of resolving the disputes before us to also address Japan's other argument and perform an entirely separate and stand-alone analysis of Japan's claim under Article III:4 of the GATT 1994. Thus, we have declined Japan's request.[545]

5.92 On appeal, Japan claims that the Panel improperly exercised judicial economy when it declined to make a finding with respect to Japan's stand-alone Article III:4 claim. We note that the Panel did not use the term "judicial

---

540 Panel Reports, para. 7.166.

541 Panel Reports, para. 7.167. The Panel made the following recommendation on the basis of its earlier conclusion:

> Accordingly, we conclude that to the extent Canada has acted inconsistently with Article 2.1 of the TRIMs Agreement and Article III:4 of the GATT 1994, Canada has nullified or impaired benefits accruing to Japan.
>
> We recommend that Canada bring its measures into conformity with its obligations under the TRIMs Agreement and the GATT 1994.

(Japan Panel Report (DS412), paras. 8.4 and 8.5)

542 Panel Reports, para. 6.71.

543 *Ibid.*

544 *Ibid.*

545 Panel Reports, para. 6.72.

economy" to describe its disposition of Japan's stand-alone Article III:4 claim. The only explanation offered by the Panel is in the interim review section of the Panel Reports quoted above. While the Panel did not state explicitly that it was exercising judicial economy, the explanation offered by the Panel in the interim review suggests that is what the Panel had in mind.

5.93 The question before us, therefore, is whether the Panel's exercise of judicial economy in this case was proper. Since panels have a margin of discretion with respect to the exercise of judicial economy, to succeed in its claim on appeal Japan has to demonstrate that the Panel exceeded this discretion. In accordance with Appellate Body jurisprudence, this means that Japan would have to show that the Panel provided only a "partial resolution of the matter at issue", or that an additional finding with respect to Japan's stand-alone Article III:4 claim "is necessary in order to enable the DSB to make sufficiently precise recommendations and rulings so as to allow for prompt compliance"[546] by Canada with those recommendations and rulings.

5.94 At the outset, we emphasize that this is not a case in which the panel failed to make a finding under a provision alleged by the complainant to have been violated. The Panel in this case has made a finding of violation of Article III:4 of the GATT 1994. It is true that this finding of violation rests on an assessment of the measures at issue under the Illustrative List of TRIMs annexed to the TRIMs Agreement, and in particular on paragraph 1(a). While it is not said in so many words, paragraph 1(a) is an instance in which an imported product is treated less favourably than a like domestic product. Understood in this manner, it is not obvious what a stand-alone finding of violation of Article III:4 of the GATT 1994 would add to a finding of violation of Article III:4 that is consequential to an assessment under the Illustrative List of the TRIMs Agreement.

5.95 Japan argues that a stand-alone finding under Article III:4 would result in broader implementation obligations. Different implementation obligations have been one of the factors used in the past to assess whether the exercise of judicial economy was proper or improper. However, this is not a case like *EC – Export Subsidies on Sugar*, where the remedy available as a result of a finding of violation of the SCM Agreement[547] was different to the remedy available in relation to a finding of violation of the Agreement on Agriculture. There is no difference here between the remedy that would be available under Article 19.1

---

[546] Appellate Body Reports, *Australia – Salmon*, para. 223; and *EC – Export Subsidies on Sugar*, para. 331. See also Appellate Body Reports, *Canada – Wheat Exports and Grain Imports*, para. 133; and *US – Upland Cotton*, para. 732.

[547] Article 4.7 of the SCM Agreement provides:

> If the measure in question is found to be a prohibited subsidy, the panel shall recommend that the subsidizing Member withdraw the subsidy without delay. In this regard, the panel shall specify in its recommendation the time period within which the measure must be withdrawn.

of the DSU in the case of a stand-alone Article III:4 finding of violation and the TRIMs–Article III:4 finding of violation entered by the Panel.

5.96 At the oral hearing, Japan clarified its position on the differences in implementation obligations, explaining that Canada could lower the FIT Programme's domestic content requirements to a point where such requirements could be met exclusively through the use of local services. Japan was of the view that such a situation would not be addressed by the Panel's TRIMS–Article III:4 finding, but that such situation would have been covered had the Panel made a stand-alone finding under Article III:4 of the GATT 1994.

5.97 We note that Japan's argument is premised on a change to the Minimum Required Domestic Content Levels of the FIT Programme. Japan has not suggested that the Minimum Required Domestic Content Levels under either the FIT or microFIT stream could be fulfilled at present using services exclusively. In fact, before the Panel, Japan emphasized that the opposite was the case, explaining that, "for *all* project types, *at least some* goods manufactured, formed, or assembled in Ontario *must* be utilized in order to satisfy the Minimum Required Domestic Content Levels."[548] In other words, as the Panel noted, it was Japan's contention that "purely service activities contained in each Domestic Content Grid[] are not sufficient to meet the 'Minimum Required Domestic Content Levels'."[549] The Panel "carefully reviewed the operation of the 'Minimum Required Domestic Content Level'" and agreed with Japan "that in all of the situations described ... by Japan, at least some Ontario-sourced (and therefore Canadian-sourced) goods must be used to satisfy them."[550] Thus, Japan's argument regarding implementation is based on a measure that is different from the measure that was before the Panel. We do not believe that it was necessary or appropriate for the Panel to make an additional finding so as to anticipate that Canada would modify the measures at issue in the manner suggested by Japan.

5.98 Moreover, it does not appear that Japan asked the Panel for different kinds of relief for each of its two Article III:4 lines of argumentation. Japan simply requested that the Panel recommend that Canada "bring the FIT Programme, as well as individually executed FIT and microFIT Contracts

---

548 Japan's first written submission to the Panel (DS412), para. 173. (original emphasis) See also Panel Reports, para. 7.161.

549 Panel Reports, para. 7.161. Japan demonstrated this by showing that, under the FIT stream, the use of services would yield a maximum qualifying percentage of 20% for wind projects, and of between 22% and 28% for solar PV projects depending on the technology used. The Minimum Required Domestic Content Levels under the FIT Programme are: wind projects, 25% for 2009-2011 milestones and 50% as of 2012; and solar PV projects, 50% for 2009-2010 milestones and 60% as of 2011. As regards microFIT solar PV projects, Japan explained that the maximum qualifying percentage for services is 27% or 28% depending on the technology used, whereas the Minimum Required Domestic Content Level is 40% for 2009-2010 milestones and 60% as of 2011. (See Panel Reports, paras. 7.158 and 7.161; and Japan's first written submission to the Panel (DS412), para. 173)

550 Panel Reports, para. 7.163.

for wind and solar PV projects, into conformity with the GATT 1994 and the TRIMs Agreement, as required by Article 19.1 of the DSU."[551] In the event, the Panel recommended "that Canada bring its measures into conformity with its obligations under the TRIMs Agreement and the GATT 1994."[552] Thus, besides the short-hand way the Panel referred to the measures at issue and the order in which the agreements are listed, the Panel's recommendation closely follows what Japan requested.

5.99 Japan also relies on the Appellate Body report in *US – Tuna II (Mexico)* to support its position. In that case, the Appellate Body faulted the panel for failing to make findings on Mexico's claims under Articles I and III of the GATT 1994 having assessed the measure under Articles 2.1, 2.2, and 2.4 of the Agreement on Technical Barriers to Trade (TBT Agreement). The Appellate Body explained:

> To us, it seems that the Panel's decision to exercise judicial economy rested upon the assumption that the obligations under Article 2.1 of the *TBT Agreement* and Articles I:1 and III:4 of the GATT 1994 are substantially the same. This assumption is, in our view, incorrect. In fact, as we have found above, the scope and content of these provisions is not the same. Moreover, in our view, the Panel should have made additional findings under the GATT 1994 in the event that the Appellate Body were to disagree with its view that the measure at issue is a "technical regulation" within the meaning of the *TBT Agreement*. As a result, it would have been necessary for the Panel to address Mexico's claims under the GATT 1994 given that the Panel found no violation under Article 2.1 of the *TBT Agreement*. By failing to do so, the Panel engaged, in our view, in an exercise of "false judicial economy" and acted inconsistently with its obligations under Article 11 of the DSU.[553]

---

[551] Panel Reports, para. 3.2(b). Japan did request separate findings, asking the Panel to find that:

> (b) the domestic content requirement of the FIT Programme, as well as individually executed FIT and microFIT Contracts for wind and solar PV projects, accords less favourable treatment to Japanese renewable energy generation equipment than accorded to like products of Ontario origin, in violation of Article III:4 of the GATT 1994; and
>
> (c) the FIT Programme, as well as individually executed FIT and microFIT Contracts for wind and solar PV projects, constitute trade-related investment measures inconsistent with the provisions of Article III of the GATT 1994, and are therefore in violation of Article 2.1 of the TRIMs Agreement.

(*Ibid.*, para. 3.1(b) and (c))

[552] Japan Panel Report (DS412), para. 8.5.

[553] Appellate Body Report, *US – Tuna II (Mexico)*, para. 405 (referring to Appellate Body Report, *Australia – Salmon*, para. 223).

5.100 There is a key difference between the situation in the present case and the situation that was before the Appellate Body in *US – Tuna II (Mexico)*. In this case, the Panel made findings of violation under both Article 2.1 of the TRIMs Agreement and Article III:4 of the GATT 1994, while in *US – Tuna II (Mexico)*, the panel made no findings of violation under Articles I:1 and III:4 of the GATT 1994 or Article 2.1 of the TBT Agreement. Thus, the situation in this case and the situation in *US – Tuna II (Mexico)* are the diametrical opposite.

5.101 In our view, the circumstances of this case more closely resemble *US – Upland Cotton* rather than *US – Tuna II (Mexico)*. We recall that, in *US – Upland Cotton*, Brazil claimed that export credit guarantees provided by the United States to certain agricultural products were export subsidies prohibited under Articles 3.1(a) and 3.2 of the SCM Agreement.[554] The panel in that case determined that the export credit guarantees were indeed export subsidies prohibited under Articles 3.1(a) and 3.2 of the SCM Agreement. For purposes of its assessment, the panel relied on item (j) of the Illustrative List of Export Subsidies annexed to the SCM Agreement.[555] At the interim review stage, the panel denied Brazil's request "to make certain additional 'factual' findings regarding the parties' evidence and argumentation relating to Brazil's allegation that the ... export credit guarantee programmes at issue constitute prohibited export subsidies under the elements of Articles 1 and 3.1(a) of the *SCM Agreement*".[556]

5.102 Brazil subsequently appealed the Panel's finding, arguing that it constituted false judicial economy. The Appellate Body observed that Brazil's claim was premised "on its submission that item (j) of the Illustrative List of Export Subsides annexed to the *SCM Agreement* is a distinct obligation from that contained in Article 3.1(a), read together with Article 1.1".[557] The Appellate Body declined to decide whether the premise on which Brazil based its argument was correct, because, "even if [the Appellate Body] were to assume that such a claim were possible, [it] would conclude that the Panel was within its discretion in exercising judicial economy in respect of Brazil's claim".[558]

---

[554] Brazil also challenged the export credit guarantees under the Agreement on Agriculture.

[555] Item (j) of the Illustrative List of Export Subsides provides:

> The provision by governments (or special institutions controlled by governments) of export credit guarantee or insurance programmes, of insurance or guarantee programmes against increases in the cost of exported products or of exchange risk programmes, at premium rates which are inadequate to cover the long-term operating costs and losses of the programmes.

[556] Panel Report, *US – Upland Cotton*, para. 6.31. Brazil alleged that, "in the event one of the parties appeals and the Appellate Body reverses the Panel's conclusion on item (j), it might not have the necessary facts at its disposal to 'complete the analysis' with respect to Brazil's claims under Articles 1 and 3.1(a) of the *SCM Agreement*". (*Ibid.*)

[557] Appellate Body Report, *US – Upland Cotton*, para. 730 (referring to Brazil's other appellant's submission, para. 22).

[558] Appellate Body Report, *US – Upland Cotton*, para. 731. In fn 1139 thereto, the Appellate Body explained that the panel did not expressly state that it was exercising judicial economy. Instead, the

According to the Appellate Body, the panel's finding that US export credit guarantee programs constituted a prohibited export subsidy under Article 3.1(a) because they did not meet the criteria in item (j) was "sufficient to resolve the matter".[559] Consequently, the Appellate Body rejected Brazil's claim and found that the panel's exercise of judicial economy was proper.[560]

5.103 The circumstances described above are similar to those surrounding Japan's claim in the present case. Both cases involve findings of inconsistency that proceeded on the basis of the application of an illustrative list. In the case of item (j) of the Illustrative List of Export Subsides, fulfilment of the elements of that provision results in a finding that there is a prohibited export subsidy under Article 3.1(a) of the SCM Agreement. In the present case, fulfilment of the elements in paragraph 1(a) of the Illustrative List of TRIMs results in a finding of inconsistency with Article III:4 of the GATT 1994. In both cases, the elements that must be demonstrated under the relevant paragraphs of the Illustrative Lists are not necessarily the same as those that must be demonstrated pursuant to the underlying obligation. In addition, in both cases, the underlying obligation captures a broader set of measures than the examples in the Illustrative Lists. Thus, the Panel's decision to exercise judicial economy in the present case with respect to Japan's stand-alone Article III:4 claim is consistent with the panel's approach in *US – Upland Cotton*, which the Appellate Body found not to have been an improper exercise of judicial economy.

5.104 In sum, we are not persuaded that the Panel's failure to make a finding on Japan's stand-alone Article III:4 claim provided only a "partial resolution of the matter at issue" or that an additional finding on Japan's stand-alone Article III:4 claim "is necessary in order to enable the DSB to make sufficiently precise recommendations and rulings so as to allow for prompt compliance"[561] by Canada with those recommendations and rulings. Therefore, we *reject* Japan's claim that the Panel failed to fulfil its obligations under Article 11 of the DSU and exercised false judicial economy by declining to make a finding on Japan's stand-alone Article III:4 claim.

5.105 Japan requests, if we were to conclude that the Panel's exercise of judicial economy was false, that we complete the analysis of its stand-alone Article III:4 claim. Given that we have found that it was not improper for the Panel to have

---

panel stated that it did not believe that it was "necessary to address Brazil's additional arguments". (Panel Report, *US – Upland Cotton*, para. 6.31 (emphasis omitted)) Brazil initially described the panel's failure to make a finding as an error by the panel in the "interpretation and application of Article 3.1(a) of the *SCM Agreement*, as well as of Article 3.7 of the DSU". (Brazil's other appellant's submission in *US – Upland Cotton*, para. 22) Later in its submission, however, Brazil described the panel's error as a "misapplication of the principle of judicial economy". (*Ibid.*, para. 23; see also paras. 33 and 39-41)

[559] Appellate Body Report, *US – Upland Cotton*, para. 732.

[560] Appellate Body Report, *US – Upland Cotton*, para. 733.

[561] Appellate Body Report, *US – Tuna II (Mexico)*, para. 403 (quoting Appellate Body Report, *Australia – Salmon*, para. 223).

declined to make a finding on Japan's stand-alone Article III:4 claim, we need not further consider Japan's request.

5.5 Claims under the SCM Agreement

5.5.1 Article 1.1(a) – "Financial contribution" or "income or price support"

5.106 Japan appeals several aspects of the Panel's findings under Article 1.1(a) of the SCM Agreement. In particular, Japan argues that the Panel erred in its interpretation and application of Article 1.1(a) in finding that the FIT Programme and related FIT and microFIT Contracts constitute government "purchases [of] goods" under Article 1.1(a)(1)(iii).[562] With respect to the Panel's interpretation of Article 1.1(a)(1), Japan contends that the Panel erred in finding that subparagraphs (i) and (iii) of Article 1.1(a)(1) are mutually exclusive.[563] With respect to the application of Article 1.1(a), Japan requests us to reverse the Panel's finding that the FIT Programme and Contracts are government "purchases [of] goods" and to find instead that the measures at issue are appropriately characterized as "direct transfer[s] of funds", "potential direct transfers of funds", or "income or price support" under Article 1.1(a). In the alternative, Japan requests us to modify the Panel's finding in this regard to find that the measures at issue may *also* be characterized as "direct transfer[s] of funds", "potential direct transfers of funds", or "income or price support" under Article 1.1(a) of the SCM Agreement.[564]

5.107 In addition, Japan argues that the Panel improperly exercised judicial economy with respect to Japan's claim that the measures at issue constitute "income or price support" within the meaning of Article 1.1(a)(2) of the SCM Agreement, and thereby failed to make an objective assessment of the matter as required by Article 11 of the DSU. Japan requests us to find that the FIT Programme and Contracts may be characterized as "income or price support" and that a benefit exists with respect to this characterization of the challenged measures.[565]

5.108 We first summarize the Panel's findings under Article 1.1(a) of the SCM Agreement and then address each of Japan's claims on appeal.

5.5.1.1 The Panel's findings

5.109 Before the Panel, Japan argued that the FIT Programme and related FIT and microFIT Contracts are "direct transfer[s] of funds" and "potential direct transfers of funds" within the meaning of Article 1.1(a)(1)(i) of the

---

[562] Japan's other appellant's submission (DS412), para. 29.
[563] Japan's other appellant's submission (DS412), para. 49.
[564] Japan's other appellant's submission (DS412), para. 48.
[565] Japan's other appellant's submission (DS412), para. 59.

SCM Agreement. Alternatively, Japan submitted that the measures at issue are "income or price support" within the meaning of Article 1.1(a)(2).[566] Canada disagreed with this position and asserted that the measures at issue can only be legally characterized as financial contributions in the form of government "purchases [of] goods" within the meaning of Article 1.1(a)(1)(iii).[567]

5.110 Following an examination of the measures at issue, the Panel found that the appropriate legal characterization of the FIT Programme and Contracts is as "financial contribution[s]" in the form of government "purchases [of] goods" within the meaning of Article 1.1(a)(1)(iii) of the SCM Agreement.[568] The Panel's reasoning in reaching this conclusion was based on three key elements. First, it noted that the OPA transfers funds to FIT suppliers for "delivered electricity" into Ontario's electricity grid.[569] It is by paying a FIT Contract Price for delivered electricity that the Government of Ontario seeks to achieve the objective of securing investment in new generation facilities for the purposes of diversifying Ontario's supply-mix. Thus, in the Panel's view, there is no grant element inherent in the design and operation of the FIT Programme. The Panel highlighted that, while FIT and microFIT Contracts facilitate suppliers' search for project financing, it would be wrong to characterize the Contract Payments themselves as finance payments for the construction of a generation facility.[570]

5.111 Second, the Panel found that the Government of Ontario takes possession over electricity and thus "purchases electricity".[571] The Panel found that government "purchases [of] goods" will arise under the terms of Article 1.1(a)(1)(iii) of the SCM Agreement when a "government" or "public body" obtains possession (including in the form of an entitlement) over a good by making a payment of some kind (monetary or otherwise).[572] In particular, given the specific characteristics of electricity, the Panel preferred to characterize a purchase of electricity as involving the transfer of an *entitlement* to electricity, rather than the taking of physical possession of the electricity.[573] Moreover, the Panel rejected the European Union's argument that the notion of

[566] Panel Reports, para. 7.169. Before the Panel, the European Union submitted that the measures at issue may each be legally characterized as a "financial contribution" in the form of a "direct transfer of funds" within the meaning of Article 1.1(a)(1)(i), or as a form of "income or price support" under the terms of Article 1.1(a)(2) of the SCM Agreement. As an alternative to these two lines of argument, the European Union maintained that the challenged measures might also be characterized as "potential direct transfers of funds" under Article 1.1(a)(1)(i), or as governmental action that involves "entrust[ment] or direct[ion]" in the sense of Article 1.1(a)(1)(iv). (*Ibid.*, para. 7.176)

[567] Panel Reports, para. 7.181.

[568] Panel Reports, paras. 7.222 and 7.243.

[569] Panel Reports, paras. 7.223 and 7.224.

[570] Panel Reports, para. 7.224. In particular, the Panel found that "[t]he OPA does not pay for renewable energy equipment or facilities. It does not make any upfront lump-sum advances to the FIT generators". (*Ibid.*, para. 7.223)

[571] Panel Reports, paras. 7.239.

[572] Panel Reports, para. 7.231.

[573] Panel Reports, para. 7.229. (original emphasis)

government "purchases [of] goods" implies that the government is the entity being supplied with something for *its use*.[574]

5.112 The Panel then observed that government "purchases [of] goods" require the involvement of the "government" or a "public body". In the Panel's view, this is exactly what happens through the FIT Programme and Contracts, where the combined actions of all three "public bodies" involved (i.e. the OPA, Hydro One Inc., and the IESO) demonstrate that the Government of Ontario purchases electricity within the meaning of Article 1.1(a)(1)(iii) of the SCM Agreement.[575]

5.113 Third, the Panel found that the legislative and regulatory framework of the FIT Programme and Contracts supports the conclusion that the challenged measures are perceived by the Government of Ontario and by others in Ontario as governmental activity that involves the procurement or purchase of electricity.[576]

5.114 Next, the Panel explained why it disagreed with the complainants' proposed legal characterizations of the measures at issue. It recognized that the challenged measures exhibit some of the basic features of certain forms of "direct transfer[s] of funds", in that the measures involve an exchange of rights and obligations that includes the payment of money.[577] However, the Panel did not agree with the complainants that this means that they can also be legally characterized as "direct transfer[s] of funds" for the purposes of the SCM Agreement. For the Panel, to conclude that government "purchases [of] goods" can also be legally characterized as "direct transfer[s] of funds" would infringe the principle of effective treaty interpretation, as this reading would result in reducing subparagraph (iii) of Article 1.1(a)(1) to "redundancy or inutility".[578] The Panel disagreed that the complainants' request was supported by the Appellate Body's interpretation in *US – Large Civil Aircraft (2nd complaint)* that "[t]he structure of [Article 1.1(a)(1)] does not expressly preclude that a transaction could be covered by more than one subparagraph."[579] In the Panel's view, this statement "does not amount to a *finding* that transactions properly characterized as 'purchases [of] goods' can also constitute 'direct transfer[s] of funds'".[580] In addition, the Panel concluded that the measures at issue cannot be "potential direct transfers of funds" under Article 1.1(a)(1)(i) or a form of financial contribution involving government "entrust[ment] or

---

[574] Panel Reports, para. 7.230.

[575] Panel Reports, paras. 7.231-7.239.

[576] Panel Reports, para. 7.242.

[577] Panel Reports, para. 7.243.

[578] Panel Reports, para. 7.246 (quoting Appellate Body Report, *US – Gasoline*, p. 23, DSR 1996:I, p. 21).

[579] Panel Reports, para. 7.247 (quoting Appellate Body Report, *US – Large Civil Aircraft (2nd complaint)*, fn 1287 to para. 613).

[580] Panel Reports, para. 7.247. (original emphasis)

direct[ion]" within the meaning of Article 1.1(a)(1)(iv) of the SCM Agreement.[581]

5.115 Moreover, the Panel decided to exercise judicial economy with respect to the complainants' allegation that the measures at issue may be legally characterized as "income or price support" under Article 1.1(a)(2) of the SCM Agreement. The Panel considered that such finding was not necessary to resolve the complainants' claims under the SCM Agreement given that: (i) the Panel majority ultimately rejected the complainants' allegations regarding "benefit" as they relate to government "purchases [of] goods"; and (ii) when the challenged measures are characterized as "income or price support", the complainants' arguments regarding "benefit" are "essentially the same" as those rejected by the Panel majority in its assessment of the measures at issue as government "purchases [of] goods".[582]

5.5.1.2 Whether the Panel erred in finding that the FIT Programme and Contracts are government "purchases [of] goods" under Article 1.1(a)(1)(iii) of the SCM Agreement

5.116 On appeal, Japan challenges the Panel's interpretation and application of Article 1.1(a)(1) of the SCM Agreement. First, we examine Japan's challenge to the Panel's interpretation of Article 1.1(a)(1) and then we turn to address Japan's claim regarding the Panel's application of this provision. With respect to the interpretation of Article 1.1(a)(1), Japan argues that the Panel erred in finding that subparagraphs (i) and (iii) are "mutually exclusive".[583] In Japan's view, after concluding that the measures at issue are properly characterized as government "purchases [of] goods", the Panel, in effect, made such finding of mutual exclusivity by rejecting the complainants' argument that the measures at issue may *also* be legally characterized as "direct transfer[s] of funds" or "potential direct transfers of funds". For Japan, this finding mainly derives from the Panel's observation that "[w]e see no way of reading Articles 1.1(a)(1)(i) and (iii) in a way that enables us to conclude that government 'purchases [of] goods' could also be legally characterized as 'direct transfer[s] of funds'".[584] Japan argues that nothing precludes a panel from determining that a measure may be characterized in multiple ways under Article 1.1(a)(1) of the SCM Agreement, as long as the panel's findings are based on a proper understanding of the measure's relevant characteristics and an objective assessment of the facts. Japan submits that this conclusion follows from the Appellate Body's findings in *US – Large Civil Aircraft (2nd complaint)* that Article 1.1(a)(1) "does not explicitly spell out the

[581] Panel Reports, para. 7.248.

[582] Panel Reports, para. 7.249.

[583] Japan's other appellant's submission (DS412), para. 49.

[584] Japan's other appellant's submission (DS412), para. 49 (quoting Panel Reports, para. 7.246 (fn omitted)).

intended relationship between the constituent subparagraphs" and that its structure "does not expressly preclude that a transaction could be covered by more than one subparagraph".[585]

5.117 Canada argues that there is no merit to Japan's claim that the Panel erred by finding that subparagraphs (i) and (iii) of Article 1.1(a)(1) are mutually exclusive. Canada submits that the Panel correctly found that the FIT Programme and Contracts could not be properly characterized as "direct transfer[s] of funds" as well as government "purchases [of] goods", and that this finding is entirely consistent with the Appellate Body report in *US – Large Civil Aircraft (2nd complaint)*. In particular, Canada argues that, while in a general sense the structure of Article 1.1(a)(1) does not preclude that a transaction could be covered by more than one subparagraph, the same aspects of the same measure cannot at the same time be properly characterized as government "purchases [of] goods" and "direct transfer[s] of funds".[586]

5.118 We begin by providing an overview of the relevant findings by the Panel regarding the interpretative issue raised by Japan. In addressing the legal characterization of the FIT Programme and Contracts under the SCM Agreement, the Panel found the measures at issue to be government "purchases [of] goods" under subparagraph (iii) of Article 1.1(a)(1). Then, the Panel rejected the complainants' argument that the challenged measures could *also* be legally characterized as "direct transfer[s] of funds" under subparagraph (i).[587] In rejecting the complainants' argument, the Panel recognized that the measures at issue exhibit some of the basic features of certain forms of "direct transfer[s] of funds", in that they involve an exchange of rights and obligations that includes the payment of money.[588] In addition to rejecting the complainants' request regarding the characterization of the measures at issue, the Panel went on to make the interpretative finding that it could not conclude that "government 'purchases [of] goods' could also be legally characterized as 'direct transfer[s] of funds' without infringing [the] principle [of effective treaty interpretation]".[589] Moreover, the Panel disagreed that the complainants' request was supported by the Appellate Body's interpretation in *US – Large Civil Aircraft (2nd complaint)* that "[t]he structure of [Article 1.1(a)(1)] does not expressly preclude that a transaction could be covered by more than one subparagraph. There is, for

---

[585] Japan's other appellant's submission (DS412), para. 50 (quoting Appellate Body Report, *US – Large Civil Aircraft (2nd complaint)*, para. 613 and fn 1287 thereto, respectively). (emphasis added by Japan omitted)

[586] Canada's appellee's submission, para. 117.

[587] Panel Reports, para. 7.243. We note that, although the Panel rejected Japan's claim that the measures at issue constitute "direct transfer[s] of funds" and "potential direct transfers of funds", the Panel's arguments mainly focused on explaining why the challenged measures do not constitute "direct transfer[s] of funds". (Panel Reports, paras. 7.243-7.248)

[588] Panel Reports, para. 7.243.

[589] Panel Reports, para. 7.246.

example, no 'or' included between the subparagraphs."[590] In the Panel's view, this statement "does not amount to a *finding* that transactions properly characterized as 'purchases [of] goods' can also constitute 'direct transfer[s] of funds'".[591]

5.119 To the extent that this finding by the Panel means that the coverage of subparagraphs (i) and (iii) of Article 1.1(a)(1) is mutually exclusive, we disagree. We recall that, in *US – Large Civil Aircraft (2nd complaint)*, the Appellate Body found that Article 1.1(a)(1) "does not explicitly spell out the intended relationship between the constituent subparagraphs"[592] and that the structure of this provision "does not expressly preclude that a transaction could be covered by more than one subparagraph".[593] In that dispute, the Appellate Body also found that "a direct transfer of funds" under subparagraph (i) "may involve reciprocal rights and obligations"[594], given that it covers situations where the recipient assumes obligations to the government in exchange for the funds provided, such as loans and equity infusions.[595] The Appellate Body further held that the term "purchase" under subparagraph (iii) usually means "that the person or entity providing the goods will receive some consideration in return".[596]

5.120 When determining the proper legal characterization of a measure under Article 1.1(a)(1) of the SCM Agreement, a panel must assess whether the measure may fall within any of the types of financial contributions set out in that provision. In doing so, a panel should scrutinize the measure both as to its design and operation and identify its principal characteristics.[597] Having done so, the transaction may naturally fit into one of the types of financial contributions listed in Article 1.1(a)(1). However, transactions may be complex and multifaceted. This may mean that different aspects of the same transaction may fall under different types of financial contribution. It may also be the case that the characterization exercise does not permit the identification of a single category of financial contribution and, in that situation, as described in the *US – Large Civil Aircraft (2nd complaint)* Appellate Body report, a transaction may fall under more than one type of financial contribution. We note, however, that the fact that a transaction may fall under more than one type of financial contribution does

---

[590] Panel Reports, para. 7.247 (quoting Appellate Body Report, *US – Large Civil Aircraft (2nd complaint)*, fn 1287 to para. 613).

[591] Panel Reports, para. 7.247. (original emphasis) The Panel indicated that, while it may be possible to characterize different aspects of the same measure as different types of financial contributions (e.g. a governmental programme involving loans and government purchases of goods), the customary rules of interpretation do not lend support to the position advanced by the complainants. (*Ibid.*)

[592] Appellate Body Report, *US – Large Civil Aircraft (2nd complaint)*, para. 613.

[593] Appellate Body Report, *US – Large Civil Aircraft (2nd complaint)*, fn 1287 to para. 613.

[594] Appellate Body Report, *US – Large Civil Aircraft (2nd complaint)*, para. 617.

[595] Appellate Body Report, *US – Large Civil Aircraft (2nd complaint)*, para. 617. The Appellate Body indicated that, in the case of grants, "the conveyance of funds will not involve a reciprocal obligation on the part of the recipient". (*Ibid.*)

[596] Appellate Body Report, *US – Large Civil Aircraft (2nd complaint)*, para. 619.

[597] Appellate Body Reports, *China – Auto Parts*, para. 171. See also, Appellate Body Report, *US – Large Civil Aircraft (2nd complaint)*, para. 586.

not mean that the types of financial contributions set out in Article 1.1(a)(1) are the same or that the distinct legal concepts set out in this provision would become redundant, as the Panel suggests.[598] We further observe that, in *US – Large Civil Aircraft (2nd complaint)*, the Appellate Body did not address the question of whether, in the situation described above, a panel is under an obligation to make findings that a transaction falls under more than one subparagraph of Article 1.1(a)(1).

5.121 In the light of these considerations, we believe that the Panel's finding that subparagraphs (i) and (iii) are mutually exclusive is not consistent with the Appellate Body's interpretations in *US – Large Civil Aircraft (2nd complaint)*. Consequently, we *declare moot and of no legal effect* the Panel's finding, in paragraph 7.246 of the Panel Reports, that "government 'purchases [of] goods' could [not] also be legally characterized as 'direct transfer[s] of funds' without infringing [the] principle [of effective treaty interpretation]", inasmuch as it negates the possibility that a transaction may fall under more than one type of financial contribution under Article 1.1(a)(1) of the SCM Agreement.

5.122 Turning to the application of Article 1.1(a)(1) of the SCM Agreement, Japan challenges on appeal the Panel's finding that the FIT Programme and Contracts are government "purchases [of] goods" within the meaning of Article 1.1(a)(1)(iii). Japan requests us to reverse this finding and to find instead that the measures at issue are appropriately characterized as "direct transfer[s] of funds", "potential direct transfers of funds", or "income or price support" under Article 1.1(a) of the SCM Agreement, or alternatively modify the Panel's finding in this regard to find that these measures may *also* be characterized as "direct transfer[s] of funds", "potential direct transfers of funds", or "income or price support" under Article 1.1(a) of the SCM Agreement.[599]

5.123 We recall that the Panel found that government "purchases [of] goods" within the meaning of Article 1.1(a)(1)(iii) of the SCM Agreement occur "when a 'government' or 'public body' obtains possession (including in the form of an entitlement) over a good by making a payment of some kind (monetary or otherwise)".[600] At the oral hearing, Japan clarified that it is not challenging this interpretation by the Panel on appeal. Nor does Japan dispute the Panel's findings that: (i) the OPA pays for delivered electricity; (ii) the Government of Ontario through Hydro One takes possession of the electricity during its transmission to end consumers; and (iii) the legislative, regulatory, and contractual framework of the FIT Programme characterizes the challenged measures as procurements or purchases of electricity.[601] Rather, Japan submits that the Panel failed to determine the proper legal characterization of the

[598] Panel Reports, para. 7.246.

[599] Japan's other appellant's submission (DS412), paras. 48 and 189 (referring to Panel Reports, paras. 7.243 and 7.328(i)).

[600] Panel Reports, para. 7.231.

[601] Japan's other appellant's submission (DS412), paras. 30 and 31.

challenged measures on the basis of an evaluation of their "principal and relevant characteristics".[602] In Japan's view, this requires a panel to appreciate fully all relevant facts and surrounding circumstances, which may include whether, and to what extent, a measure would serve to achieve a stated policy goal. In particular, Japan claims that the Panel overlooked the Government of Ontario's policy decision to unbundle the generation, transmission, and distribution of electricity to achieve its goal of ensuring a stable supply of electricity in Ontario, as well as the design and operation of the FIT Programme and Contracts within the framework of the Ontario electricity market.[603] On this basis, Japan puts forward the following arguments to support its assertion that the Panel erred in characterizing the measures at issue as government "purchases [of] goods".

5.124 First, Japan argues that, given the Government of Ontario's policy choice of unbundling the different functions of electricity supply, the role of the OPA should be central for the proper characterization of the FIT Programme and Contracts under Article 1.1(a)(1). In particular, Japan alleges that the characterization of the measures at issue should be informed by the fact that one government entity (the OPA) makes the payments for electricity, while a different government entity (Hydro One) receives and transmits electricity delivered by suppliers. Thus, in Japan's view, the OPA serves as a financing entity, not a purchasing entity, because it never takes possession of electricity.[604] We do not consider this argument to be persuasive. Ontario's policy decision to unbundle its electricity system and to allocate responsibilities between different government entities does not undermine the conclusion that the Government of Ontario purchases electricity through the FIT Programme and Contracts. While it is true that the OPA is the entity charged with paying FIT suppliers for delivered electricity and Hydro One is the entity transmitting electricity, both entities were found by the Panel to be "public bod[ies]" within the meaning of Article 1.1(a)(1) of the SCM Agreement.[605] Similarly, the Panel found the IESO

[602] Japan's other appellant's submission (DS412), para. 31. (emphasis omitted)

[603] Japan's other appellant's submission (DS412), para. 31.

[604] Japan's other appellant's submission (DS412), para. 39.

[605] Panel Reports, paras. 7.234, 7.235, 7.239, and fn 464 thereto. We note that the Panel found that the OPA and the IESO are agents of the Government of Ontario and noted that there is no dispute between the parties that they are a "public bod[ies]" for the purpose of Article 1.1(a)(1) of the SCM Agreement. (*Ibid.*, fn 464 to para. 7.239) We observe that the Panel found that "Hydro One is an agent of the Government of Ontario", thereby being "a provincial government organization ... to which the government has assigned or delegated authority and responsibility, or which otherwise has statutory authority and responsibility to perform a public function or service". (*Ibid.*, para. 7.234 (referring to and quoting Government of Ontario webpages, "All Agencies List" (Panel Exhibit JPN-49), available at: <*http://www.pas.gov.on.ca/scripts/en/BoardsList.asp*>; and "Agencies: Boards, Commissions, Councils, Authorities and Foundations" (Panel Exhibit JPN-51), available at: <*http://www.ontario.ca/en/your_government/ONT06_018949.html*>, p. 1)) The Panel further found that Hydro One's status as an agent of the Government of Ontario and the fact that "the Government of Ontario has 'meaningful control' over Hydro One's activities" demonstrate that it is a "public body" within the meaning of Article 1.1(a)(1) of the SCM Agreement. (*Ibid.*, paras. 7.234 and 7.235)

to constitute a "public body" under Article 1.1(a)(1).[606] Since in the present case all the entities involved are public bodies and thus their activities are attributable to the government, it is not relevant whether the Government of Ontario acts through one or several of these entities. Indeed, the Panel found that "the *combined actions* of all three 'public bodies'"[607] – the OPA, Hydro One, and the IESO – demonstrate that the Government of Ontario purchases electricity within the meaning of Article 1.1(a)(1)(iii) of the SCM Agreement. The Panel's findings that the OPA, Hydro One, and the IESO are public bodies under Article 1.1(a)(1) have not been appealed by Japan. Consequently, Japan's argument that the OPA itself does not take possession over electricity does not undermine the Panel's finding that the Government of Ontario purchases electricity through the FIT Programme and Contracts. This is so because Hydro One, which is the entity transmitting electricity, was also found to be a public body, and the Panel found that the "combined actions" of the OPA, Hydro One, and the IESO demonstrate that the Government of Ontario purchases electricity.

5.125 Japan's second argument on appeal is that the Government of Ontario's goals of achieving a stable supply of electricity and stimulating renewable energy are not addressed through purchases of electricity by the government, but rather through the allocation of distinct roles to the entities operating in Ontario's electricity system and the implementation of certain programmes.[608] Although it may be correct that the Government of Ontario seeks to meet its goals of achieving a stable supply of electricity and stimulating renewable energy through various entities and programmes, Japan's argument disregards that the Government of Ontario implements these policies through, *inter alia*, programmes involving purchases of electricity by the government.[609] This is the case of the FIT Programme. We recall that the OPA, a public body under the SCM Agreement, enters into FIT and microFIT Contracts with suppliers participating in the FIT Programme. As found by the Panel, the function of these contracts is the delivery of electricity by FIT and microFIT suppliers and, in return, the OPA undertakes to pay the supplier remuneration in the form of a Contract Price.[610] We highlight that "[t]he FIT Rules provide that the OPA is responsible for making all Contract Payments to the Supplier."[611] Similarly, "ultimate liability for [payments of the Contract Price] under the microFIT Contract lies with the OPA."[612] Moreover, we note that, as part of

606 Panel Reports, para. 7.239 and fn 464 thereto.

607 Panel Reports, para. 7.239. (emphasis added; fn omitted)

608 Japan's other appellant's submission (DS412), para. 40.

609 In addition to generators participating in the FIT Programme, other generators in Ontario receive prices that are set under different types of electricity supply contracts, including under the RES Requests for Proposals I, II, and III and the RESOP. (Panel Reports, paras. 7.27 and 7.28)

610 Panel Reports, paras. 7.208 and 7.214.

611 Panel Reports, para. 7.204 (referring to FIT Rules (version 1.5.1), Sections 6.3(a) and 8.4; and FIT Contract (version 1.5.1), Section 3.1).

612 Panel Reports, para. 7.213 (referring to microFIT Contract (version 1.6.1), Section 4.4.1).

Ontario's policy decision of unbundling responsibilities and functions between different governmental entities within its electricity system, Japan has not identified any financing provided by the OPA to FIT and microFIT suppliers beyond the remuneration provided in exchange for delivering electricity into the system. As stated above, this remuneration constitutes the payment for electricity delivered into the system by FIT and microFIT suppliers. Hence, the fact that Ontario's goals to ensure a stable supply of electricity and to provide renewable energy are pursued through several entities and programmes does not change the fact that the Government of Ontario purchases electricity pursuant to the FIT Programme and Contracts.

5.126 Moreover, Japan argues that the existence of private entities supplying electricity to consumers in Ontario shows that it is unnecessary for a governmental agency to take possession over (i.e. purchase) electricity in order to achieve its objectives.[613] We disagree that this is of particular relevance for the proper characterization of the FIT Programme and Contracts under the SCM Agreement. Determining the proper legal characterization of the measures at issue under Article 1.1(a)(1) does not require assessing whether it is *necessary* for government entities to take possession of electricity to achieve Ontario's objectives or whether or not private entities are permitted to supply electricity to consumers in Ontario. The issue is whether the FIT Programme and Contracts in fact involve purchases of electricity by the Government of Ontario and thus fall within subparagraph (iii) of Article 1.1(a)(1). In the present case, the Panel concluded that the *combined actions* of the OPA, Hydro One, and the IESO demonstrate that the Government of Ontario purchases electricity within the meaning of Article 1.1(a)(1)(iii) of the SCM Agreement.[614] Japan's argument, in our view, does not undermine this finding by the Panel.

5.127 Finally, Japan suggests that the Panel erred by assuming that, if a measure is characterized in a particular manner under domestic law (e.g. as a government purchase), it can never be characterized in a different manner under WTO law.[615] We understand Japan to be arguing that the Panel erred in finding that the characterization of a measure under domestic law is dispositive of its legal characterization under WTO law. Japan is correct in arguing that the manner in which municipal law characterizes a measure is not determinative for its characterization under the covered agreements. We recall that the Appellate Body has found that "a panel may examine the municipal law of a WTO Member for the purpose of determining whether that Member has complied with its obligations under the *WTO Agreement*"[616] and that "[t]he label given to an instrument under municipal law ... is not dispositive and cannot be the end of

[613] Japan's other appellant's submission (DS412), para. 41.
[614] Panel Reports, para. 7.239.
[615] Japan's other appellant's submission (DS412), para. 43.
[616] Appellate Body Report, *US – Section 211 Appropriations Act*, para. 105.

our analysis".[617] However, we do not consider that, in reaching its conclusion as to the proper characterization of the measures at issue under the SCM Agreement, the Panel relied exclusively on their characterization under Ontario law, as Japan contends. On the contrary, the Panel recognized that the label given to an instrument under municipal law is not dispositive of the analysis under WTO law and found that the measures at issue constitute government "purchases [of] goods" under Article 1.1(a)(1)(iii) for three main reasons. First, the OPA pays for electricity that is delivered into Ontario's electricity grid.[618] Second, the Government of Ontario takes possession over electricity and therefore purchases electricity.[619] Third, only as "a relevant factor" in its analysis, the Panel took into account that "the *Electricity Act of 1998*, the Ministerial Direction, the FIT and microFIT Contracts and other documents, all in one way or another characterize the challenged measures as a procurement or purchase of electricity".[620] The Panel concluded that the legislative and regulatory framework of the FIT Programme, as well as the language found in certain clauses of the FIT and microFIT Contracts, "leave no doubt that the challenged measures are perceived by the Government of Ontario, and others in Ontario, as governmental activity that involves the procurement or purchase of electricity".[621] Consequently, we disagree with Japan that the Panel's analysis was based on the proposition that the characterization of a measure under domestic law is dispositive of its legal characterization under WTO law.

5.128 For these reasons, we do not consider that the Panel erred in its characterization of the measures at issue under Article 1.1(a)(1) of the SCM Agreement. Accordingly, we *uphold* the Panel's finding, in paragraphs 7.243 and 7.328(i) of the Panel Reports, that the FIT Programme and related FIT and microFIT Contracts are government "purchases [of] goods" within the meaning of Article 1.1(a)(1)(iii) of the SCM Agreement.

5.129 Having upheld the Panel's finding that the measures at issue are properly characterized as government "purchases [of] goods" under Article 1.1(a)(1)(iii), we turn to examine Japan's alternative claim that we modify the Panel's finding in this regard to find that these measures may *also* be characterized as "direct transfer[s] of funds" or "potential direct transfers of funds" under Article 1.1(a)(1)(i) of the SCM Agreement.[622] Japan also requests us to find that the FIT Programme and Contracts may be characterized as "income or price

---

617 Appellate Body Report, *US – Large Civil Aircraft (2nd complaint)*, para. 593. Similarly, in *US – Softwood Lumber IV*, the Appellate Body found that "it would be inappropriate to characterize, for purposes of applying any provisions of the WTO covered agreements, the same thing or transaction differently, depending on its legal categorization within the jurisdictions of different Members." (Appellate Body Report, *US – Softwood Lumber IV*, para. 56)

618 Panel Reports, para. 7.223.

619 Panel Reports, paras. 7.231 and 7.239.

620 Panel Reports, para. 7.242.

621 *Ibid.*

622 Japan's other appellant's submission (DS412), paras. 48 and 189.

support" under Article 1.1(a)(2) of the SCM Agreement.[623] We note that Japan also claims that the Panel acted inconsistently with Article 11 of the DSU by exercising false judicial economy with respect to its claim that the challenged measures constitute "income or price support". We will thus address Japan's request to find that the measures at issue may be characterized as "income or price support" once we have made a determination on whether the Panel exercised false judicial economy regarding this claim of Japan.

5.130 As a preliminary matter, we note that the characterization of a transaction under Article 1.1(a) of the SCM Agreement may have implications for the manner in which the assessment of whether a benefit is conferred is to be conducted. For instance, the context provided by Article 14 of the SCM Agreement presents different methods for calculating the amount of a subsidy in terms of benefit to the recipient depending on the type of financial contribution at issue. However, although different characterizations of a measure may lead to different *methods* for determining whether a benefit has been conferred, the issue to be resolved under Article 1.1(b) remains to ascertain whether a "financial contribution" or "any form of income or price support" has conferred a benefit to the recipient.[624]

5.131 With this in mind, we do not believe that the arguments advanced by Japan are sufficient to demonstrate that the measures at issue are "direct transfer[s] of funds" or "potential direct transfers of funds". We recall that Japan argued that the challenged measures are "direct transfer[s] of funds" because the OPA distributes funds to FIT generators from the amounts collected from consumers through the GA. Japan further argues that the fact that FIT and microFIT generators are entitled to guaranteed payments for all electricity generated for the duration of the FIT and microFIT Contracts makes the payments under these contracts "potential direct transfers of funds".[625] Japan's arguments in this respect do not present any new characteristics of the measures at issue that go beyond, or are different from, the payment of consideration by the Government of Ontario through the OPA in exchange for electricity delivered into the grid by FIT and microFIT suppliers during a 20-year contract. To us, Japan's arguments merely underscore and reiterate certain specific aspects of the FIT Programme and Contracts, such as the conveyance of funds in exchange for delivered electricity and the fact that the OPA commits to pay for such electricity for the duration of the contracts. Japan overlooks that all these aspects are part of a broader transaction that involves an exchange of rights and obligations, that is, the payment of consideration in return for electricity

---

[623] *Ibid.*

[624] In the context of examining a financial contribution, the Appellate Body found in *Canada – Aircraft* that the analysis under Article 1.1(b) of the SCM Agreement requires assessing whether a financial contribution "makes the recipient 'better off' than it would otherwise have been, absent that contribution". (Appellate Body Report, *Canada – Aircraft*, para. 157)

[625] Japan's other appellant's submission (DS412), para. 46.

delivered into Ontario's electricity system. Pursuant to this composite transaction, the Government of Ontario, through the OPA, enters into 20-year contracts with FIT and microFIT suppliers and pays them a Contract Price as consideration in exchange for electricity delivered into the system. We do not see in Japan's arguments any aspects different from, or in addition to, those characteristics that led us to agree with the Panel that the transactions at issue constitute government "purchases [of] goods". We are not persuaded that, on the basis of these arguments and features of the challenged measures, Japan has established that these measures should in addition be characterized as "direct transfer[s] of funds" or "potential direct transfers of funds".

5.132 For these reasons, we *reject* Japan's appeal that the FIT Programme and FIT and microFIT Contracts may also be characterized as "direct transfer[s] of funds" or "potential direct transfers of funds" under Article 1.1(a)(1)(i) of the SCM Agreement.

5.5.1.3 Did the Panel err in exercising judicial economy with respect to the allegations that the measures at issue constitute "income or price support"?

5.133 Japan argues that the Panel improperly exercised judicial economy with respect to Japan's claim that the FIT Programme and related FIT and microFIT Contracts constitute "income or price support" under Article 1.1(a)(2) of the SCM Agreement, and thereby failed to make an objective assessment of the matter as required by Article 11 of the DSU. Japan requests us to find that the challenged measures may be characterized as "income or price support", and to find that a benefit exists with respect to this characterization of the FIT Programme and Contracts.[626]

5.134 We recall that the Appellate Body has found in relation to the principle of judicial economy that "[a] panel need only address those claims which must be addressed in order to resolve the matter in issue in the dispute."[627] The Appellate Body has, however, cautioned that "panels may refrain from ruling on every claim as long as it does not lead to a 'partial resolution of the matter'."[628] In this regard, the Appellate Body has found that "[a] panel has to address those claims on which a finding is necessary in order to enable the DSB to make sufficiently precise recommendations and rulings ... 'in order to secure effective resolution of disputes to the benefit of all Members.'"[629]

---

[626] Japan's other appellant's submission (DS412), paras. 57-59.

[627] Appellate Body Report, *US – Wool Shirts and Blouses*, p. 19, DSR 1997:I, p. 340. (fn omitted)

[628] Appellate Body Report, *US – Upland Cotton*, para. 732 (quoting Appellate Body Report, *Australia – Salmon*, para. 223).

[629] Appellate Body Report, *Australia – Salmon*, para. 223 (quoting Article 21.1 of the DSU). See also, Appellate Body Reports, *Canada – Wheat Exports and Grain Imports*, para. 133; and *EC – Export Subsidies on Sugar*, para. 335.

5.135 On appeal, Japan contends that the Panel failed to explain why the Panel's findings with respect to Japan's benefit argument in connection with its financial contribution claim under Article 1.1(a)(1) would also be applicable to Japan's benefit argument in connection with its income or price support claim under Article 1.1(a)(2). Japan argues that whether the measures confer a benefit must be examined in relation to the particular subparagraph of Article 1.1(a) at issue. In Japan's view, it is not clear why the Panel's rejection of Japan's benefit argument in connection with its financial contribution claim necessarily implies rejection of its benefit argument in relation to income or price support claim.[630]

5.136 We observe that Japan's request for findings before the Panel did not distinguish between situations where the measures would be characterized as a "financial contribution" and as "income or price support". Rather, Japan focused on requesting the Panel to make a recommendation that Canada "withdraw its prohibited subsidies without delay".[631] Thus, the thrust of Japan's claim concerned the existence of prohibited subsidies and the specific remedy associated with such finding, rather than the specific characterization of the challenged measures as financial contribution and/or income or price support.

5.137 Moreover, although the characterization of a transaction under Article 1.1(a) may have implications for the manner in which the determination of benefit under Article 1.1(b) of the SCM Agreement is conducted, Japan has not elaborated whether and in which way the benefit analysis would have been different, or would have led to a different outcome, if the Panel had characterized the FIT Programme and Contracts as "income or price support" instead of as a "financial contribution". Rather, as argued by Canada, Japan's benefit argument before the Panel relied on the same benchmarks in both situations, in particular, the HOEP and the average wholesale rate for electricity in competitive markets outside of Ontario.[632] We note that the Panel rejected these benchmarks for the purposes of determining whether the measures at issue confer a benefit.[633]

5.138 Thus, given that the basis of Japan's benefit arguments in both instances was "essentially the same"[634], and that the Panel rejected Japan's benefit arguments as they relate to Article 1.1(a)(1), we do not believe that an additional finding by the Panel that the challenged measures constitute "income or price support" within the meaning of Article 1.1(a)(2) was necessary to resolve fully the dispute. Accordingly, we *reject* Japan's claim that the Panel failed to fulfil its obligations under Article 11 of the DSU and exercised false judicial economy by

---

630 Japan's other appellant's submission (DS412), para. 58.

631 Japan's first written submission to the Panel (DS412), para. 304.

632 Canada's appellee's submission, para. 125. See also, Japan's first written submission to the Panel (DS412), paras. 219, 220, 222, 234, and 244.

633 Panel Reports, paras. 7.313 and 7.319.

634 Panel Reports, paras. 7.249.

declining to make a finding on Japan's claim that the measures at issue constitute "income or price support" under Article 1.1(a)(2) of the SCM Agreement.

5.139 Given that we have rejected Japan's claim that the Panel exercised false judicial economy by declining to make a finding on Japan's claim that the measures at issue constitute "income or price support", we *decline* to make a finding on whether the FIT Programme and Contracts may be characterized as "income or price support" under Article 1.1(a)(2) of the SCM Agreement.

5.5.2 Article 1.1(b) – "Benefit"

5.140 In this section we address the claims by the European Union and Japan that the Panel erred in finding that the complainants failed to establish that the challenged measures confer a benefit within the meaning of Article 1.1(b) of the SCM Agreement, as well as their alternative claim that the Panel acted inconsistently with Article 11 of the DSU.

5.141 Japan claims that the Panel erred both in the interpretation and in the application of Article 1.1(b) of the SCM Agreement. Japan argues, first, that the Panel erred in interpreting Article 1.1(b) because it failed to analyze the question of benefit from a perspective other than the framework of Article 14(d) of the SCM Agreement. Second, Japan claims that the Panel erred because it wrongly rejected benchmarks of the current Ontario electricity market and chose an improper benchmark for its alternative counterfactual analysis, which was based on costs and ignored the demand-side of the market.[635]

5.142 The European Union claims that the Panel wrongly applied Article 1.1(b) of the SCM Agreement to the facts of this case by engaging into the examination of market counterfactuals when it was an uncontested fact that FIT generators would not have obtained any remuneration from the market in Ontario absent the FIT Programme. According to the European Union, the conclusion as to the existence of a benefit should have been made "with little difficulty"[636] by the Panel without the need to examine market counterfactuals or proxies.

5.143 The European Union and Japan request that we reverse the Panel's finding that the complainants failed to establish that the challenged measures confer a benefit, within the meaning of Article 1.1(b) of the SCM Agreement, and that we complete the legal analysis and find that the challenged measures confer a benefit, based on the factual findings made by the Panel and uncontested facts on the Panel record. This evidence shows that, absent the FIT Programme, FIT generators would not have obtained the remuneration provided by the FIT Programme on the basis of the prevailing market conditions in Ontario.[637] Moreover, the European Union requests us to declare moot and of

[635] Japan's other appellant's submission (DS412), para. 110.

[636] European Union's other appellant's submission (DS426), para. 162. (fn omitted)

[637] European Union's other appellant's submission (DS426), para. 171; Japan's other appellant's submission (DS412), para. 118.

no legal effect the Panel's findings and observations, in paragraphs 7.276 to 7.327 of the Panel Reports, concerning hypothetical counterfactuals and market proxies.[638]

5.144 In the alternative, should we agree with the Panel's finding under Article 1.1(b) of the SCM Agreement, the European Union and Japan claim that the Panel failed to make an objective assessment of the matter, under Article 11 of the DSU, in concluding that there was not enough evidence on the record that would allow it to make findings on the existence of benefit under Article 1.1(b) of the SCM Agreement, based on its own approach to the question of benefit.[639] The European Union and Japan request that we complete the analysis based on the factual findings by the Panel and uncontested facts on the record and find that the challenged measures confer a benefit within the meaning of Article 1.1(b) of the SCM Agreement.

5.145 Whether we reverse the Panel's findings under Article 1.1(b) of the SCM Agreement or find that the Panel failed to make an objective assessment under Article 11 of the DSU, both the European Union and Japan request that we complete the analysis and find that the challenged measures amount to subsidies prohibited under Articles 3.1(b) and 3.2 of the SCM Agreement.[640]

5.146 Canada requests that we reject the cross-appeals of the European Union and Japan and uphold the Panel's finding that the complainants failed to establish that the challenged measures confer a benefit within the meaning of Article 1.1(b) of the SCM Agreement and constitute prohibited subsidies inconsistent with Articles 3.1(b) and 3.2 of the SCM Agreement.[641] In particular, Canada contends that the European Union's and Japan's approach to benefit ignores the Panel's findings that the IESO-administered wholesale market is not a "market" appropriate for the purposes of a "benefit" analysis and that, absent the FIT Programme, new entrants into the market would probably negotiate a price for wind- and solar PV-generated electricity.[642] Canada also considers that the complainants' criticisms on appeal of the Panel majority's observations about an alternative constructed benchmark are misplaced, because these were simply the Panel majority's views about an alternative approach to benefit, made at the complainants' urging and were not legal findings by the Panel.[643]

---

[638] European Union's other appellant's submission (DS426), para. 170.

[639] European Union's other appellant's submission (DS426), para. 173; Japan's other appellant's submission (DS412), para. 119.

[640] European Union's other appellant's submission (DS426), paras. 172 and 205; Japan's other appellant's submission (DS412), para. 126.

[641] Canada's appellee's submission, para. 214.

[642] Canada's appellee's submission, para. 189.

[643] Canada's appellee's submission, para. 205.

5.5.2.1 The Panel's findings

5.147 The Panel found that Japan and the European Union failed to establish that the challenged measures confer a benefit within the meaning of Article 1.1(b) of the SCM Agreement.[644]

5.148 The Panel began its analysis by setting out the legal standard for determining the existence of a benefit under Article 1.1(b) of the SCM Agreement. The Panel recalled that a financial contribution will confer a benefit within the meaning of Article 1.1(b) when it provides an advantage to its recipient, and that the existence of any such advantage is to be determined by comparing the position of the recipient in the marketplace with and without the financial contribution. The Panel pointed out that Article 14(d) of the SCM Agreement, although not intended to define the circumstances when a government's purchase of goods will confer a benefit within the meaning of Article 1.1(b), provides useful context for such a determination.[645]

5.149 The Panel then reviewed the Ontario electricity market and its 2002 market opening experience. Based on the evidence submitted by the parties, the Panel found that there is no effective competition in Ontario's current wholesale electricity market. Rather, in the Panel's view, Ontario's wholesale electricity market is better characterized as a part of an electricity system that is defined by the Government of Ontario's policy decisions and regulations. These decisions and regulations govern the supply-mix (including electricity generated from renewable sources) that is necessary to ensure a safe, reliable, and long-term supply of electricity in Ontario, and the process to recover the electricity system's costs.[646]

5.150 Regarding the specific market benchmarks proposed by the complainants, the Panel found, first, that electricity wholesale prices in Ontario (i.e. the HOEP) result from the operation of forces of supply and demand that are significantly affected by government intervention in a way that renders them an inappropriate benchmark to conduct the present benefit analysis. In particular, the Panel found that generators' price offers in the IESO-administered wholesale market are not motivated by the need to cover marginal costs of production, but rather by the need to be chosen to supply electricity into the Ontario grid in order to receive the contracted or regulated prices. Thus, the HOEP is not an "equilibrium price" determined by the forces of supply and demand, but rather "a tool for the IESO to make the dispatch decisions needed to balance *physical* supply and demand for electricity".[647]

---

[644] Panel Reports, para. 7.328(ii).

[645] Panel Reports, para. 7.271.

[646] Panel Reports, para. 7.308.

[647] Panel Reports, para. 7.298 (referring to Canada's first written submission to the Panel (DS426), para. 71; opening statement at the first Panel meeting, para. 83; and Hogan Report, pp. 37-41). (original emphasis)

5.151 Therefore, the Panel concluded that the Ontario prices on the basis of which the complainants had made their case of benefit – namely, the HOEP and all of the HOEP-derivatives advanced by the complainants, such as the weighted-average wholesale rate for generators other than FIT or RESOP[648] in 2010, retail prices under the RPP in 2010, and import and export prices – could not serve as appropriate benchmarks for the purpose of the benefit analysis.[649]

5.152 The Panel also rejected four benchmarks from out-of-province electricity markets – Alberta, in Canada, and New York State, New England, and the Mid-Atlantic region (PJM Interconnection), in the United States – submitted by the complainants as proxies for the wholesale electricity market price in Ontario. As regards Alberta, the Panel considered that the "market approach"[650] introduced in Alberta could not be reproduced in Ontario with the same degree of success in the light of the particular conditions of supply and demand in Ontario and of the renewable and non-renewable generating capacity that would need to be renewed, replaced, or added to the Ontario electricity system by 2030.[651] As for the other three markets, the Panel was persuaded by evidence on the record showing that these markets do not provide participating generators with all of the revenues they need to be present on the market. Thus, these three markets do not represent competitive wholesale electricity markets that are capable, on their own, of attracting sufficient investment in generation capacity to secure a reliable system of electricity supply.[652]

5.153 Moreover, the Panel was not persuaded of the premise underlying the complainants' arguments – namely, that, in the absence of the FIT Programme, FIT generators would be faced with having to opera0te in a competitive wholesale electricity market. The Panel considered that competitive wholesale electricity markets will only rarely remunerate the mix of generators needed to secure a reliable electricity system with enough revenue to cover all their costs (including fixed and sunk costs), let alone a system that ensures the inclusion of facilities using solar PV and windpower technologies in the supply-mix.[653]

5.154 The Panel was of the view that, under the prevailing conditions of supply and demand in Ontario, a competitive wholesale electricity market would fail to attract the degree of investment in generating capacity needed to secure a reliable supply of electricity. Therefore, the Panel did not consider it appropriate to determine whether the FIT Programme and related FIT and microFIT Contracts confer a benefit, within the meaning of Article 1.1(b) of the SCM Agreement, by comparing the terms and conditions of participation in the

[648] Renewable Energy Standard Offer Program (RESOP).
[649] Panel Reports, para. 7.308.
[650] Panel Reports, para. 7.306.
[651] Panel Reports, para. 7.310.
[652] *Ibid.*
[653] Panel Reports, para. 7.309.

FIT Programme with those that would be available to generators participating in a wholesale electricity market where there was effective competition.[654]

5.155 At the end of its benefit benchmark analysis, the Panel rejected Canada's argument that the relevant "market" for the purpose of the benefit analysis should be the market for electricity produced from solar PV and windpower technologies. The Panel observed that consumers of electricity in Ontario do not distinguish electricity on the basis of different generation technologies, either by way of price or usage, and that no arguments had been advanced to suggest that the physical properties of electricity change depending upon how it is generated. Accordingly, the Panel found that, in Ontario, there is only one single market for electricity that is generated from all sources of energy.[655]

5.156 Having rejected the benchmarks proposed by the complainants, the Panel made its own suggestion as to what it considered could be an appropriate benchmark in the circumstances of this case. The Panel explained that one way to determine whether the challenged measures confer a benefit, within the meaning of Article 1.1(b) of the SCM Agreement, would involve testing them against the types of arm's-length purchase transactions that would exist in a wholesale electricity market whose broad parameters are defined by the Government of Ontario. In the circumstances of the present case, this could be done by comparing the terms and conditions of the challenged FIT and microFIT Contracts with those that would be offered by commercial distributors of electricity that acquire electricity pursuant to a governmental obligation from solar PV and windpower generator facilities of a comparable scale to those functioning under the FIT Programme.[656]

5.157 According to the Panel, this approach could be used to determine whether the challenged measures confer a benefit by comparing the rate of return obtained by FIT generators under the terms and conditions of the FIT and microFIT Contracts with the average cost of capital in Canada for projects with a comparable risk profile in the same period. The Panel observed that such a comparison would allow for an immediate and clear determination of whether FIT generators are being overcompensated by the government, and therefore receive a benefit within the meaning of Article 1.1(b) of the SCM Agreement.[657] The Panel then assessed whether there was sufficient factual information on the record to apply its own proposed benchmark. After reviewing the evidence on the record, the Panel found that the information available was insufficient to determine the average cost of capital in Canada for projects with a risk profile comparable to the challenged FIT and microFIT Contracts during the relevant period.[658]

---

[654] Panel Reports, para. 7.312.
[655] Panel Reports, para. 7.318.
[656] Panel Reports, para. 7.322.
[657] Panel Reports, para. 7.323.
[658] Panel Reports, para. 7.326.

5.5.2.2 Whether the Panel erred in finding that the European Union and Japan failed to establish that the challenged measures confer a benefit within the meaning of Article 1.1(b) of the SCM Agreement

5.158 In addressing the claims by the European Union and Japan under Article 1.1(b) of the SCM Agreement, we begin by reviewing the legal standard adopted by the Panel in its Article 1.1(b) analysis. We then address the Panel's analysis of the relevant market followed by an analysis of the appropriate benchmark for the remuneration of wind- and solar PV-generated electricity. Finally, in the light of the appropriate market benchmark, we consider the Panel's assessment of the benefit benchmarks submitted by the complainants.

5.5.2.2.1 The legal standard for the determination of benefit under Article 1.1(b) of the SCM Agreement

5.159 We begin our analysis of the Panel's finding under Article 1.1(b) of the SCM Agreement by reviewing the legal standard adopted by the Panel for the determination of benefit. Relying on the jurisprudence of the Appellate Body under Article 1.1(b), the Panel considered that a financial contribution confers a benefit within the meaning of Article 1.1(b) when it confers an advantage on its recipient, and that such an advantage is to be determined by comparing the position of the recipient in the marketplace with and without the financial contribution.[659] The Panel further observed that Article 14(d) of the SCM Agreement – which establishes guidelines for calculating the amount of subsidy for the purpose of countervailing duties investigations under Part V of the SCM Agreement in cases involving purchases of goods by a government – provides useful context for the determination of benefit in the present disputes.[660]

5.160 According to the Panel, *one way* to assess whether the challenged measures confer a benefit within the meaning of Article 1.1(b) is to examine whether, under the benchmark provided in Article 14(d) of the SCM Agreement, the remuneration obtained by windpower and solar PV generators under the FIT Programme is "more than adequate" when compared to the remuneration the same generators would, in the light of the "prevailing market conditions", otherwise receive on the relevant "market" for electricity in Ontario.[661] The Panel noted that the relevant market need not be one that is "undistorted by

---

[659] Panel Reports, para. 7.271 (referring to Appellate Body Reports, *US – Softwood Lumber IV*, para. 51; and *Canada – Aircraft*, para. 157).

[660] Panel Reports, para. 7.271 (referring to Appellate Body Report, *Canada – Aircraft*, paras. 157 and 158).

[661] Panel Reports, para. 7.272.

government intervention", or that is devoid of any degree of government intervention.[662] Nevertheless, the Panel recalled that, where the role of the government in the market is so predominant that it effectively determines prices, there would be no way of telling whether the recipient is better off absent the financial contribution, and the market that is the object of the government intervention cannot serve as an appropriate benchmark under Article 14(d).[663]

5.161 Japan argues that the Panel erred in interpreting Article 1.1(b) because it failed to analyze the question of benefit from a perspective other than the framework of Article 14(d) of the SCM Agreement. Japan points out that, while Article 14(d) provides a particular methodology for calculating the amount of the benefit for the purpose of the imposition of countervailing measures, no precise quantification of the benefit is required in a prohibited subsidy dispute under Article 3.1 of the SCM Agreement, where a complainant merely needs to demonstrate that a benefit exists.[664] The European Union does not challenge the Panel's interpretation of Article 1.1(b), but, in the context of its challenge of the Panel's application of Article 1.1(b), it also remarks that, in a prohibited subsidies case, the issue of the amount of the subsidy is irrelevant, such that, in these disputes, there is no need to identify the relevant benchmark in order to establish the amount of the benefit conferred by the FIT Programme.[665]

5.162 We are not persuaded that, by analyzing whether a benefit is conferred on the basis of the guidelines contained in Article 14(d), the Panel erred in the interpretation of Article 1.1(b) of the SCM Agreement. We observe that the Panel stated at the beginning of its analysis that Article 14(d) is "not intended to define the circumstances when a government purchase of goods will confer a benefit in disputes involving Part[s II and] III of the SCM Agreement"[666], but that it provides useful context in a benefit analysis under Article 1.1(b). Moreover, the Panel clarified that Article 14(d) simply suggests *one way* to demonstrate that the challenged measures confer a benefit.[667]

5.163 The Appellate Body has stated in previous disputes that whether a benefit has been conferred should be determined by assessing whether the recipient has received a "financial contribution" on terms more favourable than those available to the recipient in the market.[668] Moreover, in previous disputes under both Parts II and III of the SCM Agreement, the Appellate Body has relied on Article 14 as the relevant context for the interpretation of benefit under

---

[662] Panel Reports, para. 7.274 (quoting Appellate Body Report, *US – Softwood Lumber IV*, para. 87; and referring to Panel Report, *US – Softwood Lumber IV*, paras. 7.50-7.51).

[663] Panel Reports, para. 7.274 (referring to Appellate Body Report, *US – Softwood Lumber IV*, paras. 157 and 158).

[664] Japan's other appellant's submission (DS412), para. 98.

[665] European Union's other appellant's submission (DS426), para. 162 and fn 170 thereto.

[666] Panel Reports, para. 7.271.

[667] Panel Reports, paras. 7.271-7.273.

[668] Appellate Body Report, *Canada – Aircraft*, para. 157.

Article 1.1(b).[669] Article 14(d) contains guidelines for determining whether government purchases of goods make a recipient "better off" than it would otherwise be in the marketplace. Article 14 is used in countervailing duties cases to calculate the amount of the subsidy in terms of the benefit to the recipient. Although Article 14 is in Part V of the SCM Agreement, the Panel was correct in pointing out that it is relevant context to the interpretation of Article 1.1(b) for the purpose of Part II of the SCM Agreement, and that it can be used as relevant context to determine whether a subsidy exists.[670]

5.164 We do not think that a different approach should be adopted when, as in the case of prohibited subsidies, one has to determine whether a benefit exists as opposed to its precise quantification. A market benchmark can tell us whether a benefit exists and usually its size. However, in the absence of a market benchmark, it will not be possible to establish if a subsidy exists at all. That a financial contribution confers an advantage on its recipient cannot be determined in absolute terms, but requires a comparison with a benchmark, which, in the case of subsidies, derives from the market. This is so, in our view, regardless of whether the advantage needs to be precisely quantified or not.

5.165 We thus consider that the Panel's interpretative approach to the question of benefit under Article 1.1(b) of the SCM Agreement, including the reliance on the context found in Article 14(d), is the correct one. We do not consider that the determination of the mere existence, as opposed to the amount, of the subsidy calls for a different interpretation of how to determine benefit under Article 1.1(b). A determination of the existence of a benefit under Article 1.1(b), read in the context of Article 14(d) of the SCM Agreement, requires a comparison between actual remuneration and a market-based benchmark or proxy, and thus between amounts, in order to determine the existence of a benefit.

5.166 In the light of the above, we do not consider that the Panel committed an error in the interpretation of the legal standard for the determination of benefit under Article 1.1(b) of the SCM Agreement.

5.5.2.2.2 The relevant market

5.167 Having identified the legal standard applicable to the benefit analysis, the Panel first reviewed the economics of wholesale electricity markets and the

---

[669] Appellate Body Reports, *Canada – Aircraft*, para. 155; and *EC and certain member States – Large Civil Aircraft*, paras. 972-975.

[670] In *Canada – Aircraft*, the Appellate Body noted that:

> [a]lthough the opening words of Article 14 state that the guidelines it establishes apply "[f]or the purposes of Part V" of the *SCM Agreement*, which relates to "countervailing measures", our view is that Article 14, nonetheless, constitutes relevant context for the interpretation of "benefit" in Article 1.1(b).

(Appellate Body Report, *Canada – Aircraft*, para. 155) See also Appellate Body Report, *EC and certain member States – Large Civil Aircraft*, para. 703.

Ontario 2002 market opening experience to conclude that "competitive wholesale electricity markets will only rarely attract sufficient investment in the generation capacity needed to secure a reliable supply of electricity" and that this "could not have been achieved in Ontario in 2002 solely on the basis of the operation of a competitive wholesale electricity market".[671] Then the Panel reviewed several in-province and out-of-province benchmarks that were put forward by the complainants and which were all based on the assumption that the relevant market for the benefit comparison was a single market for electricity generated from all sources of energy. As we consider further below, the Panel considered all these benchmarks to be distorted, and thus not appropriate, for a proper benefit analysis.

5.168 The Panel undertook and completed a full benefit benchmark analysis before it reached a conclusion on the definition of the relevant market. The Panel defined the relevant market only in paragraph 7.318, after it had rejected all the benchmarks proposed by the complainants. In defining the relevant market, the Panel stated that "[t]here is ... no basis to accept that a separate wholesale market for electricity generated from solar PV and windpower technologies would be the appropriate focus of the benefit analysis in the present disputes", considering that, "at present, consumers of electricity in Ontario, whose demand instantaneously determines the purchases made at the wholesale level, do not distinguish electricity on the basis of different generation technologies, either by way of price or usage"[672], and that no arguments had been advanced to suggest that the physical properties of electricity change depending upon how it is generated. Accordingly, the Panel agreed with the complainants that the relevant market for the purpose of the benefit analysis was the market for electricity generated from all sources of energy.[673]

5.169 We see two main problems with the Panel's analysis of the relevant market for the purpose of the benefit comparison in these disputes. First, we are of the view that the Panel should have started, rather than concluding, its benefit analysis with the definition of the relevant market. The definition of the relevant market is central to, and a prerequisite for, a benefit analysis under Article 1.1(b) the SCM Agreement. The existence of a benefit can properly be established only by comparing the prices of goods and services in the relevant market where they compete. It would seem logical for a panel that is tasked with a benefit determination to begin its analysis by defining the relevant market, which will be used for the purposes of undertaking the benefit analysis. Instead, in this case, the Panel took note of the parties' divergent views on the relevant market[674], and proceeded to analyze the benefit benchmarks put forward by the complainants, before taking a position on the relevant market for the benefit comparison. At the

[671] Panel Reports, para. 7.292.
[672] Panel Reports, para. 7.318. (fns omitted)
[673] Panel Reports, para. 7.318.
[674] Panel Reports, para. 7.278.

end of its benefit analysis, the Panel defined the relevant market for the benefit analysis as a single market for electricity generated from all sources of energy, but concluded that the competitive wholesale electricity market could not be the appropriate focus of the benefit analysis in these disputes.[675]

5.170 Second, we observe that, on the one hand, the fact that electricity is physically identical, regardless of how it is generated, suggests that there is high demand-side substitutability between electricity generated through different technologies. On the other hand, however, there are additional factors that may be used to differentiate on the demand-side, which the Panel did not consider in its analysis of the relevant market. Factors such as the type of contract, the size of the customer, and the type of electricity generated (base-load *versus* peak-load) may differentiate the market.[676]

5.171 In addition, the Panel did not analyze supply-side factors in the definition of the relevant market. In *EC and certain member States – Large Civil Aircraft*, in addressing market definition for the purposes of Articles 6(3)(a) and 6(3)(b) of the SCM Agreement, the Appellate Body found that both demand-side and supply-side considerations should be taken into account in the definition of the relevant market. The Appellate Body found:

> Demand-side substitutability – that is, when two products are considered substitutable by consumers – is an indispensable, but not the only relevant, criterion to consider when assessing whether two products are in a single market. Rather, a consideration of substitutability on the supply-side may also be required. For example, evidence on whether a supplier can switch its production at limited or prohibitive cost from one product to another in a short period of time may also inform the question of whether two products are in a single market.[677]

5.172 Had the Panel undertaken an analysis of demand-side and supply-side factors, and in particular supply-side factors, the significance of government intervention in the electricity market to the definition of the relevant market would have become evident. Such an analysis would have permitted the Panel to reach different conclusions, particularly if, as it explained later in its Reports, it was of the view that the competitive wholesale electricity market was not the appropriate focus of the benefit analysis in these disputes.

5.173 The Panel recognized that "Ontario's wholesale electricity market is perhaps better characterized as a part of an electricity system that is defined in

[675] Panel Reports, para. 7.320.

[676] For instance, certain customers, due to their size, operation, and contract, may require electricity at certain times of the day or night, thus increasing demand for base-load or peak-load electricity. Large industrial-sized customers are likely to be able to negotiate more favourable contract conditions than will be offered to household customers. The market may also be differentiated by contract type – i.e. its duration or whether prices are hedged or flexible.

[677] Appellate Body Report, *EC and certain member States – Large Civil Aircraft*, para. 1121.

almost all aspects by the Government of Ontario's policy decisions and regulations pertaining to the supply mix".[678] However, considerations as to the relevance of regulatory intervention in the Ontario electricity market are entirely absent from the definition of the relevant market, which the Panel used for the purpose of the benefit analysis.

5.174 In the present disputes, supply-side factors suggest that windpower and solar PV producers of electricity cannot compete with other electricity producers because of differences in cost structures and operating costs and characteristics. Windpower and solar PV technologies have very high capital costs (as compared to other generation technologies), very low operating costs, and fewer, if any, economies of scale. Windpower and solar PV technologies produce electricity intermittently (depending on the availability of wind and sun) and cannot be relied on for base-load and peak-load electricity. Differences in cost structures and operating costs and characteristics between windpower and solar PV technologies, on the one hand, and other technologies, on the other hand, make it very unlikely, if not impossible, that the former may exercise any form of price constraint on the latter. In contrast, conventional generators produce an identical commodity that can be used for base-load and peak-load electricity. They have larger economies of scale and exercise price constraints on windpower and solar PV generators.[679]

5.175 In circumstances where the supply of electricity from different sources is blended and, for as long as the differences in costs for conventional and renewable electricity are so significant, markets for wind- and solar PV-generated electricity can only come into existence as a matter of government regulation. It is often the government's choice of supply-mix of electricity generation technologies that creates markets for wind- and solar PV-generated electricity. A government may choose the supply-mix by setting administered prices (based on the principles of cost recovery and reasonable margin) for technologies that would not otherwise be able to recover their costs on the spot market. Alternatively, a government may require that private distributors or the government itself buy part of their requirements of electricity from certain specified generation technologies. As we consider further below, in both instances, the definition of a certain supply-mix by the government cannot *in and of itself* be considered as conferring a benefit within the meaning of Article 1.1(b) of the SCM Agreement.

5.176 We also note that the Panel's analysis of the relevant market focused on the preferences of the final consumers and ignored that electricity is purchased by the Government of Ontario at the wholesale level and then resold to consumers at the retail level. Final consumers at the retail level may not distinguish between electricity on the basis of generation technology, because all

---

678 Panel Reports, para. 7.308.

679 See Hogan Report, pp. 6-8.

electricity fed into the grid is blended regardless of the energy generation technology used. However, at the wholesale level, the government's purchase decisions are shaped by its definition of the energy supply-mix. The decisions taken by the government on the energy supply-mix as including wind- and solar PV-generated electricity necessarily dictate its electricity purchase decisions at the wholesale level. In this respect, where government decisions require a certain supply-mix, electricity from different generation technologies is not substitutable at the wholesale level. Had the Panel distinguished between the conditions of supply and demand at the wholesale and retail levels, it would have reached conclusions on the relevant market definition that took into account the Government of Ontario's choice of energy supply-mix.

5.177 A government's definition of the energy supply-mix will generally reflect a variety of policy imperatives that inform governmental action. As we discuss further below, among these is reducing reliance on fossil fuels to secure the sustainability of electricity markets in the long term, as well as addressing the negative and positive externalities that are associated with conventional and renewable electricity production. Moreover, the government definition of the energy supply-mix may reflect the fact that consumers are ready to purchase electricity that results from the combination of different generation technologies, even if this is more expensive than electricity that is produced exclusively from conventional generation sources.

5.178 In our view, not only should the Panel have defined the relevant market at the outset of its benefit analysis, but, in its analysis of the relevant market, it should also have considered that in Ontario the government definition of the energy supply-mix for electricity shapes the markets in which generators of electricity through different technologies compete. We recall that Canada had argued before the Panel that the relevant market for the purpose of the benchmark analysis should be the market for electricity produced from windpower or solar PV technology.[680] Had the Panel more thoroughly scrutinized supply-side factors, it would have come to the conclusion that, even if demand-side factors weigh in favour of defining the relevant market as a single market for electricity generated from all sources of energy, supply-side factors suggest that important differences in cost structures and operating costs and characteristics among generating technologies prevent the very existence of windpower and solar PV generation, absent government definition of the energy supply-mix of electricity generation technologies. This, in turn, would have lead the Panel to conclude that the benefit comparison under Article 1.1(b) should not be conducted within the competitive wholesale electricity market as a whole, but within competitive markets for wind- and solar PV-generated electricity, which are created by the government definition of the energy supply-mix.

[680] Panel Reports, paras. 7.277 and 7.318.

5.179 Bearing in mind the relevant market in the light of the Government of Ontario's definition of the energy supply-mix and the prevailing market conditions for wind- and solar PV-generated electricity in Ontario, we now turn to the identification of what we consider would be in the circumstances of these disputes the appropriate benchmark for the benefit comparison under Article 1.1(b) of the SCM Agreement.

5.5.2.2.3 Identification of a benefit benchmark for electricity produced from windpower and solar PV technologies

5.180 Although the Panel defined the relevant market as a single market for electricity generated from all energy sources and, as we consider further below, engaged in an in-depth analysis of all market benchmarks for blended electricity put forward by the complainants, the Panel stated in its conclusions on benefit that, in the case of electricity, the competitive wholesale electricity market is not an appropriate benchmark, given that government intervention is required to achieve certain policy goals, such as ensuring a stable and reliable supply of electricity, including from renewable sources. The Panel's finding that the complainants failed to establish benefit was based on two fundamental considerations.

5.181 First, the Panel remarked that "competitive wholesale electricity markets, although a theoretical possibility, will only rarely operate in a way that remunerates the mix of generators needed to secure a *reliable* electricity system with enough revenue to cover their all-in costs, let alone a system that pursues *human health and environmental* objectives through the inclusion of facilities using solar PV and wind technologies into the supply-mix."[681] Second, the Panel remarked that the prevailing conditions of supply and demand in Ontario suggest that a competitive wholesale electricity market would fail to attract the degree of investment in generating capacity needed to secure a reliable supply of electricity. The Panel was of the view that, "at present, this goal can only be achieved by means of government intervention in what would otherwise be unacceptable competitive market outcomes."[682]

5.182 These considerations by the Panel on the determination of benefit in electricity markets, and specifically in Ontario, stand in contrast to the Panel's definition of the relevant market for the benefit comparison as a single market for electricity generated from all sources of energy, and to its analysis of the blended electricity benchmarks submitted by the complainants. We understand these statements by the Panel to suggest that a benchmark for wind- and solar PV-generated electricity in Ontario should take into account the government's

[681] Panel Reports, para. 7.309. (original emphasis)
[682] Panel Reports, para. 7.312.

definition of the energy supply-mix as including windpower and solar PV generation. However, we do not consider that these statements should be interpreted as suggesting that the policy objectives underlying electricity production and supply entirely prevent a market-based approach to the determination of benefit. To do so would mean to read an exception into Article 1.1(b) based on the rationale of the subsidy that has no textual basis in the Agreement.

5.183 A benefit analysis under Article 1.1(b), read in the context of Article 14(d) of the SCM Agreement, involves a comparison with a market benchmark or proxy. Article 14(d) states, on the one hand, that purchases of goods should be considered as conferring a benefit if "the purchase is made for more than adequate remuneration" and, on the other hand, that the adequacy of remuneration has to be determined in relation to the "prevailing market conditions" for the good or service in question in the country of purchase. The adequacy of remuneration is only one aspect of the Article 14(d) comparison, the other being the "prevailing *market* conditions"[683] in the country of purchase, which requires a comparison with a market benchmark.

5.184 That Article 14(d) requires a comparison with *market* conditions was confirmed by the Appellate Body in *US – Softwood Lumber IV*. The Appellate Body found that, in cases where the private prices of the goods in question in the country of provision are distorted, it is possible to resort to an out-of-country benchmark or to a constructed benchmark, provided that the necessary adjustments are made to reflect conditions in the market of purchase.[684] The very purpose of resorting to an out-of-country or to a constructed benchmark is to replicate competitive market conditions that are absent in the country of purchase. Thus, resorting to a benchmark that does not reflect market conditions would not be consistent with the guidelines of Article 14(d), as interpreted by the Appellate Body in *US – Softwood Lumber IV*.

5.185 Nevertheless, while introducing legitimate policy considerations into the determination of benefit cannot be reconciled with Article 1.1(b) of the SCM Agreement, we do not think that a market-based approach to benefit benchmarks excludes taking into account situations where governments intervene to create markets that would otherwise not exist. For example, governments create electricity markets with constant and reliable supply. By regulating the quantity and the type of electricity that is supplied through the network (base-load, intermediate-load, or peak-load) and the timing of such supply, governments ensure that there is a continuous supply-demand balance between generators and consumers, thus avoiding imbalances that would destabilize the network and cause interruptions of power supply. Although this type of intervention has an effect on market prices, as opposed to a situation

683 Emphasis added.

684 Appellate Body Report, *US – Softwood Lumber IV*, para. 103.

where prices are determined by unconstrained forces of supply and demand, it does not exclude *per se* treating the resulting prices as market prices for the purposes of a benefit analysis under Article 1.1(b) of the SCM Agreement. In fact, in the absence of such government intervention, there could not be a market with a constant and reliable supply of electricity.[685]

5.186 Similarly, considerations relating to the choice of energy supply-mix by a government, including wind- and solar PV-generated electricity, may be crucial to the viability and sustainability of the electricity market in the long term. Governments intervene by reducing reliance on fossil energy resources and promoting the generation of electricity from renewable energy resources to ensure the sustainability of electricity markets in the long term. Fossil energy resources are exhaustible, and thus fossil energy needs to be replaced progressively if electricity supply is to be guaranteed in the long term. Government intervention in favour of the substitution of fossil energy with renewable energy today is meant to ensure the proper functioning or the existence of an electricity market with a constant and reliable supply of electricity in the long term. Like the government regulation that ensures the stability and reliability of supply in the electricity market, a government's choice to include windpower and solar PV generation in the energy supply-mix should not be considered as preventing the identification or adaptation of competitive benefit benchmarks for purposes of an analysis under Article 1.1(b) of the SCM Agreement.

5.187 Government intervention ensures that electricity markets may exist in the current form where consumers have a constant and reliable access to electricity. However, the regulation of electricity markets by governments is guided not only by immediate and short-term considerations relating to the nature of electricity and electricity systems, and requiring the management of "dispatchable" and "non-dispatchable" generators and loads, but also by long-term considerations aimed at ensuring that consumers have stable access to electricity in the coming years and increasingly from renewable sources. It is in the latter situation that the government's management of the energy supply-mix plays a key role.

5.188 Nevertheless, a distinction should be drawn between, on the one hand, government interventions that create markets that would otherwise not exist and, on the other hand, other types of government interventions in support of certain players in markets that already exist, or to correct market distortions therein. Where a government creates a market, it cannot be said that the government intervention distorts the market, as there would not be a market if the government had not created it. While the creation of markets by a government

[685] In particular, the Panel points out that, if supply and demand were not continuously balanced between generators and consumers, this would destabilize the networks, "leading to brownouts, blackouts or, in extreme cases, the interruption of power to all consumers". (Panel Reports, para. 7.11 (referring to Hogan Report, p. 13))

does not *in and of itself* give rise to subsidies within the meaning of the SCM Agreement, government interventions in existing markets may amount to subsidies when they take the form of a financial contribution, or income or price support, and confer a benefit to specific enterprises or industries.

5.189 We further note that a comparison between renewable energy electricity generators and conventional energy electricity generators requires consideration of the full costs associated with the generation of electricity. In this respect, if, on the one hand, higher prices for renewable electricity have certain positive externalities, such as guaranteeing long-term supply and addressing environmental concerns, on the other hand, lower prices for non-renewable electricity generation have certain negative externalities, such as the adverse impact on human health and the environment of fossil fuel energy emissions and nuclear waste disposal. Considerations related to these externalities will often underlie a government definition of the energy supply-mix and thus be the reason why governments intervene to create markets for renewable electricity generation. On this point, we agree with the Panel's statement that, where government intervention that internalizes social costs and benefits is limited to defining the broad parameters of the market, "significant scope will remain for private actors to operate within those parameters on the basis of commercial considerations".[686]

5.190 In the light of the above, and in particular in view of the fact that the government's definition of the energy supply-mix for electricity generation does not *in and of itself* constitute a subsidy, we believe that benefit benchmarks for wind- and solar PV-generated electricity should be found in the markets for wind- and solar PV-generated electricity that result from the supply-mix definition. Thus, where the government has defined an energy supply-mix that includes windpower and solar PV electricity generation technologies, as in the present disputes, a benchmark comparison for purposes of a benefit analysis for windpower and solar PV electricity generation should be with the terms and conditions that would be available under market-based conditions for each of these technologies, taking the supply-mix as a given.

5.191 Having determined that an appropriate benefit benchmark for windpower and solar PV generators should take into account the government definition of the energy supply-mix, we now turn to consider the Panel's analysis of the benefit benchmarks submitted by the complainants.

5.5.2.2.4 The Panel's benefit benchmark analysis

5.192 After setting out the interpretative framework of Articles 1.1(b) and 14(d) of the SCM Agreement and before defining the relevant market, the Panel proceeded to examine various Ontario blended electricity market benchmarks

[686] Panel Reports, fn 633 to para. 7.322.

put forward by the complainants. The Panel examined: (i) the HOEP – that is, the price for electricity sold at the wholesale level in the IESO-administered market; (ii) the retail prices offered under the RPP; and (iii) the export and import prices to and from neighbouring provinces and the United States. The Panel rejected all these benchmarks, as it had found that they were distorted by the government intervention in the market, and thus not suitable.[687]

5.193 Having rejected all Ontario prices as distorted, the Panel, following the Appellate Body's finding in *US – Softwood Lumber IV*, examined as possible benchmarks prices in four out-of-province electricity markets: Alberta, New York State, New England, and the PJM Interconnection. The Panel rejected Alberta because of the differences in the conditions of supply and demand as compared to Ontario. It rejected New York State, New England, and the PJM Interconnection because it found that generators in these markets also receive capacity payments.[688] As we have considered above, after it had rejected all the benchmarks put forward by the complainants, the Panel found that the relevant market for the benefit comparison was the wholesale market in Ontario for electricity generated from all sources of energy.[689]

5.194 The European Union claims that the Panel wrongly applied Article 1.1(b) of the SCM Agreement to the facts of this case. The Panel should not have engaged in the examination of market counterfactuals in order to make a comparison to determine the adequacy of the remuneration provided to FIT generators through the FIT Programme.[690] In the view of the European Union, recourse to hypothetical market counterfactuals or proxies was not necessary, as it was uncontested that FIT generators would not have obtained any remuneration from the market in Ontario in view of the "prevailing market conditions" where the same good (electricity) produced by using other generating technologies was much less remunerated. In the light of this, the European Union argues that the conclusion as to the existence of benefit should have been made "with little difficulty" by the Panel without the need to examine market counterfactuals or proxies.[691]

5.195 Japan agrees with the dissenting opinion in the Panel Reports that the history of the Ontario electricity market and the design, structure, and operation of the FIT Programme demonstrate that solar PV and windpower generators would not be able to operate in the Ontario market without the FIT Programme,

---

687 Panel Reports, paras. 7.293-7.302 and 7.317. The Panel also rejected the weighted-average wholesale rate during 2010 for generators other than FIT and RESOP generators, as a "HOEP-derivative[]". (Panel Report, para. 7.308 and fn 610)

688 Panel Reports, paras. 7.305-7.307.

689 Panel Reports, para. 7.318.

690 European Union's other appellant's submission (DS426), para. 168.

691 European Union's other appellant's submission (DS426), para. 162. (fn omitted)

and that this fact alone is sufficient to establish the existence of benefit under Article 1.1(b) of the SCM Agreement.[692]

5.196 We observe that the arguments of the European Union and Japan on appeal are very similar to those put forward in the dissenting opinion in the Panel Reports. We understand the European Union and Japan to argue that the Panel erred under Article 1.1(b) of the SCM Agreement because it embarked in a full benefit benchmark analysis instead of establishing the existence of benefit based on a simple "but for" test. Under such a test, the history, structure, and objectives of the FIT Programme, as well as the uncontested fact that, absent the FIT Programme, solar PV and windpower generators would not operate in the Ontario electricity market, would reveal the existence of a benefit.

5.197 We first observe that if, as the Panel acknowledged, windpower and solar PV energy generation would not occur in Ontario absent the government's definition of the energy supply-mix, a "but for" approach would be inapposite for establishing benefit, because such an approach would, by definition, not measure what the recipient could obtain in the marketplace for windpower and solar PV energy generation. Benefit cannot be established on the basis of a "but for" market counterfactual, which presupposes that the relevant market is electricity generated from all energy sources, in a situation where the government defines its energy supply-mix as including wind- and solar PV-generated electricity, and accordingly creates separate markets for wind- and solar PV-generated electricity. Assuming that benefit could be established by determining whether or not windpower and solar PV generators would have entered the market "but for" the FIT Programme, the fundamental question that needs to be answered is "what" market provides the appropriate benchmark. Before answering the question of whether windpower and solar PV generators would have entered the market, the relevant market in which they would operate needs to be defined. It is in this market that the appropriate benchmark would need to be identified.

5.198 We further observe that Canada states that what it has accepted is that the HOEP and its derivatives are insufficient to attract investment in new generation technology of any kind and that, absent the FIT Programme, prospective windpower and solar PV generators would most probably agree on a negotiated price with the Government of Ontario.[693] This is different from accepting that windpower and solar PV FIT generators would not be in the market absent the FIT Programme, as Japan and the European Union argue Canada did. Canada argued before the Panel that the relevant market for the purpose of the benefit analysis is electricity generated through solar PV and windpower technologies. Although the Panel rejected Canada's argument that the relevant market from an economic perspective is wind- and solar PV-generated electricity, it seems to

[692] Japan's other appellant's submission (DS412), para. 76.

[693] Canada's appellee's submission, para. 170 and fn 190 thereto.

have agreed with Canada that, absent the FIT Programme, FIT generators would not have to operate in a competitive wholesale electricity market, but would negotiate their rates with the government.[694]

5.199 We have disagreed with the relevant market definition underpinning the Panel's benefit analysis. We consider, for the reasons given above, that markets for wind- and solar PV-generated electricity exist in Ontario only because of government intervention. Thus, we do not consider that the Panel could have determined that benefit exists because FIT generators would not have entered the Ontario wholesale blended electricity market "but for" the FIT Programme. This is so because, as we have explained above, we do not consider that the relevant benchmark is to be found in the wholesale market for electricity generated from all sources of energy, but rather in the markets for wind- and solar PV-generated electricity, which are defined by the Government of Ontario's choice of the energy supply-mix. Therefore, in our view, the relevant question is whether windpower and solar PV electricity suppliers would have entered the wind- and solar PV-generated electricity markets absent the FIT Programme, not whether they would have entered the blended wholesale electricity market.

5.200 Japan also considers that the conclusion that benefit exists because FIT generators would not have been on the market absent the FIT Programme is also supported by comparisons with market benchmarks based on Article 14(d) of the SCM Agreement. Specifically, Japan refers to the weighted-average wholesale rate and the commodity portion of Ontario retail prices under the RPP (RPP retail prices). These prices, which are significantly lower than the FIT rates, do not depend on the HOEP, as they are fixed by contract or regulation.[695]

5.201 Japan contends that the Panel wrongly rejected these benchmarks because they were distorted by government intervention. It argues that a market price to be used as a benchmark in a subsidy determination can be influenced by government intervention without resulting in a circular comparison, as affirmed by the Appellate Body in *US – Softwood Lumber IV*, particularly where the question is about the existence of the subsidy, not its size.[696] The European Union does not directly address on appeal the Panel's rejection of in-province and out-of-province electricity prices as a benefit benchmark. As considered above, in the view of the European Union, the Panel erred in engaging in a benefit benchmark analysis when it could have determined easily the existence of benefit based on a "but for" test. Accordingly, the European Union asks us to determine the existence of benefit and to declare the

---

[694] Panel Reports, para. 7.315.

[695] According to Japan, the weighted-average wholesale rate in 2010 was between 7.02 and 7.13 cents/kWh, while the highest commodity portion of RPP retail prices was 10.8 cents/kWh. 2009 FIT prices for wind-generated electricity were 13.5 cents/kWh for on-shore and 19 cents/kWh for off-shore. 2009 FIT prices for solar PV-generated electricity ranged from 44.3 to 80.2 cents/kWh. (Japan's other appellant's submission (DS412), paras. 90-92; Panel Reports, para. 7.30)

[696] Japan's other appellant's submission (DS412), para. 104 (referring to Appellate Body Report, *US – Softwood Lumber IV*, para. 93).

Panel's findings on the in-province and out-of-province market benchmarks "moot and with no legal effect".[697]

5.202 In addressing the market benchmarks put forward by the complainants, the Panel found that there is no effective competition in Ontario's wholesale electricity market, and that this market is better characterized as a part of an electricity system defined by the Government of Ontario's policy decisions and regulations governing the supply-mix (including electricity generated from renewable sources) that is necessary to ensure a safe, reliable, and long-term supply of electricity in Ontario, and the process to recover the electricity system costs.[698]

5.203 The Panel found that generators' price offers in the IESO-administered wholesale market are not motivated by the need to cover marginal costs of production, but rather by the need to be chosen to supply electricity into the Ontario grid in order to receive the contracted or regulated prices. Thus, the HOEP, the wholesale electricity price in the IESO-administered market, is not an "equilibrium price" determined by the forces of supply and demand, but rather "a tool for the IESO to make the dispatch decisions needed to balance *physical* supply and demand for electricity".[699] The Panel observed that 92% of generators do not receive the HOEP, but a contracted or regulated price that is higher than the HOEP, and that contracted or regulated prices have been constantly above the HOEP since at least 2009.[700] Therefore, the Panel concluded that the HOEP and all of the HOEP-derivatives (such as the weighted-average wholesale rate for generators other than FIT or RESOP in 2010, the RPP retail prices in 2010, and import and export prices) advanced by the complainants as benefit benchmarks could not serve as appropriate benchmarks for the purpose of the benefit analysis.[701]

5.204 We recall that we have considered above that the proper benchmark for wind- and solar PV-generated electricity should take into account the Government of Ontario's definition of the energy supply-mix as including wind- and solar PV-generated electricity, which implies the existence of separate markets for wind- and solar PV-generated electricity. The weighted-average wholesale rate and the RPP retail prices are prices for blended electricity, that is, electricity generated from all sources of energy. As such, we consider that the weighted-average wholesale rate and the RPP retail prices are not appropriate benchmarks to determine whether the FIT Programme confers a benefit on windpower and solar PV generators. For the same reason, we consider that all the other in-province and out-of-province blended electricity benchmarks that were submitted to the Panel are not appropriate benefit benchmarks.

---

[697] European Union's other appellant's submission (DS426), para. 170. (emphasis omitted)

[698] Panel Reports, para. 7.308.

[699] Panel Reports, para. 7.298. (original emphasis; fn omitted)

[700] Panel Reports, para. 7.55.

[701] Panel Reports, para. 7.308.

5.205 Both Japan and the European Union also argue that the Panel's error under Article 1.1(b) of the SCM Agreement is underscored by the fact that the Panel found that mere participation in the FIT Programme confers an "advantage" within the meaning of the *chapeau* of paragraph 1(a) of the Illustrative List of the TRIMs Agreement, based on the objective, design, and operation of the FIT Programme, while it did not consider that, for the same reasons, it confers a "benefit" within the meaning of Article 1.1(b) of the SCM Agreement.[702] Japan considers that this contradiction also evidences a lack of objective assessment by the Panel and thus constitutes a violation of Article 11 of the DSU.[703]

5.206 In its analysis of the compatibility of the challenged measures with the GATT 1994 and the TRIMs Agreements, the Panel found that, in the light of the fixed price to be paid over a period of 20 years, "*mere participation* in [the] FIT Programme may be viewed as obtaining an 'advantage' within the meaning of the chapeau of Paragraph 1(a) of the Illustrative List."[704] Under the SCM Agreement, the Panel, however, found that Japan and the European Union failed to establish that the challenged measures confer a benefit within the meaning of Article 1.1(b).[705]

5.207 Article 1.1(b) of the SCM Agreement does not refer to "advantage", but to "benefit". However, in *Canada – Aircraft*, the Appellate Body noted that "[t]he dictionary meaning of 'benefit' is 'advantage', 'good', 'gift', 'profit', or, more generally, 'a favourable or helpful factor or circumstance'."[706] The Appellate Body further stated that "the ordinary meaning of 'benefit' clearly encompasses some form of advantage".[707]

5.208 In *Canada – Aircraft* and in its later jurisprudence, the Appellate Body did not equate the notions of "benefit" and "advantage". The Appellate Body's interpretation of "benefit" in Article 1.1(b) of the SCM Agreement clearly suggests that, while benefit involves some form of advantage, the former has a more specific meaning under the SCM Agreement. "Benefit" is linked to the concepts of "financial contribution" and "income or price support", and its existence requires a comparison in the marketplace. The same cannot be said about an "advantage" within the meaning of the TRIMs Agreement. Paragraph 1 of the Illustrative List of the TRIMs Agreement simply refers to TRIMs that are

---

[702] European Union's other appellant's submission (DS426), para. 169; Japan's other appellant's submission (DS412), para. 117.

[703] Japan's other appellant's submission (DS412), para. 117.

[704] Panel Reports, para. 7.165. (original emphasis)

[705] Panel Reports, para. 7.328(ii).

[706] Appellate Body Report, *Canada – Aircraft*, para. 153 (quoting *The New Shorter Oxford English Dictionary*, 4th edn, L. Brown (ed.) (Clarendon Press, 1993), Vol. 1, p. 214; *The Concise Oxford Dictionary*, 9th edn, D. Thompson (ed.) (Clarendon Press, 1995), p. 120; and *Webster's Third New International Dictionary* (unabridged) (William Benton, 1966), Vol. I, p. 204).

[707] Appellate Body Report, *Canada – Aircraft*, para. 153. (fn omitted)

necessary to obtain an advantage.[708] The concept of "advantage" in the TRIMs Agreement has to be interpreted in the context of this Agreement and, without entering into the merit of such an interpretation, it seems to us that "advantage" under the TRIMs Agreement may take other forms than a "financial contribution" or a "benefit" under the SCM Agreement. In any event, a finding of an "advantage" under the TRIMs Agreement does not require a comparison with a benefit benchmark in the relevant market, as required for a benefit analysis under the SCM Agreement.

5.209 Thus, while we do not exclude that certain measures that provide an advantage within the meaning of paragraph 1 of the Illustrative List of the TRIMs Agreement may also confer a benefit within the meaning of Article 1.1(b) of the SCM Agreement, it is conceivable that a measure that confers an advantage within the meaning of paragraph 1 of the Illustrative List of the TRIMs Agreement be found not to confer a benefit within the meaning of Article 1.1(b) of the SCM Agreement.

5.210 In sum, we do not consider that the Panel finding that mere participation in the FIT Programme constitutes an advantage within the meaning of paragraph 1 of the Illustrative List of TRIMs while, at the same time, not finding that benefit exists under Article 1.1(b) of the SCM Agreement demonstrates that the Panel committed an error under Article 1.1(b). Neither are we persuaded that, in doing so, the Panel entered into a contradiction, which Japan argues would constitute a violation of Article 11 of the DSU.

5.211 In the light of all of the above, we consider that the approach and the benefit benchmarks advanced by the European Union and Japan are not appropriate to determine the existence of benefit for windpower and solar PV generation under the FIT Programme.

5.5.2.2.5 Conclusions under Article 1.1(b) of the SCM Agreement

5.212 In its benefit analysis, on the one hand, the Panel correctly considered that the need to secure a reliable supply of electricity through an energy supply-mix that included windpower and solar PV generation rendered inappropriate a comparison of the FIT remuneration with the terms and conditions available on the competitive wholesale electricity market.[709] On the other hand, the Panel accepted the complainants' line of argument, including their market definition, and proceeded to evaluate whether a benefit had been conferred based on benefit

---

[708] The *chapeau* to paragraph 1 of the Illustrative List of the TRIMs Agreement states that:

> TRIMs that are inconsistent with the obligation of national treatment provided for in paragraph 4 of Article III of GATT 1994 include those which are mandatory or enforceable under domestic law or under administrative rulings, or compliance with which is necessary to obtain an advantage, …

[709] Panel Reports, para. 7.312.

benchmarks for a single market for electricity generated from all sources of energy.

5.213 Further, in its "observations on one approach to the question of benefit"[710] made after its finding under Article 1.1(b) of the SCM Agreement, the Panel proposed to compare FIT remunerations for windpower and solar PV generators with the remuneration that windpower and solar PV generators would obtain on competitive markets for wind- and solar PV-generated electricity. The benchmark under the Panel's approach was "the terms and conditions that would be offered by commercial distributors of electricity acting under a government-imposed obligation to acquire electricity from generators operating solar PV and windpower plants of a comparable scale to those functioning under the FIT Programme".[711] This approach clearly suggests that the benefit comparison should take place within markets for windpower and solar PV technologies that result from the government's definition of the energy supply-mix. Thus, while the Panel first conducted a benefit benchmark analysis that presupposed a single market for electricity generated from all sources of energy, it then proposed an alternative approach to assessing benefit, which required a comparison within the windpower and solar PV generation technologies, respectively.

5.214 It seems to us that, in its "observations on one approach to the question of benefit", the Panel identified the proper market for the benefit comparison in respect of windpower and solar PV generation in Ontario that would not exist absent government definition of the energy supply-mix. We fail to understand, however, why the Panel did not then choose to conduct its benefit analysis on the basis of a benchmark that reflected the energy supply-mix. Instead, the Panel reviewed the complainants' line of argument that was based on a single wholesale electricity market and limited itself to making some *obiter dicta* observations on the appropriate benchmark only after it had found that the complainants had failed to demonstrate the existence of benefit under an approach that the Panel considered to be incorrect.

5.215 We note that, in making a claim, a complainant has the responsibility of providing evidence and arguments that the panel must objectively assess. While a panel cannot make the case for a complainant, it has the competence "freely to use arguments submitted by any of the parties – or to develop its own legal reasoning – to support its own findings and conclusions on the matter under its consideration".[712] Panels also have broad fact-finding powers and may seek information from any source. We do not think that the Panel should have limited its analysis to the proposed benefit approach, and/or to the benchmarks that were part of the complainants' principal argument, in a situation where the evidence and the arguments presented by the complainants, and the arguments in response

---

[710] Panel Reports, para. 7.321. (emphasis omitted)

[711] Panel Reports, para. 7.322.

[712] Appellate Body Report, *EC – Hormones*, para. 156. See also Appellate Body Report, *US – Certain EC Products*, para. 123.

by Canada, may have allowed it to develop its own reasoning and to make findings based on a benchmark that took into account the government's definition of the energy supply-mix. Provided the complainants had presented relevant evidence and arguments to make a *prima facie* case, it was for the Panel to analyze the appropriate benchmark or proxy. We observe that arguments and evidence were presented before the Panel that could have been useful in identifying a benefit benchmark that took into account the Government of Ontario's definition of the energy supply-mix, including wind- and solar PV-generated electricity.

5.216 In making a *prima facie* case of benefit under Article 1.1(b) of the SCM Agreement, the burden was on the complainants to identify a suitable benchmark and to make adjustments, where necessary. While the complainants focused their main arguments before the Panel on blended electricity market benchmarks (the HOEP, the average wholesale rate, retail rates, import and export prices, as well as out-of-province rates), the European Union also presented arguments and evidence on electricity rates from renewable sources in Ontario and in Quebec in response to Canada's argument that the relevant markets for the benefit comparison were the markets for wind- and solar PV-generated electricity. The European Union argued in its second written submission and in its opening oral statement at the second meeting of the Panel that benefit could be demonstrated by comparing the FIT remuneration with the terms and conditions under the Request for Proposals of Renewable Energy Supply (RES) I, II, and III and with the Quebec 2005 and 2008 competitive contracts for wind farms.[713] Thus, if the Panel believed, as is evident from its Reports, that the appropriate benefit comparison could not take place in the competitive wholesale electricity market, it could have explored instead these arguments.

5.217 In its "observations on one approach to the question of benefit", the Panel proposed a benefit benchmark based on the Government of Ontario's choice of the energy supply-mix as including wind- and solar PV-generated electricity. The Panel attempted to apply such benchmark by comparing the rates of return obtained by FIT generators with the average cost of capital in Canada for projects having a comparable risk profile in the same period, but found that there was not enough evidence on the record to make such a comparison. We express no views about the merits of a comparison between FIT rates of return and the average cost of capital in Canada. However, we note that the Panel did not even explore the possibility of an electricity supply-mix benchmark based on the evidence submitted by the complainants regarding previous renewable energy programmes in Ontario (RES) and out-of-province (Quebec).

[713] European Union's second written submission to the Panel (DS426), paras. 82-84; and opening statement at the second Panel meeting, paras. 25 and 26.

5.218 The complainants' principal benefit claims focused on benchmarks in the competitive wholesale blended electricity market. However, the European Union also presented arguments and evidence that would have allowed the Panel to compare the FIT remuneration with a benchmark reflecting competitive prices in generation technology-specific markets, provided that appropriate adjustments would have been proposed by the European Union and reviewed by the Panel. This could have allowed the Panel to conduct its benefit analysis on the basis of the appropriate benefit benchmark that it evoked in paragraphs 7.309 to 7.313 of its Reports and that it later developed in its *obiter dicta* observations on an alternative approach to the question of benefit.

5.219 In the light of the above, we consider that the Panel committed an error in not conducting the benefit analysis on the basis of a market that is shaped by the government's definition of the energy supply-mix, and of a benchmark located in that market reflecting competitive prices for windpower and solar PV generation. We, therefore, *reverse* the Panel's findings, in paragraph 7.328(ii) of the Panel Reports, paragraph 8.3 in the Japan Panel Report, and paragraph 8.7 in the EU Panel Report, that Japan and the European Union failed to establish that the challenged measures confer a benefit within the meaning of Article 1.1(b) of the SCM Agreement and thereby that Canada acted inconsistently with Articles 3.1(b) and 3.2 of the SCM Agreement.

5.220 Having reversed the Panel's finding that the complainants failed to establish the existence of benefit, no determination exists as to whether or not the challenged measures confer a benefit within the meaning of Article 1.1(b) of the SCM Agreement. We shall consider further below, whether, on the basis of factual findings of the Panel and undisputed facts on the Panel record, we can complete the analysis and determine whether the challenged measures confer a benefit within the meaning of Article 1.1(b) of the SCM Agreement and whether Canada acted inconsistently with Articles 3.1(b) and 3.2 of the SCM Agreement.

5.5.2.3 Whether the Panel acted inconsistently with Article 11 of the DSU in finding that the European Union and Japan failed to establish that the challenged measures confer a benefit within the meaning of Article 1.1(b) of the SCM Agreement

5.221 Both the European Union and Japan claim, in the alternative, should we agree with the Panel's findings under Article 1.1(b) of the SCM Agreement, that the Panel failed to make an objective assessment of the matter, under Article 11 of the DSU, in concluding that there was not enough evidence on the record that would allow it to reach conclusions on benefit under Article 1.1(b) of the

SCM Agreement, based on its own approach to the question of benefit.[714] Moreover, the European Union and Japan also claim that the fact that the Panel first defined the relevant market as the market for electricity that is generated from all sources of energy, but later developed its own counterfactual relying on a separate market for solar PV- and wind-generated electricity, constitutes a contradiction, which is itself a violation of Article 11 of the DSU.[715]

5.222 We have reversed the Panel's findings that the European Union and Japan failed to demonstrate that the challenged measures confer a benefit within the meaning of Article 1.1(b) of the SCM Agreement. Thus, the condition for us to consider the European Union's and Japan's alternative claims under Article 11 of the DSU is not met. Therefore, we do not address the alternative claims that the Panel failed to make an objective assessment of the matter according to Article 11 of the DSU. We further note that, having reversed the Panel's finding under Article 1.1(b) of the SCM Agreement, there is no need for us to address the alternative claims under Article 11 of the DSU to provide a positive solution to these disputes.

5.5.2.4 Completion of the analysis

5.223 Both Japan and the European Union have requested, should we reverse the Panel's "benefit" finding, that we complete the legal analysis on the basis of the factual findings made by the Panel and uncontested evidence on the Panel's record and find that the challenged measures confer a benefit within the meaning of Article 1.1(b) of the SCM Agreement and constitute prohibited subsidies inconsistent with Articles 3.1(b) and 3.2 of the SCM Agreement.[716]

5.224 Therefore, having reversed the Panel's "benefit" finding, we now turn to consider whether we can complete the legal analysis and determine first whether the FIT Programme and related FIT and microFIT Contracts confer a benefit within the meaning of Article 1.1(b) of the SCM Agreement. In previous disputes, the Appellate Body has completed the analysis with a view to facilitating the prompt settlement and effective resolution of the dispute.[717] However, the Appellate Body has held that it can do so only if the factual findings of the panel and the undisputed facts on the panel record provide it with a sufficient basis for its own analysis.[718] The Appellate Body has found it

---

[714] European Union's other appellant's submission (DS426), para. 173; Japan's other appellant's submission (DS412), para. 119.

[715] European Union's other appellant's submission (DS426), para. 199; Japan's other appellant's submission (DS412), para. 111.

[716] Japan's other appellant's submission (DS412), para. 118; European Union's other appellant's submission (DS426), para. 171.

[717] See e.g. Appellate Body Reports, *Australia – Salmon*, paras. 117-118; *US – Wheat Gluten*, paras. 80-92; and *Canada – Aircraft (Article 21.5 – Brazil)*, paras. 43-52.

[718] See Appellate Body Reports, *Australia – Salmon*, paras. 209, 241, and 255; *Korea – Dairy*, paras. 91 and 102; *Canada – Autos*, paras. 133 and 144; and *Korea – Various Measures on Beef*, para. 128. The Appellate Body has indicated that it may complete the analysis only if the provision

impossible to complete the legal analysis due to insufficient factual findings in the panel report or a lack of undisputed facts on the panel record.[719] Also among the reasons that have prevented the Appellate Body from completing the legal analysis are the complexity of the issues, the absence of full exploration of the issues before the panel, and, consequently, considerations for parties' due process rights.[720]

5.225 In the present disputes, the assessment of whether benefit is conferred would require completing the analysis. This would involve conducting a comparison with a benefit benchmark to determine whether the remuneration obtained by FIT generators confers on them an advantage as compared to the remuneration they would otherwise have been able to obtain in the marketplace. However, as explained above, the parameters of the marketplace would need to take into account the energy supply-mix defined by the Government of Ontario. We also recall that we have agreed with the Panel that Article 14(d) constitutes relevant context for the determination of the existence of benefit under Article 1.1(b) of the SCM Agreement. A determination of benefit in the framework of Article 14(d) requires a comparison between actual remuneration and a market-based benchmark or proxy. For the purposes of that comparison in these disputes, the market-based, price-discovery mechanism would have to take as a given the supply-mix defined by the government.

5.226 Article 14(d) requires that the adequacy of remuneration in a benefit comparison be determined in relation to the prevailing market conditions for the good or service in question in the country of provision or purchase. Nevertheless, the Appellate Body has held in previous disputes that a benchmark other than private prices in the country of provision under Article 14(d) can be used "if it is first established that private prices in that country are distorted because of the government's predominant role in providing those goods".[721] The Appellate Body has stated that it is possible to resort to both out-of-country benchmarks and constructed benchmarks, provided adjustments are made "to ensure that the resulting benchmark relates or refers to, or is connected with, prevailing market conditions in the country of provision, and must reflect price,

---

that a panel has not examined is "closely related" to a provision that the panel has examined, and that the two are "part of a logical continuum". (Appellate Body Report, *Canada – Periodicals*, p. 24, DSR 1997:I, p. 469) See also Appellate Body Reports, *EC – Asbestos*, para. 79; and *EC – Export Subsidies on Sugar*, para. 337.

[719] See Appellate Body Reports, *US – Section 211 Appropriations Act*, para. 343; and *EC – Asbestos*, para. 78. In *US – Large Civil Aircraft (2nd complaint)*, the Appellate Body completed the analysis "assuming that the evidence submitted by the United States [was] accurate and uncontested" (Appellate Body Report, *US – Large Civil Aircraft (2nd complaint)*, para. 662), or, in other words, on the basis of what the losing party had admitted or submitted. (*Ibid.*, fn 1561 to para. 741)

[720] Appellate Body Report, *EC – Export Subsidies on Sugar*, fn 537 to para. 339.

[721] Appellate Body Report, *US – Softwood Lumber IV*, para. 90. (fn omitted)

quality, availability, marketability, transportation and other conditions of purchase or sale, as required by Article 14(d)".[722]

5.227 We have considered above that the appropriate benchmark to establish whether the FIT remuneration confers a benefit within the meaning of Article 1.1(b) of the SCM Agreement should take into account that the Government of Ontario defines the energy supply-mix for electricity generation as including wind- and solar PV-generated electricity and the progressive phase-out of fossil fuels, in particular coal-based electricity generation. This is so because, as explained above, creating a market by defining the energy supply-mix as including windpower and solar PV generation cannot *in and of itself* be considered as conferring a benefit. Accordingly, an appropriate benefit benchmark for windpower and solar PV electricity generation in Ontario should be one that, within the parameters of the Government of Ontario's definition of the energy supply-mix, reflects what a market benchmark would yield for wind- and solar PV-generated electricity. Moreover, based on the guidelines contained in Article 14(d), an appropriate benchmark should first be sought in the windpower and solar PV generation markets in Ontario. If no suitable benchmark is available in Ontario, an appropriate benchmark outside Ontario or a proxy may also be considered.

5.228 Government-administered prices such as FIT may or may not reflect what a hypothetical market would yield. Thus, the fact that the government sets prices does not in itself establish the existence of a benefit. In challenging a benefit comparison under Article 1.1(b) of the SCM Agreement, a complainant would have to show that such prices do not reflect what a market outcome would be. An analysis of the methodology that was used to establish the administered prices may provide evidence as to whether the price does or does not provide more than adequate remuneration. There may be circumstances where there is no information about the methodology that was used or the methodology used does not assist in determining whether the administered price is or is not reflective of what a market would yield. If it becomes necessary to identify a market benchmark or to construct a proxy, such benchmark or proxy may be administered prices for the same product (in the country of purchase or in other countries, subject to adjustments), provided that it is determined based on a price-setting mechanism that ensures a market outcome. Alternatively, such benchmark may also be found in price-discovery mechanisms such as competitive bidding or negotiated prices, which ensure that the price paid by the government is the lowest possible price offered by a willing supply contractor.

5.229 With these considerations in mind, we turn to the relevant facts and arguments submitted by the participants and assess to what extent they are undisputed or the Panel has made pertinent factual findings. Evidence submitted

[722] Appellate Body Report, *US – Softwood Lumber IV*, para. 106. See also Appellate Body Report, *US – Anti-Dumping and Countervailing Duties (China)*, para. 486, regarding the use of proxies under Article 14(b) of the SCM Agreement.

by Canada before the Panel shows that "[t]he weighted average price for the winning projects [under RES II] was disclosed to be 8.64 cents per kWh" and that "the highest accepted bid could be in the range of 9.4 cents per kWh."[723] In responding to Panel question No. 4 following the second meeting with the parties, Canada stated that "[r]ates for wind projects under the [three] RES request[s] for proposal process range from $0.08/kWh to $0.11/kWh."[724]

5.230 In its second written submission to the Panel, the European Union submitted that, "even if the cost of generating wind and solar electricity would have to be taken into account, as Canada alleges, ... the structure of the FIT Programme leads to payments in excess of costs".[725] The European Union argued that the structure of the FIT Programme, and in particular the standardized rates, leads to payments in excess of the cost of production, as compared to RES I (2004), RES II (2005), and RES III (2008), which were administered based on the best prices offered by generators through a bidding process.[726] In its opening oral statement at the second meeting of the Panel, the European Union also submitted evidence regarding prices outside Ontario, namely, the prices for wind-generated electricity in Quebec. The European Union observed that competitive contracts for wind-generated electricity in Quebec in 2005 and 2008 showed average rates of 6.5 cents and 8.7 cents per kWh respectively, which it argued demonstrated that the FIT Programme did not reflect the costs of generation.[727]

5.231 In its closing oral statement at the second meeting of the Panel, Canada stated that "an analytical approach based on Appellate Body jurisprudence ... might have been used to arrive at an appropriate benchmark in this case" and that, "even if a private price for wind and solar electricity in Ontario could not be found, there might have been appropriate alternative in-jurisdiction benchmarks proposed in this case"[728], but that no such evidence had been presented to the Panel. In its comments on the responses of Japan and the European Union to the Panel's questions following the second meeting with the parties, Canada contends that, while "both Japan and the European Union admit that the

---

723 OPA, Joint Report to the Minister of Energy: Recommendations on a Standard Offer Program for Small Generators connected to a Distribution System (RESOP), 17 March 2006 (Panel Exhibit CDA-55), p. 20.

724 In the light of the Panel's question about "prices paid for electricity", we understand these rates to refer to the prices for wind-generated electricity resulting from the bidding process. (See Canada's response to Panel question No. 4 (second set), para. 16)

725 European Union's second written submission to the Panel (DS426), para. 82.

726 European Union's second written submission to the Panel (DS426), paras. 82-85.

727 European Union's opening statement at the second Panel meeting (DS426), paras. 25 and 26. We further note that, in its response to Panel question No. 34 (second set), the European Union restated its views that the FIT standard rate overcompensated FIT generators, as compared to the terms and conditions available under the RES initiatives that were the result of a bidding process, or as compared to rates of wind-generated electricity in Quebec that also resulted from a bidding process. (European Union's response to Panel question No. 34 (second set), paras. 45-53)

728 Canada's closing statement at the second Panel meeting, para. 27.

benchmark or comparator that should be used is one for renewable electricity", the complainants have not constructed "any benchmark for wind or solar electricity based on costs of production and other relevant prevailing market conditions in Ontario".[729]

5.232 The Panel found that, under the RES initiative, "the OPA awarded supply contracts through a competitive bidding process which set prices for delivered electricity at the levels of the lowest bids meeting the specified conditions."[730] The parties did not seem to dispute the accuracy of the evidence concerning various prices under RES and in Quebec. The Panel, however, did not make any factual findings on this evidence, or draw conclusions on whether these prices can serve as appropriate benefit benchmarks for windpower and/or solar PV electricity generators in Ontario, or whether any adjustments within the meaning of Article 14(d) were necessary.

5.233 The RES initiative, like the FIT Programme, reflects the Government of Ontario's choice of energy supply-mix as including renewable energy generation sources. Moreover, under the RES initiative, prices are not fixed by the government, but determined by a competitive bidding process, which is a market-based, price-discovery process. A bidding process that is competitive will ensure that the price paid by the government is the lowest possible price offered by a willing supply contractor. As we have noted above, market-based price discovery is not necessarily tied to a competitive bidding process. The methodology adopted to determine government-administered prices may also show that these do not provide more than adequate remuneration and thus reflect what a market would yield.

5.234 We have noted above that government-administered prices may or may not reflect what a hypothetical market would yield. In the case of FIT, however, while FIT prices were intended to cover costs plus a reasonable rate of return[731], there are no undisputed facts on the record or factual findings by the Panel that would allow us to assess whether the methodology the OPA used to establish the FIT prices resulted in prices that provide more than adequate remuneration. Indeed, the only factual finding by the Panel regarding this methodology is that the FIT prices were determined using a discounted cash flow model taking into account "reasonable" capital costs, "reasonable" operating and maintenance costs, and "reasonable" connection costs.[732] Evidence adduced by Canada shows that the FIT Price Schedule was designed with a view to balancing several

[729] Canada's comments on the European Union's and Japan's responses to Panel questions (second set), paras. 30 and 63.

[730] Panel Reports, para. 7.29.

[731] Panel Report, para. 7.202.

[732] Panel Report, para. 7.202 (referring to OPA Proposed FIT Price Schedule Presentation, slides 22-28). The Panel defined capital costs as "project development, construction and equipment costs"; operating and maintenance costs as "project staffing and maintenance costs, including on-going capital expenditures and property taxes"; and connection costs as "project connection costs, no significant upgrade costs assumed". (*Ibid.*, para. 7.202)

objectives. These objectives include promoting broad participation in the FIT Programme (e.g. different technologies, project sizes, and proponents), providing price stability necessary to promote the investment objectives of the Green Energy and Green Economy Act of 2009, and encouraging efficient project development.[733] Such evidence further indicates that the OPA used a cost-based price methodology to enable a wide range of technologies to participate in the FIT Programme.[734] Moreover, in order to develop the FIT Price Schedule, the OPA had to make assumptions about the costs and performance characteristics of a "typical" project.[735] For these reasons, we are not in a position to determine whether the FIT prices represent what a market would have yielded by analyzing the methodology by which they are established.

5.235 Turning to RES, while in principle RES I, II, and III prices, which resulted from competitive bidding, may represent a market outcome for renewable electricity generation, in order to carry out a meaningful comparison of the FIT Programme and the RES initiative, it is necessary to ensure that the comparison is made between prices referring to the same period, the same type of generation technology, the same overall supply-mix, projects of the same or similar scale, and supply contracts of the same duration.[736] If any of these conditions are not met by the proposed benchmark, adjustments in the light of the factors listed in Article 14(d) and of the supply-mix defined by the government may be necessary to ensure comparability. We believe that, on the basis of this approach, it should be possible to determine whether prices under RES constitute an appropriate benchmark for a comparison with FIT prices in order to establish the existence of benefit consistently with Article 1.1(b) of the SCM Agreement.

5.236 Although the RES initiative was also open to solar PV generators, there does not seem to be any evidence on the Panel record that solar PV generators were awarded contracts under any of the three RES initiatives. Rather, Canada's Hogan Report asserts that the RES experience demonstrates that solar PV generators cannot compete with other less-costly technologies. To promote investment in solar PV technology through the RESOP and the FIT Programme, prices for solar PV-generated electricity were cost-based and set by the OPA.[737] Japan submitted as an exhibit a "Progress Report on Electricity Supply" by the OPA that contains a table that sets out the different renewable energy contracts in force as of the fourth quarter 2010, which indicates that there were no solar

---

733 OPA Proposed FIT Price Schedule Presentation, slide 5.

734 OPA Proposed FIT Price Schedule Presentation, slide 21.

735 OPA Proposed FIT Price Schedule Presentation, slide 6.

736 Canada did not make specific arguments as to what extent and in what manner adjustments would be necessary. The complainants submitted no evidence or arguments on adjustments that might have been necessary to ensure the comparability of the prices under the FIT and RES programmes.

737 Hogan Report, p. 34.

RES Contracts recorded as of that date.[738] Against this background, it does not appear that the FIT remuneration for solar PV generators can be compared to prices under the RES initiative to establish whether the FIT Programme confers a benefit in respect of solar PV energy generation.[739]

5.237 We note, in respect of windpower generation, that the requests for proposals under the three RES initiatives were issued in 2004 (RES I), 2005 (RES II), and 2008 (RES III). The European Union argued before the Panel that the costs of windpower generation had decreased in the years preceding the launch of the FIT Programme. The European Union submitted various documents suggesting that, due to technological advancements, costs of wind-generated electricity have decreased rather than increased in recent years.[740] While we have found no specific evidence on the record regarding the evolution of windpower generation costs in Ontario between 2004 and 2009, we note that the latest RES initiative was launched in 2008 – that is, only one year before the FIT Programme – and that the RES prices submitted by Canada for the period 2004 to 2008 range from 8 cents to 11 cents per kWh.[741] It is thus conceivable that RES III (2008) contracts for windpower generators, concluded less than a year before the launch of the FIT Programme in 2009, received a remuneration of 11 cents per kWh or less *versus* the lowest FIT remuneration for windpower generators of 13.5 cents per kWh.[742]

5.238 Several contracts for wind-generated electricity were awarded under the three RES initiatives, although, according to Canada, for "much smaller capacity than the capacity provided by wind projects under the FIT Programme".[743] While the RES initiative and FIT Programme overlap for projects between 500 kW and 200 MW, the FIT Programme has a broader scope than the RES initiative, covering also projects of smaller capacity than 500 kW and greater than 200 MW.[744] RES contracts, like FIT Contracts for windpower and solar PV

---

[738] OPA, A Progress Report on Electricity Supply – Fourth Quarter 2010 (Panel Exhibit JPN-26), Table at p. 4.

[739] The Quebec prices referred to by the European Union are also only for windpower generation and not for solar PV generation.

[740] See European Wind and Energy Association, *The Economics of Wind Energy* (March 2009) (Panel Exhibit EU-20), pp. 13 and 15; and European Union's opening statement at the second Panel meeting (DS426), para. 26. See also Government of Ontario, *Ontario's Long-Term Energy Plan* (Queen's Printer for Ontario, 2010) (Panel Exhibit CDA-6) ; and Electricity Conservation & Supply Task Force, Tough Choices: Addressing Ontario's Power Needs, Final Report to the Minister of Energy (January 2004) (Panel Exhibit CDA-59), p. 50.

[741] Hogan Report, p. 32; Canada's response to Panel question No. 4 (second set), para. 16.

[742] Panel Reports, para. 7.30.

[743] Canada's response to Panel question No. 4 (second set), para. 16.

[744] RES I (2004) was open to renewable generators with a capacity range of 0.5 to 100 MW; RES II (2005) to generators with a capacity range of 20 to 200 MW; and RES III (2008) to generators with a capacity range of 10.1 to 199.9 MW. (Hogan Report, p. 32) We recall that, under the FIT Programme, FIT Contracts are for qualifying generators with capacity over 10 kW, while generators with capacity of up to 10 kW are eligible for microFIT Contracts. (*Ibid.*) It is not clear whether RES contracts of

generation, were concluded for the duration of 20 years[745] and, thus, significant overlap exists between the duration of the RES contracts awarded in 2004, 2005, and 2008 and the FIT Contracts awarded in 2009.

5.239 We do not consider that a comparison of FIT prices with the prices of wind-generated electricity in Quebec would be possible for the purposes of completing the analysis in this appeal, considering that the standard of comparability that would be required for such an out-of-province benchmark was not raised before the Panel, or before us. In this respect, we recall that the Appellate Body has considered in previous disputes that, while it may be possible to resort to external benchmarks, it is necessary to ensure that such benchmarks reflect the prevailing market conditions in the country of provision or purchase.[746] We, therefore, conclude that we are not able to consider the prices for wind-generated electricity in Quebec in our attempt at completing the analysis under Article 1.1(b) of the SCM Agreement.

5.240 In contrast, we are of the view that it would be, in principle, possible to make a comparison of the FIT remuneration of windpower generators with the remuneration that windpower generators obtain under the RES initiative to determine whether the former confers a benefit. We observe that there are clearly no factual findings by the Panel or undisputed evidence on the Panel record that would allow us to complete the analysis with respect to the remuneration for solar PV electricity generation under the FIT Programme.

5.241 Nevertheless, while a comparison between prices under FIT and RES seems to suggest that the former confers a benefit, we do not consider that we are able to complete the analysis on that basis alone. We recall that both complainants' main line of argumentation with respect to benefit was focused on a single electricity market and on an approach that sought to establish the existence of benefit by reference to other electricity generation technologies. The complainants also submitted a number of in-province and out-of-province benchmarks based on a single electricity market definition. In other words, all these benchmarks were not based on the Government of Ontario's definition of the energy supply-mix. Only at the second Panel meeting, and especially in written responses and comments to questions after the second meeting, did the

---

specific scale and prices can be matched with FIT Contracts of similar size, and thus we are not in a position to make a comparison of RES and FIT prices and contract size.

[745] Ontario Ministry of Energy, Request for Proposals for 300 MW of Renewable Energy Supply (RES I), issued 24 June 2004 (Panel Exhibit CDA-52), p. 41; Request for Proposals for 1,000 MW of Renewable Energy Supply (RES II), issued 17 June 2005 (Panel Exhibit CDA-53), p. 56; Request for Proposals for approximately 500 MW of Renewable Energy Supply (RES III), issued 22 August 2008 (Panel Exhibit CDA-54), p.2.

[746] Appellate Body Report, *US – Softwood Lumber IV*, para. 103. We observe that, while Ontario and Quebec are in the same "country", that is, Canada, they have separate regional markets for electricity. Thus, the "prevailing market conditions" in the country of purchase within the meaning of Article 14(d) of the SCM Agreement is to be read in this case as referring to the Ontario regional market as opposed to other out-of-province markets, within Canada or in another country.

parties engage in argumentation on benefit benchmarks for renewable energy generation.

5.242 We further recall that the Panel made very limited findings regarding benchmarks that take into account the Government of Ontario's definition of the energy supply-mix. The Panel considered in its conclusions under Article 1.1(b) of the SCM Agreement that an appropriate benchmark could not, and should not, be found in the competitive wholesale electricity market, and then, after its finding under Article 1.1(b), it developed in its "observations on one approach to the question of benefit"[747] a benchmark that took into account the Government of Ontario's definition of the energy supply-mix. The Panel attempted to apply its alternative benchmark by comparing the FIT rates of return with the average cost of capital in Canada for projects having a comparable risk profile in the same period.

5.243 The Panel, however, did not make a finding on whether RES constituted an appropriate benchmark in the light of the Government of Ontario's definition of the energy supply-mix. Nor did it consider conducting a comparison of the FIT remuneration with the remuneration under the RES initiative. Indeed, the Panel's only finding in respect of RES was a factual finding concerning the price-discovery mechanism, which the Panel found was based on competitive bidding.[748] Finally, we observe that the applicability to the challenged measures of a benefit benchmark based on a supply-mix including wind- and solar PV-generated electricity was not sufficiently debated in this appeal, so as to provide us with further elements that would allow us to complete the analysis.

5.244 We recall that the Appellate Body has refrained from completing the legal analysis in the light of the complexity of the issues and in the absence of full exploration of the issues before the panel, which raised concerns about the parties' due process rights.[749] We believe that these elements are present in the benefit issues raised in this appeal. The identification of a benchmark that takes into account the government's definition of the energy supply-mix involves consideration of the fact that the government has created markets for wind- and solar PV-generated electricity, and is a more complex exercise than evaluating benchmarks in the wholesale electricity market as the Panel did. The Panel has made no findings on the adequacy of proposed benchmarks for wind- and solar PV-generated electricity. In these circumstances, completing the analysis would raise due process concerns for the parties.

5.245 In sum, we have found evidence on the Panel record that is relevant to a benefit analysis based on a benchmark that takes into account the Government of Ontario's definition of the energy supply-mix. Based on this evidence, we have considered that RES prices for windpower generation contracts awarded through

---

[747] Panel Reports, para. 7.321. (emphasis omitted)

[748] Panel Reports, para. 7.29.

[749] Appellate Body Report, *EC – Export Subsidies on Sugar*, fn 537 to para. 339.

competitive bidding may qualify as benchmarks for a benefit comparison and seem to suggest that benefit may exist in the case of FIT windpower generation contracts. We conclude, however, that such evidence was neither sufficiently debated before the Panel, nor before us. Moreover, the Panel did not make factual findings on this evidence that would assist us in completing the analysis.

5.246 In the light of the above, we do not consider that there are sufficient factual findings by the Panel and uncontested evidence on the Panel record that would allow us to complete the legal analysis and conduct a benefit benchmark comparison between the prices of wind-generated electricity under the FIT Programme and the prices for wind-generated electricity under the RES initiative. Consequently, we cannot determine whether the challenged measures confer a benefit within the meaning of Article 1.1(b) of the SCM Agreement and whether they constitute prohibited subsidies inconsistent with Articles 3.1(b) and 3.2 of the SCM Agreement.

6. FINDINGS AND CONCLUSIONS IN THE APPELLATE BODY REPORT WT/DS412/AB/R

6.1 In the appeal of the Panel Report, *Canada – Certain Measures Affecting the Renewable Energy Generation Sector* (WT/DS412/R) (Japan Panel Report), for the reasons set out in this Report, the Appellate Body:

a. *declines* Japan's request to commence its evaluation with Japan's allegations of error relating to the SCM Agreement;

b. as regards Article III:8(a) of the GATT 1994:

    i. *reverses* the Panel's findings, in paragraphs 7.127, 7.128, and 7.152 of the Japan Panel Report, that the Minimum Required Domestic Content Levels of the FIT Programme and related FIT and microFIT Contracts are laws, regulations, or requirements governing the procurement by governmental agencies of electricity within the meaning of Article III:8(a) of the GATT 1994;

    ii. *declares moot and of no legal effect* the other intermediate findings made by the Panel, in particular in paragraphs 7.136, 7.145, and 7.151;

    iii. *finds* that the Minimum Required Domestic Content Levels prescribed under the FIT Programme and related FIT and microFIT Contracts do not meet the conditions of the derogation in Article III:8(a) of the GATT 1994; and

    iv. in the light of this finding, *does not find it necessary to address* Canada's claim that the Panel failed to fulfil its obligations under Article 11 of the DSU by exercising judicial economy; and

v. *finds* that the FIT Programme and related FIT and microFIT Contracts are not covered by Article III:8(a) of the GATT 1994 and that, consequently, the Panel's conclusion, in paragraph 8.2 of the Japan Panel Report, that the Minimum Required Domestic Content Levels prescribed under the FIT Programme and related FIT and microFIT Contracts are inconsistent with Article 2.1 of the TRIMS Agreement and Article III:4 of the GATT 1994, *stands*;

c. *rejects* Japan's claim that the Panel failed to fulfil its obligations under Article 11 of the DSU and exercised false judicial economy by declining to make a finding on Japan's stand-alone claim under Article III:4 of the GATT 1994;

d. as regards Article 1.1(a) of the SCM Agreement:

i. *declares moot and of no legal effect* the Panel's finding, in paragraph 7.246 of the Japan Panel Report, that "government 'purchases [of] goods' could [not] also be legally characterized as 'direct transfer[s] of funds' without infringing [the] principle [of effective treaty interpretation]", inasmuch as it negates the possibility that a transaction may fall under more than one type of financial contribution under Article 1.1(a)(1) of the SCM Agreement;

ii. *upholds* the Panel's finding, in paragraphs 7.243 and 7.328(i) of the Japan Panel Report, that the FIT Programme and related FIT and microFIT Contracts are government "purchases [of] goods" within the meaning of Article 1.1(a)(1)(iii) of the SCM Agreement;

iii. *rejects* Japan's appeal that the FIT Programme and FIT and microFIT Contracts may also be characterized as "direct transfer[s] of funds" or "potential direct transfers of funds" under Article 1.1(a)(1)(i) of the SCM Agreement;

iv. *rejects* Japan's claim that the Panel failed to fulfil its obligations under Article 11 of the DSU and exercised false judicial economy by declining to make a finding on Japan's claim that the measures at issue constitute "income or price support" under Article 1.1(a)(2) of the SCM Agreement; and

v. *declines* to make a finding on whether the FIT Programme and Contracts may be characterized as "income or price support" under Article 1.1(a)(2) of the SCM Agreement; and

e. as regards Article 1.1(b) of the SCM Agreement:

i. *reverses* the Panel's finding, in paragraphs 7.328(ii) and 8.3 of the Japan Panel Report, that Japan failed to establish that the challenged measures confer a benefit within the meaning of Article 1.1(b) of the SCM Agreement and thereby that Canada acted inconsistently with Articles 3.1(b) and 3.2 of the SCM Agreement;

ii. in the light of these findings, *does not find it necessary to address* Japan's alternative claim that the Panel acted inconsistently with Article 11 of the DSU; and

iii. *is unable to complete the analysis* as to whether the challenged measures confer a benefit within the meaning of Article 1.1(b) of the SCM Agreement and whether Canada acted inconsistently with Articles 3.1(b) and 3.2 of the SCM Agreement.

6.2 The Appellate Body recommends that the DSB request Canada to bring its measures found in this Report, and in the Japan Panel Report as modified by this Report, to be inconsistent with the TRIMs Agreement and the GATT 1994 into conformity with its obligations under those Agreements.

6. FINDINGS AND CONCLUSIONS IN THE APPELLATE BODY REPORT WT/DS426/AB/R

6.1. In the appeal of the Panel Report, *Canada – Measures Relating to the Feed-in Tariff Program* (WT/DS426/R) (EU Panel Report), for the reasons set out in this Report, the Appellate Body:

a. as regards Article III:8(a) of the GATT 1994:

   i. *upholds* the Panel's finding, in paragraph 7.121 of the EU Panel Report, that paragraph 1(a) of the Illustrative List in the Annex to the TRIMs Agreement did not obviate the need for the Panel to undertake an analysis of whether the challenged measures are outside of the scope of application of Article III:4 of the GATT 1994 by virtue of the operation of Article III:8(a) of the GATT 1994;

   ii. *reverses* the Panel's findings, in paragraphs 7.127, 7.128, and 7.152 of the EU Panel Report, that the Minimum Required Domestic Content Levels of the FIT Programme and related FIT and microFIT Contracts are laws, regulations, or requirements governing the procurement by governmental agencies of electricity within the meaning of Article III:8(a) of the GATT 1994;

   iii. *declares moot and of no legal effect* the other intermediate findings made by the Panel, in particular in paragraphs 7.136, 7.145, and 7.151;

   iv. *finds* that the Minimum Required Domestic Content Levels prescribed under the FIT Programme and related FIT and microFIT Contracts do not meet the conditions of the derogation in Article III:8(a) of the GATT 1994; and

   v. in the light of this finding, *does not find it necessary to address* Canada's claim that the Panel failed to fulfil its obligations under Article 11 of the DSU by exercising judicial economy; and

   vi. *finds* that the FIT Programme and related FIT and microFIT Contracts are not covered by Article III:8(a) of the GATT 1994 and that, consequently, the Panel's conclusion, in paragraph 8.6 of the EU Panel Report, that the Minimum Required Domestic Content Levels prescribed under the FIT Programme and related FIT and microFIT Contracts are inconsistent with Article 2.1 of the TRIMS Agreement and Article III:4 of the GATT 1994, *stands*; and

b. as regards Article 1.1(b) of the SCM Agreement:

i. *reverses* the Panel's finding, in paragraphs 7.328(ii) and 8.7 of the EU Panel Report, that the European Union failed to establish that the challenged measures confer a benefit within the meaning of Article 1.1(b) of the SCM Agreement and thereby that Canada acted inconsistently with Articles 3.1(b) and 3.2 of the SCM Agreement;

ii. in the light of these findings, *does not find it necessary to address* the European Union's alternative claim that the Panel acted inconsistently with Article 11 of the DSU; and

iii. *is unable to complete the analysis* as to whether the challenged measures confer a benefit within the meaning of Article 1.1(b) of the SCM Agreement and whether Canada acted inconsistently with Articles 3.1(b) and 3.2 of the SCM Agreement.

6.2. The Appellate Body recommends that the DSB request Canada to bring its measures found in this Report, and in the EU Panel Report as modified by this Report, to be inconsistent with the TRIMs Agreement and the GATT 1994 into conformity with its obligations under those Agreements.

ANNEX 1

WORLD TRADE ORGANIZATION

WT/DS412/10
WT/DS426/9

6 February 2013

(13-0616)

Page: 1/1

Original: English

CANADA – CERTAIN MEASURES AFFECTING THE RENEWABLE ENERGY GENERATION SECTOR

CANADA – MEASURES RELATING TO THE FEED-IN TARIFF PROGRAM

Notification of an Appeal by Canada under Article 16.4 and Article 17 of the Understanding on Rules and Procedures Governing the Settlement of Disputes (DSU), and under Rule 20(1) of the Working Procedures for Appellate Review

The following notification, dated 5 February 2013, from the Delegation of Canada, is being circulated to Members.

Pursuant to Article 16.4 and Article 17 of the *Understanding on Rules and Procedures Governing the Settlement of Disputes* (DSU) and Rule 20 of the *Working Procedures for Appellate Review*, Canada notifies its appeal of certain issues in the Reports of the Panel in *Canada – Certain Measures Affecting the Renewable Energy Generation Sector* (WT/DS412/R) and *Canada – Measures Relating to the Feed-In Tariff Program* (WT/DS426/R) and certain legal interpretations developed by the Panel in these Reports.

Canada seeks review by the Appellate Body of the Panel's findings and conclusion that the Government of Ontario's FIT Program, as implemented through the FIT and MicroFIT Contracts[1], is not covered by the terms of Article III:8(a) of GATT 1994.[2] This conclusion is in error and is based on erroneous findings on issues of law and legal interpretation including the Panel's finding that the Government of Ontario purchases renewable electricity "with a view to commercial resale".[3]

Canada also requests the Appellate Body to find that the Panel acted inconsistently with Article 11 of the DSU by failing to make an objective assessment of the facts related to this issue, specifically with respect to the Panel's finding that the resale of electricity purchased under the FIT Program is "commercial" in nature, and by using this faulty factual finding to support its conclusion about the applicability of Article III:8(a) of GATT 1994 to the FIT Program.[4]

Canada also requests the Appellate Body to find that the Panel failed to find that the Government of Ontario does not purchase renewable electricity "with a view to use in the production of goods for commercial sale".

---

1 For a summary of the measure at issue, see paras. 7.6 and 7.7 of the Panel Reports.

2 See e.g., para. 7.152 of the Panel Reports.

3 See e.g., paras. 7.147-7.151 of the Panel Reports.

4 *Ibid.*

ANNEX 2

WORLD TRADE ORGANIZATION

WT/DS412/11

15 February 2013

(13-0863)

Page: 1/3

Original: English

CANADA – CERTAIN MEASURES AFFECTING THE RENEWABLE ENERGY GENERATION SECTOR

Notification of an Other Appeal by Japan under Article 16.4 and Article 17 of the Understanding on Rules and Procedures Governing the Settlement of Disputes (DSU), and under Rule 23(1) of the Working Procedures for Appellate Review

The following notification, dated 11 February 2013, from the Delegation of Japan, is being circulated to Members.

Pursuant to Article 16.4 and Article 17 of the Understanding on Rules and Procedures Governing the Settlement of Disputes ("DSU") and Rule 23(1) of the Working Procedures for Appellate Review ("Working Procedures"), Japan hereby notifies its decision to appeal to the Appellate Body certain issues of law covered in the Panel Report in *Canada – Certain Measures Affecting the Renewable Energy Generation Sector* (WT/DS412/R) ("Panel Report"), and certain legal interpretations developed by the Panel in this dispute.

For the reasons to be elaborated in its submissions to the Appellate Body, Japan appeals the following errors of law and legal interpretation contained in the Panel Report, and requests the Appellate Body to reverse, modify, or declare moot and of no legal effect the related findings, conclusions and recommendations of the Panel, and where indicated to complete the analysis.[1]

1. With respect to Japan's claims under the Agreement on Subsidies and Countervailing Measures ("SCM Agreement"):

   a. The Panel erred in its interpretation and application of Article 1.1(a) of the SCM Agreement in concluding that the appropriate legal characterization of the FIT Program and Contracts[2] is "government ... purchases [of] goods".[3] Japan requests the Appellate Body to reverse the Panel's finding in this regard, and complete the analysis to find instead that the FIT Program and Contracts are appropriately characterized as "a government practice [that] involves a direct transfer of funds ... [or] potential direct transfers of funds" or "any form of income or price support" or alternatively modify the Panel's finding in this regard to find that these measures may also be characterized as "direct transfer[s] of funds", "potential direct transfer of funds", or "income or price support" under Article 1.1(a) of the SCM Agreement.

   b. The Panel erred in its interpretation and application of Article 1.1(a)(1) of the SCM Agreement by concluding that government "purchases [of] goods" under Article 1.1(a)(1)(iii) could not also be legally characterized as "direct transfer[s] of funds" or "potential direct transfers of funds" under Article 1.1(a)(1)(i).[4] Japan requests that the Appellate Body declare this finding to be moot and of no legal effect, and to find that the Government of Ontario provides financial contributions in the form of "direct transfer[s] of funds" or "potential direct transfers of funds" through the FIT Program and Contracts, regardless of whether they may be characterized as government "purchases [of] goods".

---

[1] Pursuant to Rule 23(2)(c)(ii)(C) of the Working Procedures, this Notice of Other Appeal includes an indicative list of the paragraphs of the Panel Report containing the alleged errors, without prejudice to the ability of Japan to refer to other paragraphs of the Panel Report in the context of its appeal.

[2] Throughout this Notice of Other Appeal, Japan uses the term "FIT Program and Contracts" to refer to the Government of Ontario's feed-in tariff program (including microFIT), and the FIT and microFIT contracts entered into by the Government of Ontario under that program, that are at issue in this dispute – i.e., the "challenged measures".

[3] Panel Report, paras. 7.220-7.249.

[4] Panel Report, paras. 6.83-6.85, 7.243-7.248, particularly paras. 7.246-7.247.

c. The Panel failed to make an objective assessment of the matter as required by Article 11 of the DSU by improperly exercising judicial economy, and failing to make findings with respect to Japan's claim that the FIT Program and Contracts may be legally characterized as "income or price support" under Article 1.1(a)(2) of the SCM Agreement.[5] Japan requests the Appellate Body to find that the Government of Ontario provides "income or price support" through the FIT Program and Contracts, regardless of whether they may be characterized as government "purchases [of] goods".

d. The Panel erred in its interpretation and application of Article 1.1(b) of the SCM Agreement, and failed to make an objective assessment of the matter as required by Article 11 of the DSU, when it found that it cannot resolve whether the challenged measures confer a benefit by applying a benchmark derived from the conditions for purchasing electricity in a competitive wholesale electricity market, particularly in disregarding Japan's argument that the challenged measures confer a benefit because the objective design, structure and operation of the FIT Program demonstrates that solar PV and wind generators would not be present in Ontario's wholesale electricity market absent the FIT Program.[6] Japan requests the Appellate Body to reverse these findings by the Panel and instead to find that the challenged measures confer a "benefit".

e. The Panel failed to make an objective assessment of the matter, including an objective assessment of the facts of the case, as required by Article 11 of the DSU, in failing to resolve the question of benefit under Article 1.1(b) of the SCM Agreement based on its preferred comparison between the relevant rates of return of the challenged FIT and microFIT Contracts with the relevant average cost of capital in Canada.[7] Japan requests the Appellate Body to complete the analysis, and find that the FIT Program and Contracts confer a benefit under the Panel's preferred approach. However, this appeal is conditional on the Appellate Body rejecting Japan's argument that the challenged measures confer a benefit pursuant to item 1.d above.

---

[5] Panel Report, paras. 6.88, 7.249.

[6] Panel Report, paras. 6.94-6.95, 7.271-7.313, 7.315, 7.317, and 7.319-7.320, particularly paras. 7.308-7.313.

[7] Panel Report, paras. 7.322-7.327.

f. Should the Appellate Body find the FIT Program and Contracts to be a subsidy within the meaning of Article 1.1 of the SCM Agreement, Japan requests the Appellate Body to complete the analysis, and find the FIT Program and Contracts to be inconsistent with Articles 3.1(b) and 3.2 of the SCM Agreement.

g. In addition to its error in failing to find the FIT Program and Contracts to be prohibited subsidies, the Panel erred in failing to recommend, pursuant to Article 4.7 of the SCM Agreement, that Canada withdraw the subsidies without delay, by eliminating the domestic content requirement of the FIT Program and Contracts, and erred in failing to specify the time period within which the measures must be withdrawn. Accordingly, if the Appellate Body completes the analysis and makes the findings requested by Japan in item 1.f above, Japan further requests that the Appellate Body make the recommendation, and specify the time period within which the measure must be withdrawn, pursuant to Article 4.7 of the SCM Agreement.

2. With respect to Japan's claims under the General Agreement on Tariffs and Trade 1994 ("GATT 1994"):

a. The Panel failed to make an objective assessment of the matter as required by Article 11 of the DSU by exercising false judicial economy and failing to separately examine Japan's claims under Article III:4 of the GATT 1994.[8] Japan requests the Appellate Body to complete the analysis, and find that the FIT Program and Contracts are inconsistent with the terms of Article III:4 independent of the Panel's findings under the Agreement on Trade-Related Investment Measures ("TRIMs Agreement").

b. The Panel erred in its interpretation and application of Article III:8(a) of the GATT 1994 in the following respects:

i. The Panel erred when it found the FIT Program and Contracts to involve "procurement by governmental agencies of products purchased" under Article III:8(a) of the GATT 1994, based on its conclusion that these

[8] Panel Report, paras. 6.72, 7.155-7.167. *See also id.*, para. 7.70 ("in the section that follows we will simultaneously evaluate the merits of both of the complainants' claims under Article 2.1 of the TRIMs Agreement and Article III:4 of the GATT 1994").

measures are "government ... purchases [of] goods" under Article 1.1(a) of the SCM Agreement.[9]

ii. The Panel erred when it interpreted the term "governmental purposes" in isolation, rather than the entire term "purchased for governmental purposes", and failed to separately assess whether purchases under the FIT Program and Contracts were "for" governmental purposes.[10] Japan requests the Appellate Body to complete the analysis, and find that the FIT Program and Contracts are not "purchase[s] [by governmental agencies] for governmental purposes". However, this appeal is conditional on the Appellate Body rejecting Japan's argument pursuant to item 2.b.i above.

iii. The Panel erred when it found evidence of profit earned by the Government of Ontario and Ontario's municipal governments may be a relevant consideration in determining that the FIT Program is undertaken "with a view to commercial resale".[11] In this regard, Japan seeks only modification of the Panel's findings to conclude that the Government of Ontario's procurement of electricity under the FIT Program and Contracts is undertaken "with a view to commercial resale" by virtue of the fact that the electricity "is resold to retail consumers through Hydro One and the LDCs"[12], without regard to whether those entities make profits. However, this appeal is conditional on the Appellate Body rejecting Japan's arguments pursuant to items 2.b.i and 2.b.ii above.

---

9 Panel Report, paras. 7.129-7.136, particularly paras. 7.135-7.136.

10 Panel Report, paras. 7.138-7.145, particularly paras. 7.140, 7.144-7.145.

11 Panel Report, paras. 7.146-7.151, particularly paras. 7.149-7.151.

12 Panel Report, para. 7.147.

ANNEX 3

WORLD TRADE ORGANIZATION

WT/DS426/10

15 February 2013

(13-0866)

Page: 1/3

Original: English

CANADA – MEASURES RELATING TO THE FEED-IN TARIFF PROGRAM

Notification of an Other Appeal by the European Union under Article 16.4 and Article 17 of the Understanding on Rules and Procedures Governing the Settlement of Disputes (DSU), and under Rule 23(1) of the Working Procedures for Appellate Review

The following notification, dated 11 February 2013, from the Delegation of the European Union, is being circulated to Members.

Pursuant to Article 16.4 and Article 17.1 of the *DSU* the European Union hereby notifies to the Dispute Settlement Body its decision to appeal to the Appellate Body certain issues of law covered in the Panel Report and certain legal interpretations developed by the Panel in the dispute *Canada – Measures Relating to the Feed-In Tariff Program* (WT/DS426). Pursuant to Rule 23(1) of the *Working Procedures for Appellate Review*, the European Union simultaneously files this Notice of Other Appeal with the Appellate Body Secretariat.

For the reasons to be further elaborated in its submissions to the Appellate Body, the European Union appeals, and requests the Appellate Body to modify, reverse and/or declare moot and with no legal effect the findings and conclusions of the Panel and complete the analysis with respect to the following errors of law and legal interpretations contained in the Panel Report.[1]

- The European Union submits that the Panel erred in the interpretation and application of Articles 2.1 and 2.2 of the TRIMs Agreement read in conjunction with Paragraph 1(a) of the Illustrative List in the Annex to the TRIMs Agreement when finding that they do not preclude the application of Article III:8(a) of the GATT 1994 to the challenged measures.[2]
- The European Union requests the Appellate Body to reverse the Panel's finding in paragraph 7.121, complete the analysis and find that Article III:8(a) of the GATT 1994 was not applicable in the present case. As a consequence, the European Union requests the Appellate Body to uphold, although modifying the reasoning, the Panel's ultimate finding in paragraph 7.166 that the challenged measures are TRIMs falling within the scope of Paragraph 1(a) of the Illustrative List, and that in the light of Article 2.2 and the chapeau to Paragraph 1(a) of the Illustrative List, they are inconsistent with Article III:4 of the GATT 1994, and thereby also inconsistent with Article 2.1 of the TRIMs Agreement.
- The Panel erred in its interpretation and application of Article III:8(a) of the GATT 1994 when finding that that the "Minimum Required Domestic Content Level" contained in the FIT Programme should be properly characterised as one of the "requirements governing" the alleged procurement of electricity for the purpose of Article III:8(a) of the GATT 1994.[3]
- The European Union requests the Appellate Body to reverse such finding, complete the analysis and find instead that the "Minimum Required Domestic Content Level" are not "requirements governing the procurement ... of the products purchased" in the present case. As a consequence of the Appellate Body's reversal of the Panel's finding in paragraph 7.128, the European Union requests the Appellate Body to reverse the Panel's finding in paragraph 7.152 that "(ii) the "Minimum Required Domestic Content Level" prescribed under the FIT Programme, and effected through the FIT and microFIT Contracts, is one of the "requirements governing" the Government of Ontario's "procurement" of electricity", and find

---

[1] Pursuant to Rule 23(2)(c)(ii)(C) of the Working Procedures for Appellate Review this Notice of Other Appeal includes an indicative list of the paragraphs of the Panel Report containing the alleged errors, without prejudice to the ability of the European Union to refer to other paragraphs of the Panel Report in the context of its appeal.

[2] Panel Report, paras. 7.114-7.121, and in particular, paras. 7.119 and 7.120.

[3] Panel Report, paras. 7.126-7.128, and 7.152.

instead that the "Minimum Required Domestic Content Level" does not constitute "requirements governing the procurement ... of the products purchased" in the present case.

- The Panel erred in its interpretation of Article III:8(a) of the GATT 1994 when stating that the ordinary meaning of the terms "governmental purposes" is relatively broad and may encompass the meaning proposed by Canada, i.e., that a purchase for "governmental purposes" may exist whenever a government purchases a product for a stated aim of the government.[4] The European Union requests the Appellate Body to reverse this statement or, at the very least, to declare it moot and with no legal effect. In addition, should the Appellate Body reverse the Panel's finding that the Government of Ontario's procurement of electricity under the FIT Programme is undertaken "with a view to commercial resale",[5] the European Union requests the Appellate Body to modify and/or reverse the Panel's reasoning[6] as to the meaning of "governmental purposes" in view of the arguments raised by the European Union as to the proper interpretation of those terms, complete the analysis and find that the Government of Ontario's procurement of electricity under the FIT Programme is not undertaken for "governmental purposes". As a consequence, the Panel's findings in paragraph 7.152 should also be amended accordingly to reflect another reason why Canada could not rely on Article III:8(a) of the GATT 1994 to exclude the application of Article III:4 of the GATT 1994 to the "Minimum Required Domestic Content Level".
- The Panel erred in its application of Article 1.1(b) of the SCM Agreement as well as did not make an objective assessment of the matter in accordance with Article 11 of the DSU when finding that the European Union had failed to established that the FIT Programme and its related contracts confer a "benefit" under Article 1.1(b) of the SCM Agreement.[7] In particular:

  (a) the Panel erred in the application of Article 1.1(b) of the SCM Agreement to the facts of this case.[8] The "prevailing market conditions" in Ontario, as evidenced by the purpose of the FIT Programme, showed that the FIT generators would not be

---

4 Panel Report, para. 7.139, first sentence (and the follow-up statement in para. 7.140, second sentence).

5 Panel Report, para. 7.151.

6 Panel Report, paras. 7.138-7.145.

7 Panel Report, para. 7.328(ii).

8 Panel Report, paras. 7.276-7.327.

able to obtain the necessary remuneration to be present in such marketplace;

(b) the Panel did not make an objective assessment of the matter in accordance with Article 11 of the DSU by failing to consider the totality of the evidence, by providing incoherent reasoning and exercising false judicial economy, when finding that, even on the basis of a hypothetical "market" counterfactual as the one suggested in its observations, the European Union had failed to establish the existence of "benefit".[9]

In view of these errors, the European Union requests the Appellate Body to *reverse* the Panel's finding in paragraph 7.328(ii) that the European Union failed to establish the existence of benefit in the present case, that the challenged measures conferred a "benefit" under Article 1.1(b) of the SCM Agreement, *complete the analysis* on the basis of the Panel's findings and uncontested facts on the record, and *find* that the challenged measures conferred a "benefit" under Article 1.1(b) of the SCM Agreement. As a consequence, the Panel's ultimate conclusion that the European Union had failed to establish that the FIT Programme and its related contracts constitute subsidies or envisage the granting of subsidies inconsistent with Articles 3.1(b) and 3.2 of the SCM Agreement is also in error.[10] The European Union requests the Appellate Body to also *reverse* such a conclusion, *complete the analysis* on the basis of the Panel's findings and uncontested facts on the record, and *find* that the challenged measures amount to subsidies prohibited under Articles 3.1(b) and 3.2. Accordingly, the European Union requests the Appellate Body to *recommend* that Canada withdraws its prohibited subsidies without delay (and, in no case, no more than within 90 days), as required by Article 4.7 of the SCM Agreement. Should the Appellate Body be unable to complete the analysis under any of the requests made by the European Union, the European Union requests the Appellate Body to declare *moot and with no legal effect* the Panel's findings and conclusions in paragraphs 7.328(ii) and 8.7.[11]

---

[9] Panel Report, paras. 7.322-7.328(ii).

[10] Panel Report, para. 8.7.

[11] The European Union observes that on 11 February 2013 Japan appealed the panel report in Canada – Certain Measures Affecting the Renewable Energy Generation Sector (WT/DS412). That report contains identical findings and conclusions as those contained in para. 7.328(ii) and para. 8.7 in the Panel Report in DS426. The European Union incorporates hereto Japan's Notice of Other Appeal dated 11 February 2013 with respect to the errors of law and legal interpretations, including any request for completing the analysis, made in connection with para. 7.328(ii) of the panel report in DS412.

ANNEX 4

ORGANISATION MONDIALE DU COMMERCE **ORGANIZACIÓN MUNDIAL DEL COMERCIO**

WORLD TRADE ORGANIZATION

Appellate Body

Canada – Certain Measures Affecting the Renewable Energy Generation Sector
Canada – Measures Relating to the Feed-in Tariff Program

AB-2013-1

Procedural Ruling

1. On 12 February 2013, we received letters from Canada, Japan, and the European Union requesting that the Appellate Body Division hearing the above appeal allow observation by the public of the oral hearing in these appellate proceedings.

2. Specifically, Canada requested that the Division allow public observation of the oral statements and answers to questions of the participants, as well as those of third participants that agree to make their statements and responses to questions public. Canada proposed that public observation be permitted via simultaneous closed-circuit television broadcasting with the option for the transmission to be turned off should the participants find it necessary to discuss confidential information, or if a third participant has indicated its wish to keep its oral statement confidential.

3. In its letter, Japan supported Canada's request, indicating that it also wished to make public its statements and answers to questions by the Division in the course of the Appellate Body hearing, and that it agreed with Canada's request that the Division hold an open hearing in this appeal. Japan further agreed that public observation be allowed by means of simultaneous closed-circuit video broadcasting. For its part, the European Union stated that it agreed and associated itself with Canada's request for an open hearing. The

participants referred to the rulings by the Appellate Body in nine previous proceedings authorizing public observation of the oral hearing.[1]

4. On 13 February 2013, we invited the third parties to comment in writing on the requests of the participants. On 18 February 2013, we received responses from Australia, Brazil, China, El Salvador, India, Mexico, Norway, the Kingdom of Saudi Arabia, Turkey, and the United States. No comments were received from Honduras, Korea, or the Separate Customs Territory of Taiwan, Penghu, Kinmen and Matsu. In their respective comments, Brazil, China, India, Mexico, and Turkey stated that they do not object to allowing public observation of the oral hearing in these disputes, but emphasized that this is without prejudice to the systemic views each has on the issue of public observation of panel and Appellate Body hearings. India and China stated that they wished to keep their oral statements and responses to questions confidential. The Kingdom of Saudi Arabia stated that it does not object to allowing public observation of the oral hearing in these disputes, but also exercised its right to keep its oral statement and responses to questions confidential. El Salvador stated that it does not object to allowing public observation of the oral hearing in these disputes, based on the conditions and modalities set out in Canada's request.

5. Norway and Australia stated their support for the participants' request to allow public observation of the oral hearing, including their statements and answers to questions as third participants. The United States supported the participants' request to allow public observation of the oral hearing, arguing that opening hearings to public observation serves to strengthen the legitimacy of the

---

[1] These proceedings are:

- *United States / Canada – Continued Suspension of Obligations in the EC – Hormones Dispute* (WT/DS320/AB/R / WT/DS321/AB/R);
- *European Communities – Regime for the Importation, Sale and Distribution of Bananas – Second Recourse to Article 21.5 of the DSU by Ecuador* (WT/DS27/AB/RW2/ECU) and *Recourse to Article 21.5 of the DSU by the United States* (WT/DS27/AB/RW/USA);
- *United States – Continued Existence and Application of Zeroing Methodology* (WT/DS350/AB/R);
- *United States – Laws, Regulations and Methodology for Calculating Dumping Margins ("Zeroing") – Recourse to Article 21.5 of the DSU by the European Communities* (WT/DS294/AB/RW);
- *United States – Measures Relating to Zeroing and Sunset Reviews – Recourse to Article 21.5 of the DSU by Japan* (WT/DS322/AB/RW);
- *Australia – Measures Affecting the Importation of Apples from New Zealand* (WT/DS367/AB/R);
- *European Communities and Certain Member States – Measures Affecting Trade in Large Civil Aircraft* (WT/DS316/AB/R);
- *United States – Measures Affecting Trade in Large Civil Aircraft (Second Complaint)* (WT/DS353/AB/R); and
- *United States – Certain Country of Origin Labelling Requirement* (WT/DS384/AB/R / WT/DS386/AB/R).

WTO dispute settlement system and that increased confidence in the dispute settlement process can translate into a great acceptance of the outcome of a dispute settlement proceeding. It further noted that past experience in holding open Appellate Body hearings has been positive. The United States confirmed that, should the Appellate Body authorize public observation of the oral hearing in this appeal, the United States would make its oral statement and answers to questions open to observation by the public.

6. We recall that requests to allow public observation of the oral hearing have been made, and have been authorized, in nine previous appellate proceedings.[2] In its rulings, the Appellate Body has held that it may authorize such requests by the participants, provided that this does not affect the confidentiality in the relationship between the third participants and the Appellate Body, or impair the integrity of the appellate process. We consider that the reasons previously expressed by the Appellate Body, and its interpretation of Article 17.10 of the Understanding on Rules and Procedures Governing the Settlement of Disputes (DSU) in this regard, apply equally to the circumstances prevailing in these appellate proceedings.

7. In this appeal, the participants have suggested that the Appellate Body allow observation by the public of the oral hearing by means of simultaneous closed-circuit television broadcasting. They have further suggested that provision be made for the transmission to be turned off should the participants find it necessary to discuss confidential information or if a third participant should wish to keep its oral statement or responses to questions confidential. We agree that such modalities would operate to protect confidential information in the context of a hearing that is open to public observation, and would not have an adverse impact on the integrity of the adjudicative function performed by the Appellate Body. We also consider that, during public observation in previous appeals, the rights of those third participants that did not wish to have their oral statements made subject to public observation were fully protected.

8. For these reasons, the Appellate Body Division in these appellate proceedings authorizes the public observation of the oral hearing on the terms set out below. Accordingly, pursuant to Rule 16(1) of the Working Procedures for Appellate Review, we adopt the following additional procedures for the purpose of this appeal:

---

[2] See fn 1.

a. The oral hearing will be open to public observation by means of simultaneous closed-circuit television broadcast, shown in a separate room to which duly registered delegates of WTO Members and members of the general public will have access.

b. Oral statements and responses to questions by the third participants that have indicated their wish to maintain the confidentiality of their submissions will not be subject to public observation.

c. Any request by a third participant – that has not already done so – wishing to maintain the confidentiality of its oral statements and responses to questions should be received by the Appellate Body Secretariat *no later than 17:00 Geneva time on Thursday, 7 March 2013*.

d. An appropriate number of seats will be reserved for delegates of WTO Members in the room where the closed-circuit television broadcast will be shown. WTO delegates wishing to observe the oral hearing are requested to register in advance with the Appellate Body Secretariat.

e. Notice of the oral hearing will be provided to the general public on the WTO website. Members of the general public wishing to observe the oral hearing will be required to register in advance with the Appellate Body Secretariat, in accordance with the instructions set out in the WTO website notice.

Geneva, 19 February 2013

CANADA - CERTAIN MEASURES AFFECTING THE RENEWABLE ENERGY GENERATION SECTOR /

CANADA - MEASURES RELATING TO THE FEED-IN TARIFF PROGRAM

Reports of the Panel

WT/DS412/R and Add.1, WT/DS426/R and Add.1*

Adopted by the Dispute Settlement Body
on 24 May 2013
*as Modified by the Appellate Body Reports***

TABLE OF CONTENTS

* The Annexes of this report can be found in DSR 2013:II.

** Note by the Secretariat:
The Panels issue these Reports in the form of a single document constituting two separate Panel Reports: WT/DS412/R and WT/DS426/R. Each Panel Report relates to one of the two complaints in these disputes. The cover page, preliminary pages, Sections I through VII, Section IX and the Annexes are common to both Panel Reports. The page header throughout the document bears two document symbols, WT/DS412/R and WT/DS426/R, with the following exceptions: Section VIII on page JPN-429, which bears the document symbol for and contains the Panel's conclusions and recommendations in the Panel Report WT/DS412/R; and Section VIII on page EU-429, which bears the document symbol for and contains the Panel's conclusions and recommendations in the Panel Report WT/DS426/R.

LIST OF ANNEXES

ANNEX A

FIRST AND SECOND WRITTEN SUBMISSIONS OF THE PARTIES, RESPONSES TO QUESTIONS AND ORAL STATEMENTS OF THE PARTIES AT THE FIRST AND SECOND SUBSTANTIVE MEETINGS OF THE PANEL

Contents	
Annex A-1	Integrated Executive Summary of Japan
Annex A-2	Integrated Executive Summary of the European Union
Annex A-3	Integrated Executive Summary of Canada

ANNEX B

WRITTEN SUBMISSIONS AND ORAL STATEMENTS OF THE THIRD PARTIES

Contents	
Annex B-1	Integrated Executive Summary of Australia
Annex B-2	Integrated Executive Summary of Brazil
Annex B-3	Integrated Executive Summary of China
Annex B-4	Integrated Executive Summary of El Salvador
Annex B-5	Integrated Executive Summary of the European Union (in WT/DS412)
Annex B-6	Integrated Executive Summary of Japan (in WT/DS426)
Annex B-7	Integrated Executive Summary of Korea
Annex B-8	Integrated Executive Summary of Mexico
Annex B-9	Norway's Third-Party Statement
Annex B-10	Integrated Executive Summary of Saudi Arabia, Kingdom of
Annex B-11	Integrated Executive Summary of the United States

ANNEX C

REQUESTS FOR THE ESTABLISHMENT OF A PANEL

Contents	
Annex C-1	Request for the Establishment of a Panel by Japan
Annex C-2	Request for the Establishment of a Panel by the European Union

TABLE OF CASES CITED IN THESE REPORTS

Short Title	Full Case Title and Citation
Canada – Aircraft	Appellate Body Report, *Canada – Measures Affecting the Export of Civilian Aircraft*, WT/DS70/AB/R, adopted 20 August 1999, DSR 1999:III, 1377
Canada – Autos	Appellate Body Report, *Canada – Certain Measures Affecting the Automotive Industry*, WT/DS139/AB/R, WT/DS142/AB/R, adopted 19 June 2000, DSR 2000:VI, 2985
Canada – Dairy	Appellate Body Report, *Canada – Measures Affecting the Importation of Milk and the Exportation of Dairy Products*, WT/DS103/AB/R, WT/DS113/AB/R and Corr.1, adopted 27 October 1999, DSR 1999:V, 2057
China – Auto Parts	Appellate Body Reports, *China – Measures Affecting Imports of Automobile Parts*, WT/DS339/AB/R / WT/DS340/AB/R / WT/DS342/AB/R, adopted 12 January 2009, DSR 2009:I, 3
China – Raw Materials	Appellate Body Reports, *China – Measures Related to the Exportation of Various Raw Materials*, WT/DS394/AB/R / WT/DS395/AB/R / WT/DS398/AB/R, adopted 22 February 2012
EC – Bananas III	Appellate Body Report, *European Communities – Regime for the Importation, Sale and Distribution of Bananas*, WT/DS27/AB/R, adopted 25 September 1997, DSR 1997:II, 591
EC – Hormones	Appellate Body Report, *EC Measures Concerning Meat and Meat Products (Hormones)*, WT/DS26/AB/R, WT/DS48/AB/R, adopted 13 February 1998, DSR 1998:I, 135

Short Title	Full Case Title and Citation
EC – Salmon (Norway)	Panel Report, *European Communities – Anti-Dumping Measure on Farmed Salmon from Norway*, WT/DS337/R, adopted 15 January 2008, and Corr.1, DSR 2008:I, 3
EC – Sardines	Appellate Body Report, *European Communities – Trade Description of Sardines*, WT/DS231/AB/R, adopted 23 October 2002, DSR 2002:VIII, 3359
EC – Selected Customs Matters	Panel Report, *European Communities – Selected Customs Matters*, WT/DS315/R, adopted 11 December 2006, as modified by Appellate Body Report WT/DS315/AB/R, DSR 2006:IX-X, 3915
EC and certain member States – Large Civil Aircraft	Appellate Body Report, *European Communities and Certain Member States – Measures Affecting Trade in Large Civil Aircraft*, WT/DS316/AB/R, adopted 1 June 2011
India – Patents (US)	Appellate Body Report, *India – Patent Protection for Pharmaceutical and Agricultural Chemical Products*, WT/DS50/AB/R, adopted 16 January 1998, DSR 1998:I, 9
Indonesia – Autos	Panel Report, *Indonesia – Certain Measures Affecting the Automobile Industry*, WT/DS54/R, WT/DS55/R, WT/DS59/R, WT/DS64/R and Corr.1 and 2, adopted 23 July 1998, and Corr. 3 and 4, DSR 1998:VI, 2201
Japan – Agricultural Products II	Appellate Body Report, *Japan – Measures Affecting Agricultural Products*, WT/DS76/AB/R, adopted 19 March 1999, DSR 1999:I, 277
Japan – Alcoholic Beverages II	Appellate Body Report, *Japan – Taxes on Alcoholic Beverages*, WT/DS8/AB/R, WT/DS10/AB/R, WT/DS11/AB/R, adopted 1 November 1996, DSR 1996:I, 97
Japan – DRAMs (Korea)	Appellate Body Report, *Japan – Countervailing Duties on Dynamic Random Access Memories from Korea*, WT/DS336/AB/R and Corr.1, adopted 17 December 2007, DSR 2007:VII, 2703

Short Title	Full Case Title and Citation
Korea – Various Measures on Beef	Panel Report, *Korea – Measures Affecting Imports of Fresh, Chilled and Frozen Beef*, WT/DS161/R, WT/DS169/R, adopted 10 January 2001, as modified by Appellate Body Report WT/DS161/AB/R, WT/DS169/AB/R, DSR 2001:I, 59
Thailand – Cigarettes (Philippines)	Panel Report, *Thailand – Customs and Fiscal Measures on Cigarettes from the Philippines*, WT/DS371/R, adopted 15 July 2011, as modified by Appellate Body Report WT/DS371/AB/R
US – Anti-Dumping and Countervailing Duties (China)	Appellate Body Report, *United States – Definitive Anti-Dumping and Countervailing Duties on Certain Products from China*, WT/DS379/AB/R, adopted 25 March 2011
US – Anti-Dumping and Countervailing Duties (China)	Panel Report, *United States – Definitive Anti-Dumping and Countervailing Duties on Certain Products from China*, WT/DS379/R, adopted 25 March 2011, as modified by Appellate Body Report WT/DS379/AB/R
US – COOL	Panel Reports, *United States – Certain Country of Origin Labelling (COOL) Requirements*, WT/DS384/R / WT/DS386/R, adopted 23 July 2012, as modified by Appellate Body Reports WT/DS384/AB/R / WT/DS386/AB/R
US – FSC	Appellate Body Report, *United States – Tax Treatment for "Foreign Sales Corporations"*, WT/DS108/AB/R, adopted 20 March 2000, DSR 2000:III, 1619
US – FSC	Panel Report, *United States – Tax Treatment for "Foreign Sales Corporations"*, WT/DS108/R, adopted 20 March 2000, as modified by Appellate Body Report WT/DS108/AB/R, DSR 2000:IV, 1675
US – FSC (Article 21.5 – EC)	Appellate Body Report, *United States – Tax Treatment for "Foreign Sales Corporations" – Recourse to Article 21.5 of the DSU by the European Communities*, WT/DS108/AB/RW, adopted 29 January 2002, DSR 2002:I, 55

Short Title	Full Case Title and Citation
US – FSC (Article 21.5 – EC)	Panel Report, *United States – Tax Treatment for "Foreign Sales Corporations" – Recourse to Article 21.5 of the DSU by the European Communities*, WT/DS108/RW, adopted 29 January 2002, as modified by Appellate Body Report WT/DS108/AB/RW, DSR 2002:I, 119
US – Gasoline	Appellate Body Report, *United States – Standards for Reformulated and Conventional Gasoline*, WT/DS2/AB/R, adopted 20 May 1996, DSR 1996:I, 3
US – Large Civil Aircraft (2nd complaint)	Appellate Body Report, *United States – Measures Affecting Trade in Large Civil Aircraft (Second Complaint)*, WT/DS353/AB/R, adopted 23 March 2012
US – Large Civil Aircraft (2nd complaint)	Panel Report, *United States – Measures Affecting Trade in Large Civil Aircraft (Second Complaint)*, WT/DS353/R, adopted 23 March 2012, as modified by Appellate Body Report WT/DS353/AB/R
US – Softwood Lumber IV	Appellate Body Report, *United States – Final Countervailing Duty Determination with Respect to Certain Softwood Lumber from Canada*, WT/DS257/AB/R, adopted 17 February 2004, DSR 2004:II, 571
US – Softwood Lumber IV	Panel Report, *United States – Final Countervailing Duty Determination with Respect to Certain Softwood Lumber from Canada*, WT/DS257/R and Corr.1, adopted 17 February 2004, as modified by Appellate Body Report WT/DS257/AB/R, DSR 2004:II, 641
US – Tuna II (Mexico)	Panel Report, *United States – Measures Concerning the Importation, Marketing and Sale of Tuna and Tuna Products*, WT/DS381/R, adopted 13 June 2012, as modified by Appellate Body Report WT/DS381/AB/R
US – Upland Cotton	Appellate Body Report, *United States – Subsidies on Upland Cotton*, WT/DS267/AB/R, adopted 21 March 2005, DSR 2005:I, 3
US – Upland Cotton	Panel Report, *United States – Subsidies on Upland Cotton*, WT/DS267/R, Corr.1, and Add.1 to Add.3, adopted 21 March 2005, as modified by Appellate Body Report WT/DS267/AB/R, DSR 2005:II, 299

Short Title	Full Case Title and Citation
US – Wool Shirts and Blouses	Appellate Body Report, *United States – Measure Affecting Imports of Woven Wool Shirts and Blouses from India*, WT/DS33/AB/R, adopted 23 May 1997, and Corr.1, DSR 1997:I, 323
US – Zeroing (EC)	Panel Report, *United States – Laws, Regulations and Methodology for Calculating Dumping Margins ("Zeroing")*, WT/DS294/R, adopted 9 May 2006, as modified by Appellate Body Report WT/DS294/AB/R, DSR 2006:II, 521

GATT PANEL REPORTS

Short Title	Full Case Title and Citation
US – Sonar Mapping	GATT Panel Report, *United States – Procurement of a Sonar Mapping System*, GPR.DS1/R, 23 April 1992, unadopted

TABLE OF ABBREVIATIONS USED IN THESE REPORTS

Abbreviation	Full Reference
CAD	Canadian dollar
CES	Clean Energy Supply
CHP	Combined Heat and Power
DSB	Dispute Settlement Body
DSU	Understanding on Rules and Procedures Governing the Settlement of Disputes
ECSTF	Electricity Conservation and Supply Task Force
FIT	Feed-in tariff
GA	Global Adjustment
GATT 1994	General Agreement on Tariffs and Trade 1994
GPA	Agreement on Government Procurement
GWh	Gigawatt hour

Abbreviation	Full Reference
HCI	Hydroelectric Contract Initiative
HEPCO	Hydro-Electric Power Commission of Ontario
HOEP	Hourly Ontario Electricity Price
IESO	Independent Electricity System Operator
IPPs	Independent Power Producers
kV	Kilovolts
kWh	Kilowatt hour
LDC	Local distribution company
MCP	Market clearing price
MW	Megawatt
NUGs	Non-Utility Generators
OEB	Ontario Energy Board
OEFC	Ontario Electricity Financial Corporation
OPA	Ontario Power Authority
OPG	Ontario Power Generation
PV	Photovoltaic
RES	Renewable Energy Supply
RESOP	Renewable Energy Standard Offer Programme
RPP	Regulated Price Plan
SCM Agreement	Agreement on Subsidies and Countervailing Measures
TRIMs	Trade-related investment measures
TRIMs Agreement	Agreement on Trade-Related Investment Measures

I. INTRODUCTION

A. Complaints of Japan and the European Union

1.1 On 13 September 2010, Japan requested consultations with Canada pursuant to Article 4 of the Understanding on Rules and Procedures Governing the Settlement of Disputes (the "DSU"), Article XXII:1 of the General Agreement on Tariffs and Trade 1994 (the "GATT 1994"), Article 8 of the Agreement on Trade-Related Investment Measures (the "TRIMs Agreement"), and Articles 4.1 and 30 of the Agreement on Subsidies and Countervailing Measures (the "SCM Agreement")[1]. On 11 August 2011, the European Union requested consultations with Canada pursuant to the same, above-mentioned provisions[2]. In both complaints, the consultations concerned certain measures relating to domestic content requirements in the feed-in tariff programme (the "FIT Programme"), established by the Canadian Province of Ontario. These measures included the following: (i) the *Electricity Act of 1998*; (ii) the *Green Energy and Green Economy Act of 2009*; (iii) the *Electricity Restructuring Act of 2004*; (iv) the *Ontario Regulation 578/05*; (v) the Independent Electricity System Operator (the "IESO") Market Manual; (vi) the IESO Market Rules; (vii) the FIT direction dated 24 September 2009 from the Deputy Premier and Minister of Energy and Infrastructure; (viii) individual FIT and microFIT Contracts executed by the Ontario Power Authority (the "OPA"); (ix) the FIT Rules and microFIT Rules issued by the OPA; (x) the FIT and microFIT Contracts issued by the OPA; (xi) the FIT Application Form and the online microFIT Application issued by the OPA; (xii) the FIT and microFIT Price Schedules issued by the OPA; (xiii) the FIT Programme Interpretations of the Domestic Content Requirements; and (xiv) any amendments or extensions of the foregoing, any replacement, renewal, implementing or related measures[3].

1.2 Consultations were held between Japan and Canada on 25 October 2010, and between the European Union and Canada on 7 September 2011. These consultations failed to resolve the disputes.

1.3 Japan and the European Union each requested, respectively on 1 June 2011 and 9 January 2012, the establishment of a panel pursuant to Articles 4.7 and 6 of the DSU, Article XXIII of the GATT 1994, Article 8 of the TRIMs Agreement, and Articles 4.4 and 30 of the SCM Agreement[4].

---

1 WT/DS412/1.

2 WT/DS426/1 and WT/DS426/1/Add.1.

3 WT/DS412/1; WT/DS426/1 and WT/DS426/1/Add.1. Japan's request for consultations did not expressly refer to the *Ontario Regulation 578/05*, the IESO Market Manual and the IESO Market Rules. However, these measures were included in Japan's request for the establishment of a panel (WT/DS412/5).

4 WT/DS412/5 and WT/DS426/5.

B. Establishment and composition of the Panels

1.4 At its meetings on 20 July 2011 and 20 January 2012, the Dispute Settlement Body (the "DSB") established two Panels pursuant to, respectively, Japan's request in document WT/DS412/5, and the European Union's request in WT/DS426/5, in accordance with Article 6 of the DSU.

1.5 The terms of reference for the respective disputes are the following:

> To examine, in the light of the relevant provisions of the covered agreements cited by the parties to the dispute, the matter referred to the DSB by Japan in document WT/DS412/5 and to make such findings as will assist the DSB in making the recommendations or in giving the rulings provided for in those agreements.
>
> To examine, in the light of the relevant provisions of the covered agreements cited by the parties to the dispute, the matter referred to the DSB by the European Union in document WT/DS426/5 and to make such findings as will assist the DSB in making the recommendations or in giving the rulings provided for in those agreements.

1.6 On 26 September 2011, Japan requested the Director-General to determine the composition of the Panel in WT/DS412, pursuant to Article 8.7 of the DSU. On 6 October 2011, the Director-General composed the Panel as follows:

Chairperson: Mr Thomas Cottier

Members: Mr Alexander Erwin

Mr Daniel Moulis

1.7 With respect to WT/DS426, following the agreement of the parties, the Panel was composed with the same persons on 23 January 2012. Following consultations with the parties, the Panels in the two disputes decided to harmonize their timetables to the greatest extent possible, in accordance with Article 9.3 of the DSU[5].

1.8 Australia, Brazil, China, El Salvador, India, Korea, Mexico, Norway, the Kingdom of Saudi Arabia, Chinese Taipei, and the United States reserved their rights to participate in the Panel proceedings as third parties in both disputes. In addition, the European Union and Honduras reserved their rights to participate as third parties with respect to WT/DS412, and Japan and Turkey reserved their third party rights to participate in the Panel proceedings with respect to WT/DS426[6].

---

5 For the reader's convenience, the Panels in WT/DS412 and WT/DS426 are herein collectively referred to as the "Panel".

6 WT/DS412/6 and WT/DS426/6/Rev.1.

1.9 The Panel met with the parties to the disputes on 27-28 March 2012 and 15-16 May 2012, and with the third parties on 28 March 2012. At the request of the parties, the Panel's meetings with the parties were open to the public. A portion of the Panel's meeting with the third parties was also open to the public.

1.10 The Panel submitted its interim report to the parties on 20 September 2012 and submitted its final report to the parties on 16 November 2012.

C. Enhanced third-party rights

1.11 At Canada's request, and as accepted by Japan and the European Union, enhanced third-party rights were granted to all third parties. Third parties in both disputes had the right to: (i) attend the entirety of all substantive meetings between the parties and the Panel; and (ii) receive copies of the parties' written submissions made in advance of the issuance of the interim report to the parties, including first written submissions, written rebuttals, and responses to questions from the Panel at the time that they were submitted to the Panel[7].

D. Amicus curiae briefs

1.12 On 14 May 2012, the Panel received an unsolicited *amicus curiae* brief relating to both disputes from the following organizations: Blue Green Canada; the Canadian Auto Workers (CAW); the Communications, Energy and Paperworkers Union of Canada (CEP); the Canadian Federation of Students (CFS); the Council of Canadians; the Canadian Union of Public Employees (CUPE); and the Ontario Public Service Employees Union (OPSEU). On 15 May 2012, the Panel in WT/DS412 received a second unsolicited *amicus curiae* brief from the following organizations: the International Institute for Sustainable Development (IISD); the Canadian Environmental Law Association (CELA); and Ecojustice Canada.

1.13 During the second substantive meeting of the Panel with the parties, Japan, the European Union and Canada recalled that it is within the discretion of the Panel to accept or reject the unsolicited *amicus curiae* briefs[8]. Subsequently, and consistent with the approach taken by previous panels[9], the Panel informed the parties that it would take the briefs into account only to the extent the parties decided to incorporate them into their own submissions. Canada informed the Panel that it had no comments to add on this issue beyond what Canada had already stated at the second substantive meeting with the Panel, namely that it is within the discretion of the Panel to accept or reject the unsolicited *amicus curiae* briefs. Japan and the European Union (the "complainants") informed the

---

[7] Working Procedures for the Panel, paras. 14 and 18.

[8] Appellate Body Report, *US – Shrimp*, para. 108.

[9] Panel Reports, *US – COOL*, para. 2.10; *US – Tuna II (Mexico)*, para. 7.2; *Thailand – Cigarettes (Philippines)*, para. 2.5; *EC – Salmon (Norway)*, para. 1.13; *US – Zeroing (EC)*, para. 1.7; and *US – Softwood Lumber IV*, fn. 75.

Panel that they did not consider it necessary to incorporate any of the observations made in the *amicus curiae* briefs. In the light of the parties' views, the Panel did not find it necessary to take the briefs into account in its analysis of the claims and arguments made in these disputes.

E. Preliminary ruling on the Panels' terms of reference

1.14 On 4 November 2011, Canada submitted to the Panel in WT/DS412 a request for a preliminary ruling concerning the consistency of Japan's request for the establishment of a panel (WT/DS412/5) with Article 6.2 of the DSU. In particular, Canada argued that the claims made under the SCM Agreement described in Japan's request for the establishment of a panel failed to provide a "brief summary of the legal basis" that is "sufficient to present the problem clearly", and should therefore be struck out of the Panel's terms of reference[10]. On 17 November 2011, Japan responded to Canada's preliminary ruling request rejecting Canada's arguments. On 21 November 2011, the Panel announced to the parties that, without prejudice to any views that the Panel may develop on Canada's request during the course of the proceeding, it was not convinced of the merit of Canada's request at that time. On 14 February 2012, Canada submitted to the Panel in WT/DS426 a request for a preliminary ruling concerning the consistency of the European Union's request for the establishment of a panel (WT/DS426/5) with Article 6.2 of the DSU, on the basis of essentially the same arguments used to justify its request for a preliminary ruling in WT/DS412[11]. On 21 February 2012, the European Union responded to Canada's request for a preliminary ruling. The Panel announced its conclusions on the merits of Canada's requests for preliminary rulings at the opening session of the first substantive meeting with the parties on 27 March 2012. The Panel subsequently issued its preliminary rulings to the parties in written form on 11 May 2012. After consulting with the parties, the Panel decided: (a) to circulate its preliminary rulings to all Members; and (b) that the circulated preliminary rulings would form an integral part of the final Panel Reports, subject to any revisions necessary in the light of comments received from the parties during interim review. The Panel's preliminary rulings were circulated on 25 May 2012 in documents WT/DS412/8 and WT/DS426/7.

II. FACTUAL ASPECTS

2.1 These disputes concern the domestic content requirements attached to the FIT and microFIT Contracts, granted under the FIT Programme established by

---

[10] Canada's request for a preliminary ruling (DS412), paras. 2 and 25; and first written submission (DS412), paras. 102-113.

[11] Canada's letter to the Panel of 14 February 2012 (DS426); and first written submission (DS426), paras. 48-50.

the Canadian Province of Ontario, for certain wind and solar photovoltaic ("PV") electricity generation projects. The complainants challenge the WTO consistency of these specific measures:

(1) the FIT Programme, as evidenced by the following measures[12]:

i. the *Electricity Act of 1998*, as amended, including in particular Part II (Independent Electricity System Operator), Part II.1 (Ontario Power Authority) and Part II.2 (Management of Electricity Supply, Capacity and Demand) thereof, including in particular Section 25.35 (Feed-in tariff program);

ii. an Act to enact the Green Energy Act of 2009 and to build a green economy, to repeal the Energy Conservation Leadership Act of 2006 and the Energy Efficiency Act and to amend other statutes (the "Green Energy and Green Economy Act of 2009"), including in particular Schedule B amending the Electricity Act of 1998;

iii. an Act to amend the *Electricity Act of 1998* and the *Ontario Energy Board Act of 1998* and to make consequential amendments to other Acts (the "*Electricity Restructuring Act of 2004*"), including in particular Schedule A, Sections 29-32, enacting Part II.1 of the *Electricity Act of 1998*, and Sections 33-38, enacting Part II.2 of the *Electricity Act of 1998*, and Schedule B, Sections 17-18, enacting Sections 78.3-78.4 of the *Ontario Energy Board Act of 1998*;

iv. the *Ontario Regulation 578/05* made under the *Ontario Energy Board Act of 1998* entitled "Prescribed Contracts Re Sections 78.3 and 78.4 of the Act";

v. the Independent Electricity System Operator ("IESO") Market Manual, including in particular Part 5.5 (Physical Markets Settlement Statements);

vi. the IESO Market Rules, including in particular Chapter 7 (System Operations and Physical Markets), Chapter 9 (Settlements and Billing) and Chapter 11 (Definitions);

vii. the FIT direction dated 24 September 2009, from George Smitherman, Deputy Premier and Minister of Energy and Infrastructure, to Colin Andersen, Chief Executive Officer, OPA, directing OPA to develop a FIT Program and include a requirement that the applicant submit a plan for meeting the domestic (i.e. Ontario) content goals in the FIT rules;

---

12 WT/DS412/5 and WT/DS426/5.

viii. all versions of the FIT Rules, and the microFIT Rules, issued by the OPA since the inception of the FIT Programme;

ix. all versions of the FIT Contract, including General Terms and Conditions, Exhibits, and Standard Definitions; and the microFIT Contract, including Appendices, and the Conditional Offer of microFIT Contract, issued by the OPA since the inception of the FIT Programme;

x. all versions of the FIT Application Form, and online microFIT Application, issued by the OPA since the inception of the FIT Programme;

xi. all versions of the FIT Price Schedule, and the microFIT Price Schedule, issued by the OPA since the inception of the FIT Programme;

xii. all versions of the FIT Program Interpretations of the Domestic Content Requirements, issued by the OPA since the inception of the FIT Programme;

(2) the individual FIT Contracts for wind or solar PV sources, executed by the OPA since the inception of the FIT Programme; and

(3) the individual microFIT Contracts for solar PV source, executed by the OPA since the inception of the FIT Programme.

III. PARTIES' REQUESTS FOR FINDINGS AND RECOMMENDATIONS

A. Complainants

1. Japan

3.1 Japan requests the Panel to find that:

(a) through the FIT Programme, as well as individually executed FIT and microFIT Contracts for wind and solar PV projects, Canada grants and maintains prohibited subsidies that are contingent upon the use of domestic over imported goods, in violation of Articles 3.1(b) and 3.2 of the SCM Agreement;

(b) the domestic content requirement of the FIT Programme, as well as individually executed FIT and microFIT Contracts for wind and solar PV projects, accords less favourable treatment to Japanese renewable energy generation equipment than accorded to like products of Ontario origin, in violation of Article III:4 of the GATT 1994; and

(c) the FIT Programme, as well as individually executed FIT and microFIT Contracts for wind and solar PV projects, constitute trade-related investment measures inconsistent with the provisions of Article III of the GATT 1994, and are therefore in violation of Article 2.1 of the TRIMs Agreement.

3.2 Japan requests that the Panel recommend that Canada:

(a) withdraw its allegedly prohibited subsidies without delay, as required by Article 4.7 of the SCM Agreement, by eliminating the domestic content requirement of the FIT Programme, as well as that of individually executed FIT and microFIT Contracts for wind and solar PV projects; and

(b) bring the FIT Programme, as well as individually executed FIT and microFIT Contracts for wind and solar PV projects, into conformity with the GATT 1994 and the TRIMs Agreement, as required by Article 19.1 of the DSU.

3.3 Japan also requests that the Panel reject Canada's request for preliminary rulings with respect to any alleged failure on Japan's part to comply with Article 6.2 of the DSU.

2. *European Union*

3.4 The European Union requests the Panel to find that:

(a) Canada violates Articles 3.1(b) and 3.2 of the SCM Agreement since the FIT Programme and its related contracts established by the Government of Ontario are subsidies within the meaning of Article 1.1 of the SCM Agreement that are provided contingent upon the use of domestic over imported goods, namely contingent upon the use of equipment and components for renewable energy generation facilities produced in Ontario over such equipment and components imported from other WTO Members, including the European Union;

(b) Canada violates Article 2.1 of the TRIMs Agreement, in conjunction with Paragraph 1(a) of its Annex, because the FIT Programme and its related contracts established by the Government of Ontario are TRIMs that require the purchase or use by enterprises of equipment and components for renewable energy generation facilities of Ontario origin or source; and

(c) Canada violates Article III:4 of the GATT 1994 because the FIT Programme and its related contracts established by the Government of Ontario are TRIMs falling under Paragraph 1(a) of the Annex to the TRIMs Agreement and, in any event, because they impose domestic content requirements on wind and solar PV electricity generators that affect the internal sale, purchase or use of renewable energy generation equipment and components, according less favourable treatment to like products of European Union origin.

3.5 The European Union requests that the Panel recommend that Canada:

(a) withdraw its allegedly prohibited subsidies without delay (and, in no case, no more than within 90 days), as required by Article 4.7 of the SCM Agreement; and

(b) bring the FIT Programme and its related contracts into conformity with the covered agreements as required by Article 19.1 of the DSU.

3.6 The European Union also requests that the Panel reject Canada's request for preliminary rulings with respect to any alleged failure on the European Union's part to comply with Article 6.2 of the DSU.

B. Canada

3.7 Canada requests that the Panel reject the complainants' claims, finding instead that Canada has not acted inconsistently with Article III:4 of the GATT 1994 and Article 2.1 of the TRIMs Agreement. Canada also requests that the Panel find, by means of a preliminary ruling, that it does not have jurisdiction over the complainants' claims under the SCM Agreement or, in the alternative, that Canada has not acted inconsistently with Articles 3.1(b) and 3.2 of the SCM Agreement.

IV. ARGUMENTS OF THE PARTIES

4.1 The arguments of the parties, as set forth in the executive summaries of their submissions provided to the Panel, are attached to these Reports as annexes (see List of Annexes, page vi).

V. ARGUMENTS OF THE THIRD PARTIES

5.1 The arguments of the third parties, as set forth in the executive summaries of their submissions provided to the Panel, are attached to these Reports as annexes (see List of Annexes, page vi)[13].

VI. INTERIM REVIEW

A. Introduction

6.1 The Interim Reports in these disputes were issued to the parties on 20 September 2012. The parties submitted written requests for review of precise

[13] Australia, Brazil, China, El Salvador, the European Union (in WT/DS412), Japan (in WT/DS426), Korea, Mexico, Norway, the Kingdom of Saudi Arabia, and the United States provided written submissions and/or made oral statements at the meeting of the Panel with the third parties.

aspects of the Interim Reports on 4 October 2012. Written comments on the written requests were submitted by the parties on 17 October 2012. None of the parties requested an additional meeting with the Panel.

6.2 The Panel's response to issues of a substantive nature raised by the parties in their requests and comments on the Interim Reports is set out below following the organization of the reports themselves, with the parties' requests for review and comments addressed sequentially. Due to changes made as a result of our review, the numbering of paragraphs and footnotes in the Final Reports has changed from the Interim Reports. The text below refers to the paragraph and footnote numbers in the Interim Reports, with the corresponding paragraph or footnote numbers in the Final Reports (if different) in parentheses for ease of reference.

6.3 In addition to the modifications made as a result of the interim review requests that are discussed below, we have corrected a number of typographical errors and made other non-substantive changes (including in relation to misdescriptions of facts and arguments identified by the parties) throughout the Final Reports.

B. Parties' requests for changes to the interim reports and Panels' evaluation

1. Paragraph 2.1

6.4 The European Union requests that the Panel add a footnote the first time the "FIT Programme" is cited in paragraph 2.1 to clarify that the references to the FIT Programme also include the "microFIT Programme". Canada has not commented on this request.

6.5 The Panel has decided not to accommodate the European Union's request. Paragraph 2.1 reflects the requests for establishment of a panel by Japan and by the European Union, and no reference to a "microFIT Programme" was made. In addition, it is clear from paragraph 2.1 that FIT and microFIT Contracts are granted under the FIT Programme.

2. Paragraph 7.8

6.6 Japan requests that the Panel set forth in paragraph 7.8 its preliminary rulings as circulated on 25 May 2012 in documents WT/DS412/8 and WT/DS426/7, in order to enhance the clarity of those preliminary rulings. Canada has not commented on Japan's request.

6.7 In our view, it is not necessary to incorporate the body of our preliminary rulings in the Final Reports. Paragraph 7.8 already includes a reference to documents WT/DS412/8 and WT/DS426/7, in which the preliminary rulings were set out in full and circulated. However, for the sake of clarity, we have added a sentence to paragraph 7.8 summarizing our conclusions from the preliminary rulings.

3. Paragraphs 7.9, 7.64, 7.124, 7.165, 7.166, 7.216 and 7.322-7.324

6.8 Japan and the European Union request that the Panel delete the term "small-scale" in the first sentence of paragraph 7.9, and in paragraphs 7.64, 7.124, 7.165, 7.166, 7.216, and 7.322-7.324, because they argue that the FIT Programme and the "Minimum Required Domestic Content Level" do not apply solely to "small-scale" solar PV and wind facilities. The complainants recall that there is no maximum capacity for wind projects, and state that it would be inappropriate to qualify solar PV projects as "small-scale", since the maximum capacity for these projects is 10 MW. Canada has not commented on this request.

6.9 We have decided to accept the complainants' requests and have accordingly made a number of adjustments to the relevant paragraphs.

4. Paragraphs 7.11-7.13 and 7.32

6.10 Japan requests the Panel to revise the facts stated in paragraphs 7.11-7.13 and 7.32. Japan submits that the adjectives "large", "vast" and "massive, respectively in the second, sixth and seventh sentences of paragraph 7.11 should be struck from the Reports, as they are highly subjective, not supported in the record, and do not accurately describe the type or size of a system or infrastructure required to maintain electricity systems. In addition, Japan requests a series of changes to paragraphs 7.11-7.13 and 7.32, as it is clear that not all electricity consumers obtain electricity through the systems described by the Panel. Canada submits that these requests should be rejected because the inclusion of the relevant adjectives to describe aspects of electricity systems is amply supported by the record[14].

6.11 The Panel has reflected on the terminology used in paragraphs 7.11-7.13 and 7.32 and, where appropriate, has made some adjustments in the light of Japan's requests and Canada's comments.

5. Paragraph 7.12

6.12 The European Union requests the Panel to add a footnote to the second sentence of paragraph 7.12, mentioning the fact that, in the specific case of Ontario, the IESO Market Rules foresee the possibility of entering into bilateral electricity supply contracts, under certain conditions (Chapter 8 of the Market

---

[14] Canada refers to the European Union's requests. However, we understand that Canada intended to refer to Japan's requests.

Rules). Canada considers that the European Union's request is unnecessary, noting that the Panel's statement is qualified by the word "generally" and, as such, means that it was clearly not intended to be comprehensive. Moreover, Canada submits that while the European Union's understanding of the IESO Market Rules is correct, there is no evidence of any such contracts in the record.

6.13 The Panel has decided to decline the European Union's request. As noted by Canada, the second sentence in paragraph 7.12 is qualified by the term "generally". Thus, this sentence is not meant to include the possibility referred to in Chapter 8 of the IESO Market Rules.

6. Paragraph 7.21

6.14 Canada requests that the Panel change the word "recognized" to "establish" in the third sentence of paragraph 7.21. The European Union submits that this request should be rejected, arguing that Canada has not justified its request on any evidence available to the Panel. Japan has not commented on Canada's request. The Panel has decided not to accommodate Canada's request. Paragraph 7.21 cites Ontario's Long-Term Energy Plan, Exhibit CDA-6, p. 5, and the same term found therein ("recognized") has been used by the Panel.

7. Paragraph 7.22

6.15 Japan requests that the Panel revise paragraph 7.22 to clarify the facts stated therein, and to add a sentence at the end indicating that the OEB was designated the regulator of the new electricity market. Canada has not commented on Japan's request. The Panel has decided to accommodate most of Japan's requests and has made the adjustments sought, albeit not in the precise manner proposed by Japan.

8. Paragraphs 7.23, 7.24, and 7.285-7.292

6.16 The European Union alleges that the descriptions in paragraphs 7.23, 7.24, and 7.285-7.292 do not reflect uncontested facts, in particular regarding the question whether "Ontario's competitive wholesale electricity market" started and ended in 2002. Were the Panel to consider these paragraphs to set out its factual findings on the nature and operation of Ontario's wholesale market before and after November 2002, the European Union requests that the Panel identify the specific qualitative changes which took place at that specific moment in time.

6.17 Canada submits that the Panel should reject the European Union's request. Canada notes that throughout paragraphs 7.23, 7.24, and 7.285-7.292, the Panel has carefully relied on evidence in the record to support its factual findings. Moreover, Canada recalls that the Panel has already set out the specific qualitative changes that took place after November 2002 in paragraphs 7.285 to 7.292, and that the European Union has apparently agreed that the current IESO market mechanism may not be the classical competitive market where supply and demand meet, as described in paragraph 7.294 of the Interim Reports.

6.18 Paragraphs 7.23 and 7.24 provide a brief description of Ontario's experience with the competitive wholesale market that was opened in 2002. In our view, none of what is stated in these paragraphs has been contested by the parties. In this regard, we note that the European Union has not denied that it has asserted that the market which operated in Ontario in 2002 was competitive. Neither has the European Union contested that the operation of this market was put to an end by the Government of Ontario following a period of relatively high prices. The European Union has also not disputed that the *Electricity Restructuring Act of 2004* was a response to the failed 2002 market opening experience. Thus, we see no reason to make any modifications to paragraphs 7.23 and 7.24.

6.19 Paragraphs 7.285-7.291 set out a more detailed description of the events that took place around Ontario's 2002 competitive market opening experience, based on a number of pieces of evidence that are referenced in this passage. Paragraph 7.292 articulates the Panel's conclusion that the evidence demonstrates that the competitive market opening experience failed to attract sufficient investment in electricity production into Ontario. In addition, we note that paragraphs 7.293-7.298 describe and evaluate the nature of the IESO-administered wholesale electricity market that replaced the 2002 competitive market on the basis of the parties' arguments and submitted evidence. Here the Panel concludes that the IESO-administered wholesale electricity market produces the HOEP, which the Panel considers cannot be used as an appropriate benchmark for what the price of electricity would be in Ontario in a competitive wholesale electricity market. In our view, the factual descriptions and findings made in these passages are sufficiently clear and referenced to the relevant pieces of evidence. Therefore, again, we see no reason to accommodate the European Union's requested changes to paragraphs 7.285-7.292.

9. Paragraph 7.24

6.20 Japan requests that the Panel revise the second sentence of paragraph 7.24 in order to clarify the description of the reforms introduced by the *Electricity Restructuring Act of 2004*. In particular, Japan requests that the terms "responsibility for" be replaced with "engaging in". Canada submits that the Panel should reject Japan's request. The Panel's description relies upon and is consistent with Section 25.2(1) of the *Electricity Act of 1998,* as amended by the *Electricity Restructuring Act of 2004*. According to Canada, this Section demonstrates that the OPA does more than just "engage in" overall long-term system planning.

6.21 We consider that the wording of the second sentence of paragraph 7.24 is appropriate in the light of the facts that are before us, as evidenced by the record. Thus, we have declined Japan's requested modifications.

10. Paragraph 7.25

6.22 Japan requests that the second sentence of paragraph 7.25 be struck from the Reports, because it is vague and not supported by the record before the Panel. Canada submits that the Panel should reject Japan's request. Canada points out that Japan does not state which particular aspect of this sentence is supposedly "vague and not supported by the record". In any case, Canada submits that each aspect of the second sentence of paragraph 7.25 is specific and amply supported by the record.

6.23 Paragraph 7.25 follows the description in paragraphs 7.21-7.24 of the essentially government-owned and managed electricity system that existed in Ontario from 1906 to 2002 and Ontario's experience with a liberalized wholesale market in 2002. Paragraph 7.25 is an introduction to section VII.A.4(c)(iii) of the Panel's findings which describes Ontario's *current* "hybrid" system and must be read in the light of these preceding paragraphs. It is intended to emphasize the fact that Ontario's electricity system continues today to be characterized by a significant degree of government involvement. The Government of Ontario's role in generation, transmission, distribution and regulation is described in the paragraphs that follow paragraph 7.25. Thus, we do not find paragraph 7.25 vague and unsupported by the record of facts. We therefore have declined Japan's requested modifications.

11. Paragraph 7.28

6.24 Canada suggests that the Panel amend the second sentence of paragraph 7.28 in order for it to read as follows: "Of these, the IPPs, which generate around 40% of Ontario's electricity supply, receive prices ... including: NUG contracts; contracts with Bruce Power; the Clean Energy Supply ("CES") contracts for natural gas ...". Neither Japan nor the European Union has commented on Canada's request.

6.25 As we understand it, Canada asks the Panel to modify paragraph 7.28 in such a way that would lead it to explain that the prices for electricity produced by IPPs are set under OPA initiatives and contracts which include NUG contracts and contracts with Bruce Power. However, Canada has not explained how the prices for IPPs are set under NUG contracts or contacts with Bruce Power. Moreover, Canada has not pointed to any factual source to support its requested change. As such, we have declined Canada's requested modifications.

12. Paragraphs 7.29 and 7.202

6.26 The European Union requests the Panel to include footnotes in paragraphs 7.29 and 7.202 recording the fact that the European Union has argued that the alleged 11% rate of return on equity is an abstract construct that does not correspond to the actual rates of return of individual projects.

Moreover, the European Union requests that the Panel modify paragraph 7.202 to clarify that whether the FIT Programme is construed in such a way as to cover generation costs plus a reasonable rate of return on investment is a contested issue.

6.27 Canada objects to the European Union's requests, recalling that the relevant passage in the Interim Reports uses language that is almost identical to that found in the exhibits upon which it relies. In addition, Canada notes that paragraph 7.29 is contained in the Panel's factual background section and not in its summary of the parties' arguments. Moreover, in Canada's view, the specific argument the European Union refers to does not address whether the rate of return was 11%. Rather, the European Union seems to be instead raising arguments about whether a particular generator can actually achieve such a return on equity. Finally, Canada submits that the Interim Reports adequately summarize the European Union's argument that the 11% rate of return on equity is an abstract construct in paragraph 7.258, and therefore, according to Canada, there is no need to add the footnotes requested by the European Union.

6.28 We have modified paragraph 7.29 to more accurately reflect the facts surrounding the 11% rate of return used by the OPA to determine the FIT prices. However, we have declined the European Union's other requests because, as Canada notes, the factual assertion made in the sentence the European Union submits must be changed is based on record evidence cited in footnote 372 (now footnote 392) found in paragraph 7.202. This information explicitly states that "prices in the [FIT] Price Schedule are intended to cover development costs plus a reasonable rate of return for Projects meeting certain assumptions relating to cost and efficiency". The language used in paragraph 7.202 repeats this text almost verbatim. On the other hand, we have decided to add a reference to the European Union's arguments concerning the allegedly "abstract" nature of the 11% rate of return used to determine the FIT Price Schedule in paragraph 7.325 of the Reports. We have also decided to add a reference to Exhibit CDA-46, slide 30, in footnote 374 (now footnote 394). This exhibit clearly discloses that an after tax return on equity rate of 11% was included in the Discounted Cash Flow model used to determine the FIT Price Schedule.

13. Paragraph 7.30

6.29 The European Union requests that the abbreviation "PV" be struck from the second sentence of paragraph 7.30. In addition, the European asks the Panel to add the relevant figures concerning aboriginal and community projects, in order for paragraph 7.30 to be entirely accurate as regards FIT prices. Canada has not commented on this request. The Panel has deleted "PV" from paragraph 7.30. However, we see no need to add any information about Aboriginal and Community Projects in this paragraph, as this information is already set out in paragraph 7.202.

14. Paragraph 7.31

6.30 The European Union submits that the third sentence in paragraph 7.31 should start with "Canada has not provided precise prices for these contracts", instead of "[w]hile precise prices for these contracts are not publicly available", given that the information exists and is available to the Canadian authorities. The European Union asserts that, despite several questions asked by the Panel, Canada has failed to provide the relevant information. Alternatively, the European Union asks the Panel to reflect in a footnote the fact that Canada failed to provide those precise prices in the course of these proceedings, even upon the Panel's request.

6.31 Canada asks the Panel to reject the European Union's request. Canada notes that precise rates for electricity are subject to the privacy and commercial interests of the counter-party to the relevant NUG contract. However, Canada has provided the Panel with an average NUG contract rate, and the European Union does not explain why this average is insufficient evidence of the rates NUGs earn for their sale of electricity to the OEFC.

6.32 The Panel has reflected on the phrasing of the third sentence in paragraph 7.31, and considers it appropriate in the light of the record. Thus, we have declined the European Union's request.

15. Paragraph 7.46

6.33 Canada asserts that while it is true that certain consumers of electricity can vary their electricity consumption, this is the case for only a very small number of consumers. Thus, Canada asks the Panel to add the following after the first sentence in paragraph 7.46: "The consumers that can easily vary their electricity consumption are very small in number".

6.34 The complainants ask the Panel to reject Canada's request. Japan disagrees with Canada's comments that only a very small number of consumers can vary their electricity consumption. Japan refers to Ontario's Long-Term Energy Plan where it is anticipated that all types of consumers can vary their consumption through innovative conservation or demand response-type programmes[15]. The European Union considers that the reference to "very small number" is vague. Finally, the complainants point out that Canada has not justified its requests on any evidence available to the Panel.

6.35 We note that Canada does not challenge the accuracy of what is described in paragraph 7.46, but rather asks for the factual description to be elaborated so as to provide more detail about the alleged nature of the consumers of electricity

[15] Government of Ontario, "Ontario's Long-Term Energy Plan", 2010, ("Ontario's Long-Term Energy Plan"), Exhibit CDA-6, p. 40.

in Ontario. We see no need to make such a change, and have therefore declined Canada's request.

16. Paragraph 7.50

6.36 Canada asks the Panel to replace the word "most" with "almost all" in the fourth sentence of paragraph 7.50 for greater accuracy. The complainants point out that Canada has not justified its request on any evidence available to the Panel, and ask the Panel to reject Canada's request. While we recognize the qualitative difference between using the words "most" and "almost all", we do not think that the choice of these words in the context of paragraph 7.50 would have any bearing on the relevance of the description of the IESO stack system that is described in this part of the Reports. Moreover, we note that Canada has not justified its request on the basis of evidence from the record of these proceedings. Thus, we have declined to make the requested modification to paragraph 7.50.

17. Paragraph 7.54

6.37 Japan asks the Panel to delete the words "market rate" from the first sentence of paragraph 7.54, in order to conform with the language used in paragraph 7.53. Canada has not commented on Japan's request. We see no need to make the requested change given that the words "market rate" are immediately followed by "(i.e. MCP/HOEP)". We have therefore declined Japan's request.

18. Paragraph 7.55

6.38 Canada suggests that the Panel replace the terms "a charge to generators" with "a credit to consumers" in the second sentence of paragraph 7.55 because, according to Canada, the GA is always either a charge or payment to the consumer depending on fluctuations in the HOEP. Canada submits that generators will always receive their contracted or regulated rates – or in the instance of unregulated OPG assets, the HOEP – regardless of HOEP/GA fluctuations. Finally, Canada notes that Exhibit JPN-1, which is referenced at the end of the second sentence, does not use such a phrase.

6.39 Japan submits that Canada provides no support in the record for its assertion, and that the Panel would be justified in using either phrase because the GA is both a charge to generators and a credit to consumers. Japan notes that where the OPA contract is a contract for differences – e.g. contracts for gas-fired facilities – and the contracted price is less than HOEP, the generator is "charged" the difference, thus reducing the GA and resulting in a credit to consumers. Were the Panel to accept Canada's proposed modification, Japan requests that the Panel cite evidence from the record to support such modification. The European Union has not commented on Canada's request.

6.40 We have decided to modify paragraph 7.55 to reflect the fact that, as Canada and Japan have highlighted, the GA can be both a charge to generators and a credit to consumers, and vice versa, depending upon the level of the HOEP.

19. Paragraph 7.56

6.41 The European Union requests the Panel to clarify that the GA is not collected from all consumers according to the same methodology, contrary to what the European Union asserts is suggested by the first sentence of paragraph 7.56. Canada submits that the European Union's request is unnecessary, and argues that the Panel's statement is true as the GA is allocated to *all* consumers in proportion with the electricity they consume. Nevertheless, Canada proposes language that it considers could be inserted before the last sentence in paragraph 7.56 to address the European Union's concern.

6.42 The Panel has decided to accommodate the European Union's request and has made the appropriate adjustments on the basis of the language proposed by Canada.

20. Paragraph 7.57

6.43 Canada asks the Panel to modify the first sentence of paragraph 7.57, with a view to increasing accuracy, in order for it to read as follows: "Prices paid by retail consumers are generally determined by adding to the wholesale price (i.e. the total of MCP/HOEP), the GA, other fees and charges, plus an additional distribution charge to cover the cost of delivering electricity to consumer".

6.44 Japan asks the Panel to reject Canada's request. Japan notes that the wholesale price is comprised of not only the MCP/HOEP but also GA and other fees and charges. Japan also points out that Canada fails to explain why it would be necessary for the Panel to single out distribution charges in the manner suggested by Canada.

6.45 The Panel has modified paragraph 7.57 to clarify the first sentence.

21. Paragraph 7.70

6.46 Japan requests that the Panel provide an explanation in paragraph 7.70 of its reasons to conclude that the TRIMs Agreement is the WTO agreement that deals most directly, specifically and in detail with the FIT Programme. In addition, Japan requests that the Panel provide its reasons for rejecting the complainants' arguments that the claim under the SCM Agreement should be examined first in the Panel's order of analysis of their complaints. Canada has not commented on Japan's request.

6.47 In response to Japan's requests, we note that paragraph 7.70 already sets out: (i) that the complainants assert (and Canada has not contested) that the challenged measures are TRIMs; and (ii) that, in the Panel's view, this suggests that the TRIMs Agreement deals most directly, specifically and in detail, with the challenged measures. The Panel therefore considers that its reasons for deciding to begin its evaluation of the complainants' claims with those made under the TRIMs Agreement (as opposed to those made under the SCM Agreement) are sufficiently clear. Thus, we have declined Japan's requested modifications.

22. Paragraph 7.73

6.48 Japan requests that the Panel insert the phrase "before addressing its claims under the TRIMs Agreement" after "Japan also argues" at the beginning of the first sentence of paragraph 7.73, in order to clarify that Japan considers its claim under the GATT 1994 to be the primary claim when compared to Japan's claim under the TRIMs Agreement. Japan also requests that the terms "internal" and "sale" should be set off separately in quotation marks to accurately reflect Japan's arguments. Canada has not commented on Japan's request.

6.49 We have summarized the parties' arguments following the order of analysis adopted in the Reports. Therefore we do not consider it necessary to insert the phrase requested by Japan. Nothing in paragraph 7.73 suggests that Japan's claim under the GATT 1994 was presented as a subsidiary claim to the one made under the TRIMs Agreement. Furthermore, in our view, the insertion of the language Japan has requested be added to paragraph 7.73 would not address the relationship between Japan's claims under the GATT 1994 and the TRIMs Agreement. As to Japan's second requested change, the Panel has made the appropriate adjustment.

23. Paragraph 7.78

6.50 The European Union requests that the Panel insert the phrase "in conjunction with Paragraph 1(a) of its Annex" after "Article 2.1 of the TRIMs Agreement", and make a minor change to the wording in paragraph 7.78, in order to better reflect the European Union's claims, as summarized in paragraph 3.4 of the Interim Reports. Canada has not commented on the European Union's request.

6.51 The Panel has made an adjustment to paragraph 7.78, albeit not in the precise manner proposed by the European Union.

24. Paragraph 7.120

6.52 The European Union asks the Panel to insert a series of sentences into paragraph 7.120 in order to better reflect the European Union's arguments. Canada considers that the European Union's request is unnecessary, as the Interim Reports accurately record the European Union's submissions. Were the

Panel to accept the European Union's requested additions, Canada asks that the Panel also address Canada's argument that the European Union's interpretation is inconsistent with the texts of the TRIMs Agreement and Article XI:2 of the GATT 1994.

6.53 We have modified the wording of paragraph 7.120 (and consequently also paragraph 7.80) in order to more accurately reflect the European Union's argument, albeit not in the precise manner proposed by the European Union. Given that we have rejected the European Union's argument, we do not find it necessary to address Canada's argument relating to Article XI:2 of the GATT 1994 in order to resolve the disputes. We have therefore made no change to paragraph 7.120 in response to Canada's comment and request.

25. Paragraph 7.124

6.54 Canada agrees with the Panel's conclusion that the "Minimum Required Domestic Content Level" is a "requirement[] governing" the procurement of electricity for purposes of Article III:8(a) of the GATT 1994. Canada requests that the Panel also conclude that Section 25.35 of the *Electricity Act of 1998*, the Ministerial Direction and the FIT and microFIT Rules and Contracts are laws and requirements that govern the procurement of electricity for the purposes of Article III:8(a).

6.55 The European Union does not consider Canada's request appropriate since this section of the Interim Reports refers to the Panel's understanding of the matter. The European Union observes that Canada's arguments are well reflected in paragraph 7.88 of the Interim Reports and, thus, there is no need for the Panel to make a reference to those arguments therein.

6.56 As noted by the European Union, Canada's arguments relating to this matter are summarized in paragraph 7.88 of the Interim Reports. Moreover, paragraph 7.124, and our findings in general on this point, are focused only on the question whether the "Minimum Required Domestic Content Level" is a "requirement[]" for purposes of Article III:8(a) of the GATT 1994. Thus, we see no need to make the requested changes.

26. Paragraph 7.125

6.57 The European Union requests (i) some minor changes to the wording of the fifth sentence of paragraph 7.125 and (ii) that the Panel insert an additional sentence at the end in order to better reflect the European Union's argument. Canada does not consider these amendments necessary, because the Interim Reports accurately record the European Union's arguments. In case the Panel accepts the European Union's requested modifications, Canada requests that the Panel also address Canada's argument that the European Union's interpretation is inconsistent with the scope of the Agreement on Government Procurement.

6.58 The Panel has decided to partly accommodate the European Union's request and has made the minor adjustments sought to the wording of the fifth sentence of paragraph 7.125. As the European Union's argument was already accurately described in the second, third and fourth sentences, the Panel has decided not to insert the additional sentence proposed by the European Union. With respect to Canada's comments and request, we recall that in the subsequent paragraphs we have explained our difficulty in accepting the European Union's interpretation and stated our conclusion that the "Minimum Required Domestic Content Level" should be properly characterized as one of the "requirements governing" the alleged procurement of electricity for the purpose of Article III:8(a) of the GATT 1994. Thus, it is not necessary for us to address Canada's argument relating to the Agreement on Government Procurement in order to resolve the disputes before us. We have made no change to this paragraph in response to Canada's comments and request.

27. Paragraph 7.134

6.59 Japan requests that the Panel explain why the fact that the GATT panel report in *US – Sonar Mapping* was not adopted diminishes the relevance of that GATT panel's findings, in the light of the Appellate Body's understanding in *Japan – Alcoholic Beverages II*, that "a panel could nevertheless find useful guidance in the reasoning of an unadopted panel report that it considered to be relevant"[16]. Japan also requests the Panel to explain the particular facts of this case that have led the Panel to conclude that the reasoning of the unadopted GATT panel report in *US – Sonar Mapping* is not relevant.

6.60 Canada does not consider that the Reports need to be supplemented in response to Japan's request. Canada recalls that the Appellate Body in *Japan – Alcoholic Beverages II* simply stated that the reasoning of an unadopted panel report could be useful if it was relevant. Canada stresses that the Panel in these disputes extensively explained why the GATT panel report in *US – Sonar Mapping* did not provide relevant guidance for these disputes.

6.61 Paragraph 7.134 sets out a number of features of the facts and law at issue in *US – Sonar Mapping* which, in our view, significantly diminish its relevance in these disputes. Therefore, we consider this paragraph to sufficiently explain why we were not persuaded by Japan's references to this GATT panel. Moreover, in the last sentence, we have simply noted "that the GATT panel report was not adopted". As this last sentence is not strictly necessary to our reasoning, we have deleted it.

[16] Appellate Body Report, *Japan – Alcoholic Beverages II*, p. 15.

28. Paragraph 7.138

6.62 Japan requests the Panel to revise this paragraph, and proposes a series of changes. Japan explains that its argument relating to the interpretation of the terms "governmental purposes" in Article III:8(a) of the GATT 1994 does not take issue with whether the meaning of "governmental purposes" is broad or narrow. Thus, Japan considers that it is highly misleading to simply qualify Japan's arguments as the narrowest compared to the other parties' arguments. Canada has not commented on Japan's request.

6.63 The Panel has decided not to accommodate Japan's request. We have carefully reviewed Japan's arguments and, in particular, its view that "a Vienna Convention analysis of the term 'for governmental purposes' suggests that it means for *government use, consumption, or benefit*, where again Japan uses the term 'benefit' to refer to that of using the product allegedly procured"[17]. Based on this statement, we do not believe it is inaccurate to characterize Japan's interpretation of the expression "governmental purposes" as the "narrowest meaning", when compared to the other parties' interpretations.

29. Paragraphs 7.139 and 7.140

6.64 The European Union understands that the Panel's statements with regards to the terms "governmental purposes" refer to the English version of the GATT 1994, since the Panel has not specifically addressed the meaning of the terms used in the Spanish and French versions, which in the European Union's view differ from the English version. Thus, the European Union requests that the Panel modify these paragraphs to remove the reference that the ordinary meaning of "governmental purposes" is "relatively broad" or to clarify that the Panel's understanding refers only to the English version of the GATT 1994.

6.65 Canada does not consider the European Union's request appropriate at this stage of the proceedings, since the European Union is asking the Panel to reverse its view that the ordinary meaning of "governmental purposes" is relatively broad. Canada notes that there is nothing in the Interim Reports that confines the Panel's statement on the ordinary meaning of "governmental purposes" to the English version of the GATT 1994.

6.66 We have adjusted the first sentence of paragraph 7.139 to clarify that our understanding is not limited to the English language version of the GATT 1994.

30. Paragraph 7.149

6.67 Canada submits that Hydro One and LDCs are intended to make returns from the transmission and distribution *assets*, as explained in Exhibit CDA-64.

---

[17] Japan's opening statement at the second meeting of the Panel, para. 33. (footnote omitted)

Thus, Canada requests that the Panel amend the fifth sentence of paragraph 7.149 by replacing the term "activities" with "assets".

6.68 Japan does not agree with Canada's request. Japan states that, notwithstanding Canada's assertion, Exhibit CDA-64 does not explain that the returns made are from transmission and distribution assets owned by Hydro One and LDCs, rather than their transmission and distribution activities. Moreover, Japan argues that Hydro One and LDCs are intended to make profits from all of their regulated activities, and not just from transmission and distribution. For example, Japan explains that any party has the right to connect to the system if that party meets all required legal and other standards. Hydro One and the LDCs respectively conduct the System Impact Assessments and Connection Impact Assessments, receiving payments from generators, including FIT generators[18].

6.69 The European Union considers that the Panel should reject Canada's request. First, it is unclear what the relevance of the distinction between "activities" and "assets" is in the present case. Pursuant to the European Union, it is undisputed that Hydro One and the LDCs are engaged in the transmission and distribution of electricity as their principal activity or business, and that they obtain their returns out of the transmission and distribution of electricity in Ontario. Second, the language suggested by Canada would appear to indicate that Hydro One and the LDCs do not generate their revenue from their operations or business but merely from their assets, e.g. such as renting their premises or infrastructure, which is clearly not the case.

6.70 The Panel has reflected on the terminology used in paragraph 7.149 and, where it considers appropriate, has made some adjustments in the light of the interim review requests and comments.

31. Paragraphs 7.163 and 7.166

6.71 Japan recalls that it made two distinct arguments to establish that the "Minimum Required Domestic Content Level" is inconsistent with Canada's national treatment obligation under Article III:4 of the GATT 1994. However, Japan notes that the Panel's evaluation of Japan's claim has only addressed one of those arguments. Japan asks that the Panel address Japan's other argument and that it do so by undertaking a separate analysis of Article III:4 of the GATT 1994. Japan considers that this separate analysis is necessary in order for the Panel to discharge its responsibilities under Articles 3 and 11 of the DSU. Canada has not commented on Japan's request.

[18] Japan cites the following Exhibits: Transmission-connected Generators, Hydro One website, ("Transmission-connected Generators"), Exhibit JPN-39; Transmission System Code, Ontario Energy Board, 10 June 2010, ("Transmission System Code"), Exhibit JPN-69, Section 4.3.3; Distribution System Code, Ontario Energy Board, 1 October 2011, ("Distribution System Code"), Exhibit JPN-70, Section 6.2.11; and Ontario Power Authority, Feed-in Tariff Contract, Version 1.5.1, 15 July 2011, ("FIT Contract"), Exhibit JPN-127, Article 2.4(b)(iv).

6.72 Paragraph 7.163 sets out our conclusions on the extent to which the "Minimum Required Domestic Content Level" requires the purchase or use of products of Canadian origin or from a Canadian source, as part of our analysis of whether the challenged measures fall within the scope of Paragraph 1(a) of the Illustrative List in the Annex to the TRIMs Agreement. On the basis of these and other conclusions (including those made in paragraph 7.166), we have found that the challenged measures are TRIMs falling within the scope of Paragraph 1(a) of the Illustrative List, and that in the light of Article 2.2 of the TRIMs Agreement and the chapeau to Paragraph 1(a) of the Illustrative List, the challenged measures are inconsistent with both Article 2.1 of the TRIMs Agreement and Article III:4 of the GATT 1994. Having made this finding, we do not believe it is necessary for the purpose of resolving the disputes before us to also address Japan's other argument and perform an entirely separate and stand-alone analysis of Japan's claim under Article III:4 of the GATT 1994. Thus, we have declined Japan's request.

32. Paragraph 7.165

6.73 The European Union requests that the Panel start the third sentence in paragraph 7.165 with the words "According to Canada". Canada states that this request should be rejected, as the Panel's statement that the European Union seeks to change is a finding of fact that is amply supported by the record.

6.74 The Panel has decided not to accommodate the European Union's request. The relevant sentence reflects our understanding of the facts and, as summarized in paragraph 7.68, it is properly supported by the evidence submitted in these disputes.

33. Paragraph 7.174

6.75 Japan requests that the language in the second sentence of this paragraph be changed to clarify that the submission made by Japan that is described in this sentence is not a conditional one but rather an argument that is true in all cases. To support this request, Japan asserts that the Appellate Body made clear in *US – Large Civil Aircraft (Second Complaint)* that a transaction may be covered by multiple subparagraphs of Article 1.1(a)(1). Canada asks the Panel to reject Japan's request, arguing that Japan is incorrect to argue that the Appellate Body's ruling that Japan relies upon is "true in all cases". According to Canada, the Appellate Body's ruling should be understood as indicating that a transaction "may" be covered by multiple subparagraphs of Article 1.1(a)(1) of the SCM Agreement. If the proper characterization of the challenged measure is under only one sub-paragraph, as Canada recalls the Panel has found in the present disputes, then that is the end of the matter.

6.76 We have declined Japan's requested modification. The focus of Japan's request is the phrase "would be" that is found in the second sentence of paragraph 7.174. This phrase refers to a possibility that depends upon the Panel making a particular finding - namely, the possibility that the challenged measures could be characterized under multiple subparagraphs of Article 1.1(a)(1) of the SCM Agreement even *if the Panel were to conclude that they could be legally characterized as a "government purchases [of] goods" under the terms of Article 1.1(a)(1)(iii) of the SCM Agreement.* As such, we consider the use of the conditional phrase "would be" to be correct and appropriate.

34. Paragraph 7.206

6.77 Japan submits that the characterization of the global adjustment in paragraph 7.206 is inaccurate because it does not reflect the fact that all OPA contracts (including non-FIT contracts) that have a contract price in excess of HOEP cause increases to the global adjustment to the extent of the excess, and that other expenses associated with procurement contracts, such as expenses for conservation measures and programmes, also directly increase the global adjustment. To this end, Japan requests that paragraph 7.206 be modified and has submitted text for this purpose. Canada has not commented on Japan's requested modification. We accept Japan's requested changes and have modified paragraph 7.206 accordingly.

35. Paragraph 7.223

6.78 The European Union requests that the Panel modify paragraph 7.206 to clarify that whether the FIT Programme is construed in such a way to cover generation costs plus a reasonable rate of return on investment is a contested issue. Canada asks the Panel to reject the European Union's request on the same grounds Canada advanced to justify its objection to the European Union's similar request with respect to paragraph 7.202 (see above). We have declined the European Union's request for the same reason we rejected the European Union's requested modification to paragraph 7.202.

36. Paragraph 7.242

6.79 Japan requests that the Panel address in paragraph 7.242 the argument presented by Japan that basing the interpretation of WTO obligations on the characterization of terms in municipal law "would be tantamount to enabling the responding Member to determine whether the measures are consistent with its WTO obligations". In addition, Japan requests that the Panel provide its reasoning that the characterization of the Government of Ontario was not "contrived" in light of the concern regarding the adoption of protectionist policies that was raised in a debate before the Ontario Legislative Assembly. Canada submits that there is no need for the Panel to make the changes requested by Japan, arguing that paragraph 7.242 already addresses Japan's argument concerning the interpretation of WTO obligations in the light of the characterization of the challenged measures under municipal law. Furthermore,

Canada argues that the Panel's conclusion that the message articulated in various instruments that the Government of Ontario "purchases" electricity through the FIT Programme is "by no means contrived" is supported by evidence that is on the record including documents emanating from the private sector. As such, Canada submits that the Panel need not make the requested changes.

6.80 We believe that paragraph 7.242 already addresses Japan's first concern in that it explicitly states that the Panel's consideration of the municipal law characterization of the challenged measures "is not dispositive of the analysis that we must undertake for the purpose of WTO law". Moreover, we see no need to explain why we find that the references to "purchases" and "procurement" contained in various Government of Ontario instruments are not "contrived" in light of the evidence Japan has submitted in Exhibit JPN-106. We fail to see how the suggestion in the record of the debate before the Ontario Legislative Assembly that is contained in Exhibit JPN-106 has any bearing on determining whether the description of the OPA's powers and responsibilities (which include the "purchase" and "procurement" of electricity) in various legal instruments is contrived. In particular, the fact that a member of Ontario's Legislative Assembly suggested that a local content rule may be protectionist does not, in our view, imply that the Government of Ontario's decision to grant the OPA the power to "purchase" and "procure" electricity (including under the FIT Programme) cannot be characterized as one that is not contrived. Thus, we have decided not to make any changes to paragraph 7.242.

37. Paragraphs 7.245 and 7.247

6.81 Japan makes a number of requests for the Panel to clarify the reasoning articulated in paragraphs 7.245 and 7.247 in support of its conclusion that a transaction properly characterized as involving "government purchases [of] goods" under Article 1.1(a)(1)(iii) of the SCM Agreement cannot also be a "direct transfer of funds" under Article 1.1(a)(1)(i) of the SCM Agreement. First, Japan asks the Panel to explain the reasoning behind its conclusion in paragraph 7.245 in the light of the finding of the Appellate Body in *US – Large Civil Aircraft (Second Complaint)* that the "examples" referred to in Article 1.1(a)(i) are illustrative and non-exhaustive. Secondly, Japan asks the Panel to provide additional explanations, in the light of certain alleged findings of the Appellate Body in *US – Large Civil Aircraft (Second Complaint)*, for what it describes as the Panel's finding in paragraph 7.247 that "Article 1.1(a)(1) does not explicitly spell out the relationship between subparagraphs (i) and (iii)". In this regard, Japan considers that the Panel has failed to provide an adequate explanation as to how its finding is consistent with the Appellate Body's conclusions in *US – Large Civil Aircraft (Second Complaint)*, or any explanation as to why the Appellate Body's alleged findings in footnotes are any less important than its findings in the body of its reports. Finally, Japan asks the Panel to explicitly state whether it is rejecting the Appellate Body's findings in *US – Large Civil Aircraft (Second Complaint)*, and if so, to adequately explain its rationale for doing so.

6.82 Canada submits that Japan's requests should be rejected, arguing that the Panel has thoroughly explained its findings and reasons with respect to the issue Japan raises in paragraphs 7.245-7.248. As regards Japan's particular concerns about paragraph 7.247, Canada is of the view that the Panel's statements are in accordance with the Appellate Body's general findings in *US – Large Civil Aircraft (Second Complaint)*. In particular, Canada argues that in this paragraph, the Panel notes that the Appellate Body's finding is permissive (i.e. the Appellate Body said "does not expressly preclude" and did not say, as Japan seems to imply, "permits" or "allows"). In addition, according to Canada, the Panel properly interprets the relationship between "purchases [of] goods" and "direct transfer[s] of funds". Thus, according to Canada, Japan is wrong to suggest that the Panel has not adequately explained its legal reasoning.

6.83 Japan's first request for review relates to paragraph 7.245. As we understand it, Japan takes issue with the following statement:

> In this regard, we observe that the only two examples of 'direct transfer[s] of funds' involving reciprocal rights and obligations that Article 1.1(a)(1)(i) identifies are 'loans' and 'equity infusion[s]'. Government 'purchases of goods' could have easily been added to these examples had the drafters considered that they should also be viewed as falling within the scope of Article 1.1(a)(1)(i) of the SCM Agreement, particularly given that they are explicitly mentioned in Article 1.1(a)(1)(iii) of the SCM Agreement.

Japan asks us to explain this statement in the light of the Appellate Body's finding in *US – Large Civil Aircraft (Second Complaint)* that the "examples" in Article 1.1(a)(1)(i) of the SCM Agreement are illustrative and non-exhaustive. In our view, there is no need to provide the requested explanation because there is no contradiction between our statements in this paragraph and the Appellate Body's finding that is cited by Japan. In particular, the fact that the "examples" set out in Article 1.1(a)(1)(i) of the SCM Agreement are illustrative and non-exhaustive does not detract from our observation that the words "purchases of goods" could have easily been added to the text of Article 1.1(a)(1)(i) *given that such transactions are "explicitly mentioned in Article 1.1(a)(1)(iii) of the SCM Agreement"*. Indeed, in our view, it would be expected that having explicitly referred to "government purchases [of] goods" in Article 1.1(a)(1)(iii) of the SCM Agreement, the drafters of the SCM Agreement would, in the light of the principle of effective treaty interpretation, have also made an explicit reference to such transactions in Article 1.1(a)(1)(i) of the SCM Agreement had they considered them to fall under both sub-paragraphs. Finally on this point, it must be recalled that our reasons for finding that transactions properly characterized as "government purchases [of] goods" cannot also be "direct transfer[s] of funds" are not only set out in paragraph 7.245 but also in paragraphs 7.246-7.247.

6.84 With respect to Japan's comments regarding paragraph 7.247, we note that contrary to Japan's contentions, the Panel did not find in this paragraph that Article 1.1(a)(1) "explicitly spell[s] out the relationship between subparagraphs (i) and (iii)". Moreover, the Panel has nowhere in this paragraph stated that Appellate Body findings are "less important" when they are set out in footnotes compared with the body of reports. Rather, as pointed out by Canada, in paragraph 7.247 the Panel notes that when it comes to the relationship between the sub-paragraphs of Article 1.1(a)(1) of the SCM Agreement, the Appellate Body statements set out in a footnote in *US – Large Civil Aircraft (Second Complaint)* do not express any definitive conclusion. Moreover, consistent with the Appellate Body's observations in *US – Large Civil Aircraft (Second Complaint)*, the Panel recognizes in paragraph 7.247 that it may be possible in certain circumstances to characterize a measure as different types of "financial contributions". However, in our view, the customary rules of interpretation of public international law (and in particular the principle of effective treaty interpretation) do not allow for such an outcome *on the basis of the facts of the present disputes*. It is therefore incorrect to suggest that the Panel disagrees or rejects the Appellate Body's observation that it may be possible to characterize a measure under more than one sub-paragraph of Article 1.1(a)(1) of the SCM Agreement.

6.85 Finally, footnote 453 (now footnote 473) explicitly states that the extract from the panel's reasoning in *US – Large Civil Aircraft (Second Complaint)* that was rejected by the Appellate Body is referred to in the present proceedings only as a "useful exposition of the interpretative problem that we believe is created by the complainants' arguments in these proceedings". Thus, we are not relying upon or agreeing with the panel's *finding* in *US – Large Civil Aircraft (Second Complaint),* which related to the question whether government purchases of services (transactions that are not explicitly mentioned in Article 1.1(a)(1) of the SCM Agreement) could be characterized as "direct transfer[s] of funds". Rather, by recalling the panel's *reasoning* on this question in *US – Large Civil Aircraft (Second Complaint)* our focus is on the interpretative dilemma that the panel draws attention to, namely, the consequence for the utility of the "purchases goods" language in Article 1.1(a)(1)(iii), in the light of the principle of effective treaty interpretation, of an interpretation that would allow transactions involving government purchases of goods to be characterized as both government "purchases [of] goods" under Article 1.1(a)(1)(iii) and as "direct transfer[s] of funds" under Article 1.1(a)(i) of the SCM Agreement.

38. Paragraph 7.249

6.86 Japan requests that the Panel make findings with respect to its arguments concerning the question whether the challenged measures amount to "income or price support" within the meaning of Article 1.1(a)(2) of the SCM Agreement, and consequently, to undertake a separate review of the merits of its related benefit arguments. While Japan agrees with the Panel that the benefit arguments it has advanced are "essentially the same" irrespective of whether the challenged measures are characterized as "financial contributions" or "income or price support", Japan emphasizes that they are not identical. Japan believes that Panel findings with respect to its "income or price support" line of argument could have a material impact on any review conducted by the Appellate Body, and are necessary in order to not only achieve the prompt settlement of its dispute with Canada but also to secure a positive resolution to the dispute in accordance with Articles 3.3 and 3.7 of the DSU.

6.87 Canada submits that Japan's request is without merit as it relies upon the same set of inappropriate benefit benchmarks that the Panel rejected in subsequent parts of its findings. Moreover, according to Canada, the interim review stage is not the appropriate point in these proceedings to ask for new factual and legal findings or attempt to re-argue one's case. Thus, Canada submits that Japan's request should be rejected.

6.88 We have once again closely reviewed the arguments that Japan has advanced to support its contention that the challenged measures confer a "benefit" within the meaning of Article 1.1(b) of the SCM Agreement when they are characterized as a form of "income or price support" under Article 1.1(a)(2) of the SCM Agreement. While the arguments are not identical to those Japan has advanced in relation to its contention that the challenged measures confer a "benefit" when characterized as "financial contributions", they do, by explicit cross-reference, rely upon the same "market rates" to establish the alleged existence of benefit. Because the very same "market rates" are rejected by the Panel majority in its benefit analysis, the outcome of the Panel's evaluation of the merits of Japan's "income or price support" arguments, *and therefore the merits of Japan's claims concerning prohibited subsidization*, would be the same irrespective of whether the Panel examined Japan's contention that the challenged measures should be legally characterized as a form of "income or price support" under Article 1.1(a)(2) of the SCM Agreement. Thus, we see no compelling reason to grant Japan's request for review.

39. Paragraphs 7.251, 7.308, 7.313(a) and footnote 588

6.89 Japan requests that the Panel make a number of modifications to paragraph 7.251 in order to ensure that it more accurately reflects Japan's arguments in respect of the electricity price benchmarks that it has advanced in these proceedings for the purpose of establishing the existence of benefit. First, Japan submits that the Panel incorrectly characterized one of the price benchmarks that it advanced as the "weighted average HOEP" when Japan had in fact described this benchmark as the "weighted average 'wholesale rate'". Secondly, Japan states that contrary to what is described in paragraph 7.251, Japan did not refer to the "price offered by two private retail operators" in its arguments as "alternative" benchmarks. Rather, Japan argues that this evidence was advanced to "confirm" that the retail rate functions as a "ceiling" price. Japan asks the Panel to revise the fourth sentence of paragraph 7.251

accordingly and submits draft text for this purpose. Thirdly, Japan finds that the fifth sentence in paragraph 7.251 is inaccurate when it states that Japan has asserted that retail prices in Ontario represent a "proxy" for the maximum level of the wholesale price of electricity in Ontario. Japan asks the Panel to delete this sentence. Finally, to reflect the above requests for review, Japan asks the Panel to modify the first sentence of paragraph 7.251 to include a reference to not only wholesale market prices but also retail market prices. Japan suggests a small modification to this sentence for this purpose.

6.90 Japan makes another request for review that is related to the changes it seeks to paragraph 7.251. In particular, Japan asks the Panel to consider making separate and additional findings to those made in paragraphs 7.308 and 7.313(a) with respect to whether the Regulated Price Plan ("RPP") prices are an appropriate market benchmark for the purpose of establishing the existence of benefit. Japan submits that it has made a distinct and "alternative" argument with respect to the RPP prices that the Panel has not evaluated. According to Japan, it has argued that the RPP prices confirm the existence of benefit because "they act as a ceiling for what consumers actually pay for electricity within the regulated Ontario market, taking into account all the various sources of electricity produced in Ontario, and all the subsidies that may be provided by the government to electricity generators in Ontario".

6.91 Canada explains that it understands Japan's arguments concerning the electricity price benchmarks it has advanced to include the following two proposed benchmarks: "the weighted average 'wholesale rate' during 2010 for generators other than FIT and RESOP generators" and "the commodity charge portion of retail prices". Canada asserts that contrary to Japan's suggestions, a more accurate fourth sentence in paragraph 7.251 should refer to these benchmarks. As regards Japan's requests for modifications to paragraphs 7.308 and 7.313(a) and footnote 588 (now footnote 610), Canada recalls that the purpose of interim review is not to request further factual or legal findings. In any case, Canada submits that it has answered Japan's assertion that the RPP prices "serve as a ceiling on the market price of electricity" recalling that the RPP is "simply a regulated price for Ontario electricity consumers that aggregates the cost of paying for all electricity generated for the province".

6.92 We have revised paragraph 7.251 (and consequently also footnote 588 (now footnote 610)) to correct the misdescription of Japan's argument concerning the "weighted average 'wholesale rate'" benchmark. The first sentence of paragraph 7.251 has also been amended to indicate that Japan has advanced not only wholesale level prices but also prices at the retail level of trade as suggested benchmarks for the benefit analysis. We have also taken note of Japan's clarification that it did not submit the evidence referred to in paragraph 7.251 on private retail prices for the purpose of advancing an alternative benchmark, but rather only to confirm that the RPP acts as a ceiling on the electricity price. Thus, we have deleted the fifth sentence of paragraph 7.251, and described Japan's alternative benchmark argument that is based on RPP prices in more detail. Japan's clarification means that there is no longer any need for the Panel to evaluate the merits of the evidence concerning private retail prices as alternative electricity price benchmarks. However, because Japan has clarified that the basis of its alternative retail price argument was *RPP* prices (and not *private* retail prices), we have revised paragraph 7.317 so that it now addresses the correct scope of Japan's alternative benefit argument. We have also made consequential changes to paragraph 7.319.

40. Paragraph 7.252

6.93 Japan notes that in paragraph 7.252, the Panel recognizes Japan's argument that the existence of benefit can also be demonstrated by the history of the electricity market in Ontario and the design and structure of the FIT Programme. However, according to Japan, the Panel has not addressed this argument in its findings. Japan therefore asks the Panel to do so. In addition, Japan asks the Panel to modify the language used to describe the argument that is summarized in paragraph 7.252 in order to more accurately reflect what Japan has actually stated in its submissions. To this end, Japan proposes a number of modifications. Canada submits that Japan's request asks the Panel to make additional findings despite the fact that the interim review stage of proceedings is limited to verifying precise aspects of the Interim Reports. Thus, Canada urges the Panel to reject Japan's request because, Canada's view, it amounts to the improper use of the interim review process to re-litigate Japan's case.

6.94 We have modified paragraph 7.252 to more accurately reflect Japan's argument. However, we disagree with Japan when it asserts that the Panel did not address this line of argument in its findings. It is clear from Japan's submissions that it is arguing that the recent history of the electricity market in Ontario and the design and structure of the FIT Programme demonstrate the existence of benefit because both of these factors show that Ontario's *wholesale electricity market* could not support the existence of renewable electricity generators on the basis of the terms and conditions (including price) available to electricity generators. This point is made in a number of places by Japan, but most clearly in Japan's opening statement at the second meeting of the Panel where, after recalling Ontario's market opening experience in 2002, the enactment of the *Electricity Restructuring Act of 2004* and the 2009 Ministerial Direction establishing the FIT Programme, Japan states: "This history demonstrates that the market price of MCP/HOEP is insufficient to support the existence of FIT generators in the Ontario market. The Government's intervention, through the OPA, to offer prices above those available in the market is the only reason FIT generators operate in the Ontario market today"[19]. Japan elaborated on this statement in its comments on Canada's response to

[19] Japan's opening statement at the second meeting of the Panel, paras. 10-13.

Panel question No. 42 following the second substance meeting, where it explained:

> In the present case, the history of Ontario's electricity market confirms that FIT generators would not have received anything like the terms they receive under FIT contracts absent the FIT Program.{} This was Japan's point at paragraphs 10-13 of its opening statement at the second meeting of the Panel. Canada confirmed this point as early as its first written submission, where it wrote: 'The experience with a competitive market in 2002 demonstrated that *the market alone would not be sufficient* to encourage the construction of new generation facilities [(e.g., wind and solar PV facilities)] able to provide the additional long-term supply needed by Ontario residents'.{} Canada has again just confirmed this point in response to question 1 above, where it explained that the Government of Ontario decided to put an end to the period of liberalization in November 2002 because '[s]upply was hampered by the [liberalized] market structure, which *did not encourage sufficient entry of new generators*', and in order to '*facilitate investment in new generation*'[20].

6.95 Thus, the premise underlying Japan's historical and objective design and structure argument is that these two factors demonstrate that the FIT generators would not exist in the absence of the Government of Ontario's intervention in the wholesale electricity market. This line of argument is recognized in paragraph 7.276 and subsequently addressed by the Panel, in particular, in paragraphs 7.309-7.313. There is therefore no basis for Japan's request to make additional findings.

41. Paragraph 7.259

6.96 Canada submits that the references to its submission in footnote 471 (now footnote 492) are not exhaustive concerning Canada's arguments as to why the complainants' proposed benchmarks are inappropriate. Canada asks that this be reflected in footnote 471 (now footnote 492) by adding the words "See for instance" at the beginning. In addition, Canada asks that a reference be added in footnote 471 (now footnote 492) to paragraphs 136-142 of Canada's opening statement at the second meeting of the Panel because this passage is where its comments on the analytical approach that might have been taken in this case are most comprehensively discussed. Neither Japan nor the European Union has commented on Canada's request. We have made the requested changes to footnote 471 (now footnote 492).

---

[20] Japan's comments on Canada's response to Panel question No. 1 (second set) (footnotes omitted, emphasis original).

42. Paragraphs 7.272 and 7.308

6.97 Canada argues that the description of the challenged FIT generators that is set out in paragraphs 7.272 and 7.308 is overly broad and captures electricity generators operating under the FIT Programme whose activities have not been challenged by the complainants. To correct this misdescription, Canada proposes two textual modifications to the respective paragraphs. The European Union proposes its own modifications for the same purpose. Japan has not commented on Canada's request. We have made the appropriate amendments to the text of these two paragraphs to address Canada's concern.

43. Footnote 503

6.98 The European Union observes that footnote 503 (now footnote 524) reproduces the same content in terms of the background of Professor Hogan as stated in footnote 30 (now footnote 47) and suggests that the Panel eliminate this repetition. Canada has not commented on the European Union's suggestion. We have made an appropriate modification to footnote 503 (now footnote 524).

44. Paragraph 7.297

6.99 Canada submits that the last sentence in paragraph 7.297 is incorrect to the extent that it states that the OPG's "unregulated assets" receive the HOEP because they have been "directed by the Government of Ontario to accept whatever price is set regardless of whether this meets marginal costs". In particular, Canada objects to the use of the "whatever price is set" language, and requests that the sentence be revised to explain that the OPG's "unregulated assets" receive the HOEP because the Government of Ontario considers, as a matter of policy, that the HOEP is sufficient for "these older, largely depreciated assets". The European Union considers that the Panel's statement is factually correct, but that it could be drafted in a different manner to account for Canada's concerns without needing to add an explanation of the policy reason behind the Government of Ontario's direction. Japan has not commented on Canada's requested change. We have modified paragraph 7.297 to more accurately explain that the OPG's unregulated assets receive the HOEP, regardless of whether this price covers their marginal costs.

45. Paragraph 7.304

6.100 Canada requests that the first sentence in paragraph 7.304 be redrafted in a way that recognizes that Canada's arguments concerning the complainants' attempts to use out-of-jurisdiction benchmarks included the submission that neither party has satisfied the standards set in WTO case law for their application in the present disputes. Canada does not, however, challenge the accuracy of what is stated in the first sentence of paragraph 7.304. In other words, Canada asks that the description in paragraph 7.304 of Canada's position *vis-à-vis* the complainants' out-of-jurisdiction benchmarks be amplified to capture the full range of its arguments. Japan submits that Canada's request is inapposite to the subject addressed by the Panel in paragraph 7.304, and suggests that the Panel disregard them. Similarly, the European Union considers that Canada's request for clarification relates to an issue that is different to that addressed by the Panel in paragraph 7.304. We agree with Japan and the European Union. The subject matter of paragraphs 7.303-7.307 is the extent to which the out-of-Province benchmarks that have been advanced by the complainants are *derived from competitive wholesale electricity markets*. As all of the parties agree, paragraph 7.304 is accurate when it explains that on this specific issue, Canada has not challenged the complainants' allegations. Thus, we see no need to accept Canada's requested modifications.

46. Footnote 599

6.101 The European Union argues that its submissions concerning the "guarantee element" in the FIT Contract or the provision of more than reasonable remuneration on the basis of "construed" prices, may help to substantiate a finding that the challenged measures confer a benefit regardless of whether the Panel accepts or rejects Canada's contentions on the relevant market. Thus, the European Union asks the Panel to reconsider its conclusions on the merits of these arguments. Canada submits that the European Union's request goes beyond the scope of interim review, and should therefore be rejected.

6.102 The arguments the European Union refers to in its request for review were advanced on the basis of an approach to the question of benefit that requires acceptance of Canada's view that electricity produced by FIT generators is sold on a wholesale market that is separate from all other electricity. Although the European Union suggests in its interim review request that it made these arguments in the alternative, this is not at all clear from the actual submissions made during the proceedings. Rather, it appears that the European Union advanced the relevant arguments only in response to Canada's benefit submissions *in the event that the Panel were to follow them in its evaluation of the question of benefit*[21]. As we have rejected Canada's contentions in this regard (indeed, in part on the basis of the European Union's own arguments), it is unnecessary for us to determine the merits of the European Union's arguments. There is therefore no basis for the Panel to reconsider its conclusions with respect of the European Union's arguments.

---

[21] See, for example, European Union's second written submission, paras. 72, 78 and 82; and opening statement at the second meeting of the Panel, paras. 24-25.

47. Paragraph 7.321

6.103 Japan asks the Panel to recognize in paragraph 7.321 that Japan has requested the Panel to provide guidance on the proper benchmark for determining the existence of benefit in the event that the Panel were to reject the benefit arguments it has advanced. The European Union also asks the Panel to more accurately reflect its own request for the Panel not to limit its analysis to rejecting the arguments it has advanced to substantiate its allegations of benefit. Canada finds the complainants' requests inappropriate because, in Canada's view, they are not supported by any authority under WTO law.

6.104 We agree with Canada that there is no authority in WTO law *requiring* a panel to consider alternative arguments to substantiate a claim when those arguments have not been advanced by the parties. However, we do not believe that the absence of any such *obligation* prevents the Panel majority in these proceedings from setting out its own *observations* on how the question of benefit could have been approached, provided, of course, that in doing so the Panel majority does not end up making the case for any of the parties[22]. In this regard, we note that the complainants have explicitly asked the Panel to provide additional guidance on the question of benefit, an issue that has been at the centre of substantial debate between the parties in the context of a dense and complicated fact pattern. In this light, and bearing in mind our duties and responsibilities under the DSU[23] as well as the objectives of the WTO dispute settlement system[24], we do not believe that the absence of any authority in WTO law compelling panels to consider the merits of arguments that have not been made by parties to a dispute prevents the Panel majority from outlining its own observations on the question of benefit in these proceedings, as requested by the complainants. We have therefore decided to accept the changes to paragraph 7.321 that have been requested by the European Union and Japan.

48. Paragraph 7.322

6.105 Canada suggests that the Panel should replace the words "those that currently exist" at the end of paragraph 7.322 with "prevailing market conditions". Japan submits that Canada has offered no explanation as to why the term from Article 14(d) of the SCM Agreement should be used in paragraph 7.322. In Japan's view, the terms advanced by Canada are not necessarily synonymous with those used by the Panel. Thus, in the absence of any explanation on the part of Canada as to why the language chosen by the Panel should be modified, Japan requests that the Panel reject Canada's request. The European Union also notes that there is a difference between the terms

[22] See, e.g. Appellate Body Report, *Japan – Agricultural Products II*, para. 129.

[23] Article 11, DSU.

[24] See, in particular, Articles 3.2, 3.3 and 3.7 of the DSU.

"prevailing market conditions" and "those that currently exist" in that the former refers to the prevailing market conditions (i.e. qualifying them as "prevailing") whereas the latter refers to those conditions (all or most, without qualifying them) that currently exist in Ontario. Therefore, not unlike Japan, the European Union asks the Panel to decline the changes that Canada has requested.

6.106 Japan submits that the exhibits cited in footnote 603 (now footnote 632) do not support the proposition that the Government of Ontario has decided that part of its additional generating capacity must come "in particular" from "small-scale projects using solar PV and wind power technologies". Thus, Japan requests that the Panel remove the references to "small-scale" from this paragraph. Canada argues that Exhibits CDA-55 and CDA-45 refer to the scale of the projects referred to by the Panel, and therefore considers the Panel's statement justified and based on record evidence.

6.107 Turning first to Canada's requested modification, there is, in our view, very little, if any, difference between the expressions "current" or "prevailing" conditions of supply and demand in a particular market. Indeed, one of the definitions of the word "prevail" is "current". Nevertheless, it was not the Panel's intention to articulate in paragraph 7.322 the test for determining the amount of a subsidy in terms of benefit that is described under Article 14(d) of the SCM Agreement. We have therefore declined Canada's request.

6.108 As regards Japan's request for review, we have modified the language of the relevant passage in paragraph 7.322 as well as the references in footnote 603 (now footnote 632) to more accurately reflect the point the Panel intended to make.

49. Paragraphs 7.322-7.326 and 8.7

6.109 The European Union requests that the Panel complete the benefit analysis allegedly performed by the Panel in paragraphs 7.322-7.325 (now paragraphs 7.322-7.327) by undertaking any one or more of three specific actions. First, the European Union submits that the Panel may complete the benefit analysis on the basis of the existing set of facts that are on the record of these disputes. In this regard, the European Union points to: (i) the information it has provided on the costs of solar PV and windpower generation; (ii) the prices that windpower generators have offered in bidding processes in Quebec in 2008; (iii) its submissions on the "reasonable" rate of return offered to FIT generators; and (iv) its arguments relating to the possibility of obtaining electricity supply via an auction process or by direct negotiation with individual generators. Secondly, the European Union submits that even if the Panel were to consider that the facts on the record were insufficient to complete its analysis, it may find the existence of benefit by drawing adverse inferences in the light of what the European Union describes as the Panel's view that Canada has failed to sufficiently explain several pieces of information necessary to understand the 11% rate of return. Thirdly, and in any event, the European Union maintains that the Panel should exercise its authority under Article 13 of the DSU and seek the information necessary for it to complete its benefit analysis. In this regard, the European Union fails to see how the Panel's analysis could serve the purposes described in Articles 3.4 and 3.7 of the DSU if it were to stop at a given point because the Panel considers there are insufficient facts on the record to complete its work. The European Union finds particular support for this latter request in *US – Large Civil Aircraft (Second Complaint)*, where the Appellate Body found that "by failing to exercise its authority to seek out relevant information to satisfy its predominance approach in assessing the claim before it, the Panel acted inconsistently with its obligations under Article 11 of the DSU..."[25]. According to the European Union, the Panel in the present proceedings is in the same position as the panel in *US – Large Civil Aircraft (Second Complaint)*, which developed an alternative approach to examine one of the issues at stake but did not complete the analysis since neither party was given the opportunity to provide the necessary evidence based on the panel's approach. Finally, in the event that the Panel were to reject the previous three requests, the European Union asks the Panel to make a number of changes to paragraphs 7.326(ii) and 8.7 (now paragraphs 7.328(ii) and 8.7) to reflect its view on what would be a more accurate description of the Panel's findings.

6.110 Not unlike the European Union, Japan submits that there is sufficient evidence on the record of these disputes for the Panel to complete its benefit analysis and asks the Panel to do so. In particular, Japan points to a series of facts that it argues demonstrate that solar PV and windpower FIT projects, although carrying principally sovereign risk, have a targeted pre-tax rate of return on equity of 15.8%, whereas the long-term Canadian government bond yield is 4.25%. Moreover, Japan notes that while Ontario's regulated utilities, which do not operate on the basis of a price that is guaranteed for 20 years, were set a target rate of return for 2009 of 9.75%, the actual rate of return obtained by such entities in 2011 was 5%, whereas the pre-tax rate of return for FIT generators was, according to Japan, set at 15.8%. Thus, Japan argues that the record contains sufficient evidence for the Panel to complete its benefit analysis and find the existence of benefit.

6.111 Canada points out that there is nothing in WTO law requiring a panel to consider alternative approaches to an issue that have not been proposed by the parties, particularly after a panel has found that the complainant(s) have failed to make their case regarding that issue. Canada emphasizes that a panel is not entitled to make the case for any of the parties. Moreover, referring *inter alia* to *EC – Sardines* and *Japan – DRAMs*[26], Canada submits that it is well established that the interim review stage of a proceeding is not intended to be used to change a panel's decision, re-argue a case, introduce new evidence or make new arguments. Rather, in Canada's view, interim review is limited to reviewing

[25] Appellate Body Report, *US – Large Civil Aircraft (Second Complaint)*, para. 1145.

[26] In particular, Appellate Body Report, *EC – Sardines*, para. 301; and Panel Report, *Japan – DRAMs (Korea)*, para. 6.2.

"precise aspects" of a report. Finally, Canada maintains that the European Union's reliance on *US – Large Civil Aircraft (Second Complaint)* to support its contention that the Panel must seek new information is misplaced. In this regard, Canada notes that in the present proceedings, the panel's analysis amounts to a "discussion of theoretical benchmarks after its findings on the issue of benefit have been made", whereas in *US – Large Civil Aircraft (Second Complaint)*, the panel used a methodology that was not suggested by a party, nor discussed with the parties before the panel used it to make its findings. Thus, for all of these reasons, Canada submits that the complainants' requests for review should be rejected in their entirety.

6.112 The complainants requests for interim review of paragraphs 7.322-7.326 (now paragraphs 7.322-7.328) are focused on the Panel majority's observations that are set out in these paragraphs on how they consider the question of benefit could have been addressed in these disputes. As already explained[27], the Panel is of the view that there is no authority in WTO law *requiring* a panel to consider alternative arguments to substantiate a claim when those arguments have not been advanced by the parties. Nevertheless, in the light of the complainants' explicit requests for the Panel to explain its own position with respect to the question of benefit were it to reject the substantial and diverse range of submissions they themselves have made on the issue, the Panel majority decided to set out its own observations on one approach it considers could have been validly pursued in these proceedings. The Panel majority did so bearing in mind its duties and responsibilities under the DSU[28], which include the obligation not to make a *prima facie* case for a party that bears the burden of making it[29].

6.113 As is evident from the language used by the Panel to draft its overall conclusions and recommendations in Section 8 of the respective Reports, the Panel majority's observations in paragraphs 7.322-7.326 (now paragraphs 7.322-7.328) do not and should not be considered to form part of the Panel majority's *findings and conclusions* on the question of benefit. Rather, they should be viewed as an attempt by the Panel majority to respond to the complainants' specific requests in a manner that is consistent with a panel's tasks and obligations under WTO law. In other words, the Panel majority's observations do not form part of the Panel majority's "benefit analysis" *for the purpose of determining the merits of the complainants' claims*. For this reason, there is no basis for the Panel to accept the complainants' requests for review. Thus, to the extent that the complainants' requests for interim review are premised on the view that the Panel majority's observations represent actual *findings* on the merits of their subsidization arguments that should be elaborated or further developed with a view to "completing the benefit analysis", they cannot be accepted. In any case, we are of the view that certain aspects of the

27 See above, para. 6.104.

28 Article 11, DSU.

29 See, for example, Appellate Body Report, *Japan – Agricultural Products II*, para. 129.

complainants' requests that the Panel take account of particular facts that are allegedly already on the record, as well as the European Union's request for the Panel to seek additional information, go beyond the scope of interim review proceedings. In this respect, we agree with Canada that it is well established that the interim review stage of a proceeding is not intended to be used to re-argue a case, make new arguments or to introduce new evidence. Thus, we have rejected the complainants' requests also for this reason.

6.114 In order to clarify that the Panel majority's observations are not *findings* on the merits of the complainants' subsidization arguments, we have made a number of changes to paragraphs 7.321 and 7.325 (now paragraphs 7.321 and 7.325-7.327). In addition, we have made changes to paragraph 7.325 (now paragraphs 7.325-7.327) to reflect some of the facts the complainants have pointed to in their interim review comments that were not previously fully taken into account by the Panel majority.

VII. PANEL FINDINGS

A. *Introduction*

1. *General principles of treaty interpretation, the applicable standard of review and burden of proof*

(a) Treaty interpretation

7.1 With respect to the question of legal interpretation, Article 3.2 of the DSU provides that Members recognize that the dispute settlement system serves to clarify the provisions of the covered agreements "in accordance with customary rules of interpretation of public international law". Article 31 of the Vienna Convention on the Law of Treaties ("Vienna Convention")[30] is generally accepted to be one such customary rule. Paragraph 1 of this rule reads as follows:

> A treaty shall be interpreted in good faith in accordance with the ordinary meaning to be given to the terms of the treaty in their context and in the light of its object and purpose.

7.2 There is a considerable body of WTO case law dealing with the application of Article 31 of the Vienna Convention in WTO dispute settlement. It is clear that interpretation must be based above all on the text of the treaty[31], but that the context of the treaty also plays an important role. It is also well-established that customary principles of treaty interpretation "neither require nor condone the imputation into a treaty of words that are not there or the

[30] The Vienna Convention on the Law of Treaties, done at Vienna, 23 May 1969, 1155 United Nations Treaty Series 331 (1980); 8 International Legal Materials 679 (1969).

[31] Appellate Body Report, *Japan – Alcoholic Beverages II*, p. 11.

importation into a treaty of concepts that were not intended"[32]. Furthermore, panels "must be guided by the rules of treaty interpretation set out in the Vienna Convention, and must not add to or diminish rights and obligations provided in the WTO Agreement"[33].

(b) Standard of review

7.3 Panels generally are bound by the standard of review set forth in Article 11 of the DSU, which provides, in relevant part, that:

> [A] panel should make an *objective assessment of the matter* before it, including an objective assessment of the facts of the case and the applicability of and conformity with the relevant covered agreements ... (emphasis added)

7.4 The obligation imposed by Article 11 of the DSU includes the consideration of all aspects of the matter, both factual and legal, and implies *inter alia* that a panel should consider the issues raised, without overstepping its terms of reference. Article 11 further provides that panels should also make such other findings as will assist the DSB in making the recommendations or in giving the rulings provided for in the covered agreements.

(c) Burden of proof

7.5 The general principles applicable to the allocation of the burden of proof in WTO dispute settlement require that a party claiming a violation of a provision of a WTO Agreement must assert and prove its claim[34]. Therefore, the complainants bear the burden of demonstrating that the challenged measures are inconsistent with the SCM Agreement, the TRIMs Agreement and the GATT 1994. The Appellate Body has stated that a complaining party will satisfy its burden when it establishes a *prima facie* case, namely a case which, in the absence of effective refutation by the defending party, requires a panel, as a matter of law, to rule in favour of the complaining party[35]. Finally, it is generally for each party asserting a fact to provide proof thereof[36].

2. *Measures at issue and summary of claims*

7.6 The complainants have brought these disputes against Canada in order to challenge the WTO-consistency of the "Minimum Required Domestic Content Level" prescribed under the FIT Programme adopted by the Government of the

---

[32] Appellate Body Report, *India – Patents (US)*, para. 45.

[33] Appellate Body Report, *India – Patents (US)*, para. 46.

[34] Appellate Body Report, *US – Wool Shirts and Blouses*, p. 14.

[35] Appellate Body Report, *EC – Hormones,* para. 104.

[36] Appellate Body Report, *US – Wool Shirts and Blouses*, p. 14.

Province of Ontario[37] in 2009, as well as all individual FIT and microFIT Contracts implementing this requirement since the FIT Programme's inception ("the measures at issue" or "the challenged measures"). According to the complainants, the "Minimum Required Domestic Content Level" renders the FIT Programme, and all relevant FIT and microFIT Contracts involving electricity generation projects using solar PV or windpower technology[38], measures incompatible with Article III:4 of the General Agreement on Tariffs and Trade 1994 ("GATT 1994"), trade-related investment measures ("TRIMs") inconsistent with Article 2.1 of the Agreement on Trade-Related Investment Measures ("TRIMs Agreement"), and prohibited subsidies under the terms of Articles 3.1(b) and 3.2 of the Agreement on Subsidies and Countervailing Measures ("SCM Agreement").

7.7 Throughout these proceedings, however, the complainants have emphasized that in contesting the WTO-consistency of the challenged measures, they do not question the legitimacy of the objectives pursued by the Government of Ontario through the FIT Programme of reducing carbon emissions and promoting the generation of electricity from renewable energy sources. In particular, Japan has explained that "Japan does not take issue with Ontario's stated goal of enhancing renewable energy generation"[39] or "the government's intervention as such to internalize the positive externalities of renewable energy generation technologies"[40]. Likewise, the European Union does not "contest the general purpose of the FIT Program, as helping to promote electricity supply from renewable energy sources", highlighting that "[s]uch a purpose is legitimately valid and ... WTO Members can and should actively support it"[41]. What the complainants call into question is limited to the alleged trade-distortive element of the challenged measures, which they identify to be the "Minimum Required Domestic Content Level" given effect through the FIT Programme and the FIT and microFIT Contracts. According to the complainants, this aspect of the challenged measures affords a form of WTO-inconsistent protection to producers of certain types of equipment used to generate electricity from solar and wind energy ("renewable energy generation equipment") that are based in Ontario to the detriment of competing industries in other WTO Members, and

---

37 It is not disputed that, under public international law, Canada is responsible for the actions of the Government of the Province of Ontario ("Government of Ontario").

38 The "Minimum Required Domestic Content Level" is prescribed for solar PV facilities operating under either a FIT or microFIT Contract, as well as windpower facilities operating under a FIT Contract. A more detailed description of the FIT Programme and the FIT and microFIT Contracts, including the "Minimum Required Domestic Content Level", is set out below at paras. 7.64-7.68, 7.158-7.166, and 7.195-7.219.

39 Japan's first written submission, para. 3.

40 Japan's response to Panel question No. 44 (first set).

41 European Union's first written submission, para. 2; and opening statement at the first meeting of the Panel, para. 3.

should therefore be eliminated[42]. Thus, as Japan has declared[43], these disputes cannot be properly characterized as "trade and environment" disputes, but rather, they should be thought of as "trade and investment" disputes.

3. *Preliminary rulings*

7.8 The Panel announced its conclusions on the merits of Canada's requests for preliminary rulings at the opening session of the first substantive meeting with the parties on 27 March 2012. The Panel dismissed Canada's requests finding that the legal bases of the complainants' prohibited subsidy claims were described with sufficient clarity in their respective Panel Request to "present the problem clearly". The Panel subsequently issued its preliminary rulings to the parties in written form on 11 May 2012. After consulting with the parties, the Panel decided: (a) to circulate its preliminary rulings to all Members; and (b) that the circulated preliminary rulings would form an integral part of the final Panel Reports, subject to any revisions necessary in the light of comments received from the parties during interim review. The Panel's preliminary rulings were circulated on 25 May 2012 in documents WT/DS412/8 and WT/DS426/7.

4. *Factual background*

(a) Introduction

7.9 As already mentioned, these disputes are about the "Minimum Required Domestic Content Level" that is applied by the Province of Ontario under the FIT Programme, and the FIT and microFIT Contracts, in relation to certain electricity generation facilities utilizing solar PV and windpower technology. In order to fully understand these measures and properly evaluate the merits of the complainants' claims, it is, in our view, essential to comprehend the role they play in Ontario's electricity system. In order to do so, we believe it is important to appreciate not only how Ontario's electricity system currently operates and has evolved over time, but also the main characteristics and features of electricity and electricity systems in general. The complexity of electricity systems and how electricity prices are determined in Ontario are germane to much of our analysis of the complainants' claims. Thus, in the following section of our Reports, we set out what we consider to be the overall factual background against which we will review and evaluate the parties' arguments[44]. We start by outlining the key characteristics of electricity and electricity systems in general, before briefly describing the history of Ontario's electricity system, and then

---

[42] Japan's first written submission, paras. 1-3; opening statement at the first meeting of the Panel, para. 5; European Union's first written submission, paras. 2-6; and second written submission, para. 1.

[43] Japan's first written submission, para. 3.

[44] The facts that are described in this section will, to the extent necessary, be further explained and elaborated in the course of our evaluation of the parties' arguments in the remainder of these Reports.

turning to explain the structure and operation of the electricity system that exists in Ontario at present drawing largely from the description provided by Japan in its first written submission[45]. The section ends with a short summary of the key features of the challenged measures – the FIT Programme, and the FIT and microFIT Contracts.

(b) Electricity and electricity systems

7.10 Electricity is the lifeblood of modern society. Yet it is invisible to the naked eye and often unnoticed in the day-to-day lives of billions of people. There is little doubt, however, that reliable systems of electricity are the engines that drive economies world-wide, bringing power to a host of consumers for a myriad of uses and applications including in homes, factories, offices, farms, transportation systems and telecommunications networks. Most goods depend upon electricity for their production, as do essential services ranging from health-care to banking. Few discoveries can boast such wide-ranging impacts on the quality of human life as electricity.

7.11 Electricity has a number of specific properties compared to other goods[46]. The provision of a secure, safe, reliable and sustainable supply of electricity requires a large system that has to be in continuous operation to ensure that it remains energised. In general, electricity is a reliable form of energy but it is also extremely dangerous if the system is not secured against accidental leakage. A critical physical characteristic of electricity is that it is intangible and, with certain limited exceptions, cannot be effectively stored[47]. It is particularly

---

[45] We note that Japan's factual description of Ontario's electricity system was adopted by the European Union as part of its arguments in these proceedings, and to a large extent, has not been contested by Canada.

[46] We note that it is not contested in these disputes that electricity produced from electricity generation facilities (what the parties refer to as "commodity" electricity) is a good and a product for the purpose of the covered agreements that are at issue. Indeed, both the European Union and Canada argue this to be the case. In doing so, the European Union explains that a number of WTO Members (including the European Union and the United States) have relied upon the optional heading for "electrical energy" contained in the Harmonized Commodity Description and Coding System to take tariff commitments with respect to electricity in their GATT Schedules, or as in the case of Canada, simply include the relevant tariff line without setting a tariff binding. Although explicitly stating that Japan does not take a position on whether electricity qualifies as a good or a product, Japan describes electricity produced from generating facilities as a "commodity", and recognizes that it is treated as a good in the optional heading contained in the Harmonized Commodity Description and Coding System. Significantly, in our view, Japan has at no stage in these proceedings responded to Canada's argument that the challenged measures involve government purchases of *goods* by rejecting Canada's contention that electricity is a good and a product. See Japan's response to Panel questions No. 43 (first set) and No. 51 (second set); first written submission, paras. 85, 96-97, 99 and 224; European Union's response to Panel question No. 51 (second set); and Canada's response to Panel question No. 51(second set).

[47] Pumped-storage hydroelectric facilities provide a limited means of storing electricity. Such facilities use electricity to pump water into reservoirs at higher elevations when demand is low, and release it through turbines to generate electricity during peak-demand periods. William W. Hogan, "Overview of the Electricity System in the Province of Ontario", 21 December 2011, Exhibit CDA-2,

because of the latter characteristic that electricity must be generated at precisely the time that it is consumed by end-users. Electricity is delivered to consumers through the operation of a vast integrated infrastructure of high-voltage transmission lines (connecting generators to distributors and large consumers) and lower-voltage distribution lines that ultimately link to individual consumers[48]. This is generally referred to as a grid and requires a massive infrastructure of complementary equipment to ensure that it functions. Access to this grid either to supply electricity into it or to take electricity out of it has to be tightly controlled to ensure the integrity of the system as a whole. Electricity delivery networks will fail if the quantity of electricity demanded (known as "load" in industry terminology) is greater or less than the quantity of electricity supplied for any length of time[49]. It is therefore necessary to maintain a continuous supply-demand balance between generators and consumers, a task complicated by the daily fluctuations in electricity demand as well as the physical capacity limits of transmission and distribution lines. When important imbalances occur, electricity networks can be destabilized, leading to brownouts, blackouts or, in extreme cases, the interruption of power to all consumers[50]. In the event of a major failure in a grid its restarting can take a significant period of time which is massively disruptive to modern economies and societies.

7.12 One important consequence of the need to maintain a continuous supply-demand balance across an entire electricity system is that uncoordinated bilateral trades between buyers and sellers of electricity cannot take place. In other words, because of the nature of how electricity must be produced and consumed, it is generally not possible for an individual consumer to enter into an individual supply contract with one or more specific generators. As a result, electricity systems require some kind of central coordination mechanism to ensure that the output of generators is exactly equal to the amount demanded by consumers (plus inevitable transmission losses) and that the physical limitations of the electricity system are not violated[51].

7.13 The fact that there are no close substitutes for electricity, combined with a lack of easily observable price signals for end users in general, implies that electricity demand is largely unresponsive to prices in the short run (i.e. it is relatively price inelastic). Thus, global electricity demand will fluctuate over the

("Hogan Report"), fn. 6. Professor William W. Hogan is the Raymond Plank Professor of Global Energy Policy at Harvard University where he is *inter alia* the Research Director of the *Harvard Electricity Policy Group*. Professor Hogan has been actively engaged in the design and improvement of competitive electricity markets in many regions of the United States, as well as around the world, from England to Australia. His activities include designing the market structures and market rules by which regional transmission organizations, in various forms, coordinate bid-based markets for energy, ancillary services, and financial transmission rights.

[48] Electricity may also be obtained through cogeneration facilities. See Ontario' Long-Term Energy Plan, Exhibit CDA-6.

[49] Hogan Report, Exhibit CDA-2, p. 13.

[50] *Ibid.*

[51] Hogan Report, Exhibit CDA-2, p. 12.

course of a day, week, month or year, as factors other than price (e.g. air temperature and hours of daylight) cause the demand for electricity to change. A typical pattern of electricity demand on a weekday in Ontario would show that most electricity is consumed during daylight hours, with consumption steadily increasing from 5.00 a.m. until reaching its peak at around 5.00 p.m.[52].

7.14 The fact that electricity cannot be stored in large quantities and that demand for electricity fluctuates over any day means that specific forms of generating capacity have to be developed to provide for this fluctuation. In addition, to keep a grid functional it has to be kept operational or "live" continuously. Therefore, in order to satisfy demand, electricity systems utilize a mix of generation technologies, each with different cost structures and operational requirements. According to industry practice, the different types of facilities may be described as "base-load", "intermediate" or "peaking", depending upon when and for how long they operate, whether they can raise or lower their output rapidly in a controlled manner ("dispatchability"), and whether their costs are mostly fixed or variable. The reliability of a generation facility's output is measured by its "capacity factor", which is defined as the percentage of hours during the year that it is able to operate.

7.15 Base-load generation is that portion of an electricity system's supply mix that is expected to be able to operate at all times, i.e. during both low and high demand periods. Base load generation is typically characterized by high fixed costs, low marginal costs, and high capacity factors. Hydroelectric and nuclear stations, both of which have large sunk capital costs and minimal fuel costs, are quintessential examples of base-load power, but this function may also be performed by other technologies (e.g. coal) depending on the supply mix in a given jurisdiction and on the cost of fuel. Although base-load generators have high capacity factors, they tend to have more limited dispatchability. Hydroelectric plants are an exception in that their output can be raised or lowered on relatively short notice.

7.16 Intermediate-load generation supplies power when system demand is above its minimum level but still below its maximum level. It is generally characterized by moderate fixed and marginal costs. Coal plants are frequently used for intermediate generation, but improvements in the efficiency of natural gas plants and falling fuel prices have made natural gas a viable option for intermediate supply. Coal-fired generation is less dispatchable than natural gas but more dispatchable than nuclear.

7.17 Peak-load generators tend to have lower fixed costs than other types of facilities, as well as relatively high marginal costs, and a high degree of dispatchability. Peaking generators may only run infrequently, usually at times when demand is near the system-wide capacity limit.

[52] A graphical depiction of the patterns of weekday demand for electricity in Ontario in Summer and Winter can be found below at para. 7.279.

7.18 Up until fairly recent times, a mix of the above-mentioned "conventional" generation technologies has traditionally been considered to provide for the most economically efficient way of producing power for the purpose of reliable electricity systems. However, concerns over the environmental impact and cost of certain technologies have increasingly emerged as key considerations in the choice of supply mix[53]. To address these concerns, electricity systems around the world have gradually begun to include renewable technologies into their production mix.

7.19 Generation facilities utilizing renewable energy technologies, such as solar PV and windpower, resemble base-load generation in that most of their costs are capital costs, with fuel costs being minimal or non-existent. However, they differ from base-load generation in that their capacity utilization is lower due to intermittent output. Wind turbines only produce electricity when the wind is blowing, which may or may not coincide with consumer demand. In contrast to the uncertainty of wind generation, solar PV is more predictable, producing all of its output during the day and none at night. A downside of solar generation is that its output falls just when daily demand is increasing as the sun sets and households and businesses turn on their lights. The fact that solar production runs counter to daily load profiles forces conventional generators to ramp up their production at night in order to make up for lost output from solar generators. As a result, generation facilities utilizing solar PV and windpower technologies may need to be paired with conventional generation in order to minimize the potential for supply disruptions[54].

7.20 Until the 1970s, electricity generation in most countries was dominated by vertically integrated monopolies, structured as either state-owned enterprises or regulated private monopolies. Monopolies were tolerated due to the belief that economies of scale in electricity could only be captured by a single, large producer. Advances in generation technology and the desire of private suppliers to gain full access to transmission networks eventually broke down this consensus. Since the 1970s, many countries have restructured their electricity systems to incorporate various elements of competition.

(c) Electricity in Ontario

(i) 1906 to 2002

7.21 The origins of Ontario's electricity system can be traced back to 1906, when the Government of Ontario established the Hydro-Electric Power Commission of Ontario ("HEPCO") as "the world's first publicly owned electric utility"[55]. In its early years, Ontario's electricity system relied almost entirely

[53] Hogan Report, Exhibit CDA-2, p. 6.
[54] Hogan Report, Exhibit CDA-2, p. 11.
[55] Ontario's Long-Term Energy Plan, Exhibit CDA-6, p. 5.

upon hydroelectric power, but as demand for electricity grew, the Province chose to diversify its supply mix, adding coal-fired power stations during the 1950s and nuclear power in the 1970s[56]. In 1974, HEPCO was recognized as a "crown corporation" and renamed Ontario Hydro.

7.22 As a vertically integrated public utility with generation, transmission and distribution functions, Ontario Hydro dominated the electricity sector until the *Energy Competition Act of 1998*, which enacted the *Electricity Act of 1998*, authorized its "unbundling" into five successor entities[57]. By this time, much of Ontario's electricity infrastructure, including its coal-fired power plants, needed to be refurbished or replaced[58]. In addition, cost overruns in Ontario Hydro's nuclear programme had left the utility heavily indebted, and provided a strong incentive to pursue market-oriented reforms along similar lines to what had been tried in other jurisdictions[59]. The successor entities to Ontario Hydro were: (i) the Independent Market Operator (subsequently renamed the Independent Electricity System Operator in 2005 (see below)), charged with administering Ontario's wholesale electricity market and directing the flow of electricity from generators to consumers through the transmission system; (ii) Ontario Power Generation ("OPG"), which inherited Ontario Hydro's generation assets, at the time accounting for approximately 90% of Ontario's electricity capacity; (iii) Hydro One Inc. ("Hydro One"[60]), which assumed Ontario Hydro's transmission network and rural local distribution businesses; (iv) the Ontario Electricity Financial Corporation ("OEFC"[61]), which inherited other Ontario Hydro assets and liabilities, including contracts with Non-Utility Generators ("NUGs"[62]) and CAD 20 billion in stranded debt; and (v) the Electrical Safety Authority, which was given responsibility for regulating the system's safety[63]. In addition, the *Ontario Energy Board Act of 1998* designated the OEB as the regulator of the new electricity market, with the authority to, *inter alia*, approve certain rates and prices applicable in the market[64].

---

56 *Ibid.*

57 Ontario's Long-Term Energy Plan, Exhibit CDA-6, p. 5.

58 Ontario's Long-Term Energy Plan, Exhibit CDA-6, p. 5; and Hogan Report, Exhibit CDA-2, p. 19.

59 See e.g. Hogan Report, Exhibit CDA-2, pp. 18-19; and Report of the Advisory Committee on Competition in Ontario's Electricity System to the Ontario Minister of Environment and Energy, "A Framework for Competition", May 1996, ("A Framework for Competition"), Exhibit CDA-3, pp. 27-28.

60 The basic corporate structure of Hydro One and the nature of its current operations in Ontario are discussed further below at paras. 7.34-7.35 and 7.234-7.238.

61 The basic corporate structure of the OEFC and the nature of its current operations in Ontario, to the extent relevant to the arguments made in the present proceedings, are discussed further below at para. 7.43.

62 The role of NUGs in Ontario's power system is explained below at paras. 7.26 and 7.31.

63 Hogan Report, Exhibit CDA-2, pp. 20-21.

64 Ontario Energy Board Act of 1998, Exhibit JPN-6.

(ii) The 2002 competitive wholesale market[65]

7.23 After several years of preparation, Ontario's competitive wholesale electricity market opened in May 2002. It was hoped that the restructuring of the electricity sector would attract private investment into the generation business, but despite a 30% rise in the price of electricity in the months following the market opening, the anticipated investment failed to materialize. Instead, the relatively high electricity prices, caused by increased demand due to record high temperatures in Ontario over the summer of 2002, led the Government of the day to temporarily freeze electricity prices for residential, institutional and small business consumers[66].

7.24 As a result of the problems encountered during the 2002 market opening experience, the Government of Ontario decided to once again restructure Ontario's electricity system in 2004, and to this end enacted the *Electricity Restructuring Act of 2004* in order to "restructure Ontario's electricity sector, to promote the expansion of electricity supply and capacity, including supply and capacity from alternative and renewable energy sources, facilitate load management and electricity demand management, encourage electricity conservation and the efficient use of electricity and to regulate prices in part of the electricity sector"[67]. One of the key reforms introduced under the *Electricity Restructuring Act of 2004* was the creation of the Ontario Power Authority ("OPA"), which was given a number of important tasks including responsibility for overall long-term system planning, activities in support of ensuring an adequate, reliable and secure electricity supply, and the promotion of the diversification of Ontario's electricity supply with a particular emphasis on renewable and clean energy[68]. The *Electricity Restructuring Act of 2004* laid the foundations for the electricity system that currently operates in Ontario.

(iii) Ontario's current "hybrid" electricity system

7.25 In its current incarnation, Ontario's electricity system has been described as a partially liberalized "hybrid"[69] system where both public and private entities participate in core generation, transmission, distribution and retail activities. Although far from the government-dominated system that characterized its first eight decades of operation, the Government of Ontario continues to play a

[65] A more detailed description and analysis of Ontario's competitive wholesale market opening experience are set out below at paras. 7.285-7.292.

[66] Ontario Energy Board, "History of the OEB" ("History of the OEB"), Exhibit CDA-17, p. 2.

[67] Highlights of the *Electricity Restructuring Act of 2004*, OEB website, ("Highlights of the *Electricity Restructuring Act of 2004*"), Exhibit JPN-9. See also *Electricity Restructuring Act of 2004*, S.O. 2004, c. 23, ("*Electricity Restructuring Act of 2004*"), Exhibit CDA-18, Section 1(a).

[68] *Electricity Act of 1998*, Chapter 15, Schedule A, as amended, ("*Electricity Act of 1998*"), Exhibit JPN-5, Section 25.2.

[69] Hogan Report, Exhibit CDA-2, p. 21.

critical role in all aspects of the system's functioning. The key participants in this system and their interactions are described in the following sections.

Generation

7.26 As of year-end 2010, there were approximately 34,700 MW of installed generation capacity in Ontario[70]. This capacity can be roughly separated into three groups of generators[71]: (i) the government-owned assets of OPG, which as already mentioned are the former generation assets of Ontario Hydro; (ii) NUGs, which are private generators that entered into supply contracts with Ontario Hydro in the 1980s and 1990s; and (iii) Independent Power Producers ("IPPs"), which comprise all the other generators in Ontario that have started to operate since the wholesale market was restructured. The IPPs include generators operating under the FIT Programme.

7.27 OPG is a wholly-owned corporation of the Government of Ontario that owns three nuclear, five thermal, 65 hydroelectric and two windpower generation facilities[72]. In 2010, the OPG produced approximately 58% of all electricity generated in Ontario. The OPG's nuclear and base-load hydroelectric generation facilities are classified as "OPG Regulated Assets". The prices received by the OPG for electricity produced by these facilities are set by the Ontario Energy Board ("OEB"[73]) on the basis of the principle of "cost recovery and a margin of return"[74]. For 2011, the return on equity for the OPG's regulated assets was set by the OEB at 9.43%[75]. However, payments to the OPG for the supply of electricity from its other "unregulated" hydroelectric and coal-fired facilities, which account for 8% of electricity generation in Ontario, are not guided by the principle of cost recovery and margin. These assets receive the Hourly Ontario Electricity Price ("HOEP"[76]), which is generally lower than the

---

[70] Power Outlook: Winter 2010-2011, ("IESO Power Outlook"), Exhibit JPN-10.

[71] Overview of Electricity Regulation in Canada, Blakes, ("Overview of Electricity Regulation in Canada"), Exhibit JPN-7, pp. 11-13; and Quick Takes: Electricity Pricing, Issue 19, IESO website, ("Quick Takes: Electricity Pricing"), Exhibit JPN-3, pp. 2-3.

[72] The OPG was established under Part IV.1 of the *Electricity Act of 1998*, Exhibit JPN-5. See also Investor Relations, OPG website, ("OPG Investor Relations"), Exhibit JPN-14.

[73] The nature of the OEB's operations and its relationship with the Government of Ontario are discussed below at para. 7.42.

[74] Canada's response to Panel question No. 26 (first set).

[75] OEB, "In the Matter of an Application by Ontario Power Generation Inc., Payment Amounts for Prescribed Facilities for 2011 and 2012: Decision with Reasons", EB-2010-0008, 10 March 2011 ("OEB Decision on Payment Amounts for Prescribed Facilities for 2011 and 2012"), Exhibit CDA-65, p.122. As of 1 March 2011, the OPG was paid CAD 5.59 cents and CAD 3.41 cents for each kWh of electricity that was generated, respectively, by its regulated nuclear and hydroelectric assets. See, Japan's first written submission, para. 36 and Payment Amounts Order (EB 2010-0008), Ontario Energy Board, 11 April 2011, ("OEB Payment Amounts Order"), Exhibit JPN-19, pp. 4-5.

[76] The HOEP is the price for electricity that is bought and sold through the operation of the IESO-administered wholesale electricity market. The average HOEP received by the OPG's unregulated assets in 2010 was CAD 3.7 cents/kWh. OPG Fact Sheet: Year End 2010, ("2010 OPG Fact Sheet"), Exhibit JPN-15. The mechanisms used to determine the HOEP as well as its relevance to the prices

regulated price obtained by the OPG's regulated assets. Canada explains that the OPG's unregulated assets receive the HOEP because "most of these are state-owned facilities [that] are over 60 years old, and the capital costs of these facilities have largely been depreciated"[77]. Similarly, the OPG's coal-fired facilities either receive the HOEP because, again, they are facilities "whose costs have largely been depreciated" or a price under contract with the OEFC which allows the OPG to recover its costs[78]. The operations of these unregulated coal-fired assets will be shut down in 2014[79].

7.28 The remaining generators operating in Ontario account for 42% of electricity supply. Of these, the IPPs, which generate around 40% of Ontario's electricity supply, receive prices that are negotiated or set under different types of OPA initiatives and contracts including: the Clean Energy Supply ("CES") contracts for natural gas[80]; the Renewable Energy Supply ("RES") Requests for Proposals I, II and III[81]; the Hydroelectric Contract Initiative ("HCI") for grid-connected non-OPG-owned hydro facilities[82]; the Combined Heat and Power ("CHP") Requests for Proposals I, II, III[83]; the Renewable Energy Standard Offer Programme ("RESOP")[84]; and the FIT Programme.

7.29 Under the CES and RES initiatives, the OPA awarded supply contracts through a competitive bidding process which set prices for delivered electricity at the levels of the lowest bids meeting the specified conditions. Prices paid to generators operating under the HCI and CHP initiatives were negotiated with the OPA and, according to Canada, generally guided by the rates paid under competitive contracts determined through a request for proposal85. Under the RESOP, the prices paid to solar PV generators are based primarily on the principle of cost recovery. For non-solar RESOP generators, prices are based on those applied under the RES initiative. As regards the FIT Programme, the price

---

paid to generators for electricity delivered to Ontario's electricity grid are discussed below at paras. 7.45-7.53.

[77] Canada's response to Panel question No. 26 (first set).

[78] The average HOEP received by these assets in 2010 was CAD 4.3 cents/kWh. 2010 OPG Fact Sheet, Exhibit JPN-15.

[79] Canada's response to Panel question No. 26 (first set).

[80] Canada's first written submission (DS412), para. 31, referring to Direction from Dwight Duncan, Minister of Energy, to Jan Carr, Chief Executive Officer of the OPA, 24 March 2005, ("Direction from Minister of Energy to CEO of the OPA from March 2005"), Exhibit CDA-25.

[81] Hogan Report, Exhibit CDA-2, pp. 30-32; and Progress Report on Electricity Supply: Second Quarter 2011, Ontario Power Authority, ("OPA Progress Report: Second Quarter 2011"), Exhibit JPN-28, p. 1.

[82] OPA, Hydroelectric Contract Initiative, OPA website, ("OPA, Hydroelectric Contract Initiative"), Exhibit CDA-26.

[83] OPA, Combined Heat and Power, OPA website, ("OPA, Combined Heat and Power"), Exhibit CDA-27.

[84] OPA, Standard Offer Program – Renewable Energy for Small Electricity Generators, An Introductory Guide, ("OPA's Standard Offer Program – Renewable Energy for Small Electricity Generators"), Exhibit JPN-206, p. 1.

[85] Canada's response to Panel question No. 26 (first set).

received by qualified generators is guided by the principle of cost recovery and margin86. The after tax rate of return on equity used to develop the FIT Price Schedule in 2009 was 11%.

7.30 According to Japan, generators that do not operate under the RESOP or FIT Programme will receive between CAD 5.0 cents/kWh to CAD 23.9 cents/kWh[87]. Under the OPA's RESOP contracts, non-solar generators are paid CAD 11.04 cents/kWh with an additional payment of CAD 3.52 cents/kWh for electricity delivered during peak hours; while solar PV generators are paid CAD 42.0 cents/kWh[88]. The FIT Price Schedule provides for payments in a range from CAD 10.3 cents/kWh to CAD 80.2 cents/kWh. Windpower projects receive either CAD 13.5 cents/kWh (onshore) or CAD 19.0 cents/kWh (offshore) with a provision for 20% of the rate to "escalate" in accordance with inflation, and solar PV projects receive from CAD 44.3 cents/kWh to CAD 80.2 cents/kWh (depending on size and technology) with no escalation. All of the OPA's contracted rates "are generally higher than the [HOEP]"[89].

7.31 Finally, the prices paid to NUGs for delivered electricity were negotiated 20 years ago and are not based on the principle of "cost recovery and a margin". Instead, the prices paid to these generators are tied to the prices paid by large consumers of electricity[90]. While precise prices for these contracts are not publicly available[91], they are known to be "generally higher than HOEP"[92]. The average contract rate is estimated to be CAD 8.0 cents/kWh[93]. According to Japan, significant NUG contracts will begin to expire in 2012, with most contracts expiring by 2017[94].

Transmission and distribution

7.32 As already mentioned, electricity systems that use integrated networks of high-voltage transmission lines and relatively lower-voltage distribution lines deliver electricity from generating stations to the general end-user. In Ontario,

---

86 Directive from Minister of Energy and Infrastructure to Ontario Power Authority Regarding FIT Program, 24 September 2009, ("Minister's 2009 FIT Direction"), Exhibit JPN-102, p. 2.

87 Generation Procurement Cost Disclosure, OPA website, ("OPA Generation Procurement Cost Disclosure"), Exhibit JPN-29. Prices as of March 2009.

88 OPA Generation Procurement Cost Disclosure, Exhibit JPN-29.

89 OPA Cash Flows from the Global Adjustment Mechanism, OPA, November 2010, ("OPA Cash Flows: November 2010"), Exhibit JPN-23, p. 5.

90 Canada explains that prior to 2002, the prices paid to NUGs were known as the "Direct Customer Rate", but has since become known as the "Direct Customer Rate new". Canada's response to Panel question No. 26 (first set).

91 NUG contract rates are indexed to the "total market cost" of electricity, which is comprised of HOEP, the GA, and various service charges. See OEFC: Management of Power Supply Contracts, OEFC website, ("OEFC: Management of Power Supply Contracts"), Exhibit JPN-22.

92 OPA Cash Flows: November 2010, Exhibit JPN-23, p. 5.

93 Ontario Electricity Market: The Good, the Bad, and the Ugly, Energy Exchange, 11 May 2010, ("Ontario Electricity Market: Energy Exchange"), Exhibit JPN-24.

94 OEFC: Management of Power Supply Contracts, Exhibit JPN-22.

high-voltage transmission lines carry electricity at voltages above 50 kilovolts ("kV") and are used to move electricity over long distances from generating stations to load or population centres to reduce power losses[95]. Once the electricity nears a distribution hub, voltage is reduced at a transformer station and carried to customers over distribution lines at voltages 50 kV and under[96].

7.33 Generators typically connect to the transmission system or to the distribution system based on their capacity. In particular, generators with capacity greater than 10 MW (including large-capacity FIT generators) typically connect to the transmission system, and generators with capacity of 10 MW or less (including small-capacity FIT and microFIT generators) typically connect to the distribution system[97]. Generators that connect to the transmission system must deliver electricity at voltages above 50 kV, while generators connected to the distribution system must deliver electricity at voltages of 50 kV or less.

7.34 Transmission-connected generators register with the IESO[98], and connect to the high-voltage transmission system, which is almost completely owned and operated by Hydro One[99]. Hydro One was established under Part IV of the *Electricity Act of 1998* as a holding company with the objective of owning and operating transmission systems and distribution systems through one or more subsidiaries[100]. The company is wholly owned and controlled by the Government of Ontario[101]. It is also an "agency" of the Government of Ontario[102]. A Hydro One subsidiary, Hydro One Networks Inc., owns and operates 97% of the

---

95 Electricity Transmission and Distribution in Ontario – A Look Ahead, Ontario Ministry of Energy, 21 December 2004, ("Electricity Transmission and Distribution in Ontario"), Exhibit JPN-36, p. 4.

96 Electricity Transmission and Distribution in Ontario, Exhibit JPN-36, p. 4.

97 Ontario Power Authority, Feed-in Tariff Program: Program Overview, ("FIT Programme Overview"), Exhibit JPN-37, p. 18; and Ontario Power Authority, Micro Feed-In Tariff Program: Program Overview, ("microFIT Programme Overview"), Exhibit JPN-38, p. 8.

98 The IESO administers the flow of electricity across Ontario's electricity grid. The basic corporate structure of the IESO and the nature of its operations are discussed below at paras. 7.39-7.40.

99 Transmission-connected Generators, Exhibit JPN-39; and Quick Facts, Hydro One website, ("Hydro One Quick Facts"), Exhibit JPN-40.

100 *Electricity Act of 1998*, Exhibit JPN-5, Section 48(1).

101 News Release: Hydro One Releases 2010 Year-End Financial Results Hydro One website, ("Hydro One Releases 2010 Year-End Financial Results"), Exhibit JPN-41.

102 All Agencies List, Government of Ontario website, ("Government of Ontario: All Agencies List"), Exhibit JPN-49. The Government of Ontario defines "agency" as "a provincial government organization: [i] which is established by the government, but is not part of a ministry; [ii] which is accountable to the government; [iii] to which the government appoints the majority of the appointees; and, [iv] to which the government has assigned or delegated authority and responsibility, or which otherwise has statutory authority and responsibility to perform a public function or service". Agencies: Boards, Commissions, Councils, Authorities and Foundations, Government of Ontario website, ("Government of Ontario: Agencies"), Exhibit JPN-51.

transmission system in Ontario[103]. Four other private companies own and operate the remaining 3%[104].

7.35 Distribution-connected generators are connected to the distribution system via a local distribution company ("LDC")[105]. Hydro One owns and operates approximately one quarter of Ontario's distribution system through a number of subsidiaries serving 1.3 million of a total 4.7 million customers, mostly in rural areas[106]. The remainder of Ontario's distribution system is presently operated by 80 LDCs, 77 of which are owned by municipal governments[107].

Regulation and administration

7.36 Ontario's electricity system is currently administered and regulated by a number of public entities. Among the most important, for the purpose the present disputes, are the OPA, the IESO, the OEFC and the OEB.

- Ontario Power Authority

7.37 The OPA is an "agency"[108] of the Government of Ontario responsible for managing Ontario's electricity supply and resources in order to meet its medium and long-term needs. The OPA was established under the *Electricity Restructuring Act of 2004* as "[a] corporation without share capital"[109], and operates its business and affairs on a not-for-profit basis[110]. It falls within the "legislative responsibility" of the Government of Ontario's Ministry of Energy[111], and receives and executes directives from the Minister of Energy[112]. Among its statutory objectives are the goals of engaging in:

> [A]ctivities in support of the goal of ensuring adequate, reliable and secure electricity supply and resources in Ontario; [and]

---

[103] Our Subsidiaries, Hydro One website, ("Hydro One: Our Subsidiaries"), Exhibit JPN-43.

[104] These companies are: Great Lakes Power; Canadian Niagara Power; Five Nations Energy; and Cat Lake Power Utility. IESO, The Power System, ("The Power System"), Exhibit JPN-44.

[105] Distribution-connected Generators, Hydro One website, ("Distribution-connected Generators"), Exhibit JPN-45; and Electricity Transmission and Distribution in Ontario, Exhibit JPN-36, p. 4.

[106] Hydro One: Our Subsidiaries, Exhibit JPN-43; Delivering Safe, Reliable and Environmentally Responsible Electricity to Ontarians, Electricity Distributors Association, July 2010, ("EDA: Delivering Electricity to Ontarians"), Exhibit JPN-46; and Overview of Electricity Regulation in Canada, Exhibit JPN-7, pp. 11 and 16.

[107] Find Your Local Utility, IESO website, ("LDCs operating in Ontario"), Exhibit JPN-47; and EDA: Delivering Electricity to Ontarians, Exhibit JPN-46.

[108] Government of Ontario: All Agencies List, Exhibit JPN-49; and Agency Details, Ontario Power Authority, Government of Ontario website, ("Agency Details, OPA"), Exhibit JPN-50.

[109] *Electricity Act of 1998*, Exhibit JPN-5, Section 25.1(1).

[110] *Electricity Act of 1998*, Exhibit JPN-5, Section 25.2(2).

[111] About the Ministry of Energy, Ministry of Energy website, ("About the Ministry of Energy"), Exhibit JPN-52.

[112] Directives to OPA from Minister of Energy, OPA website, ("Directives to OPA from Minister of Energy"), Exhibit JPN-55.

> ... activities to facilitate the diversification of sources of electricity supply by promoting the use of cleaner energy sources and technologies, including alternative energy sources and renewable energy sources; ...[113]

To achieve these and other objectives, the OPA was given the power to *inter alia*:

> [E]nter into contracts relating to the procurement of electricity supply and capacity in or outside Ontario; [and]
>
> ... enter into contracts relating to the procurement of electricity supply and capacity using alternative energy sources or renewable energy sources to assist the Government of Ontario in achieving goals in the development and use of alternative or renewable energy technology and resources; ...[114]

7.38 The OPA's supply contracts provide guaranteed prices over a long-term period that is typically 20 years[115]. The OPA has used its contracting powers to secure actual and future electricity supply from a variety of private and publicly-owned generation facilities including those utilizing nuclear, gas, hydro, wind, solar and bioenergy technologies[116]. As of 30 June 2011, the OPA had 19,090 MW of electricity supply capacity under contract, of which 12,426 MW was in commercial operation[117].

- The Independent Electricity System Operator

7.39 The IESO is another "agency" of the Government of Ontario[118]. Like the OPA, the IESO is a not-for-profit "corporation without share capital"[119] and falls under the "legislative responsibility" of the Government of Ontario's Ministry of Energy[120]. Similarly, pursuant to the *Electricity Act of 1998*, the IESO is also controlled by the Government of Ontario.

7.40 The IESO administers Ontario's electricity markets and operates and maintains the IESO-controlled grid to ensure real-time coordination between

---

[113] *Electricity Act of 1998*, Exhibit JPN-5, Sections 25.2(1)(c) and (d).

[114] *Electricity Act of 1998*, Exhibit JPN-5, Section 25.2(5)(c). This authority is repeated in Section 25.32(1)(a); while Section 25.32(4.1) reveals that the "Minister may direct the OPA to undertake ... any other initiative or activity that relates to, (a) the procurement of electricity supply or capacity from renewable energy sources..."

[115] Canada's first written submission (DS412), para. 31.

[116] The range of supply contracts that the OPA has entered into or taken over from the OEFC are identified above at para. 7.28.

[117] OPA Progress Report: Second Quarter 2011, Exhibit JPN-28, p. 1.

[118] Government of Ontario: All Agencies List, Exhibit JPN-49; and Agency Details, Independent Electricity System Operator, Government of Ontario website, ("Agency Details, IESO"), Exhibit JPN-57.

[119] *Electricity Act of 1998*, Exhibit JPN-5, Sections 4(1) and 5(2).

[120] About the IESO, IESO website, ("About the IESO"), Exhibit JPN-59; and About the Ministry of Energy, Exhibit JPN-52.

electricity supply and demand[121]. In particular, the IESO manages Ontario's wholesale electricity market (the "physical market"), bringing together generators, traders, utilities, and large volume consumers[122]. This not only involves the IESO monitoring and directing the movement of electricity across the IESO-controlled grid, but also the settlement of payments between market participants. In this latter respect, the IESO explains its role as follows: "In the physical market, we collect funds from buyers and transfer funds to sellers. We do not actually take title to energy, and we are, by law, revenue neutral"[123]. The settlement process in the physical market comprises four steps: (i) gathering and processing metering data to produce settlement-ready data; (ii) using the settlement-ready data to determine revenue owed to suppliers, costs for consumers, and various overhead costs payable by market participants; (iii) invoicing participants; and (iv) transferring funds between energy purchasers and suppliers[124].

7.41 The IESO also oversees the reliable operation of the provincial transmission system[125], and makes and approves the Market Rules, which define the IESO-administered markets and describe how they operate, and the Market Manuals, which provide detailed guidelines for various activities of market participants[126].

- Ontario Energy Board

7.42 The OEB is an "agency"[127] of the Government of Ontario that regulates Ontario's electricity and natural gas sectors in conformity with the public interest[128]. In the electricity sector, this regulation is done through the OEB's authority to set transmission and distribution rates, as well as its authority to license all market participants. As already noted[129], the OEB determines the prices at which the "regulated" assets of OPG are to be paid for electricity

[121] *Electricity Act of 1998*, Exhibit JPN-5, Section 5.

[122] IESO, Marketplace Training: Settlement Statements and Invoices, December 2010, ("IESO: Settlement Statements and Invoices"), Exhibit JPN-62, p. 1. The "physical market" refers to the real-time markets for the delivery and use of electricity. The IESO also administers a "financial market" for buying and selling transmission rights.

[123] IESO: Settlement Statements and Invoices, Exhibit JPN-62, p. 1.

[124] IESO: Settlement Statements and Invoices, Exhibit JPN-62, p. 1. The processes used to settle payments between wholesale market participants are explained in more detail below at paras. 7.60-7.63.

[125] About the IESO, Exhibit JPN-59; and The Power Grid, IESO website, ("IESO: The Power Grid"), Exhibit JPN-60.

[126] Rules, Manuals and Forms, IESO website, ("IESO: Rules, Manuals and Forms"), Exhibit JPN-61.

[127] Government of Ontario: All Agencies List, Exhibit JPN-49; and Agency Details, Ontario Energy Board, Government of Ontario website, ("Agency Details, OEB"), Exhibit JPN-63.

[128] What We Do, OEB website, ("OEB functions"), Exhibit JPN-64.

[129] See above at para. 7.27.

delivered into Ontario's electricity grid[130]. The OEB also maintains the Regulated Price Plan ("RPP"), which establishes the prices paid by retail consumers that purchase electricity from LDCs. As of 1 November 2011, the prices applied under the RPP ranged from CAD 7.1 cents/kWh to CAD 8.3 cents/kWh for customers with standard meters, and from CAD 6.2 cents/kWh to CAD 10.8 cents/kWh for customers with smart meters[131]. Finally, among other functions of the OEB is its responsibility for establishing, *inter alia*, codes for the transmission system, distribution system and retail settlement[132]. The Transmission System Code sets out the minimum standards that an electricity transmitter (i.e. Hydro One Networks Inc. and other smaller transmission companies) must meet in designing, constructing, managing and operating its transmission system[133]. The Distribution System Code sets out the minimum obligations that a licensed electricity distributor (i.e. LDCs, including Hydro One subsidiaries) must comply with in distributing electricity within the service area under its license[134]. The Retail Settlement Code sets out the minimum obligations that an electricity distributor (i.e. LDCs, including Hydro One subsidiaries) and retailer (i.e. entities that are licensed to re-sell electricity) must meet in conducting financial settlements[135].

- Ontario Electricity Financial Corporation

7.43 The OEFC was established by the *Electricity Act of 1998* as a "corporation without share capital"[136] and is another "agency"[137] of the Government of Ontario. The OEFC is mandated to, *inter alia*, manage the contracts for the supply of electricity with NUGs[138]. The OEFC's contracts with NUGs were concluded prior to the establishment of the OPA in 2004.

[130] *Ontario Energy Board Act of 1998*, S.O. 1998, Chapter 15, Schedule B, as amended, ("*Ontario Energy Board Act of 1998*"), Exhibit JPN-6, Section 78.1; *Ontario Regulation 53/05, Payments Under Section 78.1 of the Act*, 19 February 2008, as amended, ("*Ontario Regulation 53/05, Payments Under Section 78.1 of the Act*"), Exhibit JPN-65, Section 6; and OPG – Payment Amounts, OEB website, ("OPG – Payment Amounts"), Exhibit JPN-17.

[131] Electricity Prices, OEB website, ("OEB: Electricity Prices"), Exhibit JPN-66; and Ontario Energy Board, Electricity Prices for Consumers on the Regulated Price Plan (April 2005 – November 2011), ("OEB: Electricity Prices for Consumers on the RPP"), Exhibit JPN-67.

[132] Rules, Codes, Guidelines and Forms, OEB website, ("OEB: Rules, Codes, Guidelines and Forms"), Exhibit JPN-68.

[133] Transmission System Code, Exhibit JPN-69.

[134] Distribution System Code, Exhibit JPN-70.

[135] Retail Settlement Code, Ontario Energy Board, 1 October 2011, ("Retail Settlement Code"), Exhibit JPN-71.

[136] *Electricity Act of 1998*, Exhibit JPN-5, Section 54(1).

[137] Government of Ontario: All Agencies List, Exhibit JPN-49; and Agency Details, Ontario Electricity Financial Corporation, Government of Ontario website, ("Agency Details, OEFC"), Exhibit JPN-72.

[138] Ontario Electricity Financial Corporation – Mandate and Governing Legislation, OEFC website, ("OEFC: Mandate and Governing Legislation"), Exhibit JPN-73.

Significant OEFC contracts will begin to expire in 2012[139]. The OPA has been directed to pursue new contracts with the NUGs upon the expiry of the existing contracts with the OEFC or where an NUG and the OEFC have mutually agreed to end an existing arrangement before its contractual expiry date[140].

Wholesale prices and retail prices

- Wholesale prices

7.44 The price of electricity at the wholesale level varies based on the cost of the electricity, which is determined by adding together the "commodity" charge (made up of the HOEP plus the Global Adjustment[141]) and the costs associated with the services of transmission and market operation[142]. The wholesale price is paid to the IESO by all wholesale consumers, including LDCs and large industrial consumers directly connected to the IESO-controlled transmission grid.

The Hourly Ontario Energy Price

7.45 The Hourly Ontario Energy Price ("HOEP") is the price for electricity sold at the wholesale level that is established by the IESO through the operation of a computer-automated market mechanism that uses supply and demand "stacks" to determine for every five-minute interval: (i) which generators supply electricity and which consumers consume electricity; (ii) the amount of electricity to be supplied and consumed; and (iii) the "market clearing price" ("MCP") and the HOEP for that electricity.

7.46 The IESO "stack system" is established on the premise that certain generators are capable of easily varying their electricity production while others are not, and likewise that certain consumers are capable of easily varying their electricity consumption while others are not. Generators and consumers that can easily vary their electricity production or consumption are termed "dispatchable", and receive "dispatch" instructions from the IESO every five minutes stating the quantity to be supplied or consumed. Those generators and consumers that cannot easily vary their electricity production or consumption are termed "non-dispatchable"; they do not receive "dispatch" instructions from the

[139] OPA Generation Procurement Update, OPA website, ("OPA Generation Procurement Update"), Exhibit JPN-21, p. 15.

[140] Directive from Minister of Energy to Ontario Power Authority Regarding Negotiating New Contracts with Non-Utility Generators, 23 November 2010, ("Minister's Directive Regarding Negotiating New Contracts with NUGs"), Exhibit JPN-74.

[141] The nature and operation of the Global Adjustment is explained below at paras. 7.54-7.56.

[142] The latter charges include, *inter alia*, hourly uplift settlement charges and monthly uplift charges, IESO and OPA administration fees, and wholesale transmission charges to LDCs and large consumers. A full list of the other fees and charges can be found in A Guide to Electricity Charges – Market Participants, IESO website, ("IESO Guide to Electricity Charges"), Exhibit JPN-1.

IESO, but rather their supply and demand is considered fixed and automatically placed by the IESO at the front of the supply and demand stacks.

7.47 To determine which generators are to be physically dispatched, the IESO uses "security constrained economic dispatch" software that employs an optimization algorithm to find the least costly way of supplying forecast demand with available generation resources[143]. The software also utilizes a model of the transmission grid to discover whether this least-cost mix of generation might overload the transmission network. If the software observes that any transmission constraints have been violated, it iterates an optimization routine until it finds the least-cost solution that does not violate any constraints. Non-dispatchable generators do not receive any instruction from the IESO, but their expected supply is considered fixed and taken into account by the optimization routine.

7.48 Following the physical dispatch of electricity, the MCP and HOEP are calculated without taking into account transmission constraints[144]. First the IESO creates a supply stack by ranking supply offers in increasing order of cost, starting with non-dispatchable generators which are placed at the beginning of the stack[145]. Non-dispatchable generators do not submit formal "offers" for electricity they are willing to supply at every five-minute interval, but must still submit schedules of production (for self-scheduling generators) or forecasts of production (for intermittent generators), so that the IESO may take their quantity of supply into account at the beginning of the stack.

7.49 After taking into account such fixed supply, the IESO then turns to the variable supply offered by dispatchable generators. Again, supply by dispatchable generators is considered variable because such supply can be "dispatched on" or "dispatched off" upon instructions from the IESO. Dispatchable generators must submit price/quantity "offers" for every five minute interval. Although many dispatchable generators will in fact receive regulated or contracted prices for the electricity they deliver into the system, they must nonetheless submit price offers to the IESO to indicate the quantity they are willing to supply in a given five minute interval. These price offers by dispatchable generators serve as a dispatch signal – i.e. a mechanism for the IESO to select electricity supply – and not as the price that these generators actually receive. The IESO ranks the price offers from dispatchable generators in ascending order to complete its supply stack. This process is illustrated in the following diagram submitted by Japan[146].

---

[143] Hogan Report, Exhibit CDA-2, p. 38.

[144] *Ibid.*

[145] Fixed supply also includes imports, i.e. supply that is scheduled to enter Ontario from another jurisdiction, as imports are scheduled an hour ahead and will therefore flow for that entire hour regardless of the rate. IESO, Marketplace Training: Introduction to Ontario's Physical Markets, October 2010, ("IESO: Ontario's Physical Markets"), Exhibit JPN-80, p. 20.

[146] Japan's first written submission, Appendix II.

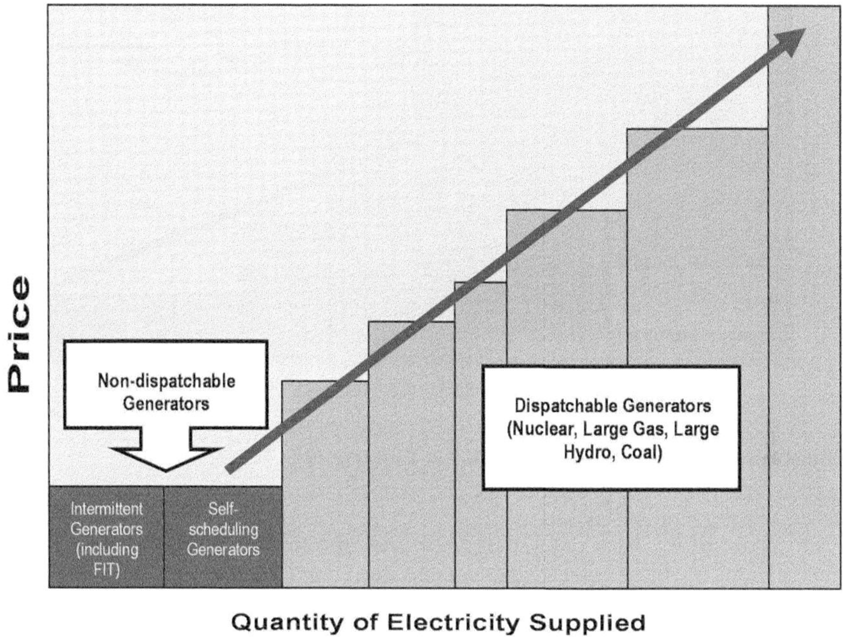

Diagram 1: IESO Supply Stack for Electricity

7.50 Similarly, the IESO stacks electricity demand, beginning with non-dispatchable loads followed by dispatchable loads. Non-dispatchable loads are those that simply draw electricity from the grid as needed and therefore cannot easily vary their consumption. Accordingly, they are considered by the IESO as fixed demand[147] that is automatically placed at the beginning of the stack. Non-dispatchable loads account for most of the energy consumed in Ontario. Dispatchable loads are those that may vary their electricity consumption; therefore, they submit "bids" to the IESO stating the price and quantity of the electricity they are willing to purchase. The IESO stacks these bids in descending order according to the price bid. This process is illustrated in the following diagram submitted by Japan[148].

---

[147] Fixed demand also includes exports (which, like imports, are fixed within the hour time window) and losses from moving electricity through the transmission and distribution systems (which create a need for an additional amount of energy). IESO: Ontario's Physical Markets, Exhibit JPN-80, p. 21.
[148] Japan's first written submission, Appendix II.

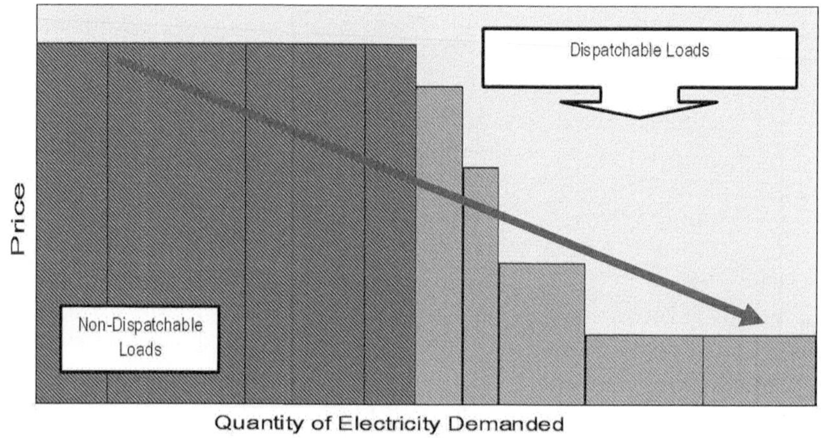

Diagram 2: IESO Demand Stack for Electricity

7.51 The IESO then sets the MCP for the five-minute interval at the intersection of these electricity supply and demand stacks. The HOEP is calculated as an average of the twelve MCPs determined over the course of a given hour. The weighted average HOEP based on Ontario demand for calendar year 2010 was CAD 3.79 cents/kWh[149]. The process used to arrive at the MCP is illustrated in the following diagram submitted by Japan[150].

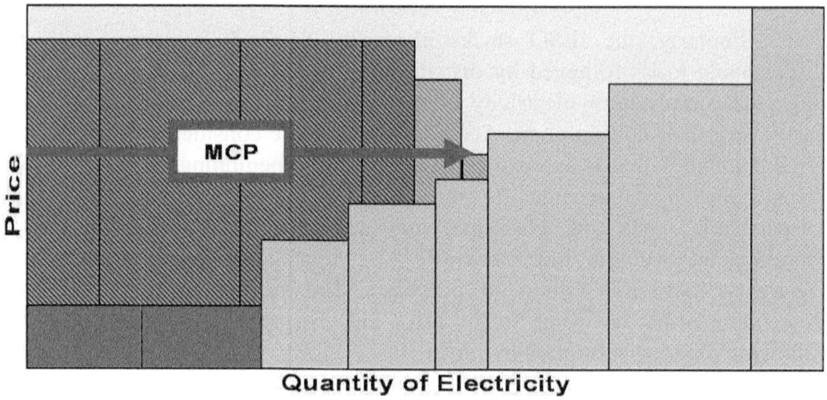

Diagram 3: Determination of Market Clearing Price by the IESO

---

[149] IESO Monthly Average Prices, Average Weighted Hourly Price, ("IESO: Average Weighted Hourly Price"), Exhibit JPN-83.
[150] Japan's first written submission, Appendix II.

7.52 The MCP/HOEP is an "unconstrained" price in that its calculation does not consider transmission constraints. As a result, it may not accord with dispatch orders, which do take transmission constraints into account. From time to time the IESO may compel a generator to run despite the fact that the MCP is below the generator's offer price. On other occasions the IESO may prevent a generator from operating even though its bid was below the MCP. To align the economic incentives of generators with those the system operator, the former are paid Congestion Management Settlement Credits whenever they are dispatched uneconomically[151].

7.53 All generators operating through the IESO-administered wholesale market will receive the MCP/HOEP for the electricity they deliver into the system[152]. In addition, for those generators that have additional arrangements – i.e. generators that receive regulated prices set by the OEB or contracted prices set by the OEFC or OPA – the prices they receive are subject to an adjustment to reconcile the difference between the MCP/HOEP and the generator's regulated or contracted price. This is done through the Global Adjustment[153].

The Global Adjustment

7.54 The purpose of the Global Adjustment ("GA") is to ensure that payments by consumers reflect the amounts payable to generators under regulated or contracted rates that differ from the market rate (i.e. MCP/HOEP). Statutory authority for the GA is found in Section 25.33 of the *Electricity Act of 1998*[154]. Part 5.5, Sections 1.6.7 and 1.6.11 of the IESO Market Manual provide detailed instructions on how the GA is to be determined and settled[155]. In particular, the GA is a monthly amount set to reflect the difference between MCP/HOEP and: (i) regulated prices paid to OPG's regulated assets; (ii) contracted prices paid to

151 Hogan Report, Exhibit CDA-2, pp. 40-41.

152 IESO, Market Rules for the Ontario Electricity Market, 12 October 2011, ("IESO: Market Rules"), Exhibit JPN-79, Chapters 7 and 9; General IESO Frequently Asked Questions, IESO website, ("General IESO FAQ"), Exhibit JPN-81 ("Dispatchable facilities will be settled at [the] five-minute [market clearing] price, non-dispatchable wholesale consumers will be settled using a weighted hourly average of these five-minute prices"); and IESO: Ontario's Physical Markets, Exhibit JPN-80, p. 23.

153 IESO Market Manual Part 5.5: Physical Markets Settlement Statements, Issue 44.0, 12 October 2011, ("IESO Market Manual Part 5.5"), Exhibit JPN-82, Sections 1.6.7 and 1.6.11.

154 *Electricity Act of 1998*, Exhibit JPN-5, Section 25.33(1). ("The IESO shall, through its billing and settlement systems, make adjustments in accordance with the regulations that ensure that, over time, payments by classes of market participants in Ontario that are prescribed by regulation reflect amounts paid, in accordance with the regulations, to generators, distributors, the OPA and the Financial Corporation, whether the amounts are determined under the market rules or under sections 78.1 to 78.5 of the *Ontario Energy Board Act of 1998*".)

155 IESO Market Manual Part 5.5, Exhibit JPN-82, Sections 1.6.7 and 1.6.11.

NUGs that have contracts with the OEFC; and (iii) contracted prices paid to generators that have contracts with the OPA[156].

7.55 Accordingly, the GA is inversely related to HOEP – i.e. an increase in the HOEP means a decrease in the GA, and vice versa[157]. Where the MCP/HOEP is below the fixed (i.e. regulated or contracted) prices, the GA will be a positive number representing the amount payable to generators (and the amount charged to consumers); conversely, where the MCP/HOEP exceeds the fixed prices, the GA will be a negative number representing a charge to generators[158] (and a credit to consumers). GA payments are affected whenever new electricity supply starts, with the GA increasing with each new contract for conservation and supply that establishes rates in excess of MCP/HOEP[159]. The GA has been consistently positive since at least 2009[160].

7.56 The total GA owed to generators is allocated to consumers pro-rata based on the amount of electricity (kWh) they consume, regardless of which generators are supplying electricity at the time of their consumption[161]. The total GA will largely be calculated by summing all adjustments to the prices owed to electricity generators, and then pro-rating this amount across consumers' purchases of electricity[162]. Since its introduction in 2005, the GA has been collected from all Ontario consumers on this basis. However, beginning in January 2011 the largest industrial consumers with average monthly demand of over 5 MW have paid the GA based on their share of consumption during the five highest demand hours of the year. Other consumers continue to be charged on the original basis[163]. The average GA for 2010 was CAD 2.718 cents/kWh[164].

- Retail prices

7.57 Prices paid by retail consumers are generally determined by adding to the total of MCP/HOEP, GA, and other fees and charges, an additional distribution charge to cover the cost of delivering electricity to the consumer. Retail consumers either purchase electricity based on use from their LDCs, or they enter into contracts for electricity with an LDC or licensed electricity retailer. The former retail consumers pay for the electricity commodity according to the

---

156 See IESO Guide to Electricity Charges, Exhibit JPN-1; and Global Adjustment, IESO website, ("IESO: Global Adjustment"), Exhibit JPN-75.

157 OPA Cash Flows: November 2010, Exhibit JPN-23, p. 6.

158 See IESO Guide to Electricity Charges, Exhibit JPN-1.

159 OPA Cash Flows: November 2010, Exhibit JPN-23, p. 6.

160 Global Adjustment Archive, IESO website, ("Global Adjustment Archive"), Exhibit JPN-11.

161 IESO, HST Guide for IESO Transactions, Issue 26.0, 12 October 2011, ("IESO: HST Guide for IESO Transactions"), Exhibit JPN-84, Section 8.11, p. 35.

162 IESO: HST Guide for IESO Transactions, Exhibit JPN-84, p. 35.

163 See Ontario Regulation 398/10, made under the *Electricity Act, 1998* (Exhibit EU-16), ss. 6 and 7.

164 Global Adjustment Archive, Exhibit JPN-11.

OEB's RPP[165], and the latter retail consumers pay for the electricity commodity according to a retail contract. In 2010, there were 77 private-sector electricity retailers in Ontario that sold "contracts to businesses and consumers"[166]. There are currently 45 licensed electricity retailers that compete with LDCs in their respective service areas[167].

7.58 RPP prices are paid by residential and small business consumers that purchase electricity from their LDCs based on use[168]. Although these RPP prices are paid to LDCs, they are reviewed and set by the OEB every six months, specifically for the periods 1 May to 31 October and 1 November to 30 April each year, and are based upon forecasts of the HOEP and the GA[169]. The GA does not appear as a separate item on an RPP customer's electricity bill because it is directly included in the rates set by the OEB[170]. RPP prices vary according to the type of meter used by the customer[171]. Effective 1 November 2011, the prices for customers with conventional meters (tier pricing) were CAD 7.1 cents/kWh (low-tier) and CAD 8.3 cents/kWh (high-tier)[172]; and the prices for customers with smart meters (time-of-use pricing) were CAD 6.2

[165] A retail consumer seeking to purchase electricity through the RPP will establish an account with the local distributor to be connected to its distribution system, and by doing so, the consumer assumes responsibility for taking or using the electricity delivered by the LDC. RPP customers do not have a formal contract with the LDC; pursuant to Section 6.1.2 of the Distribution System Code, however, "[a] distributor has an implied contract with any customer that is connected to the distributor's distribution system and receives distribution services from the distributor. The terms of the implied contract are embedded in the distributor's Conditions of Service, the Rate Handbook, the distributor's rate schedules, the Distributor's licence and the Distribution System Code". Distribution System Code, Exhibit JPN-70, Section 6.1.2; and Conditions of Service, Hydro One website, ("Hydro One: Conditions of Service"), Exhibit JPN-87.

[166] Ontario's Long-Term Energy Plan, Exhibit CDA-6, p. 63.

[167] *Electricity Act of 1998*, Exhibit JPN-5, Section 29; Retail Settlement Code, Exhibit JPN-71, Sections 1.1, 2.7, 10.1, and 12; and OEB Licensed Electricity Retailers (http://www.ontarioenergyboard.ca/html /licences/all_issuedlicences_read.cfm?showtype=Electricity %20Retailer) referred to in Retail Contracts, IESO website, ("IESO: Retail Contracts"), Exhibit JPN-90.

[168] IESO: Global Adjustment, Exhibit JPN-75; and IESO, LDC Settlement of RPP and Global Adjustment, 28 September 2009, ("LDC Settlement"), Exhibit JPN-88, p. 9.

[169] Ontario Energy Board, Regulated Price Plan Price Report: November 1, 2011 to October 31, 2012, 17 October 2011, ("RPP Price Report: 1 November 2011 to 31 October 2012"), Exhibit JPN-89, p. 1.

[170] IESO: Global Adjustment, Exhibit JPN-75.

[171] RPP Price Report: 1 November 2011 to 31 October 2012, Exhibit JPN-89, pp. 3-5.

[172] OEB: Electricity Prices, Exhibit JPN-66. The conventional meter plan sets a lower fixed price for energy consumption up to a monthly threshold amount, with consumption above this level at a higher price. As of 1 November 2011, customers pay CAD 7.1 cents/kWh for a lower tier (which ranges from 600 kWh to 1,000 kWh per month depending on the season and the type of customer) and CAD 8.3 cents/kWh for an upper tier (all consumption per month above the lower tier). See also IESO Market Manual Part 5.5, Exhibit JPN-82, Section 1.6.7.7.

cents/kWh (off-peak), CAD 9.2 cents/kWh (mid-peak), and CAD 10.8 cents/kWh (on-peak)[173].

7.59 Retail consumers not under the RPP may enter into a retail contract with an LDC or licensed electricity retailer, paying a contracted price for electricity for a fixed period, plus the GA[174].

Settlement of payments to generators

7.60 The IESO is responsible for settling the "physical" electricity market in which participants buy and sell energy[175]. Settlement of the physical market involves a four-step process of gathering and processing data, reconciling the markets, invoicing participants, and transferring funds[176]. During this process, the IESO will collect electricity payments from consumers and distribute these funds to electricity generators.

7.61 In general, the MCP/HOEP portion of the payments it receives from consumers will be sent directly to generators, while the GA portion will be transferred to generators through the OPA or on behalf of the OPA. However, when the MCP/HOEP is negative, the IESO will receive a MCP/HOEP payment from generators. Accordingly, the IESO will determine the amount of money to be received or paid by a market participant based on the MCP/HOEP during its hours of participation in the IESO-administered markets[177].

7.62 The IESO will collect the GA from consumers and distribute it to generators through the OPA or on behalf of the OPA pursuant to Part 5.5, Sections 1.6.7 and 1.6.11 of the IESO Market Manual[178]. The settlement rules for the GA are complex and vary according to the different components of the GA and the class of market participant. However, typically, monthly invoices are issued by the IESO indicating the amounts to be paid or received by the market participant and the payment due date[179], and market participants must pay these invoices by the specified due date[180]. These invoices will include a line item for the settlement difference between the MCP/HOEP and the regulated or contracted prices received by certain generators, i.e. the GA[181]. If the GA is

---

173 See OEB: Electricity Prices, Exhibit JPN-66. The smart meter plan establishes prices for energy based on the time that energy is consumed. As of 1 November 2011, customers pay CAD 6.2 cents/kWh off-peak, CAD 9.2 cents/kWh mid-peak, and CAD 10.8 cents/kWh on-peak. See also IESO Market Manual Part 5.5, Exhibit JPN-82, Section 1.6.7.7.

174 IESO: Global Adjustment, Exhibit JPN-75.

175 IESO: Settlement Statements and Invoices, Exhibit JPN-62, p. 1.

176 *Ibid.*

177 IESO: Market Rules, Exhibit JPN-79, Chapter 7, Section 8.3; and Chapter 9, Sections 3.1.1, 3.1.3, 3.3, 6.10.2, and 6.11.1.

178 IESO Market Manual Part 5.5, Exhibit JPN-82, Sections 1.6.7 and 1.6.11.

179 See IESO: Market Rules, Exhibit JPN-79, Chapter 9, Section 6.10.2.

180 See IESO: Market Rules, Exhibit JPN-79, Chapter 9, Section 6.11.1.

181 OPA, 2006 Business Plan, 30 September 2005, ("OPA's 2006 Business Plan"), Exhibit JPN-92, p. 26.

positive, it is collected from the consumer; if negative, the IESO will pay the consumer the GA from its settlement clearing account[182]. The IESO then sends part of the total GA collected to the OPA to settle contract payments with transmission-connected generators, and uses the remainder to settle contract payments with distribution-connected generators on behalf of the OPA[183].

7.63 Although the settlement process for transmission-connected generators operating under the FIT Programme is the same as that described above, distribution-connected generators operating under the FIT Programme will receive their full contract payments (i.e. the HOEP plus GA) from the LDC to which they are connected. The relevant LDC will then seek reimbursement of the GA from the OPA via the IESO[184].

(iv) The FIT Programme and the FIT and microFIT Contracts[185]

7.64 The FIT Programme can be generally described as a scheme implemented by the Government of Ontario and its agencies through which generators of electricity, produced from certain forms of renewable energy, are paid a guaranteed price per kWh of electricity delivered into the Ontario electricity system under 20-year or 40-year contracts with the OPA. In the case of windpower projects having a capacity to produce electricity that is greater than 10 kW, and solar projects with a capacity of up to 10MW, a "Minimum Required Domestic Content Level" must be satisfied in the development and construction of the qualifying electricity generation facility.

7.65 The FIT Programme was formally launched by the OPA on 1 October 2009 pursuant to the Direction of the Ontario Minister of Energy and Infrastructure[186] acting under the authority of the *Electricity Act of 1998*[187], as amended by the *Green Energy and Green Economy Act of 2009*[188]. The FIT Programme is the third in a series of initiatives adopted by the Government of Ontario since 2004 to increase the supply of electricity produced from renewable sources of energy into the Ontario electricity system in order to diversify its

---

182 See IESO: Market Rules, Exhibit JPN-79, Chapter 9, Section 6.11.

183 See IESO Market Manual Part 5.5, Exhibit JPN-82, Section 1.6.7.8. IESO Guide to Online Data Submission via the IESO Portal, March 2011, ("IESO Guide to Online Data Submission"), Exhibit JPN-93, pp. 20-21.

184 The settlement process for payments made to generators operating under the FIT Programme is discussed further at paras. 7.204-7.207.

185 A more detailed description and analysis of the FIT Programme and the FIT and microFIT Contracts are set out below at paras. 7.195-7.248, where we evaluate the merits of the parties' arguments concerning the proper factual and legal characterization of the challenged measures under Article 1.1(a) of the SCM Agreement.

186 Minister's 2009 FIT Direction, Exhibit JPN-102.

187 *Electricity Act of 1998*, Exhibit JPN-5, Sections 25.32 and 25.35, as amended by the *Green Energy and Green Economy Act of 2009*, S.O. 2009, c. 12, Schedule B, ("*Green Energy Act of 2009*"), Exhibit JPN-101.

188 *Green Energy Act of 2009*, Exhibit JPN-101, Sections 5(2) and 7.

supply-mix and help replace coal-fired facilities[189]. As described by the Ontario Minister of Energy and Infrastructure, its four objectives are to: (i) "increase capacity of renewable energy supply to ensure adequate generation and reduce emissions"; (ii) "introduce a simpler method to procure and develop generating capacity from renewable sources of energy"; (iii) "enable new green industries through new investment and job creation"; and (iv) "provide incentives for investment in renewable energy technologies"[190].

7.66 Participation in the FIT Programme is open to facilities located in Ontario that generate electricity exclusively from one or more of the following sources of renewable energy: wind, solar photovoltaic ("PV"), renewable biomass, biogas, landfill gas or waterpower[191]. The Programme is divided into two streams: (i) the FIT stream - for projects with a capacity to produce electricity that exceeds 10 kW, but is no more than 10 MW for solar PV projects or 50 MW in the case of waterpower projects; and (ii) the microFIT stream - for projects having a capacity to produce up to 10 kW of electricity (typically small household, farm or business generation projects)[192].

7.67 The FIT Programme is administered by the OPA and is implemented through the application of a standard set of rules, standard contracts and, for each class of generation technology, standard pricing. The standard rules are found in a number of instruments, with the most specific being the FIT Rules and the microFIT Rules developed by the OPA. Other relevant rules are found in

---

[189] See, for example, Ontario's Long-Term Energy Plan, Exhibit CDA-6, pp. 7, 9-10, 19, and 31. The two earlier initiatives were the *Request for Proposals for Renewable Energy Supply I* (2004), *II* (2005) and *III* (2008), and the *Renewable Energy Standard Offer Program* (2006). See Ontario Ministry of Energy, Request for Proposals for 300 MW of Renewable Energy Supply (RES I), issued 24 June 2004, ("RES I"), Exhibit CDA-52; Ontario Ministry of Energy, Request for Proposals for 1,000 MW of Renewable Energy Supply (RES II), issued 17 June 2005, ("RES II"), Exhibit CDA-53; Ontario Ministry of Energy, Request for Proposals for approximately 500 MW of Renewable Energy Supply (RES III), issued 22 August 2008, ("RES III"), Exhibit CDA-54; and Ontario Power Authority, Joint Report to the Minister of Energy Recommendations on a Standard Offer Program for Small Generators connected to a Distribution System (RESOP), 17 March 2006, ("RESOP"), Exhibit CDA-55.

[190] Minister's 2009 FIT Direction, Exhibit JPN-102, p. 1. More specifically, the OPA explains that the Programme was developed:

> [T]o encourage and promote greater use of renewable energy sources including wind, waterpower, Renewable Biomass, Bio-gas, landfill gas and solar (PV) for electricity generating projects in Ontario. The fundamental objective of the FIT Program, in conjunction with the Green Energy and Green Economy Act, 2009 is to facilitate the increased development of Renewable Generating Facilities of varying sizes, technologies and configurations via a standardized, open and fair process.(Ontario Power Authority, Feed-in Tariff Programme Rules, Version 1.5.1, 15 July 2011, ("FIT Rules"), Exhibit JPN-119, Section 1.1).

[191] FIT Rules, Exhibit JPN-119, Section 2.1(a); and Ontario Power Authority, Feed-in Tariff Appendix 1, Standard Definitions, Version 1.5.1, 15 July 2011, ("FIT Standard Definitions"), Exhibit JPN-135, Definitions Nos. 215 and 216.

[192] FIT Rules, Exhibit JPN-119, Section 2.1(a)(iii); and Ontario Power Authority, microFIT Rules, Version 1.6.1, 10 August 2011, ("microFIT Rules"), Exhibit JPN-157, Section 2.1(a)(iv).

the IESO Market Rules, the IESO Market Manual, the Transmission System Code, the Distribution System Code, and the Retail Settlement Code.

7.68 Only projects that satisfy all of the specific eligibility requirements set out in the FIT and microFIT Rules[193], and that can be connected to the Ontario electricity system[194], will be offered a Contract, and thereby permitted to participate in the Programme. By entering into a FIT or microFIT Contract, a qualifying entity will be required to *inter alia* build, operate and maintain the approved renewable energy electricity generation facility, in accordance with all relevant laws and regulations, and deliver the produced electricity into the Ontario electricity system. In return for performing these and other contractual obligations, the same entity will be remunerated, over the term of the particular Contract, in accordance with a formula that is based on a standard Contract Price established by the OPA[195]. This is done through the application of similar mechanisms to those used to settle the payments to generators supplying electricity into the Ontario electricity system under non-FIT contracts[196]. Thus, while the OPA has ultimate contractual liability for all FIT and microFIT Contract Payments[197], in practice, the actual payments are made by a combination of the OPA, the IESO and relevant LDCs.

5. *Order of analysis*

7.69 The complainants claim that Canada acts inconsistently with its obligations under the SCM Agreement, the TRIMs Agreement and the GATT 1994 by reason of the "Minimum Required Domestic Content Level" adopted by the Province of Ontario under the FIT Programme, and implemented through the FIT and microFIT Contracts. According to the complainants, the Panel should evaluate the merits of these claims by first focusing on those made under the SCM Agreement. The complainants justify this submission by arguing that of the three covered agreements that are relied upon in these disputes, the SCM Agreement deals most specifically and in detail with the measures at issue, including with respect to the nature of the remedy that is available in the event of

---

[193] FIT Rules, Exhibit JPN-119, Sections 2-3; and microFIT Rules, Exhibit JPN-157, Sections 2-3.

[194] In particular, for FIT projects, the OPA must first confirm that there are resources available to connect the proposed renewable energy electricity facility to the relevant transmission or distribution network. FIT Rules, Exhibit JPN-119, Sections 5.2 ("Transmission Availability Test") and 5.3 ("Distribution Availability Test"). Similarly, for microFIT projects, a Connection Agreement between a Local Distribution Company and the microFIT facility must exist and be operational. microFIT Rules, Exhibit JPN-157, Section 4.1.

[195] FIT Rules, Exhibit JPN-119, Sections 7.1(a), 7.1(b), and 10.1(a); FIT Price Schedule, 3 June 2011, ("2011 FIT Price Schedule"), Exhibit JPN-30; FIT Contract, Exhibit JPN-127, Article 3.1 and Exhibit B; and microFIT Price Schedule, 13 August 2010, ("2010 microFIT Price Schedule"), Exhibit JPN-31.

[196] FIT Rules, Exhibit JPN-119, Sections 8.1 and 8.2; and FIT Contract, Exhibit JPN-127, Articles 4.2-4.4 and Exhibit B.

[197] FIT Rules, Exhibit JPN-119, Section 6.3(a).

a finding of violation. Canada, on the other hand, considers that the Panel should first address the complainants' claims under Article III:4 of the GATT 1994 because, in its view, this provision deals most specifically and in detail with the focus of the complainants' challenge, namely, the "Minimum Required Domestic Content Level".

7.70 We note that the complainants assert, and Canada does not contest, that the measures at issue are trade-related investment measures affecting imports of renewable energy generation equipment and components. This suggests that, compared with the SCM Agreement and Article III:4 of the GATT 1994, it is the TRIMs Agreement that deals most directly, specifically and in detail[198], with the aspects of the FIT Programme, and the FIT and microFIT Contracts, that are at the centre of the complainants' concerns. In this light, we will commence our evaluation of the complainants' claims by focusing on those made under the TRIMs Agreement. However, it is apparent from the terms of Article 2.1 of the TRIMs Agreement that, in undertaking this evaluation[199], we will also necessarily have to come to a view about the merits of the complainants' allegations concerning the consistency of the challenged measures with Article III:4 of the GATT 1994. Thus, in the section that follows we will simultaneously evaluate the merits of both of the complainants' claims under Article 2.1 of the TRIMs Agreement and Article III:4 of the GATT 1994.

B. Whether Canada acts inconsistently with Article 2.1 of the TRIMs Agreement and Article III:4 of the GATT 1994

1. Arguments of the parties

(a) Japan

7.71 Japan claims that the FIT Programme, and the FIT and microFIT Contracts are (i) trade-related investment measures inconsistent with Canada's obligation under Article 2.1 of the TRIMs Agreement; and (ii) measures inconsistent with Canada's national treatment obligation under Article III:4 of the GATT 1994.

7.72 Japan argues that the FIT Programme, and the FIT and microFIT Contracts, are TRIMs falling within the scope of the TRIMs Agreement because, through the operation of the prescribed domestic content requirements, they (i) "encourage investment in the production of renewable energy and associated equipment in Ontario"[200]; and (ii) by definition, favour the use of domestic over imported products (i.e. wind and solar energy generation equipment) and are

[198] Appellate Body Report, *EC – Bananas III*, para. 204.

[199] The text of Article 2.1 of the TRIMs Agreement is set out and discussed below, at paras. 7.114-7.121.

[200] Japan's first written submission, para. 298, citing the Minister's FIT Directive of 24 September 2009, which refers to new investment in renewable energy technologies. See Minister's 2009 FIT Direction, Exhibit JPN-102, p. 1.

thereby "trade-related"[201]. Japan recalls that a TRIM will be in violation of Article 2.1 of the TRIMs Agreement when it is inconsistent with Article III or Article XI of the GATT 1994[202]. Thus, to the extent they are inconsistent with Article III:4 of the GATT 1994, Japan submits that the FIT Programme, and the FIT and microFIT Contracts, must also be inconsistent with Article 2.1 of the TRIMs Agreement[203]. In any case, Japan submits that the challenged measures' inconsistency with Article 2.1 is also apparent from the terms of Paragraph 1(a) in the Annex to the TRIMs Agreement, which describe one category of TRIMs that is deemed to be inconsistent with the obligation of national treatment found in Article III:4 of the GATT 1994[204].

7.73 Japan also argues that the FIT Programme, and FIT and microFIT Contracts, are inconsistent with Article III:4 of the GATT 1994 because they impose requirements on renewable energy generators affecting the internal sale, purchase, and use of renewable energy generation equipment, and accord imported equipment treatment less favourable than like products of Ontario origin[205]. First, renewable energy generation equipment manufactured domestically in Ontario and imported from Japan are "like products" because they are in a directly competitive situation in the market and there is no substantial difference between domestic and imported equipment in terms of their physical properties, end-uses, consumer perceptions, and tariff classifications. Second, the domestic content rules of the FIT Programme and Contracts are "requirements" in that they are conditions with which FIT generators voluntarily comply in order to obtain an advantage. Third, the domestic content rules of the FIT Programme and Contracts "affect" the "internal" "sale", "purchase" or "use" of renewable energy equipment in that they provide an incentive to wind and solar PV energy generators in Ontario to choose renewable energy equipment manufactured in Ontario. Finally, the domestic content rules of the FIT Programme and Contracts accord less favourable treatment to imported renewable energy generation equipment than that accorded to like products of Ontario origin because they modify the conditions of competition to the detriment of imported products[206].

7.74 In this connection, Japan submits that Article III:8(a) of the GATT 1994 does not apply to the measures at issue base on the following three main arguments.

7.75 First, Japan argues that FIT Contracts are not "procurement by governmental agencies of products purchased". In Japan's view, the OPA does

---

201 Japan's first written submission, para. 299, citing the Panel Report, *Indonesia – Autos*, para. 14.82.

202 Japan's first written submission, para. 296.

203 Japan's first written submission, paras. 295 and 300.

204 Japan's first written submission, paras. 295 and 301-302.

205 Japan's first written submission, para. 262.

206 Japan's first written submission, paras. 262-283.

not "purchase" electricity "for governmental purposes". Moreover, according to Japan, even if it were possible to conclude that products were "purchased" under the FIT Contracts, such purchases could not amount to "procurement" by governmental agencies, under Article III:8(a) of the GATT 1994, in the light of the proper interpretation of the term "procurement" under customary international law rules of treaty interpretation[207].

7.76 Second, Japan argues that the FIT Contracts are not entered into "for governmental purposes". Properly interpreted in accordance with customary rules of treaty interpretation, Japan is of the view that the expression "for governmental purposes" means for governmental use, consumption or benefit. Japan contends that the Government of Ontario does not use, consume or benefit from the electricity delivered pursuant to FIT Contracts[208].

7.77 Finally, Japan submits that the FIT Contracts are entered into "with a view to commercial resale". Properly interpreted, Japan argues that the expression "with a view to commercial resale" means with a view to being sold into the stream of commerce or trade, as opposed to being used or consumed by the government. Because the electricity delivered pursuant to the FIT Contracts is injected into the transmission grid and delivered almost instantaneously to consumers in Ontario for their use, Japan maintains that to the extent that electricity may be considered to have been purchased by the Government of Ontario under FIT Contracts, that electricity is purchased with a view to commercial resale[209].

(b) European Union

7.78 The European Union argues that the FIT Programme, and the FIT and microFIT Contracts are (i) trade-related investment measures that are inconsistent with Article 2.1 of the TRIMs Agreement, in conjunction with paragraph 1(a) of its Annex; and (ii) measures inconsistent with Article III:4 of the GATT 1994[210].

7.79 According to the European Union, the challenged measures are TRIMs because: (i) they aim at encouraging the development of a local manufacturing capability for equipment and components for renewable energy generation

---

[207] Japan's opening statement at the first meeting of the Panel, paras. 49-58; second written submission, paras. 54 and 60; and opening statement at the second meeting of the Panel, paras. 27-28 and 32.

[208] Japan's first written submission, fn. 457; opening statement at the first meeting of the Panel, paras. 53 and 69-75; second written submission, para. 61; opening statement at the second meeting of the Panel, para. 33; and response to Panel question No. 47 (second set).

[209] Japan's opening statement at the first meeting of the Panel, paras. 78-85; second written submission, paras. 64-71; opening statement at the second meeting of the Panel, paras. 36-39; and response to Panel question No. 48 (second set).

[210] European Union's first written submission, paras. 98-106.

facilities in Ontario[211]; and (ii) the "Minimum Required Domestic Content Level" affects trade in wind and solar energy generation equipment and components, as it creates an incentive to purchase or use Ontario's products to the detriment of imported like products[212].

7.80 The European Union submits that it is possible to establish that a TRIM is inconsistent with Article 2.1 of the TRIMs Agreement by either: (i) adducing evidence to demonstrate the existence of any of the situations described in the Illustrative List of TRIMs; or (ii) otherwise demonstrating a violation of Article III:4 of the GATT 1994 on the basis of the terms of that provision[213]. The European Union makes both these arguments in the present disputes. Thus, the European Union argues that the challenged measures are inconsistent with Article 2.1 of the TRIMs Agreement when read in the light of Article 2.2 of the TRIMs Agreement and Paragraph 1(a) of its Annex, because in its view they are TRIMs requiring the purchase or use by entities of equipment and components for renewable generation facilities of Ontario origin or from a source in Ontario[214]. In addition, the European Union argues that the FIT Programme and its related contracts are inconsistent with the terms of Article III:4 of the GATT 1994 because, through the operation of the "Minimum Required Domestic Content Level", they accord less favourable treatment to imported equipment and components for renewable energy generation facilities than that accorded to like products originating in Ontario[215]. In this regard, the European Union agrees with, and adopts as its own, the arguments advanced by Japan as to why the measures at issue are inconsistent with Article III:4 of the GATT 1994[216].

7.81 The European Union submits that Article III:8 of the GATT 1994 does not apply to the measures at issue on the basis of four main arguments.

7.82 First, the European Union argues that Article III:8(a) of the GATT 1994 is not applicable because Article III:8(a) only covers requirements directly relating to the product purchased by the government. In the case under consideration, the European Union submits that the product allegedly procured by the Government of Ontario is electricity produced by FIT generators. However, the "Minimum Required Domestic Content Level" at issue relates to different products, i.e. renewable energy generation equipment and components, the sourcing of which does not add anything to and is completely disconnected from the basic nature of the product procured or purchased, electricity. Thus, the European Union argues that the "Minimum Required Domestic Content Level"

---

211 European Union's first written submission, para. 100, referring to the evidence submitted by Japan in its first written submission, paras. 121-128, and the objectives mentioned by the Minister's Directive to the OPA. (Minister's 2009 FIT Direction, Exhibit JPN-102, pp. 1-2).

212 European Union's first written submission, paras. 101-102.

213 European Union's first written submission, paras. 151 and 156-157.

214 European Union's first written submission, paras. 141 and 153.

215 European Unions' first written submission, paras. 156 and 158-162.

216 European Union's first written submission, paras. 106 and 158.

does not "govern" the alleged procurement of electricity because it is not related to the subject matter of the alleged procurement[217].

7.83 Second, the European Union argues that Article III:8(a) of the GATT 1994 is not applicable because the FIT Programme does not involve a "purchase" or "procurement". According to the European Union, the term "procurement" in Article III:8(a) means "acquisition". In its view, the OPA does not acquire electricity from the FIT generators under the FIT Programme. Rather, the European Union asserts that the OPA facilitates the production of electricity from renewable sources of energy and directs the FIT generators to supply their electricity into the grid[218].

7.84 Third, the European Union argues that Article III:8(a) of the GATT 1994 is not applicable because even assuming that the measures involve a "purchase" or "procurement" of electricity, such conduct is not undertaken "for governmental purposes". For the European Union, the key question in this respect is whether the electricity purchased by the OPA is acquired with a view to covering the needs of the Government of Ontario. According to the European Union, the fact that the OPA purchases electricity from FIT generators to secure a sufficient and reliable supply of electricity from clean sources, in pursuit of a public policy, is irrelevant since the electricity is neither used by nor covers the needs of the OPA or the Government of Ontario to perform any of its public service functions[219].

7.85 Finally, the European Union argues that Article III:8(a) of the GATT 1994 is not applicable because any purchase of electricity through the FIT Programme is "with a view to commercial resale and/or with a view to be used in the production of goods for commercial sale"[220]. In this respect, the European Union submits that a "commercial resale" in the sense of Article III:8(a) does not necessarily require that the product in question be resold for a *profit*. Rather, the European Union submits that Article III:8(a) merely requires that the purchased product is sold, traded or introduced into the market for that particular product. The European Union asserts that the electricity produced by the FIT generators is introduced into the market and sold to all consumers at commercial prices. Moreover, the European Union also argues that

---

[217] European Union's response to Panel question No. 22 (first set); and opening statement at the first meeting of the Panel, para. 41.

[218] European Union's first written submission, paras. 57 and 115; response to Panel question No. 49 (first set); and opening statement at the second meeting of the Panel, para. 12.

[219] European Union's first written submission, paras. 116-132; opening statement at the first meeting of the Panel, paras. 36-37; second written submission, paras. 125-133; opening statement at the second meeting of the Panel, paras. 41-49; and responses to Panel questions Nos. 46 and 47 (second set).

[220] European Unions' first written submission, para. 133.

since the electricity produced by the FIT generators is fed into the grid, the purchased product is used in the production of goods for commercial sale[221].

(c) Canada

7.86 Canada argues that the FIT Programme is not subject to the obligations of Article III of the GATT 1994 because the laws and requirements that create and implement the FIT Programme are laws and requirements that govern the procurement of renewable electricity for the governmental purpose of securing electricity supply for Ontario consumers from clean sources, and not with a view to commercial resale or with a view to use in the production of goods for commercial sale[222]. Thus, Canada states, considering that the FIT Programme is not subject to Article III of the GATT 1994, it cannot be inconsistent with Article 2.1 of the TRIMs Agreement[223].

7.87 In support of its view that Article III:8(a) of the GATT 1994 applies to the measures at issue, Canada submits four main arguments.

7.88 First, Canada contends the challenged measures are law, regulations or requirements governing the procurement of electricity. Canada considers that Section 25.35 of the *Electricity Act of 1998*; the Ministerial Direction; and the FIT and microFIT Rules and Contracts are laws or requirements for the purposes of Article III:8(a). In addition, Canada argues that the scope of Article III:8(a) is not confined to the purchase of products that are the focus of a claim under Article III of the GATT 1994[224]. Canada contends that its understanding is supported by the Government Procurement Agreement ("GPA") and academic literature on the GPA[225]. Finally, Canada states that nothing in the wording of Article III:8(a) prescribes that the "domestic content requirement" must "govern" the procurement. Alternatively, Canada argues that the domestic content requirement does "govern" the OPA's procurement of wind and solar electricity[226].

7.89 Second, Canada asserts the OPA is procuring electricity. Canada points out that there is no dispute between the parties that the OPA is a governmental agency[227]. Canada also explains that several sections of the challenged measures

---

221 European Union's first written submission, paras. 128-132; opening statement at the first meeting of the Panel, paras. 38-40; second written submission, paras. 134-149; opening statement at the second meeting of the Panel, paras. 50-59; and response to Panel question No. 48 (second set).

222 Canada's first written submission (DS412), para. 67.

223 Canada's first written submission (DS412), para. 101.

224 Canada's first written submission (DS412), para. 68; first written submission (DS426), para. 13; opening statement at the first meeting of the Panel, paras. 10 and 46-48; response to Panel question No. 22 (first set); and opening statement at the second meeting of the Panel, paras. 62 and 69.

225 Canada's opening statement at the first meeting of the Panel, paras. 49-51; and response to Panel question No. 22 (first set).

226 Canada's opening statement at the second meeting of the Panel, paras. 64-65.

227 Canada's first written submission (DS412), para. 70.

expressly state that the OPA is procuring renewable electricity[228]. In any case, Canada argues that the ordinary meaning of "procurement" is "[t]he action of obtaining something; acquisition [...]"[229]. Canada contends that this meaning is confirmed by its context in Article III:8(a), since it refers to the procurement of products "purchased", and the ordinary meaning of "purchase" is "[t]o acquire in exchange for payment in money or an equivalent; to buy"[230]. Thus, according to Canada, "Article III:8(a) applies to the governmental acquisition of products by payment"[231]. Canada contends that the OPA purchases renewable electricity for the following reasons: (i) the challenged measures state that the OPA is purchasing renewable electricity; (ii) the OPA only pays money in exchange for renewable electricity that is produced and delivered into the grid[232]; (iii) the OPA also purchases the by-products from the production of renewable electricity, including carbon credits and "future contract related products"[233]; and (iv) the OPA pays sales tax under the FIT Contracts, which in Ontario is paid by the acquirer of goods and services[234].

7.90 Third, Canada argues that the ordinary meaning of a "purchase for governmental purposes" is a purchase for an aim of the government. The OPA's purchase of renewable electricity furthers the aim of the Government of Ontario to secure the supply of adequate and reliable electricity from clean sources[235].

---

[228] Canada's first written submission (DS412), paras. 71-75. See also Canada's first written submission (DS426), para. 16; opening statement at the first meeting of the Panel, para. 29; closing oral statement at the first meeting of the Panel, para. 3; second written submission, para. 19; and opening statement at the second meeting of the Panel, para. 20.

[229] Canada's first written submission (DS412), para. 76, quoting the OED Online Dictionary, definition of "procurement" (OED Online Dictionary, definition of "procurement", ("OED Online Dictionary: procurement"), Exhibit CDA-39). See also Canada's second written submission, para. 24.

[230] Canada's first written submission (DS412), para. 76, quoting the OED Online Dictionary, definition of "purchase" (OED Online Dictionary, definition of "purchase", ("OED Online Dictionary: purchase"), Exhibit CDA-40).

[231] Canada's first written submission (DS412), para. 77. See also, Canada's response to Panel question No. 56 (first set).

[232] Canada's first written submission (DS412), paras. 77-80. See also Canada's first written submission (DS426), para. 16; second written submission, paras. 16 and 43; opening statement at the second meeting of the Panel, para. 20; and closing statement at the second meeting of the Panel, para. 2.

[233] Canada's first written submission (DS426), para. 16; opening statement at the first meeting of the Panel, paras. 17-20, referring to FIT Contract, Exhibit JPN-127, Article 2.10(a); and second written submission, para. 15.

[234] Canada's first written submission (DS426), para. 17, referring to Canada Revenue Agency, How GST/HST works, ("How GST/HST Works"), Exhibit CDA-56; FIT Contract, Exhibit JPN-127, Article 3.5; and FIT Rules, Exhibit JPN-119, Section 7.3(d). See also Canada's opening statement at the first meeting of the Panel, para. 21.

[235] Canada's first written submission (DS412), paras. 86-88; first written submission (DS426), paras. 23-34; closing statement at the first meeting of the Panel, para. 9; response to Panel question No. 28 (first set); second written submission, paras. 50-67; opening statement at the second meeting of the Panel, paras. 33-46; closing statement at the second meeting of the Panel, paras. 5-12; and response to Panel question No. 47 (second set).

7.91 Finally, Canada submits that OPA's purchase of renewable electricity is not with a view to commercial resale as it is not a purchase with an aim to resell for profit. Similarly, the OPA is not purchasing renewable electricity with a view to using the product in the production of goods for commercial sale as neither the OPA nor any other part of the Government of Ontario uses the electricity to produce goods[236].

2. *Arguments of the third parties*

(a) Australia

7.92 Referring to the term "governmental purposes" in Article III:8(a) of the GATT 1994, Australia notes that the ordinary meaning of the term "purpose" may be "practical advantage or use"[237]. Although this ordinary meaning may not be as common as the one suggested by Canada, Australia submits that it appears to be more appropriate when one considers the reference to "*les besoins*" in the French version of Article III:8(a) of the GATT 1994. With respect to the term "with a view to commercial resale", Australia notes that the ordinary meaning of "commercial" is "concerned with or engaged in 'commerce'; commerce is defined as the activity of buying and selling"[238]. In Australia's view, the concept of profit in both definitions is a secondary consideration. Australia considers that to interpret "with a view to commercial resale" as meaning a purchase with an aim to resell for profit would be an overly narrow definition – one that would expand the possible exemptions to the national treatment obligations in Article III. Australia submits that Article III:8(a) was not intended to cover the situation where a government enters into contracts for the supply or purchase of electricity at fixed prices, which it then sells on a market for general consumption[239].

(b) Brazil

7.93 Brazil considers that the complainants unduly limit the scope of the expression "for governmental purposes" in Article III:8(a) of the GATT 1994, by maintaining that it only covers purchases for the government's own use or benefit. In Brazil's view, the complainants' interpretation seems to indicate that the sole purpose of the government is to provide for the maintenance and the

---

[236] Canada's first written submission (DS412), paras. 90-97; first written submission (DS426), paras. 35-47; opening statement at the first meeting of the Panel, paras. 54-72; response to Panel question No. 25(a) (first set); second written submission, paras. 68-83; opening statement at the second meeting of the Panel, paras. 47-59; closing statement at the second meeting of the Panel, paras. 13-16; and response to Panel question No. 48 (second set).

[237] Australia's third-party submission (DS412), para. 20; and third-party submission (DS426), para. 20.

[238] Australia's third-party submission (DS412), para. 30; and third-party submission (DS426), para. 30.

[239] Australia's third-party submission (DS412), paras. 16-35; third-party submission (DS426), paras. 16-35; and third-party statement (DS412 and DS426), paras. 21-24.

regular functioning of its bureaucracy, disregarding the fact that state bureaucracy is only a means to achieve a myriad of ends, as defined by each society. Brazil contends that the purpose of a government cannot be conceptually construed, and can only be understood on a case-by-case basis and informed by the specific function performed by a given government in each sector of the economy. However, Brazil considers that the definition of "governmental purposes" cannot be as broad as suggested by Canada, as it would significantly undermine the scope of the national treatment obligation set out in Article III of the GATT 1994[240].

(c) China

7.94 China considers that the terms "purchased for governmental purposes" in Article III:8(a) of the GATT 1994 mean that (i) the government is the reason for the purchase; (ii) the government shall benefit from the result or effect of the purchase; or (iii) the government is the aim or the end of the purchase. In these disputes, China considers that the electricity purchased by the OPA is not for governmental purposes because it is injected into the grid for sale to end consumers. Moreover, China notes that the electricity sold to business operators will be used in the production of goods for commercial sale[241].

(d) European Union (in WT/DS412)

7.95 As a third party in WT/DS412, the European Union considers that the renewable energy generation equipment manufactured in Ontario and the one imported from Japan and from other countries are "like products" in the sense of Article III:4 of the GATT 1994. The European Union contends that the contested measures are "requirements" in the sense of Article III:4, and that it may be reasonably expected that the challenged measures will adversely modify the conditions of competition between the domestic and imported like products. The European Union recalls that the FIT Programme creates incentives among Ontario-based wind and solar PV energy generators to use renewable energy generation equipment produced within Ontario. With regards to Article III:8(a), the European Union considers that there is no "procurement" in the sense of this provision; and even if the Government of Ontario did procure electricity, it would be with a view to commercial resale or use in the production of goods for commercial sale[242].

7.96 Turning to the claims under the TRIMs Agreement, the European Union underlines that the TRIMs Agreement is a fully fledged agreement, which applies independently to Article III of the GATT 1994. The European Union

240 Brazil's third-party statement (DS412 and DS426), paras. 2-8.

241 China's third-party submission (DS412), paras. 8-22; and third-party statement (DS412 and DS426), paras. 2-3.

242 European Union's third-party submission (DS412), paras. 27-42.

also notes that the measures at issue would be covered by Paragraph 1(a) of the Annex to the TRIMs Agreement. A finding that a measure falls under Paragraph 1(a) results, in and of itself, in a finding of violation of Article 2.1 of the TRIMs Agreement and, consequently, in a finding of violation of Article III:4 of the GATT 1994. Thus, in the European Union's view, the Panel need not examine first whether there is a violation of Article III:4 of the GATT 1994 to then conclude that there is a violation of Article 2.1 of the TRIMs Agreement[243].

(e) Japan (in WT/DS426)

7.97 As a third party in WT/DS426, Japan contends that the characterization and treatment provided under domestic law cannot have any bearing on the application or interpretation of provisions of the covered agreements, or more generally on the determination of whether any WTO obligation has been violated. For similar reasons, Japan considers that the manner in which a Member chooses to administer its tax system has little relevance for whether a particular transaction is a "procurement" or "purchase" for purposes of Article III:8(a) of the GATT 1994[244].

(f) Korea

7.98 Korea considers that the text of Article III:8(a) of the GATT 1994, when read as a whole, suggest that the meaning of "procurement" is not completely identical to the meaning of "purchase", since this provision uses both terms in the same sentence in a manner that suggests that there may be types of procurement that do not involve purchases. The term "procurement" would appear to encompass any form of governmental acquisition, including but not limited to "purchase"[245].

7.99 Moreover, Korea considers that electric power is not a material object, but a form of energy typically generated when coils of wire are turned in a magnetic field to cause a quantity of electrons (the electric current) to flow as a result of a difference in potential (the voltage). Korea contends that it remains open whether, in the circumstances of these disputes, (i) electricity should be considered a "product", and (ii) a definition of "product" (referring to renewable energy from wind, solar PV, or other "clean" alternatives) that considers the methods used to produce the electric power would be appropriate where the definition is intended to achieve important environmental objectives[246].

7.100 Turning to the expression "governmental purposes", Korea contends that Canada's interpretation of "governmental purposes" would result in all

---

243 European Union's third-party submission (DS412), paras. 43-47.

244 Japan's third-party submission (DS412), paras. 13-15.

245 Korea's third-party submission (DS412), paras. 16-18.

246 Korea's third-party submission (DS412), paras. 22-26.

procurements made by a government being considered "for governmental purposes", which would render this expression inutile. In addition, Korea notes that Canada appears to suggest that "governmental purposes" can be discerned from the societal interest in the alleged aim of the governmental action. Korea considers that Canada is correct in stressing the importance of adequate and reliable electrical energy supplies to the public welfare. However, Korea notes that the same description could be applied to almost any other field of economic activity. Thus, Korea contends that a test under Article III:8(a) that requires only some connection of the purchase to some matter relevant to public welfare would appear to be inadequate[247].

(g) Mexico

7.101 Mexico considers that when a subsidy contingent upon the use of domestic over imported goods is found to be prohibited under the SCM Agreement, a violation of the national treatment obligation under Article III of the GATT 1994 will necessarily exist. In addition, measures conditioned upon the use of domestic goods constitute investment measures, and being inconsistent with Article III of the GATT 1994, will also automatically result in a violation of Article 2.1 of the TRIMs Agreement. However, Mexico considers that in the case of governmental purchases measures will be excluded from the scope of Article III of the GATT 1994 and Article 2.1 of the TRIMs Agreement[248].

(h) Norway

7.102 Norway agrees with the complainants that the crucial issue in these disputes is whether the OPA is actually "purchasing" electricity, or whether it functions solely as a "clearing house". In this respect, Norway argues that it is not sufficient to consider whether the OPA's activities are referred to as "procurement". With regards to Canada's interpretation of "governmental purposes", Norway considers that it would in practice include every single purchase made by a government. This would result in the terms "governmental purposes" being made inutile, and also allow Members to circumvent the obligation included in Article III:4 of the GATT 1994[249].

(i) United States

7.103 With respect to the "likeness" analysis under Article III:4 of the GATT 1994, the United States recalls that several panels have found significant the fact that a measure distinguishes between a domestic and an imported

[247] Korea's third-party submission (DS412), paras. 31-34.

[248] Mexico's third-party submission (DS412), paras. 16-19; and third-party submission (DS426), paras. 16-19.

[249] Norway's third-party statement (DS412 and DS426), paras. 2-6.

product solely on the basis of origin[250]. Turning to Article III:8(a), the United States addresses the following three issues.

7.104 First, the United States contends that Canada has improperly assigned an "object and purpose" to Article III:8(a) of the GATT 1994. The United States recalls that Article 31 of the Vienna Convention provides that the interpretation of treaty provisions shall be informed by the object and purpose *of the treaty*. Thus, according to the United States, the proper identification of the object and purpose of an agreement is not derived by reviewing an isolated subsection of that agreement[251].

7.105 Second, the United States argues that Canada has employed an overly broad interpretation of "governmental purposes" in Article III:8(a). The United States argues that Canada's interpretation renders meaningless the phrase "purchase for governmental purposes" because of two reasons: (i) nearly every government procurement is "directed by" a government document of some sort; and (ii) Canada's interpretation is circular, as it is difficult to conceive of a situation in which a government would say it is not acting with a governmental aim in mind[252].

7.106 Finally, the United States considers that Canada has incorrectly identified the relevant product for purposes of Article III:8(a). The particular purchases to which the FIT local content requirement apply – sales of equipment by manufacturers to private power generators – appear to differ in nature and by contract from the purported government procurement of electricity that is at the core of Canada's Article III:8(a) defence. In other words, although Canada consistently identifies *electricity* as the "product" covered by Article III:8(a), it seeks to justify local content requirements that apply to *equipment*. According to the United States, it does not follow that a purported government procurement of one class of goods under Article III:8(a) justifies a local content requirement covering private purchases of a different class of goods. The United States considers that the interpretation advanced by Canada would extend the scope of Article III:8(a) well beyond its ordinary meaning, effectively broadening it to permit a government procurement of a good to be used to leverage all manner of domestic content requirements[253].

3. *Evaluation by the Panel*

(a) Introduction

7.107 In the sections that follow, we begin our evaluation of the merits of the parties' arguments by first determining whether the complainants have established that the challenged measures amount to TRIMs within the meaning

---

[250] United States' third-party submission (DS412 and DS426), paras. 3-5.
[251] United States' third-party submission (DS412 and DS426), paras. 6-12.
[252] United States' third-party submission (DS412 and DS426), paras. 13-15.
[253] United States' third-party submission (DS412 and DS426), paras. 16-20.

of Article 1 of the TRIMs Agreement. We subsequently examine whether the complainants have also demonstrated that the FIT Programme, and the FIT and microFIT Contracts, are inconsistent with Article 2.1 of the TRIMs Agreement by virtue of being inconsistent with the national treatment obligation provided for in Article III:4 of the GATT 1994. In this connection, the key question that we will have to resolve, given Canada's line of defence[254], is whether Article III:8(a) of the GATT 1994 may apply to remove the challenged measures from the scope of Article III:4 of the GATT 1994, and thereby also the disciplines found in Article 2.1 of the TRIMs Agreement.

(b) Whether the measures at issue are trade-related investment measures

7.108 Article 1 of the TRIMs Agreement stipulates that it "applies to investment measures related to trade in goods only". However, the TRIMs Agreement does not define trade-related investment measures ("TRIMs"). The complainants argue that the measures at issue are TRIMs because they (i) encourage investment in the local production of renewable energy generation equipment and components in Ontario; and (ii) affect trade in wind and solar energy generation equipment by favouring Ontario products over imported products[255]. Canada does not advance any arguments on whether the challenged measures constitute TRIMs.

7.109 With respect to whether the challenged measures constitute "investment" measures, the evidence before us reveals that, as argued by the complainants, one of the aims of the FIT Programme, and the FIT and microFIT Contracts, is to encourage investment in the local production of equipment associated with renewable energy generation in the Province of Ontario. Thus, for example, the objectives of the FIT Programme include enabling "new green industries through new investment and job creation" and the provision of "incentives for investment in renewable energy technologies"[256].

7.110 The evidence before us also discloses that the FIT Programme has been a key factor motivating a number of manufacturers to establish facilities for the production of renewable energy equipment in Ontario. For instance, Siemens has reported that by becoming a local manufacturer of inverters for solar PV technology, "Siemens will allow its customers investing in commercial and solar farm applications to meet the 'minimum required domestic level' requirement by

[254] We note that apart from Canada's reliance on Article III:8(a) of the GATT 1994, Canada has not advanced any specific arguments to reject the complainants' claims under Article 2.1 of the TRIMs Agreement and Article III:4 of the GATT 1994.

[255] Japan's first written submission, paras. 298-299; and European Union's first written submission, paras. 100-102; and 151-152.

[256] Minister's 2009 FIT Direction, Exhibit JPN-102, p. 1.

the Ontario government's feed-in tariff (FIT) program"[257]. In addition, another company, Automation Tooling Systems, "announced plans in October 2009 to manufacture solar modules in Ontario to take advantage of the province's Green Energy Act, which guarantees a higher price for solar energy through its feed-in tariff program"[258]. Similarly, two other firms, ENERCON and Niagara Region Wind Corporation, have signed a contract pursuant to which ENERCON will supply and maintain wind turbines for the Niagara Region Wind Power Project. It has been reported that "[a] key component of this agreement is ENERCON's commitment to build a manufacturing facility in the Niagara Region ... [which] will allow NRWC to fulfill its domestic content requirements, as required by the Ontario Power Authority"[259]. The new facility "would be the first of its kind in the North American market and for ENERCON outside of its home market of Germany"[260].

7.111 As to whether the measures are "trade-related", we note that the FIT Programme imposes a "Minimum Required Domestic Content Level" on electricity generators utilising solar PV and windpower technologies that, for the reasons we explain elsewhere in this section[261], compels them to purchase and use certain types of renewable energy generation equipment sourced in Ontario in the design and construction of their facilities. To this extent, we see the "Minimum Required Domestic Content Level" that is at issue in these disputes to be not unlike the domestic content requirements challenged in *Indonesia – Autos*, where the panel opined that "by definition, [domestic content requirements] always favour the use of domestic products over imported products, and therefore affect trade"[262].

7.112 Thus, based on the foregoing analysis, we find that the FIT Programme, and the FIT and microFIT Contracts, to the extent they envisage and impose a "Minimum Required Domestic Content Level", constitute TRIMs within the meaning of Article 1 of the TRIMs Agreement. Having established that the challenged measures amount to TRIMs, we now turn to examine whether they are inconsistent with Article 2.1 of the TRIMs Agreement.

---

[257] Siemens invests in Solar Inverter Manufacturing in Canada, Siemens Canada, Press Release, 3 June 2010, ("Siemens invests in Canada"), Exhibit JPN-112.

[258] Chuck Howitt, "ATS lifts curtain on green wing", *Waterloo Region Record*, 26 November 2010, ("ATS lifts curtain on green wing"), Exhibit JPN-113.

[259] "Niagara Region Wind Corporation selects turbine manufacturer", Canada NewsWire, 27 September 2011, ("Niagara Region Wind Corporation selects turbine manufacturer"), Exhibit JPN-117.

[260] Niagara Region Wind Corporation selects turbine manufacturer, Exhibit JPN-117.

[261] The "Minimum Required Domestic Content Level" is described and examined in more detail below at paras. 7.158-7.165.

[262] Panel Report, *Indonesia – Autos*, para. 14.82.

(c) Whether the measures at issue are inconsistent with Article 2.1 of the TRIMs Agreement because they are allegedly inconsistent with Article III:4 of the GATT 1994

7.113 As already noted, we see the core issue that is contested in these disputes in relation to the complainants' claims under the TRIMs Agreement and the GATT 1994 to be whether the challenged measures are outside the scope of application of Article III:4 of the GATT 1994 by virtue of the operation of Article III:8(a) of the GATT 1994[263]. In this regard, the key questions that we must resolve are: (i) whether Paragraph 1(a) of the Illustrative List in the Annex to the TRIMs Agreement precludes the application of Article III:8(a) to the challenged measures; and (ii) to the extent that Paragraph 1(a) of the Illustrative List does not remove the possibility of applying Article III:8(a) to the challenged measures, whether those measures are of the kind described in Article III:8(a). We now address each of these questions in turn.

[263] We agree with the European Union's characterization of Article III:8(a) of the GATT 1994 as a "scope" provision rather than an exception. (European Union's response to Panel Question No. 14 (first set); and opening statement at the second meeting of the Panel, para. 29). We recall that the Appellate Body in *China – Raw Materials* considered the different nature of Articles XI:2 and XX of the GATT 1994, and stated that:

> Members can resort to Article XX of the GATT 1994 as an exception to justify measures that would otherwise be inconsistent with their GATT obligations. By contrast, Article XI:2 provides that the general elimination of quantitative restrictions *shall not extend to* the items listed under subparagraphs (a) and (c) of that provision. This language seems to indicate that the scope of the obligation not to impose quantitative restrictions itself is limited by Article XI:2(a). Accordingly, where the requirements of Article XI:2(a) are met, there would be no scope for the application of Article XX, because no obligations exists. (Appellate Body Report, *China – Raw Materials*, para. 334).

We note that, pursuant to Article III:8(a), the provisions of Article III *shall not apply to* laws, regulations or requirements governing certain type of procurement. Thus, consistent with the Appellate Body's view relating to the relationship between Articles XI:2 and XX of the GATT 1994, the language in Article III:8(a) seems to indicate that the scope of the national treatment obligation under Article III is limited by Article III:8(a). In other words, if a measure is covered by Article III:8(a), it will not fall within the scope of Article III of the GATT 1994.

(i) Whether the challenged measures are outside the scope of Article III:4 of the GATT 1994 by virtue of the operation of Article III:8(a) of the GATT 1994

Whether Paragraph 1(a) of the Illustrative List in the Annex to the TRIMs Agreement precludes the application of Article III:8(a) of the GATT 1994 to the challenged measures

7.114 We begin by setting out and reviewing the relevant legal provisions, which stipulate as follows:

> *Article 2*
>
> *National Treatment and Quantitative Restrictions*
>
> 1. Without prejudice to other rights and obligations under GATT 1994, no Member shall apply any TRIM that is inconsistent with the provisions of Article III or Article XI of GATT 1994.
>
> 2. An illustrative list of TRIMs that are inconsistent with the obligation of national treatment provided for in paragraph 4 of Article III of GATT 1994 and the obligation of general elimination of quantitative restrictions provided for in paragraph 1 of Article XI of GATT 1994 is contained in the Annex to this Agreement.

7.115 Paragraph 1(a) of Illustrative List in the Annex to the TRIMs Agreement provides:

> 1. TRIMs that are inconsistent with the obligation of national treatment provided for in paragraph 4 of Article III of GATT 1994 include those which are mandatory or enforceable under domestic law or under administrative rulings, or compliance with which is necessary to obtain an advantage, and which require:
>
> (a) the purchase or use by an enterprise of products of domestic origin or from any domestic source, whether specified in terms of particular products, in terms of volume or value of products, or in terms of a proportion of volume or value of its local production; or
>
> ...

7.116 Article III:8(a) of the GATT 1994 stipulates that:

> The provisions of this Article shall not apply to laws, regulations or requirements governing the procurement by governmental agencies of products purchased for governmental purposes and not with a view to commercial resale or with a view to use in the production of goods for commercial sale.

7.117 The text of Article 2.1 of the TRIMs Agreement imposes an obligation on Members not to apply any TRIM that is inconsistent with the "provisions of Article III or Article XI of GATT 1994". The "provisions of Article III" include the national treatment obligation found in Article III:4. It follows that any measure found to be inconsistent with Article III:4 of the GATT 1994 that is also a TRIM will be incompatible with Article 2.1 of the TRIMs Agreement.

7.118 It is important to note that the "provisions of Article III" that are referred to in Article 2.1 of the TRIMs Agreement include Article III:8(a). This provision precludes the application of the obligations set out in Article III to "laws, regulations or requirements governing" certain types of government procurement[264]. Consequently, any government procurement transactions covered by the terms of Article III:8(a) of the GATT 1994 will be removed from the scope of the obligations set out in Article III, including Article III:4. Thus, where a particular TRIM involves the same kind of government procurement transactions described in Article III:8(a), it cannot be found to be inconsistent with the obligation in Article 2.1 of the TRIMs Agreement.

7.119 Article 2.2 of the TRIMs Agreement does not impose any obligations on Members, but rather informs the interpretation of the prohibition set out in Article 2.1. In particular, Article 2.2 explains that the TRIMs described in the Illustrative List of the Annex to the TRIMs Agreement are to be considered inconsistent with Members' specific obligations under Articles III:4 and XI:1 of the GATT 1994. It does not follow, however, that TRIMs having the same characteristics as those described in Paragraph 1(a) of the Illustrative List must be automatically found to be inconsistent with Article III:4 of the GATT 1994 *when they would otherwise be covered by the terms of Article III:8(a) of the GATT 1994*. Such a reading of Article 2.2 would be inconsistent with the clear terms of Article 2.1, which explicitly state that there will be a violation of Article 2.1 of the TRIMs Agreement whenever a measure is inconsistent with Article III of the GATT 1994. This refers to *the whole of Article III, including Article III:8(a)*.

7.120 In our view, the European Union's argument that Paragraph 1(a) of the Illustrative List, read in conjunction with Article 2.2 of the TRIMs Agreement, may be determinative of whether a measure violates Article III:4 of the GATT 1994, and thereby also Article 2.1 of the TRIMs Agreement, does not reflect the proper sequence of the legal analysis that is envisaged under Articles 2.1 and 2.2 of the TRIMs Agreement. We consider this sequence to be the following. Where in a particular case it is found that the national treatment obligation in Article III:4 applies to a challenged measure, the Illustrative List may be used to determine whether the challenged measure is inconsistent with that obligation through the operation of Article 2.1 of the TRIMs Agreement.

---

[264] The obligation in Article 2.1 of the TRIMs Agreement is further qualified by the statement that it is "without prejudice to other rights and obligations under the GATT 1994".

Where such a measure has the characteristics that are described in Paragraph 1(a) of the Illustrative List, it follows from the clear language of this provision that it will be in violation of Article III:4 of the GATT 1994, and thereby also Article 2.1 of the TRIMs Agreement. Given the language of Article 2.1, it would, in our view, be inappropriate to infer from Paragraph 1(a) of the Illustrative List that TRIMs having the characteristics described in that paragraph will *always* be inconsistent with Article III:4 of the GATT 1994, irrespective of whether they may be covered by the terms of Article III:8(a) of the GATT 1994.

7.121 In the light of the foregoing considerations, we conclude that Paragraph 1(a) of the Illustrative List in the Annex to the TRIMs Agreement does not obviate the need for us to undertake an analysis of whether the challenged measures are outside of the scope of application of Article III:4 of the GATT 1994 by virtue of the operation of Article III:8(a) of the GATT 1994.

Whether the challenged measures are of the kind described in Article III:8(a) of the GATT 1994

7.122 These proceedings are the first where a panel has been asked to interpret and apply Article III:8(a) of the GATT 1994. A plain reading of this provision, which we have already set out above, suggests that it can be broken up into a number of cumulative elements. The parties' arguments appear to raise issues with respect to the following three questions:

(i) whether the challenged measures can be characterized as "laws, regulations or requirements *governing* procurement";

(ii) whether the challenged measures involve "*procurement* by governmental agencies"; and

(iii) whether any "procurement" that exists is undertaken "for *governmental purposes* and not with a view to *commercial resale* or with a view to use in the production of goods for commercial sale".

"Laws, regulations or requirements *governing* procurement" of electricity

7.123 The complainants' claims under Article 2.1 of the TRIMs Agreement and Article III:4 of the GATT 1994 are focused on the "Minimum Required Domestic Content Level" imposed under the FIT Programme, and the FIT and microFIT Contracts, which they allege results in less favourable treatment of imported renewable energy generation equipment compared with the treatment accorded to domestic like products[265]. Canada argues that it has no national treatment obligations with respect to the "Minimum Required Domestic Content Level" because it is part of the "laws, regulations or requirements *governing* the procurement" of electricity under the FIT Programme. In other words, Canada submits that the "Minimum Required Domestic Content Level" is removed from the scope of Article III by operation of Article III:8(a) of the GATT 1994[266].

7.124 As we explain in more detail elsewhere in these Reports[267], the evidence before us reveals that the "Minimum Required Domestic Content Level" is a condition that *must* be satisfied by electricity generators utilizing solar PV or windpower technologies wanting to participate in the FIT Programme. In other words, the "Minimum Required Domestic Content Level" compels the purchase and use of certain renewable energy generation equipment that is sourced in Ontario as a necessary prerequisite for the alleged procurement by the Government of Ontario to take place. We agree with Canada that a measure "governing" procurement is one that controls, regulates or determines that procurement[268]. It follows that the "Minimum Required Domestic Content Level" is a "requirement[] governing" the alleged procurement of electricity by the Government of Ontario under the FIT Programme, and the FIT and microFIT Contracts, for purposes of Article III:8(a).

7.125 The European Union does not contest that compliance with the "Minimum Required Domestic Content Level" is a necessary condition for the alleged procurement of electricity to take place. Nevertheless, according to the European Union, "the domestic content requirements imposed by the Government of Ontario do not 'govern' the alleged procurement of electricity, within the meaning of Article III:8(a), *because they are not requirements related to the subject-matter of the procurement, which is electricity*"[269]. The European Union submits that "the text of Article III:8(a) is structured in a manner that the term 'products' is directly qualified by the term 'purchased', which implies that the requirements [must] govern the products purchased by governmental agencies and not other products that do not have any relationship with the object or subject-matter of the procurement contract"[270]. In other words, the European Union argues that the "laws, regulations or requirements" referred to in Article III:8(a) of the GATT 1994 can only be understood to refer to "laws,

---

265 Japan's first written submission, paras. 272-283 and 295-297; and European Union's first written submission, paras. 106, 152-153, 156, and 158-162.

266 Canada's first written submission (DS412), paras. 62, 67, and 101; first written submission (DS426), paras. 3 and 11; opening statement at the first meeting of the Panel, paras. 5 and 9; second written submission, paras. 2 and 13; and opening statement at the second meeting of the Panel, paras. 5 and 12.

267 See below at paras. 7.164-7.166.

268 See Canada's first written submission (DS412), para. 83 referring to the ordinary meaning of "govern" endorsed in the Panel Report, *EC – Selected Customs Matters*, para. 7.529.

269 European Union's response to Panel question No. 22 (first set), para. 88. (emphasis added)

270 European Union's second written submission, para. 113. See also European Union's response to Panel question No. 56 (first set).

regulations or requirements" that *directly relate to the product* procured by the government. Thus, because the "Minimum Required Domestic Content Level" is imposed with respect to products (certain renewable energy generation equipment) that are different to the product allegedly procured (electricity), the European Union argues that the "Minimum Required Domestic Content Level" cannot be said to actually "govern" the alleged procurement. For this reason, the European Union asserts that the challenged measures cannot be covered by the terms of Article III:8(a)[271].

7.126 We have difficulty accepting the European Union's interpretation. The words "laws, regulations or requirements governing" in Article III:8(a) are not linked directly to the "products purchased" but to the "procurement" of such products. In this light, we cannot accept that the reference to "laws, regulations or requirements governing the procurement" can *only* be read to mean "laws, regulations or requirements" that *directly* affect a product that is identical to the product that is the subject of the alleged procurement. In our view, it is apparent from the text of Article III:8(a) that the focus of the analysis must be the "laws, regulations or requirements governing" the alleged *procurement* of electricity.

7.127 As already mentioned, the "Minimum Required Domestic Content Level" is a necessary prerequisite for the alleged procurement by the Government of Ontario to take place, and to this extent, we are of the view that such requirements "govern" the alleged procurement. Furthermore, we observe that the electricity allegedly procured by the Government of Ontario under the FIT Programme is produced using the renewable energy generation equipment that is the subject of the "Minimum Required Domestic Content Level". Thus, to the extent that the "Minimum Required Domestic Content Level" relates to the very same equipment that is needed and used to produce the electricity that is allegedly procured, there is very clearly a close relationship between the products that are affected by the relevant "laws, regulations or requirements" (renewable energy generation equipment) and the product that is allegedly procured (electricity).

7.128 Thus, for the above reasons, we find that the "Minimum Required Domestic Content Level" should be properly characterized as one of the "requirements governing" the alleged procurement of electricity for the purpose of Article III:8(a).

---

271 In its third-party submission, the United States also raised the issue of the legal implications of the difference between the product subject to the "Minimum Required Domestic Content Level" and the product that is the subject of the alleged procurement. See United States' third-party submission, paras. 18-19.

"*Procurement* by governmental agencies"

7.129 We now proceed to examine whether the measures at issue involve "*procurement* by governmental agencies of products *purchased*" within the meaning of Article III:8(a) of the GATT 1994.

7.130 The European Union and Canada consider that the ordinary meanings of the words "procurement" and "purchased" should be understood, in the context of Article III:8(a) of the GATT 1994, to imply the same governmental action of *acquiring* a product[272]. Although agreeing with the view that a "procurement" can be defined as "[t]he action of obtaining something; acquisition"[273], Japan submits that the notion of "procurement" referred to in Article III.8(a) is not entirely captured by the meaning of "purchased" that is advanced by the European Union and Canada. In Japan's view, a number of contextual elements suggest that the proper interpretation of the term "procurement", and thus a finding that "procurement by governmental agencies" exists, involves consideration of the following four factors, "none of which alone may be decisive": (i) governmental payment for the procurement; (ii) governmental use, consumption or benefit; (iii) governmental obtainment, acquisition, or possession; and (iv) governmental control over the obtaining of the product[274].

7.131 We have some difficulty accepting Japan's interpretation of the term "procurement". In our view, Japan's argument that "procurement" implies "governmental use, benefit, or consumption" does not sit well with the immediate context within which the term "procurement" is used in Article III:8(a) of the GATT 1994. As the parties have explained, the ordinary meaning of the word "procurement" includes "[t]he action of obtaining something; an acquisition"[275]. Article III:8(a) refers to "procurement by governmental agencies of products *purchased*". The ordinary meanings of the word "purchase" advanced by the parties include "to obtain; to gain possession of" and "to acquire in exchange for payment in money or an equivalent; to buy"[276]. The notion of governmental *use, benefit or consumption* is not immediately apparent from the ordinary meanings of these terms. Rather, in our view, to the extent that the ordinary meanings of both words refer to the action

---

272 European Union's first written submission, para. 114; response to Panel question No. 56 (first set); Canada's first written submission (DS412), para. 76; and response to Panel question No. 56 (first set).

273 Japan's first written submission, para. 51.

274 Japan's opening statement at the first meeting of the Panel, paras. 49-58; second written submission, para. 54; and opening statement at the second meeting of the Panel, para. 28.

275 The French and Spanish texts of Article III:8(a) of the GATT 1994 confirm this understanding of the meaning of "procurement", respectively providing in the relevant part: "*produits achetés pour les besoins des pouvoirs publics*" and "*productos comprados para cubrir las necesidades de los poderes públicos*".

276 Japan's second written submission, para. 38; Canada's second written submission, para. 93; opening statement at the second meeting of the Panel, paras. 22-23; European Union's first written submission, para. 114; and opening statement at the second meeting of the Panel, para. 38.

of "obtaining" or "acquiring" something, they support a conclusion that "procurement" and "purchase" should be given the same meaning. Indeed, the fact that Article III:8(a) describes the "*procurement* ... of products" as "products *purchased*" would seem to confirm the view that the term "procurement" in Article III:8(a) should be given the same essential meaning as the word "purchased" and *vice versa*.

7.132 Moreover, if the notion of "procurement" that is referred to in Article III:8(a) were interpreted to necessarily include "governmental use, consumption, or benefit" of the product at issue, there would have been no need to exclude government procurement of products "with a view to commercial resale or with a view to use in the production of goods for commercial sale" from the types of government procurement covered under Article III:8(a). This is because government procurement of a product for its own use, consumption or benefit cannot, by definition, amount to procurement "with a view to commercial resale or with a view to use in the production of goods for commercial sale". Had negotiators intended for the notion of "procurement" to be understood to include purchases of products for a government's own use, consumption or benefit, it would have been sufficient to end Article III:8(a) with the words "procurement by governmental agencies of product purchased for governmental purposes".

7.133 We also are not persuaded that the references made by Japan to the GATT Panel in *US – Sonar Mapping* and to Canada's Appendix I to the GPA support Japan's interpretation of the term "procurement" in Article III:8(a) of the GATT 1994. Starting with the latter, we agree with Canada that Appendix I to the GPA is not intended to provide a general definition of the term procurement, nor an interpretation of the term "procurement" within the meaning of Article III:8(a) of the GATT 1994. It is evident that the definition Canada has agreed to be bound by for the purpose of the GPA is not intended to define the scope of its rights and obligations under Article III:8(a) of the GATT 1994.

7.134 As to the GATT panel in *US – Sonar Mapping*, we believe there are a number of features of the facts and law at issue in that dispute which significantly diminish the relevance, for these disputes, of the panel's findings Japan relies upon. First, we note that the GATT panel in *US - Sonar Mapping* examined whether a contract between two private companies regarding the acquisition of a sonar mapping system constituted "government procurement" under Article I:1(a) of the Tokyo Round Agreement on Government Procurement. Thus, it was within the very specific context of an alleged government procurement effected through purchases made by two private companies that the GATT panel identified the four elements that Japan refers to in these proceedings[277]. Second, we note that the wording and structure of

[277] GATT Panel Report, *US – Sonar Mapping*, para. 4.7, as cited by Japan in its opening statement at the first meeting of the Panel, para. 50.

Article I:1(a) of the Tokyo Round Agreement on Government Procurement is fundamentally different from Article III:8(a). In particular, Article I:1(a) refers to several methods of procurement, including lease, rental or hire-purchase, with or without an option to buy, which are not found in Article III:8(a). Indeed, it was because these methods of procurement referred to in Article I:1(a) "were all means of obtaining the use or benefit of a product", that the GATT panel concluded that "the word 'procurement' could be understood to refer to the obtaining of such use or benefit"[278].

7.135 Thus, in our view, the term "procurement", when interpreted in its immediate context, should be understood to have the same meaning as the term "purchase". We can find no support in the text of Article III:8(a) and the context of the term "procurement" to accept Japan's argument that this term must necessarily involve governmental use, consumption or benefit of the procured product[279].

7.136 As already noted, the ordinary meanings of the word "purchase" advanced by the parties include "to obtain; to gain possession of" and "to acquire in exchange for payment in money or an equivalent; to buy"[280]. For the reasons explained in Section VII.C.2(c)(iii) of these Reports, where we evaluate the parties' arguments concerning the proper legal characterization of the measures at issue under Article 1 of the SCM Agreement, we interpret government "purchases" of goods to mean the action by which a government obtains possession (including via obtaining an entitlement) over goods through some kind of payment (monetary or otherwise). In our view, this interpretation of the notion of a government "purchase" of goods is equally applicable to guide our analysis of the parties' claims under Article III:8(a) of the GATT 1994. Thus, we find that for the purpose of Article III:8(a) of the GATT 1994, a "procurement by governmental agencies of products purchased" should be understood to refer to the action of a government of obtaining possession (including via obtaining an entitlement) over products through some kind of payment (monetary or otherwise). Moreover, in the light of this interpretation and our finding, set out in Section VII.C.2(c)(iii) of these Reports, that the challenged measures may be properly characterized as "government purchases [of] goods" within the meaning of Article 1.1(a)(1)(iii) of the SCM Agreement, we conclude that the measures at issue also involve "*procurement* by governmental agencies of products purchased" for the purpose of Article III:8(a) of the GATT 1994.

---

278 GATT Panel Report, *US – Sonar Mapping*, para. 4.5.

279 With respect to the other elements considered by the GATT panel in *US – Sonar Mapping* – payment by government; governmental possession; and governmental control over the obtaining of the product – we consider them to be met when a governmental agency "purchases" a product. Thus, they do not support Japan's understanding that there is a difference in meaning between "procurement" and "purchased" in Article III:8(a) of the GATT 1994.

280 Japan's second written submission, para. 38; Canada's second written submission, para. 93; opening statement at the second meeting of the Panel, paras. 22-23; European Union's first written submission, para. 114; and opening statement at the second meeting of the Panel, para. 38.

Procurement "for *governmental purposes* and not with a view to *commercial resale* or with a view to use in the production of goods for commercial sale"

7.137 We now proceed to examine whether the procurement by the Government of Ontario is "for governmental purposes and not with a view to commercial resale or with a view to use in the production of goods for commercial sale". The main issues raised in the parties' arguments relate to the meanings of the expression "governmental purposes" and the term "commercial resale" in Article III:8(a) of the GATT 1994.

- "Governmental purposes"

7.138 With respect to the ordinary meaning of the expression "governmental purposes", we first note that the parties have advanced a range of different meanings. At one end of the spectrum, Canada proposes the broadest meaning of the parties, suggesting that a purchase for "governmental purposes" may exist whenever a government purchases a product for a stated aim of the government[281]. At the other extreme, Japan advances the narrowest meaning, submitting that a purchase for "governmental purposes" must be limited to purchases of products for governmental use, consumption or benefit[282]. The European Union takes an intermediate position, proposing a meaning of "governmental purposes" that refers to government purchases for governmental needs, which include both the purchase of goods consumed by the government itself and those necessary for a government's provision of public services[283].

7.139 As we understand it, the ordinary meaning of "governmental purposes" ("*les besoins des pouvoirs publics*" and "*las necesidades de los poderes públicos*", respectively in the French and Spanish versions) is relatively broad, and may encompass all three of the meanings advanced by the parties. We must, however, interpret this expression within its context. In this regard, we find it

---

[281] Canada's first written submission (DS412), para. 86; first written submission (DS426), para. 23; closing statement at the first meeting of the Panel, para. 9; response to Panel question No. 28 (first set); second written submission, para. 50; opening statement at the second meeting of the Panel, para. 33; closing statement at the second meeting of the Panel, para. 5; and response to Panel question No. 47 (second set).

[282] Japan's first written submission, paras. 284 and 287; opening statement at the first meeting of the Panel, paras. 53, 69; 71, 74-75; second written submission, para. 61; opening statement at the second meeting of the Panel, para. 33; and response to Panel question No. 47 (second set).

[283] European Union's first written submission, paras. 116 and 118; second written submission, paras. 128 and 130; opening statement at the second meeting of the Panel, para. 48; response to Panel question No. 47 (second set); and comments on Canada's response to Panel question No. 45 (second set). Japan considers that this may also be a plausible reading of "governmental purposes" (Japan's opening statement at the second meeting of the Panel, para. 33). The European Union finds support for its interpretation in the French and Spanish versions of Article III:8(a) of the GATT 1994, which respectively provide in the relevant part: "*produits achetés pour les besoins des pouvoirs publics*" and "*productos comprados para cubrir las necesidades de los poderes públicos*".

particularly instructive to observe that the expression "governmental purposes" is immediately followed by the words "and not with a view to commercial resale or with a view to use in the production of goods for commercial sale." Canada argues that the "requirement that the purchase is not with a view to commercial resale is a requirement *in addition* to the requirement that the purchase is for governmental purposes"[284]. Thus, Canada is of the view that the "governmental purposes" and "not with a view to commercial resale" language establishes *two* separate requirements that must *both* be satisfied for a law, regulation or requirement to fall within the scope of Article III:8(a). Canada concludes from this observation that "the meaning of a purchase for 'governmental purposes' cannot be confined to a purchase for governmental consumption, and the meaning of a purchase 'with a view to commercial resale' cannot be confined to a purchase with the aim to resell"[285]. The complainants, however, submit that the expression "not with a view to commercial resale" should be contrasted with the expression "for governmental purposes"[286].

7.140 In our view, the plain language of Article III:8(a) suggests that a "procurement … of products purchased for governmental purposes" *cannot* also be a "procurement … of products purchased … with a view to commercial resale or with a view to use in the production of goods for commercial sale". In this regard, we see the expression "and not with a view to commercial resale …" as serving to specifically inform and limit the otherwise relatively broad ordinary meaning of the term "governmental purposes". We are not convinced by Canada's arguments that the "governmental purposes" and "not with a view to commercial resale" language establishes *two* separate and cumulative requirements. In our view, the fact that Article III:8(a) includes the words "*and not*" after "governmental purposes" qualifies this expression by indicating that the "procurement … of products purchased … with a view to commercial resale" are excluded from the operation of Article III:8(a).

7.141 The parties have argued that Article XVII:2 of the GATT 1994 also serves as relevant context for the interpretation of Article III:8(a), with Japan and the European Union, in addition, submitting that the negotiating history of the two provisions supports their own interpretations of Article III:8(a). According to Canada, Article XVII:2 helps to demonstrate not only that "governmental purposes" in Article III:8(a) is not confined to "governmental consumption or use", but also that the "governmental purposes" and "not with a view to commercial resale" language establishes two cumulative conditions[287]. Japan, on the other hand, submits that Article XVII:2, together with its

---

[284] Canada's second written submission, para. 75.

[285] Canada's second written submission, para. 76. See also Canada's closing statement at the second meeting of the Panel, para. 14; and comments on Japan's and the European Union's responses to Panel questions Nos. 45 and 48 (second set).

[286] Japan's opening statement at the first meeting of the Panel, para. 82; and European Union's opening statement at the first meeting of the Panel, para. 39.

[287] Canada's response to Panel question No. 45 (second set).

negotiating history, reveals that the two provisions exclude the same type of "procurement", namely procurement that is for "governmental consumption or use", from the scope of their other operative subparagraphs[288]. Likewise, the European Union considers that the negotiating history of Articles III:8(a) and XVII:2 shows that, despite differences in language, both provisions were meant to address the same matter, concluding that the words "'for governmental purposes' or 'government needs' are conterminous with 'products for immediate or ultimate consumption in governmental use'"[289].

7.142 Article XVII:2 reads as follows:

> The provisions of paragraph 1 of this Article shall not apply to imports of products for immediate or ultimate consumption in governmental use and not otherwise for resale or use in the production of goods* for sale. With respect to such imports, each contracting party shall accord to the trade of the other contracting parties fair and equitable treatment.

7.143 As the European Union observes[290], both Article III:8(a) and Article XVII:2 describe the circumstances when purchases of products undertaken by governmental agencies under Article III:8(a), or imports of products by State Trading Enterprises for purposes of Article XVII:2, shall be removed from their main respective disciplines. Thus, measures covered by Article III:8(a) will be automatically removed from the scope of the national treatment obligations set out elsewhere in Article III. Similarly, the kind of purchases identified in Article XVII:2 will be removed from the scope of Article XVII:1, which imposes an obligation on State Trading Enterprises to conduct its purchasing activities involving either imports or exports in a manner consistent with the principles of non-discrimination found in the GATT 1994. The latter includes the national treatment obligations found in Article III of the GATT 1994[291]. To this extent, it can be concluded from the text of Articles III:8(a) and XVII:2 that both provisions are intended to define the scope of the national treatment obligations in the context of two particular types of purchases: (i) purchases of products by governmental agencies (Article III:8(a)); and (ii) purchases of products through State Trading Enterprises (Article XVII:2).

7.144 The kind of government purchases covered under the terms of Article III:8(a) are those that are "for governmental purposes and not with a view to commercial resale or with a view to use in the production of goods for commercial sale". On the other hand, Article XVII:2 applies to purchases of

---

[288] Japan's first written submission, fn. 457; opening statement at the first meeting of the Panel, paras. 56 and 74; and response to Panel question No. 45 (second set).

[289] European Union's response to Panel question No. 45 (second set), para. 75.

[290] European Union's response to Panel question No. 45 (second set).

[291] Panel Report, *Korea – Various Measures on Beef*, para. 753.

products "for immediate or ultimate consumption in governmental use and not otherwise for resale or use in the production of goods for sale". At first sight, the distinct language used to describe the types of relevant purchases that are covered by the two provisions could be interpreted to signify that Articles III:8(a) and XVII:2 were intended to cover a different range of transactions (not only because of the differences in the entities covered by the provisions). However, in our view, such a conclusion would not be completely accurate as it is evident from the language used in both provisions that there is, at the very least, significant overlap with respect to the types of purchases that are *excluded* from their terms of operation, namely, purchases "not with a view to commercial resale ..." (under Article III:8(a)) and purchases "not otherwise for resale ..." (under Article XVII:2). Thus, to the extent that the language of Article XVII:2 may serve as context for the interpretation of Article III:8(a), we find that it helps to confirm that a "procurement ... of products purchased for governmental purposes" under Article III:8(a) cannot also be a "procurement ... of products purchased ... with a view to commercial resale or with a view to use in the production of goods for commercial sale".

7.145 In the light of the foregoing analysis, we find that the term "governmental purposes" should be interpreted in juxtaposition to the expression "not with a view to commercial resale or with a view to use in the production of goods for commercial sale" that appears in Article III:8(a). In other words, we conclude that a purchase of goods for "governmental purposes" cannot at the same time amount to a government purchase of goods "with a view to commercial resale" under the terms of Article III:8(a). Thus, if we find that the procurement of electricity by the Government of Ontario under the FIT Programme is undertaken "with a view to commercial resale or with a view to use in the production of goods for commercial sale", such procurement will not be covered by Article III:8(a)[292]. With this finding in mind, we now turn to examine whether the measures at issue involve a government purchase "with a view to commercial resale".

- "Commercial resale"

7.146 The parties have advanced different meanings of the expression "with a view to commercial resale" that appears in Article III:8(a) of the GATT 1994. On the one hand, Canada argues that it means a purchase with the aim to resell for profit[293]. The complainants, on the other hand, submit that "with a view to

[292] We note that even pursuant to Canada's own interpretation of "governmental purposes" and "commercial resale" as cumulative and separate requirements, a government procurement will not be covered by Article III:8(a) of the GATT 1994, if it is undertaken "with a view to commercial resale", regardless of whether such procurement can be said to be for "governmental purposes".

[293] Canada's first written submission (DS412), para. 90; first written submission (DS426), paras. 35-39; opening statement at the first meeting of the Panel, paras. 55 and 57; response to Panel question

commercial resale" means with a view to being sold or introduced into the stream of commerce, trade or market, regardless of any profit[294].

7.147 We recall that the Government of Ontario purchases electricity under the FIT Programme, through the FIT and microFIT Contracts. The purchased electricity is injected by generators into Ontario's electricity grid via transmission and distribution networks, and is eventually sold to consumers by Hydro One, LDCs and private-sector licensed electricity retailers. Hydro One is a holding company wholly-owned by the Government of Ontario and an "agent" of the Government of Ontario. As explained in more detail below[295], Hydro One is also a "public body" for the purpose of Article 1 of the SCM Agreement. Of the 80 LDCs that currently operate in Ontario, 77 are owned by municipal governments. The private-sector licensed retailers "sell contracts to businesses and consumers"[296]. We understand there are currently 45 licensed electricity retailers operating in Ontario that compete with LDCs in their respective service areas[297]. Thus, it is evident that the electricity purchased by the Government of Ontario under the FIT Programme is resold to retail consumers through Hydro One and the LDCs in competition with private-sector retailers. We are not convinced by Canada's argument that electricity purchased under the FIT Programme is not *resold* because of the fact that it is injected into Ontario's electricity grid, where it is pooled with electricity from other sources[298]. As we see it, the fact that electricity purchased under the FIT Programme is consumed through precisely the same channels as electricity supplied from all other generating sources supports the view that it is resold by the Government of Ontario and the municipal governments through Hydro One and the LDCs in competition with private-sector electricity retailers.

7.148 Thus, to the extent that the notion of commerce should, as the complainants argue, be understood to simply encompass the buying and selling or trading of products into a market, the Government of Ontario's purchases of electricity, through the FIT Programme, may be considered to be a first step in

---

No. 25(a) (first set); second written submission, para. 69; and opening statement at the second meeting of the Panel, para. 48.

294 Japan's opening statement at the first meeting of the Panel, paras. 78 and 85; second written submission, para. 66; opening statement at the second meeting of the Panel, para. 36; and European Union's first written submission, para. 139; opening statement at the first meeting of the Panel, para. 39; second written submission, para. 135; opening statement at the second meeting of the Panel, para. 54; and response to Panel question No. 48 (second set).

295 See below at paras. 7.234-7.239.

296 Ontario's Long-Term Energy Plan, Exhibit CDA-6, Appendix One.

297 *Electricity Act of 1998*, Exhibit JPN-5, Section 29; Retail Settlement Code, Exhibit JPN-71, Sections 1.1, 2.7, 10.1, and 12; and OEB Licensed Electricity Retailers (http://www.ontarioenergyboard.ca/html/licences/all_issuedlicences_read.cfm?showtype=Electricity%20Retailer) referred to in IESO: Retail Contracts, Exhibit JPN-90.

298 Canada's opening statement at the first meeting of the Panel, para. 56; response to Panel question No. 25(a) (first set); second written submission, para. 68; and opening statement at the second meeting of the Panel, para. 47.

the resale of electricity to retail consumers, and thereby the introduction of electricity into commerce. Canada, however, argues that even under the complainants' interpretation of the term "commercial resale", the purchases of electricity by the Government of Ontario under the FIT Programme cannot be qualified as being made "with a view to commercial resale". In particular, Canada argues that the OPA cannot be said to sell or introduce products into the "*market*", because a "*market*" "where supply and demand freely meet" does not exist in the Ontario electricity system[299]. We are not persuaded by Canada's argument. In our view, the consideration of whether Ontario's electricity system is, as a whole, highly regulated or made up entirely of competitive markets at the different levels of trade does not change the basic fact that electricity purchased by the Government of Ontario under the FIT Programme is bought from generators and sold to retail consumers through the same channels as all other electricity by Hydro One and LDCs *in competition with private sector electricity retailers*. Therefore, consistently with the complainants' interpretation of "commercial resale", the purchased electricity is introduced into commerce.

7.149 Canada submits that the Government of Ontario's purchases of electricity under the FIT Programme are not "with a view to commercial resale" because the OPA does not profit from the resale of electricity but simply recovers the cost of purchasing renewable electricity[300]. However, whether the *OPA* profits from the Government of Ontario's purchases of electricity under the FIT Programme is not conclusive of whether any profit is made by the *Government of Ontario* on the resale of electricity to consumers. In this regard, we note that Hydro One distributes electricity to almost one third of electricity consumers in Ontario. The Memorandum of Agreement between the Government of Ontario and Hydro One provides that Hydro One "will operate as a commercial enterprise with an independent Board of Directors that will, at all times, exercise its fiduciary responsibility and a duty of care to act in the best interests of [Hydro One]"[301]. Canada has acknowledged that both Hydro One and the 77 LDCs owned by the municipal governments are intended to make returns from their electricity transmission and distribution activities and/or assets on the basis of OEB-approved prices that are "just and reasonable"[302]. In this connection, in

---

299 Canada's first written submission (DS426), para. 43, referring to European Union's first written submission, paras. 129-130.

300 Canada's first written submission (DS412), para. 92; and response to Panel question No. 25(a) (first set).

301 Memorandum of Agreement between Her Majesty the Queen in Right of the Province of Ontario as Represented by the Minister of Energy and Hydro One Inc., 27 March 2008 ("Memorandum of Agreement between the Government of Ontario and Hydro One"), Exhibit CDA-107, p. 1.

302 Canada's response to Panel question No. 13(b) (second set); citing OEB, "Report of the Board on the Cost of Capital for Ontario's Regulated Utilities, EB-2009-0084, 11 December 2009, ("OEB Report on the cost of capital for Ontario's regulated utilities"), Exhibit CDA-64, p. 8. Canada also states that the rates received by LDCs allow for cost recovery and a rate of return that is "just and reasonable". (Canada's response to Panel question No. 13(a) (second set)).

2010, Hydro One paid CAD 28 million in dividends to its shareholder, the Province of Ontario[303].

7.150 Therefore, although the OPA does not profit from the resale of electricity through Hydro One and the LDCs, it is evident that the Government of Ontario and Ontario's municipal governments will profit from these operations. We are not convinced by Canada's argument that the Government of Ontario does not profit from the resale of electricity because "[d]istributors profit from their service of distributing electricity to the end-user, rather than any on-sale of the renewable electricity, itself"[304]. To the extent that the service of electricity distribution is necessarily tied to and inseparable from the sale of electricity as a "commodity", there is no basis to conclude that the resale activities of Hydro One and almost all of the LDCs do not result in making profits.

7.151 Having found that Hydro One and the LDCs sell electricity in competition with private-sector licensed retailers and that the Government of Ontario and the municipal governments profit from the resale of electricity purchased under the FIT Programme to consumers, it is clear to us, for purposes of these disputes, that the nature of the resale of electricity purchased under the FIT Programme is "commercial". In coming to this conclusion, we emphasize that this does not mean we agree with Canada's understanding that a "commercial resale" will always necessarily involve profit, as there may well be situations where a resale of a product purchased by a governmental agency may not involve a profit but still may be "commercial" for the purpose of Article III:8(a) of the GATT 1994. Indeed, it is a fact that loss-making sales can be, and often are, a part of ordinary commercial activity. However, in the present factual situation, we have concluded that it is sufficient, for the purpose of finding that the Government of Ontario purchases electricity under the FIT Programme "with a view to commercial resale", that the Government of Ontario and the municipal governments not only profit from the resale of electricity that is purchased under the FIT Programme, but also that electricity resales are made in competition with licensed electricity retailers. In the light of the foregoing considerations, we find that the Government of Ontario's procurement of electricity under the FIT Programme is undertaken "with a view to commercial resale".

303 Hydro One Releases 2010 Year-End Financial Results, Exhibit JPN-41, p. 2. Hydro One operates through its subsidiaries in electricity transmission and distribution, and telecom businesses. Total revenues for 2010 were CAD 5,124 million, from which CAD 5,061 million represented transmission and distribution revenues. Hydro One Releases 2010 Year-End Financial Results, Exhibit JPN-41, pp. 2-3.

304 Canada's opening statement at the second meeting of the Panel, para. 55.

Conclusion with respect to whether the challenged measures fall outside the scope of Article III:4 of the GATT 1994 by virtue of the operation of Article III:8(a) of the GATT 1994

7.152 We have concluded above that: (i) the Government of Ontario's purchases of electricity under the FIT Programme constitute "procurement", within the meaning of that term in Article III:8(a); (ii) the "Minimum Required Domestic Content Level" prescribed under the FIT Programme, and effected through the FIT and microFIT Contracts, is one of the "requirements governing" the Government of Ontario's "procurement" of electricity; and (iii) the Government of Ontario's "procurement" of electricity under the FIT Programme is undertaken "with a view to commercial resale". In the light of this latter conclusion, we find that the measures at issue are not covered by the terms of Article III:8(a), and that consequently, Canada cannot rely on Article III:8(a) of the GATT 1994 to exclude the application of Article III:4 of the GATT 1994 to the "Minimum Required Domestic Content Level" that the complainants challenge.

7.153 In coming to this conclusion, we express no opinion about the legitimacy of the Government of Ontario's objective of promoting the use of renewable energy in the production of electricity through the FIT Programme. Our conclusion that the Government of Ontario purchases electricity under the FIT Programme "with a view to commercial resale", within the meaning of Article III:8(a), must be understood only as a judgement about the extent to which Canada is entitled to rely upon Article III:8(a) of the GATT 1994 to maintain a measure that is alleged to discriminate against imported products under the terms of Article III:4.

7.154 Having found that the challenged measures are not removed from the obligations prescribed under Article III:4 by virtue of the operation of Article III:8(a), it follows that they must also be subject to the obligations in Article 2.1 of the TRIMs Agreement, as elaborated and informed by Article 2.2 and the Illustrative List contained in the Annex to the TRIMs Agreement. In this connection, we recall that one of the arguments that has been advanced by both Japan and the European Union is that the challenged measures may be found to be inconsistent with Article 2.1 of the TRIMs Agreement by virtue of the operation of Paragraph 1(a) of the Illustrative List in the Annex to the TRIMs Agreement, which describes one category of TRIMs that is deemed to be inconsistent with the obligation of national treatment found in Article III:4 of the GATT 1994. We now turn to evaluate the merits this argument.

(ii) Whether the measures at issue are inconsistent with Article III:4 of the GATT 1994, and thereby also Article 2.1 of the TRIMs Agreement, by virtue of the operation of Article 2.2 of the

TRIMs Agreement and Paragraph 1(a) of the Illustrative List in the Annex to the TRIMs Agreement

7.155 As we have previously explained[305], Article 2.2 of the TRIMs Agreement prescribes that the TRIMs identified in Paragraph 1(a) of the Illustrative List in the Annex to the TRIMs Agreement are inconsistent with Article III:4 of the GATT 1994. Thus, where it is established that a measure falls within the scope of the obligations in Article III:4 of the GATT 1994, that measure may be found to be inconsistent with those obligations, and thereby also Article 2.1 of the TRIMs Agreement, if it shares the characteristics of the TRIMs described in Paragraph 1(a) of the Illustrative List.

7.156 The European Union argues that the measures at issue are covered by Paragraph 1(a) of the Illustrative List because: (i) compliance with the "Minimum Required Domestic Content Level" is necessary for generators to participate in the FIT Programme; and (ii) the "Minimum Required Domestic Content Level" requires generators to purchase or use domestic renewable energy equipment and components[306]. Similarly, Japan argues that the measures at issue are of the type explicitly listed in Paragraph 1(a) of the Illustrative List because the "Minimum Required Domestic Content Level" requires wind and solar PV generators to use generation equipment produced in Ontario in order to take advantage of the rates offered by the FIT Programme[307]. Canada has not advanced any arguments to reject the complainants' allegations that the challenged measures are of the kind described in Paragraph 1(a) of the Illustrative List.

7.157 Given the parties' arguments and the language of Paragraph 1(a) of the Illustrative List[308], we are of the view that in order to determine whether the complainants have established that the challenged measures share the characteristics of the TRIMs described in Paragraph 1(a) of the Illustrative List, we must ascertain: (i) whether the "Minimum Required Domestic Content Level" that is applied under the FIT Programme requires electricity generators using solar PV and windpower technology to purchase or use renewable energy generation equipment and components that are of Canadian origin or from a Canadian source; and (ii) whether compliance with the "Minimum Required Domestic Content Level" is necessary in order to obtain an "advantage". Below we examine each of these elements in turn.

---

305 See above at para. 7.119.

306 European Union's first written submission, paras. 141, 143, 152, and 156-157. See also European Union's opening statement at the first meeting of the Panel, para. 43; response to Panel question No. 14(a) (first set); second written submission, para. 152; and opening statement at the second meeting of the Panel, para. 61.

307 Japan's first written submission, paras. 295 and 301-302.

308 The relevant text of Paragraph 1(a) of the Illustrative List is set out above at para. 7.115.

Whether the "Minimum Required Domestic Content Level" requires the purchase or use of products of Canadian origin or from a Canadian source

7.158 The FIT Rules define the "Minimum Required Domestic Content Level" as the minimum percentage of domestic content level set out on the FIT Contract cover page that should be achieved by contract facilities utilizing windpower with a contract capacity greater than 10 kW, or contract facilities utilizing solar PV[309]. Japan has presented the following table to summarize the Minimum Required Domestic Content Levels that are prescribed under the FIT Programme.

Table 1: Minimum Required Domestic Content Levels Prescribed under the FIT Programme

	Wind (FIT)		**Solar PV (FIT)**		**Solar PV (microFIT)**	
Milestone Date for Commercial Operation	2009-2011	2012-	2009-2010	2011-	2009-2010[310]	2011-
Minimum Required Domestic Content Level	25%	50%	50%	60%	40%	60%

7.159 The domestic content level of a contract facility is calculated pursuant to the methodology set out in Exhibit D of the FIT Contract[311]. This Exhibit contains four different "Domestic Content Grids", each of which identifies a range of different "Designated Activities" and an associated "Qualifying Percentage", with respect to each of the categories of renewable energy generation falling within the scope of the FIT Programme[312]. These categories are (i) windpower projects greater than 10 kW; (ii) solar PV projects greater than 10 kW utilizing crystalline silicon PV technology; (iii) solar PV projects greater than 10 kW utilizing thin-film PV technology; and (iv) solar PV projects less than or equal to than 10 kW. The Domestic Content Grids identified for the latter

[309] Ontario Power Authority, Feed-in Tariff Programme Rules, Version 1.5.1, 31 October 2011, ("FIT Rules"), Exhibit EU-4, Section 6.4(a).

[310] Solar PV microFIT applications received by the OPA on or before 8 October 2010 may satisfy the 40% domestic content requirement.

[311] FIT Rules, Exhibit EU-4, Section 6.4(b).

[312] Ontario Power Authority, Feed-in Tariff Contract, Version 1.5.1, 31 October 2011, ("FIT Contract"), Exhibit EU-5, Exhibit D.

two categories of solar PV projects apply equally to microFIT projects under the microFIT Rules[313].

7.160 For each "Designated Activity" that is performed in relation to the Contract Facility, an associated "Qualifying Percentage" will be achieved. For example, where the wind turbine blades of a windpower project have been "cast in a mould in Ontario" and the "instrumentation that is within the blades has been assembled in Ontario", the Contract Facility will achieve a Qualifying Percentage of 16%. The FIT Contract explains that a project's Domestic Content Level will be determined by adding up the Qualifying Percentages associated with all of the Designated Activities performed in relation to that particular project.

7.161 Japan, argues that "for *all* projects", the effect of the Domestic Content Grids is to require that "*at least some* goods manufactured, formed, or assembled in Ontario *must* be utilized in order to satisfy the Minimum Required Domestic Content Levels"[314]. Japan contends that purely service activities contained in each Domestic Content Grids are not sufficient to meet the "Minimum Required Domestic Content Levels". In particular, Japan submits that the Minimum Required Domestic Content Levels cannot be achieved, in the light of the relevant Domestic Content Grids, without the use of domestic over imported goods for the following reasons[315]:

> In the FIT Contract, Exhibit D, Table 1 for Wind Power Projects Greater than 10 kW, the only designated activities that are purely service activities are line item 17 relating to construction costs (with a qualifying percentage of 15%) and line item 18 relating to consulting services (with a qualifying percentage of 5%). Thus, services may contribute at most 20% to the Domestic Content Level. In other words, where the Minimum Required Domestic Content Level is greater than 20% (as it has always been for these Wind Power Projects ...), at least some Ontario-sourced goods must be used to satisfy the Minimum Required Domestic Content Level.
>
> In the FIT Contract, Exhibit D, Table 2 for Solar (PV) Power Projects Greater than 10 kW Utilizing Crystalline Silicon PV Technology, the only designated activities that are purely service activities are line item 8 relating to construction costs (with a qualifying percentage of 18%) and line item 9 relating to consulting services (with a qualifying percentage of 4%). Thus, services may contribute at most 22% to the Domestic Content Level. In other words, where the Minimum Required Domestic

313 microFIT Rules, Exhibit JPN-157, Definitions, pp. 14-16.

314 Japan's first written submission, para. 173.

315 *Ibid.*

Content Level is greater than 22% (as it has always been for these Solar (PV) Power Projects, ...), at least some Ontario-sourced goods must be used to satisfy the Minimum Required Domestic Content Level.

In the FIT Contract, Exhibit D, Table 3 for Solar (PV) Power Projects Greater than 10 kW Utilizing Thin-Film PV Technology, the only designated activities that are purely service activities are line item 15 relating to construction costs (with a qualifying percentage of 24%) and line item 16 relating to consulting services (with a qualifying percentage of 4%). Thus, services may contribute at most 28% to the Domestic Content Level. In other words, where the Minimum Required Domestic Content Level is greater than 28% (as it has always been for these Solar (PV) Power Projects, ...), at least some Ontario-sourced goods must be used to satisfy the Minimum Required Domestic Content Level.

In the FIT Contract, Exhibit D, Table 4 for Solar (PV) Power Projects Less than or Equal to 10 kW, the only designated activity that is purely a service activity is line item 24 relating to labour and services (with a qualifying percentage of 27%). Thus, services may contribute at most 27% to the Domestic Content Level. In other words, where the Minimum Required Domestic Content Level is greater than 27% (as it has always been for these Solar (PV) Power Projects, ...), at least some Ontario-sourced goods must be used to satisfy the Minimum Required Domestic Content Level.

In the microFIT Contract, Appendix C, Table 1 for Micro-Scale (≤10kW) Solar Photovoltaic Power Projects, the only designated activity that is purely a service activity is line item 8 relating to labour and services (with a qualifying percentage of 27%). Thus, services may contribute at most 27% to the Domestic Content Level. In other words, where the Minimum Required Domestic Content Level is greater than 27% (as it has always been for these Solar Photovoltaic Power Projects, ...), at least some Ontario-sourced goods must be used to satisfy the Minimum Required Domestic Content Level.

In the microFIT Contract, Appendix C, Table 2 for Micro-Scale (≤10kW) Solar Photovoltaic Power Projects Utilizing Thin-Film PV Technology, the only designated activity that is purely a service activity is line item 6 relating to labour and services (with a qualifying percentage of 28%). Thus, services may contribute at most 28% to the Domestic Content Level. In other words, where the Minimum Required Domestic Content Level is greater than 28% (as it has always been for these Solar Photovoltaic Power

Projects ...), at least some Ontario-sourced goods must be used to satisfy the Minimum Required Domestic Content Level[316].

7.162 The European Union agrees with Japan's description of how this aspect of the challenged measures operates, and has adopted all of Japan's arguments in this context as its own[317].

7.163 We have carefully reviewed the operation of the "Minimum Required Domestic Content Level" and agree with the complainants that in all of the situations described above by Japan, at least some Ontario-sourced (and therefore Canadian-sourced) goods must be used to satisfy them. Thus, we find that the "Minimum Required Domestic Content Level" that is applied under the FIT Programme requires FIT and microFIT electricity generators using solar PV technology and FIT generators using windpower technology to purchase or use a certain percentage of renewable energy generation equipment and components that are sourced in Ontario, and therefore "from a domestic source" within the meaning of Paragraph 1(a) of the Illustrative List.

Whether compliance with the "Minimum Required Domestic Content Level" is necessary in order to obtain an advantage

7.164 The 2009 Ministerial Direction that called upon the OPA to establish the FIT Programme, also directed the OPA to include minimum domestic content requirements and ensure that any failure to comply with such requirements "should be subject to significant commercial consequences under the FIT contract"[318]. To this end, Section 6.4(b) of the FIT Rules stipulates that "[i]f a Contract Facility does not meet the Minimum Required Domestic Content Level, the Supplier will be in default under the FIT Contract." Sections 9.1(b) and (d) of the FIT Contract define a Supplier's failure to perform "any material covenant or obligation" set forth in the Contract, as well as a Supplier's representation that is "not true or correct in any material respect" as events that would place the Supplier in default. Other provisions of the FIT Contract suggest that such events may relate to a Supplier's obligations with respect to the "Minimum Required Domestic Content Level". For instance, Article 2.4(b)(iii) of the FIT Contract requires that a Supplier's "Notice to Proceed Request" include a "Domestic Content Plan" as defined therein. Article 2.2(f) of the FIT Contract stipulates that "[w]here the FIT Contract Cover Page identifies the Renewable Fuel of the Contract Facility as windpower or solar (PV), the Supplier shall develop and construct the Contract Facility such that the Domestic Content Level is equal to or greater than the Minimum Required Domestic Content Level." Furthermore, Article 2.11(c) of the FIT Contract requires that a Supplier must provide the OPA with a "Domestic Content Report" detailing how the

---

316 *Ibid.*

317 European Union's first written submission, para. 16.

318 Minister's 2009 FIT Direction, Exhibit JPN-102, pp. 1-2.

Contract Facility has satisfied the Domestic Required Content Level within 60 days of its Commercial Operation Date.

7.165 It is evident from the above that compliance with the "Minimum Required Domestic Content Level" is a necessary condition and prerequisite for electricity generators to participate in the FIT Programme. As we have explained elsewhere in these Reports, the FIT Programme guarantees a fixed price for every kWh of electricity delivered into the Ontario electricity system over a period of 20 years by qualifying generators of electricity using solar PV and windpower technology[319]. The prices paid under the FIT Programme were established by the OPA with a view to ensuring that participants are able to cover "typical" development costs and obtain a reasonable rate of return. Thus, generators participating in the FIT Programme will be remunerated for each kWh of electricity delivered into Ontario's electricity system at a price calculated to ensure economically viable operations for "typical" facilities for a 20-year period. We agree with the complainants that, on the basis of these conditions, *mere participation* in FIT Programme may be viewed as obtaining an "advantage" within the meaning of the chapeau of Paragraph 1(a) of the Illustrative List. Moreover, because a failure to comply with the "Minimum Required Domestic Content Level" will place FIT and microFIT generators in default of their contractual obligations, it may also be concluded that the "Minimum Required Domestic Content Level" renders the FIT and microFIT Contracts TRIMs that are "enforceable under domestic law", and they must also for this reason fall within the scope of the chapeau to Paragraph 1(a) of the Illustrative List.

7.166 Thus, on the basis of the foregoing analysis, we find that compliance with the "Minimum Required Domestic Content Level" not only involves the "purchase or use" of products from a domestic source, within the meaning of Paragraph 1(a) of the Illustrative List, but also that such compliance "is necessary" for electricity generators using solar PV and windpower technologies to participate in the FIT Programme, and thereby "obtain an advantage", within the meaning of Paragraph 1 of the Illustrative List. We are therefore satisfied that the challenged measures are TRIMs falling within the scope of Paragraph 1(a) of the Illustrative List, and that in the light of Article 2.2 and the chapeau to Paragraph 1(a) of the Illustrative List, they are inconsistent with Article III:4 of the GATT 1994, and thereby also inconsistent with Article 2.1 of the TRIMs Agreement.

[319] See paras. 7.64, 7.203, 7.213, 7.217, and 7.219.

(d) Conclusion with respect to the claims under Article 2.1 of the TRIMs Agreement and Article III:4 of the GATT 1994

7.167 In the light of the findings we have made in this Section of these Reports, we conclude that the FIT Programme, and the FIT and microFIT Contracts, are inconsistent with Article 2.1 of the TRIMs Agreement and Article III:4 of the GATT 1994.

C. Whether the challenged measures constitute subsidies within the meaning of Article 1.1 of the SCM Agreement

1. Introduction

7.168 In the following sections we evaluate the merits of the complainants' arguments that the FIT Programme, and the FIT and microFIT Contracts, constitute subsidies within the meaning of Article 1.1 of the SCM Agreement. We start by examining whether the complainants have established that the challenged measures each constitute a "financial contribution" and/or "income or price support" within the meaning of Article 1.1(a) of the SCM Agreement. We then turn to assess the parties' arguments concerning the existence of "benefit" within the meaning of Article 1.1(b) of the SCM Agreement.

2. Whether the challenged measures constitute a "financial contribution" and/or "income or price support" within the meaning of Article 1.1(a) of the SCM Agreement

(a) Arguments of the parties

(i) Japan

7.169 Japan argues that the challenged measures each amount to a "financial contribution" in the form of a "direct transfer of funds" or a "potential direct transfer of funds" under Article 1.1(a)(1)(i) of the SCM Agreement, or *alternatively*, a form of "income or price support" within the meaning of Article 1.1(a)(2) of the SCM Agreement[320].

7.170 Recalling that the Appellate Body has observed that a "direct transfer of funds" may take the form of a transaction prescribing "reciprocal rights and obligations" or a "conditional grant", and that "what is captured in [Article 1.1(a)(1)(i)] is a government's provision ... of funds, irrespective of

---

[320] Japan's first written submission, paras. 185-214; response to Panel question No. 5 (first set); opening statement at the first meeting of the Panel, para. 24; second written submission, paras. 26-51; and responses to Panel questions Nos. 21 and 25 (second set). Japan submits, *in the alternative*, that the measures at issue could also be characterized as governmental action involving entrustment or direction, within the meaning of Article 1.1(a)(1)(iv) of the SCM Agreement. Japan's first written submission, fn. 367.

whether this is done gratuitously or in exchange for consideration"[321], Japan submits that the challenged measures may be best characterized as "direct transfers of funds" because they involve payments on the part of the OPA that are analogous to a "conditional grant". In this regard, Japan identifies the following features of the FIT and microFIT Contracts, which Japan submits demonstrate that the FIT payments are nothing other than government financing provided to FIT generators on the condition of (i) the construction of a renewable energy generating facility that satisfies a specified Minimum Domestic Content Level; and (ii) the delivery of electricity generated from this facility to the grid for use by all Ontarians[322]:

(a) under the FIT and microFIT Contracts, FIT generators must build a generation facility while satisfying a requirement to use Ontario-made wind and solar PV generation equipment in constructing the facility;

(b) in return, the OPA promises to pay a price which is alleged to be above a market price that guarantees the recovery of costs plus a reasonable return on investment over a 20-year period;

(c) the OPA pays that price to the generator upon the generator delivering electricity to the grid, or upon the generator withholding such delivery pursuant to instructions from the IESO, up to the contract capacity; and

(d) the electricity injected into the grid goes straight to consumers, without the OPA or any other governmental agency taking possession of the electricity, having the right to take possession of the electricity, using or intending to use the electricity, or seeking any profit from the resale of the electricity[323].

7.171 According to Japan, the same features also demonstrate that, independent of any actual payments made under the challenged FIT and microFIT Contracts, the challenged measures may be characterized as "potential direct transfer[s] of funds" because they guarantee payments for all electricity generated (or foregone as per IESO instruction) for the entirety of the contract period, which for solar PV and windpower projects is 20 years. Thus, Japan argues that the OPA's commitment to making the envisaged disbursements under the challenged measures constitutes a governmental practice involving a "potential direct transfer of funds"[324].

---

321 Japan's second written submission, para. 43, referring to Appellate Body Report, *US – Large Civil Aircraft (Second Complaint)*, paras. 617-618 and fn. 1292.

322 Japan's second written submission, para. 45; and responses to Panel questions Nos. 5 (first set) and 25 (second set).

323 Japan's second written submission, para. 36; and response to Panel question No. 25 (second set).

324 Japan's first written submission, paras. 192-194.

7.172 *Alternatively*, Japan argues that the measures at issue constitute "any form of income or price support in the sense of Article XVI of GATT 1994", within the meaning of Article 1.1(a)(2) of the SCM Agreement. According to Japan, the challenged measures may be properly characterized as such because they "contribute" to the income and prices received by FIT generators while at the same time operate to reduce imports of renewable energy generation equipment into Ontario, distorting international trade[325]. Japan submits that two particular aspects of the FIT and microFIT Contracts are consistent with this characterization: (i) the allegedly above-market prices paid by the Government of Ontario for electricity; and (ii) the long-term contract period (20 years). Japan argues that the combined effect of these two contractual terms is to enable "FIT generators to construct and operate their generating facilities in the first place, assured of achieving a return that they would not otherwise achieve in the market". Thus, Japan argues that the Government of Ontario "quite literally 'supports' the 'income' received by generators and the 'price' paid to them for their electricity output"[326].

7.173 Japan rejects Canada's argument that the challenged measures can *only* be legally characterized as financial contributions in the form of government purchases of goods. Recalling that "the classification of a transaction under municipal law is not 'determinative' of whether that measure can be characterized as a financial contribution under Article 1.1(a)(1) of the *SCM Agreement*", Japan argues that the fact that the FIT and microFIT Contracts appear to be described as government "purchases" under Canadian law is not dispositive of the legal characterization of the challenged measures for the purposes of WTO law[327]. In addition, Japan asserts that the OPA never takes possession of, or exercises control over, or takes title to the electricity supplied under the FIT and microFIT Contracts, and as such, it does not "purchase" electricity[328]. In this regard, Japan maintains that the FIT Programme is not aimed at promoting renewable energy generation in order to supply electricity solely to the OPA or other agencies of the Government of Ontario, or to allow the Government of Ontario to sell electricity to local distributors and/or consumers. Rather, Japan argues that the purpose of the FIT Programme is to provide electricity to all consumers in Ontario.

7.174 In any case, Japan argues that even if the Panel were to conclude that the FIT and microFIT Contracts may be characterized as "purchases [of] goods", the Panel may still find them to be characterized as "direct transfer[s] of funds",

---

[325] Japan's first written submission, paras. 205-214.

[326] Japan's first written submission, para. 212.

[327] Japan's opening statement at the first meeting of the Panel, para. 25, referring to Appellate Body Report, *US – Large Civil Aircraft (2nd Complaint)*, para. 586 (quoting Appellate Body Report, *US – Softwood Lumber IV*, para. 56); and second written submission, paras. 29-34.

[328] Japan's opening statement at the first meeting of the Panel, para. 23; second written submission, para. 39; and comments on Canada's response to Panel question No. 47 (second set).

"potential direct transfers of funds", or "income or price support"[329]. According to Japan, this would be possible because, in Japan's view, the Appellate Body made clear in *US – Large Civil Aircraft (Second Complaint)* that a transaction may be covered by multiple subparagraphs of Article 1.1(a)(1), and that the presence of the word "or" that exists between Article 1.1(a)(1) and Article 1.1(a)(2) of the SCM Agreement need not necessarily imply that the two provisions are mutually exclusive.

7.175 Finally, were the Panel to find that the challenged measures could *only* be properly characterized as government purchases of goods, as Canada contends, Japan submits that it would still have met its burden of showing that they satisfy the first element of the subsidy definition, recalling that a government purchase of goods constitutes a "financial contribution" under Article 1.1(a)(1) of the SCM Agreement[330].

(ii) European Union

7.176 Not unlike Japan, the European Union submits that the challenged measures may each be legally characterized as a "financial contribution" in the form of a "direct transfer of funds" within the meaning of Article 1.1(a)(1)(i) of the SCM Agreement, or as a form of "income or price support" under the terms of Article 1.1(a)(2) of the SCM Agreement. However, for the European Union, the most appropriate legal characterization, and the European Union's "primary" submission in these proceedings, is that the FIT Programme and related contracts constitute a form of "income or price support". As an *alternative* to these two lines of argument, the European Union maintains that the challenged measures might also be characterized as "potential direct transfer[s] of funds" under Article 1.1(a)(1)(i) of the SCM Agreement, or as governmental action that involves entrustment and direction in the sense of Article 1.1(a)(1)(iv) insofar as private LDCs make settlement payments on behalf of the OPA under the terms of the FIT and microFIT Contracts[331].

7.177 The European Union asserts that the FIT Programme operates as a price support system whereby the Government of Ontario, through its agency, the OPA, contractually agrees with the FIT generators a price for the electricity they will produce (or will be directed not to produce) and then pays that price directly (through another agency, the IESO) or indirectly (through LDCs) to the FIT generators. Moreover, the European Union submits that the nature of the FIT Programme's local content requirements reduces or even eliminates imports of

---

[329] Japan's opening statement at the first meeting of the Panel, para. 28; opening statement at the second meeting of the Panel, para. 7, referring to Appellate Body Report, *US – Large Civil Aircraft (2nd Complaint)*, para. 613 and fn. 1287; and comments on Canada's response to Panel question No. 24 (second set).

[330] Japan's response to Panel question No. 22 (second set).

[331] European Union's first written submission, paras. 43-44; and opening statement at the first meeting of the Panel, paras. 18-19.

equipment and components for renewable energy generation facilities into Ontario. As such, the European Union argues that the long-term, guaranteed and allegedly above-market prices paid to the FIT generators under the challenged FIT and microFIT Contracts provide a "form of income or price support in the sense of Article XVI of GATT 1994", within the meaning of Article 1.1(a)(2) of the SCM Agreement[332].

7.178 According to the European Union, the challenged measures may be characterized as "direct transfer[s] of funds" because, apart from the expected delivery of electricity into the Ontario electricity grid, they involve the OPA making payments to the FIT generators on an unconditional basis. The European Union submits that for the purpose of the financial contribution analysis, the payments committed under the legally binding FIT and microFIT Contracts should be seen as "granted" or "transferred" payments, even though physically those payments have not yet taken place[333]. Recalling that the Appellate Body has observed that a "direct transfer of funds" may exist in the form of a "conditional grant" and that "what is captured in [Article 1.1(a)(1)(i)] is a government's provision ... of funds, irrespective of whether this is done gratuitously or in exchange for consideration", the European Union submits that the essence of the FIT Programme and its related contracts is that the FIT generators assume a set of obligations (including the construction of a generation facility and the delivery of electricity into the grid) in return for which they will receive payment from the OPA. The European Union maintains that this renders the challenged measures "direct transfer of funds"[334].

7.179 The European Union advances two additional *alternative* arguments to support its view that the measures amount to "financial contributions". First, relying upon the same arguments advanced in Japan's first written submission, the European Union submits that the challenged measures may also be characterized as "potential direct transfer[s] of funds"[335]. Secondly, the European Union argues that the disbursements made by the LDCs pursuant to the FIT and microFIT Contracts on behalf of the OPA result in a "financial contribution", in any of the forms discussed above, because they involve entrustment or direction

---

332 European Union's first written submission, paras. 32-42; opening statement at the first meeting of the Panel, para. 14-17; response to Panel question No. 20 (first set); and second written submission, paras. 5-18 and 33-38.

333 European Union's first written submission, para. 48. The European Union's arguments in relation to the existence of a financial contribution in the form of a "direct transfer of funds" explicitly incorporated all of the arguments made by Japan in its first written submission. European Union's first written submission, fn. 51.

334 European Union's first written submission, paras. 49-50; opening statement at the first meeting of the Panel, para. 18; second written submission, paras. 42-43; and opening statement at the second meeting of the Panel, para. 11, referring to Appellate Body Report, *US – Large Civil Aircraft (Second Complaint)*, para. 617.

335 The European Union explicitly incorporated all of the arguments made by Japan in its first written submission on this point. European Union's first written submission, para. 53 and fn. 65.

in the sense of Article 1.1(a)(1)(iv) of the SCM Agreement[336]. However, in this regard, the European Union maintains that because the OPA is ultimately liable for making these payments, the challenged measures would probably be better characterized as a "direct transfer of funds"[337].

7.180 Finally, although the European Union considers that the most appropriate characterization of the challenged measures would not be as a government "purchase [of] goods" within the meaning of Article 1.1(a)(1)(iii) of the SCM Agreement[338], it argues that such a conclusion would not be an obstacle to finding that the challenged measures could also be characterized as "any form of income or price support". In this regard, the European Union maintains that the use of the term "or" between Paragraphs (1) and (2) in Article 1.1(a) of the SCM Agreement does not exclude the possibility that a measure can fall at the same time under one or the other sub-element. According to the European Union, the word "or" merely provides for a choice or alternative characterisations to meet the first element of the definition of "subsidy". The European Union also notes that the terms of Article 1.1(a)(2) of the SCM Agreement are broad enough to capture domestic programmes involving *a combination of* various forms of financial contribution, bundled together with other features[339]. Similarly, the European Union argues that the challenged measures may be characterized as several types of financial contributions within the sub-headings of Article 1.1(a)(1), recalling certain observations of the Appellate Body in *US – Large Civil Aircraft (Second Complaint)*[340]. In any event, were the Panel to consider that the OPA actually "purchases" electricity pursuant to the FIT Contract, the European Union considers that this would amount to a financial contribution in the form of purchases of goods under Article 1.1(a)(1)(iii) of the SCM Agreement[341].

(iii) Canada

7.181 Canada submits that the complainants have mischaracterized the challenged measures as financial contributions in the form of "direct transfer[s]

336 European Union's first written submission, para. 44.

337 European Union's first written submission, paras. 59-61.

338 European Union's second written submission, paras. 41-51. The European Union maintains that the OPA acts more like an intermediary (an agent or a clearing house) than an actual purchaser of electricity. According to the European Union, other market operators purchase electricity either at market rates or above (i.e. at "regulated" rates), while the OPA pays the allegedly above-market rates agreed contractually with the FIT generators. European Union's opening statement at the first meeting of the Panel, para. 20; and opening statement at the second meeting of the Panel, para. 12.

339 European Union's opening statement at the first meeting of the Panel, paras. 10-13; second written submission, paras. 5-18; and opening statement at the second meeting of the Panel, paras. 5-10.

340 European Union's opening statement at the first meeting of the Panel, para. 19, citing Appellate Body Report, *US – Large Civil Aircraft (Second Complaint)*, fn. 1287.

341 European Union's opening statement at the first meeting of the Panel, paras. 20 and 21; and second written submission, para. 53.

of funds" or "potential direct transfer[s] of funds", or as a form of "income or price support". Canada argues that the FIT Programme and its related contracts can only be properly legally characterized as financial contributions in the form of "government purchases [of] goods" within the meaning of Article 1.1(a)(iii) of the SCM Agreement[342].

7.182 Canada asserts that the FIT programme, and the FIT and microFIT Contracts, involve the payment of money by the OPA, which it describes as the "agent" of the Government of Ontario[343], to renewable electricity generators for the supply of electricity into the Ontario transmission grid[344]. Thus, according to Canada, the measures at issue operate to enable the OPA to *purchase* electricity from generators using solar PV and wind technology. Canada submits that its legal characterization of the measures as a government purchase of goods is substantiated by certain sections of the *Electricity Act, 1998*, the Ministerial Direction, various aspects of the FIT and microFIT Rules, the terms and conditions of the FIT and microFIT Contracts, and a number of other documents and sources[345].

7.183 Canada argues that a transaction properly characterized as a purchase of goods must be treated as only a purchase of goods for the purpose of Article 1.1(a)(1)(iii) of the SCM Agreement, even though it will invariably involve a "direct transfer of funds" or a "potential direct transfer of funds"[346]. Relying upon a line of reasoning developed by the panel in *US – Large Civil Aircraft (Second Complaint)*, Canada argues that to maintain that a transaction properly characterized as a government purchase of goods could also be characterized as a direct transfer of funds would be inconsistent with the principle of effective treaty interpretation[347].

7.184 Canada rejects the view advanced by the complainants that a product can only be "purchased" if the purchaser takes physical possession, control or title over the product, referring to two examples of product purchasers that do not possess these characteristics in support of its position[348]. In addition, Canada submits that the examples of electricity "aggregators" and "marketers", which Japan presents as entities that actually purchase electricity in contrast to the

---

342 Canada's first written submission (DS412), paras. 116-122; and first written submission (DS426), paras. 54-63.

343 Canada's first written submission (DS412), paras. 1 and 70; and first written submission (DS426), para. 2.

344 Canada's first written submission (DS412), paras. 70-81; first written submission (DS426), paras. 16-22; and responses to Panel questions Nos. 1 and 2 (first set).

345 Canada's first written submission (DS412), fns. 135 and 141, and para. 73; first written submission (DS426), paras. 16-22; opening statement at the first meeting of the Panel, paras. 11-44; second written submission, paras. 15-22; opening statement at the second meeting of the Panel, para. 20; and response to Panel question No. 25 (second set).

346 Canada's first written submission (DS412), para. 120.

347 Canada's first written submission (DS412), paras. 117-119; and first written submission (DS426), para. 55.

348 Canada's opening statement at the first meeting of the Panel, para. 41.

OPA, merely highlight that it is possible to purchase and take title to electricity without physically possessing it[349]. In any case, Canada asserts that to the extent that the electricity produced by FIT generators is delivered into Ontario's transmission and distribution networks, the Government of Ontario does take physical possession over it by virtue of Hydro One owning 97% of the transmission lines and the fact that all but three of 80 LDCs are owned by municipal governments[350]. Canada also notes that FIT generators have never been directed by the IESO to refrain from delivering electricity into the system, explaining that the particular clauses in the FIT Contracts that the complainants focus upon are standard and that, in any case, the IESO cannot make such requests for smaller FIT generators or for any microFIT generators[351].

7.185 Finally, Canada maintains that the complainants' legal characterization of the challenged measures as "income or price support" is misplaced for two main reasons. First, relying on the same reasoning mentioned above from the panel in *US – Large Civil Aircraft (Second Complaint)*, Canada argues that Article 1.1(a)(2) cannot be interpreted as applying to transactions that are properly characterized as government purchases of goods because this would render Article 1.1(a)(1)(iii) meaningless, and thereby infringe the principle of effective treaty interpretation. Thus, in the same way that Canada dismisses the complainants' assertions that the measures at issue involve "direct transfers of funds", Canada argues that the FIT programme and individual contracts cannot amount to a form of "income or price support" because this would render Article 1.1(a)(1)(iii) redundant[352]. Secondly, Canada submits that the reference to "any product" in Article XVI of the GATT is not a reference to unsubsidized input goods, but rather a reference to an increase in exports of "any product" that is the subject of the alleged subsidy being notified under this provision or a decrease in imports of foreign products impacted by the notified subsidy. Thus, in order for the FIT Programme to be properly characterized as a form of "income or price support", Canada argues that complainants would need to show that trade in electricity (the allegedly subsidized good) is affected by the alleged subsidy, not trade in renewable electricity generation equipment[353].

---

[349] Canada's opening statement at the second meeting of the Panel, para. 26.

[350] Canada's response to Panel question No. 21 (first set); and opening statement at the second meeting of the Panel, paras. 30-32.

[351] *Ibid.*

[352] Canada's first written submission (DS412), paras. 121-122; and first written submission (DS426), paras. 59-60.

[353] Canada's first written submission (DS426), para. 62.

(b) Arguments of the third parties

(i) Australia

7.186 Australia agrees with the arguments of the complainants with respect to the classification of the FIT Contracts as a form of income or price support under Article 1.1(a)(2) of the SCM Agreement. Alternatively, Australia submits that the Panel may characterize the FIT Contracts as "purchases of goods" under Article 1.1(a)(1)(iii). Australia argues that in determining whether a financial contribution is a purchase of goods, it is not necessary for the government to use the goods purchased. Rather, a purchase of goods within the meaning of Article 1.1(a)(1(iii) occurs where a government pays a person or entity for the provision of goods. Thus, according to Australia, in these disputes the contract rate received by FIT generators could be characterized as consideration for the electricity supplied to the Ontario electricity market[354].

(ii) China

7.187 China disagrees with the European Union's use of export restrictions as examples of "income or price support", within the meaning of Article 1.1(a)(2) of the SCM Agreement, for the following reasons. First, this phrase "does not exhaust all government interventions that may have an effect on income or price, such as tariffs and quantitative restrictions." Second, the application of the "effect" test to the existence of an "income or price support" would exaggerate the reasonable scope of this phrase. Third, as Article XI of the GATT 1994 provides for the "general elimination of quantitative restrictions", it is questionable whether the concept of "income or price support" seeks to place such governmental actions within the scope of the SCM Agreement. Fourth, the concept of "market price support" included in Annex 3 of the Agreement on Agriculture indicates that direct control by the government over the domestic price is required to demonstrate the existence of "price support". Thus, in China's view, the analysis should focus on the nature of the direct governmental action, rather than on the movement in prices. Finally, the European Union's reliance on Paragraph 7.430 of the Panel Report in *China – Raw Materials* fails to observe the footnote stating that the term "subsidy" included in that paragraph does not implicate a legal conclusion under the SCM Agreement[355].

(iii) El Salvador

7.188 El Salvador emphasizes the role played by LDCs within the FIT Programme, and the importance of deciding whether they are owned by the

---

[354] Australia's third-party submission (DS412), paras. 4-10; third-party submission (DS426), paras. 4-10; and third-party statement (DS412 and DS426), paras. 3-10.

[355] China's third-party submission (DS426), paras. 3-10; and third-party statement (DS412 and DS426), paras. 5-8.

government. El Salvador considers that the Appellate Body Report in *US – Anti-Dumping and Countervailing Duties (China)* may contribute to the Panel's examination of this matter. Turning to the notion of "income or price support", El Salvador considers that the Panel should be provided with objective parameters to determine whether a reduction of imports of renewable energy generation equipment has occurred. El Salvador suggests that methodologies used for purposes of other WTO rules may be employed by the Panel to determine "income or price support", citing as an example the methodology used in the field of safeguards to examine the correlation between increased injury and industry[356].

(iv) European Union (in WT/DS412)

7.189 As a third party in WT/DS412, the European Union considers that the FIT Programme amounts to a subsidy as defined in Article 1.1 of the SCM Agreement. In the European Union's view, the FIT Programme implies a financial contribution by the Government of Ontario either as a direct transfer of funds or a potential direct transfer of funds. The European Union contends that the commitment by the Canadian Province of Ontario to pay the agreed price for the electricity generated by FIT generators would be better characterised as a "direct transfer of funds" in the sense of Article 1.1(a)(1)(i) of the SCM Agreement because future payments are made unconditionally. Alternatively, the European Union considers that the FIT Programme provides a form of income or price support to FIT generators through guaranteed prices in the sense of Article 1.1(a)(2)[357].

(v) Japan (in WT/DS426)

7.190 As a third party in WT/DS426, Japan argues that, to the extent Article XVI:1 of the GATT 1994 may serve as relevant context for interpreting "income or price support" under Article 1.1(a)(2) of the SCM Agreement, it does not support Canada's view that the "income or price support" must be provided to the goods, the trade of which is actually impacted by the support. Japan claims that Canada offers no basis for its interpretation that the term "any product" is a reference to the "subject of the alleged subsidy", and may not be a reference to "unsubsidized input goods". Japan notes that Article XVI:1 uses the term "*any* product", and not a term such as "*like* product" (emphasis added). Japan considers that the term "any product" in Article XVI:1 refers to every product, including unsubsidized input goods, the exports or imports of which may increase or decrease as a result of the income or price support provided. Thus, Japan contends that "income or price support" provided to a product will fall

---

[356] El Salvador's third-party submission (DS426), paras. 5-16; and third-party statement (DS412 and DS426), paras. 3-11.

[357] European Union's third-party submission (DS412), paras. 19-20.

within the definition of a "subsidy" if it increases exports or decreases imports of *any product*[358].

(vi) Mexico

7.191 Mexico notes that the SCM Agreement does not contain a provision similar to Article III:8(a) of the GATT 1994 to exclude governmental purchases from its scope. However, Mexico contends that it is questionable whether a governmental purchase, in which the government receives something in return for a payment, will amount to a financial contribution within the meaning of the SCM Agreement[359].

(vii) Norway

7.192 Norway expresses support for the position advanced by the Kingdom of Saudi Arabia urging the Panel to respect the principles defined by the Appellate Body with regards to the terms "public body" and "governmental control"[360].

(viii) The Kingdom of Saudi Arabia

7.193 Saudi Arabia refers to the Appellate Body Report in *US – Anti-Dumping and Countervailing Duties (China)*, setting out that a "public body", within the meaning of Article 1.1(a)(1) of the SCM Agreement, is an entity that possesses, exercises or is vested with governmental authority. Saudi Arabia contends that the unique defining element of "governmental authority" is the power to command or compel private bodies. Saudi Arabia considers that if an entity's role is merely to follow a governmental mandate and it is powerless as to the manner in which it pursues governmental functions, then it has no "governmental authority" and is instead merely acting at the direction of the government. Saudi Arabia contends that the government's exercise of "meaningful control" over an entity alone is not sufficient to determine that the entity is a public body, as governmental control is merely one element of evidence that may be consider when determining "governmental authority"[361].

(c) Evaluation by the Panel

(i) Introduction

7.194 The complainants' assertions about the proper legal characterization of the challenged measures under Articles 1.1(a)(1) and 1.1(a)(2) of the

---

358 Japan's third-party submission (DS426), paras. 16-18.

359 Mexico's third-party submission (DS412), para. 20; and third-party submission (DS426), para. 20.

360 Norway's third-party statement (DS412 and DS426), para. 7.

361 Saudi Arabia's third-party submission (DS412), paras. 2-17; third-party submission (DS426), paras. 2-17; and third-party statement (DS412 and DS426), paras. 2-7.

SCM Agreement are largely in contrast to those advanced by Canada. Recent WTO jurisprudence suggests that when faced with such a situation, a panel should first determine the proper factual characterization of the measures at issue, before turning to examine whether those measures, in the light of their proper factual characterization, fall within the scope of Article 1.1(a) of the SCM Agreement[362]. In undertaking the task of properly characterizing a challenged measure, a panel "must thoroughly scrutinize the measure before it, both in its design and in its operation, and identify its principal characteristics"[363]. Moreover, "[i]n making its objective assessment of the applicability of specific provisions of the covered agreements to a measure properly before it, a panel must identify *all* relevant characteristics of the measure, and recognize which features are the most central to that measure itself, and which are to be accorded the most significance for purposes of characterizing the relevant [measure] and, thereby, properly determining the discipline(s) to which it is subject under the covered agreements"[364]. While the classification of a transaction under municipal law may inform a panel's assessment, it is not "determinative"[365] of a challenged measure's proper legal characterization under WTO law. With these considerations in mind, we proceed to evaluate the merits of the parties' arguments.

(ii) Factual characterization of the measures

The legal bases of the FIT Programme[366] and the mandate and powers of the OPA

7.195 We recall that the FIT Programme was formally launched by the OPA on 24 September 2009 pursuant to the Direction of the Ontario Minister of Energy and Infrastucture[367] acting under the authority of the *Electricity Act of 1998*[368], as amended by the *Green Energy and Green Economy Act of 2009*[369]. Section 25.35(1) of the amended *Electricity Act of 1998* provides that the "Minister may direct the OPA to develop a feed-in tariff program that is designed to procure energy from renewable energy sources". The same section defines a "feed-in tariff program" as a "program for procurement, providing standard program rules, standard contracts and standard pricing ..."[370]. Pursuant to this statutory

---

362 Appellate Body Report, *US – Large Civil Aircraft (Second Complaint)*, paras. 585 and 589.

363 Appellate Body Reports, *China – Auto Parts*, para. 171.

364 Appellate Body Reports, *China – Auto Parts*, para. 171 (emphasis original).

365 Appellate Body Report, *US – Softwood Lumber IV*, para. 56.

366 A more general description of the FIT Programme, including its objectives and how it is intended to operate, is set out in the introduction to our findings at paras. 7.64-7.68.

367 Minister's 2009 FIT Direction, Exhibit JPN-102.

368 *Electricity Act of 1998*, Exhibit JPN-101, Sections 25.32 and 25.35.

369 *Green Energy Act of 2009*, Exhibit JPN-101, Sections 5(2) and 7.

370 *Electricity Act of 1998*, Exhibit JPN-101, Section 25.35(4). More generally, Section 25.32(4.1) of the *Electricity Act of 1998* provides that the "Minister may direct the OPA to undertake ... any

authority, the Minister of Energy and Infrastructure called upon the OPA to establish a "feed-in tariff ("FIT") program that is designed to procure energy" through "a 20-year power purchase agreement in respect of all renewable fuels other than waterpower ..."[371]. This direction specified that the FIT Contract "should require the developer to design, build and operate a renewable generating facility and in exchange should provide for guaranteed, long-term pricing for the output of the renewable generating facility"[372].

7.196 The OPA's power to enter into such "contracts" is set out in section 25.35(4) of the amended *Electricity Act of 1998*, which grants the OPA authority to enter into "contracts relating to the procurement of electricity supply and capacity using alternative energy sources or renewable energy sources to assist the Government of Ontario in achieving goals in the development and use of alternative or renewable energy technology and resources". This authority is repeated in Section 25.35(1)(a); and, confirming the OPA's power to enter into "contracts relating to the procurement of electricity", Section 25.20(3) of the amended *Electricity Act of 1998* grants the OPA the right to "recover from consumers its costs and payments under procurement contracts"[373]. These powers are intended to enable the OPA to pursue its mandated activities, which include "to engage in activities to facilitate the diversification of sources of electricity supply by promoting the use of cleaner energy sources and technologies, including alternative sources and renewable sources" and "to establish system-wide goals for the amount of electricity to be produced from alternative energy sources and renewable energy sources"[374].

7.197 That the OPA has the mandate and power to enter into "procurement" contracts for the supply of electricity is also evident from various documents prepared by the OPA and other Ontario governmental agencies[375].

---

other initiative or activity that relates to, (a) the procurement of electricity supply or capacity from renewable energy sources..."

[371] Minister's 2009 FIT Direction, Exhibit JPN-102, pp. 1-2.

[372] Minister's 2009 FIT Direction, Exhibit JPN-102, p. 2.

[373] The OPA's powers to enter into "procurement" contracts for electricity under the amended *Electricity Act of 1998* are also referred to in Sections 78.3 and 78.4 of the *Ontario Energy Board Act of 1998* and *Ontario Regulation 578/05*. *Ontario Regulation 578/05*, as amended, ("*Ontario Regulation 578/05*"), Exhibit JPN-154.

[374] *Electricity Act of 1998*, Exhibit JPN-101, Section 25.2(1).

[375] For example, see OPA Generation Procurement Update, Exhibit JPN-21; A Progress Report on Electricity Supply, Fourth Quarter 2010, Ontario Power Authority, ("OPA Progress Report: Fourth Quarter 2010"), Exhibit JPN-26, p. 1 (disclosing that "4,709 MW were procured from existing generating facilities"); OPA Progress Report: Second Quarter 2011, Exhibit JPN-28, p. 1 (disclosing that "4,716 MW were procured from existing generating facilities"); OPA's Generation Procurement Cost Disclosure, Exhibit JPN-29 (stating that "[t]he OPA has procured a generation portfolio consisting of various generation technologies and capacities for the province of Ontario"); Highlights of the *Electricity Restructuring Act of 2004*, Exhibit JPN-9, p. 2 (stating that "[t]he OPA is responsible for developing an integrated power system plan and procurement process for electricity supply"); and OEFC: Management of Power Supply Contracts, Exhibit JPN-22, p. 2 (referring to "Ontario Power Authority supply procurements"). See also from the private sector, Overview of

The FIT Contract

7.198 The FIT Contract describes the contractual relationship between the OPA and the legal entity or entities responsible for the approved renewable energy electricity project (the "Supplier"). It is comprised of a project-specific cover page (which provides a summary of a number of key project facts and characteristics including, where applicable, the relevant "domestic content level"), a set of general terms and conditions[376], a series of exhibits addressing a range of formal and substantive matters relating to each project, and an appendix of standard definitions. By entering into the FIT Contract, the OPA and the Supplier "mutually agree to be bound" by its terms and conditions "[f]or valuable consideration"[377]. The Standard Definitions Appendix suggests that the FIT Contract is a "power purchase agreement"[378].

7.199 In order to fully understand the contractual parties' rights and obligations, the FIT Contract must be read together with the FIT Rules. These set out, in varying degrees of detail over 42 pages comprising thirteen sections and four exhibits, the rules and procedures that govern the operation of the FIT Programme. In particular, the FIT Rules describe the project eligibility and application requirements, the application review and acceptance procedures, and the tests for determining what kind of connection, if any, can be established between the relevant generation facility and the Ontario electricity system[379]. They also provide an overview of the form of the FIT Contract and how it should be executed, including an explanation of some of its key provisions such as, for example, those relating to the "Minimum Required Domestic Content Level" that must be achieved by qualifying solar PV and windpower projects[380]. In addition, the FIT Rules identify the relevant prices and describe the processes to be used for settling the Contract Payments[381].

7.200 Apart from the delivery of electricity into the Ontario power grid, one of the fundamental obligations undertaken by the Supplier under a FIT Contract is to design, build and own or lease a qualifying renewable energy electricity generation facility ("Contract Facility") and to operate and maintain it in

---

Electricity Regulation in Canada, Exhibit JPN-7, p. 18 (stating that "[t]he OPA ... is ... primarily responsible for ... procuring new generation through various forms of procurement processes").

[376] The FIT Contract also envisages the possibility that, where necessary, a "Special Terms and Conditions" schedule could be added to the Contract. FIT Contract, Exhibit JPN-127, Schedule 2.

[377] FIT Contract, Exhibit JPN-127, Cover Page.

[378] The Standard Definitions Appendix defines "Pre-COD Facilities" as "the Facility, or the Facility and other generation facilities that are the subject of a *FIT Contract or other power purchase agreement* with the OPA similar in nature to the FIT Contract ..." (emphasis added). FIT Standard Definitions, Exhibit JPN-135, Definition No. 192.

[379] FIT Rules, Exhibit JPN-119, Sections 2-5.

[380] FIT Rules, Exhibit JPN-119, Section 6.

[381] FIT Rules, Exhibit JPN-119, Sections 7-8. In addition, the FIT Rules set out requirements in respect of "program review and amendments", "confidentiality", and "program launch".

accordance with all relevant IESO Market Rules, laws and regulations[382]. These requirements not only serve to ensure that the Supplier delivers electricity into the grid but they also assure the OPA that the conditions for its delivery are satisfied according to the relevant standards. When building a Contract Facility that utilizes solar PV or windpower technology that has a capacity to produce more than 10 kW of electricity, the Supplier must additionally ensure that it is developed and constructed in such a way that satisfies the "Minimum Required Domestic Content Level"[383].

7.201 Other notable obligations on the Supplier include assigning all Environmental Attributes associated with the Contract Facility to the OPA[384], transferring half of all payments received from the Canadian Government under the "ecoENERGY for Renewable Power Program" to the OPA[385], paying all taxes on the electricity delivered up to the relevant Connection Point[386], and ensuring that the Contract Facility is appropriately connected to the Ontario electricity system. With particular respect to the latter, Articles 2.3(a) and 2.7(b) of the FIT Contract direct the Supplier to arrange, at its own cost, for the Contract Facility to be connected to the relevant connection point in order to permit the successful delivery of the electricity it produces into the IESO-

---

[382] FIT Contract, Exhibit JPN-127, Articles 2.1(a) and 2.7(a); and FIT Rules, Exhibit JPN-119, Section 6.3(a). The relevant laws and regulations include those found in the Distribution System Code, the Transmission System Code and the Connection Agreement.

[383] FIT Contract, Exhibit JPN-127, Article 2.2(f).

[384] FIT Rules, Exhibit JPN-119, Section 7.3(c); and FIT Contract, Exhibit JPN-127, Article 2.10. "Environmental Attributes" are defined as *inter alia* "the interests and rights arising out of attributes or characteristics relating to the environmental impacts associated with a Renewable Generating Facility or the output of a Renewable Generating Facility, now or in the future, and the right to quantify and register these with competent authorities, including: (a) all right, title, interest and benefit in and to any renewable energy certificate, credit, reduction right, offset, allocated pollution right, emission reduction allowance or other proprietary or contractual right, whether or not tradable, resulting from the actual or assumed displacement of emissions by the production of Electricity from the Contract Facility as a result of the utilization of renewable energy technology; (b) rights to any fungible or non-fungible attributes or entitlements relating to environmental impacts, whether arising from the Contract Facility itself, from the interaction of the Contract Facility with the IESO-Controlled Grid, a Distribution System or the Host Facility ...; (c) any and all rights, title and interest relating to the nature of an energy source (including a Renewable Fuel) as may be defined and awarded through Laws and Regulations or voluntary programs, including all Emission Reduction Credits; and (d) all revenues, entitlements, benefits and other proceeds arising from or related to the foregoing..." FIT Standard Definitions, Exhibit JPN-135, Definition No. 85.

[385] FIT Rules, Exhibit JPN-119, Section 7.3(b); and FIT Contract, Exhibit JPN-127, Article 3.2 ("If the Supplier receives any payments under the ecoENERGY for Renewable Power Program attributable to the Contract Facility, the Supplier, within 30 days of receipt of such payment, shall pay to the OPA 50% of the amount of such payment, failing which, the OPA may set off any such payments due to the OPA against any amounts payable by the OPA to the Supplier").

[386] FIT Contract, Exhibit JPN-127, Article 3.4. In essence, the "Connection Point" is defined as the point where electricity from the Contract Facility directly or indirectly enters the Distribution System or the IESO-Controlled Grid. FIT Standard Definitions, Exhibit JPN-135, Definition No. 54. All taxes payable on the Delivered Electricity from the Connection Point onwards are to be paid by the OPA. In addition, the OPA is liable for any Sales Taxes payable in connection with the Delivered Electricity. FIT Contract, Exhibit JPN-127, Article 3.5.

controlled transmission grid or the distribution system[387]. In order to do this, the Supplier must first identify a proposed connection point, from the available options identified by the OPA on a semi-annual basis[388], that matches the particular characteristics of the Contract Facility. However, it is the OPA that decides, together with the IESO as well as the relevant licensed transmitters or distributors, whether any particular Contract Facility can be connected to the proposed connection point. FIT projects may be connected to the IESO-controlled transmission grid or the distribution system[389]. However, typically, FIT Projects with a capacity greater than 10 MW will be connected to the IESO-controlled transmission grid[390].

7.202 The FIT Contract Price is established by the OPA and, in principle, revised once every two years for unexecuted projects[391]. Such prices are intended to cover the development costs plus a reasonable rate of return over the term of the FIT Contract for projects meeting specific assumptions relating to cost and efficiency[392]. The Contract Prices applicable to the measures at issue were determined using a discounted cash flow model taking into account "reasonable" capital costs (i.e. "project development, construction and equipment costs"), "reasonable" operating and maintenance costs (i.e. "project staffing and maintenance costs, including on-going capital expenditures and property taxes") and "reasonable" connection costs (i.e. "project connection costs, no significant upgrade costs assumed")[393]. In 2009, the rate of return used to establish the FIT Price Schedule was "approximately 11%"[394]. For certain technologies, a specified percentage of the Contract Price will escalate annually based on increases in the consumer price index[395]. In addition, qualifying Aboriginal[396] and Community[397] Participation Projects will receive a "Price Adder" depending upon their respective Aboriginal and Community

387 FIT Contract, Exhibit JPN-127, Articles 2.3(a) and 2.7(b).

388 FIT Rules, Exhibit JPN-119, Section 5.1(a).

389 FIT Rules, Exhibit JPN-119, Section 2.1(a)(vii).

390 FIT Programme Overview, Exhibit JPN-37, p. 18.

391 FIT Rules, Exhibit JPN-119, Sections 7.1(a), 7.1(b), and 10.1(a).

392 FIT Rules, Exhibit JPN-119, Section 7.1(a). The Contract Price does not include any Sales Taxes payable by the OPA in connection with the Delivered Electricity. As already noted, where Sales Tax is payable, it shall be paid by the OPA. FIT Contract, Exhibit JPN-127, Article 3.5.

393 Proposed Feed-In Tariff Price Schedule, Stakeholder Engagement - Session 4, OPA, ("Proposed FIT Price Schedule Presentation"), Exhibit CDA-46, Slides 22-28.

394 Canada's responses to Panel questions Nos. 26 (first set) and 12 (second set); Proposed FIT Price Schedule Presentation, Exhibit CDA-46, Slide 30.

395 FIT Rules, Exhibit JPN-119, Section 7.2.

396 Section 9.1(a) of the FIT Rules, Exhibit JPN-119, defines an "Aboriginal Community" as *inter alia* "(i) a First Nation that is a 'Band' as defined in the Indian Act (Canada); (ii) the Métis Nation of Ontario or any of its active Chartered Community Councils; ..."

397 Section 9.1(e) of the FIT Rules, Exhibit JPN-119, defines an "Community Investment Member" as *inter alia* "(i) one or more individuals Resident in Ontario; (ii) a Registered Charity with its head office in Ontario; (iii) a Not-For-Profit Organization with its head office in Ontario; ..."

Participation Levels[398]. All relevant prices are published by the OPA on its website in the FIT Price Schedules[399], and these define the Contract Prices under the FIT Contract.

7.203 For each kWh of electricity that is delivered into the Ontario electricity system (or not delivered under the instruction of the IESO), a Supplier will receive the Contract Payment (or the Additional Contract Payment) defined in Exhibit B of the FIT Contract as a function of the FIT Contract Price[400]. Put simply, where a Contract Facility is an "IESO market participant", because, for example, it is connected to the IESO-controlled grid (i.e. connected to the transmission network[401]), the Contract Payment is defined as the relevant Contract Price multiplied by the Hourly Delivered Electricity[402], minus the HOEP, minus 80% of the total net revenues that a Supplier may receive from the sale of Future Contract Related Products[403]. Where, on the other hand, the Contract Facility is not an "IESO market participant", and is directly or indirectly connected to the distribution network, the Contract Payment is defined as the relevant Contract Price multiplied by the Hourly Delivered Electricity, minus 80% of the total net revenues that a Supplier may receive from the sale of Future Contract Related Products[404]. However, for Contract Facilities connected

---

398 Section 9.1(b) of the FIT Rules, Exhibit JPN-119, defines the "Aboriginal Participation Level" as "the percentage of the Economic Interest in the Applicant or the Supplier that is held by an Aboriginal Community." Similarly, Section 9.1(f) of the FIT Rules, Exhibit JPN-119, defines the "Community Participation Level" as *inter alia* "the percentage of the Economic Interest in the Applicant or the Supplier that is held by Community Investment Members ..."

399 2011 FIT Price Schedule, Exhibit JPN-30; and 2010 microFIT Price Schedule, Exhibit JPN-31.

400 All transmission-connected Suppliers and distribution-connected Suppliers with a capacity of more than 5 MW will receive the Additional Contract Payment for electricity they are directed by the IESO *not* to deliver into the Ontario electricity grid for system safety and reliability reasons. FIT Contract, Exhibit JPN-127, Exhibit B, Types 1, 2, and 3A, Article 1.5. ("Insofar as the IESO issues instructions to reduce all or part of the output of the Contract Facility on an economic basis in order to mitigate over generation on the entire IESO-Controlled Grid ..." an Additional Contract Payment shall be made to the Supplier).

401 Approximately 97% of transmission lines are owned and maintained by Hydro One, an agent of the Government of Ontario. Canada's opening statement at the second meeting of the Panel, para. 27; and response to Panel question No. 13 (second set).

402 In essence, "Hourly Delivered Electricity" is the electricity generated by the Contract Facility that is successfully injected into the transmission or distribution system during any hour. FIT Standard Definitions, Exhibit JPN-135, Definition No. 118.

403 FIT Contract, Exhibit JPN-127, Exhibit B, Types 1 and 2, Article 1.4. "Future Contract Related Products" are defined as "all Related Products that relate to the Contract Facility and that were not capable of being traded or sold by the Supplier in the IESO-Administered Markets or other markets on or before the Contract Date". FIT Standard Definitions, Exhibit JPN-135, Definition No. 106. "Related Products" are defined as products and services, including transmission rights, "that may be provided by the Contract Facility from time to time, ... that may be traded or sold in the IESO-Administered Markets or other markets, or otherwise sold, and which shall be deemed to include products and services for which no market may exist, such as capacity reserves." Article 3.3 of the FIT Contract, Exhibit JPN-127, provides that the Supplier "shall sell, supply or deliver all Future Contract Related Products as requested, directed or approved by the OPA".

404 FIT Contract, Exhibit JPN-127, Exhibit B, Type 3A, Article 1.4(a)(i) and (b); and Type 3B, Article 1.4.

to the distribution network that have a capacity greater than 5 MW, the Contract Payment, in situations when the HOEP is negative, is defined as the relevant Contract Price multiplied by the Hourly Delivered Electricity, minus the absolute value of the HOEP, minus 80% of the total net revenues that a Supplier may receive from the sale of Future Contract Related Products[405].

7.204 The FIT Rules provide that the OPA is responsible for making all Contract Payments to the Supplier[406]. However, the typical settlement processes through which a Supplier will be paid (either explicitly or implicitly referred to in the FIT Contract and FIT Rules) envisage that in addition to the OPA, the IESO and relevant LDCs acting on behalf of the OPA will also play a role. In particular, for transmission-connected Contract Facilities, the FIT Rules specify that payments under the FIT Contract "will be adjusted by subtracting the greater of the [HOEP] and zero in respect of all Hourly Delivered Electricity to account for either payments made in accordance with the IESO Market Rules or benefits conferred on the Host Facility, as applicable"[407]. The IESO Market Rules govern the IESO-controlled grid, including the terms and conditions pursuant to which payments due to electricity generators participating in the "IESO-administered markets" will be settled. For a Contract Facility that is connected to the IESO-controlled transmission grid this means that whenever the HOEP is positive, the relevant Supplier will receive the (HOEP) portion of the Contract Price *from the IESO*. When the HOEP is less than the Contract Price, the outstanding portion of the Contract Price minus 80% of any Future Contract Related Product sales (i.e. the GA) will be paid *by the OPA*. On the other hand, it will be for the Supplier to pay the GA to the OPA when the HOEP is greater than the Contract Price[408].

7.205 For distribution-connected Contract Facilities, the FIT Rules stipulate that the OPA "will pay the Supplier any amounts owing under the FIT Contract through settlement between the Supplier and the applicable LDC on a periodic basis in accordance with the applicable LDCs monthly, quarterly or other periodic billing cycle"[409]. In other words, distribution-connected projects will be paid directly by the LDC to which they are connected. However, after making this payment, the relevant LDC will, in accordance with the Retail Settlement Code and the IESO Market Manual[410], seek to recover any amounts paid in

---

405 FIT Contract, Exhibit JPN-127, Exhibit B, Type 3A, Article 1.4(a)(ii) and (b).

406 FIT Rules, Exhibit JPN-119, Section 6.3(a) and 8.4; and FIT Contract, Exhibit JPN-127, Article 3.1.

407 FIT Rules, Exhibit JPN-119, Section 8.1(a). This is reflected in FIT Contract, Exhibit JPN-127, Exhibit B, Types 1 and 2, Article 1.4(a).

408 FIT Rules, Exhibit JPN-119, Section 8.1(b), reflected in FIT Contract, Exhibit JPN-127, Exhibit B, Types 1 and 2, Article 1.4(c).

409 FIT Rules, Exhibit JPN-119, Section 8.2(a). See also FIT Contract, Exhibit JPN-127, Exhibit B, Type 4, Article 1.4.

410 IESO Market Manual Part 5.5, Exhibit JPN-82, Section 1.6.11.2.

excess of the wholesale price[411] of electricity for the electricity delivered by the Supplier in question, from the OPA, through the IESO[412].

7.206 The FIT Contract envisages that for Contract Facilities connected to the IESO-controlled transmission grid, the HOEP portion of the Contract Price will be paid by the IESO through the operation of the settlement process regulated by the IESO Market Rules. The same generators will receive the outstanding portion of the Contract Price minus 80% of net revenues from the sale of Future Contract Related Products (i.e. the Contract Payment) from the OPA , which will form part of the global adjustment. In other words, the Contract Payment for transmission-connected projects will be included in the global adjustment; and the difference between the Contract Payment and the Contract Price will, in the absence of any net revenues from Future Contract Related Products, be the HOEP, which will be paid to a FIT Supplier by the IESO as a result of its status as an "IESO market participant". On the other hand, for Contract Facilities that are directly or indirectly connected to the distribution system, the Contract Payment (i.e. the Contract Price multiplied by the Hourly Delivered Electricity, minus 80% of net revenues from the sale of Future Contract Related Products) will be made by the associated LDC, on behalf of the OPA, and will also be included in the global adjustment.

7.207 Notwithstanding these settlement arrangements, the OPA may decide "at its sole discretion" to change them "at any time and from time to time" for the Programme as a whole or in respect of one or more projects or LDCs[413]. Moreover, whatever settlement arrangements may operate, the OPA will remain liable to make the Contract Payments[414].

7.208 Thus, although there is no specific provision in the FIT Contract that explicitly defines its object, it is evident when it is read as a whole, in the light of the FIT Rules, that its fundamental purpose is the *delivery of electricity* produced from a Contract Facility that satisfies the "Minimum Required Domestic Content Level" into the Ontario electricity system, in return for which, the OPA undertakes to pay the Supplier the remuneration defined under the Contract through the operation of one or more different settlement mechanisms for a period of 20 years[415]. Article 3.5 of the FIT Contract appears to describe this transaction as a "purchase" of electricity[416].

---

411 The wholesale price is the price that the relevant LDC should pay on the "wholesale market" for the electricity in question.

412 This settlement process is more fully described by Japan in its first written submission. See Japan's first written submission, paras. 145-147.

413 FIT Rules, Exhibit JPN-119, Section 8.4.

414 FIT Rules, Exhibit JPN-119, Sections 6.3(a) and 8.4.

415 This understanding is also consistent with how the FIT Contract and Settlement process is described in the FIT Programme Overview: "The [FIT] contract requires the OPA to pay the contract holder for the electricity produced by the project"; for distribution-connected projects, "the local distribution company will make payments to the proponents on a regular basis according to the normal billing cycle of the local distribution company"; and for transmission-connected projects,

The microFIT Contract

7.209 The microFIT Contract "governs [the] OPA's procurement of electricity"[417] from the entity or entities responsible for an approved project (the "Supplier"). It defines the contractual relationship between the OPA and the Supplier on the basis of a set of standard terms and conditions that are much simpler and less detailed when compared with those used in the FIT Contract. This reflects the OPA's stated intention of providing, through the operation of the microFIT stream of the FIT Programme, "a simplified approach for enabling the development of renewable micro-generation projects in Ontario", with a view to attracting participants such as homeowners, farmers and small businesses[418].

7.210 As with the FIT Contract, the microFIT Contract must be read together with the microFIT Rules in order to be fully understood. The microFIT Rules set out the basic rules and procedures that must be followed by microFIT Project applicants and participants. They describe the relevant eligibility requirements and the application and project connection processes, and outline some of the key provisions of the microFIT Contract with respect to duration, price and the settlement of payments[419].

7.211 A Supplier operating a microFIT Project must own or lease a "micro-generation project" (the "Facility") for the term of the microFIT Contract, and ensure that it delivers electricity into the Ontario electricity system in accordance with all relevant laws and regulations[420]. In addition, when the Facility is based on solar PV technology, the Supplier must ensure that it is developed and constructed in such a way that satisfies the "Minimum Required Domestic Content Level"[421].

---

payments will be "settled directly by the OPA and the Independent Electricity System Operator". FIT Programme Overview, Exhibit JPN-37, Section 6.4.

[416] In particular, Article 3.5 of the FIT Contract, Exhibit JPN-127, reads in relevant part: "If any Sales Tax is payable in connection with the Delivered Electricity ... *purchased hereunder*, such Sales tax shall be paid by the OPA" (emphasis added). Article 3.4 of the FIT Contract, Exhibit JPN-127, indicates that the Supplier "sells" electricity under the transaction: "The Supplier is liable for ... all Taxes applicable to the Delivered Electricity ... *sold hereunder* ..." (emphasis added). The "Delivered" electricity is defined as the "Electricity ... delivered to the Connection Point". FIT Standard Definitions, Exhibit JPN-135, Definition No. 65.

[417] Ontario Power Authority, microFIT Contract, Version 1.6.1, 10 August 2011, ("microFIT Contract"), Exhibit JPN-164, Article 2.1.

[418] microFIT Programme Overview, Exhibit JPN-38, p. 1 and Section 1.2(a); and microFIT Rules, Exhibit JPN-157, Section 1.1.

[419] microFIT Rules, Exhibit JPN-157, Sections 1-5.

[420] microFIT Contract, Exhibit JPN-164, Articles 6.2 and 6.4; and microFIT Rules, Exhibit JPN-157, Sections 2.1(a) and 6.1(a).

[421] microFIT Contract, Exhibit JPN-164, Article 6.4.4.

7.212 A microFIT Supplier must assign all Environmental Attributes associated with the Facility to the OPA[422]. It must also, at its own cost, enter into a Connection Agreement with a relevant LDC[423], in the absence of which, it will not be offered a microFIT Contract[424]. A microFIT Facility cannot be directly connected to the IESO-controlled transmission grid – it must be connected to the Ontario electricity system via a distribution system[425].

7.213 The microFIT Contract Price is established by the OPA in the same way as the FIT Contract Price[426] and is listed in the FIT and microFIT Price Schedules[427]. The microFIT Contract Price is guaranteed for 20 years. For each kWh of electricity that a Supplier successfully delivers into the Ontario electricity system, it will receive the Contract Price (the "Generation Payment") from the relevant LDC in accordance with the Retail Settlement Code and the Connection Agreement[428]. In other words, the LDC connected to the microFIT Facility, acting on behalf of the OPA, will make the Generation Payment in accordance with a similar settlement process used to pay distribution-connected FIT Suppliers[429]. As with the FIT Contract, ultimate liability for Generation Payments under the microFIT Contract lies with the OPA[430].

7.214 Thus, not unlike the FIT Contract, when the microFIT Contract is read as a whole and in the light of the microFIT Rules, it is apparent that its fundamental purpose is the *delivery of electricity* produced from a Facility that satisfies the "Minimum Required Domestic Content Level" into the Ontario electricity

---

[422] microFIT Contract, Exhibit JPN-164, Article 5. "Environmental Attributes" are defined as "the interests and rights arising out of attributes or characteristics relating to the environmental impacts associated with the Facility, now or in the future, and the right to quantify and register these with competent authorities, including: (a) all right, title, interest and benefit in and to any renewable energy certificate, credit, reduction right, offset, allocated pollution right, allowance, emission reduction allowance or allowance set aside or other proprietary or contractual right, whether or not tradable; (b) rights to any fungible or non-fungible attributes or entitlements relating to environmental impacts, however arising; (c) any and all rights, title and interest relating to the nature of an energy source as may be defined and awarded through applicable laws and regulations or voluntary programs; and (d) all revenues, entitlements, benefits and other proceeds arising from or related to the foregoing. ...". microFIT Contract, Exhibit JPN-164, Appendix A, Definitions.

[423] microFIT Rules, Exhibit JPN-157, Sections 1.2(4), 3.1(xi), and 6.1(c). A "Connection Agreement" is defined as "a 'Micro-Embedded Generation Facility Connection Agreement' as prescribed by the Distribution System Code entered into between an LDC and a Supplier." microFIT Rules, Exhibit JPN-157, Definition No. 6. It is the standard agreement used by all LDCs and is prescribed by the OEB. microFIT Programme Overview, Exhibit JPN-38, Section 1.2(d).

[424] microFIT Rules, Exhibit JPN-157, Sections 1.2(10) and 4.1(b).

[425] microFIT Rules, Exhibit JPN-157, Section 2.1(a)(v).

[426] microFIT Rules, Exhibit JPN-157, Section 5.2 and Definitions. The FIT Contract Price is discussed above at para. 7.202.

[427] 2011 FIT Price Schedule, Exhibit JPN-30; and 2010 microFIT Price Schedule, Exhibit JPN-31. See also microFIT Programme Overview, Exhibit JPN-38, Section 1.2(e).

[428] microFIT Contract, Exhibit JPN-164, Sections 4.4 and 4.4.2; and microFIT Rules, Exhibit JPN-157, Section 5.2.

[429] See above discussion at para. 7.205.

[430] microFIT Contract, Exhibit JPN-164, Section 4.4.1.

system, in return for which the OPA undertakes to pay the Supplier the remuneration defined under the Contract through the operation of a similar mechanism used to settle payments owed to distribution-connected FIT Projects. Section 2.1 of the microFIT Contract characterizes this transaction as the "OPA's procurement of electricity"[431]. Similarly, Appendix A to the microFIT Contract describes it as a "sale" of electricity[432].

Conclusion

7.215 Having carefully scrutinized the challenged measures, and recalling the descriptions of the challenged measures set out elsewhere in these Reports[433], we conclude that the principle characteristics of the FIT Programme, and of the FIT and microFIT Contracts, can be described in the following terms:

The FIT Programme

7.216 The FIT Programme has very clearly two fundamental objectives: First, to encourage the participation of new generation facilities using renewable sources of energy into Ontario's electricity system in order to diversify Ontario's supply-mix and help replace the generation capacity that has been (and will be) lost as a result of the closure of Ontario's coal-fired facilities by 2014, and thereby also reduce greenhouse gas emissions; and secondly, to stimulate local investment in the production of renewable energy generation equipment needed to design and construct qualifying generation facilities using solar PV and windpower technologies. These objectives are pursued through the execution of the FIT and microFIT Contracts, which involve an exchange of performance obligations on the part of the OPA and qualifying Suppliers. There is no inherent grant element to the FIT and microFIT transactions.

The FIT and microFIT Contracts

7.217 In essence, the FIT and microFIT Contracts envisage an exchange of the following core performance obligations between Suppliers and the OPA:

7.218 A Supplier must:

(a) design, construct, own (or lease) and operate a qualifying facility in accordance with all relevant IESO Market Rules, laws and regulations;

(b) comply with the "Minimum Required Domestic Content Level" when designing and constructing a solar PV or a microFIT windpower facility;

---

431 microFIT Contract, Exhibit JPN-164, Section 2.1.

432 microFIT Contract, Exhibit JPN-164, Appendix A, Definitions: "'Settlement Price' means the price at which *electricity sales pursuant to this agreement* will be settled." (emphasis added)

433 See above paras. 7.64-7.68 and 7.158-7.165

(c) deliver the electricity that is produced into the Ontario electricity system in accordance with all relevant IESO Market Rules, laws and regulations;

(d) participate in a defined electricity payment processes to settle Contract Payments that is not unlike that used generally in Ontario's electricity system; and

(e) assign all Environmental Attributes associated with the Contract Facility to the OPA, pay the OPA 50% of all payments received by the Supplier under the "ecoENERGY for Renewable Power Program"[434], and effectively transfer to the OPA 80% of total net revenues from the sale of Future Contract Related Products[435].

7.219 In return, the OPA agrees to make the Contract Payments, which are defined in such a way that ensures each Supplier will be remunerated via defined settlement processes at the guaranteed FIT Contract Price for each kWh of Delivered Electricity for 20 years.

(iii) Legal characterization of the measures

7.220 We recall that the complainants have argued that the challenged measures may be properly characterized as one or multiple types of the "financial contribution[s]" defined in Article 1.1(a)(1) of the SCM Agreement and/or a form of "income or price support" within the meaning of Article 1.1(a)(2) of the SCM Agreement. On the other hand, Canada has argued that the only appropriate characterization of the measures at issue is as "financial contribution[s]" in the form of "government purchases [of] goods" under the terms of Article 1.1(a)(1(iii) of the SCM Agreement. Because there is no dispute between the parties about whether each of the challenged measures amount to a "financial contribution", we begin by assessing the merits of the parties' arguments concerning the specific *types* of "financial contribution" they each consider match the salient characteristics of the challenged measures.

The challenged measures as financial contributions

7.221 Article 1.1(a)(1) of the SCM Agreement defines a "financial contribution" in the following terms:

> (a)(1) there is a financial contribution by a government or any public body within the territory

[434] Although explicitly excluded from the definition of Environmental Attributes found in the microFIT Rules, ecoENERGY payments are neither excluded from, nor included in, the definition of Environmental Attributes that is contained in the microFIT Contract. Thus, it is unclear whether any ecoENERGY payments made to microFIT Suppliers would not have to be transferred to the OPA by virtue of being Environmental Attributes. See above para. 7.212 and fn. 422.

[435] This obligation is only explicitly found in the FIT Contract, Exhibit JPN-127.

> of a Member (referred to in this Agreement as "government"), i.e. where:
>
> (i) a government practice involves a direct transfer of funds (e.g. grants, loans, and equity infusion), potential direct transfers of funds or liabilities (e.g. loan guarantees);
>
> (ii) government revenue that is otherwise due is foregone or not collected (e.g. fiscal incentives such as tax credits);
>
> (iii) a government provides goods or services other than general infrastructure, or purchases goods;
>
> (iv) a government makes payments to a funding mechanism, or entrusts or directs a private body to carry out one or more of the type of functions illustrated in (i) to (iii) above which would normally be vested in the government and the practice, in no real sense, differs from practices normally followed by governments[.]

7.222 Having carefully considered the parties' arguments, we agree with Canada that the appropriate legal characterization of the FIT Programme and the FIT and microFIT Contracts is as "financial contribution[s]" in the form of "government purchases [of] goods" within the meaning of Article 1.1(a)(1)(iii) of the SCM Agreement. We come to this conclusion on the basis of the following considerations.

The OPA pays for "delivered electricity"

7.223 First, in evaluating how the challenged measures should be legally characterized it is, in our view, important to recall that one of the fundamental objectives of the FIT Programme is to secure investment in new generation facilities *for the purposes* of diversifying Ontario's supply-mix and helping to fill the supply gap that is expected from the closure of Ontario's coal-fired facilities by 2014. It is by offering a Contract Price and making Contract Payments *for Delivered Electricity* that the Government of Ontario endeavours to achieve this objective. In other words, although the construction of a certain type of renewable energy generation facility is one of the objectives (and indeed, one of the conditions) of the challenged measures, the provisions of the FIT and microFIT Contracts expressly confirm that the funds transferred to qualifying Suppliers are intended to pay *for the electricity that is delivered* into Ontario's electricity grid. That the Contract Price is set at a level that is intended to provide a reasonable return on investment for the overall project does not alter the fact that under the express terms of the FIT and microFIT Contracts, Contract Payments will be made to solar PV and windpower generators *only* if electricity is delivered[436]. Thus, there is no grant element inherent in the design and operation of the FIT Programme. The OPA does not pay for renewable energy equipment or facilities. It does not make any upfront lump-sum advances to the FIT generators: the OPA's payment liability will arise only as and when electricity is produced and delivered into the system pursuant to the terms of the FIT and microFIT Contracts.

7.224 Likewise, while a FIT and microFIT Contract will facilitate a Supplier's search for appropriate project financing, it would be wrong to characterize the Contract Payments themselves as finance payments for the construction of the Contract Facility. Indeed, whereas an entity that provides project financing accepts the risk of losing money if it obtains insufficient security, the OPA accepts no comparable risk because it is only by way of the provision of electricity – the goods in this case – that any money is paid to a FIT Supplier.

The Government of Ontario takes possession over electricity and therefore "purchases" electricity

7.225 Secondly, we are not convinced by the European Union's argument that the notion of government "purchases [of] goods" that is referred to in Article 1.1(a)(1)(iii) of the SCM Agreement, must be interpreted to mean that the "term 'purchase' implies that the government is the entity being supplied with something for *its use*"[437]. In our view, the correct interpretation of these terms is closer to that advanced by Japan, which is derived from the following two ordinary meanings of the verb to "purchase" obtained from The Oxford English Dictionary (OED Online): (i) "to obtain; to gain possession of"; and (ii) "to acquire in exchange for payment in money or an equivalent; to buy"[438].

7.226 On the basis of the above two definitions, the act of purchasing a good might be described in terms of gaining possession of, acquiring, buying or obtaining a good. Among the definitions of the verbs to "acquire", to "buy" and to "obtain", found in the same dictionary used by Japan and Canada are, respectively: (i) to "gain possession of through skill or effort; to obtain, develop,

[436] The relevance to our legal characterization of the challenged measures of the fact that Exhibit B of the FIT Contract, Exhibit JPN-127, provides that a FIT generator will be given an "Additional Contract Payment" when it is directed by the IESO *not* to deliver electricity is discussed below at paras. 7.240 and 7.241.

[437] European Union's second written submission, para. 13. (emphasis added)

[438] Japan's second written submission, para. 38. Similar ordinary meanings can be found in the dictionary definitions of the terms used to describe a government "purchase" of goods in the French and Spanish language versions of Article 1.1(a)(1)(iii) of the SCM Agreement (respectively, "*achètent*" and "*compre*"). In particular, "*acheter*" is defined as "*obtenir contre paiement la propriété et l'usage*" (Le Trésor de la Langue Française Informatisé, online version at http://atilf.atilf.fr/); while "*comprar*" is defined as "*obtener algo con dinero*" (Real Academia Española, online version at http://www.rae.es/rae.html).

or secure in a careful, concerted, often gradual manner"[439]; (ii) to "get possession of by giving an equivalent, usually in money; to obtain by paying a price; to purchase"[440]; and (iii) to "come into the possession of; to procure; to get, acquire, or secure"[441].

7.227 The fact that the notion of "possession" is central to all three of the above definitions suggests that irrespective of the particular term used to explain what is meant by a "purchase", it should necessarily be understood as an act that, in the context of Article 1.1(a)(1)(iii) of the SCM Agreement, will result in the government "possessing" the good that is purchased. Furthermore, it follows from most of the above formulations, that the notion of a "purchase" for the purpose of Article 1.1(a)(1)(iii) should involve some kind of payment (usually monetary) in exchange for a good. This latter proposition finds support in *US – Large Civil Aircraft (Second Complaint)*, where the Appellate Body observed that "[t]he second sub-clause [of Article 1.1(a)(1)(iii) of the SCM Agreement] uses the term 'purchase', which is usually understood to mean that the person or entity providing the goods will receive some consideration in return"[442]. Thus, we find that the ordinary meaning of the term "purchase" suggests that for the purpose of Article 1.1(a)(1)(iii) of the SCM Agreement, government "purchases [of] goods" will arise when a government obtains possession over a good through some kind of payment (monetary or otherwise).

7.228 Having said that, like Canada[443], we observe that nothing in the ordinary meanings we have reviewed suggests that a "purchase" must involve obtaining *physical* possession over something. Although a purchase of goods may exist when an entity takes physical possession over of a good in exchange for a payment of some kind, it may also arise in other situations when a purchaser does not physically possess the purchased good. Canada has presented the following two examples of such purchases: (i) a book that is bought on the internet by an entity that directs the seller to deliver it to somebody else as a gift; and (ii) a product on a ship at sea that is bought and sold by means of its bill of lading[444]. In both examples, a purchase of goods is effected by means of an exchange of performance obligations involving the transfer of an *entitlement* to

[439] Shorter Oxford English Dictionary, online version at http://www.oed.com/view/Entry/1731.

[440] Shorter Oxford English Dictionary, online version at http://www.oed.com/view/Entry/25484.

[441] Shorter Oxford English Dictionary, online version at http://www.oed.com/view/Entry/130002.

[442] Appellate Body Report, *US – Large Civil Aircraft (Second Complaint)*, para. 619. We note that the notion of "consideration" is derived from common law, where it plays a critical role in determining the existence of a contract. However, the word "consideration" does not appear in the above dictionary definitions. Moreover, the notion of "consideration" is not a necessary element of contracts executed under civil law (and possibly other legal) systems. Thus, to the extent that the concept of "consideration" may inform the meaning of the term "purchase [of] goods" under Article 1.1(a)(1)(iii) of the SCM Agreement, it needs to be recalled that it is a legal construct that cannot be found in the legal systems of many WTO Members.

[443] Canada's second written submission, para. 93; and opening statement at the second meeting of the Panel, paras. 22-23.

[444] Canada's opening statement at the first meeting of the Panel, paras. 41-42.

the purchased product from the seller to the purchaser. No actual physical possession of the product purchased is necessary.

7.229 That a purchase of goods may take place through the transfer of an entitlement to a product is particularly important when considering what it means to purchase *electricity*, which, as we have previously explained[445], is an intangible good that, in general, cannot be stored and must be consumed almost at the same time it is produced. Thus, given the specific characteristics of electricity, it is perhaps best to conceive of a purchase of electricity as involving the transfer of an *entitlement* to electricity, rather than the taking of physical possession over electricity. This appears to accord with Japan's view that "[d]espite the nature of electricity, which is drawn 'almost instantaneous[ly]" by consumers when consumers turn on their electronic devices, intermediaries in the transmission and distribution process (such as wholesalers and retailers) can and do take title to, and accordingly possess, the electricity on its way to the end consumer"[446].

7.230 Turning to the context of the term "purchases goods", the European Union argues that the language of Article 1.1(a)(1)(iii) opposes the word "purchase" to the term "provision", and that this is instructive for the purpose of interpreting the former. Specifically, the European Union suggests that this juxtaposition means that just as "the term 'provision' implies that the government is the entity supplying something for the use of the recipient, the term 'purchase' implies that the government is the entity being supplied with something for its use"[447]. We are not persuaded by this argument. In our view, there is little interpretative guidance to be drawn from the fact that the words "provides goods" and "purchases goods" appear in the same sub-paragraph. Certainly, we cannot see how the different language used in the two clauses of Article 1.1(a)(1)(iii) assists us in understanding whether "purchases [of] goods" must necessarily involve *using* the goods in question.

7.231 It is important to recall that Article 1.1(a)(1)(iii) refers to "*government* ... purchases goods". The first paragraph of Article 1.1 clarifies that the term "government" is to be understood to mean "government" or "public body". Thus, in the light of the foregoing analysis, it follows that "government purchases [of] goods" will arise under the terms of Article 1.1(a)(1)(iii) of the SCM Agreement when a "government" or "public body" obtains possession (including in the form of an entitlement) over a good by making a payment of some kind (monetary or otherwise). In our view, and for the reasons we explain in the following paragraphs, this is exactly what happens through the FIT Programme and its related FIT and microFIT Contracts.

---

445 See above para. 7.11.

446 Japan's second written submission, para. 39.

447 European Union's opening statement at the second meeting of the Panel, para. 13.

7.232 We recall that the provisions of the FIT and microFIT Contracts expressly confirm that the funds transferred to qualifying Suppliers are intended to pay *for the electricity that is delivered* into Ontario's electricity grid[448]. Once a Supplier delivers electricity into the grid, it loses all rights and entitlements to that electricity, but it will be paid for the kWhs that are injected into the system. According to Japan and the European Union, the OPA does not take any form of possession over the electricity that is supplied. Canada has not contradicted the complainants' assertions as they relate to the OPA[449]. Nevertheless, Canada has argued that the "Government" of Ontario does take physical possession over the electricity delivered under the FIT Programme through the transmission and distribution operations of Hydro One and 77 of the 80 LDCs that currently operate in Ontario[450].

7.233 In *US – Anti-Dumping and Countervailing Duties (China)*, the Appellate Body explained that the term "government" is defined as the "continuous exercise of authority over subjects; authoritative direction or regulation and control", recalling that in *Canada – Dairy*, it had found that "the essence of government is that it enjoys the effective power to regulate, control, or supervise individuals, or otherwise restrain their conduct through the exercise of lawful authority"[451]. The Appellate Body went on to find that "public body" must be understood to mean "an entity that possesses, exercises or is vested with governmental authority"[452]. The Appellate Body has explained the nature of "governmental authority" in the following terms:

> There are many different ways in which government in the narrow sense could provide entities with authority. Accordingly, different types of evidence may be relevant to showing that such authority has been bestowed on a particular entity. Evidence that an entity is, in fact, exercising governmental functions may serve as evidence that it possesses or has been vested with governmental authority, particularly where such evidence points to a sustained and systematic practice. It follows, in our view, that evidence that a government exercises meaningful control over an entity and its conduct may serve, in certain circumstances, as evidence that the

---

448 See above, paras. 7.203-7.213.

449 Although Canada maintains that the fact that the IESO does not take title to electricity "says nothing of the obtaining or acquisition by the OPA" (Canada's second written submission, para. 47), Canada has not specifically refuted Japan's allegation that "no provision of a FIT Contract ... gives the OPA the right to take title to the renewable electricity delivered". Japan's second written submission, para. 39.

450 Canada's response to Panel question No. 21 (first set); and opening statement at the second meeting of the Panel, paras. 30-32.

451 Appellate Body Report, *US – Anti-Dumping and Countervailing Duties (China)*, para. 290, referring to the Shorter Oxford English Dictionary, 6th Edition, A. Stevenson (ed.) (Oxford University Press, 2007), Vol. 1, p. 1139; and Appellate Body Report, *Canada – Dairy*, para. 97.

452 Appellate Body Report, *US – Anti-Dumping and Countervailing Duties (China)*, para. 317.

> relevant entity possesses governmental authority and exercises such authority in the performance of governmental functions. We stress, however, that, apart from an express delegation of authority in a legal instrument, the existence of mere formal links between an entity and government in the narrow sense is unlikely to suffice to establish the necessary possession of governmental authority. Thus, for example, the mere fact that a government is the majority shareholder of an entity does not demonstrate that the government exercises meaningful control over the conduct of that entity, much less that the government has bestowed it with governmental authority. In some instances, however, where the evidence shows that the formal indicia of government control are manifold, and there is also evidence that such control has been exercised in a meaningful way, then such evidence may permit an inference that the entity concerned is exercising governmental authority[453].

7.234 Hydro One is an agent of the Government of Ontario[454]. As we have previously noted, the Government of Ontario describes a governmental "agent" as "a provincial government organization: [i] which is established by the government, but is not part of a ministry; [ii] which is accountable to the government; [iii] to which the government appoints the majority of the appointees; and [iv] to which the government has assigned or delegated authority and responsibility, or which otherwise has statutory authority and responsibility to perform a public function or service"[455]. It is particularly the last point included in the Government of Ontario's definition of a governmental agent that makes Hydro One a "public body" within the meaning of Article 1.1(a)(1) of the SCM Agreement.

7.235 That the Government of Ontario has "meaningful control" over Hydro One's activities in a way that confirms it is a "public body" within the meaning of Article 1.1(a)(1) of the SCM Agreement is evident from a number of more formal indicators. Starting with the statutory basis of Hydro One's incorporation, the *Electricity Act of 1998*, we note that the Government of Ontario has not only imposed a *duty* on Hydro One to "operate generation facilities and distribution systems" and "distribute electricity" in "such communities" as the Government may prescribe, but it has also granted itself broad powers to define the "conditions and restrictions" pursuant to which such operations must be conducted. Thus, Section 48.1(1) of the *Electricity Act of 1998* provides that:

> Hydro One Inc. shall, through one or more subsidiaries, operate generation facilities and distribution systems in, and shall distribute electricity within, such communities as may be

[453] Appellate Body Report, *US – Anti-Dumping and Countervailing Duties (China)*, para. 318.

[454] Government of Ontario: All Agencies List, Exhibit JPN-49.

[455] Government of Ontario: Agencies, Exhibit JPN-51, p. 1.

> prescribed by regulation, whether or not the community is connected to the IESO-controlled grid, and shall do so in accordance with such conditions and restrictions as may be prescribed by regulation[456].

Likewise, Section 48.2(1) of the *Electricity Act of 1998* reveals that the Government of Ontario has the power to prescribe mandatory provisions in Hydro One's articles of incorporation "governing the creation and issuance of one or more classes of special shares to be issued to the Minister, to hold on behalf of Her Majesty in right of Ontario", governing "constraints on the issue, transfer and ownership, including joint ownership, of voting securities of the corporation", and "with respect to the enforcement of the constraints"[457]. The scope of this power is clarified in Section 53(1)(c); while Section 53(2) identifies "[w]ithout limiting the generality of" Section 53(1)(c), the following examples of the areas where the Government may choose to intervene:

> (a) the mandatory disclosure of information in documents issued or published by the applicable corporation;
>
> (b) the duties and powers of the directors to refuse to issue or register transfers of shares in accordance with the articles of the corporation;
>
> (c) the limitations on voting rights of any shares held contrary to the articles of the corporation;
>
> (d) the powers of the directors to require disclosure of beneficial ownership of shares of the corporation and the rights of the corporation and its directors, employees or agents to rely on the disclosure and the effects of the reliance;
>
> (e) the manner of determining how much of the equity of a corporation a person or class of persons owns.

Finally as regards the *Electricity Act of 1998*, we note that Sections 50.4(1) and 50.4(4) require that Hydro One report to the Minister on the following basis:

> Hydro One Inc. shall, within 90 days after the end of every fiscal year, submit to the Minister an annual report on its affairs during that fiscal year, signed by the chair of the board of directors.
>
> Hydro One Inc. shall give such other reports and information to the Minister of Finance or to the Minister as each of them may require from time to time.

---

[456] The government's power to prescribe the communities to be targeted by Hydro One's generation and distribution activities, as well as the conditions and restrictions of such operations, is repeated in Section 53(1)(a) and (b) of the *Electricity Act of 1998*, Exhibit JPN-5.

[457] This power is repeated and clarified in Section 53(1)(c) of the *Electricity Act of 1998*, Exhibit JPN-5.

7.236 The 2008 Memorandum of Agreement ("MOU") between the Government of Ontario and Hydro One reveals how some of the above-mentioned government's powers and Hydro One duties have been implemented. Although directed to operate as a "commercial enterprise with an independent Board of Directors"[458], Hydro One must comply with the Government of Ontario's direction to undertake "special initiatives" in relation to "governance" issues. Hydro One must also "prioritize investments in transmission and distribution capacity to support projects necessary to maintain ongoing grid security and reliability". In this regard, Hydro One is directed to "prepare a three to five year investment plan for new projects", which after being approved by its Board of Directors, "will be submitted to the Minister of Energy and Minister of Finance for concurrence". Moreover, Hydro One "will obtain the approval of the Minister of Energy and Minister of Finance in advance with respect to: (i) any proposal to issue or transfer shares in the Corporation or any of its subsidiaries; (ii) any proposed acquisition or divestment of assets"[459].

7.237 In terms of communications and reporting, Hydro One's Board of Directors must meet the Minister of Energy "as needed" "to enhance mutual understanding of interrelated strategic matters". Hydro One's Chair, President and Chief Executive Officer will meet with the Minister of Energy "on a regular basis". Moreover, Hydro One's senior management is also required to meet with senior officials of the Ministry of Energy and the Ministry of Finance "on a regular basis and as needed to discuss ongoing issues and clarify expectations or to identify and address emergent issues"[460].

7.238 Finally, as regards Hydro One's "performance expectations", "[k]ey measures are to be agreed upon with the Minister of Energy and the Minister of Finance", and once approved by Hydro One's Board of Directors, annual performance targets "will be submitted to the Minister of Energy and the Minister of Finance for concurrence"[461].

7.239 Thus, apart from the Government of Ontario's explicit description of Hydro One as its "agent", the above indicia of the Government of Ontario's "meaningful control" over Hydro One's corporate and business operations lead to the conclusion that Hydro One is a "public body" for the purpose of Article 1.1(a)(1) of the SCM Agreement. In this light, the fact that Hydro One owns and operates 97% of the transmission lines combined with the fact that it distributes electricity to 1.3 million customers, strongly suggests that the Government of Ontario purchases the electricity that is delivered into the grid under the FIT

---

[458] Memorandum of Agreement between the Government of Ontario and Hydro One, Exhibit CDA-107, p. 1.

[459] Memorandum of Agreement between the Government of Ontario and Hydro One, Exhibit CDA-107, p. 2.

[460] *Ibid.*

[461] Memorandum of Agreement between the Government of Ontario and Hydro One, Exhibit CDA-107, p. 3.

Programme[462]. In this regard, it is also important to recall that while the IESO (another "agent" of the Government of Ontario) has stated that it does not take any "title" to the electricity in the Ontario power grid[463], it nevertheless *controls* how electricity flows through that grid. Thus, the Government of Ontario not only contracts with FIT Programme generators through the OPA to supply electricity into the grid, but it also directs the movement of that electricity to and throughout that grid by means of IESO instructions, and then finally, through the operations of Hydro One, transmits and distributes the delivered electricity to end-user customers. In our view, the combined actions of all three "public bodies"[464] (but especially Hydro One and the OPA) demonstrate that the Government of Ontario purchases electricity within the meaning of Article 1.1(a)(1)(iii) of the SCM Agreement.

7.240 Although both Japan and the European Union have identified the fact that FIT and microFIT generators will be paid for electricity they are directed by the IESO *not to supply* as evidence to support the conclusion that the OPA does not purchase electricity[465], Canada, as already noted, has explained that: (i) FIT generators have never been directed by the IESO to refrain from delivering electricity into the system; (ii) the IESO cannot make such requests of smaller FIT and microFIT generators because they are not connected to the IESO-controlled transmission grid; and (iii) supply contracts with generators that are "non-dispatchable" (such as the FIT solar PV and windpower generators) will typically include a clause allowing the IESO to direct a facility not to supply as a mechanism to prevent the oversupply of electricity into the grid[466].

7.241 To the extent that the FIT Contracts contemplate the possibility of FIT generators being paid for electricity that is not produced and delivered into the transmission grid by virtue of the IESO's instruction, it is clear to us that the

---

[462] In this regard, we note that the European Union argues that the purchaser of the electricity under the FIT Programme is not the OPA *but the distributors.* European Union's first written submission, para. 56. Similarly, Japan argues that the purchasers of electricity in Ontario are the *"intermediaries in the transmission and distribution process such as wholesalers and retailers"*. Moreover, Japan has submitted evidence suggesting that an electricity "marketer" takes title to electricity (and therefore in our view possession), by virtue of purchasing electricity for resale from power generators and wholesalers. Japan's second written submission, fn. 48 quoting from Ohio Electric Utility Institute, Glossary, ("Glossary of the Ohio Electric Utility Institute"), Exhibit JPN-224; Delaware Code, Title 26, Section 1001, ("Delaware Code"), Exhibit JPN-225; and Pennsylvania Code, Title 52, Section 54.2, ("Pennsylvania Code"), Exhibit JPN-226.

[463] IESO: Settlement Statements and Invoices, Exhibit JPN-62, p. 1.

[464] The OPA and the IESO are "agents" of the Government of Ontario. See Government of Ontario: All Agencies List, Exhibit JPN-49; Agency Details, OPA, Exhibit JPN-50; and Government of Ontario: Agencies, Exhibit JPN-51. There is no dispute between the parties that the OPA and the IESO are "public bodies" for the purpose of the SCM Agreement.

[465] Japan's response to Panel question No. 21 (first set); second written submission, para. 42; European Union's opening statement at the first meeting of the Panel, para. 18; and second written submission, para. 44.

[466] Canada's response to Panel question No. 21 (first set); and opening statement at the second meeting of the Panel, paras. 30-32.

OPA is paying for the existence of an exceptional mechanism that is needed to manage the risks of system overload. Given the inherent characteristics of electricity and the complexities of operating a safe and reliable electricity system[467], it seems to us that such a contractual clause would be a *sine qua non* to the purchase of electricity from non-dispatchable generators. Thus, in our view, the fact that the FIT Contract contemplates the payment of generators for electricity supply that is foregone under IESO direction, does not take away from the characterization of the challenged measures as "government purchases [of] goods".

Legislation, regulations and contracts

7.242 Finally, the third consideration that has led us to the conclusion that the challenged measures constitute government purchases of goods is the legislative and regulatory framework of the FIT Programme as well as the language found in certain clauses of the FIT and microFIT Contracts themselves[468]. In our view, these documents leave no doubt that the challenged measures are perceived by the Government of Ontario, and others in Ontario, as governmental activity that involves the procurement or purchase of electricity. This is the consistent and repeated message articulated in the legal instruments we have reviewed, and it is by no means contrived. We recognize, however, that as the complainants have emphasized, the label given to an instrument under municipal law is not dispositive of the analysis that we must undertake for the purpose of WTO law. Nevertheless, it is equally the case that such evidence cannot simply be ignored and it must form part of our analysis. Thus, while this evidence "cannot be the end of our analysis"[469], the fact that the *Electricity Act of 1998*, the Ministerial Direction, the FIT and microFIT Contracts and other documents, all in one way or another characterize the challenged measures as a procurement or purchase of electricity, is a relevant factor that we take into account in our analysis.

Conclusions

7.243 Thus, for all of the foregoing reasons, we conclude that the appropriate legal characterization to be given to the FIT Programme, and the FIT and microFIT Contracts, is as "government purchases [of] goods" under Article 1.1(a)(1)(iii) of the SCM Agreement. Although we recognize that the challenged measures exhibit some of the basic features of certain forms of "direct transfer[s] of funds", in that they involve an exchange of rights and obligations which includes the payment of money, we do not agree with the complainants that this means they can *also* be legally characterized as such for the purposes of the SCM Agreement.

---

[467] See above paras. 7.11-7.18.

[468] See above paras. 7.195-7.214.

[469] Appellate Body Report, *US – Large Civil Aircraft (Second Complaint)*, para. 593.

7.244 In *US – Large Civil Aircraft (Second Complaint)*, the Appellate Body observed that a purchase of goods "is usually understood to mean that the person or entity providing the goods will receive some consideration in return"[470]. The ordinary meaning of the word "purchase" suggests that a government purchase of goods will arise when it makes some kind of payment in the form of "money or an equivalent" in exchange for taking possession (including by obtaining an entitlement) over a good[471]. Thus, we see two major differences between a "direct transfer of funds", in the form of a transaction involving an exchange of rights and obligations, and government "purchases [of] goods". First, a government providing a "direct transfer of funds" must transfer financial resources of some kind; whereas a government may use money *or an equivalent* to purchase goods. Second, whereas Article 1.1(a)(1)(iii) identifies only one object of a government's purchases, i.e. *goods*; Article 1.1(a)(1)(i) does not specify the particular object of a government's direct transfer of funds (when this involves an exchange of rights and obligations).

7.245 In our view, the fact that Article 1.1(a)(1)(iii) specifically identifies "goods" as the objects that a government will purchase is significant and reveals an intention on the part of the drafters to focus the relevant sub-clause of this provision on *only* this form of financial contribution. It is difficult to imagine that the drafters expressly referred to "purchases [of] *goods*" in Article 1.1(a)(1)(iii) of the SCM Agreement intending that such transactions should also be properly covered under Article 1.1(a)(1)(i) as "direct transfers of funds". In this regard, we observe that the only two examples of "direct transfer[s] of funds" involving reciprocal rights and obligations that Article 1.1(a)(1)(i) identifies are "loans" and "equity infusion[s]". Government "purchases of goods" could have easily been added to these examples had the drafters considered that they should also be viewed as falling within the scope of Article 1.1(a)(1)(i) of the SCM Agreement, particularly given that they are explicitly mentioned in Article 1.1(a)(1)(iii) of the SCM Agreement.

7.246 Furthermore, finding that the challenged measures may be legally characterized as "direct transfer[s] of funds" would, in our view, be contrary to the principle of effective treaty interpretation, which requires an interpreter to refrain from adopting "a reading that would result in reducing whole clauses or paragraphs of a treaty to redundancy or inutility"[472]. We see no way of reading Articles 1.1(a)(1)(i) and (iii) in a way that enables us to conclude that government "purchases [of] goods" could also be legally characterized as "direct transfer[s] of funds" without infringing this principle[473]. While we recognize that

---

[470] Appellate Body Report, *US – Large Civil Aircraft (Second Complaint)*, para. 619.

[471] See above paras. 7.225 and 7.227.

[472] Appellate Body Report, *US – Gasoline*, p. 23.

[473] The same conclusion led the panel in *US – Large Civil Aircraft (Second Complaint)* to state that it was "not free to accept the argument that transactions involving purchases of services (along with transactions involving purchases of goods) are covered by other sub-paragraphs and elements of Article 1.1(a)(1)", finding therefore that "transactions properly characterized as purchases of services

one way the two provisions could be read together would be to limit the types of purchases covered under Article 1.1(a)(1)(iii) to only those effected through a payment that is *not monetary* in nature, we can find no support for such a restrictive interpretation of the ordinary meaning of the word "purchase" in the language of Article 1.1(a)(1)(iii) or its immediate context; and, indeed, the complainants have not ventured any.

7.247 Finally, the complainants claim that support for their views comes from the following observation made by the Appellate Body *in a footnote* in *US – Large Civil Aircraft (Second Complaint)*: "The structure of [Article 1.1(a)(1)] does not expressly preclude that a transaction could be covered by more than one subparagraph. There is, for example, no 'or' included between the subparagraphs"[474]. It is apparent that the content of this footnote does not amount to a *finding* that transactions properly characterized as "purchases [of] goods" can also constitute "direct transfer[s] of funds". On this specific issue, the Appellate Body did not come to any definitive conclusion. Thus, while we can see that it may be possible to characterize different aspects of the same measure as different types of "financial contributions" (for example, a governmental programme involving loans and purchases of goods), we do not believe that customary rules of interpretation of public international law allow us to accept the interpretation advanced by the complainants.

7.248 Having found that the challenged measures should be legally characterized as "government purchases of goods", and thereby rejecting that they amount to "direct transfer[s] of funds", we also find that they cannot be "potential direct transfers of funds". Equally, to the extent that Japan and the European Union may have argued that the challenged measures could be legally characterized as a form of "financial contribution" involving government entrustment or direction within the meaning of Article 1.1(a)(1)(iv) of the SCM Agreement, we also reject this argument.

The Challenged measures as a form of income or price support

7.249 Both complainants in these proceedings have advanced essentially parallel arguments focused around the wholesale market for electricity to substantiate their assertions concerning the existence of "benefit", irrespective of whether the challenged measures are legally characterized under Articles 1.1(a)

are excluded from the scope of Article 1.1(a)(1)(i) of the SCM Agreement". Panel Report, *US – Large Civil Aircraft (Second Complaint)*, paras. 7.956 and 7.970. While the Appellate Body Report declared the panel's *finding* "moot and of no legal effect" (Appellate Body Report, *US – Large Civil Aircraft (Second Complaint)*, para. 620), we consider the panel's reasoning, as it relates to the concept of "purchases of goods", nevertheless a useful exposition of the interpretative problem that we believe is created by the complainants' arguments in these proceedings.

[474] Appellate Body Report, *US – Large Civil Aircraft (Second Complaint)*, fn. 1287.

or 1.1(a)(2) of the SCM Agreement[475]. In the section that follows, the Panel majority rejects the entirety of the complainants' "benefit" arguments as they relate to Article 1.1(a)(1)(iii). It follows that the complainants' subsidy claims must also fail regardless of whether the Panel majority agrees with their contentions that the FIT Programme, and the FIT and microFIT Contracts, constitute a form of "income or price support" within the meaning of Article 1.1(a)(2) of the SCM Agreement. In other words, the arguments the complainants have advanced to support their allegations about the extent to which the challenged measures confer a "benefit", when they are characterized as "income or price support" within the meaning of Article 1.1(a)(2) of the SCM Agreement, are essentially the same as those examined and rejected by the Panel majority in the following section of these Reports. In this light, we do not believe it is necessary, for the purpose of satisfactorily resolving the complainants' subsidy claims, to also decide whether the FIT Programme, and the FIT and microFIT Contracts, amount to "income or price support" under the terms of Article 1.1(a)(2) of the SCM Agreement. Therefore, on the grounds of judicial economy, we make no findings in respect of the complainants' allegations that the challenged measures may be legally characterized as "income or price support" under Article 1.1(a)(2) of the SCM Agreement.

3. *Whether the challenged measures confer a "benefit" within the meaning of Article 1.1(b) of the SCM Agreement*

(a) Arguments of the parties

(i) Japan

7.250 Recalling that the Appellate Body and WTO panels have consistently found that a "financial contribution" confers a "benefit" when it is provided on terms that are better than those available to the recipient on the relevant market, Japan submits that the measures at issue confer a benefit within the meaning of Article 1.1(b) of the SCM Agreement for two main reasons[476].

7.251 First, according to Japan, the challenged measures confer a benefit because they guarantee that FIT and microFIT generators will receive a price for the electricity[477] they produce that exceeds the price of electricity on the

[475] See e.g. Japan's first written submission, paras. 219-247; and European Union's first written submission, paras. 63-89.

[476] Japan's first written submission, paras. 216-247; and second written submission, paras. 3-16.

[477] The focus of Japan's argument is on the "commodity charge" portion of wholesale electricity prices, which it describes as the "portion of the prices paid by consumers that serves as the payment for the electricity itself, as opposed to payment for services associated with the delivery of that electricity to consumers", or the "price that relates to payment for the electricity itself (as opposed to payment for the services of transmission/distribution and market operation)". Japan's first written submission, paras. 11 and 77.

wholesale and/or retail markets in Ontario, or alternatively, in any one of four jurisdictions outside of Ontario ("out-of-Province jurisdictions"). To substantiate its view that the FIT and microFIT generators are remunerated in excess of the price of electricity on the wholesale electricity market, Japan advances seven wholesale "commodity" electricity price benchmarks. The first of the proposed benchmarks is what Japan considers to be the actual weighted average of the wholesale price of electricity in Ontario during 2010, namely, the weighted average HOEP[478]. The second and third proposed benchmarks Japan advances are the weighted average "wholesale rate" during 2010 for generators other than FIT and RESOP generators[479], and the "commodity portion" of the price paid by retail consumers under the Regulated Price Plan ("RPP") in 2010[480]. The remaining four wholesale electricity price benchmarks that Japan presents allegedly represent the 2010 average wholesale prices in the deregulated/competitive markets of Alberta, New York, New England and the Mid-Atlantic United States[481]. Japan submits that the Panel may turn to these out-of-Province benchmarks if it determines that the Ontario-based electricity price benchmarks are distorted in any way[482]. Finally, Japan argues that the RPP prices it has advanced may also serve as a benchmark against which to measure whether the challenged measures confer a benefit because, in Japan's view, they establish a ceiling for the amount that Ontario consumers will be willing to pay for electricity. According to Japan, no generator of electricity in Ontario should expect to receive a rate in excess of the price paid by retail consumers in the commodity portion of their bill[483]. Thus, to the extent that FIT and microFIT generators receive prices for delivered electricity that are in excess of the RPP prices, Japan submits that the challenged measures must confer a benefit.

7.252 The second argument that Japan makes to substantiate its allegations concerning benefit is based on the history of the Ontario electricity market, and the objective design and structure of the FIT Programme. In particular, Japan submits that the history of the Ontario electricity market demonstrates that Ontario established its present market structure, including the OPA and

---

478 Japan's first written submission, paras. 219-220.

479 Japan's first written submission, para. 221. This rate is calculated by finding the weighted average of the prices received for each kWh of electricity delivered into Ontario's electricity system in 2010 by "assets whose rates are not regulated or contracted (i.e., OPG's unregulated assets with no OPA contracts and IPPs with no OPA contracts)" and "assets that receive a regulated or contracted rate (i.e., OPG's regulated assets, OPG's unregulated assets with OPA contracts, NUGs, and most IPPs)". Japan explains that the former category of generators receive the same price – the HOEP – and that the second category of generators receive a price which is in part based on the level of the HOEP. Japan's first written submission, para. 32.

480 Japan's first written submission, paras. 223-224.

481 Japan's first written submission, para. 222.

482 Japan's response to Panel question No. 7 (first set); second written submission, paras. 8-12; opening statement at the second meeting of the Panel, paras. 14-19; and response to Panel question No. 31 (second set).

483 Japan's first written submission, paras 223-224; opening statement at the second meeting of the Panel, para. 19; responses to Panel question 28 (second set).

ultimately the FIT Programme, because the liberalized market that operated in 2002 did not attract sufficient electricity supply, in particular from renewable sources, to cover the needs of the Province[484]. According to Japan, the Government of Ontario decided to internalize the positive externalities of renewable energy by guaranteeing payments that cover the production costs and reasonable profits of the FIT and microFIT generators over a period of 20 years. Japan submits that such payments would not have been otherwise available to renewable electricity generators because the wholesale electricity market that would exist in the absence of the FIT Programme would have exposed them not only to lower pricing but also other less advantageous contractual terms and conditions. Thus, Japan argues that the history of the Ontario electricity and the objective design and structure of the FIT Programme shows that, in the absence of the FIT Programme, the FIT and microFIT generators would be unable to operate in today's wholesale electricity market[485].

7.253 In response to Canada's submission that the proper market benchmark should be a price that reflects the higher costs of production of renewable electricity, Japan argues that Canada has not established that a distinct market for renewable electricity actually exists in Ontario, and therefore, Canada's contention must be rejected. On the contrary, Japan emphasizes that there is no such separate market because electricity is a commodity, and consumers in Ontario find one unit of electricity indistinguishable from another unit of electricity. Moreover, Japan notes that the FIT Programme does not give consumers the option to choose a renewable source for the electricity they use, and to pay a higher price for that electricity. Rather, according to Japan, the higher prices owed to FIT generators are distributed across all consumers via the Global Adjustment to establish a single price paid by consumers for electricity produced from all production technologies[486].

7.254 Finally, Japan calls the Panel's attention to the distinction between: (i) *regulated* prices that cover production costs plus reasonable profit; and (ii) *subsidized* prices that cover production costs plus reasonable profit. Japan submits that in a market environment, the most efficient producer of electricity (for example due to economies of scale) should be able to sell its electricity at a price covering its production cost plus reasonable profit, and should be the dominant generator. According to Japan, the market may even support this generator charging a higher price, but this generator may not be permitted to sell at any higher price by virtue of governmental *regulation*. By contrast, Japan argues that, in a market environment, less cost-efficient generators, such as

---

[484] Japan's second written submission paras. 5-6; opening statement at the second meeting of the Panel, paras. 11-12; comments on Canada's responses to Panel questions Nos. 1 and 42 (second set).

[485] Japan's second written submission, paras. 3-7; opening statement at the second meeting of the Panel, paras. 10-13; and comments on Canada's responses to Panel questions Nos. 1 and 42 (second set).

[486] Japan's opening statement at the first meeting of the Panel, paras. 30-45; and second written submission, para. 23.

renewable energy generators, would be unable to survive competition with the dominant generator. In order to enable such less cost-efficient generators to survive in the market despite their inferior cost-efficiency, Japan submits that the government must *subsidize* them, which in Japan's view, is precisely what the FIT Programme does in Ontario[487].

(ii) European Union

7.255 Like Japan, the European Union advances two main lines of arguments to support its allegations of benefit. First, relying on the same wholesale electricity price market benchmarks advanced by Japan, the European Union submits that the challenged measures confer a benefit because they guarantee that FIT and microFIT generators will receive a price for the electricity they produce that exceeds the price of electricity on the wholesale electricity market in Ontario, or alternatively, in any one of the four out-of-Province jurisdictions referred to by Japan[488]. Secondly, the European Union argues that the inherent nature of the FIT Programme demonstrates the existence of benefit because it reveals that the Programme is intended to facilitate private investment in new renewable electricity generation that the wholesale market in Ontario is incapable of attracting. In this regard, the European Union points to two main features of the FIT Programme: (i) the allegedly above-market pricing for electricity that is produced by FIT generators; and (ii) the guaranteed 20-year duration of such allegedly above-market pricing (including "generous" price escalation at various intervals). According to the European Union, either of these features would not be available to the same renewable electricity generators if they had to operate on the wholesale electricity market in Ontario. Thus, the European Union submits that in the absence of the FIT Programme, the FIT generators would have been unable to participate in Ontario's wholesale electricity market[489].

7.256 The European Union rejects Canada's argument that the proper market benchmark should be a price that reflects the higher costs of production of renewable electricity. Like Japan, the European Union emphasizes that electricity is a commodity, and that regardless of whether it is generated from a renewable or non-renewable source of energy, it is physically alike in all respects and perfectly substitutable. Moreover, the European Union observes that the electricity prices paid by consumers in Ontario do not distinguish between the different generating technologies. Thus, according to the European Union, in the context of the present disputes, there can be only one relevant product market for the purpose of the benefit analysis - the Ontario wholesale

---

487 Japan's response to Panel question No. 33 (second set).

488 European Union's first written submission, paras. 65-88; second written submission, paras. 86-102.

489 European Union's second written submission, paras. 69-70, 103 and 105; opening statement at the first meeting of the Panel, paras. 23 and 27.

market for electricity that is generated from all sources of energy (i.e. renewable and non-renewable energy)[490].

7.257 Were the Panel to decide that the relevant market benchmark should take into account the existence of a distinction between electricity generated from renewable and non-renewable sources of energy, the European Union considers that the Panel could also determine the existence of benefit on the basis of the different prices that are guaranteed to FIT generators. In this regard, the European Union notes that the FIT Price Schedule reveals that the prices offered to generators using, for example, waterpower, biomass or biogas technologies, are lower than the prices offered to wind and solar PV generators. Thus, even assuming that there were a separate market for electricity produced from renewable energy sources, the higher prices paid to generators using wind and solar PV technologies compared with other "clean" technologies under the FIT Programme, demonstrate that the challenged measures confer a benefit to the generators using wind and solar PV technology.

7.258 Finally, the European Union submits that even if, as Canada argues, the cost of generating wind and solar electricity were an appropriate benchmark for the Panel's benefit analysis, the FIT Programme would nevertheless confer a benefit because it offers standardized prices to all generators regardless of their *actual* costs of production. According to the European Union, the fact that the location of a generating plant using solar or wind energy will influence its productivity implies that facilities in good locations will have relatively lower overall costs of production given that capital costs between different plants will be very similar. This, in turn, means that the standard pricing applied under the FIT Programme will inevitably exceed the costs of production of producers with facilities in good locations, and for this reason, will confer a benefit upon such generators. In this regard, the European Union recalls that the predecessor to the FIT Programme (the RESOP) functioned on the basis of the best prices offered by generators through a bidding process. Thus, the European Union submits that it is possible for Ontario to obtain electricity produced from renewable energy sources at lower cost compared with what is guaranteed under the FIT Programme[491].

(iii) Canada

7.259 Canada argues that the complainants have failed to establish that the challenged measures confer a benefit because their proposed electricity price benchmarks ignore the fundamental condition underlying the Government of Ontario's purchase of electricity under the FIT Programme, namely, that the

---

490 European Union's second written submission, paras. 72-77; and opening statement at the first meeting of the Panel, para. 24.

491 European Union's second written submission, paras. 82-85. The European Union also advances the use of import/export prices as a commercial benchmark in the present case. See, European Union's second written submission, para. 95.

purchased electricity is generated from renewable sources of energy. According to Canada, the appropriate electricity price benchmark for the purpose of the Panel's benefit analysis must be found on the "market" for electricity produced from wind and solar PV technology, reflecting the fact that it is the Government of Ontario (not the end-consumer) that is the purchaser of the electricity supplied under the FIT Programme. Canada suggests that such a benchmark may, in the first instance, be found in the prices paid in Ontario by private purchasers of electricity produced using windpower and solar PV technology. However, in Canada's view, the complainants have failed to advance any such benchmarks of this kind, including any alternatives based on, for example, the constructed costs of producing electricity generated using wind and solar PV technology or appropriate out-of-Province electricity prices adjusted for the conditions in Ontario[492].

7.260 Canada emphasizes that it would be inappropriate to use an electricity price benchmark that reflects a single price for blended or co-mingled commodity electricity, such as the HOEP, because there is no single market for such electricity in Ontario and the different generating technologies do not compete with each other. In this regard, Canada asserts that because of the range of factors that must be taken into account in order to secure a reliable and clean supply of electricity in Ontario, the varying cost structures and inherent attributes of the different generation technologies needed to achieve this objective must be taken into account and ultimately reflected in differential pricing. Canada explains that, for the most part, this is done by the Ontario Government through the application of regulated and contracted prices that are higher than the HOEP[493]. According to Canada, this approach to securing a sufficient electricity supply recognizes the limitations of wholesale markets worldwide in offering adequate incentives to new generation. This dilemma, known as the "missing money" problem, arises in electricity systems in which wholesale prices do not provide adequate compensation to pay for the fixed costs of generators or the total investment costs of new generators, with the resulting effect that investors will not decide to enter the market[494].

7.261 Apart from criticizing the complainants' proposed electricity price benchmarks on the basis that they represent a price for blended or co-mingled commodity electricity that does not reflect the nature of the challenged financial contributions and the "missing money" reality of wholesale electricity markets in Ontario and other jurisdictions, Canada rejects the complainants' characterization of the IESO-administered wholesale electricity market as a "competitive"

---

[492] For instance, Canada's first written submission (DS412), paras. 125 and 136-150; first written submission (DS426), paras. 64-66; and opening statement at the second meeting of the Panel, paras. 111-120 and 136-142.

[493] Canada's first written submission (DS412), paras. 130-140; and first written submission (DS426), paras. 64-81.

[494] Canada's first written submission (DS412), para. 35; and first written submission (DS426), para. 72.

market. According to Canada, the market clearing mechanism that produces the HOEP is merely a tool created by the Government of Ontario to help the IESO make dispatch decisions in order to balance *physical* supply and demand for electricity[495]. Canada asserts that the majority of generators participate in this mechanism by offering electricity at prices that do not cover their costs of production or any amount of return. These generators do not make price and volume offers on the grounds of ordinary commercial considerations, but rather to ensure that their electricity output is accepted by the IESO in order to earn the relevant regulated or contract price[496]. Thus, according to Canada, the HOEP does not reflect the costs and other operating conditions that most producers of electricity in Ontario face. Moreover, Canada points out that FIT generators do not make bids in the IESO market-clearing mechanism.

7.262 Canada contrasts the IESO-administered market that exists today with the liberalized wholesale electricity market that existed in Ontario between May and November 2002. Whereas the latter market functioned as a "venue" where buyers and sellers met to exchange electricity at an equilibrium price balancing supply and demand, Canada explains that the IESO-administered market that exists today does not set the price received by the vast majority of generators representing 92% of Ontario's generation capacity[497]. Moreover, Canada observes that the facilities that today receive the HOEP alone are older, state-owned, hydro and coal plants that the Government of Ontario has decided do not require higher contract or regulated rates in the light of largely depreciated capital costs, as well as (in the case of the coal facilities) imminent decommissioning[498].

7.263 Finally, Canada also contests the view that in the absence of the FIT Programme, the FIT generators would be left with having to survive on the basis of the HOEP. According to Canada, this counterfactual is incorrect because "in all likelihood", a prospective renewable electricity generator would approach the Government of Ontario through the OPA and attempt to negotiate a contract for the sale of electricity at prices reflective of the prevailing market conditions, which include the generator's costs of production and the government's supply requirements[499].

---

495 Canada's first written submission (DS426), para. 8.

496 Canada's first written submission (DS426), paras. 67-81; and first written submission (DS412), para. 138.

497 Canada's opening statement at the second meeting of the Panel, paras. 113-117.

498 Canada's opening statement at the second meeting of the Panel, paras. 118-119.

499 Canada's opening statement at the second meeting of the Panel, paras. 128-129.

(b) Arguments of the third parties

(i) Australia

7.264 In Australia's view, the relevant market in these disputes, for purposes of the benefit analysis, is the electricity market. In its analysis of benefit, Canada predominantly focuses on the conditions of supply of renewable energy. However, Australia argues that the Panel should also consider the demand side of the electricity market in examining benefit, noting that consumers of electricity in Ontario do not – and cannot – distinguish between renewable and non-renewable sources of electricity. Moreover, Australia does not consider that the difference in the production costs for different energy types precludes a benefit analysis using the market price for electricity. In Australia's view, there are two possible ways in which FIT Contracts confer a benefit to FIT generators. First, the governmental support establishes a buyer for the renewable energy that would not otherwise exist. Second, FIT generators receive a higher price for their product than that which is otherwise available on the market. With regards to the second option, Australia considers that the HOEP used by the complainants is an appropriate comparator for determining benefit[500].

(ii) Brazil

7.265 Brazil considers that the appropriate benchmark in these disputes should be assessed in the light of the Appellate Body Report in *EC and certain member States – Large Civil Aircraft*. Brazil argues that the appropriate benchmark should take into account both the supply and the demand sides in the energy market, and thus cannot be based solely on the prices for which certain types of producers are willing to sell, or the prices set forth by the government. In addition, Brazil contends that the wholesale unregulated market prices in a strategic sector of an economy cannot form the basis for this benchmark[501].

(iii) China

7.266 China argues that the consideration of whether a benefit was conferred does not depend on the "proportion of non-subsidized recipients" or on the production cost of the recipient of a subsidy. With regard to the proportion of non-subsidized recipients, China considers that Canada has not addressed in detail (i) why the electricity market in Ontario is distorted due to the presence of the Government of Ontario as a "predominant" purchaser, and (ii) other factors that may affect the assessment of an appropriate benchmark. Moreover, China contends that the cost of production is not an appropriate basis to determine the benchmark price. China fails to see the reason why the HOEP is not an

---

[500] Australia's third-party submission (DS412), paras. 11-15; third-party submission (DS426), paras. 11-15; and third-party statement (DS412 and DS426), paras. 11-20.

[501] Brazil's third-party statement (DS412 and DS426), paras. 9-13.

appropriate benchmark, taking into account that electricity from renewable energy and that from other forms of energy are similar and comparable[502].

(iv) European Union (in WT/DS412)

7.267 As a third party in WT/DS412, the European Union contends that the FIT Programme will result in most cases in a benefit to FIT generators due to the difference between the market prices and the guaranteed prices. In the European Union's view, the benefit assessment should focus on the relevant market benchmark at the time the financial contribution is granted to the recipient[503].

(v) Korea

7.268 Korea notes that the selection of a "market price" for the benefit analysis at times requires a complex analysis that may involve an examination of returns over a longer period of time. Taking into account that individuals have different time horizons, rational market participants may assign different weights to the short-term and long-term consequences of a transaction, and thus value the overall return quite differently. Korea recalls that it is common for profit-maximizing businesses to accept a short-term loss in order to obtain a greater long-term profit. From this perspective, it is not simple to select an appropriate benchmark where, as in these disputes, complex long-term business and policy considerations, and investments with lengthy pay-back periods, are involved. Thus, Korea considers that a snap shot at a single moment of time may not necessarily ensure a reliable comparison that takes into account the real market situation, as mandated by Article 14 of the SCM Agreement[504].

(vi) Kingdom of Saudi Arabia

7.269 Saudi Arabia considers that, pursuant to WTO rules, the domestic market provides the most appropriate benchmark in determining the existence and magnitude of a subsidy benefit. In Saudi Arabia's view, resort to external benchmarks, such as international market prices or prices in third countries, is generally inappropriate. Saudi Arabia contends that a panel may not use external benchmarks to measure the amount of "benefit" unless it has established that private prices in the country of provision are distorted, as defined by the Appellate Body in *US – Softwood Lumber IV*[505].

---

502 China's third-party submission (DS412), paras. 23-38; and third-party statement (DS412 and DS426), para. 4.

503 European Union's third-party submission (DS412), paras. 21-22.

504 Korea's third-party submission (DS412), paras. 46-54.

505 Saudi Arabia's third-party submission (DS412), paras. 18-28; third-party submission (DS426), paras. 18-28; and third-party statement (DS412 and DS426), paras. 8-14.

(c) Evaluation of the Panel

(i) Introduction

7.270 By way of introduction, we note that although the primary purpose of the complainants' benefit arguments was to substantiate their views that the challenged measures, when characterized as *direct or potential direct transfers of funds* under the terms of Article 1.1(a)(1)(i) of the SCM Agreement, and/or *income or price support* within the meaning of Article 1.1(a)(2), confer a benefit, we understand them to have each submitted that the same arguments have equal relevance and application to any analysis that would need to be undertaken for the purpose of evaluating whether the challenged measures, when characterized as *government purchases of goods*, confer a benefit[506]. In this regard, we recall that both complainants have emphasized that were the challenged measures to be characterized as government purchases of goods, this would be consistent with their views that they amount to financial contributions[507]. Thus, although primarily submitted for the purpose of substantiating a different line of subsidization arguments, we see no legal impediment to evaluating the merits of the same contentions for the purpose of establishing whether the complainants have established that the challenged measures amount to subsidies when characterized as "government purchases [of] goods". To this end, we now turn to examine the parties' arguments by first recalling the relevant legal standard for the determination of the existence of "benefit" under the terms of Article 1.1(b) of the SCM Agreement. We then review the parties' specific assertions about how the FIT Programme, and the FIT and microFIT Contracts, confer (or do not confer) a "benefit" in the light of the relevant legal standard, directing particular attention to the extent to which the wholesale market for electricity in Ontario should be the appropriate focus of the benefit analysis. Finally, in last part of our evaluation, we set out our conclusions on the merits of the complainants' submissions in the light of our findings about the relevant focus of benefit analysis.

(ii) The legal standard for determining the existence of "benefit"

7.271 A financial contribution will confer a benefit upon a recipient within the meaning of Article 1.1(b) of the SCM Agreement when it provides an advantage to its recipient[508]. It is well established that the existence of any such advantage is to be determined by comparing the position of the recipient with and without

---

[506] European Union's opening statement at the second meeting of the Panel, para. 23; second written submission, para. 53; response to Panel question No. 21 (second set); and Japan's response to Panel question No. 22 (second set).

[507] European Union's first written submission, para. 54; response to Panel question No. 12 (first set); and Japan's response to Panel question No. 22 (second set).

[508] Appellate Body Report, *US – Softwood Lumber IV*, para. 51.

the financial contribution, and that "the marketplace provides an appropriate basis for [making this] comparison"[509]. Article 14(d) of the SCM Agreement establishes guidelines for calculating the amount of subsidy in terms of benefit when there has been a government purchase of goods for the purpose of countervailing duty investigations. Although not intended to define the circumstances when a government purchase of goods will confer a benefit in disputes involving Part III of the SCM Agreement, Article 14(d) provides useful context for the analysis that is required in the present disputes. Article 14(d) reads as follows:

> [T]he provision of goods or services or purchase of goods by a government shall not be considered as conferring a benefit unless the provision is made for less than adequate remuneration, or the purchase is made for more than adequate remuneration. The adequacy of remuneration shall be determined in relation to prevailing market conditions for the good or service in question in the country of provision or purchase (including price, quality, availability, marketability, transportation and other conditions of purchase or sale).

7.272 On its face, Article 14(d) stipulates that a government purchase of goods will not confer a benefit upon a recipient unless it is made for "more than adequate remuneration", and that the adequacy of this remuneration must be evaluated in relation to the "prevailing market conditions" for the good in question in the country of purchase, including "price, quality, availability, marketability, transportation and other conditions of purchase or sale". Thus, in the context of the present disputes, Article 14(d) suggests that *one* way to demonstrate that the challenged measures confer a benefit is by showing that the remuneration provided to FIT generators using windpower and solar PV technology to produce the electricity purchased by the OPA is "more than adequate" compared with the remuneration the same generators would receive on the "market" for electricity in Ontario, in the light of the "prevailing market conditions". As we see it, the starting point for this analysis is the identification of the relevant "market".

7.273 In *US – Upland Cotton*, the Appellate Body defined a "market" as "the area of economic activity in which buyers and sellers come together and the

---

[509] Appellate Body Report, *Canada – Aircraft*, para. 157. We note that to date, the "marketplace" has not been explicitly used as a benchmark to determine whether financial contributions taking the form of the measures described in Article 1.1(a)(ii) of the SCM Agreement (i.e. where "government revenue that is otherwise due is foregone or not collected (e.g. fiscal incentives such as tax credits)") confer a benefit. Panel Reports, *US – FSC*, para. 7.103; and *US – FSC (Article 21.5 – EC)*, paras. 8.44-8.48; and Appellate Body Reports, *US – FSC*, para. 140; and *US – FSC (Article 21.5 – EC)*, para. 198.

forces of supply and demand affect prices"[510]. Similarly, in *EC and certain member States – Large Civil Aircraft*, the Appellate Body clarified that the "marketplace to which the Appellate Body referred in *Canada – Aircraft* reflects a sphere in which goods and services are exchanged between willing buyers and sellers"[511]. Moreover, the Appellate Body has explained that:

> The terms of a financial transaction must be assessed against the terms that would result from unconstrained exchange in the relevant market. The relevant market may be more or less developed; it may be made up of many or few participants. ... In some instances, the market may be more rudimentary. In other instances, it may be difficult to establish the relevant market and its results. But these informational constraints do not alter the basic framework from which the analysis should proceed. ... There is but one standard—the market standard ... [512]

7.274 In the specific context of Article 14(d), however, the relevant "marketplace" need not be one that is "undistorted by government intervention" or that excludes "situations in which there is government involvement"[513]. The relevant "market" need not be a "pure" marketplace that is devoid of any degree of government intervention[514]. Nevertheless, in previous disputes involving a government *provision* of goods, it has been held that where a "government's role in providing a financial contribution is so predominant that it effectively determines the price at which private suppliers will sell the same or similar goods, ... the comparison contemplated by Article 14 would become circular"[515]. In other words, where a government's involvement as a provider of a particular good in a given market is such that "there is no way of telling whether the recipient is 'better off' absent the financial contribution"[516], the market that is the object of the government intervention cannot serve as an appropriate benchmark for the purpose of Article 14(d). We see no reason why the same considerations should not also apply to situations involving government *purchases* of goods.

7.275 Thus, as we understand the relevant jurisprudence, the "market" against which to evaluate whether a financial contribution in the form of a government

---

[510] Appellate Body Report, *EC and certain member States – LCA*, para. 1122, referring to Appellate Body Report, *US – Upland Cotton*, para. 408. The Appellate Body also noted that "The term 'market' has been defined as '{g}enerally, any context in which the sale and purchase of goods and services takes place' and '{a} collection of homogenous transactions. A market is created whenever potential sellers of a product are brought into contact with potential buyers and a means of exchange.'" Appellate Body Report, *EC and certain member States – LCA,* fn. 2467.

[511] Appellate Body Report, *EC and certain member States – LCA*, para. 981.

[512] Appellate Body Report, *Japan – DRAMs (Korea)*, para. 172.

[513] Appellate Body Report, *US – Softwood Lumber IV*, para. 87; and Panel Report, *US – Softwood Lumber IV*, paras. 7.50-7.51.

[514] *Ibid.*

[515] Appellate Body Report, *US – Softwood Lumber IV*, para. 93.

[516] *Ibid.*

purchase of goods confers a benefit need not be one that is necessarily "perfectly competitive" in the sense of economic theory[517]. However, it must nevertheless be a market where there is effective competition, in the sense that prices for the purchased good must be established through the operation of unconstrained forces of supply and demand, and not by means of government intervention of a kind that renders "the comparison contemplated by Article 14 ... circular"[518]. With this legal standard in mind, we turn to evaluate the merits of the parties' arguments.

(iii) The wholesale market for electricity as the relevant focus of the benefit analysis[519]

7.276 Fundamentally, the complainants' first and main line of benefit argument is that in the absence of the FIT Programme, a competitive wholesale market for electricity in Ontario could not support commercially viable operations of the contested FIT generators because the terms and conditions, including price, that would be attached to private purchases of electricity in such a market would expose them to significantly lower revenues and higher commercial risks compared with the terms and conditions associated with participation in the FIT Programme. To substantiate this argument, the complainants advance a number of proposed competitive wholesale market electricity price benchmarks, or proxies for this benchmark, that they submit demonstrate that the FIT Programme provides "more than adequate remuneration" for the OPA's purchases of electricity under the FIT and microFIT Contracts. The complainants also focus on the long-term (20-year) guaranteed pricing that is available under the FIT Programme, arguing that no such condition would be available from a private purchaser of electricity on the relevant market. Moreover, the complainants' note that one of the key uncontested objectives of the FIT Programme is to induce new investment in renewable energy generation facilities, arguing that this alone demonstrates that relevant FIT generators would not be operating in the Ontario wholesale electricity market in the absence of the FIT Programme.

7.277 Canada accepts that "most" of the contested FIT generators would be unable to conduct viable operations in a competitive wholesale market for

[517] According to Nicholson, a perfectly competitive industry is one with the following characteristics: (a) a large number of firms producing a homogeneous product; (b) firms attempting to maximize profits; (c) firms assume that their own actions have no influence on market prices, i.e. they are price takers; (d) perfect information, i.e. prices are known by all market participants including consumers, and (e) costless transactions. W. Nicholson, *Microeconomic Theory: Basic Principles and Extension*, 8th ed. (Thomson Learning, 2002) ("Nicholson 2002"), p. 370.

[518] Unless otherwise indicated, we refer to this legal standard in the remainder of these Reports as either a "competitive" market or a market "where there is effective competition".

[519] The dissenting opinion of one of the members of the Panel with respect to whether the challenged measures confer a benefit within the meaning of Article 1.1(b) of the SCM Agreement is set out in Section IX of these Reports.

electricity in Ontario. Indeed, Canada points out that one of the objectives of the FIT Programme was to encourage the construction of new renewable energy generation facilities that would not have otherwise existed[520]. However, Canada rejects the view that this demonstrates that the OPA's purchases of electricity under the FIT Programme confer a benefit within the meaning of Article 1.1(b) of the SCM Agreement. Canada explains that the OPA's purchases of electricity, including from renewable energy generators under the FIT Programme, have been motivated by the inability of Ontario's wholesale electricity market to encourage the investment in new electricity generation facilities needed to secure a reliable and clean supply of electricity that is sufficient to meet Ontario's long-term requirements (i.e. the "missing money" problem)[521]. Canada emphasizes that given the different costs associated with the different technologies that must operate to achieve this objective, the most appropriate benchmark for the Panel's benefit analysis in relation to the FIT and microFIT Contracts must reflect what it considers to be the fundamental condition for the Government of Ontario's purchases of electricity under the FIT Programme, namely, that the electricity be produced from renewable energy sources. Thus, Canada submits that the relevant "market" comparator must be the market for electricity produced from wind and solar PV generation technologies.

7.278 The different positions held by the complainants and Canada about what should be the appropriate "market" benchmark raise a number of important questions related to the nature of competitive wholesale electricity markets and the suitability of using one or more alleged examples of such markets to determine the existence of benefit in the present disputes. It is to these questions that we now turn, starting first with the "missing money" problem.

The economics of electricity markets and the "missing money" problem

7.279 As we have previously explained[522], electricity has some specific properties compared to other types of goods. It is intangible and, with some limited exceptions, cannot be effectively stored[523]. It is also delivered to consumers through networks of transmission and distribution lines that can fail if the quantity demanded (known as load) is greater or less than the quantity supplied for any length of time. These properties imply that electricity must be produced at the time that it is consumed, and that the flow of electricity through a transmission grid cannot be left to the choices of individual market participants, but rather it must be centrally coordinated and controlled[524].

---

520 Canada's first written submission (DS412), para. 49.

521 See above para. 7.261 and below para. 7.283.

522 See above paras. 7.11-7.13.

523 As already noted, pumped-storage hydroelectric facilities provide a limited means of storing electricity. See above fn. 47.

524 Hogan Report, Exhibit CDA-2, p. 13. The credentials of Professor William W. Hogan, the author of the Hogan Report, are set out above at fn. 47.

Consumers, and therefore governments, regard electricity as an essential commodity because a safe, reliable and long-term supply is necessary for the smooth functioning of all modern economies. The fact that there are no close substitutes for electricity, combined with a lack of easily observable price signals on the demand side[525], implies that electricity demand is largely unresponsive to prices in the short run (i.e. it is relatively inelastic)[526]. Graphically, the demand curve can therefore be represented by a (nearly) vertical line in a traditional supply/demand diagram. This demand curve will shift from left to right and back again over the course of an hour, a day, a week, a month or year, as factors other than price cause the quantity demanded to change. Such factors include temperature, hours of daylight, time of the year and the structure and performance of an economy. The seasonal fluctuations in the demand for electricity in Ontario are depicted in the following diagram[527].

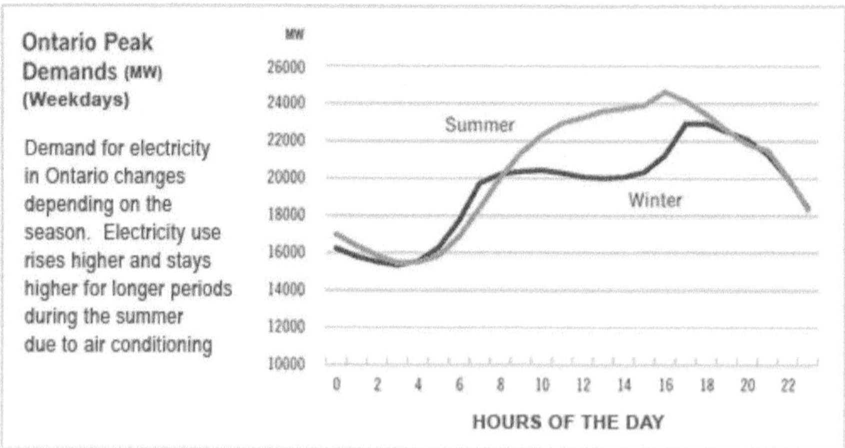

Diagram 4: Seasonal Fluctuations in the Demand for Electricity in Ontario

7.280 It is generally accepted that a diverse mix of generation technology is desirable on the supply side in the interest of securing a reliable and clean

[525] Most consumers are unaware of the price of electricity at the moment that they use it. This causes them to consume more than they otherwise would in times of scarcity, and less than they otherwise would in times of surplus. Hogan Report, Exhibit CDA-2, p. 39; and Electricity Conservation and Supply Task Force, "Tough Choices: Addressing Ontario's Power Needs", Final Report to the Minister of Energy, January 2004, ("2004 Report of the ECSTF"), Exhibit CDA-59, pp. 38-39.

[526] IESO: Ontario's Physical Markets, Exhibit JPN-80, p. 4 ("Non-dispatchable loads simply draw electricity from the grid as needed. They pay the wholesale market price for electricity at the time of consumption, regardless of what the price might be. Non-dispatchable loads account for most of the energy consumed in Ontario"). See also Hogan Report, Exhibit CDA-2, p. 16-17.

[527] Smoothing the Peaks, IESO website ("IESO: Smoothing the Peaks"): referred to in European Union's second written submission, fn. 71.

electricity system. Indeed, as we have explained elsewhere[528], the use of a range of generation technologies is a technical, economic and environmental imperative. The "conventional"[529] technologies can be separated into base-load generation (characterized by high fixed and low marginal costs, e.g. nuclear power), intermediate generation (moderate fixed and marginal costs, e.g. oil or gas-fired steam), and peak-load generation (low fixed costs and high marginal costs, e.g. single cycle gas combustion turbines)[530]. Base-load generators are designed to operate almost always[531], supplying electricity to satisfy core and sustained levels of demand in most hours of the day and, importantly, keep the grid "alive". Intermediate-load plants are used to supply electricity during periods when demand is above core minimum levels, but not at its peak. These generators typically operate during the day and evening[532]. Peak-load generators satisfy demand when it is very high, such as during the hottest days of summer, and some may operate for only a few hours per day[533]. The ability of generators to adjust their level of output quickly, known as *dispatchability*, tends to be lowest for base-load generators and highest for peak-load generators. Although hydroelectricity is usually classified as base load power, certain types of hydroelectric facilities can be dispatched[534]. Electricity generation by means of solar PV and wind technology provides variable or intermittent generation, meaning that power is produced only during certain times of the day and/or night. Typically, both types of facilities have relatively high capital costs per MW of energy produced[535], but they have little or no variable cost[536]. To replace part of the generating capacity that will be lost when Ontario's coal-fired plants will be decommissioned at the end of 2014[537], Ontario's supply mix has

---

[528] See above at paras. 7.13-7.18.

[529] Hogan Report, Exhibit CDA-2, p. 6.

[530] Hogan Report, Exhibit CDA-2, pp. 2-10; and The Tellus Institute, "Best Practice Guide: Integrated Resource Planning for Electricity", 2000, ("Best Practice Guide: Integrated Resource Planning for Electricity"), Exhibit CDA-45, pp. 13-15.

[531] According to Professor Hogan, base-load generators operate "for most hours of the year, perhaps 50% to 80% or more". Hogan Report, Exhibit CDA-2, p. 3.

[532] According to Professor Hogan, intermediate-load generators "typically achiev[e] capacity factors of 15%-50%". Hogan Report, Exhibit CDA-2, p. 5.

[533] Hogan Report, Exhibit CDA-2, p. 6.

[534] Hogan Report, Exhibit CDA-2, p. 5.

[535] In 2007, the capital cost of roof-mounted (0.5 MW) and ground-mounted (10 MW) solar facilities were, respectively, estimated to be CAD 6,690/kW and CAD 4,600/kW; and the capital cost of a "small wind farm" (10 MW) was estimated to be CAD 2,750. These figures compare with the 2007 capital costs of CAD 2,970 for nuclear (1000 MW), CAD 665 for frame single-cycle gas turbine (340 MW), and CAD 924 for combined-cycle gas turbine (500 MW) facilities. Hogan Report, Exhibit CDA-2, p. 8.

[536] Hogan Report, Exhibit CDA-2, p. 6.

[537] In 2003, coal-fired facilities accounted for 25% of Ontario's generation capacity, having increased by 127% from 1995 levels. Among the motivations for eliminating Ontario's coal-fired facilities appear to have been the conclusions reached in a 2005 study prepared for the Government ("Cost Benefit Analysis: Replacing Ontario's Coal-Fired Electricity Generation"), which found the

expanded to include renewable technologies like wind and solar PV. It is expected that these technologies will account for 11.5% of Ontario's generating capacity by 2030[538]. The mix of electricity generation that existed in Ontario in 2010 and selected characteristics are set out in the following table[539].

Table 2: Ontario Electricity Generation Mix

Generation Technology	Share of 2010 Installed Capacity	Approximate Share of 2010 Projected Generation	Type of Capacity	Relative Capital Cost	Relative Operating Cost per kWh	Relative Dispatchability
Nuclear	31%	52%	Baseload	High	Low	Low
Hydropower	22%	19%	Baseload, Peak-Load, Renewable	High	Low	Low for Run-of-River, High for Pondage
Coal	12%	8%	Intermediate	Medium	Low	High
Gas and Oil	25%	15%	Peak-Load	Low	High	High
Wind	4%	2%	Intermittent, Renewable	Very High	Very Low	Low
Solar PV	0.3%	<0.1%	Intermittent, Renewable	Very High	Very Low	Low
Bioenergy	0.7%	1%	Intermittent, Renewable	Medium	Low	Low
Conservation	5%	4%	Baseload, Peak-Load	N/A	N/A	N/A

7.281 In a wholesale electricity market where there is effective competition, the bids that generators submit to the system operator should be usually quite close to their marginal cost of production[540]. Plotting such bids against their output defines a supply curve in the traditional supply/demand framework. Given these particular characteristics, the supply curve of a typical mix of generators would appear as an upward sloping step function that rises sharply as output approaches the market's capacity limit.

7.282 As usual, the intersection of supply and demand determines the market clearing price and quantity of electricity. However the steepness of both curves in typical electricity markets suggests that prices may be extremely volatile,

annual health and environmental costs of coal at CAD 3 billion. Ontario's Long-Term Energy Plan, Exhibit CDA-6, pp. 2 and 19.

538 Ontario's Long-Term Energy Plan, Exhibit CDA-6, p. 19.

539 Hogan Report, Exhibit CDA-2, Table 2, p. 12.

540 Hogan Report, Exhibit CDA-2, p. 16. More generally, it is recognized that, as long as a firm chooses to produce a positive amount of output, equating price and marginal cost is equivalent to profit maximization behaviour. See G. Jehle and P. Reny, *Advanced Microeconomic Theory*, 2nd ed. (Addison Wesley Longman, 2001), p. 144.

rising or falling sharply in response to small changes in demand and/or supply. This is not necessarily an undesirable feature in an electricity market. As long as certain criteria are met (e.g. well informed consumers on the demand side, free entry/exit on the supply side), economic theory suggests that the outcome should be socially desirable[541]. For example, high prices should encourage households and businesses to consume less of the scarce commodity. Elevated prices also provide incentives for incumbent generators to increase their output and for new firms to enter the market by investing in new generation. Thus, in theory, "a well designed" electricity market will provide for a long-term equilibrium "built around a sequence of short-run wholesale market spot prices [that] would provide adequate incentive and compensation to support investment in new electricity generation"[542]. However, as Professor Hogan explains, "this theoretical market ideal has not yet been achieved in many electricity systems, including in Ontario"[543]. As we understand it, one of the main reasons for this is the complexity of incorporating appropriate demand-side responsiveness to supply-side price signals in times of scarcity - or, in other words, the difficulty of equipping electricity consumers with the information and means they need to respond to electricity supply constraints *in real-time*[544].

7.283 In the absence of demand that is more responsive (but not only for this reason), governments and regulators have sought to control potential/actual price volatility by intervening in the market because of the value of stable electricity prices to their economies, with the consequence that many countries have experienced insufficient investment in generation because the price achieved on their "organized" wholesale market is not allowed to rise to a level that, in the long-run, fully compensates generators for the all-in cost of their investments (including fixed and sunk costs)[545]. Private investors will not be willing to finance construction of new generation under such conditions; and in the absence of such investment, an electricity market will be unable to reliably meet future electricity demand. This is referred to as the "missing money" problem[546], and it affects not only more expensive solar PV and wind generation technologies, but also "conventional generating technologies, where energy-only markets do not support investment"[547]. To resolve this dilemma, "alternative mechanisms to wholesale spot markets have been required to provide incentives

[541] These conditions allow real-world market outcomes to approximate ideal market outcomes under perfect competition (see above fn. 517). In a partial equilibrium competitive model, the competitive outcome is "efficient" in that it maximizes overall welfare as measured by the sum of consumer and producer surplus. See Nicholson 2002, p. 402.

[542] Hogan Report, Exhibit CDA-2, p. 16.

[543] Hogan Report, Exhibit CDA-2, p. 17.

[544] Hogan Report, Exhibit CDA-2, p. 16.

[545] Hogan Report, Exhibit CDA-2, pp. 13 and 15-19.

[546] Hogan Report, Exhibit CDA-2, pp. 18-19.

[547] Hogan Report, Exhibit CDA-2, p. 17.

for long-term investment to meet forecasted demand", including power purchase agreements (as in Ontario) and "capacity" payments[548].

7.284 Thus, because of the specific features of electricity and the nature of competitive wholesale electricity markets, government intervention will often be necessary in order to secure an electricity supply that is safe, reliable and sustainable in the long-term.

Ontario's 2002 wholesale electricity market experience

7.285 The complainants assert that a competitive wholesale market for electricity existed in Ontario in 2002. Canada accepts that such a market existed between May and November 2002[549]. During this seven month period, electricity generated from facilities accounting for 94% of Ontario's generation capacity was bought and sold on the wholesale market at prices set through a market clearing mechanism administered by the Independent Market Operator[550]. As much as 90% of the generating capacity operating during this period was government owned and operated through the OPG[551], which was subject to a Market Power Mitigation Agreement imposing a price/revenue cap and other obligations to curtail its potential market power as the dominant operator[552]. Despite this, Canada explains that the wholesale market was "premised on all generators (including those owned by the government through Ontario Power Generation (OPG)) offering their electricity into the wholesale market based on their marginal costs of production"[553]. According to Canada, it was "hoped that

---

548 The Hogan Report defines electric "capacity" as "the capability of a generating unit to produce electricity (measured in kilowatts)". The Hogan Report notes that three regions in the United States – "PJM, New York and New England operate capacity markets to supplement spot market payments for electricity and ancillary services". Hogan Report, Exhibit CDA-2, pp. 13 and 18, and fn. 17 and 21.

549 Canada's first written submission, para. 25; and response to Panel question No. 1 (second set).

550 The remaining 6% was accounted for by electricity produced from NUGs, which were paid according to prices contained in pre-existing contracts with Hydro One, which were taken over by the OEFC. Canada's responses to Panel questions Nos. 1 and 26 (first set); and first written submission, para. 22(iv).

551 In 2000, that is, two years before the "competitive" market was opened, 90% of Ontario's generating capacity was controlled by Ontario Power Generation. Final Report of the Market Design Committee to the Honourable Jim Wilson, Minister of Energy, Science and Technology, 29 January 1999, ("Final Report of the Market Design Committee"), Exhibit CDA-9. In 2011, the OPG accounted for approximately 70% of Ontario's generation capacity. Ontario Power Generation, Frequently Asked Questions, OPG website ("OPG FAQ"), Exhibit CDA-8. See also Ontario Power Generation, About OPG, OPG website, ("About OPG"), Exhibit CDA-10; and About the Ministry of Energy, Exhibit JPN-52.

552 Final Report of the Market Design Committee, Exhibit CDA-9; and Ontario Energy Board, EB-2007-0905, In the Matter of an Application By Ontario Power Generation Inc., Payment Amounts for Prescribed Facilities, Decision with Reasons, 3 November 2008, ("OEB Decision on Payment Amounts for Prescribed Facilities"), Exhibit JPN-233, pp. 2-3.

553 Canada' first written submission (DS426) para. 68.

this would allow generators to recover their operating and capital costs and earn a return"[554].

7.286 The mix of electricity generation technologies that operated in 2002 included nuclear, coal, hydroelectric and oil/gas facilities, which together accounted for over 99% of total available capacity (29,523 MW) and total electricity output (149,690 GWh) in 2002[555]. Although additional nuclear capacity owned by OPG had been expected to come into operation during the course of 2001[556], this was delayed significantly and therefore was not available at the time of market opening[557]. It was partly due to events that transpired because of the unavailability of this additional generation capacity[558], as well as a pre-existing lack of investment in new sources of generation, that Ontario's wholesale electricity market was brought to an end[559].

7.287 Canada explains that over the summer of 2002, very high temperatures drove up demand to levels that could not be satisfied by existing suppliers without significant price increases. Between May and November 2002, prices rose by an average of over 30%[560]. Canada attributes the inability of suppliers to respond to the spike in demand without significant price increases to the "market structure" that existed during this period, and the delay in re-establishing production at the Pickering Unit 4 nuclear plant[561]. Japan also appears to make the former point, asserting that it was because "the established market structure did not invite the sufficient entry of new generators ... [that] the Government of Ontario enacted the Electricity Restructuring Act, 2004, amending the Electricity Act, 1998"[562].

7.288 In its Final Report to the Minister of Energy, the Electricity Conservation and Supply Task Force[563] (the "ECSTF") identified a number of events that took

---

[554] Canada' first written submission (DS426) para. 67.

[555] Other "miscellaneous" technologies accounted for less than 1% of capacity and output. Canada's response to Panel question No. 1 (second set).

[556] The first unit of the OPG's nuclear facilities at Pickering was initially expected to become available on 13 November 2001. On 17 December 2001, the IMO announced that this would be delayed until mid-2002. IMO, 18-Month Outlook: An Assessment of the Adequacy of the Ontario Electricity System from January 2002 to June 2003, ("IMO: 18-Month Outlook"), Exhibit CDA-90.

[557] According to Ontario's Long-Term Energy Plan, Exhibit CDA-6, Bruce Units 3 and 4 were returned to service in March 2004 and November 2003, respectively, while Pickering A Unit 1 was restarted in November 2005.

[558] In 1997, the Ontario Government decided to take seven nuclear reactors off-line to address "critical maintenance and repair needs". This amounted to 8% of Ontario's generation capacity. 2004 Report of the ECSTF, Exhibit CDA-59, p. 23.

[559] Canada's first written submission (DS426), para. 70; response to Panel question No. 1(g) (second set); and Government of Ontario, Action Plan to Lower Your Hydro Bill, ("Action Plan to Lower Your Hydro Bill"), Exhibit CDA-96.

[560] Ontario's Long-Term Energy Plan, Exhibit CDA-6, p. 6.

[561] Canada's response to Panel question No. 1(g) (second set).

[562] Japan's first written submission, para. 25.

[563] The Electricity Conservation and Supply Task Force was established in June 2003 and charged with developing an action plan to address Ontario's need for an affordable, reliable and

place around and during the period of the existence of the wholesale market that shaped the conditions in which it was required to operate. In particular, the ECSTF highlighted that the "financial markets expected to underwrite new capacity were severely impacted by Enron's collapse" and "the long-term energy trading market" at least temporarily ceased to function[564]. According to the ECSTF, this "loss undercut merchant generation, merchant transmission and robust emissions trading"[565]. Similarly, the ECSTF observed that the "retreat of the financial markets from the electricity industry" had the effect of slowing the development and construction of new gas-fired facilities, which were also impacted by "spiking natural gas prices and concerns over long-term supplies"[566]. Indeed, the ECSTF points out that during the period under review, gas-fired plants "became increasingly viewed as a fuel most appropriate for intermediate and peaking operations, rather than baseload"[567]. Obviously, this has implications for the economics of any future investment in gas generation, as intermediate and peaking plants would be expected to operate less than baseload plants. Finally, like Canada, the ECSTF emphasizes that "delays and cost increases in returning the four Pickering A nuclear units to service contributed to reduced supply and higher and more volatile prices", noting that this "added to concern that the Government would continue to make uneconomic investment decisions that would damage the competitive position of competing suppliers in the market"[568].

7.289 Thus, it appears that in addition to the price volatility problems associated with the inherent attributes of competitive wholesale electricity markets[569], a combination of other factors shaping the interaction of supply and demand for electricity in Ontario affected the operation of the competitive wholesale market that existed between May and November 2002, creating critical limits on what it could achieve.

7.290 According to Canada, the 2002 experience demonstrates that a competitive wholesale electricity market "would not be sufficient to encourage the construction of new generation facilities able to provide the additional long-term supply needed by Ontario residents"[570]. This is consistent with one of the

---

environmentally acceptable power supply over the period to 2020. The ECSTF "met thirty times and had detailed discussions with over 90 individuals and organizations representing all sectors of society". 2004 Report of the ECSTF, Exhibit CDA-59, pp. 1-2.

564 2004 Report of the ECSTF, Exhibit CDA-59, p. 84.

565 *Ibid.*

566 *Ibid.*

567 *Ibid.*

568 *Ibid.*

569 See discussion above at paras. 7.279-7.284. The Hogan Report explains that "[c]ost overruns in Ontario Hydro's nuclear construction program and the need to replace or refurbish much of the Province's aging electricity infrastructure provided the impetus for reform and restructuring", suggesting that supply conditions were already tight at the time that the market opened in May 2002. Hogan Report, Exhibit CDA-2, p. 19.

570 Canada's first written submission, para. 27.

main findings of the ECSTF, which concluded that "the market approach adopted in the late 1990s needs substantial enhancement if it is to deliver the new generation and conservation Ontario needs, within the timeframes we need them"[571]. In this latter regard, the ECSTF projected that in the absence of new capacity or demand reduction measures, there would be a supply shortfall in Ontario of 5000-7,000 MW by 2007 and approximately 25,000 MW by 2020. The ECSTF's projected supply and demand conditions are represented in the following table[572].

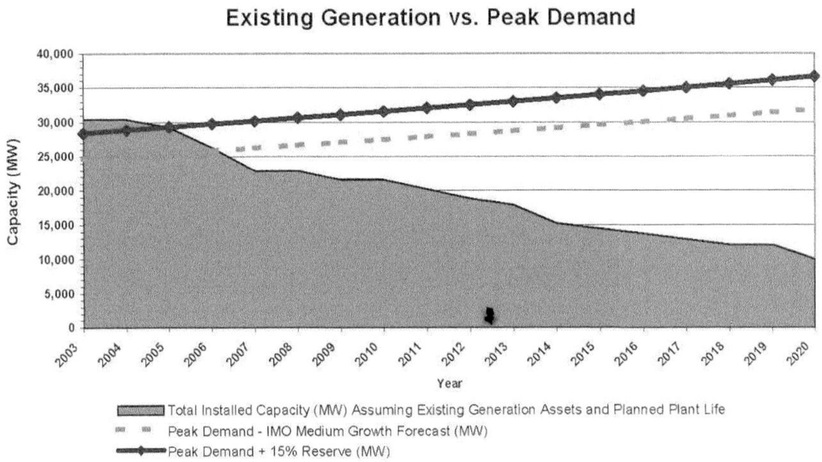

Diagram 5: Existing Generation vs. Peak Demand

7.291 After having "seriously debated" "market solutions and measures to demonstrate commitment to those solutions (such as a willingness to allow consumers to face whatever prices the market dictates and the sale of OPG's output to private traders and wholesalers)", the ECSTF opined that such a path "provides no assurance that the needed supply will be in place to replace Ontario's coal fired generation in 2007 or to ensure an early start to the process of developing effective supply and demand options to rehabilitate or replace aging nuclear plant. It does not provide the stable and predictable prices Ontario consumers demand ... [and] does not ensure that Ontario will have the diverse power mix we believe Ontario needs if its power prices are to remain

571 2004 Report of the ECSTF, Exhibit CDA-59, p. (i).

572 2004 Report of the ECSTF, Exhibit CDA-59, Figure 1A, p. 1.

competitive with neighbouring markets"[573]. The ECSTF concluded that "on balance, ... relying on market signals alone is simply too risky an approach to take, given the potential consequences of failing to achieve the needed early investments in new supply and conservation"[574]. Thus, the ECSTF recommended that there should be "less reliance on the spot market as a signal for new investment"[575].

7.292 In our view, Ontario's 2002 market opening experience confirms what is suggested in the Hogan Report, namely, that competitive wholesale electricity markets will only rarely attract sufficient investment in the generation capacity needed to secure a reliable supply of electricity. The evidence before us indicates that this universal objective of all electricity systems could not have been achieved in Ontario in 2002 solely on the basis of the operation of a competitive wholesale electricity market.

The IESO-administered wholesale electricity market

7.293 Japan asserts that the current IESO-administered wholesale electricity market is a competitive wholesale electricity market. Japan argues that normal market forces, including supply and demand, and the cost of production, come together in this market to set wholesale electricity prices (i.e. the HOEP)[576]. According to Japan, these prices serve "not only as signals for when electricity should be dispatched, but also as signals for when electricity should be consumed, just as market prices do"[577]. Japan observes that the IESO Market Rules describe the objective of the IESO-administered markets as "to promote an efficient, competitive and reliable market for the wholesale and purchase of electricity and ancillary services in Ontario"[578]. Moreover, Japan notes that the IESO itself has described the market it administers as a "competitive wholesale market", where "wholesale prices are based on supply and demand, and reflect the cost of producing electricity"[579].

---

[573] 2004 Report of the ECSTF, Exhibit CDA-59, pp. 64-65. At the time of writing the 2004 Report of the ECSTF, the Government of Ontario had indicated that it would close down coal-fired facilities by 2007. Subsequently, it was decided that the last coal-fired facility would complete operations by end of 2014.

[574] 2004 Report of the ECSTF, Exhibit CDA-59, p. 4.

[575] 2004 Report of the ECSTF, Exhibit CDA-59, p. (iii).

[576] Japan's first written submission, paras. 79-81 and 219; and response to Panel question No. 45 (first set).

[577] Japan's comments on Canada's response to Panel question No. 43 (second set).

[578] Japan's comments on Canada's response to Panel question No. 43 (second set), referring to IESO, Market Rules for the Ontario Electricity Market, ("IESO Market Rules"), Exhibit CDA-106, Chapter 1, Section 3.1.1.

[579] Japan's first written submission, para. 79, referring to Quick Takes: Electricity Pricing, Exhibit JPN-3, p. 1.

7.294 Although initially sharing many of Japan's assertions about the "competitive" nature of the IESO-administered wholesale electricity market[580], the European Union subsequently agreed with the contention that the IESO market mechanism "may not be" the "classical" competitive market where supply and demand meet[581]. Indeed, according to the European Union, "there may not be many 'classical' markets in many jurisdictions with respect to electricity or other products"[582].

7.295 We note that while Japan has argued that the IESO-administered wholesale market is competitive, it has provided the following description of how the HOEP is actually determined:

> Dispatchable generators must submit price/quantity 'offers' for every five minute interval. Although many dispatchable generators will in fact receive regulated or contracted rates for the electricity they sell, they must nonetheless submit offers to the IESO to indicate the quantity they are willing to supply in a given five minute interval, and in doing so *they must strategize about what price to offer such that their quantity will actually be selected by the IESO. Thus, the price offers by dispatchable generators serve as a dispatch signal – i.e., a mechanism for the IESO to select electricity supply* – and not as the rate that these generators actually receive. Generators for which it would be very costly to shut down, such as nuclear facilities, would likely offer a price at or near zero so they can always operate, while other generators would likely offer prices that cover their marginal costs of production[583].

7.296 Japan's description highlights two important points, the first being that most generators participating in the IESO-administered wholesale market do not receive the HOEP. In fact, facilities accounting for 92% of Ontario's 2010 generation capacity do not receive the HOEP, but a higher price established by the OEB (50% of capacity) or under contracts with the OPA or the OEFC (42% of capacity)[584]. The only generators that receive the HOEP *alone* are the OPG's unregulated hydroelectric facilities and two of its coal-fired generation facilities[585]. Canada has explained that these facilities are relatively old (most

---

580 e.g. European Union's first written submission, paras. 70-73.

581 However, the European Union nevertheless considers that "the IESO market mechanism is a market where demand, represented by the relevant competent authorities in Ontario, meets with supply (i.e., electricity generators); and it is the market mechanism chosen by the competent authorities in Ontario to regulate the exchanges of electricity". European Union's second written submission, para. 91.

582 European Union's second written submission, para. 91.

583 Japan's first written submission, Appendix II, para. 8. (footnote omitted, underline added)

584 Canada's first written submission, para. 37. See also above, paras. 7.27-7.31.

585 Canada's first written submission, para. 38.

have operated for over 60 years) with largely depreciated capital costs[586]. In addition, the coal-fired facilities will be decommissioned by the end of 2014[587]. Because of this, the Government of Ontario has decided that these unregulated facilities should receive the HOEP instead of a price "guided by the principle of cost recovery and a margin of return"[588].

7.297 The second telling feature of the IESO-administered wholesale market that is apparent from Japan's description follows from the first, namely, that the primary motivation behind a generator's price offers is to be selected to dispatch electricity, and not to cover its marginal costs of production. Canada confirms that this is exactly what happens, explaining that OPG's regulated hydroelectric and nuclear facilities (which account for the majority of generation in Ontario) make offers into the IESO market clearing mechanism that are "so low (often negative rates) that the IESO must accept" them[589]. According to Canada, the OPG makes such low price offers "to ensure its electricity is accepted", knowing that they will not affect its revenue, which depends upon the regulated price that is set by the OEB. Similarly, for one category of contract generators, the NUGs, Hogan points out that "[b]ecause the contract prices are above both marginal cost and market clearing price during off-peak periods NUGs have incentives to produce uneconomic power off-peak"[590]. Generally, costs of production are also not a consideration for OPG's "unregulated assets" receiving the HOEP, as this price, as a matter of policy, has been deemed to be sufficient for these older, largely depreciated assets, regardless of whether this enables them to cover marginal costs.

7.298 It follows from the above that the price offers attached to a generator's supply bids in the IESO-administered wholesale market are not motivated by the need to cover marginal costs of production (as would typically be the case in a competitive wholesale electricity market such as that which existed in Ontario in 2002[591]), but rather by the need for each generator to be chosen to supply electricity into the Ontario grid in order to receive its contracted or regulated prices. Thus, the IESO-administered wholesale market does not arrive at its equilibrium price (the HOEP) through forces of supply and demand that are unaffected by the policies of the Government of Ontario. To the extent that the Government of Ontario (through the OEB, the OPA and OEFC) ensures that

---

586 Professor Hogan describes these suppliers as "a small subset of old or infrequently operating generating facilities that have fully recovered their sunk costs, and thus, only need to meet their variable costs to be profitable". Hogan Report, Exhibit CDA-2, p. 10.

587 Canada's response to Panel question No. 41 (second set).

588 Canada's response to Panel question No. 26 (first set).

589 Canada's response to Panel question No. 41 (second set).

590 Hogan Report, Exhibit CDA-2, p. 30.

591 In this regard, Canada emphasizes that the IESO-administered wholesale market is qualitatively different to the wholesale market operated by the IMO during the 2002 market opening experience because in the case of the latter, electricity generators competed on the basis of both price and volume offers, whereas there is no such competition between generators operating today. Canada's responses to Panel questions Nos. 41-43 (second set).

92% of Ontario's generation capacity is remunerated at prices above the HOEP, and instructs the OPG's unregulated assets to accept the HOEP irrespective of production costs, it is clear to us that the HOEP is not a market outcome that may be used for the purpose of conducting the present benefit analysis. This is because, in many important respects, the equilibrium level of the HOEP is a direct consequence of the electricity pricing policy and supply-mix decisions of the Government of Ontario. Thus, as Canada and Professor Hogan emphasize, the IESO-administered wholesale market clearing mechanism is perhaps best characterized as a tool for the IESO to make the dispatch decisions needed to balance *physical* supply and demand for electricity[592].

7.299 The European Union submits that "one possible means to assess whether the HOEP represents the price of electricity in Ontario under market conditions" is to compare it with the prices of Ontario electricity imports and exports[593]. After reviewing the average import and export prices of electricity to and from neighbouring Provinces (including Manitoba) and the United States (Michigan, Minnesota and New York) over the past three years, the European Union concludes that the "similarity between the HOEP and the import and export prices is ... revealing of the fact that the HOEP faithfully reflects the price practiced in Ontario and neighbouring jurisdictions under market conditions"[594]. The European Union considers this to be a valid conclusion because "neither the Canadian provinces nor the US States are submitted to overarching governmental regulations" implying that "these entities trade electricity entirely based on their demand and their available supply"[595]. We have a number of problems with the inferences the European Union draws from the data.

7.300 First, we recall that the HOEP does not represent an equilibrium price that is set in a competitive wholesale market of a kind that may be used for the purpose of conducting the present benefit analysis. Rather, the HOEP is a price that is heavily influenced by the electricity pricing policy and supply-mix decisions and regulations of the Government of Ontario. Thus, to the extent that export and import prices reflect or are "tied to" the HOEP, they cannot be considered to reflect prices established in a competitive wholesale electricity market.

7.301 Secondly, if, as Professor Hogan suggests, exporters of electricity will supply to Ontario when the difference between wholesale prices in different jurisdictions is "large enough" to warrant arbitrage between the two systems, it follows that the price level in an exporter's domestic wholesale market will significantly influence the price of exports. However, apart from asserting that the relevant exporters "trade electricity entirely based on their demand and their

---

592 Canada's first written submission (DS426), para. 71; opening statement at the first meeting of the Panel, para. 83; and Hogan Report, Exhibit CDA-2, pp. 37-41.

593 European Union's second written submission, para. 92.

594 European Union's second written submission, para. 95.

595 European Union's second written submission, para. 92.

available supply", the European Union has advanced no evidence to demonstrate that the domestic wholesale electricity markets in Manitoba, Michigan, Minnesota and New York are themselves based on "market conditions" that are not significantly distorted by government intervention. In this light, the fact that the HOEP is similar to export and import prices could simply reflect the existence of less than competitive wholesale markets in the neighbouring jurisdictions. Moreover, as explained in more detail in the section that follows, the wholesale electricity market in New York is not the only source of remuneration that keeps generators participating in the New York electricity system[596].

7.302 The above features of electricity import and export exchanges suggest to us that the price of electricity that is traded between Ontario and its neighbouring jurisdictions does not, as the European Union argues, verify that the HOEP "represents the price of electricity in Ontario under market conditions".

Wholesale electricity markets outside of Ontario

7.303 The complainants argue that the price of electricity in four allegedly competitive wholesale electricity markets operating outside of Ontario could be used as a proxy for the wholesale market price of electricity in Ontario. In particular, the complainants refer to the prices established in the wholesale electricity markets of Alberta, New York State, the State of New England and the Mid-Atlantic region of the United States (the PJM Interconnection). To substantiate the alleged competitive nature of these markets, Japan, supported by the European Union[597], highlights *inter alia* the following statements made in publications from each of the four markets[598]:

> Alberta's power market is unique in Canada. It's wholesale and retail markets are open to competition … Investment in generation is at the developers' risk …[599].
>
> NYISO (and more generally, New York's competitive wholesale market) has performed extremely well on many if not most of the outcomes to which the state's restructuring of its electric industry aspired. In many respects, NYISO stands as a model of a well - functioning electric market that relies extensively on competitive markets to provide benefits to the state's electricity consumers [600].

---

596 See discussion below paras. 7.304-7.305.

597 e.g. European Union's, response to Panel question No. 27 (second set).

598 Japan's response to Panel question No. 31 (second set). See also Japan's response to Panel question No. 7 (first set).

599 Independent Power Producers Society of Alberta, Alberta's Power Market, ("Alberta's Power Market"), Exhibit JPN-208.

600 The New York Independent System Operator: A Ten-Year Review, Analysis Group, 12 April 2010, ("New York Independent System Operator"), Exhibit JPN-209, p. 3.

> To assess the competitiveness of the electric energy markets, the [Internal Market Monitor of ISO New England] examined two types of measures of market competitiveness: structural measures, which analyze the concentration of generation-resource ownership in the New England markets; and price-based measures, which compare wholesale market prices to the estimated cost of providing electric energy. The results of the concentration analyses show that the market is structurally competitive ... Market results show that electric energy prices reflect supplier costs to produce electric energy (i.e., largely fuel prices), which is consistent with the finding that the market is competitive[601].

> The overall market results support the conclusion that prices in PJM are set, on average, by marginal units operating at, or close to, their marginal costs. This is evidence of competitive behavior and competitive market outcomes[602].

7.304 Although Canada does not appear to specifically challenge the complainants' allegations concerning the competitive nature of the above-mentioned wholesale markets, we find it instructive for the purpose of evaluating the nature of the wholesale markets that exist in New York, New England and the PJM, to read in the Hogan Report that because of the "missing money" problem:

> [A]lternative mechanisms to wholesale spot markets have been required to provide incentives for long-term investment to meet forecasted demand. In some regions, such as Ontario, centralized decision makers employ purchased power contracts to finance new investment. Many organized markets in the U.S. have taken a similar path, developing parallel capacity markets and requiring ratepayers to pay additional capacity charges for their share of required levels of capacity, to meet resource adequacy requirements and provide the additional compensation to generators[603].

7.305 The Hogan Report identifies New York, New England and PJM as examples of regions that "operate capacity markets to supplement spot market revenues for electricity and ancillary services"[604]. In other words, the wholesale spot market prices for electricity in New York, New England and PJM, are not the only sources of revenue for generators supplying electricity into their

601 ISO New England, 2010 Annual Markets Report, 3 June 2011, ("New England 2010 Annual Markets Report"), Exhibit JPN-210, pp. 4-6 and 56-64.

602 Monitoring Analytics, 2010 State of the Market Report for PJM, 10 March 2011, ("2010 State of the Market Report for the PJM Interconnection"), Exhibit JPN-211, pp. 30-32.

603 Hogan Report, Exhibit CDA-2, p. 18.

604 Hogan Report, Exhibit CDA-2, fn. 21.

respective systems. Generators in these systems also receive "capacity" payments. Thus, not unlike Ontario's market opening experience in 2002, the fact that generators in New York, New England and PJM operate on the basis of more than just the revenues obtained from the wholesale spot market for electricity evidences the difficulties that competitive wholesale markets have to, *on their own*, attract sufficient investment in the generation capacity needed to secure a reliable system of electricity supply.

7.306 Turning to the complainants' reference to the Province of Alberta, we observe that the fact that a "market" approach "has had some success in Alberta" was noted by the ECSTF. However, in the light of *inter alia* the conditions of supply and demand forecast to exist in Ontario between 2003 and 2020[605], the ECSTF concluded that following the same approach in Ontario involved risks that "were simply too great"[606]. As already noted, the ECSTF found that "on balance ... relying on market signals alone is simply too risky an approach to take, given the potential consequences of failing to achieve the needed early investments in new supply and conservation"[607], and recommended that there should be "less reliance on the spot market as a signal for new investment"[608].

7.307 Although the ECSTF did not explicitly identify the specific differences between Alberta and Ontario that led it to draw the above conclusions, the contents of its Report suggest that they must, at least in part, have had to do with the conditions of supply and demand in the two Provinces. Thus, while there is no evidence before us to doubt the contention that Alberta operates a competitive wholesale electricity market, it is perhaps best characterized as one of the exceptions alluded to in the Hogan Report. Most importantly, however, the ECSTF charged with devising a plan for *Ontario's* electricity future up to 2020 concluded, in 2004, that it would not be possible to introduce a competitive wholesale market in Ontario that guaranteed the same degree of success as Alberta.

Conclusions concerning the wholesale electricity market as the relevant focus of the benefit analysis

7.308 We recall that Article 14(d) of the SCM Agreement provides useful guidance for determining whether "financial contribution[s]" in the form of "government purchases [of] goods" confer a benefit for the purpose of claims made under Part III of the SCM Agreement. According to this guidance, one

---

[605] The Electricity Conservation and Supply Task Force was established in June 2003 and was charged with "developing an action plan to address the province's need for an affordable, reliable and environmentally acceptable power supply over the period to 2020". 2004 Report of the ECSTF, Exhibit CDA-59, p. 1.

[606] 2004 Report of the ECSTF, Exhibit CDA-59, p. 64.

[607] 2004 Report of the ECSTF, Exhibit CDA-59, p. 4.

[608] 2004 Report of the ECSTF, Exhibit CDA-59, p. (iii).

way the challenged measures may be found to confer a benefit is by demonstrating that the remuneration obtained by FIT generators operating on the basis of windpower and solar PV technology under the FIT Programme is "more than adequate" compared with the remuneration the same generators would receive on the relevant "market" for electricity in Ontario, in the light of the "prevailing market conditions". Throughout these proceedings, the complainants' principal argument has been that the benchmark for "adequate remuneration" should be found in the allegedly competitive wholesale electricity market that exists in Ontario or four out-of-Province jurisdictions. However, for the reasons we have explained above, the evidence before us indicates that the wholesale electricity market that currently exists in Ontario is not a market where there is effective competition. Rather, Ontario's wholesale electricity market is perhaps better characterized as a part of an electricity system that is defined in almost all aspects by the Government of Ontario's policy decisions and regulations pertaining to the supply mix needed to ensure that Ontario has a safe, reliable and long-term sustainable supply of electricity, as well as how the costs of that system will be recuperated. We have little doubt that the HOEP results from the operation of forces of supply and demand that are significantly affected by government intervention in a way that renders it an inappropriate benchmark to conduct the present benefit analysis. In the light of the benefit standard that has thus far been applied in WTO disputes[609], we find that the HOEP and all of the HOEP-derivatives that the complainants have advanced[610], cannot serve as appropriate benchmarks for the purpose of the benefit analysis.

7.309 Importantly, the complainants have not convinced us of the premise underlying their two main lines of benefit arguments, namely, that in the absence of the FIT Programme, the FIT generators would be faced with having to operate in a competitive wholesale electricity market. The evidence before us indicates that competitive wholesale electricity markets, although a theoretical possibility, will only rarely operate in a way that remunerates the mix of generators needed to secure a *reliable* electricity system with enough revenue to cover their all-in costs, let alone a system that pursues *human health and environmental* objectives through the inclusion of facilities using solar PV and wind technologies into the supply-mix. In the specific context of Ontario, the 2002 market opening experience illustrates this point. Although intended to operate as a "classical" competitive market where generators would sell electricity at spot prices equal to marginal costs, the conditions of supply and demand that existed at that time made it impossible for the market to attract the investment in generation capacity needed to secure a reliable system of electricity supply. By saying that it was because "the established market structure did not invite the

[609] See above at paras. 7.271-7.275.

[610] Specifically, the weighted average "wholesale rate" during 2010 for generators other than FIT and RESOP generators, and the price paid by retail consumers under the Regulated Price Plan in 2010.

sufficient entry of new generators ... [that] the Government of Ontario enacted the Electricity Restructuring Act, 2004, amending the Electricity Act, 1998"[611], Japan appears to recognize the limits of the competitive market experience in Ontario.

7.310 The complainants have referred to examples of what they consider to be competitive wholesale markets existing outside of Ontario. However, as we have explained, the evidence before us suggests that because of, at least in part, the particular conditions of supply and demand that were forecast in 2003 for Ontario up to 2020, the ECSTF found that the Alberta experience could not be reproduced in Ontario with the same degree of success. Given the significant volume of generating capacity (around 43%) that it is projected will need to be renewed, replaced or added to Ontario's electricity system by 2030[612], and in the light of the limitations that are inherent to competitive wholesale electricity markets, the complainants' benefit arguments fail to convince us that the recommendations of the ECSTF do not also hold true today. With respect to the three examples of allegedly competitive wholesale markets in the United States, it appears from the Hogan Report that these markets do not, in fact, provide participating generators with *all* of the revenues they need to be present on the market. As Professor Hogan explains, the New York, PJM and New England electricity systems have developed "parallel capacity markets and [require] ratepayers to pay additional capacity charges for their share of required levels of capacity, to meet resource adequacy requirements and provide the additional compensation to generators"[613]. It follows that the allegedly competitive New York, PJM and New England wholesale electricity markets do not represent examples of competitive wholesale markets that are capable, *on their own*, of attracting sufficient investment in generation capacity to secure a reliable system of electricity supply.

7.311 We note that all parties to these proceedings agree that FIT generators using solar PV and windpower technology would be unable to conduct viable operations on the basis of the equilibrium prices that could be achieved in a competitive wholesale electricity market[614]. However, Canada has also suggested that there would be unacceptable risks to the *reliability* of Ontario's electricity

---

[611] Japan's first written submission, para. 25.

[612] Ontario's Long-Term Energy Plan reveals that 15,000 MW of Ontario's existing 35,000 MW of generation capacity will need to be renewed, replaced or added by 2030. This is due to the fact that Ontario's nuclear facilities will be temporarily shut down for maintenance between 2010 and 2020, and because coal-fired facilities will be eliminated by the end of 2014. Canada's first written submission (DS412), para. 34, referring to Ontario's Long-Term Energy Plan, Exhibit CDA-6, pp. 10 and 23. On this basis, it would appear that the potential for the same tight supply conditions that existed a decade ago, which at least in part informed the ECSTF recommendations, continues today.

[613] Hogan Report, Exhibit CDA-2, p. 18.

[614] Japan's second written submission, paras. 3-7; opening statement at the second meeting of the Panel, paras. 10-13; comments on Canada's responses to Panel questions Nos. 1 and 42 (second set); European Union's opening statement at the second meeting of the Panel, para. 18; and Canada's first written submission (DS412), paras. 27 and 39.

system if the structure of Ontario's supply-mix were left to be settled by competitive forces of supply and demand. We tend to agree. Given the technical complexities of electricity systems, the inherent limitations of competitive wholesale electricity markets, and recalling, in particular, Ontario's failed 2002 market-opening experience, as well as the current and projected conditions of supply and demand in Ontario, we are not convinced that a *reliable* supply of electricity could be secured at present in Ontario solely through the operation of a competitive wholesale electricity market.

7.312 In our view, the application of a competitive wholesale market standard in the circumstances of the present disputes would not only insufficiently respond to the considerable challenges faced by electricity systems that are caused by the specific properties of electricity, but it would also overlook the particular situation in Ontario. Importantly, it would ignore the evidence indicating that the prevailing conditions of supply and demand in Ontario suggest that a competitive wholesale electricity market would fail to attract the degree of investment in generating capacity needed to secure a reliable supply of electricity, and that, at present, this goal can only be achieved by means of government intervention in what would otherwise be unacceptable competitive market outcomes. In these circumstances, and given the critical importance of electricity to all facets of modern life, we cannot accept that it would be appropriate to determine whether the FIT Programme and the FIT and microFIT Contracts confer a benefit within the meaning of Article 1.1(b) of the SCM Agreement by comparing the terms and conditions of participation in the FIT Programme with those that would be available to generators participating in a wholesale electricity market where there is effective competition[615].

7.313 Thus, for all of the foregoing reasons, we conclude that:

(a) the HOEP is a price set through the interaction of supply and demand forces that in many critical aspects are significantly influenced by the supply-mix and pricing policy decisions and regulations of the Government of Ontario, and therefore, the HOEP and all of the related HOEP-derivatives the complainants have submitted as appropriate benchmarks for the purpose of the benefit analysis cannot be accepted;

(b) the complainants have failed to convince us that, in the absence of the FIT Programme, the FIT generators would be faced with having to operate in a competitive wholesale electricity market because: (i) the economics of competitive wholesale electricity markets suggest that they will only rarely attract the degree of investment in the generation capacity needed to secure a reliable electricity system; and (ii) the weight of the evidence before us

[615] See further in this regard at para. 7.320.

indicates that, at present, a competitive wholesale electricity market would fail to achieve this outcome in Ontario; and

(c) in the light of our conclusions in (a) and (b), and given the critical importance of electricity to all facets of modern life, we find that the question whether the challenged measures confer a benefit within the meaning of Article 1.1(b) of the SCM Agreement cannot be resolved by applying a benchmark that is derived from the conditions for purchasing electricity in a competitive wholesale electricity market.

(iv) Alternatives to the wholesale market for electricity as the relevant focus of the benefit analysis

7.314 Both Japan and the European Union have advanced a number of alternative benchmarks to the competitive wholesale electricity market which they consider may be used to demonstrate that the challenged measures confer a benefit within the meaning of Article 1.1(b) of the SCM Agreement.

7.315 First, Japan and European Union both argue that even if the HOEP is not the price established in a competitive wholesale electricity market, it is nevertheless the *actual price* that would be received by the FIT generators but for the existence of the FIT Programme[616], and for this reason, it should be used as the appropriate benchmark for the purpose of the benefit analysis. Although the complainants have not explained this argument in great detail, we understand that it is premised on a counterfactual where, in the absence of the FIT and microFIT Contracts, the non-FIT suppliers currently operating in Ontario would continue to operate in the same way, thereby maintaining the HOEP at current levels. In our view, this could only happen if the existing suppliers would continue to receive the (generally) above-HOEP prices that have been contracted with the OPA and the OEFC or regulated by the OEB. In other words, in the counterfactual posited by the complainants the Government of Ontario would continue to play the role of contracting and regulating electricity wholesale electricity prices[617]. In this light, it is difficult for us to accept that the *only* option, in the absence of the FIT Programme, for a generator using solar PV and windpower technology to enter the market would be to accept the HOEP. Rather, as Canada suggests, the most probable course of action for such new entrants would be to agree to a price negotiated with the Government of Ontario.

---

616 The European Union appears to makes this argument by characterizing the HOEP as the price that is formed in the "nominal" wholesale electricity market. European Union's second written submission, para. 88.

617 A counterfactual where the Government of Ontario is not present at all would imply the existence of a competitive wholesale market, which we have already rejected as being the appropriate focus of the benefit analysis.

7.316 The European Union also argues that an alternative to, or a proxy for, a benchmark found in the competitive wholesale electricity market could be the prices of imports and exports of electricity into and out of Ontario[618]. We respectfully disagree. As we have explained above, to the extent that such prices reflect or are "tied to" the HOEP, they cannot be considered to be competitive market prices, and therefore cannot be used for the purpose of conducting the present benefit analysis.

7.317 According to Japan, another way of determining whether the challenged measures confer a "benefit" could be by comparing the FIT and microFIT Contract Prices with the prices offered under the Regulated Price Plan ("RPP"). Although at a different level of trade to the wholesale market benchmarks it has advanced, Japan argues that RPP prices may nevertheless be taken into account as possible benchmarks because "no generator of electricity in Ontario should expect to receive a rate in excess of the price paid by retail consumers in their commodity portion of the bill"[619]. Japan argues that RPP prices represent the "ceiling" for the amount that Ontario consumers are willing to pay for electricity[620], an assertion that Japan submits is confirmed by the evidence it has advanced of the prices set in two private retail contracts offered in a recent promotion in Ontario[621]. Thus, Japan appears to argue that because the (wholesale level) Contract Prices offered under the FIT Programme are greater than RPP prices paid at the retail level, the challenged measures must confer a benefit. We are not able to share Japan's point of view. As we have already explained, RPP prices are regulated prices that are inherently linked to the HOEP, which we have found cannot serve as an appropriate benchmark for determining the existence of "benefit". In our view, in order to be used for the argument that Japan is attempting to make, the retail level prices that Japan relies upon would need to be determined in a competitive marketplace. Thus, even if we were to accept that a *retail level* electricity price may serve as an appropriate benchmark against which to determine whether the *wholesale level* prices paid to FIT generators confer a benefit within the meaning of Article 1.1(b) of the SCM Agreement, the relevant retail level prices could not be those set under the RPP because, in the same way as the HOEP, the RPP is significantly influenced by the supply-mix and pricing policy decisions and regulations of the Government of Ontario. Given these considerations, we cannot accept Japan's argument that RPP prices may serve as appropriate benchmarks for the benefit analysis.

7.318 Finally, we note that throughout these proceedings Canada has argued that the relevant "market" for the purpose of the benefit analysis should be the

618 European Union's second written submission, para. 95.

619 Japan's first written submission, para. 223.

620 Japan's opening statement at the second meeting of the Panel, para. 19.

621 Japan's response to Panel question No. 28 (second set), referring to offers made by "Canada Energy", Canada Energy website, ("Canada Energy"), Exhibit JPN-229; and "MyRate Energy", MyRate Energy website, ("MyRate Energy"), Exhibit JPN-230.

market for electricity produced from solar PV and windpower technology, reflecting the fact that it is electricity generated from renewable sources of energy that is purchased by the Government of Ontario under the FIT Programme. According to the complainants, however, there can be only *one* relevant market for the purpose of the benefit analysis, namely, the market for electricity that is generated from all sources of energy, including solar and wind energy. This is because multiple distinct electricity markets based on differences in generation technologies do not exist in Ontario. On this particular point, we agree with the complainants. As both Japan and the European Union have convincingly argued, at present, consumers of electricity in Ontario, whose demand instantaneously determines the purchases made at the wholesale level, do not distinguish electricity on the basis of different generation technologies, either by way of price or usage[622]. Moreover, there are no arguments before us to suggest that the physical properties of electricity change depending upon how it is generated. There is therefore no basis to accept that a separate wholesale market for electricity generated from solar PV and windpower technologies would be the appropriate focus of the benefit analysis in the present disputes[623].

7.319 Thus, we find that none of the alternatives that have been advanced by the complainants (or Canada) may be used as appropriate benchmarks against which to measure whether the FIT Programme and the FIT and microFIT Contracts confer a benefit within the meaning of Article 1.1(b) of the SCM Agreement. In particular, we have determined that the HOEP would not be the only option available to potential generators using solar PV and windpower technology in the absence of the FIT Programme. The HOEP cannot therefore be used to test whether the FIT and microFIT Contract Prices confer a benefit upon FIT Programme generators. The two other alternatives advanced by the complainants (electricity import and export prices, and RPP prices) are both inherently connected to the HOEP and, thereby, the electricity pricing policy decisions and regulations of the Government of Ontario. Therefore, these alternatives also cannot be relied upon to determine whether the FIT Programme confers a benefit. Finally, we have found that there is no evidence to support the existence in Ontario of a separate wholesale market for electricity that is generated solely from solar PV and windpower technology. There is therefore no factual basis to support Canada's contention that the existence of benefit could

---

622 Japan's opening statement at the first meeting of the Panel, para. 31; response to question No. 53 (first set); second written submission, para. 23; comments on Canada's response to Panel question No. 41 (second set); European Union's response to Panel question No. 64 (first set); second written submission, para. 74; and opening statement at the second meeting of the Panel, para. 25.

623 Having rejected Canada's submissions concerning the appropriate approach to determining the existence of benefit, it is not necessary for us to evaluate the merits of the European Union's alternative arguments advanced to demonstrate that even according to Canada's line of argument, the FIT and microFIT Contracts amount to financial contributions that confer a benefit upon the FIT generators within the meaning of Article 1.1(b) of the SCM Agreement.

have been determined in the present disputes by comparing FIT and microFIT Contract Prices with the prices established in such a market.

(v) Final conclusions and observations on the existence of benefit

7.320 We have carefully reviewed the parties' legal and factual arguments in the light of the legal standard for determining the existence of benefit that has to date been applied in WTO dispute settlement. In the particular circumstances of these disputes, we have concluded that determining whether the challenged measures confer a benefit on the basis of a benchmark derived from a *competitive* wholesale electricity market, would mean that the FIT and microFIT Contracts could be legally characterized as subsidies by means of a comparison with a market standard that has not been demonstrated to actually exist nor one that could be reasonably achieved in Ontario - a market standard that the complainants have not contested will only rarely, if at all, attract sufficient investment in generation capacity to secure a reliable system of electricity supply even outside of Ontario[624]. In our view, such an outcome would fail to reflect the reality of modern electricity systems, which by their very nature need to draw electricity from a range of diverse generation technologies that play different roles and have different costs of production and environmental impacts. As we have emphasized on a number of occasions, it is only in exceptional circumstances that the generation capacity needed from all such technologies will be attracted into a wholesale market operating under the conditions of effective competition. Thus, the competitive wholesale electricity market that is at the centre of the complainants' main submissions cannot be the appropriate focus of the benefit analysis in these disputes. Furthermore, for the reasons we have outlined above, the alternatives to the wholesale electricity market that have been presented to us also cannot stand as appropriate benchmarks against which to measure whether the challenged measures confer a benefit. There is therefore no basis to uphold the complainants' benefit arguments.

7.321 In coming to this conclusion, we note that the complainants have asked the Panel not to limit its analysis to rejecting the benchmarks proposed by the parties, inviting the Panel to "find the appropriate benchmark to make a finding on the existence or absence of benefit"[625] and "identify the proper benchmark to

---

[624] On this point, we note that the general descriptions the complainants have presented of their own electricity systems confirm that differing degrees of government intervention in market outcomes are also a feature of wholesale electricity markets in Japan and the European Union. For instance, the European Union explains that "some EU Member States have taken steps to make further use of nuclear power, whereas others prefer not to rely on (or to phase out) that particular source of energy". European Union's response to Panel question No. 27 (second set). Similarly, Japan states that "only GEUs may supply electricity to small-scale users, and they must do so at rates regulated by the Government. … Wholesale rates for sales of electricity to GEUs may be subject to regulation by the Government". Japan's response to Panel question No. 27 (second set).

[625] European Union's closing statement at the second meeting of the Panel, para. 19.

complete the benefit analysis"[626]. Indeed, according to the European Union, the Panel is under an obligation to do so[627]. We do not share the European Union's conviction. In our view, there is no authority in WTO law that *compels* us to review the merits of the complainants' prohibited subsidy claims on the basis of arguments that they have not themselves advanced. We are not convinced that the passages the European Union has referred to from the Appellate Body report in *Japan – DRAMS* and the panel report in *Canada – Aircraft*[628], stand for the proposition that the Panel majority in these disputes cannot limit its analysis to rejecting the complainants' benefit arguments. Moreover, we recall that it has been consistently recognized in WTO dispute settlement practice that it is for a complaining party to establish a claimed infringement of the covered agreements by presenting at least a *prima facie* case of violation on the basis of relevant legal and factual arguments[629]. Thus, while a panel has a duty to engage with and explore such arguments and make objective findings upon their merits, a panel is not entitled to make a *prima facie* case for a party that bears the burden of making it[630]. With these principles in mind, and in the light of the complainants' explicit requests for the Panel to explain its own position with respect to benefit were it to reject the substantial and diverse range of submissions they themselves have made on the issue, we set out in the following paragraphs our own *observations* on one approach to the question of benefit that we believe could have been validly pursued in these disputes.

7.322 Because we have found that the very existence of a reliable electricity supply in Ontario at present requires comprehensive government intervention in the wholesale electricity market, one way we believe it is possible to evaluate whether the challenged measures confer a benefit, that at the same time maintains a market-based discipline, is by evaluating the commercial nature of the FIT and microFIT Contracts against the actions of private purchasers of electricity in a wholesale market where the conditions of supply and demand mirror those that currently exist in Ontario. For this purpose, we believe it is important to recall that: (i) the Government of Ontario has decided to eliminate coal-fired electricity plants by the end of 2014; (ii) that because of this, and due to the scheduled maintenance of Ontario's nuclear facilities between now and 2020, approximately 43% of Ontario's generation capacity will need to be renewed, replaced or added to Ontario's electricity system by 2030[631]; and (iii) that the Government of Ontario has decided that at least part of the additional generating capacity needed to address future needs up to 2030 must come from

626 Japan's closing oral statement at the second meeting of the Panel, para. 7.

627 European Union's closing statement at the second meeting of the Panel, para. 19.

628 In particular, the European Union refers to Appellate Body Report, *Japan – DRAMs*, para. 174; and Panel Report, *Canada - Aircraft*, para. 9.312.

629 Appellate Body Report, *US – Gambling*, para. 282; Appellate Body Report, *US – Wool Shirts and Blouses*, p. 14, DSR 1997:I, 323, at 335.

630 See, for example, Appellate Body Report, *Japan – Agricultural Products II*, para. 129.

631 See above para. 7.310.

renewable sources of energy, including small and large-scale projects using solar PV and windpower technologies[632]. Thus, one way to determine whether the challenged measures confer a benefit within the meaning of Article 1.1(b) of the SCM Agreement would involve testing them against the types of arm's length purchase transactions that would exist in a wholesale electricity market whose broad parameters are defined by the Government of Ontario[633]. In the present set of circumstances, this could be done by comparing the terms and conditions of the challenged FIT and microFIT Contracts with the terms and conditions that would be offered by commercial distributors of electricity acting under a government-imposed obligation to acquire electricity from generators operating solar PV and windpower plants of a comparable scale to those functioning under the FIT Programme. We are attracted by such an approach because not only does it take into account the complexities of electricity markets and the particular conditions of supply and demand that currently exist in Ontario, but it also evaluates the Government of Ontario's actions against a commercial benchmark.

7.323 In our view, any rational distributor charged with having to purchase a volume of electricity that is not insignificant from generators (including small-scale facilities) using solar PV and windpower technology would, acting on the basis of commercial considerations, try to negotiate a supply contract with terms and conditions that ultimately enable it to maximize or optimize the overall return it makes from trading activities (i.e. buying and selling electricity). In general, this means that a distributor will endeavour to enter into a supply contract with any electricity generator that has the lowest overall net cost. By the measure of this simple standard[634], we are of the view that one approach to

---

[632] In particular, as we have already noted, Ontario's Long-Term Energy Plan envisages that electricity generated from projects using wind and solar PV technologies (including small-scale projects) should account for 11.5% of Ontario's electricity generation capacity by 2030. Ontario's Long-Term Energy Plan, Exhibit CDA-6, pp. 18 and 28. Although the OPA has observed that small-scale projects will not produce economies of scale, it also recognizes that such projects can "reduce system costs by reducing transmission losses". Moreover, because small-scale projects "can be considered to reduce marginal demand at the times that they are running", they can also be "credited with reducing marginal losses". RESOP, Exhibit CDA-55, p. 20. Small-scale solar PV and windpower projects are also among the technologies considered to be appropriate for local and dispersed power generation. See Best Practice Guide: Integrated Resource Planning for Electricity, Exhibit CDA-45, p. 14.

[633] Governments regularly intervene in markets for a variety of reasons including in order to avoid outcomes that are believed to be socially unacceptable, or to address various market failures. For instance, governments may decide to limit the availability of certain products because of human health and environmental concerns, or as the Government of Ontario has done, choose to end the use of a particular production technology (coal-fired electricity generation) for the same reasons. These kinds of actions are designed to internalize the social costs (in the case of negative externalities) and benefits (in the case of positive externalities) of certain actions in the production and consumption decisions of economic agents. However, where such government intervention is limited to defining the broad parameters of a market, significant scope will remain for private actors to operate within those parameters on the basis of commercial considerations.

[634] We acknowledge that the considerations shaping a distributor's purchases of electricity under the defined government direction would no doubt involve a range of other issues. However, in our view,

determining whether the challenged measures confer a benefit could be to compare the rate of return obtained by the FIT generators under the terms and conditions of the FIT and microFIT Contracts with the average cost of capital in Canada for projects having a comparable risk profile in the same period. In our view, such a comparison would allow for an immediate and clear determination of whether FIT generators are being overcompensated, and thereby subsidized within the terms of the SCM Agreement.

7.324 The rate of return of a particular project involving the investment of capital is a measure of the extent to which that project realizes a profit (or loss). In other words, the rate of return represents the proportion of money earned on a particular project relative to the capital actually invested. Typically, a rate of return that is at least equal to the opportunity cost of capital in a given economy for a project having a comparable risk profile will signal that an investment is an efficient use of capital. On the other hand, where the rate of return associated with a particular project is below the opportunity cost of capital, it would not make sense to invest in that project because the funds at issue could be used more efficiently by being invested elsewhere in the economy. It follows that an electricity generator in Ontario using solar PV and windpower technology will only be willing to enter into an electricity supply contract with a distributor if its terms and conditions allow the generator to achieve a rate of return on the required investment that is at least equal to the opportunity cost of capital in Canada for comparable projects (i.e., the average cost of capital in Canada). As the minimum requirement that would need to be satisfied in order for such a generator to enter into a supply contract, it is evident that the cost to the distributor of entering into a contract that delivers this desired rate of return must also represent the lowest cost outcome for the distributor. Thus, a distributor directed to purchase electricity produced by generators (including small-scale facilities) operating in Ontario on the basis of solar PV and windpower technology will, when acting under commercial considerations, seek to ensure that the terms and conditions it agrees to under the supply contract result in a rate of return for the generator that falls within an acceptable range above or below the average cost of capital in Canada for projects having a comparable risk profile. It is therefore possible, in this light, to determine whether the purchases of electricity effected by the Government of Ontario under the FIT Programme confer a benefit by examining whether the rates of return associated with the FIT and microFIT Contracts are significantly above the average cost of capital in Canada for projects having a comparable risk profile. Were this to be the case, it could be concluded that the Government of Ontario was overcompensating FIT Programme generators, relative to what they could expect to achieve under supply contracts with private distributors acting under a government instruction to purchase electricity from solar PV and windpower

---

the overall guiding principle would be that of cost minimization with a view to maximizing or optimizing returns.

plants (including small-scale generators) on the basis of commercial considerations, thereby conferring a benefit upon such generators under the terms of the SCM Agreement.

7.325 Canada has disclosed that the rate of return of the FIT Contracts used to develop the FIT Contract Price Schedule was set in 2009 at "approximately 11%"[635]. The evidence reveals that this percentage represents an *after tax* rate of return, implying that the pre-tax rate of return would be higher[636]. Canada has not explained why the 11% after tax rate of return was chosen as the appropriate target for the prices set under the FIT Programme. Moreover, the precise methodology that was used in the Discounted Cash Flow model applied to establish the FIT prices on the basis of the 11% rate of return is not entirely clear. For instance, there is no information before us about the extent to which the Discounted Cash Flow model takes account of the premium paid to Aboriginal and Community Participation projects or the potential revenues that may accrue to the Government of Ontario through the assignment of Environmental Attributes or from the sale of Future Contract Related Products[637]. In addition, the European Union questions the validity of the 11% rate of return, arguing that it underestimates the actual rates of return that could be achieved by the most efficient FIT generators on the basis of the FIT Contract Prices[638].

7.326 Turning to the evidence that is before us with respect to the average cost of capital in Canada for projects with a risk profile that is comparable to solar PV and windpower FIT projects, we note that the OEB set the target rate of return on equity for Ontario's regulated utilities in 2009 at 9.75%[639]. However, this rate was calculated on the basis of an average equity risk premium of 550 basis points for Ontario's regulated electricity *and gas* utilities. Thus, the 550 basis points figure is not specific to Ontario's electricity producing utilities. In this regard, we note that the data used by the OEB to arrive at the equity risk premium reveals that the equity risk premium for electricity utility projects on their own could be as high as 871 basis points[640], suggesting that the rate of

---

635 Canada's responses to Panel questions Nos. 26 (first set) and 12 (second set).

636 Proposed FIT Price Schedule Presentation, Exhibit CDA-46, slides 28 and 30. The latter slide reveals that the actual income tax rate used in the OPA's calculations was 30.5%.

637 A general overview of the Discounted Cash Flow model used to establish the FIT Price Schedule is described in the Proposed FIT Price Schedule Presentation, Exhibit CDA-46. This overview reveals that "[n]o credit [was] assumed for revenues from [the] federal ecoENERGY program". However, there is no indication whether the premium paid to Aboriginal and Community Participation projects or the potential revenues from the assignment of Environmental Attributes or Future Contract Related Products is, or is not, taken into account.

638 See, e.g. European Union's opening statement at the second meeting of the Panel, para. 26; response to Panel question 34 (second set); comments on Canada's response to Panel question 12 (second set).

639 OEB Report on the cost of capital for Ontario's regulated utilities, Exhibit CDA-64, p. 37.

640 OEB Report on the cost of capital for Ontario's regulated utilities, Exhibit CDA-64, pp. 38 and 40.

return on equity for regulated electricity utilities could be as high as 12.96%[641]. It is also important to recall that Ontario's regulated electricity utilities operate nuclear and hydro-electric facilities. Given the major technical differences between the latter types of operations, which it should be recalled are also long-established and government-controlled, and the solar PV and windpower projects operating under the FIT Programme, we do not think it would be appropriate to accept that the risk premium associated with Ontario's regulated electricity assets could be automatically compared with the rate of return associated with solar PV and windpower projects under the FIT Programme. It appears, therefore, that the record of these disputes does not contain any appropriate information that can be used to determine the average cost of capital in Canada for projects with a comparable risk profile to the challenged FIT and microFIT projects during the relevant period.

7.327 Thus, while we believe that a comparison between the relevant rates of return of the challenged FIT and microFIT Contracts with the relevant average cost of capital in Canada would be a useful way to determine, on the basis of the benefit standard we have outlined above, whether the challenged measures confer a benefit within the meaning of Article 1.1(b) of the SCM Agreement, a number of important questions and factual issues would need to be explored and resolved in order for any such analysis to be undertaken.

4. *Overall conclusion with respect to the claims of subsidization*

7.328 In the light of our evaluation of the merits of the parties' arguments and the findings that we have made in Sections VII.C.1 to 3 of these Reports, we conclude that:

(i) the FIT Programme, and the FIT and microFIT Contracts, amount to government purchases of goods within the meaning of Article 1.1(a)(1)(iii) of the SCM Agreement; and

(ii) Japan and the European Union have failed to establish that the challenged measures confer a benefit, within the meaning of Article 1.1(b) of the SCM Agreement.

[641] The rate of return of 9.75% was set by the OEB on the basis of the forecast long-term Canadian government bond yield (4.25%) plus the equity risk premium (550 basis points). The 12.96% figure can be calculated by adding the 4.25% forecast long-term Canadian government bond yield to the 871 basis points equity risk premium determined by one of the OEB's consultants. OEB Report on the cost of capital for Ontario's regulated utilities, Exhibit CDA-64, pp. 37 and 40.

VIII. CONCLUSIONS AND RECOMMENDATIONS

8.1 As already noted in the cover page to these Reports, our conclusions and recommendations have been set out separately with respect to each dispute in the following sections.

A. Complaint by Japan (DS412)

1. Conclusions

8.2 In the light of the findings set out in the foregoing sections of this Report, we conclude that Japan has established that the "Minimum Required Domestic Content Level" prescribed under the FIT Programme, and implemented through the individual FIT and microFIT Contracts executed since the FIT Programme's inception, places Canada in breach of its obligations under Article 2.1 of the TRIMs Agreement and Article III:4 of the GATT 1994.

8.3 On the other hand, in the light of the findings set out in the foregoing sections of this Report, we conclude that Japan has failed to establish that the FIT Programme, and the individual solar PV and windpower FIT and microFIT Contracts executed since the FIT Programme's inception, constitute subsidies, or envisage the granting of subsidies, within the meaning of Article 1.1 of the SCM Agreement, and thereby that Canada has acted inconsistently with Articles 3.1(b) and 3.2 of the SCM Agreement.

2. Recommendations

8.4 Pursuant to Article 3.8 of the DSU, in cases where there is infringement of the obligations assumed under a covered agreement, the action is considered *prima facie* to constitute a case of nullification or impairment of benefits under that agreement. Accordingly, we conclude that to the extent Canada has acted inconsistently with Article 2.1 of the TRIMs Agreement and Article III:4 of the GATT 1994, Canada has nullified or impaired benefits accruing to Japan.

8.5 We recommend that Canada bring its measures into conformity with its obligations under the TRIMs Agreement and the GATT 1994.

B. Complaint by the European Union (DS426)

1. Conclusions

8.6 In the light of the findings set out in the foregoing sections of this Report, we conclude that European Union has established that the "Minimum Required Domestic Content Level" prescribed under the FIT Programme, and implemented through the individual FIT and microFIT Contracts executed since the FIT Programme's inception, places Canada in breach of its obligations under Article 2.1 of the TRIMs Agreement and Article III:4 of the GATT 1994.

8.7 On the other hand, in the light of the findings set out in the foregoing sections of this Report, we conclude that the European Union has failed to establish that the FIT Programme, and the individual solar PV and windpower FIT and microFIT Contracts executed since the FIT Programme's inception, constitute subsidies, or envisage the granting of subsidies, within the meaning of Article 1.1 of the SCM Agreement, and thereby that Canada has acted inconsistently with Articles 3.1(b) and 3.2 of the SCM Agreement.

2. Recommendations

8.8 Pursuant to Article 3.8 of the DSU, in cases where there is infringement of the obligations assumed under a covered agreement, the action is considered *prima facie* to constitute a case of nullification or impairment of benefits under that agreement. Accordingly, we conclude that to the extent Canada has acted inconsistently with Article 2.1 of the TRIMs Agreement and Article III:4 of the GATT 1994, Canada has nullified or impaired benefits accruing to the European Union.

8.9 We recommend that Canada bring its measures into conformity with its obligations under the TRIMs Agreement and the GATT 1994.

IX. DISSENTING OPINION OF ONE MEMBER OF THE PANEL WITH RESPECT TO WHETHER THE CHALLENGED MEASURES CONFER A BENEFIT WITHIN THE MEANING OF ARTICLE 1.1(B) OF THE SCM AGREEMENT

A. Introduction

9.1 The Panel majority has undertaken a long and careful evaluation of the parties' arguments concerning the question whether the challenged measures confer a benefit, ultimately concluding that the complainants have failed to establish the existence of subsidization[642]. While I agree with parts of the Panel majority's benefit analysis, I respectfully disagree with certain key aspects of its reasoning and ultimate findings. In essence, the Panel majority has found that the circumstances of ensuring a reliable supply of electricity that achieves certain objectives sought by the Government of Ontario justifies the rejection of the competitive wholesale electricity market as the relevant focus of the benefit analysis. The Panel majority has furthermore suggested that, in these circumstances, the existence of benefit could be determined by focusing upon the rate of return associated with the FIT and microFIT Contracts and comparing this with the average cost of capital in Canada for projects having a comparable risk profile.

9.2 I respectfully disagree with these findings and the alternative benefit test. The wholesale electricity market that currently exists in Ontario is recognizable as a market for the buying and selling of electricity. It is undeniable that the

642 See above at Section VII.C.3.

supply of electricity, its price and competition between electricity generators – in particular, market entry – are very heavily regulated and conditioned in the market by the Government of Ontario. The wholesale electricity market that currently exists in Ontario is therefore not the kind of market where price is determined by the unconstrained forces of supply and demand. The regulatory impacts on the market are not simply in the nature of framework regulation, within which those forces may operate. The Government of Ontario (through Hydro One) and the municipal governments (through Local Distribution Companies) account for almost all purchases of electricity made at the wholesale level. The same product, which in this case is electricity, is purchased by these entities at different prices depending upon its method of generation or particular status in the Government of Ontario's electricity supply policy, including under the FIT Programme. In these circumstances the complainants have expressed their concern that an advantage is being given to the market participants that are receiving the highest prices for the electricity they produce, namely generators using solar PV and windpower technologies operating under the FIT Programme. The Panel's task is to test that concern according to the disciplines of the SCM Agreement.

9.3 The relevant question that a Panel in a case such as this must address is whether a benefit is conferred on the recipient of the financial contribution. The wholesale electricity market in Ontario does not allow for the discovery of a single market-clearing price established through the unconstrained forces of supply and demand. In that market the Government of Ontario and the municipal governments are the chief buyers of the goods concerned. In these circumstances the Panel must consider whether there is some appropriate frame of reference for determining if a benefit is conferred in the provision of that financial contribution. In my view, the competitive wholesale market for electricity that *could* exist in Ontario is the appropriate focus of the benefit analysis. Furthermore, I am of the view that facilitating the entry of certain technologies into the market that does exist – such as it is – by way of a financial contribution can itself be considered to confer a benefit. In the light of these considerations, it follows from the arguments and evidence presented by the complainants, as well as Canada's own statements, that the challenged measures confer a benefit, within the meaning of Article 1.1(b) of the SCM Agreement.

B. The competitive wholesale electricity market is the relevant focus of the benefit analysis

9.4 As the Panel majority explained, a financial contribution will confer a benefit within the meaning of Article 1.1(b) of the SCM Agreement when it confers an advantage upon its recipient. It is well established that the existence of any such advantage is to be determined by comparing the position of the recipient with and without the financial contribution, and that "the marketplace provides an appropriate basis for [making this] comparison"[643]. Having found that the challenged measures amount to "financial contribution[s]" in the form of "government purchases [of] goods", it follows that the relevant "marketplace" must be the competitive market where electricity is purchased at the same level of trade as the government purchases that are challenged in the present disputes, namely, the wholesale level of trade.

9.5 The Panel majority concluded that the wholesale electricity market currently operating in Ontario cannot be used for the purpose of conducting the benefit analysis. In addition, the Panel majority found that the competitive wholesale electricity market that could, in theory, exist in Ontario could also not be used as a basis for the benefit analysis because, in the light of the prevailing conditions of supply and demand, such a market would fail to attract the generation capacity needed to secure a reliable supply of electricity for the people of Ontario[644]. In my view, however, the fact that a competitive market might not exist in the absence of government intervention or that it may not achieve all of the objectives that a government would like it to achieve, does not mean it cannot be used for the purpose of conducting a benefit analysis. Indeed, it is because competitive markets do not often work the way that governments would like them to that governments will decide to influence market outcomes by, for example, becoming a market participant, regulating market participants or providing them with incentives (or creating disincentives) to behave in a particular way. A government might also choose to intervene in competitive market outcomes by granting subsidies, as defined in Article 1.1 of the SCM Agreement. Provided that such subsidies are not prohibited under Article 3 of the SCM Agreement, a government will be entitled to maintain such measures, subject to the remedies available to other WTO Members under Parts III and V of the SCM Agreement where either "adverse effects" or "material injury" is proven.

9.6 The Panel majority has come to a number of conclusions about the shortcomings of competitive wholesale electricity markets and the inability of the market to achieve the legitimate objectives of the Government of Ontario for its electricity system. However the fact that a market is imperfect in its operation or does not meet the objectives that a government might have for the goods or services which are traded in it does not shield financial contributions which take place in the market from the benefit analysis that is required under the SCM Agreement. In this regard, it is important to recall that the Appellate Body has consistently identified the "marketplace" as the relevant focus of a benefit analysis, regardless of its particular characteristics or imperfections:

> The terms of a financial transaction must be assessed against the terms that would result from unconstrained exchange in the

---

643 Appellate Body Report, *Canada – Aircraft*, para. 157.

644 See above para. 7.312.

> relevant market. The relevant market may be more or less developed; it may be made up of many or few participants. ... In some instances, the market may be more rudimentary. In other instances, it may be difficult to establish the relevant market and its results. But these informational constraints do not alter the basic framework from which the analysis should proceed. ... There is but one standard—the market standard ... [645]

9.7 On the basis of the above considerations, I now turn to examine the merits of the two lines of argument the complainants have advanced in support of their allegations of subsidization.

C. *Whether the challenged measures provide for "more than adequate remuneration" within the meaning of Article 14(d) of the SCM Agreement*

9.8 The first line of benefit argument advanced by the complainants follows the approach that is described in the guidelines for calculating the amount of subsidy in terms of benefit contained in Article 14(d) of the SCM Agreement. Although intended to guide benefit determinations for the purpose of countervailing duty investigations, previous disputes tell us that the approach adopted by the complainants may be one way of demonstrating the existence of benefit in the present proceedings[646]. Thus, the complainants have advanced a series of different prices for electricity, which they submit represent the price that a distributor or trader would have to pay for electricity in Ontario's current wholesale electricity market, or are a proxy for that price. As the complainants note, each of the proposed benchmark prices is outwardly lower than the prices received by solar PV and windpower projects under the FIT Programme.

9.9 Before evaluating the merits of the complainants' arguments, it is important to recall that the guidelines in Article 14(d) of the SCM Agreement stipulate that the amount of benefit may be calculated by identifying the extent to which "more than adequate remuneration" has been paid for a purchased product "in relation to prevailing market conditions" in the *country* of purchase. In the present disputes, the complainants have not advanced *country*-specific price benchmarks, but rather benchmarks based on prices established in regional intra-national markets operating in Canada, and also the United States. The complainants appear to have done so because there are no national electricity wholesale markets in Canada. In other words, the "prevailing market conditions" in the country of purchase (Canada) are such that there are no country-wide electricity markets. In my view Article 14(d) does not suggest that the prevailing market conditions can only be those of a national market. Market conditions in a regional market of a country are, relevantly, market conditions "in the country of

---

645 Appellate Body Report, *Japan – DRAMs (Korea)*, para. 172.

646 See above paras. 7.271-7.275.

purchase". In this light, the complainants' approach is not inconsistent with the guidelines stipulated in Article 14(d) of the SCM Agreement.

9.10 Returning to the substance of the complainant's benefit submissions, the competitive nature of the IESO-administered wholesale electricity market in Ontario was closely examined by the Panel majority, which found that the equilibrium level of the HOEP that is set in this market is directly related to the electricity pricing policy and supply-mix decisions of the Government of Ontario[647]. I agree with this finding. The Government of Ontario's intervention in the IESO-administered wholesale market price outcomes encompasses participation not only as a purchaser of electricity, but also a generator, transmitter, distributor and price-setter (for both generators and consumers). As a result, the price outcomes of the IESO-administered wholesale market (the HOEP) are significantly distorted by the actions and policies of the Government of Ontario. For this reason, the HOEP and all related derivatives advanced by the complainants cannot be used as appropriate market benchmarks for the purpose of performing a benefit analysis under the terms of Article 14(d) of the SCM Agreement[648]. They do not represent a price established on a competitive wholesale electricity market in Ontario.

9.11 The complainants also present the prices for electricity paid in four allegedly competitive wholesale electricity markets outside of Ontario as proxies for the wholesale market price of electricity in Ontario, and argue that these prices demonstrate that the challenged measures confer a benefit. They are prices in Alberta, Canada (the "Alberta benchmark") and prices in New York, New England, and the PJM Interconnection (the "US benchmarks")[649].

9.12 In *US - Softwood Lumber IV*, the Appellate Body found that where private prices for a particular good provided by a government are "distorted because of the government's predominant role in providing those goods", Article 14(d) of the SCM Agreement permits investigating authorities to use the price of the same or similar goods in a market outside of the country in question as a benchmark for conducting a benefit analysis[650]. However, the Appellate Body cautioned that when "an investigating authority proceeds in this manner, it is under an obligation to ensure that the resulting benchmark relates or refers to, or is connected with, prevailing market conditions in the country of provision, and must reflect price, quality, availability, marketability, transportation and other conditions of purchase or sale, as required by Article 14(d)". In addition, investigating authorities must keep in mind that:

---

647 See above paras. 7.298 and 7.300.

648 In this regard, I agree with the description of the relevant legal standard that is set out in the Panel majority opinion above at paras. 7.271-7.275.

649 Collectively, the "out-of-Province" benchmarks.

650 Appellate Body Report, *US – Softwood Lumber IV*, paras. 90, 103, and 115.

> [P]rices in the market of a WTO Member would be expected to reflect prevailing market conditions in that Member; they are unlikely to reflect conditions prevailing in another Member. Therefore, it cannot be presumed that market conditions prevailing in one Member, for instance the United States, relate or refer to, or are connected with, market conditions prevailing in another Member, such as Canada for example. Indeed, it seems to us that it would be difficult, from a practical point of view, for investigating authorities to replicate reliably market conditions prevailing in one country on the basis of market conditions prevailing in another country. First, there are numerous factors to be taken into account in making adjustments to market conditions prevailing in one country so as to replicate those prevailing in another country; secondly, it would be difficult to ensure that all necessary adjustments are made to prices in one country in order to develop a benchmark that relates or refers to, or is connected with, prevailing market conditions in another country, so as to reflect price, quality, availability, marketability, transportation and other conditions of purchase or sale in that other country.[]
>
> It is clear, in the abstract, that different factors can result in one country having a comparative advantage over another with respect to the production of certain goods. In any event, any comparative advantage would be reflected in the market conditions prevailing in the country of provision and, therefore, would have to be taken into account and reflected in the adjustments made to any method used for the determination of adequacy of remuneration, if it is to relate or refer to, or be connected with, prevailing market conditions in the market of provision. ...[651]

9.13 Like the Panel majority, I see no reason why the above principles that were pronounced in the context of a dispute involving a financial contribution in the form of a government *provision* of goods should not also apply in the context of the present disputes involving government *purchases* of goods.

9.14 Thus, in order for the complainants' US benchmarks to be validly applied in the benefit analysis, it must be shown that they: (i) represent prices established in competitive wholesale electricity markets – that is, wholesale electricity markets that are not significantly distorted by government intervention such as that in Ontario; and (ii) must be adjusted to reflect the "prevailing market conditions" for electricity in Ontario. The application of the Alberta benchmark is subject to the same consideration as set out in (i). Given that the Alberta benchmark is a price which does exist "in the *country* of... purchase" a question arises as to whether the consideration set out in (ii) is also applicable. In my

[651] Appellate Body Report, *US – Softwood Lumber IV*, paras. 108-109. (footnote omitted)

opinion it is equally applicable, because the "prevailing market conditions" in the country of purchase include those of both Ontario and Alberta. Determining whether a benefit is conferred "in relation to" prevailing market conditions in Canada includes a consideration of the divisions between markets in that country, and how the conditions of a regional market (that of Ontario) might need to be reflected in a price benchmark adopted from another regional market in that country (that of Alberta).

9.15 With respect to whether the prices in the out-of-Province markets are established through the unconstrained forces of supply and demand, Canada has not contested the complainants' assertions that the wholesale electricity markets in Alberta and in New York, New England and in the PJM Interconnection are competitive and would be available as market price benchmarks (were it not for the fact that they ignore the fundamental condition that the benchmark must relate to the purchase of electricity generated from renewable sources of energy). Nevertheless, the complainants have not presented the same detailed analysis of the alleged competitive nature of these markets as has been advanced in respect of the IESO-administered wholesale market in Ontario. This is an important deficiency because it is clear from the Hogan Report and other arguments and evidence presented in these proceedings that governmental regulation of electricity systems and/or markets is very pronounced across the world. There are many political, social and economic considerations underlying such regulation. Moreover, the specific characteristics of electricity (intangibility, inability to store effectively and almost simultaneous production-consumption) and its critical importance to all facets of modern life make it the type of product whose production, distribution and usage will invariably be susceptible to varying degrees of government intervention. Thus, in the absence of more detailed information about how each of the four out-of-Province markets actually operates, it is difficult to draw any definitive conclusions about their competitive nature for the purpose of conducting a benefit analysis under Article 1.1(b) of the SCM Agreement[652].

[652] Japan has referred the Panel to the website of the Independent Power Producers Society of Alberta, and also provided Exhibits containing information about the electricity markets of Alberta, New York, New England and the PJM Interconnection. (Japan's response to Panel question No. 7 (first set), introducing Exhibits JPN-208-211.) The information contained in these Exhibits suggests that competitive market benchmarks may be derived from experiences in other electricity markets. However, the information provided by Japan was not detailed enough to permit any definitive conclusions in this regard. In this respect, Japan argued that:

> Even if these benchmarks are not "perfect", they are "reasonable and objective", which as the panel explained in *US – Anti-Dumping and Countervailing Duties (China)*, is all that is required for purposes of the benefit analysis. (footnote omitted)

The comments of the panel in *US – Anti-Dumping and Countervailing Duties (China)* that Japan refers to were made in the context of its review of a decision by an investigating authority to impose a countervailing measure. The panel's comments did not, however, relate to the acceptance of an out-of-country benchmark *per se*. The comments related to the need for an investigating authority to identify a benchmark that "relates or refers to, or is connected with" the prevailing market conditions

9.16 In any case, the complainants have not made any of the adjustments to the prices in the out-of-Province markets that would need to be made in order to use them as appropriate benchmarks for assessing the existence of benefit. As already noted, such adjustments would need to take into account the "prevailing market conditions" in Ontario for electricity at the wholesale level of trade. Such conditions might include: (i) the mix of generation technologies that are currently needed to satisfy Ontario's overall baseload, intermediate load and peak load demand; (ii) Ontario's particular transmission grid characteristics; (iii) Ontario's comparative advantage (or disadvantages) with respect to accessing energy sources used to generate electricity; and (iv) key demand characteristics such as population size, industrial base as well as seasonal or daily consumption fluctuations. The complainants have failed to make any adjustments to the out-of-Province prices to account for these and other "prevailing market conditions" in Ontario, nor have they adequately explained away why such adjustments need not be made. Thus, in my view, the evidence is not in a sufficient state to enable the Panel to conduct the benefit analysis under the terms of Article 14(d) of the SCM Agreement in the way the Appellate Body has insisted that it should be conducted[653].

D. Whether the challenged measures enable solar PV and windpower generators to conduct viable operations and thereby participate in the wholesale electricity market

9.17 The second line of benefit argument advanced by the complainants is focused on the very nature and objectives of the FIT Programme. In particular, the complainants submit that the FIT Programme was created and operates for the purpose of allowing generators of electricity from renewable sources of energy, including solar and wind, to supply electricity into the Ontario electricity system because a competitive wholesale electricity market could not support such high cost producers. Thus, the complainants argue that in the absence of the

in the country of provision. It was a description of this relationship, and of the adjustments necessary to allow the acceptance of a benchmark based on out-of-country information, that were absent from the submissions of the complainant in that dispute.

[653] As made clear by the chapeau, Article 14(d) is a method for determining benefit "[f]or the purpose of Part V" of the SCM Agreement. Article 1.1(b) is in Part I of the SCM Agreement. Nonetheless, Article 14(d) strongly informs the interpretation of Article 1.1(b) in the case of the conferral of benefit from the sale or purchase of products. In every case, considering whether and how to adjust an out-of-country benchmark so that it could be said to be "in relation to prevailing market conditions" in the country concerned is a relevant consideration. The European Union made reference to "the natural conditions prevailing in Ontario" in the context of a comparison "with the rates in France and Germany, in addition to all the evidence already put forward by the European Union" (European Union's response to Panel question No. 27 (second set)). However this reference does not discharge the burden of the "strong obligation" of considering "prevailing market conditions" insisted upon by the Appellate Body in *US - Softwood Lumber IV*, para. 106.

FIT Programme, solar PV and windpower generators would be unable to support commercially viable operations in the wholesale electricity market in Ontario[654].

9.18 Canada accepts that in the absence of the FIT Programme, "most" of the contested FIT generators would be unable to conduct viable operations. Thus, Canada explains that:

> Like FIT programs in other parts of the world, the Ontario FIT Program was created to induce new renewable generation. As recognized by Japan, the Ontario 'FIT Program ... became necessary to encourage the entry into the market of renewable energy generators, most of which would not have entered the market in the absence of the FIT Program[655].

9.19 Moreover, referring to Ontario's episodic market opening experience in 2002, Canada states that "the market alone would not be sufficient to encourage the construction of new generation facilities able to provide the long-term supply needed by Ontario residents", adding that "[a]s recognized by Japan, the OPA was created 'because the market structure established immediately following the dissolution of Ontario Hydro in 1998 did not invite the sufficient entry of new generators, particularly generators using alternative and renewable energy sources'"[656]. Thus, the OPA was established with a mandate to:

> [R]estructure Ontario's electricity sector, to promote the expansion of electricity supply and capacity, including supply and capacity from alternative and renewable energy sources ... [657]

9.20 That the FIT Programme was intended to bring about the entry of new generating capacity from renewable sources of energy that would otherwise not exist in the Ontario wholesale electricity market can also be understood from the objectives of the FIT Programme described in the Ministerial Direction, which include to "[i]ncrease capacity of renewable energy supply to ensure adequate generation and reduce emissions", to "[p]rovide incentives for investment in renewable energy technologies" and "[e]nable new green industries through new investment and job creation"[658]. Similarly, the FIT Rules explain that the "fundamental objective of the FIT Program, in conjunction with the *Green Energy and Green Economy Act of 2009* is to facilitate the increased

---

[654] Japan's second written submission, paras. 3-7; opening statement at the second meeting of the Panel, paras. 10-13; comments on Canada's response to Panel questions No. 1 and 42 (second set); European Union's second written submission, paras. 69-70, 103 and 105; and opening statement at the first meeting of the Panel, paras. 23 and 27.

[655] Canada's first written submission (DS412), para. 39.

[656] Canada's first written submission (DS412), para. 27.

[657] Highlights of the *Electricity Restructuring Act of 2004*, Exhibit JPN-9.

[658] Minister's 2009 FIT Direction, Exhibit JPN-102, p. 1.

development of Renewable Generating Facilities of varying sizes, technologies and configurations ..."[659].

9.21 Professor Hogan confirms that renewable energy technologies are typically too expensive to be supported by the spot prices achieved on wholesale electricity markets[660]. Table 2 (Ontario Electricity Generation Mix) contained in the Panel majority's opinion identifies solar PV and windpower technologies as having "very high" relative capital costs, with albeit "very low" relative operating costs per kWh of electricity generated. This reflects the following specific cost data that is provided in the Hogan Report[661] (Table 3).

9.22 According to Professor Hogan, the major costs differences between solar and windpower generating facilities compared with more "conventional" technologies exist for the following reasons:

> The relatively small scale of wind and solar facilities leads to few if any economies of scale in generation in comparison with large nuclear, coal, hydro and gas plants.
>
> Wind and solar facilities have relatively low capacity factors, due to their dependence on the wind and the sun, meaning that the generating facilities produce electricity for a much smaller proportion of the hours of the year or day than conventional generating technologies.
>
> The relatively small base of experience in operating wind and solar generating facilities means that there are fewer efficiencies in operating new facilities.
>
> The lack of experience in constructing wind and solar generating facilities, leading to relatively fewer efficiencies in constructing new facilities[662].

659 FIT Rules, Exhibit JPN-119, Section 1.1.
660 Hogan Report, Exhibit CDA-2, pp. 15-18 and 36.
661 Hogan Report, Exhibit CDA-2, Table 1, p. 8.
662 Hogan Report, Exhibit CDA-2, p. 10.

Table 3: Cost and Operating Characteristics of Different Generating Technologies

Plant Type	Typical Plant Size	Capital Cost	Fixed Operating Cost	Variable Operating Cost	Fuel Cost	Heat Rate	Start Fuel	Start Cost	Project Life	Average Annual Availability	Capacity Factor
	(MW)	(2007 C$/kW)	(2007 C$/kW)	(2007 C$/MWh)	(2007 C$/MWh)	(BTU/kWh HHV)	(BTU/kW/ Start HHV)	(2007 C$/Start/Unit)	(years)	(%)	(%)
Frame Single-Cycle Gas Turbine[1]	340	$665	$16	$3.50		9,500	700	$10,000	20	97%	10-30%[3]
Aeroderivative Single-Cycle Gas Turbine[1]	93	$1,174	$34	$3.50		8,700	200	$375	20	97%	10-30%[3]
Combined Cycle Gas Turbine[1]	500	$924	$17	$2.75		7,000	800	$10,000	20	95%	
Nuclear[1]	1,000	$2,970	$89	$1.50	$6				30	90%	70-80% or higher[3]
Large Wind Farm[1]	100	$1,741	$37	$0					20	98%	13.5-43%[4]
Landfill Gas[1]	1	$2,288	$140	$0	$0	10,000			15	85%	
Wood-Residue Biomass[1]	20	$2,096	$231	$4.00	$23	14,800			20	85%	
Wastewater Biogas[1]	2	$4,215	$68	$13.00		10,000			15	85%	85%
Small Wind Farm[1]	10	$2,750	$41	$0	$0				20	98%	13.5-43%[4]
District Energy Combined Heat and Power[1]	2	$2,346	$24	$8.00		5,700	0	$0	20	95%	
Industrial Combined Heat and Power[1]	50	$1,413	$22	$3.00		6,300	150	$0	20	95%	
Gas Engine Distributed Generation[1]	0.5	$1,172	$9	$16.00		10,770	0	$0	15	85%	
Roof-mounted Solar[2]	0.5	$6,690	$12	$0					20		13%
Ground-mounted Solar[2]	10	$4,600	$5	$0					20		14%

Sources:

1 "Evaluation of Costs of New Entry, Prepared for: Ontario Power Authority", Navigant Consulting, February 21, 2007, page 35, biogas capacity factor on page 30(Exhibit CDA-49).

2 "Proposed Feed-in Tariff Price Schedule Stakeholder Engagement – Session 4", Ontario Power Authority, April 7, 2009, page 36. Shown statistics are in 2008 C$(Exhibit CDA-46).

3 IESO Monthly Generator Disclosure Report Overview, http://www.ieso.ca/imoweb/marketdata/genDisclosure.asp

4 Dr. Khaqan Kahn, Ontario IESO, "Growing Wind in Canada: An Ontario Perspective on Wind, CanWEA 2008 Annual Conference and Trade Show, October 20, 2008, p. 9 (Exhibit CDA-47).

9.23 Thus, by contracting to purchase electricity produced from solar PV and windpower technologies under the FIT Programme at a price intended to provide for a reasonable return on the investment associated with a "typical" project, the Government of Ontario ensures that qualifying generators are remunerated at a level that allows them to recoup the entirety of their "very high" capital costs. As the complainants argue and Canada accepts, such levels of remuneration would never be achieved through the unconstrained forces of supply and demand in a competitive wholesale electricity market in Ontario. Nor could they be achieved within the constrained forces of supply and demand which actually do operate within the wholesale electricity market in Ontario, without an intervention which remunerates the facilities which generate power from solar PV and windpower technologies at a higher rate than is paid in respect of electricity generated by the other technologies[1]. It follows that by bringing these high cost and less efficient electricity producers into the wholesale electricity market, when they would otherwise not be present, the Government of Ontario's purchases of electricity from solar PV and windpower generators under the FIT Programme clearly confer a benefit upon the relevant FIT generators, within the meaning of Article 1.1(b) of the SCM Agreement.

[1] Moreover, both Japan and the European Union point to the 20-year guaranteed pricing available to FIT generators as features of the FIT and microFIT Contracts that demonstrate the existence of benefit. See e.g. Japan's opening statement at the second meeting of the Panel, paras. 10-13; and European Union's opening statement at the second meeting of the Panel, para. 22.

Cumulative List of Published Disputes